From the
South African Past

Sources in Modern History Series:

Other titles forthcoming

From the
South African Past

Narratives, Documents, and Debates

John A. Williams

State University of New York
at Stony Brook

Houghton Mifflin Company
Boston   New York

To Ginger

Senior Sponsoring Editor: Jean Woy
Senior Associate Editor: Fran Gay
Project Editor: Nicole Ng
Senior Designer: Henry Rachlin
Electronic Production Supervisor: Irene V. Cinelli
Associate Production/Design Coordinator: Deborah Frydman
Manufacturing Coordinator: Michael O'Dea

Cover Design: Alwyn R. Velásquez, Lapis Design

Cover Image: Paul Sibisi, *Umzavela Unrest*, 1981

Printed in the U.S.A.
Library of Congress Catalog Card Number: 96-76977
ISBN: 0-669-28789-X

2 3 4 5 6 7 8 9-DC- 06 05 04 03 02

Preface

From the South African Past is a timely collection of documents illuminating the formation of the modern multi-racial society of South Africa. The texts span four hundred years, from European–African contracts in the Cape in the seventeenth century to the debates over the future of South Africa that continue even now. With its versatile selections, new voices, balanced attention to both the European and African experiences, and emphasis on debates, the volume offers a unique blend of qualities not found in any other collection

The volume is designed for a variety of courses. Foremost among these are classes on South African history proper. The volume may also be used by students of more general African history, especially the history of European imperialism and colonial rule in Africa. The nineteenth-century documents on the contact between different cultures and on African political systems and the documents covering twentieth-century policy debates provide strong South African case studies for such a course. In addition, the substantial coverage of the post-1948 era of apartheid makes the book well suited to courses on South African and African politics. Earlier selections of the book might also be used effectively in such courses, for the interpretation of South African history has been a battleground of debate about apartheid.

Coverage and Emphasis

With an enormously rich store of documents from which to draw, choosing what to include and what to leave out was difficult. Even though the volume spans general South African history, it cannot illustrate all the standard themes of the history in the available space. To focus the scope of the project, I have therefore limited the coverage to specific thematic threads that are part of the broader fabric of the general history. I hope that these pieces of the historical mosaic will stimulate some readers to want to learn more.

- The book does not attempt to document deeply the rich and significant history of South African societies before 1652. Considering that the sources for this early history are primarily archaeological, and their interpretation technical, a book devoted to literary sources recounting the development of modern South African society could not easily include such material. For practical purposes, therefore, the coverage begins with 1652, even though the importance of the long historical development and rich cultural heritage predating 1652 must be acknowledged for its profound contribution to modern South African society. The fact that the National party regime in part justified apartheid by denying the depth and significance of pre-1652 African history is noted and discussed in the section on the ideology of apartheid. So although I strive to show the long roots of South Africa's problems, policies, and debates in the early history of European settlement, the overall focus of this volume is *on* the more recent periods.

- The book emphasizes *South* Africa rather than southern Africa. As a result the Portuguese territories, Zimbabwe, Zambia, and Malawi, and even the former High Commission territories of Lesotho, Swaziland, and Botswana, receive scant mention. Nor was space available for the international debate over the status of Namibia or the struggle of its peoples for independence. But this limitation is not applied strictly, for certain topics beyond the definition of the term *South Africa*—for example, the Lesotho kingdom under King Moshoeshoe and his successors and the Ndebele kingdom in Zimbabwe—are integral to the history of the region.

- Throughout, I have weighted the volume more toward European–African relations than toward the nationalist debates in white politics between British and Afrikaner South Africans. White politics, of course, serves as the vital context of and occasion for debates over African status, and key events and developments are referred to; however, they are not documented in as much detail as are the debates over African policy.

- By necessity, the book devotes much space to the nature of apartheid. More than just a slogan, apartheid was a set of measures of social engineering, a grand scheme of segregation, and a strategy for preserving white supremacy. However strongly many students may condemn apartheid, to them it is often only a vaguely defined epithet. The concept of apartheid is in turn embedded in the context of ideological debates. These receive much attention in the later sections of the book, where the debates proliferate and take on new forms.

- "African voices" also recur throughout the book, especially in Parts 3, 4, and 5, where praise poems, testimony before royal commissions and trial judges, speeches, and manifestos all tellingly reveal the African experience during the various periods.

- Finally, I have tried to capture the flavor of historical debate about South Africa. To a marked degree, there is currently no consensual version of South African history by which we can identify the standard core of information, periodization, and leading points of scholarly dispute. Rather, one sees a rapidly changing set of historical explorations. *From the South African Past* seeks to contribute to those explorations. This aim makes the decision of balance and emphasis and of inclusion and exclusion in this volume both more difficult and more rewarding. Yet I hope that controversy about the very shape and texture of any synthesis of South African history will make the book that much more interesting and provocative, even beyond the merits of its individual readings.

Themes and Organization

This book contains five parts, each in turn comprising several subsections. Part 1, "Settlement and Contact in the Cape, 1652–1857," introduces three broad, standard themes in South African history. The first is the fate of the indigenous peoples under the impact of settlement. The second is the history of slavery in the Cape. Taken together, these threads weave the story of the formation of the Cape Coloured people. The third theme concerns the development of the Eastern Cape frontier, which one scholar declares *the* prototypical confrontation of European imperialist expansion with the other peoples of the world.

Part 2, "African Statecraft, Cultural Contact, and Colonialism in the Interior, 1818–1893," considers the interior regions beyond the Cape settlement, an area of particularly rich documentation. The selections here draw especially on European travelers and their meetings with the African monarchs of this region and reveal much about European attitudes, African reactions to the Europeans, and the nature of nineteenth-century African leadership.

Part 3, "Toward a White-Dominated State, 1851–1936," examines the debate about Africans that occupied white politics after the end of politically independent African states. These years witnessed the establishment of white-dominated, industrializing South Africa.

Part 4. "The Rise of the Apartheid State, 1936–1976," explores the concept and experience of apartheid: the theory, the policy, the regime, and the debate, as well as the development of African organized resistance to white domination.

Finally, Part 5, "Toward a Democratic South Africa, 1977–Present," documents the attempts to reform apartheid after 1976 and the crescendo and eventual explosion of African protest into full insurrection. The book ends with documents illustrating the process by which the apartheid regime was dismantled and a new regime installed by 1994.

Format and Features

The selections in *From the South African Past* vary in length but average roughly four pages. Excerpts of this scope are long enough to provide richness of content but short enough for close and detailed reading and discussion. Certain reading, such as extracts from laws, which tend to be dry, are very brief indeed. Other documents, especially those with some narrative content, run much longer.

Part introductions provide context for understanding the documents. For example, the industrialization of South Africa is a major component of any course on South African history. Yet the story of South African economic development by necessity does not receive full coverage in the documents. This economic theme can be detected in many of the selections, but the discovery of gold and diamonds, and the building of industries, cities, and railroads stemming from those discoveries, is not documented *as such*. The Part 3 introduction fills the gap somewhat by presenting these developments for readers in some detail.

In addition to the part introductions, selection headnotes introduce the author of each document and provide further context. They do not, however, preempt the lines of discussion that students might develop on their own.

Last, students will find helpful study and review tools in the maps, chronology, suggested further readings, and lists of key terms and principal names. Each part opens with a photograph, too, that strikingly illustrates a major theme in the documents.

Acknowledgments

I have accumulated many debts in preparing this work. Above all the editorial staff at D.C. Heath and Houghton Mifflin have been patient and helpful at every juncture. I thank especially James Miller, who signed me on to the project; David Light, who started the editorial work; Lauren Johnson, who oversaw most of the detailed editorial effort; and all the others at D.C. Heath with whom I had less direct contact but whose help was crucial.

Just as the book was moving to production, D. C. Heath was acquired by Houghton Mifflin Company, and a whole new team took over the production. The changeover was remarkably smooth and free of delay. I am thankful to Ann Barnard, Fran Gay, Nicole Ng, Jean Woy, and the rest of the HMCo. staff for a remarkably efficient and sympathetic treatment of my manuscript.

Back at the State University of New York at Stony Brook, the work's preparation was punctuated by many lively discussions with Olufemi Vaughan about teaching African materials. Seth Armus, too, kept up an always exciting argument and commentary on South African affairs.

I am grateful to Donna Sammis of the University at Stony Brook's Frank Melville Jr. Memorial Library for digging out many obscure and difficult interlibrary loan requests and to Steve Wasay, who during two stints as my research assistant located, photocopied, and collated many obscure sources. Cecile Verbaarschot helped with Afrikaans documents.

Throughout this time, Barbara Beresford did so much to make the Stony Brook history department a pleasant place to work. Ginger Roberts, a valued friend and a gifted teacher at a different level of the educational system, supplied many new ideas about how documents such as these can be used in teaching.

Finally, many thanks to the reviewers who provided helpful advice as the project took shape:

Ralph Austen
University of Chicago

John Cell
Lafayette College

R. Hunt Davis, Jr.
University of Florida

Richard Hull
New York University

Paul Landau
University of New Hampshire

Patrick Manning
Northeastern University

Elizabeth Schmidt
Loyola College

Harrison Wright
Swarthmore College

William Worger
University of California, Los Angeles

Contents

Part II
African Statecraft, Cultural Contact, and Colonialism in the Interior, 1818–1893

69

Introduction 69

Part III
Toward a White-Dominated State, 1851–1936

141

Part IV
The Rise of the Apartheid State, 1936–1976

239

Part V
Toward a Democratic South Africa, 1977–the Present

323

Chronology

ca. 500 B.C.–500 C.E.

Iron Age peoples move into southern Africa, encroaching on ancestors of Khoisan, who had lived in the region for thousands of years

FIFTEENTH CENTURY

1487 Bartholemeu Dias rounds Cape of Good Hope, discovers path to India

SIXTEENTH CENTURY

1498 Vasco da Gama reaches India by Dias's route

SEVENTEENTH CENTURY

1652 Dutch East India Company (VOC) establishes permanent settlement at Table Bay

EIGHTEENTH–NINETEENTH CENTURY

1770s Dutch Settlement contacts Xhosa near Great Fish River, or Eastern Cape Frontier
1770s–1812 "open" frontier period emerges between Europeans and Xhosa at Eastern Cape; relations between them are ambiguous; alliances possible
1795–1802 First British occupation

NINETEENTH CENTURY

1800–1820 *Mfecane* wars break out among Africans in the Interior
1806 second British occupation; British begin rule of Cape Colony
1812–1857 colonial government enforces dividing line between Europeans and Xhosa at Eastern Cape frontier; wars break out
1818 Dingiswayo of the Ndandwe dies, is succeeded by Shaka
1818–1828 Shaka rules newly formed Zulu kingdom
1828 Shaka is assassinated and succeeded by his half brother, Dingane
1830s Mzilikazi, Shaka's former regent commander, builds Ndebele kingdom in the Transvaal and southern Zimbabwe; Moshoeshoe founds kingdom of Lesotho
1836 Great Trek begins
1838 December 16, Battle of Blood River; Zulus, led by Dingane, are defeated by trekkers in Natal
1840 Dingane is killed; his brother Mpande succeeds him as Zulu king
1843 British annex Natal

1850s trekkers form new republics: Orange Free State and South African Republic, or Transvaal; republics achieve virtual autonomy under Britain; Sir George Grey makes unsuccessful bid to unify South African settlements

1850–1880 African kingdoms see the last generation of their political independence

1852 parliament established in Cape colony

1857–1870s Xhosa kill cattle following prophecy and enter period of dependency on Europeans' economy; Xhosa face final defeat by Europeans, late 1870s

1868 Mzilikazi dies; his son Lobengula succeeds him as Ndebele king; British annex Lesotho

1868–1893 Lobengula reigns as Ndebele king

1870 Moshoeshoe dies; succeeded by his son Letsie I as king of the Lesotho kingdom

1872 responsible government is granted to the Cape Province

1872 Mpande dies; is succeeded by Cetshwayo as Zulu king

1877 Lord Carnarvon carries out British annexation of the Transvaal, with the goal of uniting South Africa under British auspices

1879 Zulus, led by Cetshwayo, triumph at Isandhlwana

1881 Transvaal Boers rebel successfully against British; Pretoria Convention provides for British suzerainty over a virtually independent Transvaal

1886 gold production begins in Witwatersrand

1883–1900 Paul Kruger serves as president of Transvaal; goes into exile in 1900, just before British occupation of Pretoria

1890s responsible government is granted to Natal; Paul Kruger rules Transvaal as nationalistic Afrikaner president

1893 Cecil Rhodes's British South Africa Company defeats Ndebele kingdom

1895 British South African Company police, led by Sir Leander Starr Jameson, raid Transvaal, hoping unsuccessfully for help from an Uitlander rebellion

1899–1902 Anglo-Boer War rages between Britain and the two Boer republics

TWENTIETH CENTURY

1906–1908 Zulus rebel against poll tax

1910 Union of South Africa forms

1910–1919 Louis Botha serves as prime minister

1912 South African Native National Congress is founded; later becomes African National Congress, or ANC

1913 Native Land Act restricts Africans' squatting on white farms; divides South Africa into black and white areas

1919–1924 Jan Smuts serves as prime minister

1922 Rand revolt

1923 Urban Areas Act restricts Africans from cities

1924–1939 J. B. M. Hertzog serves as prime minister

1933 J. B. M. Hertzog and Jan Smuts form fusion government

1934 Smuts and Hertzog parties form United party

1936 African vote in the Cape is repealed; worldwide economic depression also hits South Africa

1939–1948 Jan Smuts serves as prime minister

1948 Purified National party gains control of government, Dr. D. F. Malan serves as prime minister to 1954

1948–1958 Hendrik Verwoerd serves as native minister, designs policy of apartheid

1949   Prohibition of Mixed Marriages Act proscribes marriage between individuals of
       different racial classifications
1950   Popular Registration Act requires anyone sixteen years old and older to register,
       carry card as member of a particular race; Immorality Act proscribes sexual rela-
       tions between different races
1952   ANC Defiance Campaign
1953   Liberal party forms as split-off from United party
1954–1958   J. G. Strijdom serves as prime minister
1955   ANC Freedom Charter, drafted by Congress Alliance, tilts organization toward
       universalism and away from Africanism; African district of Sophiatown razed, its
       residents expelled
1958–1966   Hendrik Verwoerd serves as prime minister
1959   opponents of ANC's universalism secede to form Pan Africanist Congress (PAC);
       Progressive party forms, seceded from United party
1960   PAC launches anti-pass campaign; March 21, Sharpeville Massacre; government
       bans the ANC and PAC
1961   ANC forms Umkhonto we Sizwe and launches armed struggle; South Africa
       proclaims a republic and is expelled from the Commonwealth
1962   Nelson Mandela arrested
1964   after raid on Rivonia farm, major leaders in the armed struggle are put on trial;
       Nelson Mandela receives life sentence
1966–1979   John Vorster serves as prime minister
1976   Soweto uprisings
1979–1983, 1983–1989   P. W. Botha serves as prime minister and state president
1982   *Conservative party formally breaks from National party*
1983   new constitution creates strong state president, with power to oppose resisters,
       and tricameral legislature excluding blacks; attempts to divide Africans by giving
       well-off blacks a stake in system; United Democratic Front founded to oppose
       new constitution
1984–1987   township insurrections
1986   American sanctions enacted against South Africa, and private measures of
       economic boycott and divestment campaigns launched
1989   Nelson Mandela released from prison; bans on ANC and other resistance
       organizations lifted and apartheid laws repealed
1989–1994   F. W. De Klerk serves as president; CODESA talks; violence between
       supporters of ANC and Inkatha Freedom Party
1994   Nelson Mandela wins presidency

Introduction: Studying South African History Through Documents

> I come here because of my deep interest and affection for a land settled by the Dutch in the mid-seventeenth century, then taken over by the British, and at last independent; a land in which the native inhabitants were at first subdued, but relations with whom remain a problem to this day; a land which defined itself on a hostile frontier; a land which has tamed rich natural resources through the energetic application of modern technology; a land which once imported slaves, and now must struggle to wipe out the last traces of that former bondage.
>
> I refer, of course, to the United States of America.

The opening phrases of Robert F. Kennedy's Day of Affirmation speech, given at the University of Cape Town on June 6, 1966, drew laughter and applause from the audience. He had been so obviously describing South Africa, but his words also fit the United States. His clever opening remarks gained the attention of his audience and put it at ease. At the time, although some welcomed Kennedy's intervention, many South Africans did not believe that an American politician had any business pronouncing on South African affairs.

In 1966 worldwide concern about South African affairs had not yet reached the pitch it would achieve after 1976 and especially in the 1980s. True, the apartheid policy of the South African National party government increasingly placed South Africa out of step with Western democracies, especially after Britain, France, and Belgium ended their colonial rule over African territories. Nevertheless, criticism of this policy had not yet gained worldwide public attention at the time of Kennedy's speech. (Robert F. Kennedy, as some white South African leaders feared, would indeed play a pioneering role in raising that concern.)

As global disapproval of apartheid gathered momentum, it became clear that the debate, especially in the United States, concerned far more than South Africa. Discussions ostensibly about South Africa gave rise to metaphors for American domestic race relations and social policies. Indeed, South African issues raise universal questions about freedom and justice for all who study them. Despite the repeal of the apartheid laws and the holding of free and democratic elections in 1994, the debate over the future course of South African society continues to resonate with the same universal concerns.

This book—a collection of documents on South African history from the beginning of European settlement to the inauguration of Nelson Mandela as president in 1994—has been prepared in the belief that knowledge of South Africa remains as vital now as it was at the height of the anti-apartheid struggle. The readings collected here document many themes of the South African past and illustrate the most important debates and conflicts from South African political history. By itself or with other textbooks and reading, the book should invite students to participate in the ongoing debate over freedom and justice in South Africa from an informed and effective position. In the late twentieth century, knowledge of South Africa and its history has become an essential ingredient in the discourse of all educated and politically conscious people.

This introduction provides background for understanding the documents; the part introductions and document headnotes provide further background. Yet the introduction also offers suggestions and guidelines for using the book and gleaning the maximum wealth of historical meaning from the documents. In the pages to come, we thus take up a series of related and indeed intertwined issues. The first concerns the benefits and pitfalls, especially in the United States, of learning South African history through comparative analysis. We also discuss the problems inherent in South African terminology, in which many words are simply unfamiliar and others, while familiar, have seen a shift in their meaning. Still other terms, though woven tightly into the fabric of the history, may strike us as ugly and demeaning racist slurs. Finally, we explore the meaning of the term *apartheid* itself, and its relationship to other policies and structures by which white settlers in South Africa have pursued the goals of white supremacy. This discussion will lead us, then to questions about the periodization of the South African past, to historiographical concerns, to rival and evolving historical interpretations, and, finally, to a discussion of techniques for fruitful discussion of the documents.

Learning South African History: The Pitfalls of Comparative Analysis

One of the most striking features of teaching South African history in the United States is the inevitability of comparative discussions. Whether they intend it or not, and whether they do it explicitly or implicitly, students familiar with American society and history tend to view South African history through American "lenses." Such reflexive comparison can lead equally to both insight and misunderstanding, Comparing the two societies openly—*while discussing the implication of any given comparative strategy*—is probably the best way to ensure insight and avoid the pitfalls of comparison. This collection of documents is not in itself a work of comparative history, but it opens opportunities to attempt such an analysis.

How can instructors and students attempt a comparative study most fruitfully? There are myriad parallels between the United States and South African history, and Robert Kennedy deftly touched on some of them. But attempts to make an equation between episodes and eras in the two histories are bound to break down or lead the observer astray. This is not to say that comparison should be avoided. It is an inevitable part of the study of any history. Rather than avoiding it because of its difficulties, we need to approach it with care.

From the early seventeenth century, European settlement—and the contact, cooperation, conflict, and conquest between the settlers and indigenous peoples—became a feature of both the North American and African continents. In this context, the indigenous African societies can be set alongside the Native Americans. Then, in the eighteenth and early nineteenth centuries, settlers in South Africa and in extensive parts of North America used the forced labor of imported slaves. This development allows us a different comparison, that between institutions of slavery in two different societies. To be sure, the comparative study of slavery is something like a historiographical industry, and has generated a wealth of useful scholarship. By the twentieth century, a modern industrial economy and modern governmental machinery—each dominated by the immigrants and their descendants—had emerged in both countries, suggesting still another point of comparison.

To compare the oppression and struggle of black South Africans and African Americans is obviously a valuable approach. It occurs to most students first, and it is often the only comparison they make. Yet we can see from the above examples that there is no one "correct" basis for comparison—those noted above, along with a great variety of others, may yield important insights. Such comparisons provide a starting point especially for those with a background in American but not South African history. Without realizing it, these students have a ready-made, if dangerous, scaffolding on which to build new information about South Africa.

Recall, too, that throughout both histories, South Africans and Americans were aware of each other. From the late nineteenth century on, black South Africans traveled to the United States, where they received education and learned rich cultural and political techniques from African Americans. In that same period, whites designing segregation measures in both societies studied each other's work. At the turn of the century, white South African liberals sometimes boasted that South Africa treated black people more justly than the violent and oppressive southern states of America did. The comparative angle that came with this mutual awareness also becomes part of the history itself, and we see evidence for it in some of the documents.

Comparison may thus help to carry American students past the burden of unfamiliar names and events to the realization that South African colonization made up part of the same movement of European overseas settlement and conquest that dominated North American history from the seventeenth century on. But comparison is not a panacea. Instead of answers, it raises yet other questions; instead of providing conclusions, it is only a field of inquiry. It can serve as a bridge for traveling from a familiar subject to a new one, but students must remember that it is above all an inquiry about *difference*. However much we see the same set of *processes* at work in South African and American histories, the timing of key events and the quality of outcomes often stand in sharp contrast. This is especially true of demographic realities. For example, in contrast to North America, only a relatively weak stream of European settlers reached the remote South African settlement. Moreover, they faced a rich array of peoples there, including the numerous, powerful, and technologically advanced society of the southern Bantu-speakers. This Iron Age, mixed-farming population had already been sufficiently exposed to the complex of Old World diseases and thus escaped the decimating epidemics that often follow initial contact—though the Khoikhoi and San peoples whom Europeans had met earlier were not so fortunate.

Thus the European settlers of South Africa never made up more than 20 percent of the population, and even that figure has declined since 1960. Africans make up over 80 percent, in contrast with African Americans, who compose just around 10 percent of the U. S. population. Comparison of racial oppression and struggle in the two societies must therefore always take these dramatic contrasts into account, though the implications of the differences are neither obvious nor easy to determine.

In short, for all its parallels with the United States, South Africa is a wholly different society. Although it is a settlement land like Canada, Australia, and the United States, all of the other countries are *demographically* dominated by peoples of European descent. South Africa does have something in common with the tropical colonized societies, in which the local inhabitants remained the vast majority even as they came under European colonial rule. But all of this aside, South Africa is markedly different from the settlement lands and the tropical societies: it is a plural society with a significant European element.

The way in which the same words can have contrasting meaning in South Africa and the United States testifies to this difference. In America, the term *minority* has become at times synonymous with *oppressed group.* This usage is clearly inappropriate for South Africa, where the *majority* has suffered under an oppressive regime. Occasionally, Americans have used the term *minority* to signify Africans suffering under apartheid; but in today's South Africa, *minority rights* designates schemes designed to prevent the hitherto dominant whites from losing their special privileges.

On Terminology

Studying and learning South African history demands more than mastering a series of names, events, and dates. Though simplistic, this observation is worth making, because the burden of unfamiliar information can sometimes overwhelm students new to the subject. The book provides a glossary of important terms, and unfamiliar language in the documents is annotated. But students face two difficulties in particular: the variant spellings of African names, and the prevalence of racially disparaging terms in South African discourse—terms that may change their meaning over time.

A standardized orthography for the various southern Bantu languages is only now being established, and older documents often show variant spellings. For example, the Ndebele people of southern Zimbabwe are often rendered *Matabele.* Their first king, Mzilikazi, is called Moselekatse in old documents. Similarly, the Tswana people of Botswana were called Bechuana, and their country Bechuanaland, in the colonial period; the Sotho of Lesotho were Basuto, their country Basutoland. Looking for the root of the word can help clear up the confusion. The prefix of group names—*Ba, Wa, Ma*—is a collective plural. As in the word *Sotho* (*Ba*suto), this prefix is often omitted today in English-language texts.

Much of South African history revolves around the concepts of race and racism. To present and discuss South African history is to discuss such matters, and this is not always easy when our own society has entangled itself in similar issues. Strong feelings can be aroused by the language used to discuss racism. In the historical documents presented here, racism is often put on display, coolly printed out in all its harshness. These usages are necessary; South African history cannot be understood without them. Moreover, strong reactions to the language and even heated arguments can be salutary and healthy. South African affairs are not and should not be made innocuous and remote for North American observers.

Even the most egregious terms can change their meaning, however. For example, the word *kaffir* derived from the Arabic word for infidel, is today an insult bearing the force of *nigger* in North America; possibly it is stronger. Yet its usage in nineteenth-century documents does not necessarily carry such force. The nineteenth-century European settler using the term may well have been an imperialist and racist conqueror. He and his fellows unilaterally named the indigenous peoples whom they met. This act itself has come to be seen as a kind of aggression; the European names are not what Africans called themselves, of course. But at the time the documents were written, there often was no other term available. Judging the connotations and nuances of such terms in early documents is therefore an important part of evaluating them.

Between the 1870s and 1950s, the most common term used by Europeans to describe the Africans of South Africa was *Native.* Insofar as this term meant simply *indigenous inhabitant,* it was undoubtedly accurate. But in this period, the word came to imply a *primitive,* backward, childlike being who needed to be ruled and controlled by the civilized Europeans. Europeans incessantly discussed the so-called Native Question, the question of what to do with the Africans, how to control them, and how to command their labor. The term *Native* was thereby discredited as overt evidence of the racist project of white supremacy. Again, this term occurs in many of the documents that date from early twentieth-century race relations in South Africa. Decoding the value and intent of the term in these documents is one important element of interpreting them.

Africans themselves rejected the term *Native,* and liberal whites quickly followed suit. Eventually white supremacists dropped it, too, when they realized that a less offensive term would be more useful to their policies. In the 1950s, they began to use the term *Bantu,* implicating the term in apartheid policy by enacting Bantu Affairs and Bantu Education. The reserves of African land became Bantustans, on their way to becoming homelands. Signs in doorways might read, "Whites Only: No Bantu or Dogs Allowed." Inevitably, then, *Bantu* became a racist and insulting term as well. But it has retained its status as a linguistic classification. Thus the classification *Bantu-speakers* is still used, although it designates only a language family and has no standing as a term of racial classification.

In addition to the names by which groups are designated, the very basis by which groups are defined also presents difficulties. Down to the 1950s, scholars thought that terms such as *Bushmen, Hottentots,* and *Bantu* represented fixed racial groups. They assumed that the cultural attributes of each of the groups—their language, technology, and all other aspects of their cultures—were firmly linked with race and indeed determined by it. In their view, the *acquired* characteristics of culture were instead *racially* inherited.

It is easy to see this error in older scholarship. But we run the danger of similar errors whenever we turn a concept, abstraction, or generalization into a palpable, concrete object. This is reification, one of the most common mental errors made in thinking about units of human social organization.

Scholars today avoid connecting race and culture in this way, for the boundaries between groups are not always clear. People can and do change their language, technology, social organization, or economic life as they make contact with one another and mingle. But inexact as group names are, we have no choice but to use them. We can, however, always recall that they are at best convenient generalizations. When we see these usages or use them ourselves, we must always be aware of the dangers of reification. We can catch ourselves in this error whenever we start to think of peoples' moving around South Africa and bumping into each other like billiard balls on a green felt table.

In South African as in other histories, we need to be able to speak of groups of peoples. The way in which the names for people become slurs through the lens of imperialist oppression makes it difficult to find an appropriate vocabulary. The reification process, by which convenient but rough divisions come to seem fixed and real, also poses a problem. These tendencies are worsened by the legally enforced group identities sanctioned under the apartheid system between 1950 and 1989, under the Population Registration Act and its many amendments. We cannot avoid using the terms and divisions described in this legislation, but it is almost impossible to do so without seeming at some level to endorse the invidious distinctions that the words make.

Remaining alert to this danger , and to the dangers of reifying the terms, can help. Beyond these measures we need to weigh two contrasting means by which groups acquire their names. Let us term one set of group names *categories;* the other, *identities.*

Categories are group names deriving (in many cases) from scholarly analysis. An example would be the designation "Bantu," or "Bantu-speakers," as applied to all of Africa. The Bantu languages are spoken in a huge triangle that reaches from the East Cape districts of South Africa, all the way north to Uganda, and then over to the Cameroons in West Africa. This is a language family whose existence is not a conscious matter among these varied people themselves but a linguistic classification made by scholars.

Identity, on the other hand, refers to a people's self-designation, the criteria of inclusion and exclusion by which they define their group, and the name or names they give themselves and prefer others to use. For example, black South Africans who want to reject the terms *Native* or *Bantu,* and who seek loyalties beyond traditional ethnicities such as *Zulu* or *Xhosa,* have called themselves Africans.

Of course, this simple distinction between category and identity is not always easy to make in practice. Identities are subject to change, and people possess multiple identities. To illustrate, the women of Phokeng interviewed in the Witwatersrand Oral Documentation Project defined themselves as women, Africans, Tswana, Lutheran Christians, Bafokeng, and elders, depending on the context of the moment. In addition, the identity that a people might regard as most central to their lives is a matter of evolving debate, even of struggle. Such choices are shaped and reshaped constantly in the ongoing political and social developments of any society. Finally, categories and identities can influence one another. For example, black South Africans had no single identity before European colonization. Their consciousness of being *African* becomes possible only when Europeans place them in that category.

These matters come up again and again in the documents in this volume, and awareness of conventions naming is essential for interpreting and understanding them. As one example of the difficulties of defining racial groupings, and of the pitfalls of comparison, American students have trouble understanding the position of the so-called "Coloured people" in South African society. The United States' racial system is usually understood as a two-tier system, and the existence of an intermediate "Coloured" group in South Africa surprises many American students. In thinking about colonial societies, too, they often reduce the situation to a confrontation between two opposed groups, the colonizer and the colonized—again a simplified bipolar model. Given such a model, the case of the Coloured people becomes a disturbing anomaly.

Expecting one story of racial confrontation, students get three, all with different outcomes. They first study the story of settler-Khoikhoi contact, so different from that of the later conflict with the Iron Age Bantu-speakers. Then they discover that it was not mainly black Africans but brown Asians who were imported as slaves. They survey the formation of the Coloured people through the mixing of Khoikhoi, slaves, and Europeans from the seventeenth to the nineteenth centuries.

The historical development of the Coloured population, with its Christian (or Muslim) religion and Afrikaans language, seems fairly clear. But many students, their attention fixed on present-day controversies, are suspicious of this third racial category. Their discomfort is shared by many journalists and scholars, who place the term "Coloured" in quotation marks and add the prefix, "so-called." Noting the imposition of racial categories under the apartheid laws and the efforts of the 1970s Black Consciousness movement to unite all oppressed groups, students often suspect "Coloured" of being an imposed *category,* not an *identity.* This is but one example of the difficulty of understanding a very different historical experience that nevertheless seems so much like our own. South African history abounds with similar difficulties, and requires careful thought and sensitive discussion. In the case of the Coloured people especially, the pitfalls of comparison and the difficulties of unfamiliar terminology intersect.

The Meaning of *Apartheid*

Before discussing another difficult term—*apartheid*—let us pause here to consider problems that can come with thinking historically. From our vantage point in the present, we know the outcomes (to this point) of past historical processes. This makes us vulnerable to several errors of hindsight bias, errors that take special effort to avoid. We commit one such error when we assume that past historical actors had no choices, that the eventual outcome was inevitable. But if they were helpless to control events, then so are we—and few of us would accept this limitation in our own lives. Another form of hindsight bias is to assume that past actors were consciously working toward some much later outcome—that, for example, a nineteenth-century Afrikaner leader was somehow purposefully building toward apartheid society. In presuming long-term purpose, we tend to collapse chronology. It is easy to assume that events decades apart were closely connected as cause and effect, if only because we encounter them on adjacent pages of a history book. These are common errors of historical thinking, but they come up especially frequently in discussions of the origins of apartheid.

Apartheid—the word, the concept, the policy—dominates all discussions of South Africa, particularly the study of South African history. For students as well as the scholars and researchers writing this history, the search for explanations and origins of apartheid dominates the consideration of every period and facet of the subject. Such a preoccupation is not always illuminating.

In many usages, the word apartheid is merely an epithet to express disapproval of racism and white domination. This usage limits our understanding. Even if we all study the past to understand the present, we need to set aside such presentist concerns at times in order to comprehend the past on its own terms.

In the South African past, expressions of racism and programs in pursuit of white domination have taken various forms, and the term *apartheid* does not cover all of them. The frontier confrontations of the nineteenth century and the paternalistic control on preindustrial white farms do not provide plausible precedents for the much later system of apartheid. For one thing, in these earlier periods, whites lacked the massive and efficient power to establish and enforce their supremacy. They often had to accommodate, compromise, and make deals with colonized groups.

It was during the period from 1910 to 1948—often called the era of segregation—that the steady growth of segregationist legislation did lay the foundation for the apartheid regime. Laws such as the Native Land Act of 1913 or the Native (Urban Areas) Act of 1923 became basic building blocks for the later apartheid system. But before 1948, segregation was only a trend and did not yet dominate policy. It had two policy rivals—*baaskap* and liberalism—and segregationists had to compete with proponents of both.

Baaskap is the enforcement of white domination, pure and simple. Under this theory, Africans would work for whites, and any concession of political rights to Africans would send everyone down a slippery slope toward social intimacy. Get rid of the chiefs, break up African landholdings, and forget bothering with schools that only raise false hopes for Africans: these were the battle cries of *baaskap* proponents. Under this system, a black man on the sidewalk, wearing shoes and a hat in the presence of whites, would be knocked down bodily.

Liberalism, by contrast, was more generous. Based on the idea of the spiritual equality of human beings under God, it aimed gradually to assimilate Africans through education. Through spiritual conversion, literacy, and hard work to accumulate individual property, a few Africans under this system would gradually qualify to participate on equal terms in modern society, and even exercise full political rights. White supremacy would be preserved by the gradual nature of the process, with whites as the sole judges of African progress toward civilized standards.

We can understand the dynamics of racial policy in twentieth-century South Africa as an interplay among these three systems: segregation, *baaskap,* and liberalism. The Nationalist victory in the apartheid election of 1948 marked the decisive defeat of liberalism. But before that, liberals had accepted increasing segregation as a way of avoiding the worse realities of *baaskap.* Some scholars have viewed apartheid as a turning of segregation toward *baaskap* goals. The architects of apartheid claimed otherwise, trumpeting it as a generous concession of African rights *in separate spheres.* Indeed, some *baaskap* proponents agreed, accusing the apartheid government of being too generous to Africans.

Apartheid, then, was one policy option among several—the carrying out of racial segregation to its logical conclusions. We can define it as a systematic policy of social engineering by which the doctrine of racial separation was applied to all aspects of South African society. Apartheid started as an electoral slogan of the National party in their 1948 campaign, and it was written into legislation over the following decades.

At the core of the policy lay a system of legally established and registered racial membership for every individual in South African society, The misdirected zeal and determination of the framers of apartheid are chillingly revealed in the definitions of the Population Registration Act of 1950 and its amendments. A white person, for example, was defined in 1962 as

> a person who (a) in appearance obviously is a white person and who is not generally accepted as a Coloured person: or (b) is generally accepted as a white person and is not in appearance obviously not a white person, but does not include any person who for purposes of his classification under this Act, freely and voluntarily admits that he is by descent a native or a Coloured person, unless it is proved that the admission is not based on fact.

Audiences hearing this passage usually laugh at first but then quickly recall the brutality with which the government enforced the system built on the definition.

We can with some irony grant that the architects of apartheid were the world's leading experts on racial classification, but we can also conclude from this definition that they set themselves an impossible task. Rigidly defined biological races simply do not exist. Racial distinctions are socially determined instead. They are akin to what the Southeast Asian specialist and historian of nationalism Benedict Anderson has called "imagined communities"—brought into reality only because people apply the distinctions to social situations. Because our own society makes so much of racial distinctions, not only through prejudice and discrimation but also through positive commitment to racial identities, many people will not or cannot accept this point.

The racial identity enforced under apartheid law in turn governed where individuals could live or own land, what jobs they could seek, what education they could receive, how they could exercise their political rights, whom they could marry or associate with. In a series of draconian enforcement measures, the full weight of the state's power came down on anyone who opposed the policy or the system. The creation of apartheid from 1948 to 1976 is documented in Part 4 of this work; its modification and ultimate repeal are laid out in Part 5.

The National party government ruled South Africa from 1948 to 1994. During this period, South Africa was the only regime in the postwar world whose social system was based on legally sanctioned racism. Proponents wanting to justify the policy, along with critics and activists seeking to condemn and change it, probed the policy's historical roots and origins. History became an important aspect of the struggle, for the interpretations that one espoused influenced one's chance of successfully opposing *or* supporting the system.

For example, one line of interpretation singled out the Afrikaners' unique history and development as the source of a particularly virulent South African racism. The seventeenth-century Calvinist settlers, as the argument went, were a fragment of the more complex ideological mix of Europe. In South Africa, they were isolated from rival viewpoints, and they missed out on subsequent European development—the Enlightenment, the Evangelical revolution with its antislavery corollaries, and the liberating transformation of industrial capitalism. Instead, they faced the challenge of the frontier conflicts with Bantu-speaking Africans—a Christian "chosen people" pitted against the unbelieving barbarian "Kaffirs."

This viewpoint, which dates from the 1930s, is no longer widely accepted, although parts of it are still occasionally stated. In its day, it offered a good deal of utility for several groups. For Afrikaner nationalists, it could be used to show that present-day Afrikaner priorities had the sanction of the people's founding fathers. It also suited English-speaking South Africans and, more generally, liberals in the Western democracies. For them, it singled out the Afrikaners and implied that this virulent racism was a particular Afrikaner problem. Hence overthrowing the domination of Afrikaner nationalism would be enough to return South Africa to a more positive course.

Some observers spoke instead of a conflict between politics and economics. Free enterprise in South Africa labored under inefficient and costly racial exclusions dictated by the political motivations of Afrikaner nationalism. Apartheid was anti-capitalist. Set enterprise free, apartheid critics reasoned, and economic growth would dissolve the pinched, poverty mentality of the nationalists. Free enterprise would mean more jobs for all, and it would no longer be necessary to reserve jobs for whites at the expense of opportunities for African workers. Better jobs for Africans would enable them to become consumers, to the benefit of all participants in the economy. In this line, more unfettered capitalism would overcome racial injustice in South Africa.

In these older interpretations, South Africa was singled out, and critics of apartheid could feel self-righteous about their opposition to racism. In their own society, whatever its problems, they could complacently believe that racism was *not* a legally enforced system but a steadily disappearing vestige of the past.

These historical arguments focused on the early development of white settlement in South Africa, the period from 1652 to 1850, but detailed work on the seventeenth and eighteenth centuries did not bear them out. Early identities and social distinctions were often based on religion, not race. Moreover, seventeenth- and eighteenth-century Cape Colony, slave society though it was, was not segregated but paternalistic, with subtle and complex gradations of status. In frontier areas, whites were too weak to assert their domination. In the frontier zones, where white settlers, indigenous peoples, and mixed-race transfrontiersmen maneuvered for resources and security, there were even alliances that cut across cultural and racial boundaries. The strict, racially based categories with which we are familiar in fact developed only after 1850.

Thus, in the 1960s and 1970s, historians supplanted the older lines of argument with new interpretations, focusing their attention on more recent historical periods. These new analyses, pursued by Marxist and liberal historians alike, depicted apartheid not as a relic from the preindustrial past but as an integral part of industrial and capitalist modernization in South Africa. The revolution brought by the mining of gold and diamonds after 1867 transformed South Africa. Vastly increasing white economic, political, and military power, it decisively ended the independence of African chiefdoms and kingdoms, and drew African labor into the orbit of the modern economy. The birth of the Industrial Age encouraged a whole new way of dividing the South African past.

Periodizing the Past and Shifting Historical Focus

Instead of periodizing South African history in terms of imperial politics—the British conquest of 1795/1806, the Great Trek of 1836, the Union of South Africa of 1910—historians in the 1960s and 1970s began dividing South African history in social and economic terms; that is between preindustrial and industrial eras.

We can note here, however, that any historical period is an interpretive device, not a rigorous reflection of some historical fact. *From the South*

African Past underscores this point by using overlapping periods in the book's five parts. For any reader, creating new periods can lead to new ways of understanding the history.

Revisionist historians in recent decades started looking for the origins of apartheid not in the preindustrial era of frontier wars and of isolated farms' controlling slaves and dependent servants, but in the processes of modern industrial change. Some historians even wrote about the "English origins" of separate development. One corollary of this shift in viewpoint stated that South African racism and white domination seemed akin both to Western imperialism and to American social development. In this view, overthrowing the Afrikaners would not be nearly enough to achieve justice in South Africa.

Other shifts in historical interest and viewpoint accompanied the above interpretations and merit brief mention. The pioneering historians of a century ago, G. M. Theal and Sir George Cory, focused heavily on the history of European settlers; in the 1930s, liberal historians such as C. W. de Kiewiet and W. M. Macmillan added detailed accounts of interaction between Africans and Europeans, recounting especially the conquest and dispossession of Africans and their subsequent entrance into the industrial economy as low paid workers. A new generation from the 1960s on delved far more deeply into the *African* history of South Africa. Examples of this trend are J. D. Omer Cooper's account of the revolutionary changes sparked by the rise of the Zulu kingdom, Shulu Marks's book on the Zulu rebellion of 1906–1908, and Terence Ranger's study of the Ndebele-Shona rising of 1896–1897. The fashion was to write African history from the "inside," emphasizing Africans as historical actors and agents who controlled and shaped their own destiny to some degree.

When Africans are suffering under the heavy burden of oppression under a government based on white domination, students are sometimes surprised to read about the extent to which they can determine their own destiny. Yet this Africanist emphasis on autonomy and effective action has been extended even to contexts of grinding oppression. Taken to their logical conclusion, rival accounts of autonomous African initiatives and of Africans as victims of overwhelming oppression are incompatible, and students are more readily attuned to the latter. For example,. studies of twentieth-century African farmers' lives by Tim Keegan, and of African gold miners by T. Dunbar Moodie, recount lives of some of the most heavily oppressed workers in the world—yet throughout the authors emphasize stratagems for survival, agency, the moral economy, and workers' pursuing their own goals. Readers of these original sources should consider the questions raised by these authors as they examine Africans' lives during the shifting phases of South African history.

Studying original documents can stimulate us to consider and test these and other contrasting historical interpretations. Of course, any selection of documents is incomplete, and what is included or excluded can play a crucial role in favoring one or shutting out another historical argument. Revisions of historical interpretation always derive in part from locating and analyzing new sources, such as the oral testimony of African workers.

But more than one might expect, new historical views arise from fresh readings of the same documents that historians have used since the pioneering days of South African historical writing over a century ago. We read the old sources in the context of present-day realities, asking new questions, and the documents yield infinite and original insights. A collection such as this one gives us a chance to hone our skills and do some historical interpreting of our own.

The distinction between primary sources and secondary accounts seems easy: the former provides firsthand historical evidence, the latter comprises accounts constructed by later writers. This volume promises a look at "original documents," or "primary sources." But the issue is more complicated than that. Documents have many uses, and an individual document's status as "primary" may well depend on how it is being used. The status and value of the information a document may yield needs to come under unceasing critical scrutiny.

The first and most obvious value in these documents is that they provide information about historical events and societies. But it is dangerous to assume that any such documents are transparent windows through which to view the society under study. The glass in the window may be wavy, distorted, or even a little clouded. It may reflect back the images of the observer. An official's diary, for example, might have been written for his superiors partly in order to justify his conduct; or a traveler's account might relate statements made to him by others; or a narrative of a battle might in some ways be a "secondary" account because the author would be criticizing the policies of men who had censored his writings. And of course, any of these accounts may be distorted by racism.

In short, we need to take care in using the documents as windows onto the past. The glass *is* indeed wavy, clouded, and reflecting. Nevertheless, however biased, documents can be used as sources of information; often, no better sources are available. The key lies in using them critically, all the while noting and discussing their dangers and distortions.

In another approach to analyzing documents, biases and distortions can become our direct topic of inquiry. When we study racism, for example, racist documents become primary sources, and the distortions actually point the way to the truth. We now are not peering through the glass but focusing intentionally on the waves and flaws of its surface. In fact, these two uses of the documents cannot be separated; to pursue either inquiry effectively, we need to carry on both.

Still a third approach, commonly described in a different kind of metaphor, is to seek in the documents an expression of one or another "voice." This kind of analysis, fashionable in the early 1990s, views documents as expressions of the identity and perspective of the author, or of the group that he or she represents. According to this approach, the best source for learning about Africans would be a document written by an African. By these standards, a European depiction of Africans is suspect and probably inferior.

Historians' success in finding and using *African* sources for African history has revolutionized the study of African history, and this volume includes many African-generated sources. But beware: African society is heterogeneous, expressing many voices. It is not one voice articulating a single perspective. African documents require the same critical scrutiny as any other primary source. To assume that one African document represents the perspective of an entire people can lead to folly. This is not to devalue African sources but rather to make them more important—and more difficult. In sum, listening for the voices of any group of people in South African society becomes one more valuable approach to documentary analysis, and not a magic key to opening up the deepest secrets of the past.

In the end, whatever answers a document depends on what questions we ask of it. The few uses noted above do not begin to exhaust the richness of any document. One can begin only by posing thoughtful questions. Historical documents call for a kind of reading that many will find unfamiliar. The challenge lies in extracting elusive meaning from the selections, and there are no right answers, no specific body of information to guide us. *From the South African Past* is presented to an American audience in the belief that knowing about South Africa is vitally important in today's world. It is important not only for its own sake but for the way it enhances our understanding of our own society—the comparative theme again. It is important, too, because South Africa's economic involvement with North America, large even now, is potentially enormous. Finally, those whose knowledge and concerns are limited to the present need more than anyone to know the history, especially if they wish to be politically active and to speak out about South Africa. An understanding of present-day South Africa and, in particular, any set of prescriptions and programs for its future, is seriously deficient unless it is built on a knowledge of the history.

Indeed, as we shall see throughout this work, arguments over the interpretation of South African history are closely related to contemporary debates about the future of this troubled country and how it might define and achieve its goals. But more than this, history in its most general sense tells the story of human contention and struggle. We seek it in justifications for our present way of life or justifications for change—a charter or a manifesto. South African issues in particular speak eloquently to American concerns and dilemmas, and can lead us to a new self-understanding through the quest to understand others.

John A. Williams
Stony Brook, NY

From the
South African Past

William Burchell's drawing of Júli, his "faithful Hottentot servant," 1812

PART 1

Settlement and Contact in the Cape,

1652–1857

The history of the Cape Colony in its first two centuries comprises many crucial developments in the unfolding of South African society. Part 1 focuses on the interaction of the European settlers with three peoples in this region: the Khoikhoi and San (sometimes combined as the Khoisan); the slaves imported into South Africa from Asia and other parts of Africa; and the Bantu-speaking Xhosa who faced the Europeans on the Eastern Cape frontier after about 1770. The Xhosa were densely settled, Iron Age mixed farmers, who both kept cattle and cultivated grains. Their use of iron tools and weapons enabled them to expand at the expense of the Khoikhoi pastoralists or San hunters. The origins and background of the Xhosa and other Bantu speakers receive fuller attention in Part 2.

The interaction of Europeans with the Khoisan and slaves gave rise to the formation of the mixed-race Cape Coloured people, who remain an important element in the population of the Western Cape region today. The settler–Xhosa confrontation in the Eastern Cape region set some of the characteristic economic, cultural, and political patterns that still shape South African race relations, even in the postapartheid era. We examine these developments in Part 1.

The Khoisan, in particular the more numerous Khoikhoi pastoralists, were the first people the Europeans met when they arrived on South African shores around 1500. In fact, European sailors had significant contact with the peoples of this region long before the establishment of the first permanent settlement by the Dutch East India Company (VOC, for Vereenigde Ostindische Compagnie) in 1652. Portuguese ships had pushed down the western coast of Africa throughout the fifteenth century. In 1497 Bartholomeu Dias rounded the Cape of Good Hope and discovered the path to India, and in 1502 Vasco da Gama reached India by this route. Over the next century, Portuguese ships passed the Cape of Good Hope with increasing frequency on their trips between Europe and Asia, and after 1600 British ships and Dutch East India Company ships joined them. Ships of all nations stopped at the Cape of Good Hope to partake of its water, fresh meat and produce, and supplies. Contact and trade with the Khoikhoi became a regular feature of these stopovers. Thus when the Dutch East India Company established a permanent settlement at Table Bay in 1652, the Khoikhoi and Europeans already knew one another and, from the first year of settlement, a few Khoikhoi served as translators or cross-cultural brokers between the indigenous people and the colonists.

The new VOC settlement was intended to serve the ships that passed between Asia and Europe. The VOC founders, interested primarily in their commercial business, attempted to restrain the settlement's expansion and to control contact with the Khoikhoi. Indeed, for a few years the VOC maintained a monopoly on all trade with the Khoikhoi. Eventually, the VOC gave a few settlers, or "free burghers" private land grants and soon lost control of the settlement's growth. In the second half of the seventeenth century, immigrants from the Netherlands, Germany, and France (exiled Huguenots) also arrived in the Cape. These settlers, numbering only two thousand by 1717, came to be called Boeren, or Boers (farmers). (Later as they developed national consciousness in the late nineteenth and early twentieth centuries, they styled themselved Afrikaners, the name by which they are known today.) The small number of settlers and the weakness of the external market for Cape products limited the settlement's expansion in the seventeenth century.

Nevertheless, during the eighteenth century the colony's territory burgeoned. By 1677 the settlement began to expand beyond the Cape peninsula. As soon as the settlers advanced past the limited Mediterranean-style, mixed-farming area of the Western Cape, they migrated into dryer country and took up the much more land-intensive activity of raising cattle. Expansion accelerated as the occupation of large cattle farms by succeeding generations of European sons became a birthright. This outward movement stretched the territory's boundaries beyond the VOC government's ability to govern or to register land claims and beyond the Dutch Reformed Church's ability to provide parish organization. By the 1770s the eastward expansion had reached the line of the Great Fish River in what came to be called the Eastern Cape frontier. A more limited and tentative growth extended northward toward the Orange River.

The lands of the Khoikhoi pastoralists were in the direct path of this expansion, and Khoikhoi–Dutch relations formed a dominant theme of early South African history. Despite the small numbers of settlers, the Khoikhoi were no match for the advancing Europeans. Khoikhoi society with its independent hordes and clans gradually disintegrated. European settlements spread to and destroyed Khoikhoi groups farther and farther from Cape Town, and the Khoikhoi population plummeted from approximately one hundred thousand people in the mid-seventeenth century to a mere ten thousand. Khoikhoi vulnerability to European childhood diseases such as measles accounted for most of this decline. The periodic epidemics caused more Khoikhoi deaths than the small wars that the VOC waged against the Khoikhoi.

Such wars and the relentless spread of European settlement wrought other kinds of disruption for the Khoikhoi: the loss of crucial resources and the consequent unraveling of their social cohesion, leadership structure, and cultural continuity. (The destruction of a people does not necessarily only mean its physical death; sometimes destruction means a people's subordination, marginalization, and impoverishment.) As European farmers encroached on and settled a district, they took over the best sources of water, leaving the Khoikhoi unable to maintain their herds. Khoikhoi who survived these scourges took jobs as servants on settler farms. Many children and grandchildren of the subjugated Khoikhoi would be of mixed race, the progeny of unions between Khoikhoi, Europeans, and imported slaves.

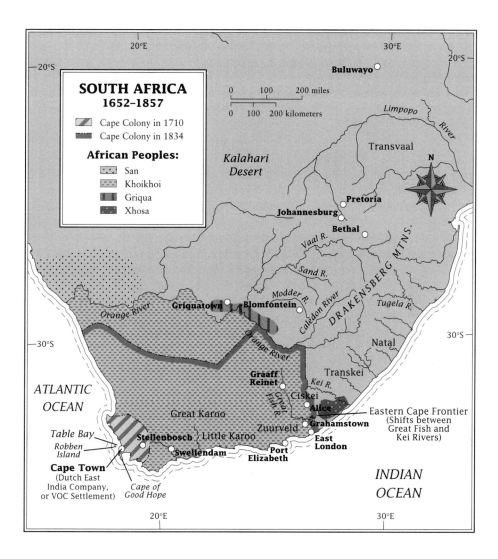

To escape servitude on the farms, some Khoikhoi simply retreated before the European advance and clung to control of their culture and resources for a generation or two longer. Even these retreating groups might already be mixed-race communities that had adopted European language, religion, and the pioneering technology of horses, guns, and wagons. The Khoikhoi groups who withdrew across the Orange River in the late eighteenth century, for example, coalesced into new communities whose members included traditional Khoikhoi, former slaves, mixed-race "Bastaards" (who later called themselves the Griqua), and even a few renegade Europeans fleeing colonial justice.

The history of Cape slavery overlaps the story of the Khoikhoi disintegration. The Khoikhoi servants and imported slaves mingled with the Europeans and with each other to form the Cape Coloured group. Although the Khoikhoi servants were not technically slaves, because the VOC government forbade the enslavement of *indigenous people, their living conditions were often indistinguishable from those of the imported slaves. In remote areas where frontier commandos attacked San bands, killing the men and capturing women and children, the farmers frankly regarded their captives as slaves.*

Overall, however, the slave population of the Cape Colony was imported. The great majority of the Cape Colony's slaves were shipped from Indonesia, with a further element coming from the Malagasy people of Madagascar, off the east coast of Southern Africa. (The Malagasy had migrated from Southeast Asia around the turn of the Christian era.) In addition , as early as 1658, Cape colony settlers purchased a few slaves in Dahomey in West Africa, in Angola in West Central Africa, and in East Africa.

The VOC itself owned many slaves who supplied Cape Town with labor for construction, hauling, dock work, and food production. Indonesian slaves, many of them Muslim, also dominated the skilled crafts of Cape Town. Soon, too, the free burghers became slaveholders, especially in the heavily agricultural region of the Western Cape. In the cattle-farming districts farther east, slaveholding proved less common, although in these regions slaves sometimes worked alongside Khoikhoi servants. By the end of the eighteenth century, the roughly twenty-five thousand settlers of the Cape Colony owned approximately the same number of slaves.

In the early decades of the eighteenth century, the distinction between Khoikhoi servants and imported slaves was especially important. Although the two groups lived under identical conditions, Khoikhoi sevants stressed the difference between their status and that of slaves. In fact, independent Khoikhoi groups often turned back slaves fleeing north or east out of the colony. Gradually, however, these distinctions blurred. The shortage of women among slaves (as among colonists) prompted marriage and sexual contact between the various groups. A mixed-race population that straddled the line between slave and free developed. Equally important, Khoikhoi servants and slaves increasingly made common cause of resisting the harsh conditions of their lives.

After over a century of growth at the expense of the weakly organized Khoikhoi, the colonists came into full contact with the Bantu-speaking Xhosa who lived along the Great Fish River, about five hundred miles east of Cape Town. The region of contact became known as the Eastern Cape frontier. The Xhosa were an expansionist people, expecting to displace or incorporate neighboring groups and to force others to conform to their language and customs. The European cattle farmers thus faced a people roughly their equal in military power across a new kind of frontier. This boundary was unlike the "moving frontier" of North American settlement in which a tide of European settlers steadily advanced as indigenous communities retreated or fell under the onslaught. The Eastern Cape frontier instead served as a permanent demographic line between black and white. The two peoples traded, fought, parleyed, and raided each others' herds. When the Xhosa lost a little ground, they tended to drift back into the districts taken from them. They did not go away, die off, or surrender.

The settlers grappled with independent Xhosa communities on this frontier from the 1770s until the 1870s. During those hundred years, nine wars broke out along this zone of contact. The entire period comprises three distinct parts. From the 1770s to 1812, the "open" frontier was characterized by ambiguity and maneuver, with the possibility of alliances across the racial divide. In this period the Xhosa pursued their traditional methods of dividing their opponents, seeking marriage alliances, and assimilating neighbors. European horses and guns, although new and threatening to the Xhosa, often proved ineffective against them in a country heavily overgrown with bush.

In the second stage, from 1812 to 1857, the frontier closed as the colonial government strove to gain military and administrative authority. British forces built lines of blockhouses, trying to enforce a sharp dividing line between Xhosa and Europeans. The alliances that some Xhosa had made with Europeans now served European, not Xhosa, purposes. The government at times tried to discourage independent settler actions in the contested areas, but it did not achieve consistent success. In these years the military balance shifted relentlessly against the Xhosa, but the decisive defeat of the Africans that many frontier settlers hoped for eluded them until the very end of this period. In spite of losing every war, the Xhosa persisted as a population and a culture, still occupying land that the settlers coveted; still numerous, independent, and militarily formidable, especially as they increasingly acquired firearms.

The question of how to stabilize the frontier and control the African population fueled endless discussion among European missionaries, soldiers, officials, traders, and settlers. The whites analyzed and attempted all the logical options— separation and buffer zones, annexation and conversion of Africans to Christianity and European culture, treaties with African kings, military settlements. Indeed, the heated debate over frontier policy unfolded both in South Africa and in Britain and at times divided South African settlers and British officials. In many documents of the time, the Xhosa and other Bantu-speaking peoples were called kaffirs (caffres or other variant spellings were common). This word means infidel in Arabic. The term has become highly derogatory in the twentieth century.

The third period of development on the Eastern Cape frontier lasted from 1857 to the 1870s. The years 1850–1853 witnessed turbulence and dislocation among the Xhosa. They suffered from the expropriation of their land and from the loss of their cattle from epidemic diseases. Worse, a new prophet, a young woman named Nongqawuse, promised a return of the ancestors and Xhosa victory and recovery if the Xhosa would kill their cattle and destroy their crops. In 1857 enough Xhosa followed these prophecies to bring disaster to the region. As many as thirty-five thousand people starved, and an equal number fled into the European colony to seek work and food.

Thus began a new era of Xhosa dependence on the European economy. Africans working for Europeans was not a new concept; young Xhosa men had long sought jobs in the colony. Work for others, whether Xhosa or European, had traditionally provided a way for a young Xhosa man to gain some economic security. Now such labor increasingly represented a new level of dependence of an entire population on another group. Even so, the Xhosa retained some aspects of independence. Although the colony had an overwhelming military advantage after 1857, it would take another war in the late 1870s to finally end Xhosa political autonomy.

The Eastern Cape frontier throughout this period and beyond became a key locus in which the South African racial system found definition. Amid war and conflict, Africans entered the colonial economy, converted to Christianity, became educated, and qualified to vote. Part 1 documents these developments through 1857.

SECTION A

Khoikhoi, Griqua, and the Formation of the Cape Coloured People

1. Jan van Riebeeck Describes His Khoikhoi Servant, Eva, 1658

The first governor of the Dutch settlement at the Cape of Good Hope, Jan van Riebeeck, kept a journal for his Dutch East India Company superiors. Van Riebeeck served from 1652 to 1662, and his journal is a prime source of information on this period. The settlement in these years was confined to a small enclave on the Cape peninsula, and the various local Khoikhoi groups retained their independence and resources. The Dutch supplied passing ships with fresh meat and produce, but they had not yet accumulated their own herds. Persuading the Khoikhoi to sell some of their cattle and sheep to the VOC became one of van Riebeeck's primary goals. The settlers also tried to use the many conflicts among Khoikhoi groups to their own advantage. At the same time some Khoikhoi, although often afraid to get too close to the Dutch settlement, sought alliance with it.

Only a few interpreters and go-betweens existed. The Khoikhoi woman Eva, who had been educated in the van Riebeeck household, performed such a function. In the following passage from van Riebeeck's journal, Eva carries messages back and forth, living in the European style at the settlement and in Khoikhoi dress among her relatives. She seems committed to serving the Europeans loyally and devotedly. Doman, another go-between mentioned in the passage, is much more suspicious of the Dutch and of Eva.

October 1658

29th In the morning it was still blowing strongly. To-day an ox and 39 sheep were bartered from some Cochoquas with whom the interpreter Eva arrived

From H. B. Thom, ed., *Journal of Jan van Riebeeck*, Vol. 2: 1656–1658, for The van Riebeeck Society. A. A. Balkema, Cape Town: Amsterdam, 1954. pp. 362–367.

at the fort in the evening. She stated that when she left the fort the Kaapmans had robbed her of everything on the way, and that her mother, living with the Kaapmans, had not taken steps to have it restored. Therefore Eva went to her sister living among the Cochoquas. She is one of the wives of Oedasoa, one of the two greatest captains, and had not seen Eva since she was a baby. Eva, who was received with great joy, told her sister's husband, Oedasoa, all about our nation and in particular explained to him our desire to live with them on friendly terms, and also that she had been educated by the Commander's (van Riebeeck's) wife in her house and had learnt our language and also partly our religion, etc. Oedasoa was likewise well-disposed towards us and to prove this had now and then sent some of his men to bring sheep and cattle to us. He desired to enter into an alliance with us, but was prevented by the Kaapmans and Gorachouquas, being afraid that we would help the latter. For that reason Oedasoa did not dare to visit the Commander, in spite of all Eva's efforts to persuade him and the examples adduced by her of the forbearance displayed by us in the face of the serious wantonness and annoyance which we had to endure from time to time from the Kaapmans and the Gorachouquas. On being asked whether it would not be advisable to send Commissioners with presents to Oedasoa, she agreed that it would and added that cinnamon, which the Hottentots had earnestly requested, should be sent, and also cloves, nut-megs, mace and pepper to see whether they liked them also, and the very strongest brandy and tobacco obtainable; also one or two persons who could play on the fiddle and other instruments, as the Hottentots were very fond thereof; in fact, whatever might serve to draw them here and amuse them.

She was told that the interpreter Doman was daily warning us against the Cochoquas, that he stated that they were very hostile towards us and wished to burn down our houses and kill the men, and that he had accordingly requested us to lend him 20 soldiers to make war on the Cochoquas and seize their cattle, as the majority of them were ill at present and they were therefore at their weakest. She replied: "Doman lies. He is a worthless fellow and speaks with a double tongue. He tries to incite the Dutch against the Cochoquas and the Cochoquas against the Dutch." For this reason, she added, Oedasoa did not dare to come here. . . .

The ensign and interpreter have been ordered to do their best to bring Oedasoa to the fort to enable us to treat him even better and bring about an interview between him and the Commander with a view to establishing last-ing friendship, as stipulated in the instructions. . . .

[P]reparations were at once set afoot for the expedition, and the ensign with his 15 men as well as Eva and 4 of Oedasoa's people left at approximately 10 o'clock in the forenoon with provisions for 6 days. They had a pack-ox which carried the presents for the chief of the Cochoquas, consisting of 7 plates of brass, 4 pieces thin wire and 4 pieces thick wire, together weighing 15 lbs., 2 maces of beads of various colours, red, lavender, violet and milky white, and some in strings, $\frac{1}{3}$ gross tobacco pipes, 7 lbs. tobacco, 1 case con-taining 4 pewter flasks of Spanish wine and brandy and another with beer, 100 lbs. of bread in two bags, some cinnamon, cloves, nutmegs, mace, pepper and ginger in paper parcels, as well as some white and black sugar. Eva had mentioned all these articles besides other matters, and neither she nor the 4 men of the Cochoquas wished that any of the Kaapmans or Gorachouquas should go or return with them, but that everything should be done without their assistance, which accorded with our view and was accordingly carried out in the hope that the Lord God would crown this venture with success in the best interests of the Hon. Company.

Meanwhile the Kaapmans tribe did not know what was going on and dared not ask what was the purpose of this expedition. Fortunately Doman was detained on board, otherwise his presence would have been a great hindrance, as he is very impertinent and pokes his nose into everything. When he landed in the afternoon and heard what had taken place, he was very angry and asked why we made friends with the Cochoquas, who were the enemies of the Kaapmans and the Gorachouquas. He was told that we desired the friendship of all the natives living here, without exception, who wished only to trade with us and be friendly. If the Kaapmans and Gorachouquas feared annoyance, they might, as had often been suggested to them, retire behind the Gevelbergen of the Cape where—as we explained—we would protect them, and where—so we hoped—we could confine them. . . .

Doman this morning again visited the Commander and told him that the ensign and his men would certainly never return but would be killed by the Cochoquas, and that we were not to suspect the Kaapmans and Gorachouquas thereof. In reply to this doubtful excuse made in advance, he was told that we knew better, that the Cochoquas and other true Saldanhars only wished to trade with us and desired our friendship, but that if our men suffered the least harm none but the Kaapmans would be held responsible and revenge would be taken against them, so that they should be careful what they did or proposed to do. Doman thereupon said: "Yes, I hear the Commander wishes to make friends with the Cochoquas and all the Saldanhars; this is not good, and it is Eva's fault." He stated that the Kaapmans were very angry with Eva, etc., but admitted that Oedasoa's chief wife was the sister of Eva—a most fortunate thing for the Hon. Company.

Meanwhile Chaihantima, one of the Chainouqua captains often mentioned before, arrived at the fort in the afternoon without any cattle, requesting to be allowed to go on board the ship *West Vrieslandt*. This was granted in order to retain his favour, as he had brought us many cattle some time before, but according to Doman he is partial towards the Cochoquas and only for our sake entered into an alliance with the Kaapmans and the Gorachouquas, as stated before.

Towards evening the ensign Jan van Herwarden with all his men and one of the Cochoquas returned, bringing 3 cows, 2 calves and 19 sheep as a present to the Commander from the great captain of the Cochoquas, named Oedasoa; they had, however, been paid for. The captain had accepted the presents sent to him with great pleasure and had treated our men well. He could not, however, make up his mind to come with them, excusing himself on the grounds that his chief wife was big with child and ill. It appeared that she was own sister to the interpreter Eva. He was a beardless man, elderly, small and thin, very stately and enjoying great authority among his people. It appeared that neither he nor any of his men had ever seen a Christian before. They had asked whether the Dutch chief was also of high descent, and what sort of people they were, and who the ensign's ancestors were, etc. Answers were given as required. The whole night was spent in providing entertainment for the ensign, who entertained them on his part with the fiddle, while a variety of tricks were performed by a certain soldier to the great amusement of the chief and all his people. Only towards daybreak did they sleep a little. After that and the enjoyment of as much sweet milk as the men desired, the party took their leave and our ensign was accompanied by Oedasoa with a following of quite a thousand people a distance of half an hour on the road. The captain declared that he desired to live in friendship with the Dutch Commander and would allow his people to sell as many cattle as they could spare, but as there was not enough pasturage in the neighbourhood for their cattle and water to drink, which the ensign confirmed, they could not come nearer, but if the Commander sent them copper and beads he would allow his people to trade, etc.

The ensign declared that in the army of the States General, where he had long served, he had never seen so many men together, distributed over a number of camps or armies, all equally strong men, living in large round huts made of mats, at least 30 or 40 feet in diameter. Oedasoa had 3 such houses for himself, much larger even, and as full of assegais, arrows and bows as if they were armour rooms. His sleeping place was on a very fine mat in a hole in the ground. Like all the Hottentots he was dressed in skins and so besmeared that the fat ran down his body, which was the highest mark of distinction.

The cattle were so numerous that no end to them could be seen. In half a day they would clear all the pastures within the whole circumference of the Cape and whatever besides the Company and freemen possessed. This morning it was observed that the sheep took 3 hours to leave the kraals [village], and the cattle not less. The latter were larger than any oxen in the Fatherland could be or that he had seen there, being, according to his account, fully $2\frac{1}{2}$ feet broad on the back and buttocks, and so high that he, a very tall person, could scarcely look over the backs of the animals or reach their backs with his elbow. In short, this was a very powerful nation, rich in cattle and able, so they said, to drive the Kaapmans into their holes if they wished. They, however, cared so little for the Kaapmans that they would take no notice of them, unless they became too troublesome. We therefore need not spare the Kaapmans on their account, and if we were inclined to go thither, we could trade freely and openly with them. For the reasons stated they were too far away to visit the fort with such large herds. The ensign further stated that if he had copper and beads with him, though he arrived there late last night, he could quickly have bought a large number of cattle, but he told them that he had come solely with gifts for the chief Oedasoa from the Dutch Commander. He was fetched in by Oedasoa, at whose command his pack-ox was at once driven among the chief's own, and orders were given for the protection of our men and their goods. . . .

2.   Lord Caledon Regulates Khoikhoi Status in the Cape, 1809

The Earl of Caledon (1777–1839) was the first British civil governor of the Cape Colony, holding office from 1807 to 1811. His term of office thus coincided with the abolition of the slave trade within the British Empire, an occurrence that may have focused attention on labor questions. Caledon also commissioned a tour of inspection by Colonel Richard Collins.

Lord Caledon's proclamation regulates the status of Khoikhoi ("Hottentots" in the document) within the Cape Colony. Under these rules, for example, William Burchell (see Document 3) attempted to recruit employees for his travels. The rules are stricter than the more frequently cited Hottentot Regulations of 1828 that so aggrieved frontier farmers in the years before the Great Trek. The later decrees sought to offer protection to the "servants" working for Dutch farmers.

Proclamation

By His Excellency, Dupre Earl of Caledon, Viscount Alexander, and Baron Caledon of Caledon, in that part of the United Kingdom of Great Britain and Ireland called Ireland, and one of the Representative Peers of that Kingdom, Governor and Commander in Chief of His Majesty's Castle, Town, and Settlement of the Cape of Good Hope in South Africa, and of the Territories and Dependencies thereof, and Ordinary and Vice Admiral of the same.

Whereas it appears, that the provisions made from time to time, for securing the fulfilling of contracts of hire between the inhabitants of this colony and Hottentots, are not sufficient for the intended purpose; and, whereas, for the benefit of this colony at large, it is necessary, that not only the individuals of the Hottentot nation, in the same manner as the other inhabitants, should be subject to proper regularity in regard to their places of abode and occupations, but also, that they should find an encouragement for preferring entering the service of the inhabitants, to leading an indolent life, by which they are rendered useless both for themselves and the community at large—

I therefore have thought proper to establish and ordain, and by these presents do establish and ordain:

1. That all and every Hottentot in the different districts of this colony, in the same manner as all inhabitants, shall have a fixed place of abode in some one of the districts, and that an entry of the same shall be made in the office of the fiscal, or the respective landdrosts [local officials], and that they shall not be allowed to change their place of abode from one district to another, without a certificate from the fiscal or landdrost of the district from which

From W. Bird, *State of the Cape of Good Hope in 1822*, Cape Town: C. Struik (Pty.) Ltd., 1966, pp. 244–248 (facsimile reprint).

they remove; which certificate they shall be bound to exhibit to the fiscal or landdrost of the district where they intend to settle, for the purpose of being entered in their office; while every Hottentot, neglecting this order, shall be considered as a vagabond, and be treated accordingly. . . .

4. That the agreement expiring on the last day of the time stipulated in the contract, the servant shall not be obliged to continue his services any longer, but be at liberty, with his wife and children, (if they are with him,) and with all his cattle and other property of whatever nature it may be, to leave the master, and enter another service, or act in any other manner the laws of this colony admit of, without being hindered by the master or any one on his part, on pain of forfeiting one hundred rds., to be divided in three shares, one-third for the treasury of the district, one-third for the magistrate who prosecutes, and the remaining third for the Hottentot thus molested.

5. The master shall be obliged to pay the wage agreed for, strictly on the periods mentioned in the agreement; and that in the case of neglect, upon the Hottentot's lodging a complaint, the case shall be tried by a committee of the court of justice, in the presence of the fiscal, if in the district of the town, and by the board of the respective landdrosts and heemraden [lesser official], if in one of the country districts, which board, upon a summary investigation, shall administer justice; and in case the complaint is well founded, the master shall not only be obliged to pay the servant his wages, but shall, over and above, forfeit all claim to the further fulfilment of the contract; as likewise all claim on account of such necessaries as he may have provided.

6. That before the said committee of the court of justice, and the board of landdrost and heemraden, in the same manner, shall be tried all cases in which a Hottentot lodges a complaint against his master for ill-treatment, when, if upon a summary investigation the fact be found true, the Hottentot shall be discharged from his service, and the master be fined in a fine not exceeding fifty rds. and not less than ten rds. according to the nature of the ill-treatment; and the Hottentot, if found to have urged his complaint wantonly or malignantly, shall receive such correction as the nature of the case shall require.

(This article is not to extend to ill-treatment, accompanied by mutilation or injury done to any part or limb of the body, by which the complainant may be deprived of the use thereof for some time, or for ever; but in these cases, the fiscal or the landdrost shall prosecute according to common law in use in this colony.)

7. That in case the Hottentot, at his own request, shall have been supplied by the master during the term of contract, with clothing or other necessaries, in deduction of the amount of his wages, the nature and value of such supplies shall, at the time of supply, be stated to the ward-master or field-cornet, who, upon the Hottentot's affirming the same, shall make a memorandum thereof, in order to be had recourse to in case of any dispute about the payment of the wages; but in case of the supplies not being stated at the time and registered in this way, no allowance for the same shall be made. This same rule is to be observed, when any claim arises between a master and Hottentot on any other account, during the term of the contract, by which the Hottentot becomes the debtor of the master.

8. That no wine, brandy, or other spirituous liquors, shall be considered as necessaries of life, and consequently no allowance shall be made for the supply thereof to a Hottentot by his master during the period of his employment.

9. That in case it is found, at the expiration of the term of contract, that the Hottentot has been supplied with more than what the amount of the wages he agreed for comes to, the master shall not have any claim, on that account, on the Hottentot's or his family's further services, but shall notwithstanding be obliged to let him or them depart, without any ways detaining him or them, and to prosecute the Hottentot before a committee of the court of justice, in the presence of the fiscal, or the board of the respective landdrosts and heemraden, who, upon finding the claim to be founded, shall condemn the Hottentot to the payment thereof, leaving to the plaintiff to carry his condemnation into effect, *ordinario modo*. . . .

13. That the Hottentots engaged in the manner prescribed in the 2d article, shall be bound diligently and honestly to serve their masters during the period of their contract, and to behave with proper submission; on penalty, that in case any founded complaints about their non-complying with their contract be lodged against them, to the fiscal or respective landdrosts, they shall, by order of the same, be subjected to domestic correction; or if their misconduct deserves a severer punishment, they shall, upon a summary investigation of the case, by a committee of the court of justice or heemraden, be punished with confiscation of the wages due to them, or part of the same, or a temporary confinement, or a more severe domestic corporal punishment, according to the exigency of the case, independent of their being bound to serve out their full time according to agreement.

14. That this however shall not extend to cases where any public criminal offence has been committed by the Hottentots, who are in such cases to be prosecuted by the fiscal or landdrost of the district, in the usual manner,

15. That no Hottentot shall be taken into service without being provided with a certificate, either of his master, or the fiscal, landdrost, or field-cornet, under whose district he did serve, containing a declaration, that he has duly served out his time, or in case he has not served out his time, that he left the service of his former master with proper consent, or upon due authority; while the Hottentots that have been in the military service, must be provided with a legal discharge, before any one whosoever shall be allowed to take them into his service; and any one taking into his service a Hottentot not provided with such certificate or discharge, shall forfeit one hundred rds., one-third for the informer, one-third for the public treasury, and one-third for the magistrate who carries on the prosecution.

16. Lastly, the Hottentots going about the country, either on the service of their masters, or on other lawful business, must be provided with a pass, either of their commanding officer, if in the military service, or the master under whom they serve, or the magistrate of the district, on penalty of being considered and treated as vagabonds; and moreover, the tenor of the proclamation of the 17th of October, 1797, respecting soldiers, sailors, servants, & c. as well as military deserters, is to be strictly attended to, in regard to Hottentots going

about the country; so that every one is to ask a pass from any Hottentot that happens to come to his place, and in case of his not being provided with it, to deliver him up to the field-cornet, landdrost, or fiscal, in order to act as, after due inquiry, they shall feel incumbent to do.

And in order to give the fullest publicity to this my intention and command, besides the usual means of making the same known, I do hereby direct each and every wardmaster of this town, to appoint and assemble one Hottentot from every house in the respective wards, and each field-cornet in the several country divisions, one Hottentot from each house in such division, as early as possible after their receipt of this proclamation, and to explain or cause to be explained to such Hottentots so assembled, the full meaning thereof; and I do further direct the wardmasters and field-cornets aforesaid, to report to his Majesty's fiscal, and to their respective landdrosts, their having complied with this instruction, as they shall answer the contrary at their peril.

Given under my hand and seal, at the Cape of Good Hope, this 1st day of November, 1809.

(Signed)   Caledon.

By his Excellency's command,

(Signed)   H. Alexander, Secr.

3. An English Traveler Praises Júli, a Khoikhoi Servant, 1812

William J. Burchell (1781–1863) was an English traveler and botanist. He lived on the South Atlantic island of St. Helena for a time, traveled in South Africa from 1811 to 1815, and later explored Brazil, making social and geographical observations and collecting specimens wherever he went. His major work is a two-volume account of his South African travels, illustrated with his own drawings. He also wrote pamphlets on emigration to South Africa.

Unlike most nineteenth-century European travelers, Burchell capably portrays the humanity of the Africans whom he encountered. In the following passage, he vividly evokes the personality and family experiences of the "faithful Hottentot" Júli, whom he wants to employ for his journey to the interior. The date is 1812, more than one-and-a-half centuries after the founding of Cape Town. Disease, conquest, and expropriation have disrupted the Khoikhoi who live within the range of the ever-expanding European settlement. Júli represents, perhaps, one of the more fortunate survivors.

William J. Burchell, *Travels in the Interior of South Africa*, Vol. 2, ed. I. Schapera, London: The Batchworth Press, 1952 (first published 1824), pp. 112–116.

It must be explained that the *tronk,* or jail, is the general receptacle, not only of convicted criminals, but of such Hottentots or slaves as are found, improperly or illegally wandering about the country, without a passport, or unable to give a credible account of themselves; and who are lodged there for examination, or until their masters or owners fetch them away. These are commonly called by the colonial term of *drossers or gedrost Hottentotten* (runaways). It is also a refuge for those who, having been illtreated by their masters, fly to the landdrost for redress: these are called *Klagt-Hottentotten,* or 'complaining Hottentots;' and are usually kept employed on the Government works, or set to labor at the drostdy, until their masters can be summoned to appear and answer to the charge. If this is clearly substantiated, the man is either released from his engagement with the boor [Dutch settler or farmer; becomes derogatory; later charged to to *Afrikaner*], or given over to another master, or retained to work as a *tronk Hottentot;* although it often happens, when the *baas's* story is heard, that he is proved to deserve punishment, instead of redress. It may therefore sometimes occur, that among these *tronk volk* (jail-people), there may be good and deserving Hottentots, as well as worthless.

Now, it happened unfortunately for me, that the selection had been made from those of the latter description: as it appeared from the best authority, that before my arrival at Graaffreynet, the landdrost and heemraden had resolved upon dismissing from the jail, nine of the least useful, or rather, the more worthless; because, as it was said, there could not be found at the drostdy work enough to employ them. Several months afterwards I discovered that one of them had been kept in jail for having, after running away from his master, joined another Hottentot of the same stamp, and lived for several months by stealing cattle. It was reported, how correctly I cannot say, that some one had remarked that such men were good enough for the Englishman, as neither he, nor they, would ever return alive. My people were often called the Englishman's *dood volk* (dead men); but they assured me that, although many persons of the village had endeavoured to deter them, by saying that I was going to take them amongst the *menschvreeters* (men-eaters), yet they considered it only as a tale invented for the purpose of frightening them.

Having, on the following day, obtained from the same quarter, the names of such *tronk Hottentots* as were recommended as fit for my journey, and whose courage and fidelity might be relied on, I immediately sent the German with some of my own men, to ascertain if they were willing to be hired. They answered without hesitation that they would gladly engage themselves. On this, I went to the landdrost and requested that I might be allowed to have these men, instead of the five whom I had seen at his house; and at the same time intimated that I had been informed by persons who knew the characters of all of them, that the first set were not such as I ought to trust myself with. His reply was, that he must refer the matter to the heemraaden: which he would do on the following Monday; that being the regular council-day. But in the mean time, he assured me, that the men he had already given, were all trustworthy people, and that, on the contrary, those whom I now wished to hire, were some of the greatest scoundrels in the district.

One of these last Hottentots deserves to be particularly noticed. He had been waggon-driver to Landdrost Stockenström, and since his death, had continued to work at the drostdy. I ascertained that his services were no longer required by that family, who spoke favorably of his character, and that he was resolved if possible to add himself to the number of my party. His name was *Júli*, a man of whose good and invaluable qualities I was not at this time aware, but who, during the three years and four months that he was constantly with me, continued always to gain on my good opinion, and prove by his fidelity, how fortunate I was in taking him into my service. I shall not, in this place, say all that could be said in his favor: as I became gradually acquainted with his value, so shall his character be gradually unfolded in the course of my journal. . . . I hope that the physiognomist will not suffer himself to be misled by the want of European beauty or proportions in a Hottentot face, to suppose that in Júli's countenance may not be seen an expression of real goodness of heart. If he has had the same experience among that race, which I have, he will discover it most clearly.

Júli was a Hottentot of the mixed race; as were also his father and mother. . . . His features do not differ very widely from those of the unmixed race. His age was, probably, nearer fifty than forty; as he was the oldest man of the party, whom I took into the Interior.

His father lived in the vicinity of Algoa-bay, but was killed by the Caffres while hunting in the Zuureveld. The mother, induced by distress at her loss, resolved to quit a district which had been fatal to her husband, and removed with her two children, a girl and a boy, to the western side of the colony. Here she was still more unfortunate; for, falling in the way of a brutal colonist who resided on the river which runs through that tract, he seized her children, then nearly grown up and strong enough to be made useful on his farm, and drove her away from the place, as she herself appeared too old to render him much service by her labor. He therefore procured Júli and his sister to be registered in the field-cornet's books, as legally bound to serve him for twenty-five years; which was in fact to make them his actual slaves for that time. The mother clung to her children, wishing to resist this unjust seizure, and desiring to be permitted either to take them away, or to live on the farm with them; but the farmer repeatedly drove her off, and at last, with a resolution to deter her fom coming there again, he one evening flogged her so unmercifully that she died the next morning! This, and the harsh treatment which he himself received, were sufficient to drive Júli to despair; and he, in consequence, took the first favorable opportunity of making his escape.

This is a tale which he several times repeated to me during my travels; but as the colonist is now dead, it rests alone upon his veracity. Yet as the word of a Hottentot gains, in general, but little credit in the Colony, so has his story, if he ever dared to make a formal complaint: which I believed he never ventured to do. If he or his wife should still be living, when this volume reaches the Cape, I hope there will be found enough humane persons to afford them protection, should they stand in need of any: it will be the greatest personal favor which can be conferred on myself.

Júli and Van Roye, who were acquainted with all the Hottentots at Graaffreynet, had found one named *Platje Zwartland,* who was very desirous of being of our party; and recommended him to me as a steady useful man. He was shepherd and herdsman to a man of the name of *Schemper,* the village butcher, and had been engaged to him for the term of one year, which had already expired some little time before: and although the Hottentot wished to quit him, the master was resolved still to detain him, contrary to a law which expressly provides, that 'as soon as the period for which he has been engaged, shall have expired, all further service shall cease, and the Hottentot, together with his wife and children and all their property, shall be allowed to depart without let or hindrance:' a wise and necessary law, which wants no other amendment than a clause decreeing punishment for the infraction of it.

Plajte informed us, that as soon as the master knew of his intention of going with us, he contrived to get him into a state of intoxication, as he little suspected the cause of his being so liberal with his brandy; and made him in that state promise to continue his servant for another year. Of all this, the man was perfectly unconscious, and declared that he never intended at any rate, to stop with him longer; but that he had always, when asked the question, persisted in his refusal. He seemed much rejoiced at being told that he should go with us, if it could be clearly made out that his story was true.

On the next day, I brought this Hottentot before the landdrost, for the purpose of ascertaining whether he was legally at liberty to enter my service. On searching the official register, nothing was found to prove the truth of the master's assertion, who was present himself; and who, finding that Maré had no power to detain the man, and hoping that the District Secretary could befriend him, referred me to that office: but neither here, could any record of proof be found. The Secretary was exceedingly warm with the Hottentot for leaving the butcher, after having promised to serve him another year; and told me that he had been credibly given to understand that he was truly, though only verbally, hired.

Still, with the strongest evidence against him, the master made another struggle to detain Platje, and persuaded the jailer or *onderschout* (under-sheriff) to send me a note certifying, fortunately for his conscience, not upon oath, that to his knowledge the man, with his wife and five children, was hired for a twelve-month at the Secretary's office, on the last day of May in the preceding year, at the sum of twenty rix dollars: wishing by this, to show that his time had not yet expired. For, after having failed to prove that he was legally, or actually, hired for another year, he thought it would answer his purpose equally well, and prevent the man's leaving the village with me, if he could induce me to believe that the period of service would not terminate till the end of May, at which time, he knew, I should long have quitted the colony.

All these endeavours, only served to convince me of the truth of the Hottentot's story; and as he was exceedingly desirous of making one of my party, and anxious lest he should be detained by the butcher, whom he was resolved at all events to leave, I determined, as much on his account as on my own, to take him with me. I therefore requested the landdrost to sign an order to the Secretary, that he should, if no legal objection could be found, prepare the usual agreement, and register him as my servant. This was accordingly done.

But on the Hottentot's demanding the arrears of his wages, of which he had only received nine rix dollars, his master not only denied his claim, but took from him some clothes, which, he said, the man had not paid for. Platje, the following day, summoned him before the landdrost; the butcher asserted that no money was due; and the Hottentot, who was unable to bring forward any witness, or to produce any written testimony, relinquished his demand, and came away, well satisfied with having gained at least his freedom.

I have related the particulars of this story, with the view of showing more forcibly than bare assertion could do, how useful and necessary a race of men the *Hottentots* are considered by the *colonists;* who feel, and by their conduct prove, that the business of the farms cannot proceed without the labor of their hands. The difficulty which I experienced, not as Graaffreynet only, but in every other part of the colony, in obtaining men for the prosecution of my travels even within the boundary, has, in conjunction with other evidence, convinced me that the demand for them is much greater than the supply: a circumstance which should obtain for this peaceable race every reasonable encouragement, and which must convince the colonists that their true interest consists in securing their fidelity by kind treatment. I do not mean to stand forward on all occasions indiscriminately, as the advocate for the Hottentots against the Boors, nor shall I undertake to defend them against many just complaints made by the latter; for I know that their conduct may sometimes be exceedingly vexatious, and sufficiently provoking to exhaust the patience of their masters. I wish merely to point out how greatly the comfort of both parties depends on a mutual good understanding; and that fidelity on one side, and justice and kindness on the other, are the only means of doing away that mutual suspicion and recrimination, which has so long subsisted between them, and which none but the worst enemies to society and good order, endeavour to cherish and perpetuate. Connected with this question, there exist among the inhabitants of the Cape two opposite parties; and, as I have had numerous opportunities of hearing the opinions of both, and have formed my own upon the evidence of facts only, and the experience of several years, I shall not make to either, any apology for saying, that I believe much blame to be due to both. For, where party spirit exists, there of course, will impartiality not be found; and where there is no impartiality, there of course can no justice dwell: for justice holds an even balance; but partiality, or party spirit, throws a deceitful preponderance into its own scale. A legislature has done but half its duty, when it has made good laws; the other half, is to watch that they are duly obeyed, or enforced.

4. Andrew Smith Depicts the Griqua, 1834

Andrew Smith (1797–1872) was a British army medical officer and later the chief medical officer for the British army. He lived in South Africa from 1820 to 1837. During his stay, he embarked on official expeditions of exploration and inquiry into Xhosa territory on the Eastern Cape frontier in 1824, into the San hunters' habitat in 1831, and across the Orange River and as far as the Ndebele court in the Transvaal on an eighteen-month scientific expedition.

The Griqua community that Smith describes in the following passage was a mixed-race community of Khoikhoi and European ancestry, but people of various origins lived in the region. The Griqua were Dutch speaking Christians who possessed firearms and wagons. They lived like the colonists and enjoyed the support and sponsorship of missionaries from the London Missionary Society. Gaining respect for their authority and property when white settlers came into their districts ranked as one of their primary diplomatic goals.

17th December 1834

On the 17th we found ourselves once more in the Griqua capital just at a most interesting period; for soon after our arrival we had an opportunity of witnessing the proceedings of the court of magistracy and also of being present at a discussion of some importance in the legislative council. When the time for these assemblies arrived considerable bustle was observed in the village and a number of strangers poured to it from all directions. We repaired to the court of justice which was held in a small building chiefly appropriated for legal proceedings. The judge we found to be a respectable looking Bastard, genteely dressed in black clothes and seated before a large table well loaded with papers and record books. At a little distance from him the clerk of the court was actively preparing various documents necessary for the proceedings that were about to commence. In the doorway stood the messenger of the court maintaining order and quiet without, and obstinately refusing entrance to anyone until the proper time of admission. On our arrival the magistrate rose from his seat, bowed respectfully, and made some remark to the clerk which was followed by the latter offering us seats. The preliminary arrangements were then resumed and, when completed, orders were given to admit the populace and to call on the first case, the particulars of which were read aloud. The persons directly concerned were summoned and, on the defendant not appearing, the magistrate inquired if he had been regularly cited. The field cornet of the district in which the man resided was called to answer if the writ had been duly served. He replied by reading the summons aloud and then the defendant's plea to the action which had been entered upon the back of the document. The

From William F. Lye, ed., *Andrew Smith's Journal of His Expedition into the Interior of South Africa: 1834–1836,* Cape Town: A. A. Balkema, 1975, pp. 137–141. Reprinted by permission of A. A. Balkema (Pty), Cape Town.

magistrate next inquired why the man had not been brought by force as, according to the records of the office, the field cornet was empowered to do, this having been the third summons the defendant had received. To this the officer replied he had not understood that the letter he received on the subject justified him to go to that extreme. The magistrate, however, thought the terms too intelligible to admit such an excuse and, therefore, fined the field cornet five rix dollars, desiring a fourth summons to be issued and ordered and the attendance of the defendant to be enforced should he not appear voluntarily.

The next case was as follows: a Griqua lost a horse, and hearing that it had strayed in a direction near which another of the tribe was about to travel, requested him to take charge of the animal should he be able to recover it. The traveller was fortunate enough to find the horse and rode it to a Coranna kraal where he happened to owe a debt he was not able to discharge. The creditor seized the horse as a guarantee for payment and refused to give it up. The owner, who was the prosecutor, therefore prayed the court to adjudge that his friend should either restore the animal or compensate him for the loss. The defendant urged that the horse was never given into his charge and, having been deprived of it by violence, he was not responsible. He then called upon the court for proof of his having been entrusted with the care of the horse and the prosecutor, not having anticipated such a line of defense, had not the necessary witnesses in readiness so that the case was adjourned for their attendance on the next court day.

22nd December 1834

The order and regularity with which the various proceedings were conducted amply justify us in considering that, as far as regards details, the Griquas possess efficient materials for dispensing justice among themselves if they had but an executive government armed with sufficient confidence and furnished with adequate means to meet the necessary expenses should such a measure prove expedient for their general interest.

In the afternoon of the same day the legislative council held its sitting in the principal chamber in the dwelling house of the chief. Eight members were present, in addition to the secretary who was also a Councillor. The chief himself appeared as president and the other members were seated on chairs around a table on which was placed several documents that bore reference to the subjects which were to engage their attention. At first some desultory conversation took place during which allusions were made to the inefficacy of several enactments that had lately been made and to the inadequacy of their present executive to maintain the existing laws: or even to carry on with success the general affairs of the tribe. In proof of this the secretary adduced the case which was that day particularly to occupy their attention. To it, therefore, the president then proposed to proceed.

The principal actor was immediately summoned before them, and, in his hearing the various reports and statements connected with the matter *sub judice* was made known to the council. From these we found that the respondent was a Coranna chief who, together with his adherents, had sometime since voluntarily placed himself as tributary to the Griquas, but had recently manifested a determination to resist the laws of the country and to return to independence, at least his having shown a disposition to oppose the authority of the field cornet of his district was considered sufficiently indicative of such a disposition. The charge having been read over to him, the chief denied having in any way opposed the field cornet in the discharge of his office, but admitted having declared he would not personally submit to the cornet's superiority; a determination he still held. The said field cornet, he here observed, had long been a member of the same kraal as himself previous to their accepting the jurisdiction of the Griquas when he was by birth as well as in other respects that officer's superior. Hence, the chief added it was impossible for him to submit to the orders of an inferior.

On this he was requested to leave the room when the subject was regularly discussed; and enough transpired to convince us of the weakness and inefficiency of the government. The want of a prescribed order of proceeding, such as existed in the magistrate's court, exhibited the many deficiencies under which the nation laboured. Here opinions required to be formed according to existing circumstances, and many collateral subjects were of necessity brought forward the importance of which were to be judged by the knowledge and discernment of the members before any determination could be arrived at relative to what ought to be the course of proceeding in the case.

The discussion brought out ample proofs of their want of confidence in their own governing power as well as the doubts they entertained of support even from their own immediate adherents. All were of opinion that for the interest of the country it was highly necessary that the independent spirit of the Coranna chief should be curbed; though it was clear a doubt existed how that could be effected should extreme measures be resorted to. It was remarked that his own people were numerous, that he was well supplied with implements of war, and that his rebellious spirit was encouraged in no small degree by the numerous colonists who were at the time grazing their flocks throughout his territory whose presence he almost courted and whose favour he had consequently gained. Nevertheless, the council felt they would have power to effect his subjugation provided their own immediate subjects would stand firm to their support: but which, we could clearly see, could not be calculated upon to an extent desirable. Under such circumstances some proposed to sanction the chief's conduct and drop the matter; others thought that he should be required to submit to the field cornet or leave the district and select another where such an objection to respect the government functionary as he had urged in the present instance did not exist. Whatever might be the decision in this case, the council resolved upon insisting that the Corannas generally should acknowledge themselves subordinate to the regularly constituted Griqua authorities.

At this stage of proceedings my own opinion was asked, and amounted to advising them not to threaten the rebel unless they were certain of being able to carry their threats into execution. If they could convince themselves they were in a condition to put them down by force, I thought they should proceed at once to the extreme, if not, that they should endeavour to make him feel the impropriety of his conduct and the injurious effects it must have upon a country in whose welfare he ought to feel as great an interest as the council themselves did, hoping that their observations might lead him to alter his course and endeavouring to convince him that the milder plan was pursued not because they would be unable to carry the harsher measure into effect but from a lenient feeling towards him.

At length the decision arrived at was that the refractory chief should be again called before the council, admonished of the impropriety of his conduct, made to understand the necessity of subordination to existing authorities, and informed he must either respect the field cornet of his district or select some other cornetcy for his residence.

On the second appearance of the chief, I proposed that if it were consistent with their regulations that my view of the case should be communicated to him, to which the council readily acceded. After a series of observations on the disreputable character which transactions similar to that of which he had been guilty would secure for him in the colony, I remarked that if I were in authority over him I should not hesitate to insist upon obedience by force of arms; although I could not but admire the inclination of the councillors to give him the opportunity of discovering his errors and, therby, of saving the lives of his own people as well as those of the Griquas.

He merely observed in reply that he could not submit to the authority of a man who till that time had been always his inferior. Upon this the council informed him that he must either concede to these terms or take up his abode in another part of the Griqua country, on hearing which the chief asked permission to call in some of his retainers whom he required to listen to the decision which was repeated, and neither himself nor his companions made any reply, but, as the business was finished, tacitly left the chamber.

From his manner we inferred that the chief had taken his final departure, but in this we were deceived for in about an hour afterwards he returned in an orderly and becoming manner to take leave of the chief, having done which he paid the same compliment to every person except the obnoxious field cornet whom he passed with the utmost disdain. It was, therefore, clearly to be seen that the principal incitement to rebellion originated in the dislike he cherished for that functionary, and it will generally be found that the chief's principal sources of disturbance in primitive societies originated more from solitary individuals than from the government of the country. It was easy to be inferred from the remarks afterwards made that none of the legislators entertained any special hopes that a change would result either in the conduct of the Coranna chief or in his place of abode. Here the discussion ended and the council proceeded to other business.

The system of surreptitiously depriving the Bushmen of their children was next discussed and stigmatized as not only highly unjust in itself, but, in the opinion of the council, extremely impolitic, inasmuch as it seldom failed to incite [t]he parents to revenge. Instances were adduced of such robberies, committed not only by the Griquas, but colonists; and, as it mattered little to the Bushmen to what nation the kidnappers belonged, it was considered extremely necessary to prevent it if possible from being practised. As a consequence of the system, it was stated that a Griqua subject while travelling with his horse-waggon had been attacked and wounded by a party of Bushmen who, after plundering the waggon, shooting seven of the horses, and disabling the eighth, assigned as a reason for the attack that the Boers, Griquas, and Corannas, through possessing horses, were better enabled to carry off the children of the Bushmen, who were determined not to leave a horse alive.

For such disclosures we were not unprepared as not many days previous we heard at a village we passed that a number of Bushmen had gone through it on their way to the colony to endeavour to regain some children stolen from them by a party of colonists. They entertained but few hopes of success feeling, as they expressed themselves, that justice was slow in reaching offenders when Bushmen were the aggrieved parties. Connected with this subject, the case was also mentioned of the sale of a Caffre lad, who had been bought for a trifling remuneration and carried into the colony. The remarks made during this discussion were in strong reprobation of the practice; yet it was evident that there was no prospect of this government being competent to check it, and, as the difficulties appeared insurmountable, the subject was almost insensibly dropped and another commenced.

The establishment of the two German missionaries with Pit Whitefoot appeared to have for some time caused some anxiety inasmuch as the council was the probability of an independent community springing up within their jurisdiction. All the councillors maintained that this new establishment was unfortunately situated, being either too near Philipolis or not near enough—too distant to effect its connexion with the missionary station at Philipolis and too near to admit of being tolerated as the foundation of a separate independence, especially owning so turbulent a head as Pit Whitefoot. It appeared that some of the councillors feared when first the station was selected that what was now threatening would be attempted, having observed that, generally speaking, an independent demeanour was assumed by the principal of a kraal or district as soon as it became the residence of a missionary. What was to be done seemed difficult to decide, but at last it was determined that the recently formed establishment should be considered as a branch of the mission at Philipolis, its inhabitants be ruled by the Griqua government, and that an answer to that effect should be dispatched to those who had intimated a wish for its independence.

These were the principal subjects that occupied the attention of the Griqua legislative council on the 22nd December 1834, at which no stranger could have been present without feeling that all that was required to make the Griqua nation an orderly and flourishing community was simply a little more strength in the executive government and a systematic mode of levying an adequate revenue to meet its expenses.

The necessary stamina might long ago with safety have been infused into the Griqua government by that of the colony at no greater expense than merely giving decided countenance to the orderly and well conducted and awarding certain advantages—valued by the whole nation—to them alone. But of this, more hereafter.

The friendly feelings entertained for the colony by this tribe and the respect evinced by them for the colonial laws were often witnessed in the course of the sitting. Frequent inquiries were made of the secretary, Henrick Henricks, who, be it understood, besides being son-in-law of the chief was the oracle of the council, as to what would be done in the "*Colonie*" in such and such points, and doubts were often expressed whether certain decisions were in keeping with the colonial laws. The Cape Town newspapers regularly reached Philipo-land and the reports of its legislative council and legal proceedings are sedulously studied at least by the secretary, who is never backward in quoting them as precedents.

5.   Two Missionaries Compare the Tswana and the "Bastaards," 1834

Thomas Arbousset (1810–1877) arrived in South Africa in 1833 as a missionary of the Paris Evangelical Missionary Society. François Daumas (1812–1871) joined Arbousset in 1835 and accompanied him on a tour of South Africa in 1836. The two men searched for the best place to establish their mission, and their book provides vivid descriptions of the peoples to the north of the colony beyond the Orange River. Arbousset and Daumas subsequently became missionaries to Moshoeshoe's Lesotho (see Part 2), with a station (missionary settlement) at Morija. The following extract reveals an interesting contrast between the Tswana people, as yet relatively little influenced by the European presence, and the "Bastaards."

New Platberg numbers about 200 inhabitants, who, thanks to the strictness of Wesleyan discipline, and to the zeal and energy of their spiritual instructor, have made no small progress in the christian life. It presents a religious aspect much more satisfactory than many a village in Europe. The day of rest is, generally speaking, well observed; the attendance on the sanctuary is in general numerous, attentive, and devotional; the meetings for prayer on the sabbath, and in the course of the week, are well attended. Oftener than once have we been surprised and refreshed by hearing the more advanced members of the church speak of their spiritual feelings with that simplicity which is so characteristic of pagan converts:—"I am a dull fellow. I understand very little of the holy truths. I have only a little love to the Lord Jesus Christ." Such is the simple way in which they express themselves in conversation, whether with one another or with strangers. The schools, also, although organised on no particular plan, present a satisfactory appearance. They follow, as they can, the

T. Arbousset and F. Daumas, *Narrative of an Exploratory Tour to the North-East of the Colony of the Cape of Good Hope*, Cape Town: C. Struik (Pty.) Ltd., 1968, pp. 9–13.

plan of mutual instruction. In the class, as in the house, the more advanced instruct the more backward; many read fluently, and begin to write; thay can also repeat many portions of the sacred volume.

The inhabitants of Platberg are Bastaards,—a designation we can never use without a painful feeling. It speaks the depravity of man; and it reminds us that wherever Europeans have carried their civilization and their industry, there they have also carried their vices. South Africa has her Bastaards, and South America her Mètis. In every country colonised by Europeans we find a mixed race,- a living testimony to the sin of their fathers. But leaving such painful reflections, we shall endeavour to make our readers acquainted with these men, with whose designation they may be familiar, but of whose character, perhaps, they know little.

The Bastaards sprung from the intercourse of the dutch settlers with the Hottentots, who originally inhabited the district of the Cape. Very few of them are the fruit of legitimate marriage, although the law of the Cape prohibiting the marriage of settlers with natives, was not passed until 1804, and, if we mistake not, it has been long since repealed. It is, then, in the ordinary sense of the term that they, or their fathers, were first called Bastaards. When these unfortunate children of the Boers had so increased as to make the white man tremble for his safety, they were driven beyond the boundary of the colony, towards the interior of the country. The greater part of them then crossed the Orange River, and located themselves in the neighbourhood of the spot where Philippolis now stands; and spreading themselves thence to the north and to the east, they are now to be found as far as Platberg, in which district some thousands of them reside. Amongst themselves they take the designation Binnelanders,—*Inhabitants of the Interior.* They have continued the use of the dutch language, cherishing at the same time, however, inveterate hatred towards the colonists.

The Bastaard is of middling stature, and rather thin in his person; he is of a tawny complexion; his hair is less crisp than that of the negro; he has a flattened nose, sunken cheek, high cheekbone, small eye deeply set, and a flat forehead—the distinctive characteristics of the hottentot race. He has no beard; a little down grows upon his upper lip, but seldom on the cheek or the chin.

In moral character he inherits the phlegmatic temperament of the dutch colonist, and the idleness of the Hottentot. Anger alone can rouse him from his habitual sluggishness. But when that passion animates him, he is a true Hottentot,—treacherous, malicious, and passionate,—and he gives himself up to unrestrained rage and revenge.

His habits are, in general, gentle and peaceful. His usual occupation is the rearing of cattle, or the cultivation of a narrow strip of corn, or of a small vegetable garden, which, if it furnish little produce, requires little care. Often out hunting, and often visiting his friends, he is exempt from avarice and ambition; and he gives himself little trouble to acquire riches, or to lay up an inheritance for his children. He has few wants, and he only looks after the absolute necessaries of life for himself and his family. If he can procure milk, some heads of indian corn, a sheep for slaughter from time to time, and occasionally an antelope, and moreover an ox to exchange with some travelling merchant from the colony for tea, or tobacco, or a piece of damaged cotton print, all his desires are satisfied. He has no further ambition. He can live; and he wants the energy necessary to lead him to seek to better his circumstances.

During his leisure time, and of that he has abundance, he finds a pleasure in lounging about the house of his missionary, whither he goes.—sometimes with, but oftener without, an object. It is seldom, if he be a pious man, that he has not some spiritual malady of which to complain to his religious instructor:—"Oh, how my peace is dried up! Oh, how cold my heart is!" Or he speaks of his debts and his loans, or oftener still of his horses and his cattle. And, if at the moment the bell summon the worshippers to the sanctuary, thither also he goes most willingly; for all possess a respect for religion, and all are more or less acquainted with its doctrines and its duties; and some, though unhappily their number is limited, love and practise these. But their habitual nonchalance is carried into their piety,—preventing its development, and paralysing its effects.

If such be the character and dispositions of those of the Binnelanders who live at the missionary stations, what can be expected of those who live on farms, or in solitary dwelling places, far from the salutary influence which these stations exert? Rude and ignorant, having little intercourse with their fellow-men, and subjecting their conduct to no law but that of their own judgment, or their own caprice, they are as despotic and as depraved as were the dutch farmers of the colony. They are subject to their chief; but they yield to him a very stinted submission. They are nominally governed by law; but their laws are obeyed neither by those for whom they were designed, nor by those who ought to see them enforced.

Those who are easy in their circumstances, and pique themselves on their civilisation, dress in european style; but many still wear the kaross, or cloak made of skins of the sheep or the jackall sewed together. The same incongruity is seen in the structure of their houses; some build them of raw brick or of clay, on a plan which is simple, and not unhealthy though very incommodious; but others content themselves with a narrow, low and smoky hut formed of mats, and into this the people and their household utensils are huddled together in the most disgusting confusion.

Brought to a state of semi-civilisation, the Bastaards are now stationary; or their progress in farming and in the mechanical arts is at best so slow that it is almost imperceptible; so that we should not be astonished if the Bechuanas [Tswana], who are as yet far behind them, should some half century hence overtake and outstrip them in the march.

In character the Bechuanas have greatly the advantage of them. They are more energetic, more resolute, more enterprising, and more persevering. There are bechuana tribes who already cultivate the ground better than do the Bastaards, and others among whom the people are more industrious than they. The bechuana female would by her diligence put the bastaard female to shame. The former is active and laborious, the latter is indolent in the extreme. The bechuana female undertakes, it may be said, the whole work of the house, the charge of the children, the cares of house keeping, and the cultivation of the ground. The bastaard female devolves the whole of these upon her bushman servants, who occupy a middle station betwixt that of slaves and that of domestics; she never leaves the house, and rarely quits the chair in which she lolls the live-long day; the utter inanity in which she passes her days does not prevent her from professing a sovereign contempt for her bechuana sister.

6.   The Treaty Between Sir Peregrine Maitland and Adam Kok, Chief of the Philippolis Griqua, 1846

Establishing treaty relations with African states beyond the Cape Colony's boundaries was one way to stabilize the frontier districts. Attempts to prevent settlers from venturing beyond the boundaries had often failed, and annexations to incorporate new settlements were expensive. The quest for stability through a treaty system coincided with missionary hopes that the Griqua state would become a "missionary kingdom" of steadily advancing "civilization." The treaty days represented the apogee of Griqua efforts to retain their independence. In the 1860s the discovery of diamonds in their territory would dash their prospects of maintaining autonomy.

The Governor aforesaid and the said Captain Adam Kok, for the purpose of settling the relations between the subjects of Her Majesty resident in the territory and the said Captain, in such a manner as to preserve therein peace and order, by protecting the quiet and well-disposed, and controlling the turbulent and ill-affected, have consented and agreed to the following articles, where they hereby respectively ratify and confirm:

Article 1. The absolute dominion of Captain Adam Kok over all the land hitherto received and regarded as belonging to him, or to his people, is hereby unreservedly recognised by the Governor, on the part of Her Majesty the Queen.

2. Without prejudice to this recognised right, Captain Adam Kok engages to make hereby a division of his territory into two portions: one division to consist of land in regard to any part of which it shall not hereafter be competent for Captain Adam Kok, or any of his people, to grant leases, or make sales, or give any right of occupation to any British subject, or generally, to any person of European birth or extraction; and the other division to consist of land which may be let on lease to British subjects, and all others indifferently; all leases to British subjects, however, to be made in the manner and under the conditions hereinafter referred to.

From G. W. Eybers, *Select Constitutional Documents Illustrating South African History, 1795–1910,* New York: Negro Universities Press, pp. 261–269.

3. Persons who are by the last preceding article prohibited from hiring or purchasing lands in the first or reserved division of the Griqua territory, may, with the express permission of the Colonial Government, but not otherwise, and then only for the purpose of religious teaching, or that of trade or business, receive leases of houses and buildings, or of building-erven, situated in the said division.

4. Captain Adam Kok binds himself, for the purpose of this treaty, to recognise as British subjects all persons of British or Colonial birth or extraction, whether born within the British dominions or not. . . .

8. It shall be the duty of the officer styled British Resident amongst the native tribes to the north-east of the Colony, as lately appointed by the said Governor, to exercise constant vigilance in regard to the state and condition of the Griqua territory, so as to secure the tranquillity thereof, to represent Her Majesty's Government upon the spot, to enforce order amongst all British subjects resident in any part of the Griqua territory, to prevent or punish all crimes or injuries meditated or committed by any such subjects, and generally to inquire into, and determine, all disputes which may arise between emigrants and Griquas, so as thereby to maintain peace, and remove all occasion of mutual apprehension and distrust.

9. In order as much as possible to co-operate with the Colonial Government in carrying out such measures as shall be necessary for the preservation of law and order amongst British subjects and all others resident in the territory of Captain Adam Kok, the following articles and provisions are consented to and agreed upon: . . . .

12. The British Resident shall have, in regard to crimes and offences committed by British subjects in any part of the Griqua territory, the like jurisdiction in all respects as a Resident Magistrate of the Colony has under, and by virtue of, the Ordinance No. 33 of 1827 in regard to crimes and offences committed within the district or place for which such Resident Magistrate shall have been appointed.

13. The British Resident may, in the exercise of the summary jurisdiction in the last preceding section mentioned, sentence any offender, when convicted, to be punished by fine not exceeding *10l.,* or by imprisonment, with or without hard labour, for any period not exceeding six months, or by such fine and such imprisonment together, as to such Resident shall seem meet. . . .

17. Captain Adam Kok engages to co-operate with the British Resident whenever so requested by him, and to give to the said Resident every support in his power in the discharge of the duties belonging to the office of such Resident. And should it so happen that part or the whole of a spot of ground which the British Resident may hereafter select for the purpose of erecting a residence shall fall within the territory of Captain Adam Kok, the said Captain hereby binds himself to allow possession to be taken and kept of such ground for the above-mentioned purpose, as long as it shall be required for the same.

18. Any act or proceeding injurious to person or property which would be a crime or offence if committed by a British subject against a Griqua, shall be deemed to be a crime or offence when committed by a Griqua against a

British subject,—and Captain Adam Kok hereby engages to have any Griqua so offending tried and punished.

19. Captain Adam Kok engages, upon complaint made to him, to cause any Griqua accused upon reasonable grounds of having committed any such crime or offence, to be secured for trial,—and the British Resident is hereby authorised to require Captain Adam Kok to fulfil this stipulation.

20. The British Resident shall be entitled to attend and be present at the trial by Captain Adam Kok, or such other person as may by him be deputed for the purpose, of any Griqua accused of any crime or offence committed against any British subject; but the said Resident will not interfere with the proceedings at such trial, otherwise than by offering such suggestions touching the right and proper conduct of the same as may seem to him to be fit and useful.

21. Whenever any Griqua shall be convicted of any such crime or offence as aforesaid, such punishment shall be awarded as Captain Adam Kok, after consultation with the British Resident (should he be at or near the spot), shall deem to be just and proper under the circumstances of the case.

22. All questions or disputes of a civil nature in which any Griqua shall bring a claim or demand against any British subject resident in the Griqua territory, shall be heard and determined by the British Resident, according to right and justice; and the contracting parties respectively hereby authorise and empower the said Resident so to do, and to enforce any decision by which he shall adjudge any British subject to pay or deliver over to any Griqua, any money or other thing, by distress and sale of the property of the person making default.

23. The British Resident shall, in regard to the manner of summoning any British subject to answer any such claim or demand, and to the summoning and compelling the attendance of witnesses, and to the manner of proceeding in the hearing of the case, to the mode of carrying his judgments into execution, and generally, in regard to the exercise of the civil jurisdiction hereby conferred upon him, act according to, and carefully observe, all such rules and regulations as shall be provided for, or prescribed to, him by the Governor aforesaid, which rules and regulations the said Captain Adam Kok engages to ratify, confirm, and establish as law within his territory.

24. All questions and disputes of a civil nature, in which any British subject shall bring any claim or demand against any Griqua, shall be heard and determined by Captain Adam Kok, according to right and justice, who engages to obtain redress for any British subject injured. . . .

28. For the purpose of this treaty, it is consented and agreed by the contracting parties, that the term Griqua shall comprehend and embrace any person who is, by birth or residence, under the authority of Captain Adam Kok.

29. The British Resident aforesaid shall be charged with the duty of settling, in conjunction with the parties interested, the conditions and duration (not exceeding forty years) of all intended leases to be granted to British subjects, of any lands situated in the territory in Article No. 6, and shall also be bound to preserve a counterpart of every such lease, and to transmit without

delay, both to the Colonial Government and the Chief of the Griquas, an abstract, showing the particulars of the same. But no such lease shall be capable of being assigned—nor shall the land leased be capable of being sub-let without the consent of the said Resident.

30. Upon every such last-mentioned lease shall be reserved a certain annual quitrent, which quitrent shall be payable to the British Resident, who shall be furnished by Captain Adam Kok with all necessary powers for recovering the same.

31. One-half the amount of all such quitrents shall annually be handed over to Captain Adam Kok, who, as often as by Griqua law or custom any of his subjects shall, as being the owner of any of the lands out of which any part of such quitrent shall have arisen, be entitled to receive any proportion of the amount so handed over, shall satisfy the demand of his said subjects according to their rights.

32. The remaining half of the said quitrents shall be retained by the British Resident, and be accounted for by him to the Colonial Government, and shall be applied to defray, as far as it will go, the expense of his establishment, together with that of a certain protective force which it is intended to form and place under his control, for the suppression of violence and crime, and maintenance of just authority. . . .

39. Captain Adam Kok upon his part engages, as often as he shall be so required by the British Resident, to arm, and place under the direction of that officer, such a number of his subjects, not exceeding 300 men, as shall be demanded by the requisition of such officer; which force shall remain at the disposal, and act under the orders, of the said officer, so long as he shall deem necessary, for the purpose of assisting to preserve peace, and repress violence and outrage, either in the territory of Captain Adam Kok or in the territory of any neighbouring tribe or nation, which tribe or nation shall itself be bound by treaty to furnish in the same manner, and according to its strength, a contingent force of the same character.

40. The Colonial Government, besides organising such a force under the command of the British Resident as shall be considered necessary, will hold itself at all times prepared, should an exigency arise, to march troops for the purpose of crushing any attempt upon the part of any portion of Her Majesty's subjects to contravene by violence any of these regulations, or resist the due authority of law, and of protecting the Griqua people while acting justly and inoffensively in the full enjoyment of their rights, their privileges, and their lands.

This done at the Government House, in Cape Town, this Fifth Day of February, in the Year of Our Lord One Thousand Eight Hundred and Forty-six.

7. Colonel Richard Collins Recommends Imperial "Benevolence" Toward the San, 1809

The history of the San hunters' contact with European settlers differs somewhat from that of the Khoikhoi peoples examined in the preceding documents. The San lived in small groups and moved frequently. Their relations with their pastoralist neighbors, both African and European, often proved rocky. Cattle owners, whether African or European, launched punitive raids against the San when the hunters stole livestock. As European settlers proliferated and became better armed, such raids approached genocide.

In the following report Colonel Richard Collins reveals a good deal about settler-hunter relations and about European conceptions and misconceptions about the San. From this passage, we might infer the likely consequences of Collins's ostensibly benevolent intentions toward the San. We might also calculate whether his policy ideas would likely be carried out.

Collins's Report on the Bosjesmen [San]. [*Omitted in the Parl. Papers.*]

My Lord,—Conceiving that the object of your Excellency's instructions might be greatly promoted by a personal communication with some part of the Bosjesmen nation, on arriving at the Hantam, I engaged as an intrepreter, a Bastard Hottentot, named Jan Tites, who speaks one of the dialects of their language, and had been visited only a few days before by one of their chiefs named Rouman. . . .

It was not to be expected that such multitudes of savages of the fiercest disposition, dispersed through such a vast extent of country, in no part of which they have a settled residence, and from which they plunder their neighbours in every direction, without the idea of any law, divine, or human, without any connection among themselves, except such as arises from the ties of parental or conjugal affection, and even without the least knowledge of the manner of cultivating corn, or rearing cattle, should at once become tractable, abandon their roving and predatory mode of life, allow themselves to be confined between the Zak River and the Karee Mountains, acquire a knowledge of the art of agriculture or the precautions for preserving and increasing herds and flocks, feel all the advantages of permanent establishments and social intercourse, and consider themselves under the protection and authority of the British government. . . .

Two or three missionaries at each station, superintended by a couple of the most respectable and intelligent inhabitants of the division, might answer the purposes of direction and instruction. It would, perhaps, be proper that

From Donald Moodie, *The Record, or a Series of Official Papers Relative to the Condition and Treatment of the Native Tribes of South Africa*, Part 5, Amsterdam & Cape Town: A. A. Balkema, 1960, pp. 33–35 (photostatic reprint).

the landdrosts should be directed occasionally, to inspect and report upon the state of the institutions at the first and last places; but the second, placed between two districts, should be independent of both, although subject, as well as the others, to an annual visit from the seat of government. This plan, would, I think, create a degree of emulation in the several establishments that would produce the happiest results.

The appointment of superintendents of the missions, is a matter of great consequence. The Bosjesmen are well acquainted with the individual character of the farmers in their neighbourhood; of whom such only should be selected as they fear, respect, and confide in. Those who appeared to me best qualified for the purpose in the districts through which I have travelled, are Mr. Jacob Louw, the elder, of Under Bokkeveld, and Mr. Jacobus Nel, of Under Roggeveld. They are both conveniently situated to superintend the western mission. The former might make arrangements for collecting a proportion of sheep and cattle to be supplied for the use of their mission, by the inhabitants of Kamies Berg, Under Bokkeveld, and the Hantam; the latter that of the Roggevelds; a subject that I shall shortly observe on more fully. I beg leave also to mention, that I have heard of a farmer named Klerk, an inhabitant of the Koup, whose family employ a great number of Bosjesmen in their service. He might, perhaps, be a fit person to act as a superintendent of the central mission, for which, I should imagine, a second might easily be procured, as well as two more for the eastern mission. Greater attention should, if possible, be directed to the selection of missionaries and superintendents for the middle institution than the others; not being under the inspection of a landdrost.

I have already mentioned several friendly kraals situated near that part of the country which I have visited, and I have been told that others are to be found on the borders of the Koup and of Sneeuwberg, where they frequently engage in the service of the farmers. I should hope they might be induced to join the establishments, of which they would serve as the foundation. Their captains should be permitted to retain their rank, and be allowed some trifling pay, which might be procured by placing them on the strength of the Cape Regiment.

The expence of cattle and sheep would be cheerfully defrayed by the farmers of the districts on the borders, who would rejoice at any plan tending to rid them of the depredations of the Bosjesmen, and procure them servants. The subscription might be settled, as already observed, by the superintendents, according to the stock of each farmer, and for that purpose thay should be invested with the necessary authority. By proper regulations these institutions might be enabled hereafter to support themselves, but I see no mode of raising the sums necessary to establish them, unless they are supplied by government or the societies to which the missionaries belong. However willing the Hernhuters might be to contribute their personal exertions, I think they would be averse to incur any pecuniary responsibility in this undertaking, as it was not without considerable hesitation, they commenced the institution at Groene Kloof; owing, I believe, to the difficulty of communicating with

Germany, in consequence of the war, which they fear also may have rendered their constituents less able to afford the means of support.

When the means of commencing these institutions are provided, there should be at each mission a depot of such things as the Bosjesmen may wish for, which should be given to them only in exchange for skins, mats, ostrich feathers, ivory, or other articles, among which may be mentioned some curious stones that are found at the Orange River. Ostrich eggs should never be purchased, in order to encourage the increase of those birds. This commerce would not only serve to give the Bosjesmen employment in their own country, but also to familiarize them with the missions, which they would thereby be the more inclined to join. It would assist to defray the expences of the institutions, an object that would also be greatly promoted by instructing the rising generation in mechanical arts, as the farmers also might then be supplied with many things, that they must procure, with considerable inconvenience, from Cape Town. This has been too little attended to at Grace Dale, and is the principal cause of the great expence of that establishment, which according to its present plan can never support itself, having no revenue except 3 or 400 dollars annually, produced by the knife manufactory. The most economical mode of procuring tradesmen, would be to get them from the army. They would also serve to maintain the police of the missions, and to defend them against the hostile Bosjesmen, and would be consequently employed in the line of their duty. If they conduct themselves satisfactorily, on their regiments being ordered from the colony, they should be transferred to others, which might give substitutes for them. Married men would be preferable, as their wives might be useful in instructing the girls in needlework, housekeeping, and other occupations.

As the population of the missions increases, the superfluous inhabitants might be gradually introduced into the colony, where their labour is much wanted, and particularly in the grazing districts, in which the difficulty of procuring Hottentots, who are there preferred to slaves, is very great. Their introduction would be promoted by the humane manner in which the farmers treat their servants, at least, in the districts that I have visited, where they are paid by a determined quantity of clothes, by food for themselves and families, and a certain number of sheep and cattle annually. This observation may appear extraordinary to those who have been led to entertain opinions of a contrary nature on this subject, opinions that the writings of the celebrated traveller, already alluded to, have served, more than the demerits of the farmers, to produce. I conceive that gentleman justly entitled to the esteem and gratitude of the public, for many just observations and valuable communication concerning Southern Africa, but in almost every thing that respects the farmers, and particularly what relates to the manner in which they treat their servants, I think he has shown the most unjustifiable prejudice, as I invariably observed them behave in the kindest manner to the Hottentots, who show them an attachment that was strongly marked by some circumstances that occurred on my late journey, an attachment not a little extraordinary, as in the service of the farmers on the borders of the colony, they are exposed to suffer, not only the severest hardships from excessive fatigue and inclemency of weather, but also the most imminent dangers from the Bosjesmen and beasts of prey.

The practice of subscribing sheep and cattle for the Bosjesmen, except for those belonging to the missions, should be put to an end. It tends to make them suppose that the colonists fear them; and besides, it would be impossiblt to supply all their nation with a sufficient number for its consumption, even were they careful of them, which they are not; and by giving them to those on the borders, such as are more distant are induced to come nearer, and consequently increase the evil.

I think the Bosjesmen should not be allowed to have any communication with the colony, except through the missions. The farmers are naturally averse to their visits, as they come merely for the purpose of discovering where they can rob with the greatest facility; and, at all event, it is a tax which falls on those who are least able to support it; their poverty forcing them to settle in the remotest part of the colony.

In return for the sheep and cattle supplied to the missions, I think the farmers should be furnished with an increased allowance of ammunition at the price paid by the government. The expenditure of powder is very considerable in that part of the country, occasioned by the necessity of arming the shepherds in all weathers, to be prepared against the attacks of the Bosjesmen and lions, and of placing trap guns for beasts of prey, &c. It might also, perhaps, be advisable to supply each farmer with the means of sending up rockets in the event of night attacks from the Bosjesmen as a signal for their neighbours to repair to their assistance.

There should be some regulations made as to the manner of repelling the attacks of the Bosjesmen. I think that when the habitations of the farmers are attacked, or their cattle stolen by them, they might be permitted to follow them as far as the borders of the colony, and put the robbers to immediate death. But they should not be allowed to proceed further without a reference to authority which might be vested in the superintendents of missions, one of whom should take charge of such parties, and be held responsible for bringing all those to punishment who should do any injury to any person whatever, except to the men of the kraal where the cattle may be found. But this is a point of considerable delicacy, and requires the coolest deliberation. It appears to me, however, that no measures can be successful in putting an end to the depredations of the Bosjesmen, unless that people are convinced that the farmers possess the power of repelling their attacks, and that the government is as much determined to punish those who conduct themselves improperly, as to protect those who are peaceable.

I have the honor to be, my Lord,
Your Excellency's most obedient humble servant,
His Excellency the Right Honorable Earl of Caledon.   R. Collins.

Slavery in the Cape

1. Captain D. M. Pasques de Chavonnes Urges an End to Slave Importation, 1717

This memorandum, whose recommendations were not followed, analyzes the economic future of South Africa with and without the continued importation of slaves. Slave imports did continue, but the kind of arguments raised by de Chavonnes nevertheless echo through subsequent South African history.

An increase in the European population in this country, if such should take place, would be to the Company's advantage and to that of the Colony, as greater trade, an increase in the Company's revenue, and an inducement to find new means of subsistence, will be the result, especially as the country is large enough to feed and carry a large population.

Such emigrants should not be encumbered with families but should be unmarried farm-labourers from Europe. They should be sent out from time to time and be placed with well-to-do persons (who have more than they can manage) for a certain number of years at a fixed wage, so that at the expiration of their term of service, their savings and their knowledge of the country and climate would enable them to make a choice of the occupation for which they are best fitted in order to provide for themselves and their future families.

For the present, from 100 to 150 farm-labourers could make a living here, without being a burden to the Company or being paupers. This might even prove a saving to the Company as it would not have to lend labourers to the burghers, and these labourers, would not, either by chance or because their

From J. X. Merriman, ed., *The Reports of Chavonnes and His Council, and of Van Imhoff, on the Cape,* Cape Town: The van Riebeeck Society, 1918, pp. 103–107.

period of service had expired, have to re-enter the Company's service and so increase the strength of the garrison beyond the ordinary and thus be a real loss and expense to the Directors.

If the further importation of slaves were prohibited, and people were gradually to accustom themselves to employ Europeans, or Dutchmen born in this country, as farm-labourers, etc., I am certain that it would be of advantage to the Company, the country and the inhabitants. This seems to me to be quite possible, if one considers the benefits derived by many of the inhabitants of Drakenstein, whose children help them in their work. These wages-earners all contribute to the revenue of the Company, and the welfare of the country. The money spent on slaves, on the other hand, goes out of the country to its loss, and no money-transactions can be expected from slaves.

Moreover, one must consider the tranquillity enjoyed by the inhabitant who is served by his own people, and the hold he would have on their wages in case of unfaithfulness and neglect. I should also like to point out the dangers, expense and troubles which residents in the country districts have to endure because of the slaves, *e.g.* conspiracies among the slaves, who run away in bands—generally in harvest time—and leave their masters in the lurch, to their loss; at the same time they are a nuisance to the farmer, his cattle and possessions and they cannot be caught without heavy loss to their owners; and then they have to be punished as our sentence-books, with their many sad examples, bear witness.

The ordinary purchase-amount of a slave is 80-150 rix dollars for a labourer , 150-300 rixdollars and more for a herdsman, mason, wagon-driver or workman's apprentice. Clothes, tobacco and food, whether in service or not, the never-ending sicknesses, accidents, maimings, deaths, burials, whatever is stolen or neglected by this class of person, and the fact that 3 slaves are required to do the work of 2 Europeans,—all add to the expense, and it will therefore be acknowledged that I am right in saying that a farm-labourer, earning 8, 9, or 10 guldens a month and his food, will be more useful to the country and a better investment for the farmer than a slave. Such a labourer would be more useful to the country too, because in time the colony would be supplied with competent people, who would have to work for the support of their households and not for wretched slaves—a canker in this province; nor would they, because of their servants, large lands and the number of their cattle be forced to increase the debt of $f.6$-700000 which rests on the country districts.

It will be of no less advantage to the landowner, to be able, in course of time, to sell to his labourers part of his huge lands (which have been the curse of many) in small holdings—holdings which were formerly given to slaves and were lost to the owner. These labourers would work the land themselves and thus provide the country with industrious people.

If the lands already sold cannot support more people, then the Honourable Company might sell or rent at a fair price, to industrious and energetic men, suitable grants of land as yet unoccupied, and so profit by the transaction.

While I judge it to be a gain for the colony and the inhabitants to be served by European labourers, it will be no less a gain for the Company to have 250 European pioneers to do the daily work here, instead of 500–600 slaves and more, consisting of male and female slaves and children. The old slaves, the pregnant and nursing slaves, and also the children, can do practically no work, and yet, year after year, they cost the Company 23,000–27,000 guldens, exclusive of the expense occasioned by death, runaway slaves, the long sea-voyage necessary to obtain slaves, the interest on the capital, the clerk of the slaves, the overseer, the school-master, school-mistress and the midwife, for all of these involve additional expense.

Not only do I believe that these people will be able to perform the Company's work well, but that they will bring security and prosperity to this province, seeing that their number, added to the usual number of Company's servants (or even a diminished number) would constitute a formidable force, which would always be at hand and would not have to be divided in order to keep a watchful eye on the slaves, and which would be able to defend this colony better than an equally great force under different conditions.

Besides the fact that the wages earned by these men would greatly increase the Company's leases and profits,—the money spent on a slave being dead money, they would help the colonists by increasing the money-circulation which is the foundation of every country's prosperity. . . .

These men would thus apparently cost much more than the slaves, but on the other hand, one must remember that at least 60–70 of the present employees could be dispensed with, and the costs, interest, etc., mentioned above, which are necessary for the upkeep of the slaves, could be saved. I dare flatter myself that my words will prove true and that 250 pioneers will be of more use and be more profitable to the Company and the country than 5–600 slaves, male, female and children. . . .

These men might, under their officers with the knowledge of His Excellency the Governor or Commander, be usefully employed for every necessary work.

The slave-lodge might conveniently be appropriated for the accommodation of the officers and men employed in the Table Valley. They would be kept under good discipline there and their meals would be supplied (for their board-money) by caterers appointed for that purpose, as is the custom in Batavia.

The Company's slaves might be sold on easy terms to the inhabitants, and those who are half or two-thirds white might be manumitted under certain conditions, while children of that class might be apprenticed for a number of years to persons who would be prepared to bring them up well during that period, after which they would be able to earn their own living, which will never fail industrious people here.

2. Crime and Punishment in the Cape, 1769–1782

This abstract summarizes the criminal sentences that were imposed during a thirteen-year period in the eighteenth century. It may tell us something about the brutality of slavery, but this brutality must be measured against the harshness of the larger Cape society at the time, and against the overall cruelty of European society in the later eighteenth century.

Abstract of Convictions before the Court of Justice in the Castle of the Cape of Good Hope, 1769–1782.

1770, Jan. 25. Thomas, slave of A. Bester, convicted of assaulting and wounding the slave Abraham; sentenced to be placed under a gallows with a rope round his neck, and thereafter to be scourged and branded, and to hard labor at Robben Island for life. Executed 27th January.

25. Baatjoe, slave of C. D. Persoon, convicted of assaulting and wounding Willem Muller; sentenced to be hanged. Executed 27th January.

25. February, slave of A. Kocleks, convicted of assaulting with intent to murder his master's son; sentenced to be broken on a cross with the coup de gras. Executed 27th January. . . .

Oct. 4. Talima, slave of A. Dzaarsz, convicted of the murder of the slave July; sentenced to be broken on a cross without the coup de gras. . . .

Dec. 13. The Hottentot Willem Stroo, convicted of the murder of the slave Sybrand; sentenced to be hanged. Executed 15th Dec.

1771, May 2. Anthony, slave of A. Schreyn, convicted of the murder of the slave Fortuyn, sentenced to be hanged. Executed 11th May.

Oct. 31. Augustus, slave of J. Le Roux, convicted of the murder of the slave Alexander; sentenced to be hanged. Executed 9th Nov.

31. 1, Akir, 2, Sacoedien, black constables; 3, Tanjanko, 4, Oensien, Chinese, convicted of theft; sentenced to be scourged and branded, and to hard labor in chains; No. 1 *ad vitam*, Nos. 2 and 3 to 50, and No. 4 to 10 years' hard labor. Executed 9th Nov.

Nov. 28. Philander, slave of A. Caldeyer, convicted of the murder of Marot; sentenced to be broken on a cross without the coup de gras. Executed 7th Dec.

1772, June 4. January, slave of J. Esterhuizen, convicted of stabbing his master with a knife; sentenced, to be hanged. Executed 13th June.

July 13. The Hottentot Louis, convicted of cattle-stealing; sentenced to be placed under a gallows with a rope round his neck, and thereafter to be scourged and branded and to hard labor at Robben Island for 50 years. Executed 8th August.

30. Panyn, slave of J. G. van Helsdingen, convicted of desertion, housebreaking, and theft; sentenced, to be placed under the gallows with a rope

From Donald Moodie, *The Record, or a Series of Official Papers Relative to the Condition and Treatment of the Native Tribes of South Africa*, Part 5, Amsterdam & Cape Town: A. A. Balkema, 1960, pp. 106–109.

round his neck and thereafter to be scourged and branded, and to 50 years' hard labor at Robben Island. Executed 8th Aug.

30. July, slave of S. Kuun, convicted of the murder of the slave Titus; sentenced to be hanged. Executed 8th August.

Oct. 22. 1, Willem, slave of F. Visser, 2, the Hottentot Fuyk, convicted of conspiring to murder and rob the christians, (the white people) and endeavouring to persuade several other slaves and Hottentots to join them; sentenced to be hanged. Executed 31st Oct. . . .

July 22. 1, Maart, 2, Ontong, slaves of the Widow Nel, convicted of the murder of their master, W. Nel, by stabbing him; sentenced,—No. 1 to be tied to a cross, and to be pinched with a red-hot pincer in eight different places, and thereafter to be broken, and his head chopped off; No. 2 to be scourged and branded, and to hard labor at Robben Island for life. (The date of execution not mentioned.)

Nov. 11. 1, The Hottentot David Paardewagter, 2, Platje Huelman, convicted of the murder of Ernst Hendrik van Billeow, by beating him to death with kirries; sentenced to be broken on a cross without the coup de gras. Executed 20th Nov. . . .

1775, March 16. January, slave of J. Radyn, convicted of culpable homicide, in killing the slave Moether, in a quarrel; sentenced to be scourged and 20 years' hard labor at Robben Island. Executed 29th March.

April 13. Absalon, slave of A. Blyenberg, convicted of assaulting and stabbing the slave Gabriel; sentenced to be scourged and branded, and to hard labor at Robben Island for life. Executed 29th April.

20. Mey, slave of D. Kepler, convicted of desertion and housebreaking and theft; sentenced to be scourged and branded, and to hard labor at Robben Island for life. Executed 29th April.

20. Moses, slave of C. Grovenewald, convicted of assaulting and stabbing the slave January; sentenced to be scourged and 20 years' hard labor at Robben Island. Executed 29th April.

July 5. Floris, slave of A. F. Koeleke, convicted of the murder of A. F. Koeleke, jun. by stabbing him with a knife; sentenced, to be broken on a cross without the coup de gras. Executed 8th July. . . .

25. 1, The Hottentot Pompoen, 2, the Hottentot Fredrick, 3, Cornelis, slave of M. A. Bergh, convicted of vagrancy and cattle-stealing; sentenced to be scourged, and to 25 years' hard labor at Robben Island. Executed 6th March.

May 6. Ontong, slave of J. Nieuwviet, convicted of attempting to stab P. Engelbrecht and the prisoner's master; sentenced to be placed under the gallows with a rope round his neck, and thereafter to be scourged and branded, and to hard labor at Robben Island for life. Executed 15th May.

Dec. 2. Dam, slave of J. Smid, convicted of assault with intent to commit a rape upon his mistress;* sentenced to be scourged and branded, and to hard labor at Robben Island for life. Executed 11th Dec.

---

*The prisoner entered the bed-room of his mistress about 12 o'clock at night.

1780. July 20. 1, Onverwagt, slave of P. van der Merwe; 2, Phoenix, slave of J. T. Mulen; 3, Jacob, 4, Charlo, 5, Fortuyn, 6, April, 7, David, 8, Domingo, 9, February, slaves of P. Heynkes; 10, Sara, slave of H. Louw; 11, Apollos, 12, Ram, slaves of W. Coetzee, convicted of desertion and forming a gang, and of the murder of the slave Solomon; sentenced,—Nos. 1, 2, 3, and 4, to be broken on a cross with the coup de gras; Nos. 5, 6, 7, 8, 10, 11, and 12, to be scourged; No. 5 to be branded; Nos. 5, 10, and 12, to twenty-five years' hard labor at Robben Island; Nos. 10, 12, 6, 7, 8, and 11, to be returned to their masters, in chains. Executed 29th July.

Oct. 12. 1, The Hottentot Marthinus, 2, the Hottentot Booy, convicted of the murder of the slaves Jacob and July, and then burning the house in which the bodies were; sentenced,—No. 1 to be broken on a cross, No. 2 to be placed under the gallows with a rope round his neck, and thereafter to be scourged and branded, and to hard labor at Robben Island for life. Executed 28th Oct.

12. Sietgoen, slave of J. T. Muller, convicted of attempting to murder his master; sentenced to be hanged. Executed 28th Oct.

12. The Hottentot Wittebooy, convicted of arson, in setting fire to the dwelling-house of Ary J. Joubert, at night; sentenced to be placed under a gallows with a rope round his neck, and thereafter to be scourged and branded, and to hard labor at Robben Island for life. Executed 29th Oct.

1781, Jan. 25. 1, Augustus, slave of D. Beukes, 2, February, slave of T. F. Dreyer, convicted of house-breaking and thefts; sentenced, No. 1 to be hanged, No. 2 to be scourged and branded, and to hard labor at Robben Island for life. Executed 1st Feb.

Aug. 2. 1, Pero, slave of J. Smook; 2, Fortuyn, 3, Immamedie, slaves of the Company; 4, Isaac, slave of J. J. Meyer; 5, Jacob, slave of Laubscher, convicted of desertion and thefts; sentenced,—Nos. 1, 2, and 3, to be scourged; Nos. 1 and 2 to be branded; No. 1 to hard labor for life; and Nos. 2 and 3 for five years; Nos. 4 and 5 to be whipped, and to three years' hard labor. Executed 11th Aug. . . . .

April 26. Java, slave of Capt. Van Heyden, convicted of wounding a Bastard Hottentot, and thereby effecting his escape; sentenced, to be scourged, and to hard labor for life. Executed 15th May.

June 6. April, slave of P. Roren, convicted of the murder of the slave woman Rosetta; sentenced to be broken on a cross. Executed 15th June.

6. 1, Marthinus, 2, Piet, 3, Goliath, Hottentots, convicted of robbery and theft: sentenced the two first prisoners to be scourged, and all three to 15 years' hard labor. Executed 15th June.

Sept. 12. Abraham de Vrees, Hottentot, convicted of culpable homicide, in killing Catryn, his concubine; sentenced to be placed under the gallows, with a rope round his neck, and thereafter to be scourged and branded, and to hard labor for life. Executed 21st Sept.

12. Ontong, slave of P. de Wet, convicted of assaulting his mistress; sentenced to be scourged and branded, and to hard labor for life. Executed 21st Sept.

12. Slammat, slave of D. Malang, convicted of disobedience to his master,

and attempting to draw a knife upon him; sentenced to be scourged and branded, and to hard labor for life. Executed 21st Sept.

Dec. 19. The Bastard Hottentot, Hans, aged 15 years, convicted of the murder of the slave Slammat; sentenced to be scourged and branded, and to hard labor for life. Executed 13th Jan. 1783.

3. A Swedish Physician Decries South African Slavery, 1776

Anders Sparrman (1748–1820), whose name is rendered Andrew in the eighteenth-century English translation of his book, was a Swedish physician. He visited South Africa to collect botanical specimens on behalf of the naturalist Linnaeus. He accompanied Captain Cook on his second voyage in 1772 and returned to South Africa in 1775. The bulk of his two-volume work describes a long journey to the interior of South Africa in 1776. The following extracts record the harshness of slavery as witnessed by a participant in the European Enlightenment.

[April 1776]

In the evening we came to *Nana rivier.* At this time there lived here a widow, whose husband had several years before met with the dreadful catastrophe of being beheaded by his own slaves. His son, then about 13 or 14 years of age, was obliged to be eye-witness to his father's fate, and was even threatened with being made to partake of it, but luckily found an opportunity of giving them the slip; and after eluding their most vigilant search, hid himself up close from the forenoon till it was dark at night; when at last he ventured forth, with a view to seek a safer asylum at a neighbouring farm, and to accuse his father's murderers. These villains had resolved likewise to murder the mother, who was expected that day home from the Cape; but fortunately for her, though very much to her dissatisfaction, she was delayed by some accident on the road till the next day. By means of her son, who made his escape, she received advice of what had happened. As the whole premises on the farm consisted merely of two houses, situated on a plain quite open on all sides, excepting that it was covered with a few straggling bushes, which grew along the little river or brook that ran close by the spot, the lad's contrivance to hide himself, though in fact extremely painful as well as singular, was the only one that could at this time save him. It consisted in this, viz. that he sat, or rather sank himself up to his nose in the river; taking care at the same time to hide his face behind the boughs that hung over the water. The murderers not being able to

From Andrew Sparrman, *A Voyage to the Cape of Good Hope, Towards, the Antarctic Polar Circle, and Round the World: But Chiefly into the Country of the Hottentots and Caffres, from the Year 1772 to 1776,* translated from the Swedish by Georg Forster, Vol. 2, printed for Messrs. White, Cash, and Byrne, Dublin, 1785, pp. 365–373.

find him any where, he having as it were entirely vanished out of their sight, immediately began to conclude, that, in order to avoid the stroke of the bloody axe, he had rather chose to put an end to his life himself, by jumping into the river: notwithstanding this, however, they attempted to make themselves certain whether he was drowned or not. The means they took in order to effect this, was to sound the brook all over with the branches of a tree; but they luckily forgot the particular place where the boy was sitting, probably as the river was in that part shallower, and had a brisker current.

I should doubtless have brought the tears into the eyes of our Hosts, and at the same time make them a bad return for their civilities, had I, by questioning them closely concerning the particulars of this story, endeavoured so unseasonably to satisfy my curiosity. For this reason, I have contented myself in taking it down, just as I have related above, from the accounts given me by Mr. Immelman and others; and consequently was not able to learn with any certainty, whether the deceased had by any unusual act of severity provoked his slaves to commit this crime, by way of revenging themselves; or else whether these latter had acted thus, from a persuasion that the same crimes and predatory practices by which violence had been offered to their persons, and they had been deprived of their liberties, might likewise lawfully be had recourse to, for the recovery of this precious right bestowed on them by nature, and might consequently be very pardonable when exercised on their tyrants.

Yet, whatever might be the real reason of the commiting this dreadful crime, I am convinced, that it has its origin in the very essence and nature of the commerce in slaves, in whatever manner, and in whatever country it may be practised; a motive which I found had as much influence among the Christians in many places, as among the Turks on the coast of Barbary, to induce the unhappy slaves, and still more their tyrannical masters, to behave very strangely; nay, sometimes to be guilty of the most horrid cruelties. I have known some colonists, not only in the heat of their passion, but even deliberately and in cool blood, undertake themselves the low office (fit only for the executioner) of not only flaying, for a trifling neglect, both the backs and limbs of their slaves by a particular slow lingering method, but likewise, exceeding the very tigers in point of cruelty, throw pepper and salt over the wounds. But what appeared to me more strange and horrible, was to hear a colonist, not only describe with great seeming satisfaction the whole process of this diabolical invention, but even pride himself in the practice of it; and rack his brains, in order to find sophisms in defence of it, as well as of the slave trade; in which occupation the important post he enjoyed in the colony, and his own interest had engaged him. He was, however, an European by birth; of a free and civilized nation; and, indeed, gave evident proofs of possessing a kind and tender heart; so that, perhaps, it would be difficult to shew any where a greater contradiction in the disposition of man, though in a world composed almost entirely of contradictions.

Many a time, especially in the mornings and evenings, have I seen in various places unhappy slaves, who, with the most dismal cries and lamentations, were suffering the immoderately severe punishments inflicted on them by their masters; during which, they are used, as I was informed, to beg, not so much for mercy, as for draught of water; but as long as their blood was still inflamed with the pain and torture, it was said that great care must be taken to avoid allowing them the refreshment of any kind of drink; as experience had shewn, that in that case, they would die in the space of a few hours, and sometimes the very instant after they had drank it. The same thing is said to happen to those who are impaled alive, after having been broken upon the wheel, or even without having previously suffered this punishment. The spike in this case is thrust up along the back-bone and the vertebrae of the neck, between the skin and the cuticle, in such a manner, that the delinquent is brought into a sitting posture. In this horrid situation, however, they are said to be capable of supporting life for several days, as long as there comes no rain; as in that case, the humidity will occasion their sores to mortify, and consequently put an end to their sufferings in a few hours.

I am glad that, during my residence in the town, no opportunity presented itself to me of seeing any one undergo this punishment; which, though it is only destined for incendiaries, or for such as are guilty of sedition or murder, aggravated with peculiar circumstances of cruelty and barbarity, yet it appears not less shocking and revolting to human nature, than the very crimes themselves, and actually irritates more than it is generally thought to do, the other slaves in the town; whom I have seen compelled to be present even at such public punishments as do not affect the life of the culprit, in order that they might take warning from it. But the slave who is punished for sedition, is always, in the eyes of his fellow-slaves a martyr, that suffers for the common cause, and for having maintained the dearest rights bestowed upon them by nature, which is their liberty. Spikes, wheels, red-hot pincers, and all the rest of the horrid apparatus employed by their executioners, will never have with the sufferers the effect of convincing them of the contrary doctrine; on the contrary, they become still more obstinate in supposing themselves tyrannized over, and in thinking that such of their fellow-slaves as have had the courage to take away the lives of their own tyrants, and prefer death and tortures to the basely grovelling and crawling any longer upon the earth in an opprobrious state of bondage, are examples worthy of imitation, and that at least they deserve to be venerated, pitied, and even revenged. . . .

. . . There is a law, indeed, existing in the colonies, which prohibits masters from killing their slaves, or from flogging or otherwise chastising them with too great severity; but how is a slave to go to law with his master, who is, as it were, his sovereign, and who, by the same laws, has a right (or at least may by dint of bribes purchase that right) to have him flogged at the public whipping-post, not absolutely to death, indeed, yet not far from it; and this merely on the strength of the master's own testimony, and without any farther inquisition into the merits of the case? The master has, besides, so far his slave's live in his hands, that by rating and abusing him day after day, as likewise by proper family discipline, as it is called, such as heavy iron chains, hoard work, and little meat, he may, without controul, by little and little, though soon enough for this purpose, worry the poor fellow out of his life. In consequence of this, the unhappy slaves, who are frequently endued with finer feelings and nobler sentiments of humanity, though for the most part actuated by stronger passions than their masters, often give themselves up totally to despondency, and commit various acts of desperation and violence. Divers circumstances and considerations may, perhaps, concur to induce a wretch in this situation to exempt this tyrant from the dagger, which he plunges in his own bosom; content with being thus able to put an end to his misery, and at the same time to disappoint his greedy master of the profits arising from the sweat of his brow. A female slave, who had been just bought at a high price, and rather prematurely, treated with severity by her mistress, who lived in *Roodezand* district, hanged herself the same night out of revenge and despair, just at the entrance of her new mistress's bed-chamber. A young man and woman, who were slaves at the Cape, and were passionately fond of each other, solicited their master, in conformity to the established custom, for his consent to their being united in wedlock, though all in vain, as from some whim or caprice he was induced absolutely to forbid it. The consequence was, that the lover was seized with a singular fit of despair; and having first plunged a dagger into the heart of the object of his dearest wishes, immediately afterwards put an end to his own life. But how many hundred instances, not less dreadful than these, might be produced to this purpose! These, however, might suffice to create all the abhorrence for the slave trade, which so unnatural a species of commerce deserves; we will, therefore, at present, dismiss this disagreeable subject.

4. A Slave Is Tried for Rebellion and Murder, 1825

In the following document, the slave Galant goes on trial for rebelling and murdering his master in 1825. This rebellion became the focus of Afrikaner novelist Andre Brink's A Chain of Voices *([pub] 1982). The document depicts the conditions of slavery and the reasons for revolt, including the ill treatment and cruel living conditions, but rumors of the pending abolition of slavery also agitate the slaves.*

The statement of the circumstances given by the 1st prisoner Galant before Commissioners from the Court on the 23rd February last is hereupon read to him, which statement is as follows:

"During the last harvest at my master's place when I and the other people, namely Isaac, Achilles, Antony, and Platje, were together, we spoke of the ill-treatment of our master towards us, and that he did

From G. M. Theal, ed., *Records of the Cape Colony,* London: Public Record Office, 1905, Vol. 20, pp. 205–211.

not give us victuals and clothes. On that occasion one Campher who lives at a little distance from my master's place was present, who said to us that when our master should beat us at the Land, we should then seize and kill him. Shortly after Master came to the Land, on which we said we could not eat the victuals he gave us. Master answered that he could not give us better victuals than he had then given us, and he went away without beating us.

"After the harvest was got in, my master rode to Mr. Jan Plessis on a visit, taking with him the Hottentots Issak Thys and Isaac Rooy and myself. We conversed with the people there also about our ill usage, when the Hottentot Jochim and Adonis spoke to us of the ill treatment they experienced from their master, on which we agreed to murder our masters and go from the one place to the other where we should be joined by the people there. When we came home in the evening we found Mr. Barend van der Merwe at my master's place with his slave Abel, with whom I also spoke, and who agreed to to kill his Master likewise. The next morning he and his master went away, but returned shortly afterwards for one of the reins that he had let fall, on which he departed again and remained away. The third day, which was on a Tuesday, he came to me in my hut in the evening and told me that he had spoken with his master's people and that they were all ready.

"I therefore rode with him to his master's place accompanied by the Hottentots Isaac Thys and Isaac Rooy and also a Hottentot named Hendrik in the service of Jan Dalree who came that evening to my master's to fetch away a mare, and he was present when Abel said that his master's people were ready.

"When we came to the place of Barend van der Merwe, the slave Klaas was busy driving back the sheep which had got out of the Kraal, and after Abel had assisted him, he came to us behind the Kraal. Mr. Barend then came from the house and asked Klaas the reason of the dogs barking so, to which he answered that they were barking at the slave Goliath, and while Mr. Barend was speaking with Klaas, I went with Abel round the corner of the house and into the kitchen. I remained at the middle door and Abel went into the room to get the guns, and came out with two that were loaded and two bandoliers with shot and horns with powder, of which he gave me one, and as soon as we went out of the kitchen door Abel fired the first shot at his master while he stood talking to the Hottentots Isaac and Hendrik whom he had found behind the house, but which missed him, on which B. van der Merwe made his escape into the house, but ran out again through the kitchen door and got up the hill along the quince hedge. I also fired a shot on that occasion at a dog, because he bit me in the trousers, but I did not hit him. The wife of Barend van der Merwe likewise made her escape, we did not do her any harm. We, namely Abel, Klaas, the two Isaacs, Hendrik, and I, thereupon rode to my master's place, while Goliath remained behind at B. van der Merwe's because he had neither gun nor horse.

"Before we came to my master's place, we first rode to the place of Jan Dalree to see whether Master Campher and the Hottentot Platje were there, but not finding them at home we proceeded to my master's place, where having arrived we turned our horses loose and waited till daybreak to murder the master. When it was day my master came out of the house and went to the kraal, on which, I, Abel, Isaac Thys, and Klaas rushed into the house in order to get possession of the guns and ran to the rack where they hung and took them away. My mistress then came towards us and laid hold of the guns, but let one of them fall, and as she held the other fast and would not give it up, the people called out to me to fire at her, and while I was about to fire the gun on one side in order to frighten her, during which she was struggling with the people to keep the gun, she suddenly turned round, through which she received the shot, and in consequence let the gun fall out of her hands. I then took up the gun and brought it out, and while I was standing at the front door, the other people came up to me, when we ran away together. When we got to the kraal we heard from the Hottentot Valentyn that Master Rensburg had mounted a horse and ridden off; Isaac Thys and Abel thereupon got before him, so that he was obliged to return. As my master was going from the kraal to the house, Abel gave him a shot which grazed him, and when Master got into the house Abel gave him a second shot through the window which passed close by his eyes, and thereupon when he opened the front door I shot him dead.

"After that, Abel came in through the back door and fired at Master Rensburg on the firehearth, who together with the schoolmaster Verlee laid hold of the muzzle of the gun, with which they struggled to the kitchen door, when I gave Verlee a shot in the arm, with which he walked to the middle door and then fell. We then went into the house, where we found a pistol near the table and another in a pot in the kitchen, and powder and ball on a table in the bedroom; after we found the pistols Klaas discovered that Verlee the Schoolmaster still lived, on which Abel gave him a second shot through the head, and as he was not yet dead, Isaac Rooy gave him a third shot with a pistol. We all then rode to the place of Dalree armed with guns, namely I, Abel Klaas, and Hendrik, but Klaas and Hendrik did not fire. When we came to Dalree's, not finding Piet Campher there, we turned back to my master's place, the Hottentots Dirk of Swanepoel, Piet Lindes, Coenraad Lieberveld, old Cobus, little Jonas of Isaac van der Merwe, and Jochim of Jan Abraham du Plessis, also knew of the plans and were to wait for us till we should come to their places, when they were to join us in order to murder their masters also.

"From Dalree's place we went back to our place, and thence to that of Barend van der Merwe, where we found Admiral Slinger, Moses, and Andries, people belonging to Piet van der Merwe of Laken Valley, who were also to have joined us, and who accompanied us to the grazing place of Piet van der Merwe where we were attacked by a Commando and dispersed, without our having made any resistance; we were then armed, namely Abel, Klaas, Hendrik, and I, with guns belonging to my master and to B. van der Merwe; the Hottentots Andries, Admiral Slinger, and Moses had their own guns."

Questions to the prisoner:

Who was the head of the gang?

Answer. Admiral Slinger was Captain provisionally, we were afterwards to have made one of the most clever amongst us Commandant.

With what intention did you assemble?

Answer. We meant to murder all the masters that did not treat their people well, to lay waste the country if we were strong enough, and then to escape to Caffreland; and if the Commando should be too strong, to remain at the places of the murdered people.

As you say in the beginning of your statement that you had spoken with Abel and the other people, had you any other conversation with them than about the ill usage?

Answer. Abel said he had heard his Master reading the newspaper about making the slaves free, and that he had heard his master say he would rather shoot all his slaves than make them free.

The above statement having been read to the prisoner Galant, his examination is continued as follows.

2. Do you persist in this statement, and have you anything to add to or take from it?

Answer. I have something more to state, namely my master told me himself that he would shoot me. My master once when I came from the work also said to me that there was a newspaper come from another country in which stood that a black cat had been hatched under a white hen. The next day my master asked me what I understood by that expression? to which I answered that I did not know. My master repeated the question, and I said again, that I did not understand it; my Master then asked Achilles and Antony if they also had an intention of going to their own Country, to which they answered yes, but said that they could not find the way there, but that they would go if the Governor would send them, . . . although they were afraid their parents were dead and that they should not be known by their nation. My master was thereupon silent, but my mistress said to my wife, a Hottentot named Betje, that a Newspaper was come from the Cape which she dare not break open, but that a time would be prescribed when it might be opened. When the Newspaper was opened my mistress said that it stood therein that there was another great nation that was unknown; that there were orders come to make the Slaves free, and that if it was not done the other nation would then come to fight against the Farmers. My mistress afterwards further told me that it was also said in the Newspapers that the Slaves must be free, but if the Farmers would not allow it then it would not take place, to which I did not say anything. Another Newspaper came afterwards, when my wife Betje told me that her mistress had said if we would go to the King for the money and bring it to her on the table, that then we might be free. I desired her to keep it quiet, which she did. Some time after, another Newspaper came, when my wife told me that her Mistress had said that the first Englishman who came to make the slaves free should be shot, as well as the slaves; upon which I again advised her to be silent, for that if our master should hear of it he would punish us, and that she must not tell it to anybody else; but I desired her to ask the Mistress why the slaves were to be free, as she spoke so often about it. She told me afterwards that she had asked her, and that her Mistress had said it was because there came too many white children among the black Negroes, and therefore that they must be free. I then desired her again not to tell it to anyone, and not to talk so much about it. Another Newspaper then came, when she informed me that her Mistress had said that the Farmers were too hardly off, and that they were obliged to put up with too much from the Blacks. My wife came to me one day to the land weeping, and on my asking her the reason she said that while she was in the kitchen she had asked for a piece of bread, and that her Master was so angry that he said he would shoot her and all the people in a lump, and leave us to be devoured by the crows and vultures. I again told her to be quiet, for that I could not well believe her although she was my wife, as she could not read or write no more than myself. Once that Barend van der Merwe was at my Master's place on his return from Worcester where he had been to fetch the slave Goliath who had made a complaint, I was in the stable preparing forage for the horses. It was dark, so that nobody could see me in the stable. My master called Barend van der Merwe out and came with him into the stable without seeing me, when I heard my master ask him whether he had had his slave flogged, to which he answered no, for that the black people had more to say with the Magistrate of late than the Christians; further saying but he shall nevertheless not remain without a flogging, for when I come home he shall have one. I also heard Barend van der Merwe say to my Master on that occasion I wish that the Secretaries or Commissioners had died rather than that they should have come here, for that since that time they had been obliged to pay so much for the *Opgaaf* [tax receipt] and also for the Slaves. My master gave for answer I wish that the first Commissioner who put his foot on the wharf from on board had broken his neck, for that it was from that time one was obliged to pay so much for the Slaves, which they were not worth. My Master likewise said to Baren van der Merwe that he must keep himself armed in order to shoot the first Commissioner or Englishman who should come to the Country to make the Slaves free, together with the Slaves all in one heap. B. van der Merwe thereupon rode home, some time after which I again heard my master speaking to Barend Lubbe who was at my Master's place, when he asked Lubbe how it was in the upper Country, to which Lubbe answered he did not know, that he

not having any slaves had not once inquired about it, and that what the gentlemen did was well done; my master replied that although he had not any
Slaves he must nevertheless stand up for his Country, further saying that he
would shoot the first Commissioner, Englishman, or magistrate who should
come to his place to make the Slaves free, but first the Slaves. Lubbe then
asked van der Merwe whether he was not afraid if he fought against the
Magistrates that the Slaves would attack him from behind, to which my master answered for that reason the Slaves must be first shot. Subsequently I heard
my master speaking for the third time with Hans Lubbe and Jan Bothma,
whom having asked how it was in their part of the Country, they answered
bad, for the black heathens have more privileges than us, and if the Christians
go to the Landdrost to complain of their slaves, the Landdrost will not even
look at us, but turns his backside to us, on which my master said the best
advice I can give you is that you remain armed and keep your powder and ball
together. Lubbe replied the first Gentleman that comes to me I will shoot with
all the Slaves in a heap. Again for the fourth time I heard my Master talking
with Schalk Lubbe, likewise at my master's place, whom he asked how it was
here in the upper Country and if he had heard anything of the Newspaper and
about the Slaves, he answered no, on which my master said lately we heard
every day of new laws. I have asked for nothing, but I keep myself armed to
shoot the first magistrate who comes to my place and the Blacks likewise.

For the fifth time I heard my Master conversing at his place with Johannes
Jansen and Jan Verlee; the former had made an ox sambok [rawhide whip]
which he brought into the house, on which my master desired me to drive in
a pig that had got out, which I accordingly did. Standing before the door of
the pigsty in order to fasten it, I heard my master say to Jansen, you must
promise me something the same as Verlee has done, namely to shoot the magistrate when he comes. Jansen answered that he would do so, for that he would
stand up for his mother Country; on that my Master said that he should give
orders to all the Slaves, and that if they did not obey them he would supple
the sambok on them the next day, for, said my Master, if you punish a slave
you must do it that he cannot be known before a magistrate. My Master
ordered us to smear the treading floor and that the floor must be well laid the
next morning when he got up, on that we made the plan to murder all the
farmers; we did not smear the floor because it was evening and was dark; we
also told my master this, but he notwithstanding would have that the floor
should be smeared against the next morning. My master did not say anything
more about it that evening, and we then immediately formed the plan, as I
have already stated.

The Emergence of the East Cape Frontier

1. Anders Sparrman and His Companions Nervously Trade with the Xhosa, 1776

This passage depicts the earliest phase in Xhosa–European contact on the Eastern Cape frontier. In the 1770s the Dutch farmers and the Xhosa tentatively began to interact. Frightened by their preconceived notions of "barbarous" Africans, Sparrman and his companions resort to imperialist bluster to avert disaster.

Very early in the afternoon, the hunting party above-mentioned went away, and about an hour before dark there arrived a hord of *caffres*. They had got within three hundred paces of us, before we discovered them, being to the number of about one hundred, all men, and each of them armed with a few *hassagais*, or a couple of *kirries*.* They marched, moreover, directly on towards our waggon, not with the careless gait of ordinary travellers, but with measured steps, as it were; and, in short, with an almost affected pride and stateliness in their deportment, as they approached nearer to us. Upon the whole, we could not well have received a visit on this spot more unexpected, nor of a more alarming nature; indeed, it occasioned a visible consternation in several of my Hottentots, at the same time that it puzzled my friend and me, to think in what manner we should receive this nation so on a sudden, so as to avoid sharing the unhappy fate which, as I have already mentioned before . . . attended Heuppenaer and his suit. In case of an attack, my Hottentots were

---

*Hassagais (assegai): an iron-pointed stabbing spear; kirrie (knobkerry): a staff or stick with a weighted rounded ball at one end which served as a club.

From Andrew Sparrman, *A Voyage to the Cape of Good Hope, Towards the Antarctic Polar Circle, and Round the World: But Chiefly into the Country of the Hottentots and Caffres, from the Year 1772 to 1776*, translated from the Swedish by Georg Forster, Vol. 2, printed for Messrs. White, Cash, and Byrne, Dublin, 1785, pp. 273–284.

too few in number, and too cowardly, to be depended upon; such of them as were of the Boshies-man's race, and had come with us from *Zondags-rivier,* would probably have assisted in plundering our waggon, had they found a convenient opportunity; and who knows, whether they were not in secret intelligence with the Boshies-men, who were at this time in the service of the Caffres, and belonged to their party. . . . [B]ut in this case, we had not a moment to lose, much less had we any spare time to fetch our horses from pasture. I therefore resolved instantly to carry matters with as high a hand as it was possible for me to assume in the situation we were in, especially as I knew from experience, that by this means the Indians might sometimes be kept in awe just like children. Accordingly, I began with my own *Hottentots,* threatening with the most terrible Dutch oaths my memory furnished me with, to shoot the first man through the head, who should stir a foot without leave, or once open his mouth to the Caffres; or, in fine, should not, at the smallest nod, perform what I might think fit to command. My companion, on his part, taking a handful of bullets, put them into a loaded gun of an uncommon length which he had brought with him; in the mean time frequently addressing himself to me, and making it out to be a very easy matter (and of the feasibility of which there could be no doubt) to kill with it the whole body of Caffres at a single shot, in case they should offer to behave in a hostile manner; and at the same time, in order to give some probability to this gasconade, did not omit to practise a few manoeuvres in the true legerdemain style. While Mr. Immelman was thus with his long gun, beyond all doubt, making a tremendous figure in the eyes of the Caffres, and I was likewise armed with my gun, and the fiercest mien I could possibly muster up, they came towards us, wedged up, as it were, into a close body, with three leaders in their front. A Hottentot interpreter in one of the wings, seemed just going to open with a long harangue; when I put a sudden stop to his sublime oratory, by accosting him with a few rough compliments in the Swedish language, and turning my back upon him.

This haughty and uncivil reception, which would only have served to irritate any other than Hottentots and Caffres, on the contrary, from the very beginning, abased their pride, so that they stood like a parcel of orderly, or rather intimidated, school-boys, and waited for my questioning them; upon which we, in quality of the principal sons of the company, ordered our interpreter to ask them what nation they were of? Whence they came? and wither they were going? For the purpose of making this examination, I called out Jan Skeper, the most alert and intelligent of all my Hottentots, and had the satisfaction to see him fly to me like a flash of lightning; a proof of his obedience, which, indeed, was at this time very agreeable to me; as it was requisite in order to excite in the Caffres a high opinion of our authority and power: but still higher ideas, and even dread which he had conceived of this nation, put his whole body into a tremor, so that even his teeth chattered in such a manner, that he could not utter a word. This unlooked for cowardly behaviour, threatened to spoil my whole plan; for which reason, both from indignation, and in order to disguise the reason of his trembling, I threatened him very hard, and accosted him in the roughest manner. I am not certain, however, whether the Caffre were not more sharp-sighted than I wished them to be; however that be, some of them fixed their eyes upon him and laughed.

Whenever the interpreter of the Caffres offered, which he did several times, to enter into a private conversation with my Hottentot, I constantly took care to prevent it. In fine, the account they gave of themselves was, "that they were Caffres from *Konaps-rivier,* and were come hither merely with a view of meeting with us, and to see whether we had brought with us a great deal of iron and copper to exchange for their cattle; for they knew from report, that we were come from a great distance, and had long resided in these plains."

In the mean while, this proposition of theirs with respect to the traffic and cattle, appeared to me extremely suspicious, inasmuch as I could not at that time perceive that they had brought any live stock along with them; and those which their herdsmen and boys brought to this place afterwards, consisted merely in a few milch cows and young steers, upon which they set an amazing high price, and, in all probability, intended them for their own support during their march.

In order to prevent their sitting down without being previously asked, I told them without delay by means of the interpreters, that they had my leave to sit down, whilst I gave my answer on the subject of their proposed commerce. Accordingly they sat themselves down in the same order as they came, viz. the three Chiefs in front of the rest. I asked, nevertheless, how many of them were captains or commanders; and the three foremost being mentioned by name as such, I gave each of them a good piece of tobacco; telling them, at the same time, that this was the way the company's sons chose to receive their friends the *Caffre captains;* but that we had already exchanged our iron and copper in these very plains with some other Caffre friends; that, however, I imagined that they had not taken their Journey in vain, in case they called at *Agter Bruntjes-boogte,* where they would get enough of these commodities from the farmers settled there.

When they saw that, in order to get tobacco, nothing more was necessary than to be a captain, they presented to me several others of the party, as being likewise *t'Ku-t'kois,* or captains, and asked for tobacco for them; but the scheme not succeeding, they themselves laughed heartily at the captains of their own creation. Neither did they shew the least inclination to distribute to these pretended chiefs, any part of the presents that had been made them. However, in order to keep these chiefs in good humour, I likewise gave them afterwards a handful of dry hemp, which they accepted as a valuable present; and mixing it with some tobacco, smoked it with a high relish, while we were talking together. . . .

When it grew dark, the Caffres stood up, and without any kind of order, or taking leave, went towards a large bush, at the distance of a musket-shot from us, where they made a great fire, near which they took up their repose for the night. Shortly after we heard a hideous roaring near that spot, and we conjectured that it proceeded from some beast they were killing. . . .

While we were standing to see the beast slaughtered, we toost notice that all the spears and hassagais, exclusive of those that were used in killing the animal, were piled up together in the middle just before one of the chiefs, who was now observed to be very busy in issuing out his orders; these orders being obeyed without delay by those who looked after the fire. Indeed, they did not seem to pay the least regard to our being present: however, as it was grown very dark, we thought it most adviseable not to make a long stay. We had scarcely got home, before their interpreter came along with two Caffres to borrow our porridge pot. This message our Hottentots interpreted to us in a sorrowful tone, adding, that the Caffres usually kept what they borrowed, else we must have a (*rusje*) or dispute with them. As our porridge pot was absolutely a treasure to us, and was particularly useful to our Hottentots, for the purpose of boiling and melting their fat, &c. and the Caffres probably could not have withstood the temptation of keeping it, I thought it was as well to have a *rusje* with them at first as at last. I endeavoured to pacify them however, by a civil answer; and sent them word, that if the company's sons had two porridge pots, they would certainly lend one of them to their friends the *Caffres;* but that we were then hungry, and were going to dress our victuals that very night: to which I added, that some skill was requisite in order to dress victuals in our pot, so that they might not be spoiled; for which reason, I would myself take care to have their meat dressed for them the next morning, as soon as ever they should send it to my Hottentots. It is true, they suffered themselves to be put off with this compliment; but we could not tell for all that, whether they might not take it in their heads to send a shower of darts in the night, before we were aware of it, through the tilt of our waggon, . . . on which account we fortified that part of our waggon with our saddles, and skins of beasts, and defended ourselves on the sides with bundles of paper, clothes, and pieces of dried rhinoceros's hides. Two guns, with their muzzles pointed in a proper position, were placed at each end of the waggon, so that we could directly, on the first rupture, discharge four pieces; moreover, in order to increase the alarm and terror of the enemy, we were then, as well as the first arrival of the Caffres on the preceding day, prepared to throw, if necessary, powderhorns and large cartouches into the fire, which was about eight or nine paces distant from us; we were likewise on this occasion to have filled our pockets without delay with loose gunpowder, in order to keep up from our firearms, a brisker, though less effectual fire, and a continual report, with a view to frighten the enemy at a distance. We considered our horses and oxen too, which, according to our constant custom, were tied to the waggon all around it, as a kind of intrenchment, having particular reason to expect, from the shyness our horses, previous notice of any attack; so that upon the whole we slept tolerably secure: and though, even after such ample preparations, for our defence, we thought ourselves happy to escape being attacked by the enemy, yet still we could not help wishing that we had been able to gratify our friends with an account of an assault on the part of the Caffres.

I cannot help thinking, however, that the instances we have of the deceitful dispositions of the barbarians in general, and of the sudden transitions which are sometimes made by them from a state of peace and tranquility to that of rapine and slaughter, are sufficient to justify all our suspicions, and the precautions we took with respect to them; and I am inclined to consider the being massacred by these fellows, as one of the species of the sudden death, against which we are taught to pray in the Litany. I have lately been informed by a letter from Mr. Immelman, dated from the Cape, 25th of March, 1781, that the *Caffres* at that time were laying waste every thing they could meet with in the districts belonging to the Christians: among others Printslo, my old worthy host, and the first I had at *Agter Bruntjes-boogte,* had had the mortification to see his new house burnt to the ground by these barbarians, after having lost his numerous herds of cattle, out of all which he had been able to save no more than six oxen. A woman of the name of Koetsje, had with great difficulty escaped the pursuit of these barbarians, having been obliged to leave one of her children behind her, which had been pierced through the body with hassagais. The loss of the Christians in the article of cattle, is said to amount to twenty-one thousand; while, on the other hand, they could not meet with the third part of the number of cattle, belonging to the Caffres, who, Mr. Immelman tells me, were led on by the Captains Mosan and Koba. I cannot say whether it was either of these that paid us a visit, as I forgot to take down their names, and therefore cannot remember them so as to be certain of them. Just after midnight it rained, with thunder and lightning.

The next morning (being the 22d) at ten o'clock, the whole party of Caffres went away without taking leave, after having, under pretence of selling a milch cow, tried to get a sight of all the iron and copper which they supposed I had brought with me: however, that I might not lead them into temptation, I shewed them nothing but plants and insects which I told them were the only commodities I had of any moderate value; these, however, I supposed they would hardly take in exchange for their cow, which we otherwise, on account of the store we set by the milk, would have been glad to have bargained with them for.

2.   Reverend John Campbell Describes the Eastern Cape Frontier After the 1812 War, 1815

The Reverend John Campbell (1766–1840) was born in Scotland. He became a director of the London Missionary Society, which first sent him to the Cape Colony in 1812–1814 to inspect its mission stations. He made a second tour of the interior in 1819–1821.

The following extract comes from the book he wrote about his first trip, which includes a "Miscellaneous Account of Kaffraria," the Eastern Cape frontier. His words, although not necessarily reliable in their details, paint a vivid picture of the complex relationships that grew out of the frontier conflict of 1812.

In the war, Gika[1] led the Rharhabe branch of the Xhosa, who occupied the Ciskei (west side of the Kei River), and his first cousin Hintsa led the Gonaqua[2] branch, who inhabited the Transkei (east side of the Kei River). Both were grandsons of Palo[3]. Gika's uncle Tzlambi[4] had gained power by backing Gika's claim and assuming the role of regent on his behalf. At seventeen, Gika rebelled and overthrew his uncle.

Chap. V

Origin of the Caffre War with the English

I had the following account of the origin of this war from a respectable quarter, many particulars of which have been corroborated by others.

A boor had taken a farm on the banks of the Great Fish River, where there was a ford, across which the Caffres frequently drove their cattle, some of which happened now and then to go into his garden, which no doubt offended the proprietor. To make the Caffres more careful, he began to demand a part of the cattle which broke into his garden. When there happened to be three, he demanded one cow or ox; when five, he required two, as a fine for the damage he had sustained. The Caffres peaceably submitted to these demands for some time. The farmer finding this to be a lucrative concern, is said to have begun to assist the Caffre cattle in getting into his garden, and then resolved to seize all he found there. The first seizure after coming to this resolution happened to be a considerable number. The Caffre complained to his chief, who instantly ordered his own cattle to be driven across the Fish River at the farmer's ford, when they all went into the boor's trap, or garden; when, like the others, they were detained by the boor. No sooner had the Caffre chief heard of what had happened, then he went with an armed force to visit the boor. On his arrival, he not only demanded the restoration of his own cattle, but also carried off all the boor's.

The other Caffres who had lost cattle by this boor, having such an example set them by their chief, determined to make up their losses in a similar way, by carrying off cattle from other boors, though they had not offended them. In this way, a thieving, plundering disposition became general among them, which afterwards made it appear necessary to the government to drive all the Caffres beyond the Great Fish River, which has been effected. But notwithstanding the number and vigilance of the military posts opposite to Caffraria, parties of the Caffres have still the audacity to penetrate many miles into the colony, and carry off great numbers of cattle from the boors.

In these plundering expeditions the Caffres never travel on the roads, but through the woods; where, in consequence of the multiplicity of obstacles, no

---

From John Campbell, *Travels in South Africa, Undertaken at the Request of the Missionary Society,* London: 1815, reprinted, Cape Town: C. Struik (Pty.) Ltd., 1974, pp. 371–375.

---

[1] = Ngqika   [2] = Phalo   [3] = Ndlambe   [4] = Gcaleka

European soldiers can come up with them; but the Hottentots shewing themselves to be as nimble travellers through the woods and bushes, government have chiefly employed the Hottentot regiment in opposing the Caffres.

Sometime after the commencement of the Caffre war, one of the chiefs desired a conference with the British Commander, who agreed to meet him in a plain, accompanied by a certain number of his men, and the Caffre to bring the like number. The chief asked, to whom that country belonged so many years ago? A Dutch boor mentioned a person to whom it had belonged. "O," said the Caffre, "I remember him, but it belonged to us before his time." Be that as it might, said the Officer, he and his people must remove beyond the Great Fish River, and he recommended their doing it in a peaceable manner. They desired time to cut down their corn, but this could not be granted; but it was promised that it should be cut down and sent after them. The Commander observing the Caffres increasing in number around, and laying hold of their assagays, thought it prudent to fall back on his main body. So long as the corn remained on the ground, it was a constant bone of contention; wherefore orders were given that all the growing corn, tobacco, &c. should be destroyed, which was accordingly done; since which they have not crossed the Fish River in such numbers as formerly; but that river is found to be a poor boundary, being sometimes completely dry. There is said to be a large and deep river about twenty days journey beyond it, which some recommend driving them beyond; else, say they, the war must be perpetual. On receiving such orders, king Gika might say, as a Canadian chief did on being ordered with his people, to remove higher up the country, to make way for fresh settlers from Europe—"Were we not born here? are not the bones of our forefathers interred here? and can we say to them, Arise and go with us to a foreign land?" But I doubt much the existence of such a river, for having afterwards travelled much higher up on the west side of the Caffre land, I did not meet with one river or stream running towards Caffraria, but all running towards the opposite side of the Continent. Should it only rise among those mountains which bound Caffraria on the westward, it is not likely to be both wide and deep.

The Caffres, being divided into many tribes, each of which has a chief, have frequent wars, among themselves; but they are never bloody, perhaps not more than one or two men are killed during a war. They prefer stealing each other's cattle, destroying fields, gardens, &c. to killing.

Most of their civil wars arise from disputes about their women, cattle, and ground. Every chief has a particular district which he considers his own, or belonging to his Kraal; others encroaching upon this occasions a war, if the intruder insists on retaining it. When one chief steals cattle from another, if he who has sustained the loss be not satisfied with the offered redress, he resorts to arms.

They take prisoners in war, but only of the higher rank, the rest are killed. The chief keeps his prisoners in close confinement, till they promise to be faithful subjects to him, when they are set at liberty.

When they march to war, each chief accompanies his people, who march in disorder; but on arriving at the field of battle, they form into a line, and first endeavour to intimidate the enemy by howling in a terrific manner, and then by threatening to cut them to pieces.

Every child is supposed to be born a soldier; wherefore all serve freely when called upon by the chief, and every one learns the art of war, or to use the assagay. When they obtain a victory, they are rewarded by their chief, and such as are wounded are kindly treated.

The Caffres are much afraid of muskets, and when they take any from the boors, they generally break them to pieces for the brass upon them, of which metal they are very fond.

Our Hottentots, who have lived some time in Caffraria, mentioned to me a battle between two Caffre tribes, the one under Congo's father, Chacca, the other under Cobella, which Chacca surrounded, when all the prisoners where either compelled to drown themselves in the sea, or were murdered on the beach; about eight or ten only escaped, and fled to the colony—of those, a father, a cousin, and three uncles of one who travelled with me, and their wives, composed that number. One of these women during this flight, was pregnant with a son who is now at Bethelsdorp, to whom the parents gave a name expressive of their circumstances at that time, as a time of trouble; indeed it is customary with the Caffres, like the ancient patriarchs, to give significant names to their posterity.

I heard of a boor, at present in the colony, who had lived a long time in Caffraria, where he married both a Caffre and a Hottentot. On the English capturing the Cape, he returning to the colony, bringing along with him his two wives, and a Mambookis girl, from the second nation beyond the Caffres. This girl he caused to be well educated, when he discarded his Hottentot and Caffre wives, and married her.

Another boor, who was in Caffraria when Dr. Vanderkemp was there, on seeing his printing press, enquired what it was. When the Doctor had described the nature and use of it, the sagacious boor requested him to print for him by the morrow a large folio bible with plates. This same boor was given to haste; for not being able in a short time to cure a sore finger of his daughter's , he cut it off, saying she would be better without it.

3.   An English Writer Protests Frontier Policies of the Cape Colony Government, 1835

Thomas Pringle (1789–1834), was an "1820 settler" who migrated from England to the Eastern Cape frontier. He eventually moved to Cape Town where he became a pioneering librarian, journalist, and literary figure. Pringle was critical of the government not only for its vacillating and

From Thomas Pringle, *Narrative of a Residence in South Africa,* London: Edward Moxon, 1835, pp. 296–307, 331–338.

double-dealing frontier policy, but also for its censorship regulations,
which denied freedom of the press. His poetry makes him one of the
founders of English-language literature in South Africa.

The councils of the confederated Caffer chiefs were at this time directed by an
extraordinary individual generally known in the colony by the title of *Links*
(or the Lefthanded), but whose native name was Makanna. He had been originally a Caffer of common rank, and without any claim to alliance with the line
of Togúh, which, with the exception of the Kongo family, constitutes the
noble blood of the Amakosa tribe; but by his talents and address he had gradually raised himself to distinction. Before the present war broke out, he was in
the habit of frequently visiting the British headquarters at Graham's Town,
and had evinced an insatiable curiosity and an acute intellect on such subjects
as fell under his observation. With the military officers he talked of war, or of
such of the mechanical arts as fell under his notice; but his great delight was to
conserve with Mr. Vanderlingen, the chaplain, to elicit information in regard
to the doctrines of Christianity, and to puzzle him in return with metaphysical subtleties or mystical ravings.

Whether Makanna had acquired any distinct view of the Christian system
seems very doubtful: but of his knowledge, such as it was, he made an extraordinary use. Combining what he had learned respecting the creation, the fall
of man, the atonement, the resurrection, and other Christian doctrines, with
some of the superstitious traditions of his countrymen and with his own wild
fancies, he framed a sort of extravagant religious medley, and, like another
Mohammed, boldly announced himself as a prophet and teacher directly
inspired from Heaven. He endeavoured to throw around his obscure origin a
cloud of religious mystery; and called himself "the brother of Christ." In his
usual demeanour he assumed a reserved, solemn, and abstracted air, and kept
himself aloof from observation; but in addressing the people, who flocked in
multitudes to hear him, he appeared to pour forth his soul in a flow of affecting and impetuous eloquence. My friend Mr. Read, the missionary, who visited him in Cafferland in 1816, describes his appearance as exceedingly imposing, and his influence both over the chiefs and the common people as most
extraordinary. He addressed the assembled multitudes repeatedly in Mr.
Read's presence with great effect: inculcating a stricter morality, and boldly
upbraiding the most powerful chiefs with their vices. At other times, instructing them in Scripture history, he adduced as a proof of the universal deluge,
the existence of immense beds of sea-shells on the tops of the neighbouring
mountains. To the Missionaries he was apparently friendly, and urged them to
fix their residence in the country under his protection; yet they were puzzled
by his mysterious demeanour, and shocked by his impious pretensions, and
could only conclude that he was calculated to do much good or mischief,
according as his influence might be ultimately employed.

By degrees he gained a complete control over all the principal chiefs, with
the exception of Gaika, who feared and hated him. He was consulted on every
matter of consequence, received numerous gifts, collected a large body of
retainers, and was acknowledged as a warrior-chief as well as a prophet. His

ulterior objects were never fully developed; but it seems not improbable that he contemplated raising himself to the sovereignty as well as to the priesthood of his nation; and proposed to himself the patriotic task (for, though a religious imposter, he certainly was not destitute of high aspirations), to elevate by degrees his barbarous countrymen, both politically and intellectually, nearer to a level with the Europeans. But, whatever were Makanna's more peaceful projects, the unexpected invasion of the country by the English troops in 1818 diverted his enterprise into a new and more disastrous channel. The confederate chiefs, in turning their arms against Gaika, though roused by their own immediate wrongs, had acted at the same time under the prophet's directions; for it was one of his objects to humble, if not to crush entirely, that chief, who was the great obstacle to his public and, perhaps personal, views of aggrandisement. With the English authorities he had assiduously cultivated terms of friendship; and had not apparently anticipated any hostile collision with them on this occasion. But after Colonel Brereton's devastating inroad, by which Makanna's followers, in common with the other confederate clans, had suffered most cruelly, his whole soul seems to have been bent upon revenging the aggressions of the colonists, and emancipating his country from their domination. He saw that this was not to be effected by mere marauding incursions, such as had always hitherto characterised Caffer warfare. The great difficulty was to concentrate the energies of his countrymen, and bring them to attempt a decisive blow; and this he at length effected. By his spirit-rousing eloquence, his pretended revelations from Heaven, and his confident predictions of complete success, provided they would implicitly follow his counsels, he persuaded the great majority of the Amakosa clans, including some of Hinza's captains, to unite their forces for a simultaneous attack upon Graham's Town, the headquarters of the British troops. He told them that he was sent by Uhlanga, the Great Spirit, to avenge their wrongs; that he had power to call up from the grave the spirits of their ancestors to assist them in battle against the English (*Amanglézi*), whom they should drive, before they stopped, across the Zwartkops river and into the ocean; "and then," said the prophet, "we will sit down and eat honey!" Ignorant of our vast resources, Makanna probably conceived that, this once effected, the contest was over for ever with the usurping Europeans.

Having called out the warriors from the various clans, Makanna and Dushàni the son of Islambi (the latter being, at least nominally, the chief captain of the host) mustered their army in the forests of the Great Fish River, and found themselves at the head of between nine and ten thousand men. They then sent (in conformity with a custom held in repute among Caffer heroes) a message of defiance to Colonel Willshire, the British commandant, announcing "that they would breakfast with him next morning."

At the first break of dawn the warriors were arrayed for battle on the mountains near Graham's Town; and before they were led on to the assault, were addressed by Makanna in an animating speech, in which he is said to have assured them of supernatural aid in the conflict with the English, which would turn the hail-storm of their fire-arms into water. Thus excited, they were led on by their various chiefs, but all under the general direction of the prophet himself, and the chief captain, Dusháni. The English were completely astonished and taken by surprise when they appeared, soon after sunrise, marching rapidly over the heights which environ Graham's Town; for Colonel Willshire had so entirely disregarded the message sent him, considering it a mere bravado, that he had taken no precautions whatever, and was himself very nearly captured by the enemy as he was taking a morning ride with some of his officers. One of those officers was Captain Harding, who communicated to me this and many other details relating to these campaigns. Had the Caffers advanced by night, they could not have failed of easily capturing the place.

All was now bustle and confusion in the little garrison, which consisted of only about three hundred and fifty European troops, and a small corps of disciplined Hottentots. The place had no regular defences, and the few field-pieces which it possessed were not quite in readiness. The Caffers rushed on to the assault with their wild war-cries. They were gallantly encountered by the troops, who poured upon them, as they advanced in dense disorderly masses, a destructive fire of musketry, every shot of which was deadly, while their showers of assagais fell short or ineffective. Still, however, they advanced courageously, the chiefs cheering them on, almost to the muzzles of the British guns; and many of the foremost warriors were then seen breaking short their last assagai, to render it a stabbing weapon, in order to rush in upon the troops, according to Makanna's directions, and decide the battle in close combat. This was very different from their usual mode of bush-fighting, but the suggestion of it evinces Makanna's judgment; for if promptly and boldly acted upon, it could not have failed of success. The great bodily strength and agility of the Caffers, as well as their vast superiority in numbers, would have enabled them to overpower the feeble garrison in a few minutes.

At this critical moment, and while other columns of the Caffer army were pushing on to assail the place in flank and rear, the old Hottentot Captain Boezak, who happened that instant to arrive at Graham's Town with a party fo his men, rushed intrepidly forward to meet the enemy. To old Boezak most of the Caffer chiefs and captains were personally known; and he was, also, familiar with their fierce appearance and furious shouts. Singling out the boldest of those, who, now in advance, were encouraging their men to the final onset, Boezak and his followers, buffalo-hunters from Theopolis, and among the best marksmen in the colony, levelled in a few seconds a number of the most distinguished chiefs and warriors. Their onset was for a moment checked. The British troops cheered, and renewed with alacrity their firing. At the same instant the field-pieces, now brought to bear upon the thickest of the enemy, opened a most destructive fire of grape-shot. Some of the warriors rushed madly forward and hurled their spears at the artillerymen; but it was in vain. The front ranks were mown down like grass. Those behind recoiled; wild panic and irretrievable rout ensued. Makanna, after vainly attempting to rally them, accompanied their flight. They were pursued but a short way; for the handful of cavalry durst not follow them into the broken ravines where they precipitated their flight. The slaughter was the great for so brief a conflict. About fourteen hundred Caffer warriors strewed the field of battle; and many more perished of their wounds before they reached their own country.

This formidable attempt, altogether unprecedented in Caffer warfare, alarmed the Colonial Government, and awakened all its vengeance. The burgher militia throughout the whole extent of the colony were called out, and marched to the eastern frontier, to assist in chastising the "savages." Colonel Willshire, collecting all the disposable British and Hottentot troops, advanced into the enemy's country in one direction, while Landdrost Stockenstrom, with a burgher commando of a thousand horsemen, swept it in another. The villages of the hostile clans were burnt, their cattle carried off, their fields of maize and millet trodden down, and the inhabitants of all classes, driven into the thickets, were there bombarded with grape-shot and congreve-rockets. Dispirited by their late failure, defeated in every attempt at resistance, their women and helpless old people often slaughtered indiscriminately with the armed men, their principal chiefs, Islambi, Kongo, Habanna,—above all, their prophet, Makanna,—denounced as "outlaws," and the inhabitants threatened with utter extermination if they did not deliver them up "dead or alive;" the Caffer people yet remained faithful to their chiefs. Among the multitudes now driven to despair, and perishing for want, not one was found willing to earn the high reward offered for their apprehension by the conquerors.

The course adopted by Makanna under these circumstances was remarkable, and gives a higher idea of his character than any other part of his history that has become known to us. He resolved to surrender himself as a hostage for his country: and I am fortunately enabled to give the authentic particulars from notes taken at the time by Captain Stockenstrom, the officer into whose hands he delivered himself up.

Captain Stockenstrom was encamped with his division of the commando on the high ground east of Trumpeter's Drift, on the Great Fish River. The rain had continued to fall in torrents for several days; and the Caffers, availing themselves of weather unfavourable to fire-arms, had repeatedly shown themselves in great force, as if contemplating a desperate attack, and rushing forward with their usual war-shout; but on being received with a brisk fire, they had as quickly retired to the wooded ravines. In the afternoon of the 15th of August, 1819, two Ghonaqua women came to the camp, and, asking to speak with the commander, informed Captain Stockenstrom that they were sent by the chief Makanna to sue for peace; and that he would himself come and treat for terms, provided his life and liberty were guaranteed. Captain Stockenstrom replied that he would pledge his solemn word that the chief's life should be safe; but that he could offer no guarantee for his liberty, because one of the principal objects of the expedition, and a strict part of his own instructions, was to take Makanna and some others "dead or alive." The women departed with this message; and Captain Stockenstrom was disposed to ascribe their errand to purposes of espionage rather than to any serious intention on Makanna's part to surrender, when, to his surprise, that chief walked unattended into the camp the next day, with an air of calm pride and self-possession which commanded involuntary respect. It appeared that the message sent by the women had been correctly delivered—"but," said the African chief, with a magnanimity which would have done honour to a Greek or Roman patriot, "people say that I have occasioned the war: let me see whether my delivering myself up to the conquerors will restore peace to my country."—He appeared to be greatly disconcerted, however, when he found that he was not speaking to the "principal man," and that Captain Stockenstrom possessed no authority to settle terms of peace. Next day Colonel Willshire, then holding the chief command, passed with the main body of the troops, and carried Makanna along with him. What follows is given from Captain Stockenstrom's notes, which he kindly placed in my possession in 1825.

"A few days afterwards, a small body of Caffers were seen at the edge of a thicket near Colonel Willshire's camp, who made signs that they desired a parley. The Colonel, attended by another officer and myself, having moved towards them unarmed, two Caffers approached, and proved to be, the one of them Islambi's, and the other Makanna's, chief councillors (*pagati*). They were, I think, as noble-looking men, and as dignified in their demeanour, as any I have ever beheld. After a few questions and answers relative to the disposal of Makanna, (who by this time had been sent into the Colony), and as to the prospects of an accommodation, the friend of the captive chief delivered himself in the following terms—in so manly a manner, with so graceful an attitude, and with so much feeling and animation, that the bald translation which I am able to furnish from my hasty and imperfect notes, can afford but a very faint and inadequate idea of his eloquence.

"'The war, 'said he,' British chiefs, is an unjust one; for you are striving to extirpate a people whom you forced to take up arms. When our fathers, and the fathers of the Boors (*Amabúlu*) first settled in the Zureveld, they dwelt together in peace. Their flocks grazed on the same hills; their herdsmen smoked together out of the same pipes; they were brothers—until the herds of the Amakosa increased so as to make the hearts of the Boors sore. What those covetous men could not get from our fathers for old buttons, they took by force. Our fathers were MEN; they lived their cattle; their wives and children lived upon milk; they fought for their property. They began to hate the colonists, who coveted their all, and aimed at their destruction.

"'Now, their kraals and our fathers' kraals were separate. The boors made commandoes on our fathers. Our fathers drove them out of the Zureveld; and we dwelt there, because we had conquered it. There we were circumcised; there we married wives; and there our children were born. The white men hated us, but could not drive us away. When there was war, we plundered you. When there was peace, some of our bad people stole; but our chiefs forbade it. Your treacherous friend, Gaika, always had peace with you; yet, when his people stole, he shared in the plunder. Have your patroles ever found cattle taken in time of peace, runaway slaves, or deserters, in the kraals of *our* chiefs? Have they ever gone into Gaika's country without finding such cattle, such slaves, such deserters, in Gaika's kraals? But he was your friend; and you wished to possess the Zureveld. You came at last like locusts. We stood: we could do no more. You said, 'go over the Fish River—that is all we want.' We yielded, and came here.

"'We lived in peace. Some bad people stole, perhaps; but the nation was quiet—the chiefs were quiet. Gaika stole—his chiefs stole—his people stole. You sent him copper; you sent him beads; you sent him horses—on which he rode to steal more. To *us* you sent only commandoes!

"'We quarrelled with Gaika about grass—no business of yours. You sent a commando—you took our last cow—you left only a few calves, which died for want, along with our children. You gave half the spoil to Gaika; half you kept yourselves. Without milk,—our corn destroyed,—we saw our wives and children perish—we saw that we must ourselves perish; we followed, therefore, the tracks of our cattle into the colony. We plundered, and we fought for our lives. We found you weak; we destroyed your soldiers. We saw that we were strong; we attacked your headquarters:—and if we had succeeded, our right was good, for you began the war. We failed—and you are here.

"'We wish for peace; we wish to rest in our huts; we wish to get milk for our children; our wives wish to till the land. But your troops cover the plains, and swarm in the thickets, where they cannot distinguish the man from the woman, and shoot all.

"'You want us to submit to Gaika. That man's face is fair to you, but his heart is false. Leave him to himself. Make peace with us. Let him fight for himself—and *we* shall not call on you for help. Set Makanna at liberty; and Islambi, Dushani, Kongo, and the rest will come to make peace with you at any time you fix. But if you will still make war, you may indeed kill the last man of us—but Gaika shall not rule over the followers of those who think him a woman.'"

This manly remonstrance, which affected some of those who heard it even to tears, had no effect in altering the destination of Makanna, or in obtaining a reprieve for his countrymen, who were still sternly called upon to deliver up those who had been *outlawed* by the Cape Government. All efforts, however, to get possession of the persons of the other chiefs were unavailing. After plundering the country, therefore, of all the cattle that could yet be found, and leaving devastation and misery behind them, our "christian commando" retired into the colony; without gaining the object for which the war was professedly commenced,—but with an additional spoil of about 30,000 head of cattle captured from the famishing and despairing natives.

Meanwhile, the treatment and fate of Makanna were briefly as follows. By order of the Colonial Government, he was forwarded by sea from Algoa Bay to Cape Town; there confined as a prisoner in the common gaol; and finally, with others of his countrymen, guilty of no other offence than fighting for their native land against its *civilised* invaders, he was condemned to be imprisoned for life on Robben Island—the Botany Bay of the Cape—a spot appropriated for the custody of convicted felons, rebellious slaves, and other malefactors, doomed to work in irons in the slate quarries. After remaining about a year in this wretched place, Makanna, with a few followers, Caffers and slaves, from among the inmates of that house of bondage, over whom he had established his characteristic ascendancy, rose upon the guard, overpowered and disarmed them; then, seizing a boat, he placed his adherents in it, and would, in all probability, have effected his escape with them, but by some mischance the overloaded pinnace, in which he was the last man to embark, was upset, in attempting to land on the iron-bound coast, and the unfortunate African chief was drowned. Several of his companions who escaped relate that Makanna clung for some time to a rock, and that his deep sonorous voice was heard loudly cheering on those who were struggling with the billows, until he was swept off and engulfed by the raging surf.

Mr. Kay, who lately resided several years in Cafferland, states, in his recent work, that such was the universal belief in Makanna's supernatural powers and character among his countrymen, that many of them would give no credit to the accounts of his death, and still confidently expected his return among them.

Upon the treatment of the Caffer people throughout the whole of these transactions, it would be difficult to comment in calm language; and any comments, indeed, would be superfluous. The *facts*, established beyond dispute by so many respectable witnesses, cannot fail to speak to the heart of every candid reader as regards the chief Makanna, it is melancholy to reflect how valuable an instrument for promoting the civilization of the Caffer tribes was apparently lost by the nefarious treatment and indirect destruction of that extraordinary barbarian, whom a wiser and more generous policy might have rendered a grateful ally to the colony, and a permanent benefactor to his own countrymen.

4.   Xhosa Writer William Gqoba Recounts the Great Cattle Killing of 1857

A. C. Jordan, a professor at the University of Cape Town, the University of Wisconsin, and University of California at Los Angeles, was a leading Xhosa literary scholar. William W. Gqoba, whose account is quoted in the Jordan translation that follows, helped to pioneer written Xhosa. He penned poems, for example, that set up debates over Christian vs. non-Christian paths for the Xhosa. In addition, he wrote historical accounts.

Born in 1840, Gqoba was a teenager when the cattle-killing episode occurred. Although a Christian, he rejected the contemporary European explanations of the event. He interviewed participants in the cattle-killing cult and in this passage provides the closest semblance of an inside account of the prophesies of Nongqawuse.

The Cause of the Cattle-Killing at the Nongqawuse Period

By: W. W. G.

It so happened that in the Thenjini region of Gcalekaland, in the ward of headman Mnzabele, in the year 1856, two girls went out to the lands to keep the birds away from the corn. One was named Nongqawuse, daughter of Mhlakaza, and the other the daughter of a sister of Mhlakaza's. Near a river known as the Kamanga two men approached them and said, "Convey our greetings to your people, and tell them we are So-and-So and So-and-So" (giving their names). And the names by which they called themselves turned out to be the names of people who were known to have died long ago. They went out to say: "You are to tell the people that the whole community is about to rise again from the dead. Then go on to say to them all the cattle living now must be slaughtered, for they are reared with defiled hands, as the people handle witchcraft. Say to them there must be no ploughing of lands, rather must the people dig deep pits (granaries), erect new huts, set up wide, strongly built cattlefolds, make milk-sacks, and weave doors from buka roots. The people must give up witchcraft on their own, not waiting until they are exposed by the witchdoctors. You are to tell them that these are the words of their chiefs,—the words of Napakade (Forever), the son of Sifubasibanzi (the Broad-chested).

On reaching home the girls reported this, but no one would listen to them. Everybody ridiculed them instead. On the following day, they went again to keep the birds away from the corn, and after some time, these men appeared again and asked if the girls had told the people at home, and what the people had said in reply. The girls reported that their message had simply been a thing of laughter, no one believing them. "The people simply said we were telling stories". This happened in Gcalekaland near the mouth of the Gxara.

The men then said: "Say to the elders that they are to call all the chiefs together from Gcaleka's, Tato's, Ngqika's and from the Gqunukhwebe, and they must tell the news to them".

On the following morning, Mhlakaza and some other men went to the lands, but these strangers did not reveal themselves. They were heard without being seen. It was only Nongqawuse and the other girl who heard them, and it was Nongqawuse who interpreted what was being said by the spirits. They said: "Tell those men to go and call the chiefs and bring them here. Only then shall we reveal ourselves".

Some men then went to Rili's royal place at Hohita, and there the strange news was related by Mhlakaza's daughter. Then Rili sent out Botomani, a minor chief, to go and verify this thing. Botomani went, but the strangers did not reveal themselves. Then Rili sent messengers to tell the chiefs that there were people who had been heard by Mhlakaza's daughter to say all the chiefs must be called together to meet the chief Mapakade, son of Sifubasibanzi, near the mouth of the Gxara.

From Tato's came Maramnco, son of Fadana, accompanied by Shele, son of Zizi. From the Ndungwane came Dulaze, son of Qwesha, related to Ndarala. From the Tshatshus came Mpeke, son of Mfeneni. From the Ngqika came Namba, great son of Maqoma. From the Gcaleka section came Rili and Lindinxiwa, sons of Hintsa, together with Ngubo, son of Mlashe, and Nxiti, son of Lutshaba. From the Ndlambes came Nowawe, son of Ndlambe. From the Gqunukwebe came Dilima, son of Pato. All these men made their way to the home of Mhlakaza near the Gxara.

On arriving there, they were told that Nongqawuse desired that the numbers to go to the Gxara be reduced, and that those who were to go must be mostly chiefs. This in truth was done.

As the people were rather fearful, it happened that as they drew near the River Kamango, their throats went dry, and they felt thirsty. Meanwhile Nongqawuse, beautifully painted with red ochre, led the way. Then those who were thirsty were heard to say: "Is one who is thirsty allowed to drink?"

Nongqawuse replied, "He who does not practice witchcraft may drink without fear".

Thereupon Dilima, hero son of Pato, removed his kaross and stooped to drink. Then one by one the other men of Nomagwayi wase Mbo followed suit.

The Vision

Just at this time, there was a tremendous crash of big boulders breaking loose from the cliffs overlooking the headwaters of the River Kamanga, whereupon, the men gazed at one another wondering, for they were seized with fear. It seemed that some unknown thing on the cliffs was going to burst into flames.

While they stood wondering, the girl was heard saying, "Just cast your eyes in the direction of the sea".

And when they looked intently at the waters of the sea, it seemed as if there were people there in truth, and there were sounds of bulls bellowing, and oxen too. There was a huge formless black object that came and went, came and went and finally vanished over the crests of the waves of the sea.

Then it was that all the people began to believe.

The army in the sea never came out to meet the chiefs, and even what they said was not heard by any besides Nongqawuse. After it had vanished, she said: "The Chiefs yonder say you are to return to your homes and slaughter all your cattle and, in order that the resurrection may hasten, you are not to rear any cattle. You are not to plough the fields, but make big new pits (granaries), and these you will suddenly find full of corn. Erect new huts and make many doors. Shut yourselves in your huts, because on the eighth day, when the community returns in the company of Napakade, son of Sifubasibanzi, all the beasts on the land and in the rivers, and all the snakes will be roaming the land. You are also to take out all the old corn in the pits and throw it away. In order to survive, you are to use many doors to close each hut, fasten every door tightly, and abstain from witchcraft".

She went on to say that there was another chief, mounted on a grey horse. His name was Grey, eitherwise known as Satan. All those who did not slaughter their cattle would become the subjects of the chief named Satan, and such people would not see the glory of our own chief, Napakade, son of Sifubasibanzi.

That then was the cause of the cattle-killing of 1856 to 1857.

In the midst of this there appeared another young girl from the house of Nkwitshi of the Kwemta clan, in the Ndlambe section near the Mpongo. Her name was Nonkosi. The message of this girl was one with Nongqawuse's. She used to lead the people to a pond there at the Mpongo, and there used to see abakweta dancing on the surface of the water, and they thought that they heard the thudding of the oxhide, accompanied by a song, to which the abakweta danced. Truly, the people were so deluded that they went so far as to claim that they had seen the horns of cattle, heard the lowing of milk-cows, the barking of dogs, and the songs of milkmen at milking time.

The Orders of the Chiefs

On reaching their homes, the chiefs assembled their subjects and made known the news of the ancestors who were expected to return to life, fresh and strong, of the promised coming-to-life again of the cattle they were about to slaughter and of those that they had slaughtered long ago.

Nongqawuse had said that anyone who, on slaughtering his ox, decided to dispose of its carcass by barter, should nevertheless engage its soul, in order that on its coming back to life it should be his property. And she had said that all those who did not slaughter their cattle would be carried by a fierce hurricane and thrown into the sea to drown and die.

The community was split in two. One section believed that the resurrection of the people would come some day, but not that of the cattle.

Thereupon, father fell out with son, brother with brother, chief with subjects, relative with relative. Two names emerged to distinguish the two groups. One group was named amaTamba (the Submissive), that is, Nongqawuse's converts. The other was called amaGogotya (the Unyielding), that is, those who were stubborn and would not kill their cattle. So some slaughtered their cattle, and others did not.

The Eighth Day

As the killing of the cattle went on, those who had slaughtered hurriedly for fear of being smelt out began to starve and had to live by stealing the livestock of others. Then everybody looked forward to the eighth day. It was the day on which the sun was expected to rise red, and to set again in the sky. Then there would follow great darkness, during which the people would shut themselves in their huts. Then the dead would rise and return to their homes, and then the light of day would come again.

On that day the sun rose as usual. Some people washed their eyes with sea-water at the mouth of the Buffalo. Some peered outside through little apertures in their huts, while those who had never believed went about their daily outdoor tasks. Nothing happened. The sun did not set, no dead person came back to life, and not one of the things that had been predicted came to pass.

Such then was the Nongqawuse catastrophe. The people died of hunger and disease in large numbers. Thus it was that whenever thereafter a person said an unbelievable thing, those who heard him, said: "You are telling a Nongqawuse tale."

Cetshwayo in British Custody at the End of the Zulu War, 1879

PART 2

African Statecraft, Cultural Contact, and Colonialism in the Interior,

1818–1893

Part 2 documents the history of the regions north and east of the Cape Colony, across the Orange River and behind the Eastern Cape frontier. This interior region comprises the twentieth-century provinces of Natal, the Orange Free State and Transvaal, and the kingdom of Lesotho. On its edges, the states of Botswana, Zimbabwe, and Swaziland also enter the story, even though they are not part of modern South Africa. Two related developments transformed the interior in the early and mid-nineteenth century, one a shift in African society and politics, the other a dramatic extension of European migration into the region.

In the first decades of the nineteenth century, African societies in the interior were torn by a widening cycle of violence and disruption. Historians have interpreted the causes of this turbulence in conflicting ways. The most familiar account tells of a series of wars among Africans, clashes of unprecedented scale and devastation called the Mfecane, *or crushing. These wars, destructive as they were, spearheaded an indigenous African revolution and the rise of several new kingdoms. The southern Bantu-speaking peoples had never before created large-scale kingdoms south of the Limpopo River. The backwash of this revolution, in fact, reached north beyond the Limpopo, as far as Zambia and Malawi.*

The story of the Mfecane *has been a dominant theme in South African historical writing for half a century, and its events and personalities have deep resonance in the consciousness and memories of South Africans of all races. The* Mfecane *has provided sources of identity, ideological symbols, and themes for imaginative literature.*

Some Africans, for example, see the rise of the Zulu and other kingdoms as a story of empowerment and militancy that retains its relevance to more recent struggles. For some whites, on the other hand, the rise of predatory and destructive militaristic African states immediately before European settlement provided sound reasons for colonialist intervention. For both Europeans and Africans, the

Mfecane was above all a chapter in African history with only marginal European participation.

Recently, some scholars launched a major reinterpretation of these events, but disagreement among historians remains deep and no new synthesis has emerged. This introduction follows a good deal of the traditional story; it is important, therefore, to note some of the ways in which that interpretation has been criticized. First, some revisionist historians have stressed the importance of European influence on this time period. In their opinion, the cycles of violence that swept the region in the first decades of the nineteenth century did not signify indigenous African political revolution. Whereas traditional scholars believe that the overseas slave trade had little impact in Southern Africa, the revisionists argue that a considerable export slave trade, reaching into the region from Mozambique, greatly intensified the level of violence. Turmoil reached the high veld (the grasslands between the Orange and Limpopo Rivers) from the Cape Colony, which imported captured "servants," often justifying its actions by claiming to rescue and convert these souls to the true faith. Peoples such as the Zulu, the victims of these slave trades, organized to defend themselves and possibly to profit by enslaving others. Overall, these revisions result in a markedly different account of these times, one in which the acts of individual leaders are less important, political and military changes more gradual and less purposeful, than in the dramatic narratives of earlier historians.

Nevertheless, the region of the high veld, the coastal plains of Natal, and the adjacent area to the north did see striking political innovations during the period. The African kingdoms of this region—most importantly, Lesotho and the Zulu, Ndebele, and Swazi kingdoms—were major participants in the nineteenth-century history of South Africa. Smaller scale but still significant states took shape among the Tswana along the western, desert edge of the region. The northern Sotho Pedi kingdom developed in the northern Transvaal.

In the older accounts of South African history, the European counterpart of the Mfecane, is the so-called Great Trek, a major migration of European settlers into this same region and their creation of new republics beyond the boundaries of the Cape Colony and British colonial control. Starting in 1836 several thousand Afrikaner migrants left the Eastern Cape Colony to found settlements across the Orange, across the Vaal, and below the Drakensberg escarpment that plummets steeply from the high veld grassland interior to the moist coastal plain of Natal.

By the early 1850s, after repeated quarrels and divisions, the trekkers had formed two republics, the Orange Free State across the Orange River from the Cape Colony and the South African Republic, or Transvaal, across the Vaal. The trekkers in Natal, after an initial defeat by Zulu regiments early in 1838, defeated the Zulu kingdom and installed a more pliant king. However, when the British annexed Natal in 1843, most of the trekkers withdrew from the area and returned to the high veld.

The story of the Great Trek and of these republics stands as the dominant theme of traditional South African history and is written as an Afrikaner nationalist saga. For our purposes, the tale serves as background; the documents that follow focus instead on the African peoples and their contact with the Europeans. A brief assessment of the Great Trek and of the strength of the European occupation that it represented introduces a fuller account of the African history of the region.

Compared with the pioneer settlement in North America, the Great Trek was a small, weak movement. Nevertheless, the trekkers covered enormous territory;

they were dispersed thinly throughout the interior, and their farms were scattered across the land. The republics' governing institutions remained feeble and primitive for years, and the whites dwelled among a vast African population.

Under these circumstances, the settlers were in no position to exploit or dominate the Africans. With their firearms and horses, the Europeans did of course have an advantage, but the African peoples, especially the residents of Lesotho and the Tswana and Griqua living along the Orange and Vaal rivers, had also acquired modern weapons. The trekkers' most formidable enemies, the Zulu and Ndebele kingdoms, retained their traditional military systems, which made full use of their overwhelming numbers. Nevertheless, the Dutch settlers, by firing from their laager, *or circled wagons, ultimately triumphed over the Ndebele and Zulu armies in 1836 and 1838, despite initial defeats.*

After such battles, however, the Europeans would return to their homes and farms and resume their tentative occupation of the country, never fully driving out the Africans who lived in the white districts. In fact, white farmers found that they needed African labor, even though the presence of this labor unnerved them. Moreover, the Africans dwelling in the vicinity of European settlements, many of them victims of decades of warfare, relied on the whites to defend them from the Ndebele and Zulu armies—at least at first.

The readings in Part 3 depict how the whites amassed enormous economic and military power after the late 1860s. Their new strength eventually upset the near parity between Africans and Europeans and opened the door for the Europeans to destroy African political—and economic—independence.

Even if the extent of the European impact in the early nineteenth century receives greater emphasis than it did in the past, one can still make an argument for the importance of autonomous African developments. Indeed, until the 1870s, Africans retained their autonomy in many respects, even as the pressure from the Europeans steadily increased. The majority of African peoples in this region kept their political independence, social cohesion, and most of their economic resources until the 1870s. (In the Orange Free State, however, some Tswana and Sotho peoples, fractured by the violence of the 1820s and 1830s, had lost their best land to the whites in the early stages of the Great Trek.)

We turn now to the development among the interior African peoples from the late eighteenth century; through the violence of the 1820s and 1830s; and on to the period of growing contact with European travelers, missionaries, traders, settlers, and soldiers in the mid-nineteenth century.

The Africans of this region speak Bantu languages and are collectively termed, the southern Bantu. The various Bantu languages prevail in much of east, central, and southern Africa, from the Eastern Cape region of South Africa, north to Uganda and northwest to the Cameroons. The migration of Bantu-speaking peoples over one-third of the continent, as historians have reconstructed it from linguistic and archaeological evidence, is a complex and technical subject. For our purposes, it is enough to note that by the early centuries of the Christian era the Bantu-speakers had filtered into southern Africa from the north. Nevertheless, they did not yet occupy the entire subcontinent. In fact, the area in which Bantu languages was spoken expanded slowly until the eighteenth century, when, as we saw in Part 1, Bantu-speakers met the Europeans on the Eastern Cape frontier.

European scholars have divided the majority of the southern Bantu into two broad linguistic and cultural groups: the Nguni and the Sotho. As a convenient generalization, we may divide these two broad groups of the southern Bantu geographically. The Nguni lived on the Indian Ocean coastal plain from Mozambique

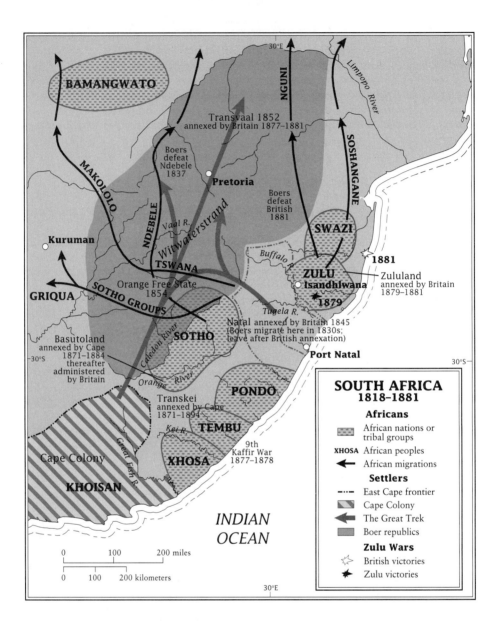

to the Eastern Cape frontier and included the Zulu and Xhosa peoples, among others. The Sotho, more diverse than the Nguni, dwelled on the high veld, to the west
of the Drakensberg mountains. The people of Lesotho and the neighboring Orange
Free State are southern Sotho; such groups as the Pedi of the Transvaal are northern Sotho; and the Tswana groups are termed western Sotho.

Overall, the southern Bantu—Nguni and Sotho alike—were Iron Age mixed
farmers who maintained large cattle herds and intensively cultivated food crops
such as maize and millet. In Tswana country, on the western desert edge of the

high veld, the chronic water shortage made people highly dependent on their herds. It also forced the population to concentrate in centralized settlements or larger towns located near permanent water supplies. These centers contrasted with the scattered small settlements of the humid Nguni country along the Indian Ocean coast.

In the late eighteenth century, southern Bantu political units typically encompassed only about two thousand persons. These units were based on kinship, with the chiefs coming from a clan's senior or royal lineage, but the political organization went beyond simple kinship. Groups often incorporated nonkin dependents and clients. Thus, the designation tribe *does not adequately describe these polities; the term* lineage state *perhaps provides a better designation.*

States of this sort continuously shifted and changed. From time to time, in response to population growth or disagreements within the group, small lineage states would split and some members would move on to new territory. By this mechanism, the Nguni especially spread south along the coast. In the late eighteenth and early nineteenth centuries, in present-day northern Natal, the abrupt end of this pattern had revolutionary consequences. In place of the splitting apart of small states, a new process emerged by which groups coalesced into large, centralized kingdoms. Historians have long debated the precise reasons for this change. It unfolded in a region well away from European settlement and intensive contact; the process seemed to originate within African society. One plausible theory postulates that a burgeoning population or local land shortages made the old split-and-expand process impossible to maintain.

Some nineteenth-century sources also credit the innovations to ambitious and gifted individuals. Naturally, in both oral tradition and written sources, events that may have broad social, economic, and ecological causes are often ascribed to exalted individuals. Although such "great-man theories" are as plausible in African as in European histories, we must nevertheless weigh such explanations carefully and grant that we can never fully explain this kind of social transformation.

At the center of this revolution in political organization is the rise of the Zulu kingdom, which sprang from a series of conflicts that erupted in the late eighteenth century. Two leaders, Dingiswayo of the Ndandwe and Zwide of the Mthethwa, had locked horns in a struggle for dominance over the region of northern Natal. Dingiswayo had hit upon an innovation: he brought the young men undergoing circumcision and initiation into manhood to his capital for the ceremony. He then retained the initiates for military service and formed them into an age-grade regiment. He thus tried to build a foundation for a larger military organization than had ever existed among the southern Bantu.

Shaka, the founder of the Zulu kingdom, became one of Dingiswayo's regimental commanders, and at Dingiswayo's death in 1818, Shaka gained control of the former leader's newly centralized state. Until then, the Zulu had been a minor clan and Shaka a junior son of the chief. Now Shaka consolidated his new power and led further military innovations. As one example, he designed an attack plan in which the regiment (impi) moved forward with interlocked shields and short stabbing spears (assegais) to envelope the enemy within the formation's horns.

The ten years of Shaka's reign (1818–1828) saw a relentless series of military campaigns, in which Shaka's armies raided and conquered to the north, to the south, and to the west onto the high veld. He built his kingdom by incorporating some of the peoples he conquered and secured it by driving others off.

To this day, Shaka embodies African militancy and serves as the subject of novels, poems, plays, and biographies. Interestingly, Shaka fought his battles against other Africans, not against European settlers. Information about him comes from oral traditions collected in the late nineteenth century. Some of the informants were supporters, others enemies, of the political tradition that the great warrior founded. The few European travelers and traders who visited the Zulu capital during Shaka's reign are another major source of information about him. Historians have depicted Shaka as everything from a raging psychopath to an esteemed and constructive leader. Such interpretations of Shaka often go far beyond what we can confidently know about him.

Shaka was assassinated by his half-brother Dingane in 1828, and it was Dingane who faced the trekkers encroaching on Natal ten years later. After Dingane's initially successful attack on the invaders, the Zulu army fell to defeat. The Battle of Blood River of December 16, 1838, became the central and formative event in Afrikaner nationalist mythology. The victory enabled the trekkers to occupy land in Natal. However, it did not destroy the Zulu kingdom.

Dingane was killed in 1840 while campaigning against the emerging kingdom of Swaziland, north of Zululand. Like the battle of 1838, his death played a key role in strengthening the position of the European settlers. Dingane had long considered his brother Mpande a cipher, and Mpande had therefore been spared in the elimination of Dingane's rivals and enemies. Now, with the help of the trekkers, Mpande succeeded to the Zulu throne. He was a weak king, and the trekkers manipulated him. But in one sense his weakness allowed the Zulu kingdom to regain its strength. After the British annexed Natal in 1843, the Zulu played a complex game of diplomacy, cultivating good terms with the British while negotiating with the Swazi and the Transvaal republic so as to avert the formation of alliances against them. For thirty years, stability reigned; the Zulu recovered from the loss of people and resources suffered in the late 1830s and early 1840s. The regimental system languished, but the tradition on which it rested survived.

Mpande's successor, Cetshwayo, became regent in the 1860s when Mpande had grown too feeble to rule. In 1873, after Mpande's death, Cetshwayo was recognized and crowned by Theophilus Shepstone, Natal's administrator of African affairs. Although the colonists seemed to dominate the Zulu kingdom, the revival of the regimental system under the new monarch strengthened the kingdom and it again became a threat to the European settlements. By the 1870s, the Europeans had made gains in both economic and military power and could no longer tolerate the presence of powerful and independent African states. The British colonial authorities, having temporarily annexed the Transvaal in 1877, forced a confrontation with the Zulu, leaving Cetshwayo no choice but to fight in 1879. After the brilliant Zulu victory at Isandhlwana in January, the war led relentlessly to Zulu defeat and the dismembering of the kingdom. But despite the end of Zulu political independence, the Zulu identity as a people was still to develop.

The rise of the Zulu kingdom had repercussions far beyond the immediate region. To avoid destruction, the societies attacked by Shaka's armies had three choices: to assimilate into the Zulu kingdom, to imitate Shaka's methods, or to flee. According to some sources, Mzilikazi, one of Shaka's regimental commanders, had had to flee when he failed to give Shaka cattle that he had won as booty. Mzilikazi led his army out of Zululand into the Transvaal, incorporating other peoples as he traveled and building a strong military kingdom similar to the Zulu state. In the mid-1830s, defeated by the trekkers, he withdrew again, crossing the Limpopo River into southern Zimbabwe. When Mzilikazi died in 1868, his son Lobengula succeeded him. Lobengula ruled the Ndebele during a period of growing European contact and pressure until the conquest by Cecil Rhodes's British South Africa Company forces in 1893.

Another major development of this period came with the great Moshoeshoe's founding of the kingdom of Lesotho. (He is called Moshesh in many books and documents.) From the 1830s he offered refuge and safety for scattered and destitute victims of the wars on the high veld, gathering them in a new kingdom in the mountains of Lesotho. A brilliant diplomat and one of the most talented South African leaders of the nineteenth century, Moshoeshoe negotiated with the British, the Afrikaners of the Orange Free State, missionary societies, and rival Africans to ensure his kingdom's survival. He lost much of his best agricultural and grazing land in wars with the Orange Free State, but he avoided conflict with the British. The kingdom was finally annexed by the British (a gain in security, as the Sotho saw it) by the time of Moshoeshoe's death in 1868.

The development of a string of small Tswana states along the edge of the desert, to the west of the trekker republics, also had significant consequences for the era. These were not military kingdoms on the Zulu model; the Tswana leaders, most notably the Ngwato leader Khama, defended their independence and adopted European techniques and alliances as means to that end. Thus in his struggle to ascend to the chiefdom, Khama maneuvered as the leader of a Christian party against conservative and traditionalist opponents.

Much of the most vivid documentation of this period comes from European travelers to the interior, visitors to the kraals and courts of Shaka or Dingane, Moshoeshoe, Mzilikazi, Khama, and other African leaders. Some of these witnesses were missionaries who hoped to convert the Africans to Christianity; others were scientists who were sent to survey flora and fauna but who took ample notice of the indigenous humans as well. Finally, there were traders who tested the commercial possibilities of the Africans and tried to outmaneuver rivals by gaining monopoly concessions from the rulers. Information from such travelers is undoubtedly biased, and scholars must read it carefully. Interestingly, however, there is no consistent bias in favor of the settlers in these writings. If anything, the missionaries, scientists, and traders describe the African peoples, more fully and sympathetically than they describe the settlers. Although we might see missionaries as precursors of imperialism or as imperialists themselves, they often accepted the legitimacy and appropriateness of African political independence. Many missionaries believed that stable polities offered a coherent society in which they could proselytize. Frequently, they grew possessive of their charges and resisted settler encroachments on "their" Africans. The two most important missionary bodies in South Africa were the London Missionary Society (LMS), an interdenominational group supporting Presbyterian and Congregationalist efforts, and the Church Missionary Society (CMS), affiliated with the Church of England. The CMS, evangelical in its theology, exhibited the typically Protestant focus on sin, conversion, and the striving for a reborn life, in contrast to high-church Anglo-Catholic emphasis on sacraments. Missionary sources offer rich information about Africans, information heavily laden with concerns about conversion and salvation.

The reports of traders and scientists also center on Africans. Traders viewed the Africans as potential customers and providers of indigenous products and sought to draw them into the orbit of the European economy. These merchants did *not regard Africans as obstacles to settlement or as mere labor units, as settlers eventually did. To the scientists, Africans constituted appropriate objects of study, and such enlightened travelers often expressed disdain for the European settlers. Scientists' attitudes toward Africans might well have been patronizing, even racist, but they were not inherently aggressive.*

Of course, these are rough generalizations about the sources: each first-hand account of nineteenth-century African life requires close critical assessment to determine its meaning and weigh its authenticity. We might also note that a tacit premise that runs through travelers' accounts: The authors seem to assume that whites could travel and sojourn safely throughout black Africa, even as conflicts between settlers and Africans simmered. Finally, the way in which these writers evaluate African society merits attention. On the one hand, they disparage it as barbarous, but on the other hand, they meet and visit with monarchs in their kingdoms and often express high regard for the dignity and character of these rulers. One piece of evidence that eloquently documents this point is the portrait of King Cetshwayo of the Zulu that the German artist Carl Sohn painted in the 1860s. Through the work's apparent reference to Holbein's portraits of Henry VIII, Sohn conveys his conviction that Cetshwayo is every inch a king.

The Coming of the Trekkers

1. A Trek Leader Explains Reasons for Leaving the Cape Colony, 1837

The Great Trek, the movement of several thousand European settlers from the eastern districts of the Cape Colony—across the Orange River, onto the high veld, and into Natal—is one of the best-known events in South African history. Indeed, as that history has been taught in the past, the trek is the central event. The meaning of the trek, of course, has changed in retrospect as part of the heritage of the Afrikaner nation.

In the document that follows, Piet Retief, an important trek leader, explains the initial reasons for leaving the Cape Colony.

Numerous reports having been circulated throughout the colony, evidently with the intention of exciting in the minds of our countrymen of prejudice against those who have resolved to emigrate from a colony where they have experienced, for so many years past, a series of the most vexatious and severe losses; and, as we desire to stand high in the estimation of our brethren, and are anxious that they and the world at large should believe us incapable of severing that sacred tie which binds a Christian to his native soil, without the most sufficient reasons, we are induced to record the following summary of our motives for taking so important a step, and also our intentions respecting our proceedings towards the native tribes which we may meet with beyond the boundary:

1. We despair of saving the colony from those evils which threaten it by the turbulent and dishonest conduct of vagrants, who are allowed to infest the country in every part; nor do we see any prospect of peace or happiness for our children in any country thus distracted by internal commotions.

From G. W. Eybers, *Select Constitutional Documents Illustrating South African History,* London: 1918, pp. 144–145.

2. We complain of the severe losses which we have been forced to sustain by the emancipation of our slaves, and the vexatious laws which have been enacted respecting them.

3. We complain of the continual system of plunder which we have ever endured from the Caffres and other coloured classes, and particularly by the last invasion of the colony, which has desolated the frontier districts and ruined most of the inhabitants.

4. We complain of the unjustifiable odium which has been cast upon us by interested and dishonest persons, under the cloak of religion, whose testimony is believed in England, to the exclusion of all evidence in our favour; and we can foresee, as the result of this prejudice, nothing but the total ruin of the country.

5. We are resolved, wherever we go, that we will uphold the just principles of liberty; but, whilst we will take care that no one shall be held in a state of slavery, it is our determination to maintain such regulations as may suppress crime, and preserve proper relations between master and servant.

6. We solemnly declare that we quit this colony with a desire to lead a more quiet life than we have heretofore done. We will not molest any people, nor deprive them of the smallest property; but, if attacked, we shall consider ourselves fully justified in defending our persons and effects, to the utmost of our ability, against every enemy.

7. We make known, that when we shall have framed a code of laws for our future guidance, copies shall be forwarded to the colony for general information; but we take this opportunity of stating, that it is our firm resolve to make provision for the summary punishment of any traitors who may be found amongst us.

8. We propose, in the course of our journey, and on arriving at the country in which we shall permanently reside, to make known to the native tribes our intentions, and our desire to live in peace and friendly intercourse with them.

9. We quit this colony under the full assurance that the English Government has nothing more to require of us, and will allow us to govern ourselves without its interference in future.

10. We are now quitting the fruitful land of our birth, in which we have suffered enormous losses and continual vexation, and are entering a wild and dangerous territory; but we go with a firm reliance on an all-seeing, just, and merciful Being, whom it will be our endeavour to fear and humbly to obey.

By authority of the farmers who have quitted the Colony,
(Signed) P. RETIEF.
Parl. Papers, C. of G. Hope (Return to
an address of the House of Commons,
dated 7 May 1838), 0.98, p. 5.

The Zulu and Ndebele Kingdoms

1. Nandi Bears a Child by Senzangakona, the Son of the Zulu Chief

James Stuart was born in Natal in 1868 and grew up among Zulu speakers. The transcriptions that he made of Africans' memories in the late nineteenth and early twentieth centuries are a fundamental source of Zulu history during early contact. In particular, historians have reconstructed the life and character of Shaka, the founder and first king of the Zulu kingdom, from sources such as the passage that follows. The evidence about Shaka's early life, however, is thin and often contradictory. Some informants had friendly ties with the monarch and the Zulu kingdom; others were hostile. We might say that historians have written much more about Shaka than is really known; indeed, the most widely read account of the warrior king is Thomas Mofolo's novel Chaka. *Nevertheless, the immense symbolic significance of Shaka's life and the meanings that it has acquired endure despite the questionable authenticity of all the stories about him.*

Interview with Zulu Notable Jantshi

After this the girls, day by day, used to come to this spot to amuse themselves and pass away their time. In the course of a few weeks Mbengi, finding that Nandi had become pregnant (she had at first stated she was suffering from an illness known as *itshaka* or *itshati*), sent a report to that effect to Mudhli. Mudhli asked why such report had been made to him. The messengers replied, 'He acquaints you of this because the girl stated she liked the *son of the chief.*' Mudhli retorted, 'Is that the case?' 'Yes', they answered. Mudhli then said, 'All right, then please look after that, in case it turns out to be a child. We of the

From C. de B. Webb and J. B. Wright, eds., *The James Stuart Archive*, Vol. 1, Pietermartzburg: University of Natal Press and Durban: Killie Campbell Africana Library, 1976, pp. 178–180. Reprinted by permission of the University of Natal Press.

Zulu tribe would be glad if it should happen to be a boy.' The *men from the Langeni* then went off *and there, for the time being, the matter rested.*

Later on, messengers again came to Mudhli to say the girl had been delivered of a child and it was a boy. Mudhli was pleased at this and said, '*On no account let his mother suckle him.*' I think this must have been done because royalty were not allowed, by custom, to be suckled by their mothers.

Mudhli secretly informed Senzangakona's mother of what had taken place. She then used to send a piece of string to where the child was in order to see how big its waist was. All this time the members of the kraal at which Senzangakona's mother lived knew nothing of what had happened. When the child had grown a little, Senzangakona's mother dispatched a man to fetch and bring it to her, which was done. But this act took place at night, and the circumstances appearing to the night guards of the *isigodhlo* of a strange character, they paid special attention. My father said to me, 'I cannot think how the persons referred to came to see that there was a child in the hut.' The persons who saw this belonged to the Zulu tribe. It was the custom to have night guards so as to detect those committing adultery etc. However the incident came to be noticed, the *guardians* of Senzangakona all came to hear of it, and an *impi* was sent to Senzangakona's mother's kraal the next day to kill off the child, seeing that, at that time, Senzangakona had not been allowed to marry. Senzangakona's mother had caused *mats* to be set up at the back of the hut behind which the child was set and where she used to play with it. It was not allowed to sit out in the open in the hut.

Before this *impi* had been sent forth, a report reached Senzangakona's mother to the effect that somehow people had come to hear of the existence of the child there and whose it was. She was advised to have it taken away and sent back to its mother among the Langeni. Senzangakona's mother acted at once on the advice given her.

Two men, on the following day, preceded the *impi* referred to and, making their way to Senzangakona's mother, asked what she had hidden away behind the mats in her hut. The *impi* at this time was close up to the kraal. The two men looked about but found nothing. Whilst they were so engaged the *impi*, in large numbers, arrived and, after searching about the kraal for the child and not finding it, they proceeded at once to destroy the kraal and the members thereof. People were put to death but Senzangakona's mother somehow escaped being killed. My father gave the very names of those who went with this *impi*, for he knew them, but I have forgotten them. Now the name of this kraal was Mfemfe (*Hamu's home kraal*), but the name was changed by Senzangakona to that of Mangeni, because lies had been told there.

The child was Tshaka [Shaka]. Now as regards the name Tshaka, I took care to question my father especially about it. He said he got the name from the ailment from which his mother Nandi was at first said to be suffering, before it became evident she was pregnant, viz. *itshaka*. My father said *itshati* by some was called *itshaka* by others in those early days. My father Nongila said that if a person had what is now known as *ikambi,* she was spoken of as having *itshaka*. The same expression was used in regard to a girl who had by accident, become *enceinte* before marriage. The *illegitimate child* she had *produced* was also spoken of as *itshaka*. My father drew my attention to the fact that we come from the north and that our dialect is different from what it used to be. He also said that some spoke of *itshaka* as *itshati*. He himself used the word *itshaka* and it was from the circumstances under which Tshaka was conceived that he was so named. The child Tshaka was taken back to the Langeni. There he grew up. When the Mfemfe (Mangeni) kraal was attacked as described, Nandi went off and married Gendeyana by whom she had a son named Ngwadi.

Senzangakona was shortly after allowed to marry. He then had the following sons: Dingana, Mpande, Ngqojana, Mfihlo, Mqubana, Mhlangano, Sigujana, Nzibe, Sankoye, and others. Tshaka at a later time said to the last-named, 'You are too ugly to be called my brother, so go away.' He, Tshaka, thereupon made him a present of cattle and Sankoye went to live a long distance off. After some years, however, Sankoye visited Tshaka, wanting to see his elder brother as he had so long been parted from him. All Tshaka said was, 'Did I not tell you not to come here?' And he thereupon gave orders for him to be put to death.

When Tshaka had grown up and become an *insizwa* [soldier] among the Langeni, Senzangakona came to hear of him and that he had become an *insizwa*. My father says Senzangakona then wanted to send to the Langeni people for Tshaka, but Mudhli, hearing of this intention, secretly dispatched a man—his *inceku*—so that Tshaka, by seeing the man, might afterwards know him. This *inceku* carried the following message to Tshaka: 'Mudhli says you are about to be summoned *to the country of the Zulu*, but do not, when you arrive there, sit down. Remain standing. You will,' the *inceku* continued, 'see me there on your arrival. *I shall wink at you* if there is any danger and, should you see me do this, you must make off immediately.'

The invitation from Senzangakona arrived in due course *among the Langeni*. Tshaka accordingly came *to the Zulu country*, accompanied by about 20 *izinsizwa* [soldiers] of his own age. All had armed themselves with *large war shields*. They found the Zulu seated outside in a semicircle. I believe this took place at the Mfemfe kraal where Senzangakona's mother lived. As soon as Tshaka and his companions arrived, they took up a position some yards off and there continued standing. Tshaka stood forth from his followers, a little in front of them. He then glanced about among the Zulu people and discovered Mudhli's *inceku* winking at him, the *inceku* being seated behind Mudhli. The *izinsizwa* with Tshaka had stood their shields *with the projecting sticks* on their feet in an upright position. On seeing the *inceku* wink, the party turned right about with their shields and made off towards their homes. When Tshaka arrived *back among the Langeni*, he did not stop there any longer but went on at once to Dingiswayo's district among the Mtetwa.

I should have remarked that whilst living among the Langeni, Tshaka had a quarrel with a cousin of his (my father mentioned the name—I forget it) about some stones. The cousin took away a stone belonging to Tshaka. On Tshaka's demanding the return of it, his cousin got angry and refused to give it up. Tshaka thereupon proceeded to the cattle belonging to the kraal at which this cousin lived and deliberately stabbed one of them to death. His cousin asked why, because of a quarrel about a stone, he should go and stab a beast. Tshaka after this *left* and went to the Qwabe. He was obliged to go because there was a good deal of ill-feeling about his killing the beast in this way. Tshaka went now and lived with a man who had *built for* Gendeyana, his mother Nandi's husband. I forgot the name of this man. Tshaka spent some time here. Here again, however, he had another quarrel. He quarrelled with a boy belonging to the man he had gone to live with. This boy retaliated by *insulting* him in the following terms: '*What sort of little Ntungwa is this, the one with the little half-cocked penis?*' Tshaka became angry, especially because these opprobrious expressions were similar to those the Lembe people had formerly used in respect of his ancestors. He then left and went back to live among the Langeni. When the quarrel above referred to between Tshaka and his cousin took place, the journey by Tshaka and his party to the Zulu on Senzangakona's invitation had not taken place.

From the Langeni Tshaka now went to the Mtetwa tribe where he grew into manhood. He lived in Ngomane's kraal, son of Mqomboli. Ngomane was already an old man when Tshaka went to the Zulu as king. I do not know if Mqomboli was living when Tshaka fled to Dingiswayo's. Tshaka here became a *warrior* and he went out with the *impi* to fight in many directions.

Tshaka went to Dingiswayo *when he was approaching the age of an insizwa*, and stayed there until he was a full-grown man. He made himself a reputation there.

2. King Shaka Converses with European Visitors, 1822

Nathaniel Isaacs (1808–1872) was shipwrecked on the Natal coast in 1822, well beyond the areas of European settlement. The survivors worked to build another ship out of the wreckage. Isaacs traveled two hundred kilometers to the court of Shaka, king of the Zulu. At the Zulu capital, the Africans compelled Isaacs and his companions to help Shaka fight one of his wars. The European firearms ensured a Zulu victory and earned Isaacs favor at the Zulu capital. Shaka made Isaacs a chief and gave him extensive land grants along the Natal coast, responsibility for the whites living in the area, and exclusive rights to trade with the Zulus. After Shaka's assassination in 1828, Dingane confirmed these grants. After the British annexation of Natal in 1843, however, Isaac failed to get colonial recognition of his claims.

From Nathaniel Isaacs, *Travels and Adventures in Eastern Africa*, Vol. 1, Cape Town: The van Riebeeck Society, 1936, pp. 58–63, 281–284. Reprinted by permission of The van Riebeeck Society, Cape Town, South Africa.

Isaacs's work to develop his land, carry on trade, and sponsor cul-
tural changes among local Africans, make him, from one point of view,
one of the first colonizers of Natal. From another point of view, however,
he is a "transfrontiersman," and Shaka and Dingane clearly regard him
as a servant and a subordinate.
   In the following selection, Isaacs recounts a conference between the
Zulu monarch and his European visitors.

3rd.—We now reached the head of the kraal, where a multitude of the natives had congregated and were seated in the form of a half circle. Chaka sat by himself on a large mat rolled up. Our natives saluted him after their manner, and I did the same, according to our European custom, and then took my seat among his people about twenty yards off. He desired me to approach him, which I did, when he immediately asked me how Mr. Farewell was, whose people we were, and if I had any knowledge of the Portuguese, mentioning that he had a Portuguese with him; at my expressing a wish to see him, Chaka sent for the individual, and I was soon most agreeably surprised to see a European in this wild and unfrequented place. The king desired me to go away, and not understanding him I was led about like a child. As his orders must be instantly obeyed, my interpreter had no time afforded him to explain the object of my visit, he therefore pulled me about from one place to the other, like a man confused and apprehensive. My natives all appeared alarmed as they approached the king, who sent for me again and presented me with a piece of paper, on which he had made some marks; these I was directed to decipher, but not being competent to do so, and my interpreter not being a very profound translator, we made but a sorry figure, and Chaka turning towards his people said, "He does not understand the ungnorty," or the letter, and they replied, "Yubo Barlu," or, "Yes father we see it." He then asked the Portuguese, who, as may be expected, was as incapable of expounding his hieroglyphics as myself. After amusing himself at our expense for some time, he directed us to retire to the hut, where the Portuguese had some ribs of beef, on which I made a sorry meal, not because I had not an appetite, but from the peculiarity of my situation, for we could not converse nor administer to each other any consolatory hopes of a more pleasing interview than the one just witnessed. I ascertained from my Portuguese inmate, however, though perhaps employed by his government in some military office, that he had arrived there for the purpose of purchasing cattle. We then retired to our mats to repose, and to which kind of rest I had now become accustomed.

   4th.—This morning I offered to his majesty the presents I had brought with me, consisting of twelve brass bangles and a bottle of sweet oil, the value of which he would be able to estimate when applied to bruises and swelled parts of the flesh. He desired me to rub his leg with some of it, an honour to which none but his subjects of rank are admitted; and during my performance none of his people dared advance to within twenty yards without danger of his displeasure. While thus engaged the Portuguese came up, whom he asked, "who were the greatest warriors," when he replied, that the English had subdued all the powers on the other side of the great water. I was apprehensive that this compliment to the gallantry of my country might incense Chaka, and lead him to fear that we might next attempt to subdue him; but to my great enjoyment he felt otherwise, and said to his people about him, "King George's warriors are a fine set of men, in fact, King George and I are brothers; he has conquered all the whites, and I have subdued all the blacks."

He asked me if "King George was as handsome as he was"; I told him, by way of flattering him, that I thought not. He then asked me to fight with the Portuguese, but I told him that, although our nation had conquered the Portuguese, we were now not only at peace with them, but were by treaties their protectors, and that were we to fight in our present situations, it might be the cause of disturbing the good understanding existing between the two countries.

"Well," said he, "what need you care? You have once conquered, and may conquer again." My Portuguese new acquaintance sat all this time and heard our conversation with concealed chagrin, and swelling with rage; but when we had left the presence of Chaka, we both laughed at the vanity of the savage. . . .

On a sudden a profound silence ensued, when his majesty uttered one or two words, at which some of the warriors immediately rose and seized three of the people, one of whom sat near me. The poor fellows made no resistance, but were calm and resigned, waiting their fate with apparently stoical indifference. The sanguinary chief was silent; but from some sign he gave the executioners, they took the criminals, laying one hand on the crown and the other on the chin, and by a sudden wrench appeared to dislocate the head. The victims were then dragged away and beaten as they proceeded to the bush, about a mile from the kraal, where a stick was inhumanly forced up the fundament of each, and they were left as food for the wild beasts of the forest, and those carnivorous birds that hover near the habitations of the natives.

After this savage execution of the criminals, the cause of which I could not discover, Chaka having given orders that his warriors should disperse, retired to his palace, and I retired to my hut with feelings not a little excited by a scene which sinks man to a level with the brute. Shortly after my departure, a fat cow was sent to me, which I killed, and, being somewhat hungry, it was a most acceptable and timely present, and no time was lost in preparing it for the table. . . .

6th.—Thus the eve of going to war was always the period of brutal and inhuman murders, in which he seemed to indulge with as much savage delight as the tiger with his prey. When he once had determined on a sanguinary display of his power, nothing could restrain his ferocity; his eyes evinced his pleasure, his iron heart exulted, his whole frame seemed as if it felt a joyous impulse at seeing the blood of innocent creatures flowing at his feet; his hands grasped, his herculean and muscular limbs exhibiting by their motion a desire to aid in the execution of the victims of his vengeance: in short, he seemed a being in a human form, with more than the physical capabilities of a man; a giant without reason, a monster created with more than ordinary power and disposition for doing mischief, and from whom we recoil as we would at the serpent's hiss or the lion's growl.

It was an invariable rule of war with him never to give his troops more cattle or provisions than would barely suffice to support them till they arrived in the country of their enemy. They had strict injunctions to fight or die, to quarter on their enemy, and not return but as victors, bringing with them the fruits of their triumph.

He was exceedingly wary, and used great precaution in concealing even from his generals or chiefs, the power or tribe with whom he designed combating; nor until the eve of marching did he make known to them the object of their expedition. By this he evinced some discretion, and precluded the possibility of his enemy being apprised of his intentions. In this particular, Chaka showed a judgment not common with the native chiefs, and peculiarly his own.

When all was ready for entering upon their march, he confided to one general his design, and to him he entrusted the command, should he not head his army in person. He, however, never confided in one man but on one occasion; upon no occasion whatever did he repeat such confidence. He made it an invariable rule always to address his warriors at their departure, and his language was generally studied to raise their expectations, and excite them in the hour of battle. He particularly detailed to them the road his spies had pointed out, inducing them to believe that they were going to attack any party but the one actually designed, and known only to the general-in-chief. This was judicious, because it kept his real object from being known, and, at the same time, prevented any treacherous communication to his enemy, who might get early intimation of his intended attack.

Chaka always kept up a system of espionage, by which he knew at all times the condition and strength of every tribe around him, both independent and tributary; and these persons were always directed to make such observations on the passes to and from the country to which they were sent, as might be useful in leading the troops to the scene of action with the surest chance of arriving at their position, without being discovered on the one hand, or surprised on the other.

At the return of his warriors from an expedition, he was usually generous to them, it must be admitted, but that only occurred in the case of their having achieved a triumph over his enemies; in such cases he gave the captured spoils liberally amongst them, as an encouragement for future exertions and enterprise: but to return without having accomplished what he had anticipated, was a signal for a scene of woe and lamentation—a massacre of no measured description.

After an expedition his troops were permitted to retire to their respective kraals for a short period, to recover from their fatigue, whence in a short time, the chiefs were called to collect the people and hear the details of those operations in which the warriors had been engaged; at which time all who had evinced cowardice were selected, brought forth, received the fiat of their ferocious master, and were led off immediately to be impaled, as an atonement for their offence, and as an example to others who should feel disposed to pursue a similar conduct. Such warriors who distinguished themselves in battle were honoured with a *nom de guerre* [war name], by which they were afterwards accosted.

The king also distinguished his regiments by giving them shields differently coloured. The great warriors have white shields with one or two black spots; the young warriors have all black shields; the middle warriors, or those that have wives, form distinct regiments, and are called Umfaudas (inferiors), have red shields.

All the regiments form three armies, and have a portion of each of three distinctions in each army. The first army is called "Umbalable, or invincibles;" the second "Umboolalio, or the slaughterers;" and the third "Toogooso, or the hide-aways." The principal chief of each regiment is a member of the "Ebarnschlo, or senate," of their own army. The king, at his pleasure, calls on them, or any part of them, to give their opinion on state affairs. In such cases they are exceedingly cautious not to decide against the wish of the king, who always submits the matter for their consideration, first making known to them his own opinion: should, however, they decide against his wish, he can call another Ebarnschlo, and if their determination accord with his views the latter then become his favourites, while the former will necessitated to "schlowoola" (make peace-offerings) for offending the king.

He can hold secret councils, and have any member killed, not excepting even the principal chief, if he fancy him opposed to his schemes. He is generally at variance with one half his chiefs, who are members of this military tribunal, and prevents their meeting by having his regiments in opposite directions and at positions at some distance apart. Although meetings are not publicly prohibited, it is well known they create Chaka's wrath and suspicion, and that they terminate with death to such as assemble without his knowledge. All meetings of this military council are held at the gateway of the king's kraal, or in the cattle-pound, which is their council-room, unless the king be present, when they meet in the palace.

Chaka had an extreme aversion to anything like commercial traffic, and forbade it among his people. Towards the Europeans he always expressed himself decidely opposed to any intercourse, having for its object the establishment of a mercantile connection with his subjects. His whole soul was engrossed by war, and he conceived that anything like commerce would enervate his people and unfit them for their military duties.

3.   Piet Retief and King Dingane Exchange Letters, 1837

Dingane killed his half-brother Shaka in 1828 and succeeded him as king. Although he condemned the violence of Shaka's regime, he carried out similar policies. Traders continued to reside at Dingane's court as before, and he gave some of them land grants. He did not regard them as settlers, but as clients subordinate to him. Missionaries also arrived at Dingane's court. When Piet Retief and the trekkers requested land cessions from Dingane, indicated in the letters that follow, the Zulu king already knew that they had defeated Mzilikazi and the Ndebele.

Port Natal, 19th October, 1837

To the Chief of the Zulus.

I take the opportunity of the return of your messengers to inform you that my great wish is to have an interview with yourself personally, in order to remove the impressions made by certain vague rumours which may have reached you respecting the intentions of the party who have quitted the colony, and who desire to establish themselves in the country which is uninhabited and adjacent to the territory of the Zulus.

Our anxious wish is to live at peace with the Zulu nation. You will, doubtless, have heard of our last rupture with Umsilikazi, resulting from the frequent and ruinous robberies committed habitually by his tribe; in consequence of which it had become absolutely necessary to declare war against him, after having in the first instance failed in every attempt to arrange our differences.

I shall set out in a few days for the country of the Zulus, in order to settle with you our future relations. The hope of always living on terms of peace and amity with the Zulu nation is the sincere wish of your true friend,

(Signed) Retief, Governor, &c.

Umgungundhlovu, 31st October, 1837

To Mr. P. Retief.

Sir,—The king desires me to say that he has taken from Moselikatzi (Umsilikazi) the sheep which the bearers of this letter have with them; that these sheep belong to the Dutch, and that he desires to restore them to their owners; that his army has taken many more than those you see, but that they have died by hundreds on the way; that many more have died since they came hither, and that he sends you their skins.

From all that he has been able to learn from a woman brought from Umsilikazi's country, there were no more than nine head of cattle belonging to the Dutch, and captured by his army; and these have all died since their

From John Bird, *The Annals of Natal, 1495 to 1845*, Vol. 1, Cape Town: T. Maskew Miller, pp. 359–366.

arrival, otherwise he would have sent them to you. Umhlala, the induna who commanded the army, says that Umsilikazi has fled with numerous herds, and he supposes that the greater number must belong to the Dutch. The king has been much grieved by the attack by Umsilikazi on the Boers. He says that he does not expect that all the sheep he is sending will reach Port Natal, for many will certainly die on the way. He says that he very much appreciates the letter sent to him by you.

I am, &c.,
(Signed) F. Owen, Missionary from England
+ Mark of the Chief

P.S.—The number of sheep leaving this place to-day is 110. The king will send the skins mentioned by his people as far as the Tugela; and, he says, you may, if you see fit, send a wagon for them, to load at that place.

Umgungundhlovu, 8th November, 1837

To Pieter Retief, Esq.,
Governor of the Dutch Emigrants.

Sir,—This is an answer to your letter of 24th October, and will inform you of the conversation that has taken place. I regret to hear that you have suffered such heavy losses by the acts of Umsilikazi. I have taken from Umsilikazi a great number of your sheep. [&c., &c. The contents of the former letter are repeated.]

Now, as regards the request you have made to me as to the territory, I am almost inclined to cede it to you; but, in the first place, I desire to say that a great number of cattle have been stolen from my country by a people having clothes, horses, and guns. The Zulus assure me that these people were Boers: that the party had gone towards Port Natal; the Zulus now wish to know what they have to expect.

My great wish, therefore, is that you should show that you are not guilty of the matters alleged against you: for at present I believe that you are. My request is that you recover my cattle and restore them to me; and, if possible, hand over the thief to me. That proceeding would remove my suspicions, and will give you reason to know that I am your friend: then I shall accede to your request. I shall give you a sufficient number of people to drive the cattle that you may re-capture for me: and they will remove all the suspicions that the stolen cattle are in the hands of the Dutch. If any cattle have been taken that were not mine, I pray you to send them to me.

(Signed) Mark + of the Chief Dingaan

Witness: (Signed) F. Owen

Port Natal, 8th November, 1837

To Dingaan, King of the Amazulu.

It is with pleasure that I recognize your friendship and justice in the matter of the flocks taken by you from Umsilikazi. I thank you also in regard to the skins that you have so obligingly offered to return to me; but I wish you to keep them for your own use and advantage. I have no difficulty in believing, as you say, that so small a number of my cattle should have been taken by your army from the possession of Umsilikazi, since, having seen a number of yours at the different villages, I found none of my own among them. Umsilikazi, I have no doubt, has fled to a distance, for he must think and feel that I shall punish his misconduct. Have I not already reason to complain that I have been constrained to kill so many men of his nation because they had been bound to execute his cruel orders?

That which has just befallen Umsilikazi gives me reason to believe that the Almighty, that God who knows all, will not permit him to live much longer. The great Book of God teaches us that kings who conduct themselves as Umsilikazi does are severely punished, and that it is not granted to them to live or reign long; and if you desire to learn at greater length how God deals with such bad kings, you may inquire concerning it from the missionaries who are in your country. You may believe what these preachers will tell you of God and His government of the world. Respecting such things, I advise you frequently to discourse with these gentlemen, who desire to preach the word of God to you, because they will teach you how justly God has ruled and still rules all the kings of the earth.

I assure you that it is an excellent thing for you to have given permission to preachers to establish themselves in your country: more than that, I certify to you that these preachers have come to you because God instilled into their hearts the idea of doing so; and they are able to show you, by reference to the Bible, that what I am now saying to you is the truth.

As a friend, I must tell you this great truth, that all, whether white or black, who will not hearken to and believe the word of God, will be unhappy. These gentlemen have not come to you to ask for land or cattle, still less to cause you trouble in any way, but only in order to preach to you and yours the word of God.

Now, I cordially thank the king for the good and favourable answer to my request, and I hope the king will remember his word and his promise when I return. You may be satisfied that I would do the same. I think it likely that, before my return, you will be disquieted by advice given you respecting my request and your promise; and I think it possible that even more will be stated to the king respecting me and my people, and that such statements may have a semblance of truth. If discourse of this kind should occur, I would ask you to inform me on my return by whom these things have been said. I have no fear of meeting, in your presence, anyone who may have spoken ill of me or my people. My desire is that it may not please you, before my return, to give ear to anyone who would seek to raise up embarrassments in your mind respecting the country in which I desire to live.

As to the thieves who have taken your cattle, and what they have said, namely, that they were Boers, it was a skillful artifice to induce you to regard me as a robber, in order that they themselves may escape with impunity. I confidently believe that I shall be able to prove to the king that I and my people are innocent of the crime. Knowing my innocence, I feel that you have imposed a severe obligation on me, which I must fulfil, in order to show that I am not guilty. As for the proceeding which you require from me, accompanied as it is by expense, by trouble, and risk of life, I must be responsible for it to you, to the world, and to God, who knows all.

I go now, placing my trust in God, who gives me hope that I shall be able to carry out this undertaking in such manner as to give a satisfactory answer. That done, I shall look forward to being satisfied that I am dealing with a king who keeps his word. I hope that some of your men, and especially those of the kraals from which your cattle have been taken will be ordered to accompany me, as have been agreed; and, moreover, that they obey my orders with precision. I thank you for the friendly reception you have given me, in return for which I shall always endeavour to show you equal good-will.

Yours obediently,

(Signed) P. Retief

Extract of a letter from Mr. P. Retief, dated Port Natal, Nov. 18, 1837:—

[From the "Graham's Town Journal."]

Dingaan received me with much kindness, but has at the same time imposed a difficult task upon me, as you will see from a copy of his letter. He finally told me, with a smile on his countenance, 'You do not know me, nor I you: and, therefore, we must become better acquainted.' The king did not give me an audience on the subject of my mission until the third day after my arrival. He said I must not be hasty, and that, as I had come from a long distance to see him, I must have rest, and partake of some amusement. During two days his people were engaged in exhibiting their national dances, and in warlike manoeuvres. The first day upwards of two thousand of his youngest soldiers were assembled; and on the following day his elder warriors were exhibited, to the number of four thousand. Their dances and manoeuvres were extremely imposing and interesting. Their sham fights are terrific exhibitions. They make a great noise with their shields and kerries, uttering at the same time the most discordant yells and cries. In one dance the people were intermingled with 176 oxen, all without horns and of one colour. They have long strips of skin hanging pendent from their foreheads, cheeks, shoulders, and under the throat, which are cut from the hides of calves. These oxen are divided in twos and threes among the whole army, which then dances in companies, each with its attendant oxen. In this way, they all in turns approach the king, the oxen turning off into a kraal, and the warriors moving in a line *from* the king. It is surprising that the oxen should be so well trained; for, notwithstanding all the shouting and yelling which accompany this dance, yet they never move faster than a slow walking pace. Dingaan showed me also, as he said, his *smallest* herd of oxen—all alike, red with white backs. He allowed two of my people to count them, and the enumeration amounted to two thousand four hundred and twenty-four. I am informed that his herds of red and black oxen consist of three to four thousand each.

The king occupies a beautiful habitation. The form is spherical, and its diameter is twenty feet. It is supported in the interior by twenty-two pillars, which are entirely covered with beads. The floor shines like a mirror. His barracks consist of 1,700 huts, each capable of accommodating twenty warriors. But since its return from the expedition against Umsilikazi, his army is at an out-post. The king behaved to me with great kindness during all the time I was with him.

Of the missionaries here in general, I cannot speak too highly of their extreme kindness and attention. I visited Capt. Gardiner on my way to and from the king, and was kindly received by him.

I must now return with my work unaccomplished, which will cause me a great deal of anxiety and fatigue. But what can I do otherwise than leave our case in the hands of the Almighty, and patiently wait His will? He will, I hope, strengthen me to acquit myself of my difficult task as becomes a Christian; and, although the duty which now devolves upon me through the misconduct of Sikonyela is by me particularly regretted, yet my hope is in God, who will not forsake those who put their trust in Him.

I perceive with astonishment that there are yet persons in the colony whose hostile feelings are still displayed towards us, and who continue to calumniate us, though so far removed. They seem to wish us evil, and to anticipate the difficulties we shall have to contend with. I can thank God that their wishes and their expectations have not yet been answered. They would act much more wisely were they first to wait and see the result of the case before they express their sentiments.

Cession of Port Natal to the Boers by Dingaan

[From a certified copy of the original, supplied to the Compiler by Mr. Jeppe.]

Umkugings Sloave, 4th February, 1838

KNOW ALL MEN BY THIS—That whereas Pieter Retief, Gouvernor of the Dutch emigrant South Afrikans, has retaken my Cattle, which Sinkonyela had stolen; which Cattle he, the said Retief, now deliver unto me: I, Dingaan, King of the Zoolas, do hereby certify and declare that I thought fit to resign unto him, Retief, and his countrymen (on reward of the case hereabove mentioned) the Place called "Port Natal," together with all the land annexed, that is to say, from Dogela to the Omsoboebo River westward; and from the sea to the north, a far as the land may be usefull and in my possession. Which I did by this, and give unto them for their everlasting property.

(Signed) De merk + van Koning Dingaan

Als Getuigen: Nwara,
                 Juliwane,   Grote Raads-Herden.
                 Manonda,
Als Getuigen: M. Oosthuyzen,   Een ware copy:
                 A. C. Greyling,   (Signed) J. G. Bantjes,
                 B. J. Liebenberg.   J. B. Roedeloff.

"We certify that the annexed contract was found by us, the undersigned, with the bones of Mr. P. Retief in Dingaan's country, on the 21st day of December, 1838, in a leather hunting-pouch. If required, we are prepared to uphold this by solemn oaths. (Signed) E. F. Potgieter."

4.   Dingane's Secretary Witnesses a Massacre, 1838

Responding to a call to open a mission for the Zulu, Reverend Francis Owen (1802–1854) traveled to South Africa in 1837 for the MS. King Dingane permitted Owen to stay at the Zulu capital but declined to take any interest in Christianity. Rather, he used Owen as a secretary and go-between. Owen served especially in the correspondence between Dingane and the Boer trek leader Piet Retief. Two months after he witnessed Dingane's massacre of Piet Retief and his party, an event recounted in the following passages from his diary, Owen withdrew the mission from the Zulu capital. He was in no danger, but he had lost all prospects of con-verts. Owen failed to open a mission elsewhere in South Africa and returned to England.

Feb. 2nd.—Dingarn sent for me at sunrise to write a letter to Mr. Retief, who with a party of the Boers is now on his way to the Zoolu capital. The letter was characteristic of the chief. He said that his heart was now content, because he had got his cattle again: he requested that the chief of the Boers would send to all his people and order them to come up to the capital with him, *but with-out their horses:* he promised to gather together all his army to sing and dance in the presence of the Dutch, who he desired would also dance: he said he would give orders that cattle should be slain for them in every place thro' which they passed on their road, and he promised to give them a country. I asked how they could come without their horses. He said tell them then that they must bring their horses and dance upon their horses in the middle of the town, that it may be known who can dance best, the Zooloos or the Abalongo,

From Sir George E. Cory, ed., *The Diary of the Rev. Francis Owen, M. A., Missionary with Dingaan in 1837–1838,* Cape Town: The van Riebeeck Society, 1926, pp. 104–111. Reprinted by permission of The van Riebeeck Society, Cape Town, South Africa.

the general term for white people. Nothing was said about the guns or horses taken from Sinkoyela. The Dutch will be too wise to expose themselves in the manner proposed, but I cannot conceive that Dingarn *meditates* any treachery, which, however, he would have the power (if he chose) to exercise toward them, should they venture to come.

Feb. 3rd.—Large parties of Zooloos in their war dress were yesterday evening entering the town. This morning when we were at family prayers the unusual sound of the muskets was heard from the west; this proved to be the arrival of the Boers who presently entered the town on horseback with their guns in their hands. An immense concourse of Zooloos were present to receive them. The deputation (in number about 60) brought with them the cattle which they had recovered from Sinkoyela. The Boers immediately shewed Dingarn the way in which they danced on horseback by making a sham charge at one another making the air resound with their guns. This was something the Zoolu chief had never witnessed. In their turn the Zooloos exhibited their agility in dancing. About noon I paid a visit to Mr. Retief, who with his party (after the amusement was over) were seated under the Euphorbia trees fronting the gate of the town. The answer he gave to Dingarn when he demanded the guns and horses was to shew the messenger his grey hairs and bid him to tell his master that was not dealing with a child. The Missionaries in Sinkoyela's country had sent away their wives in expectation of the Zoolu army. Mr. Retief had allured the chief into his tent, and here clapped him in irons, saying he had news from Dingarn. Mr. Retief called in the evening. Not only had the wives of the Missionaries fled, but they themselves had their horses ready at their door when they heard of the arrival of the Dutch. Sinkoyela called on Mr. Retief and asked what news from Dingarn. He said he would tell him next morning. Accordingly when he came he clapped him in chains. A tribe which has been nearly destroyed by the Zooloos had claimed the protection of the Boers. This is the tribe against which Dingarn sent out an army soon after the Boers left (as already related in my journal) under pretence that it was designed against Sinkoyela. He endeavoured to make me and my Interpreter believe that the cattle which had been captured from this weakened tribe had not been seized by *his* orders. Three chiefs and about 650 men, the remnant of those who have at various times been slain, have been taken at their earnest request under the protection of the Dutch: it has been the practice of Dingarn to send an army against them every 2 or 3 years by which means all their young men have been cut off. They are not cannibals as the Zooloos affirmed.

Feb. 4th, Sabbath.—With the sun the singing and dancing commenced in the town in order to afford amusement to the Dutch. It was their intention yesterday to attend Divine worship here to-day, but it does not appear that they considered it well to disappoint the Zoolu chief by postponing the amusement for a single day. I felt grieved because it would have had an amazing influence on Dingarn's mind, if they had not only resisted on this occasion his desires to entertain (saying it was Sunday) but had also come in a body to the station. Nevertheless, it is one of those things which, however much to be regretted, it is not our part rashly to censure, as I am persuaded there was no wilful or predetermined contempt of the Day or the Divine word. Our Sabbath services as usual. English service in the hut morning and evening. Our congregation composed only of 2 families my own and my Interpreter's, but of 3 nations, English, Dutch and Zoolu, part of my Interpreter's family speaking Dutch. In the afternoon instructed my native servants—2 girls and a boy—I commenced with the beginning of the Bible and have explained to them a few of the first chapters. Narratives they soon comprehended and easily remember, but to impress them with a sense of sin is at present impossible. All I can say is that, as they do not yet know God's law (the transgression of which is sin) they cannot say they are *not* sinners. So far only I can hope at present to carry their consciences with me. They seem to have now a fixed idea of the origin of man of which they knew nothing before. When I ask them to repeat any narrative (as of the fall) which I have told them they will one after another give a very good compendium of what thay have heard. There is no difficulty arising from want of parts. No less than a hundred boys from the town attended, to learn their letters and syllables. The number which attends generally varies from 20 to 40, many more than used to come; but they do not attend every day and only at certain intervals. Two or three of the boys (who are Dingarn's servants) are making some little progress and what encourages me most, they always seem interested. These boys have attended from the beginning, but all the rest are new comers and know scarcely anything. The attendance of the children depends entirely on these servants of the king. They call them out whenever they have opportunity or inclination, but in the case of non attendance they always plead the king's business to which I can say nothing. But the circumstance of their progress, apparent interest in what they learn and their great influence over the other boys is so far encouraging. The orthography of the language is not yet settled, so that only some syllables can be taught without the fear of disappointment in having to change the mode of writing in certain cases. By the time that we can produce a book or get it printed, I hope some few will be able to read. At present either some easy Zoolu words are written with a pen on a card, and we are kindly furnished with an elementary book by the American Missionaries from their own press at Port Natal. Gangetoli, my own servant, is the most forward as well as the quickest boy, but he had previously been sometime at one of the American stations.

Feb. 6th.—A dreadful day in the annals of the mission! My pen shudders to give an account of it. This morning as I was sitting in the shade of my waggon reading the Testament, the usual messenger came with hurry and anxiety depicted in his looks. I was sure he was about to pronounce something serious, and what was his commission! Whilst it shewed consideration and kindness in the Zoolu monarch towards me, it disclosed a horrid instance of perfidy—too horrid to be described—towards the unhappy men who have for these three days been his guests, but are now no more. He sent to tell me not to be frightened as he was going to kill the Boers. This news came like a thunder stroke to myself and to every successive member of my family as they heard it. The reason assigned for this treacherous conduct was that they were going to kill him, that they had come here and he had *now* learned all their plans. The messenger was anxious for my reply, but what could I say? Fearful on the one hand of seeming to justify the treachery and on the other of exposing myself and family to probable danger if I appeared to take their part. Moreover I could not but feel that it was my duty to apprize the Boers of the intended massacre whilst certain death would have ensued (I apprehended) if I had been detected in giving them this information. However, I was released from this dilemna by beholding an awful spectacle! My attention was directed to the blood stained hill nearly opposite my hut and on the other side of my waggon, which hides it from my view, where all the executions at this fearful spot take place and which was now destined to add 60 more bleeding carcases to the number of those which have already cried to Heaven for vengeance. There (said some one), they are killing the Boers *now*. I turned my eyes and behold! an immense multitude on the hill. About 9 or 10 Zoolus to each Boer were dragging their helpless unarmed victim to the fatal spot, where those eyes which awaked this morning to see the cheerful light of day for the last time, are now closed in death. I lay myself down on the ground. Mrs. and Miss Owen were not more thunderstruck than myself. We each comforted the other. Presently the deed of blood being accomplished the whole multitude returned to the town to meet their sovereign, and as they drew near to him set up a shout which reached the station and continued for some time. Meanwhile, I myself, had been kept from all fear for my personal safety, for I considered the message of Dingarn to me as an indication that he had no ill designs against his Missionary, especially as the messenger informed (me) that the Boer's Interpreter, an Englishman from Port Natal was to be preserved. Nevertheless, fears afterwards obtruded themselves on me, when I saw half a dozen men with shields sitting near our hut, and I began to tremble lest we were to fall the next victims! At this crisis I called all my family in and read the 91st Ps., so singularly and literally applicable to our present condition, that I could with difficulty proceed in it! I endeavoured to realize all its statement and tho' I did not receive it as an absolute provision against sudden and violent death, I was led to Him who is our refuge from the guilt and fear of sin, which alone make Death terrible. We then knelt down and I prayed, really not knowing but that in this position we might be called into another world. Such was the effect of the first gust of fear on my mind. I remembered the words, "Call upon me in the day of trouble and I will hear thee." But of the Boers, Dingarn, the Mission, the Providence of God, I had other thoughts. Dingarn's conduct was worthy of a savage as he is. It was base and treacherous, to say the least of it—the offspring of cowardice and fear. Suspicious of his warlike neighbours, jealous of their power, dreading the neighbourhood of their arms, he felt as every savage would have done in like circumstances that these men were his enemies and being unable to attack them openly, he massacred them clandestinely! Two of the Boers paid me a visit this morning and breakfasted only an hour or two before they were called into Eternity. When I asked them what they thought of Dingarn, they said he was good: so unsuspicious were they of his intentions. He had promised to assign over to them the whole country between the Tugala and the Umzimvubu rivers, and this day the paper of transfer was to be signed. My mind has always been filled with the notion that however friendly the two powers have heretofore seemed to be, war in the nature of things was inevitable between them, but I dreamed of the ultimate conquest of the Boers who would not indeed be the first to provoke, but who would be the sure defenders of their own property, and the dreadful antagonists of the Zoolu nation, who could hardly be kept from affronting them, not to mention that real or imaginary causes of quarrel could not fail to exist between two such powerful bodies. The hand of God is in this affair, but how it will turn out favourably to the Mission, it is impossible to shew. The Lord direct our course. I have seen by my glass that Dingarn has been sitting most of the morning since this dreadful affair in the centre of his town, an army in several divisions collected before him. About noon the whole body *run* in the direction from which the Boers came. They are (I cannot allow myself to doubt) sent to fall or to join others who have been ordered to fall unawares on the main body of the Boers who are encamped at the head of the Tugala, for to suppose that Dingarn should murder this handful and not make himself sure of the whole number with their guns, horses and cattle would be to conceive him capable of egregious folly, as he must know that the other Boers will avenge the death of their countrymen. Certain it is as far a human foresight can judge, we shall speedily hear either of the massacre of the whole company of Boers, or what is scarcely less terrible of wars and bloodshed, of which there will be no end till either the Boers or the Zoolu nation cease to be.

To Dingarn's message this morning, I sent as guarded a reply as I could, knowing it would be both foolish and dangerous to accuse him at such a season of perfidy and cruelty. Moreover, as his message to me was *kind* and well intended, shewing a regard to my feelings as well as my safety (however criminal his conduct to others) I judged it prudent and proper as well as reasonable to thank him for letting me know. Sorrow prevailed on every countenance in our little circle: my Interpreters wife wept to whom the messenger spake kindly saying, "Too-lā, too-lā musuku Ka lā," be still, be still, don't weep. As her husband is away her case is peculiarly trying, for he will not know what is become of her. We have no means at any time except thro' Dingarn of communicating either with our American Brethren, Capt. Gardiner, Port Natal or the Colony, except when Capt. G. has sent any of his own people here. Under present circumstances all communication is stopped and the Togala [River] is moreover said to be now full. I cannot have any more communication with Dingarn at present, and even if he sends for me I know not how I shall go. In my hurry this morning and under the sudden impression of my feelings, I forgot to my great grief the American Missionaries and omitted to ask Dingarn by his messenger to acquaint them with the transaction as he had done me. When the messenger was gone it was too late, as even my native servants were afraid to go down. I was quite ready to go myself, but Wm. Wood, my young Interpreter was too much petrified for me to ask him to accompany me. On the former occasion when the first reports of the massacre of the Dutch were spread (which now appear after all to have been but too true), the American Brethren said they never would have left the country themselves, as *us* in it (?) All we could do now was to recommend them in prayer to the Divine mercy, and we hope that wisdom will be given to each of us to know how to act. At present all is still as death: it is really the stillness of death, for it has palsied every tongue in our little assembly. Since writing the above Mr. Venable has arrived from Temba station on the Umhlatoosi. His coming was unexpected, as it was peculiarly seasonable for his presence administered comfort, and mutual conference under present circumstances was much to be desired. The occasion of his coming to the king, was however, very painful. Mungo, the principal Indoona of Congela had called about half a dozen of his men and enquired of them the reason why they had attended the teaching of the Missionaries. He then gave an order, that no one in furture, neither man nor woman should go to be taught and that the children should not go and learn to sew. Mr. Venable intended coming to see the king in this business, but yesterday morning about 10, four messengers arrived who had been travelling all night from the capital, in order to bring James Brownlee, the Interpreter, to interpret for the king. They said that William as well as Mr. Hully, my own Interpreter, were not here and that Thos. Halstead, the Boers Interpreter was at Capt. Gardiner's, a palpable lie, for he was here when the messenger left on Sunday evening, and I tremble to say is now amongst the number of the slain: so the natives to say tho' Dingarns servant this morning informed me he was not to be killed. The reason for this call from James Brownlee is mysterious, he is a boy and the king likes him; for what end he should have sent in so unaccountable a manner and with such haste is surprising. On Mr. V's arrival he was surprised to see the Boer guns under the trees and the natives handling them freely, but they themselves not to be found, but described as having gone a hunting, etc. At length Umthlela the Indoona told him that the Boers were killed. Mr. Venable made no reply, and the savage, remorseless Indoona asked him if he did not *thank* the king for having killed them. Before this conversation, Mr. V. had told him for what purpose he had come to see the king, and Umthlela had asked him what they wanted to teach. Being told the "Book," he asked, cannot you teach us to shoot, or to ride? At length our friend left and came to the station where as he saw no one about as usual he expected to find *us* all gone. Our conversation has been partly on the wisest course to be adopted in the present exigency. We agree that we have no security for life. The man who brings our milk informs us that the army went out to-day against the Boers. We tremble for the result. In the evening the king sent to me for some medicine heal a man who had been wounded by a spear in a quarrel with another Zoolu.

Feb. 7th.—In the morning two Indoonas with an attendant called. One of them patted his breast, a common gesticulation of friendship. No Indoona had ever been to the station before and they asked to see the hut, waggon, etc. They were remarkably civil. They had been sent by the king to inform me that it was not his intention to kill either me or the other missionaries, for we had come into his country by *fews* and *fews:* he could live in peace with us, for we were his people. All George's people, meaning the British were his, i.e., he liked them, but the Amaboro were not his people: nor where they George's. He said that all the *armies* that came into his country should be killed, that the Amaboro (Boers) were going to kill the king: they had come like an army and had fallen into a passion with him. Many other causes were then assigned for their slaughter, as that they had not brought Sinkoyela and his people prisoners. Some of the other reasons I could not well understand nor did I trouble myself about them as there was but one true reason, the dread of their power and that the whole was a premeditated preconcerted plan of Dingarn who was anxious to see in order that he might butcher them all at once, I cannot now have a reasonable doubt, tho' I could not imagine previously that his designs were so treacherous. The thought frequently entered my mind but I rejected it. I said little in reply to the king. I remarked that I had come into his country only to teach the Book: that I was not a fighting person, as those who taught the Book in my country did not handle the gun.

I did not give an adequate description of the dreadful carnage yesterday. I omitted to state that many of the Boers had children with them, some under 11 years of age, as I am informed, as these were all butchered. They also had their Hottentot servants and these were likewise slaughtered besides their Interpreter and his servant. The number of slain must have been nearer a hundred than sixty, but if there had been ten hundred it would have been all the same.

5.   Mpande Maneuvers to Become King of the Zulu, 1840

After the death of Piet Retief and his party, the Zulu army harangued the trekkers camped at the foot of the Drakensberg mountains. Later that year a new trekker party, led by Andreas Pretorius, descended into Natal to avenge the murder of Retief. On December 16, 1838, the Zulu attacked the trekkers' laager *and suffered a decisive defeat. Afrikaners have called this victory the Battle of Blood River, and its anniversary has become their national holiday. After the battle, the trekker forces pressed their pursuit of the Zulu army, and Dingane lost many rivals and enemies in the retreat.*

Dingane's brother Mpande, deemed incompetent and therefore not dangerous, survived these events. Instead of retreating with the Zulu forces, he crossed into Natal and asked for protection from the trekker republic of Natal. He gained its support and recognition, and in 1840 Mpande defeated his brother Dingane and won recognition as the third Zulu king.

During Mpande's reign, the kingdom enjoyed several decades of peace and occasionally forged alliances with the Boer republics and the

From John Bird, *The Annals of Natal, 1495 to 1845*, Vol. 1, Cape Town: T. Maskew Miller, 1965, pp. 536–541.

British colonial authorities. Even so, the Zulu military power had faded, and many of the kingdom's subjects had moved into colonial territory. Nevertheless, during Mpande's rule, from 1840 to 1872, the population grew, and the kingdom retained political independence despite its virtual client status.

In the following documents, officials of the trekker republic of Natalia examine Mpande.

Minutes of the Volksraad

15th October, 1839

[Panda (Mpande), who had come within the limits of Natal, interrogated before Council.]

What did you come here for, and why did you cross the Tugela [River]?

To escape from Dingaan [Dingane], and to seek for protection amongst you.

Why did you escape from Dingaan?

Because I heard that Dingaan wanted to proceed further into the interior, and because I did not wish to join him; and also because he would certainly cause me to be murdered, should he ascertain my unwillingness to join him.

Give us a statement of all the particulars.

I was informed that Dingaan had sent four regiments to Sapnsa, in order to encroach on the country of that chief; but he was defeated by that chief with the loss of many head of cattle, and Dingaan then sent for two other regiments.

Did these regiments go thither?

Yes, they complied with that order; and when they reached the place, they heard that Dingaan, together with his cattle, women, children, &c., had already proceeded onward. They then returned. I asked them for the reasons why they returned. They answered that they had not found Dingaan, as he had proceeded onward. Dingaan then sent to me to ascertain why I and my people had not proceeded, and whether we intended to join the white people. After that I received another message, ordering me to join Dingaan, and thank him that he had not made us suffer for our disobedience. I then told my captains that they might go if they chose. Some went. On their way they again met some messengers with cattle, who came to call me. I clearly saw from all this that Dingaan cherished hostile views against me. At last Umsela, the chief captain of Dingaan, came in person, and said to my people, "Why don't you rise and proceed onward, or do you wait for Panda? If you wait for him, I can tell you that in a short time one of Dingaan's commandos will surround him. Don't you clearly see that he has turned his face towards the whites?" Umsela having said this, part of my people joined him, but the greatest part turned back and said to me, "Will you sit here and wait until the commando surprises us?" I said, We will go. I have heard of there being white people at the Tugela;

I will immediately send a message thither. At last I arrived at the Tugela with the half of Dingaan's people, where I met Mr. De Lange.

Who was the chief of the Zulu country before Chaka?
　　His father, Senzagakona.

What were you under his orders?
　　One of the great captains, which I was until the death of Chaka.

Did you often go on commando?
　　Yes; but not once under Dingaan.

Why did you not wish to go with Dingaan?
　　Because I have heard that the white people wish to live in peace with us: and why should I allow myself to be murdered by a villain, or take to flight with him?

Where have you lived?
　　In the country near Ganzela.

What is the reason that you did not become king instead of Dingaan?
　　Chaka had sent me on a commando against a chief called Sotshangana; and when I returned I was told that Dingaan had put himself on the throne in my absence, and had murdered my father, Chaka, and all the royal family.

Has not Dingaan endeavoured to murder you when you returned?
　　No; but Hlela and Dambuza, the great captains, wished to kill me, but Dingaan would not allow it, pretending that I had not influence enough, and could do no harm.

When you sent a message to the Tugela, you were already effecting your escape?
　　Yes.

Where did you meet Mr. De Lange?
　　On this side of the Tugela.

If you had not met with the whites at the river, would you, notwithstanding, have continued your way?
　　Yes; as I was proceeding, I would not have stopped.

Do you not know that according to treaty no Zulu is allowed to come to this side of the Tugela?
　　Yes; but what is a man not capable of when his life is in danger.

Panda! this day you must be sincere.

Yes; for that reason I came hither in person to speak to you, gentlemen. I shall lay my heart open to you.

If Dingaan had acted like you, war would have been at an end.
Therefore you see that I come personally and deal with you in a more upright manner than Dingaan. I wish to be your friend and act according to your wishes.

What do you now expect of us?
As the gentlemen now give me liberty to speak, I would request of you the piece of ground between the Umhlali and Umvoti [rivers].

Why won't you live on the other side of the Tugela?
Because I am afraid of Dingaan, as I have divided the people.

Don't you know, then, that Dingaan may not murder any people?
Yes; but he will not care about that.

Do you consider yourself strong enough to wage war against Dingaan?
Not at the present moment; but if the people receive information of the peace, they will certainly come to me in crowds.

Do you know how the people are inclined?
Yes: I have also sent out spies, but as Dingaan's commando was in the bushes, they have not been able to do anything.

Do you know how many captains will join you, when they hear of the peace between you and us?
Of three I have already heard. They are on the other side of Dingaan, and cannot therefore come at present.

How many regiments has Dingaan wherewith he wages war?
This I cannot say with certainty, as many have been killed in the battle with Sapusa. He probably has many yet.

Have many of Dingaan's people been killed?
Yes; as well of his people as of those of Sapusa.

Have you received intelligence, or do you know with certainty where Dingaan now is?
No; I do not at the present moment know where he is, I cannot say with certainty. I have heard that he (Sapusa) had killed more than half of Dingaan's people in the last conflict.

Can't you send out spies, whom you as well as we may trust?
Yes, this I will do immediately; perhaps as soon as I get to my camp.

Perhaps the spies I have sent out have returned. I shall lose no time; for my heart is now full of joy; as I see that you deal with me in so good and kind a manner.

You know that we will no longer allow Dingaan to kill women, and children. You must therefore send us a report as soon as possible, so that we may take steps accordingly.

Yes; that I will do: and as the gentlemen are so kind towards me, they must open their hearts very wide for me—yes, as wide as my arm. [He lifted his arm on high.]

Promise was then made him that the land for which he had asked would be allowed him, until he should be able to live on the other side of the Tugela in safety, and that he might always calculate on the protection of the farmers as long as he behaved himself as a friend and faithful ally.

Report of the Landdrost of Tugela

[Embassy to Panda]

October, 1839.

In compliance with a request of the Assembly of the emigrants, I departed on 24th October last, accompanied by the heemraad, S. van Breda, and M. van Breda, who joined at our request, to visit the kraal of the chief Panda, where we arrived on the 26th, with four more wagons, in company with the member of the Assembly, G. Kemp; the commandant G. Fourie; the fieldcornet, J. Meyer; Mr. Morewood, Dr. Krause, Delegorgue, and many other respectable persons; the member of the Assembly, J. Moolman, and his company having also joined us, on our written application.

On the first interview of the commission with Panda, we already perceived a dejected melancholy in him, which was apparent to us during the whole time of our stay with him, and in everything he did.

After having communicated to him with what view the commission had come there, and what orders we had received from the assembly of the emigrants, he was requested to prepare himself by the next morning to be solemnly installed as the head or prince of the Zulu emigrants, and to be presented to his people as such; and the flag having been brought in his presence, he repeated in an impressive manner the solemn assurance of peace, friendship, and alliance which he had before given to the Assembly. When this was communicated by his great captains to the crowd that had collected together (which we estimated at more than 3,000 warriors, and more than an equal number of young men and women), a cry was raised three times as a sign of their approbation. The following morning having been fixed for a feast or military dance, Panda requested that after it should be finished the same honour of firing a volley of musketry might be shown him which he had received at Bosjesmansrand. On the morning of that day Panda was invited to the tent of

Mr. Breda, in front of which the national flag was offered him, also a fine blue cloak presented by Mr. Parker, and a fine officer's poignard by Mr. Delegorgue, wherewith he girded himself. Panda was then seated in our court on the right hand of the Landdrost, and the other gentlemen according to their rank, on which occasion the Landdrost repeated to him the assurance of alliance and the protection granted to him by the Assembly of the emigrants, which again having been communicated to the people, a cry of joy was again thrice raised: after which it was signified to Panda that his stay on this side of the Tugela was but of a temporary nature, and that neither the delivery of any cattle, nor anything else of a like nature, was to be considered as giving to him any right to the land now occupied by him, and that he was to leave this part of the country as soon as his own safety should in any way allow. It was also agreed with him that in the future he should allow no punishment of death for supposed witchcraft or other ridiculous superstitious pretences.

That at his death his successor should be chosen by his people, subject to our approval.

That his title should be "Reigning Prince of the Emigrant Zulus," until he should have been confirmed as Dingaan's successor.

That he will fulfil and comply with the contract entered into by the Assembly of the emigrants with Dingaan, in respect of the acknowledged boundary line, as well as in respect of the delivery of the stolen cattle, &c.

That in future he will not allow any woman, child, or defenceless aged person to be murdered; nor allow any war or hostility of his people with any neighbouring chief or tribes without the consent of the Assembly of the emigrants.

6. Cetshwayo the Zulu King Complains of Unjust Treatment, 1881

When Cetshwayo succeeded Mpande, the population of the Zulu kingdom had recovered and the Zulu still controlled ample land and resources. The regimental system revived under Cetshwayo's leadership, and Zulu military might began to intimidate neighboring white authorities—the weak, impoverished Transvaal republic and the dependent, undeveloped British colony of Natal. The diamond discoveries of 1869 buttressed white economic power in South Africa and the British annexation of the Transvaal in 1877 set the stage for the Zulu war of 1879. After the stunning Zulu victory over British forces camped at the base of Isandhlwana

From C. de B. Webb & J. B. Wright, eds., *A Zulu King Speaks: Statements Made by Cetshwayo kaMpande on the History and Customs of His People*, Pietermartzburg: University of Natal Press and Durban: Killie Campbell Africana Library, 1978, pp. 41–47.

mountain in January, British reinforcements defeated the Zulu kingdom later that year. Cetshwayo was arrested and banished, and his kingdom was broken up.

A number of British humanitarians pleaded for the Zulu and exposed the injustice of their treatment. Most notable among these were Bishop Colenso of Natal and his daughter Harriette Colenso, who helped Cetshwayo to bring his case before the British government. Cetshwayo won reinstatement as king under colonial control, but he was murdered by enemies within the kingdom shortly after his reinstatement. The Zulu kingdom remained divided, and the British paid Cetshwayo's successor a pension and closely watched him.

An extract of Cetshwayo's letter of complaint to the Cape governor follows.

Oude Molin, March 29, 1881.

I am writing to you, Sir Hercules Robinson, Governor of this land, to ask why my case is kept quiet even now, seeing that the Boers have sued for peace and their affair is quieted. I think now is the right time to hear and learn about the grounds on which the arguments for killing me (i.e. destroying my country and taking me captive) were based. I wish now to lay my case, as clearly as possible, before this Parliamentary Assembly, but specially before the Parliament in England, and the Queen. I say I died just shortly after Mr. Shepstone had been in Zululand to settle matters and crown me; but for what reasons was I killed, and what wrong had I committed? I say to you English nation, I will commence and state my case from the ground, i.e. from the very commencement.

As soon as I heard of my father's death, I sent me with an ox to report to Mr. Shepstone and to the Assembly of Natal—to whom Mpande belonged—about the death of the king. I thought it fit, on my father's death, that you the English nation should be present and witness the settlement of the Zulu country under my rule, seeing that this house, King, and country of this land are not without or outside the English nation, but within the English nation: my father, I knew, had served you well till his death. Now, it so happened that Mr. Shepstone, after settling the country under my rule, asked me the laws of the land (we having previously accepted the laws brought to us by him). We then stated the laws of the country to be as follows:

I.   If a man overleap the bounds within which are located the maids of honour, and seduce any of them, we punish him by death, since he has overleapt the throne, and thus has overleapt the King.

II. If a man take another man's wife while the man is alive, and thus cheats the husband, we say that he is a malefactor, has done wrong, is bad, and is fit to be killed; therefore all we chiefs of Zululand say that we will kill such an one.

III. We said, if a man kills and eats the cattle that the King has lent him to get milk from, he has done wrong, and we will kill such a man, since he has destroyed the cattle lent to him by the King.

IV.   If a man go about in the night time and destroy other people, we take such an one from the place in which it is reported he kills people, and we put him in another part of the country to see whether it be true or not what people say about him; if he is reported to be destroying the people in this place he is removed again to find out for certain whether he destroys people or not; if he does not stop his tricks we kill him, and say that a man like this is noxious, and must not live. He is a criminal, since he destroys people everywhere.

When we had finished giving a detail of these laws, we requested Mr. Shepstone to give the kindest respects to Queen Victoria from the Zulu nation, and to talk nicely to the Queen for us. Mr. Shepstone replied to the law about the man prowling about in the night, that it was good to try him thus— by moving him from one place to the other—and kill him when sure of his crime. He said also, that 'we' (i.e. Mr. Shepstone & Co.) 'will not break these laws of yours, since those are the laws by which malefactors are corrected and the country ruled.' Umanxele, the Induna (chief) of Mr. Shepstone, heralded Mr. Shepstone's words to us Zulus, and said, 'This is your King; take care of him, and desist from your crimes; treat him well, and do not continue in your wrong doings, since I know that you will turn on your King and kill him, as you did with Chaka and Dingane. Mpande has lived, and at last died from a natural death, he being in our keeping. The King is also ours, and we are going to watch you, because we know that you will kill him for no reason whatever, and set up a new King according to your taste.' Mr. Shepstone also said that he had been sent by the men of his country to me. Mr. Shepstone then sent some of his chiefs to see the disputed boundary of Zululand; these chiefs were Umanxele, Unombemba, Uzijula, and another white chief, the name of whom I know not. When these four chiefs came to the disputed place (the place that the Boers have robbed us of), they asked us (the chiefs) whether the Boers were living here now; we said, 'Yes.' They said, 'Even here among your houses;' we said, 'Yes.' [We, of course, means the Zulu chiefs.]

On Mr. Shepstone's departure I handed over to him three hundred head of cattle, in order to thank him and the government for coming to settle the country under my rule; I gave him also four elephant's tusks. I daily regaled the men that came up with Mr. Shepstone, and gave them cattle to slaughter every day of their stay in Zululand. Mr. Shepstone was then saluted by the whole Zulu army, as he wished, and then all the Zulu troops said, 'Bayete' (i.e. 'hail!'). Mr. Shepstone then said to me, 'Place down your shield and do not fight; a large nation does not move about; we also (viz., the English nation) do not provoke anybody and we do not make war on anybody. When you wish to take up the shield, come to me and hear what I have to say first.'

It so happened after this that, in the district of Seketwayo, the Boers shot a servant of the King, the servant of the King having done nothing beyond refusing to drag away a cow that had died in this place, a cow that belonged to the Boers, the Boers ordering him. I then sent to Mr. Shepstone and reported this; but Mr. Shepstone only said, 'Be quiet only; I see that the Boers are doing wrong.' After this, again, it so happened that while, at Qandi's kraal, an assembly was sitting and discussing some case, that a Boer party came up to them, and one of the Boers shot a young man belonging to the assembly with shot; the man fell down dead to all appearance, but in a short time got up, went home, was ill for a long time, and then got well. At this occurrence the men of the assembly jumped up, chased the Boer till he fell over, horse and all, into a donga [ditch]. They captured him, but let him go unhurt, saying that it is best to leave him, and we will be the last to do wrong, and then they cannot blame us. The Boers then came to Boza's kraal in large numbers, quite a small army, and fired outside the kraal at a hillock, saying to Boza's people, 'Get you away from here; leave this kraal, as we want to live here ourselves.' The Boers then carried on their wrong doings by driving their cattle into the Zulu gardens, and when the Zulus—men and women—tried to save their food by driving out the cattle, the Boers simply half killed these men and women by whipping them.

After a time, one Boer, by name Mayisaka, came to a kraal to steal women and children (at this time all able men were at my kraal, viz., Mahlabatini, to build it up, and only old and ill men were at home). This kraal was Tinta's, uncle to Seketwayo. The men then that had been left at home because of illness and old age, when they saw Mayisaka passing by and wishing to drive away women and children, stopped Mayisaka from doing so. Tinta, an old man, the owner of the kraal, opposed this Boer, but the Boer struck Tinta in the face with the stock of his gun, and took a small boy belonging to Tinta, put him on his horse, and intended taking him away. A young man then came forward and asked the Boer to put the boy down, but the Boer replied by simply shooting at the man, and the bullet went through the young man's shield and went into the ground. The young man then laid into the Boer with a stick, and would have very likely killed the Boer, but the elders of the kraal stopped it, and said, 'Leave him alone till the matter has been put in the light, for it will be said that we killed a white man. Leave him alone, although he has shot at us.' When Mayisaka, the Boer that we let go, came home, the other Boers started and proceeded to Tinta's kraal and asked why they had beaten Mayisaka. The Zulus said, 'What did he tell you as to the reasons why we beat him?' The Zulus then told the Boers why they beat the Boer. (At the time the Boers came to ask about this, Tinta had his face very swollen from the blow the Boer gave him with the stock of his gun.) The Zulus also showed the Boers the hole that had been made by the Boer's bullet into the man's shield (the man that the Boer shot at). The Boers were then convinced and went away.

After this the Boers came into my country in the north with many men, as if they came to war with us, surrounded the Zulu kraals, and beat the inmates, telling them to leave their homes, as they (the Boers) were going to live there. They went to Qodi's kraal and Mahlebe's kraal and did the same. When the Boers did this the Zulus got alarmed, specially because on going away the Boers said they were coming in force on the morrow, and it will be good for the Zulus to be found gathered and together; for these reasons the Zulus armed themselves and kept themselves in readiness. When the Boers came on the morrow they found the partizans of Qodi and Mahlebe sitting together in large numbers. The Boers then called on Qodi and Mahlebe to come to them (wishing to shoot them apart from the rest), but both these men refused. They (the Boers) said all this, sitting on horseback at a distance. At this juncture the Boers said, 'We are going now to enter the Zulu country, commencing at Seketwayo's, then passing on to Enkande, then passing on to Enhlazatye; we will go across all this country during the night, and in the morning we will enter Ulundi.' During the same night in which the Boers said that they would enter the country, the Zulus heard noises of Boer horses, ridden by Boers who were to reconnoitre the country. The Zulus then got alarmed, and armed. I also gave orders to the whole of Zululand to arm themselves and keep themselves in readiness till they were told whereabouts in the country the Boers are lying; but on my ascertaining that the Boers had gone back to their own country, I immediately apprised all my soldiers of it, and told them to go home, and keep quiet. This is what was called in Natal, 'Cetywayo has armed himself, and is about to fight'.

After this the Boers entered the country again, and found that Qodi, Mahlibe, and Boza had moved all their families and cattle away, when they heard that the Boers had entered the country, and left their kraals quite empty. I sent all these reports to Mr. Shepstone, but he said simply, 'Be quiet only my child, and I will settle everything for you.' I at the same time sent Umaketelela and Unombona to ask the Boers why they did all this in the Zulu country. The Boers said that there were some vagabonds that had stolen cattle and sheep from them, and that these vagabonds must be these Zulus (although they had no good proof, and had not actually caught any doing so, but had simply seen a skull of a sheep lying outside one of the small kraals in that part). I then sent up to this part, and made the people pay cattle to the Boers. All this part of the country the Boers entered, and told the owners of the soil to go away, for they (the Boers) wish to live there, and will live there. I made these men pay cattle to the Boers, not because they had been caught stealing sheep, but because I heard they had done wrong.

Very shortly after this Mr. Shepstone said that he would go up country and settle these matters, and put the country right for me. At this time the Boers quarrelled with Um Milini. This quarrel arose thus. Umtyiyane, the uncle of Milini, bolted over to the Dutch, taking with him Milini's cattle, wives, and children. Um Milini then went to the Boers, to ask them to give Umtyiyane's cattle up, but the Boers refused. Um Milini then went to Umtyiyane's position, surrounded it, and took his property away. The Boers then attacked Milini, but were beaten. Then they came to me, and asked me if I had sent Milini to kill Umtyiyane (while Milini was taking away his property from Umtyiyane some men got hurt). I then said, 'I did not send him, and I did not know of his doings; therefore, do with him what you like, and kill him as you like, since he has fought with you without my knowledge.' (Milini was son of Inswazi, the Swazi king, and had come over to Zululand with his family, because he thought and was sure his countrymen would kill him.) The Boers then attacked Milini and killed him while I was sitting down at home and saying, 'Do with him what you like, since he has fought with you by his own accord; I will have nothing to do with a man that does thus; he is simply drawing on the white men on me.'

After this I sent up to the Boers, and told them to leave my country, as they were always making noises and creating disturbances in my country by shooting my people and thrashing them with whips. I then sent up men to the Incaka, telling them to build up their kraals and keep quite quiet, even if they heard that the Boers were arming themselves (as they were only building on their own land). I am putting in these words about the kraal building because, while Mpande was alive, he sent Tyingwayo to build in the same district on his own ground, the Incaka. The Boers allowed him to build, but as soon as he had turned and gone home to tell Mpande that the kraal was done, the Boers pulled it all down, and destroyed it. I then said that this was not at all nice of the Boers. On my sending to the Boers to tell them to leave my country, they left part of it, in the two districts of Incaka and Pemvana.

After this Mr. Shepstone went up country, saying that he would settle about these lands, viz., begin by Transvaal, then Usikukuku's, then Swaziland, then return by Zululand, and settle the question for me about the boundary of Zululand that was claimed by the Boers, and finally settle about the country claimed by the Boers. When Mr. Shepstone arrived at Newcastle he sent Nkabane to me while staying at Mbonambi. This messenger came to me when I was together with Umyamane, Tyingwayo, Utuzwa, and Usityaluza, and said that he was sent by Mr. Shepstone to say, 'I am now passing on, and am about to go and arrange matters with the Boers. Tell my child (Cetwayo) that I do not know how matters will turn out, as the Boers seem about to be troublesome. I will tell him (Cetwayo) about the result when I have talked with the Boers.'

When this last message came to me, I, having already heard that the Boers intended shooting Shepstone, and then fighting with his men (all this heard by rumour), and having heard that the Boers had hung a piece of rag about Mr. Shepstone, were shooting at it, and saying that they would shoot Shepstone, I immediately sent to my kraals at the Magulasini, and told them to be on the alert, because, in case the Boers do what they say they will do, I wish the men of this place to go at once to support Mr. Shepstone.

After this I sent up to Mr. Shepstone, who was at Pretoria, Usintwangu and Maketelele, to say to Mr. Shepstone, 'Where are you now, as I have not heard from you for so long? How is it that everything is so quiet, and I do not hear about you? I, your son, feel anxious about you, and wish to hear all about you and your proceedings.' Mr. Shepstone then sent back and said, 'I am still talking with the Boers; but I do not know about the result of the conference yet. I am sure, though, that they wish to be insubordinate and inattentive, but the soldiers overawe them.' He continued and said, 'I will pass on, and try to settle Usikukuku's case, and then to the Maswaziland, and then I will return by Zululand and settle everything about the country for you.' (Usintwangu and Maketelele, of course, brought this message.) He continued and said, 'I am soon coming to Zululand. You are noisy, as I hear that you have built a kraal, and have called in Kwamaizekanye. Are you calling me then, and saying, "Well, you may come then"?'

The Zulus then got surprised, and said, 'How is it that Mr. Shepstone is sending such a message to you? About what have you quarrelled? You have only sent men to learn if anything has happened to him, and to know about his proceedings, and how comes he to talk thus?'

Usintwangu and Maketelele then came, and the above message. I was then very much surprised, and said to my chiefs, 'How can Mr. Shepstone talk thus?' I did not, however, say anything to Mr. Shepstone about it; but I must not conceal this, that I felt very surprised, and thought that Mr. Shepstone was not about to do well to the Zulu nation. . . .

7. A Missionary Struggles to Convert King Mzilikazi and the Ndebele, 1859

Robert Moffat (1795–1883) arrived in South Africa in 1817 as an LMS missionary. He served for a long time at Kuruman among the Tswana, learning the language, translating the Bible, and training Tswana converts as catechists and teachers. During several trips to the Ndebele, Moffat tried to persuade King Mzilikazi to allow the opening of the mission. Although Moffat and Mzilikazi became friends, Mzilikazi refused to permit a mission in his territory until 1859, shortly before his death. Robert Moffat's son, John Smith Moffat, served as a missionary there.

In the journal entry that follows, the elder Moffat describes his troubles in converting the Zulu king and the Ndebele to Christianity. He cannot convert others or preach to anyone without the King's blessing.

The planting a mission among the Matabele [Ndebele], I need scarcely say, weighs *very heavy* on my mind, notwithstanding my fullest convictions as to the path of duty. Everything considered, it is only what was to be expected. A succession of events has been bringing it on: 'Coming events cast their shadows before'. I could not help sometimes observing shadows of coming events, but the finances of the Society and the distant and isolated position of the Matabele would not permit me to hope. Their dreadfully savage state—this is no exaggeration—seemed sometimes to require a faith I did not possess; and, added to this, the peculiar character of their government, worshipping their king with the idea that he is superhuman. At the present moment there are about fifty naked warriors (you would say so), with clubs in hand, dancing before my waggon. They know that our arrival pleases their king, and they dance and sing with perfect enthusiasm. O what a spectacle to a Christian mind filled with thoughts of eternity!

From J. P. R. Wallis, ed., *The Matabele Journals of Robert Moffat, 1829–1860*, London: Chatto & Windus, 1945, Vol. 2, pp. 202–208, 214–215.

Whatever may be the results, I feel resigned. The commencing of a mission among the Matabele originated entirely with the Directors. The plan was natural enough after the discoveries of Livingstone, and the resolution to send missionaries to the Makololo. The Makololo removing to a more healthy region where they, and especially missionaries, might be expected to enjoy better health than in their present abode, naturally enough suggested the idea that the permanency of such a location could only be ensured by securing the friendship of Moselekatse [Mzilikazi], who could at any time order out a body of his warriors to pass the Zambesi [River] to pillage and drive the tribes from that quarter, as he had done before. . . .

Sabbath, (30th October). Had our sermon in Sechuana as usual, but Mr. Thomas was interrupted in the afternoon with rain. After the forenoon service I went in and spent a couple of hours with the king, and improved the time the best way I could with such interpreters as there are. I stated to him my deep regret at the loss of William [a former Griqua interpreter], he being the only individual through whom I could speak freely to his people on the things of God, and it was an addition to my sorrow to know that he had been murdered by his own men. As he saw at once that I knew all about the affair, he said only that he regretted [it], but at the same time threw all the blame on the *machaha.* I endeavoured to show him that it was a great loss to him as well as to myself, and it was a great sin against God. He appeared rather anxious to let the subject drop. . . .

. . . Patience is required in having to do with a despot before whom every knee must bow and every tongue be filled with adulation. It requires all the politeness and patience one can muster to have anything to do with a despot such as Moselekatse. Even his interpreters seem afraid to speak even the simplest things we wish to communicate to him. However degraded and mean he may appear to be as to externals, he possesses a fearful amount of power. His thousands of warriors start at his bidding, his slightest frown would send any one of his subjects to the horrors. I have been sitting with him a couple of hours. I found him with about ten of his wives. He was feasting them on *his* beer. They sat mute as if stricken with awe at his presence, while almost every motion or remarks made by him was received with *phesula,* (heaven), *tlamantota* (man-eater) etc. At his wink or at a single word the cup bearer, one of his wives, fills the cup and, after skimming off everything like froth or anything else, she lifts her eyes wistfully to his to know his sovereign will. A significant nod or a word will intimate to her that she must drink first (as if it might contain poison) and then he drinks or hands it to myself or any other whom he thinks worthy to drink his beer out of *his* cup. This is just a specimen of today—to you nothing new. When he thinks proper, or wishes himself to hear what he expects to be said, 'hampañ!' (Go ye!), and verily they go with bowing and humble expressions of thankful praise. Today Pule, Sechele's ambassador, sent a message to his greatness that he had been here so long and had not been called upon to communicate with him. The only reply was that he, Moselekatse, was so much taken up with endeavouring to provide for the children of Moffat, *i.e.,* to appoint them a place and that he could not at present attend to that business. *Fudge!* I am applying to him daily to point out where we are to settle for the present, that we may put seed into the ground in order to provide for the coming year. He has had warning enough of our coming and of our approach, so that he has no excuse, but, like all great folks, he likes to be waited upon. I of course, who knew the man, expected that we should have to wait some time till he should please himself as to time and place. . . .

I generally see the king once or twice each day. He tells me again and again all my wishes will be acceded to. We took into him some of our potatoes to show that they required to be put into the ground, or we should have none to eat; also the vine cuttings. They have not been attended to, and I fear they will not grow. Some of John's may, but Mr. Sykes's are hopeless. The brethren wished to try him by way of barter for native corn. Mr. Thomas bought some three or four pails, but the payment in print—rather thin stuff—was out of all character. I murmured. Mr. Sykes offered a musket for three cows. He sent one only, which of course was very properly refused. I murmured and asked why he treated my friends in that way. He only laughed, and added that he only wished to see what the value of things was, and Baas, as I suppose they call Henry Hartley, and his company, who were here some time ago, were fleeced. They submitted to all his demands out of sheer fear, and McCabe, good soul, had to deal with him on his own terms, and therefore, I hear, will not have enough to cover his expenses. McCabe will have told you before this reaches the [town of] Kuruman. I would advise no one to come here to trade without first making up his mind to pay handsomely for his visits.

Of course the liberties he takes with such he will not take with me or my friends; but the exorbitant prices he has got for everything he has to dispose of embolden him to make the same demands of others. If we are spared to reside with him and traders cease to visit, he will get his eyes opened and understand these things better than he does now. Although I can use great plainness of speech in speaking to him, yet it requires great prudence and caution in having anything to do with such a brutally despotic monarch. If ever I prayed for divine direction to teach me what to think and what to say, it is now; and I believe I am heard. So far as I am myself concerned, my faith does not waver. I know the man. His mental degradation and that of his passive imploring subjects I know well, and all the others might know who have read my first journal; and therefore a little allowance may well be made for the whims of one who has, his life long, been adored by his thousands of satraps and parasites, and before whom his nobles, if such they may be called, dare not stand upright in his presence. Even Monyébe, who seems to be one in favour, ever attendant on his presence, approaches crouching, to interpret for me, and not infrequently looks quite petrified with the idea of interpreting to his dread majesty my honest straight forward speeches and just demands. Privately the same individual will tell me, 'You are right. Do not tire, for who can speak to the king like you?' This remark was communicated to me about a half an hour ago. It is painful to one's mind to witness the crouching obsequiousness of all grades in his presence, even his wives. His subjects must think me a nondescript, as I stand as straight as a poker in his presence, or sit beside him, as he always orders a seat, or ascend at his request and sit on the forechest when he is in his waggon. Of course I give honour to whom honour is due, as Paul did to Festus, so that when I meet him, as I have occasion to do in going to his waggon (new one) to see it covered or uncovered I salute him in the usual way, and in all my interviews I endeavour to be courteous, even to a tyrant. He is to be pitied. He knows no better than to act in the way he does. We have specimens, much of the same character, in ancient times in our own now enlightened 'fatherland'. . . .

We all pity Mr. McCabe, for he must have got sadly plucked here. When we meet him I expressed a wish that he might return while I was here. I have no such wish now, for I see no trader can have anything to do with the extortions of Moselekatse without suffering loss. Mr. McCabe was timid and Hartley, who preceded him, still more so, without any cause: they only required courage. Danger there was none. Moselekatse is too wide awake [a] politician to kill white men from the south; but depend upon it, he will sponge everyone whose object is trade. He does not now seem to have a single counsellor to check him or his insatiable thirst for *things*. His waggons are groaning with weight, while the mice, moths and rain are carrying on the work of destruction. He has powder enough, from what I can learn, but he grudges a single shot to his people, as a miser would do a shilling. . . .

What Moselekatse intends to do with us we must wait and see; but he takes a long time to think about it. He will say anything for an excuse. I asked him a few days ago if he had heard any news from the Zambezi, adding that I was desirous to hear about Livingstone, if he had been heard of. He promptly replied that the party had settled somewhere and were building. I did not believe a word of this. The reply was made merely to save further enquiries. He does not appear to like the prospect of opening up a road to the Zambezi. He may be afraid of enemies arising from that quarter. There is nothing in the economy of the Matabele to excite or encourage commercial enterprise. Not an individual among all the thousands of Moselekatse's subjects can either buy or sell. This power is exclusively his own, and it would be death to transgress. A man has not even power over his own children. Shortly after entering the Matabele territory Mrs. Thomas saw a little girl whom she could have liked for a little nurse maid. The reply of the father was, 'She is the king's; we are all Moselekatse's.'

I asked him this morning if any information had reached him from his western outposts respecting Helmore and party, pointing out at the same time their probable location. 'They have gone forward. They have passed to the Makololo'. I wish it may be so, thought I, but I believe he knows nothing about them. . . .

8. King Lobengula Entertains European Guests, 1875

Frederick Hugh Barber (1847–1919) and his brother were diamond dig-gers and big-game hunters. They also prospected for gold (the Barberton reef in the Transvaal is named for them). In 1875 Frederick journeyed to Victoria Falls and back on the Zambezi River, traveling by ox wagon and visiting King Lobengula's capital of Buluwayo. During a trip in 1877, the Zulu monarch briefly held him hostage.

Barber's attitudes typify those of the many adventurers and conces-sion hunters seeking their fortunes in nineteenth-century South Africa. In his writings, we can also discern his awareness of his reading public.

Wishing goodbye to these friendly natives, we trekked on and reached Bulowayo the following day, the 20th of May [Sunday], drawing up our wagon and cart alongside the trading shop of Messrs. Clarkson and Goulding, on a slope to the east of the kraal. Here were half a dozen traders' stores and houses, belonging to Messrs. Westbeach and Phillips, Ogden and Catonby, Clarkson and Goulding, Peterson, Deans, and others.

Lobengulo was away at an outpost, Amatje umhlopi (White Rocks), so we went to see [his] sister . . . who held a small court of her own, a huge fat short block of a woman, cheerful, talkative, fond of beer, and much liked by the traders and hunters, who felt more comfortable and at home with this kindly woman than in the august presence of His Majesty the King. She gave us much good Kaffir beer, and dumplings made of maize and sweetened with sorghum. She and Clarkson kept up a stream of conversation, which was very enter-taining to those who understood it. Harry and I did not understand it, but we tried to roar with laughter in the right places, and she rewarded us with smiles.

It is imperative that hunters and traders going into the country should immediately proceed to wherever the King happens to be at the time, report themselves, exchange civilities [and] presents, eat fat meat, and drink beer with him and make friends, after which they are at liberty to come and go as they please. We were anxious to get away to the hunting country, so trekked to Amatje umhlopi next morning, accompanied by Clarkson and Goulding. Outspanning near the kraal on an open flat, we were told that [Lobengula] was down in his lands supervising his many spouses and slaves, [who were] preparing the soil for the next season's mealie crops.

Proceeding thither, we espied the burly potentate sitting on the top of a small rocky eminence, while below and about him, perched upon their hams, were about forty *majakas* (young soldiers), his body guard. It was evident that the King was in good humour, as they were chattering and laughing and nois-ily discoursing. Below them in the fields, a considerable number of women and slaves were cultivating the soil with Kaffir hoes.

From Edward C. Tabler, ed., *Zambezia and Matabeleland in the Seventies: The Narrative of Frederick Hugh Barber, 1875 and 1877–1878 and the Journal of Richard Frewen, 1877–1878*, London: Chatto & Windus, 1970, pp. 74–81.

As we approached, Clarkson was noticed by him and greeted with a cheerful '*Sakabona* (we see you) Mat.' (Short for Matthew.) 'I am glad to see you, Mat, and who are your friends?' We were introduced, and he shook hands in a friendly manner. 'You say their name is Barber? Why, that's my name.' *Baba*, signifying 'Father,' being the name he is addressed by his people. He asked us all about our journey, and whether our oxen were healthy and not affected with any contagious diseases. What was the object of our journey? Whether we were hunters or traders? And chaffingly asked us if we were not frightened to go into the hunting country, that lions and elephants were dangerous things to shoot.

After a while he got up and invited us to the kraal to drink beer and have something to eat. This we were quite ready to do. It was a hot day and the road dusty. As he strode along, followed by his shouting and signing *majakas,* we could not but admire his jaunty and dignified carriage, powerful build, and massive limbs. Around his waist was [a] great apron of cat and monkey tails, completely encircling his loins. Bar sunshine, a few ivory rings and brass armlets were his only attire. [sic] His hair was worked up to an apex, surrounded on the top by an oily shining ring. His face was pleasant in conversation, with a humourous twinkle in his eye. He was ready-witted and loved a joke, a grand savage, and every inch a king, fit ruler for the savage hordes over whom he had to wield a firm and stern sway.

Arrived at the kraal, he climbed upon his wagon and perched himself on the front wagon box, while we found sitting places where we could, on the wagon pole and stumps of trees forming the kraal. Gradually the kraal filled with indunas [councillors], headmen, and followers. Beer was handed round in closely woven baskets by maidens. A big vessel was handed to us, to which we did ample justice. The King's beer was always good! Then followed a huge flat-bottomed wooden dish with a savory joint of beef. The King cut this into chunks as big as a leg of mutton, using his left hand as a fork. A chunk was handed us. We pulled out our pocket knives and hacked it up and 'chawed.' It was splendidly cooked, we were hungry, and hearty old hunters found no difficulty in dining in this primitive manner, and by the time our hunger was appeased there was very little left. Lobengulo was pleased at the hearty manner we had disposed of his good things.

We expressed our appreciation of his cooking, and he pressed more beer upon us, which we did not refuse. After this great feed he retired for his afternoon siesta. This was a signal for a general dispersion. We returned to our wagons and made our camp snug, much pleased with our reception and easy familiarity and intimacy with royalty. We had become the friends of a king, an honour accorded to few.

II

Next morning after breakfast an extraordinary apparition approached our wagons. It was some time before we could analyze it. We thought it some new arrival, some gigantic Dutchman bound for the bush veld. It stalked into our bush fence round our wagons. Lobengulo! Lo and behold! What a metamorphosis! The cat and monkey tails had given place to a complete suit of brown moleskin, his huge limbs and feet were encased in Wellington boots, and a spreading brown wide-awake felt hat covered his sable brow. It was absurd, ridiculous. Loben in European clothes was no longer a king, the dignity of his savage majesty had gone. He was no longer picturesque, but he was quite satisfied with himself. I have no doubt but that he thought he was paying us a delicate compliment. Had it not been for the great respect, if not awe, with which we regarded him, we should have burst into laughter, but he was not a man to be laughed at, ridiculous though he make himself. We reserved our mirth for another time.

We sat him down on our strongest chair and comtemplated him nervously, lest he should go through it, and were greatly relieved when it held. We produced a bottle of French brandy, and had to sip some from his glass to show that it was not poisoned. Then we drank to our better acquaintance. Then we chatted and brought out and showed him our elephant guns and had some rifle practice with them. My brother and I gave him a silver-mounted revolver and a silver mug with a glass bottom. He was delighted with both, especially the mug, which he hugged and carried away in his hand and used all the time we were there, and was still using on our return from the hunting country. Then he wanted to see some coloured stuffs, and we pulled out a number of highly coloured plaid shawls and rugs, some of which he took a fancy to. We presented him [with these.] Having got about as much out of us as he could reasonably expect, he returned to his kraal, to drink more beer and sleep, I suppose.

Soon after some men appeared, bringing us a fat sheep and more beer. Our liberality to the King had induced other members of the royal family to visit us. In the afternoon two of his brothers with some followers arrived, fat jolly fellows, but also on the lookout for presents. Other visitors followed, of lower rank and smell, who became such a nuisance that we had to complain to the King, who sent word by the induna of the kraal that we were not to be molested, upon which our dusky visitors returned to their homes.

Our present of bright-coloured shawls had evidently been reported to the King's sister XniXni in Bulowayo, who came hurrying to our wagons to get one too. In getting some out of a box, we found a blue one, the only one of that colour. She pounced upon it, beside herself with delight, and carried it off to the kraal. A messenger from Loben came hurrying down and said the King wanted a blue one. We said we were very sorry, but that we hadn't another of that colour. Then Lobengulo came down himself, and said he must have a blue one, and wanted to know why we hadn't shown him one, and that we must look well and see if we hadn't any more. We ransacked the whole case in his presence and suggested that he should ask his sister to exchange. He said he had done so, but she wouldn't. Then he strode away in a horrid, petulant, and ill-tempered manner.

On the 24th of May rather an exciting incident happened. It was a bright moonlight night. Clarkson, Goulding, my brother, and myself were sitting on the front of our wagon. We were drinking Her Majesty's health, and were about to have a nightcap and turn in, when about a dozen *majakas* came walking across the flat from the kraal gate.Clarkson said, 'Look out, those fellows are up to some rascality.' They approached the front of our wagon. The ringleader, a tall, athletic, wiry-looking chap, carried in his hand a large piece of meat, saying in an insolent manner, '*Reka, reka!*' 'Buy, buy!' Clarkson said, 'Go home! We don't want meat. The King has given us plenty. Only wolves run about at night.' Whereupon he whispered to his campanions, stooped down, snatched up a large skin karross [cloak] that was hanging across the wagon pole, and darted away towards the kraal, followed by his companions. We gave chase, but they had twenty yards start and got into the kraal and disappeared among the huts before we could overtake them.

Next morning early we reported the occurrence to Loben, who smiled and said he was going to see about it. He sent for the induna of the kraal and told him to go and tell the young men to bring the white man's things. They denied having taken anything, saying the white men had lied. The induna was sent a second time, and came back with the same answer. Then up rose the mighty Lobengulo, seized a large rhinoceros-horn knobkerrie [club] which he always carried, and walked into the temporary camp and enclosure in which his bodyguard were lodged. As there was a high stockade round the kraal, he wasn't noticed until he had got among them, when with a rush like frightened deer they sprang over the centre fence. With a bound forward, Lobengulo hurled his heavy kerrie with tremendous force, catching a tall savage in the small of his back, who falling forward, lay all of a heap like a dead man on the open flat outside of the fence. Calling to somebody to bring back his stick, the redoubtable King marched back, climbed on to his wagon, pulled out a Martini rifle, placed a cartridge in the breech, stood towering on the wagon box overlooking the terrified delinquents, and roared out in stentorian tones, that if they did not immediately bring back the stolen articles, he would open fire promiscuously.

In a moment a dozen ash-coloured savages rushed into their huts, and in half a minute, half a dozen of them crawled through the gateway on hands and knees and placed before him the karross, two American axes, a bag of musket bullets, a box of percussion caps, and several other articles, which they had lifted from our wagons during their friendly visits. Loben now sat down on his wagon box, well pleased with himself, and amidst shouts of praise and applause from a crowd who had collected to see the fun, narrated to them how, the previous night being a bright moonlight [one], he had gone to the gate of the kraal before retiring; and, while standing in the shade of a kaffir plum tree at the gate, had been an eyewitness of the whole scene; how the thieves, in running away with the karross, had passed within two yards of him, as he stood behind the stump of the tree; and how the man who carried the karross was the identical one who had knocked it down.

Turning to us, he said, 'There, white men, are your things. Make a fence round your wagons, and shoot anybody that comes in at night. It is only wolves that run about at night.' What became of the damaged man we never heard. He was carried away limp. Some of the traders said he would be killed, but we asked the King not to hurt him any more, that it was more a joke than a real crime.

The exertion had made him thirsty, so beer was sent for. About one hundred savages had collected, indunas and others, all thirsty, and as the King was in high good humour at his proficiency as a detective and police officer, much drink was handed round to the swells, who gave their friends a sip. The King's smart deed and summary punishment were extolled with great acclamation. It was a great feather in his cap. Clarkson told me that he liked to have opportunities of this sort, as it strengthened his hold over his unruly subjects and made them respect him. Some fat cattle were killed, and a quarter of a beast was brought to our wagons in the afternoon.

A case of lynch law of a very drastic nature also occurred during our stay here. A party of natives passing during the night had stolen some pumpkins and mealie cobs from one of Loben's huts in the lands. The executioner, Mavonya, was sent in pursuit. They were spoored [tracked] to Umganen, a neighbouring kraal, where they were found and summarily strung up on the nearest trees.

Later we had the pleasure of being introduced to Mr. Mavonya. He was a sprightly, cheerful little chap, and told us many interesting anecdotes of his experiences as sheriff and hangman. He was very proud of a Colt's revolver which the King had given him, [and] carried it slung over his shoulder beneath his blanket. He said it was a beautiful instrument, so small and yet so effective, and saved so much trouble. Before he had it, he used to have so much trouble in getting malefactors killed. Some of them objected to being knocked on the head, and if they were strong he had to take men with him, and sometimes chase them for long distances, and kill them in a slovenly manner with axes, assaigais, and knobkerries. But now he had as a rule very little trouble. He would walk about with a light stick, meet his victim, ask him for snuff, and while pleasantly chatting, would whip out his handy little gun and blow their brains out before they suspected anything. Sometimes he would show them his little gun, and while they were innocently admiring it, or looking down the muzzle, he would let it off in their faces, and there was an end of them. These and many other pleasant tales he told, with an air of utter contempt of human life that was quite refreshing. He showed us his little gun, but we were careful not to look down the muzzle.

After dancing attendance on Loben for a week, much against our inclination, we became impatient to get away to the shooting country, especially as all the hunters had already gone on. So we told him one morning that we were anxious to get away, that other hunters would be shooting and driving all the elephants away. He answered, 'Oh, you can go if you like. But what is your hurry? Are you not enjoying yourselves with me? You have not half paid me a visit yet. There is still lots of fat meat and beer.' Which from a native point of view was all that man requires in this vale of tears. Don't go yet! This was all very well in a way, but we had not come eight hundred miles to hang about this dusky despot, eat meat, drink beer, smoke, and sleep. However, we had to humour him.

After dragging through two or three more weary days, we repeated our request. This time he graciously acquiesced, so we got ready to start next morning early. It is the custom that every hunter of any standing has to give the King a salted horse [horse that is immune to disease] for permission to shoot elephants and ostriches in his country. We had a strong, fleet salted pony [that] cost £100 [and] had won races in Bulowayo. Loben took a fancy to him, and we were afraid that he would insist on being paid with him, and we were trying to get him to take another. However, after a while he said, 'Never mind paying me now. Take all your horses to the shooting country and show them the game, and when you return and have no further use for them, you can give me one.' This compromise was satisfactory as far as it went, but we ultimately had to give him this valuable horse, which took practically all the ivory we shot to pay for.

On the following morning, 3rd of June [Sunday], we were up early and inspanned [with our oxen hooked up], only waiting for Loben to get up, to say goodby to him. He soon made his appearance, wished us a successful hunt and pleasant journey, and sent us a fat sheep to keep us in meat until we got among the game.

9.   Lobengula Signs a Concession, 1888

Beleaguered by whites seeking privileges and concessions, such as land grants or trade monopolies, Lobengula finally agreed to the concession that Charles D. Rudd offered. Rudd was working on behalf of Cecil Rhodes's mining and colonizing company. Lobengula's lifelong missionary friend John Smith Moffat argued that signing the following concession with Rhodes would provide the best protection for Lobengula and his kingdom. The monarch believed that the document would allow only a few whites to dig holes in the ground, not be an invitation to many whites ('a whole impi*') to come and take over his country.*

The Concession Signed by Lobengula

Know all men by these presents that WHEREAS Charles Dunell Rudd of Kimberley Rochfort Maguire of London and Francis Robert Thompson of Kimberley hereinafter called the grantees have convenanted and agreed and do hereby covenant and agree to pay to me my heirs and successors the sum of One hundred Pounds sterling British Currency on the first day of every lunar month and further to deliver at my Royal Kraal one thousand Martini-Henry

From Constance E. Fripp and V. W. Hiller, eds., *Gold and the Gospel in Mashonaland, 1888*, London: Chatto & Windus, 1949, pp. 219–220.

Breech-loading Rifles together with one hundred thousand rounds of suitable ball cartridge five hundred of the said Rifles and fifty thousand of the said cartridge to be ordered from England forthwith and delivered with reasonable despatch and the remainder of the said Rifles and Cartridge to be delivered so soon as the said grantees shall have commenced to work mining machinery within my territory and further to deliver on the Zambesi river a Steamboat with guns suitable for defensive purposes upon the said river or in lieu of the said Steamboat should I so elect to pay to me the sum of five hundred pounds sterling British Currency upon the execution of these presents I Lobengula King of Matabeleland [the land of the Ndebele] Mashonaland and certain adjoining terrotories in the exercise of my Sovereign powers and in the presence and with the consent of my Council of Indunas do hereby grant and assign unto the said grantees their heirs representatives and assigns jointly and severally the complete and exclusive charge over all metals and minerals situated and contained in my Kingdoms Principalities and dominions together with full power to do all things that they may deem necessary to win and procure the same and to hold collect and enjoy the profits and revenue if any derivable from the said metals and minerals subject to the aforesaid payment and WHEREAS I have been much molested of late by divers persons seeking and desiring to obtain grants and concessions of Land and Mining rights in my territories I do hereby authorize the said grantees their heirs representatives and assigns to take all necessary and lawful steps to exclude from my Kingdoms principalities and dominions all persons seeking land metals minerals or mining rights therein and I do hereby undertake to render them such needful assistance as they may from time to time require for the exclusion of such persons and to grant no concessions of land or mining rights from and after this date without their consent and concurrence provided that if at any time the said monthly payment of one hundred pounds shall be in arrear for a period of three months then this grant shall cease and determine from the date of the last made payment and further provided that nothing contained in these presents shall extend to or affect a grant made by me of certain mining rights in a portion of my territory south of the Ramakoban river which grant is commonly known as the Tati Concession.

This given under my hand this thirtieth day of October in the year of our Lord Eighteen hundred and Eighty-Eight at my Royal Kraal.

his

Lobengula **X**

mark

Witnesses
(*Signed*)
CHAS. D. HELM
J. G. DREYER

(*Signed*)
C. D. RUDD
ROCHFORT MAGUIRE
F. R. THOMPSON

Copy of Endorsement on the Original Concession

I hereby certify that the accompanying document has been fully interpreted and explained by me to the Chief Lobengula and his full Council of Indunas and that all the Constitutional usages of the Matabele Nation had been complied with prior to his executing same,

Dated at Umguza River this thirtieth day of October 1888.

CHAS. D. HELM

The Sotho and Tswana Peoples

1. The Missionary Robert Moffat Describes the "Battle" of Dithakong, 1823

This document and the events that it describes speak to the question of the causes and nature of disorder and violence in the nineteenth-century South African interior. The traditional view held that wild and exotic hordes of "Mantatees" invaded the region, extending the wars that originated in Zululand westward across the high veld. In this view, the Griqua and Europeans had the task of defending the mission station, and the missionaries had the task of rescuing innocents from heathen barbarism. But were the Mantatees really just people of the region? Was the one-sided slaughter a battle at all? Were the missionaries rescuing people or capturing them for use as forced labor?

26. Thursday. We all saddled our horses and proceeded before daylight, and came within sight of the enemy a little after sunrise. According to the plan, we all rode up to about 150 yards opposite, when they commenced their howl and threw out their right and left wings for an immediate attack, and discharged from their hands some of their savage weapons. Their black, dismal appearance and savage fury was calculated to daunt, and the commando on their attacking wisely retreated a few yards and again drew up. Andrews, the chief, commenced firing, and levelled one of their warriors to the ground. Several *more* shared the same fate, when the wings retired, with their shields on their backs, couching as the muskets were discharging. According to Mr. M's directions, the firing was slow, but *extremely* irregular, from a most irregular and undisciplined corps. It was expected that their courage would be daunted when they saw several of their warriors levelled by an invisible weapon. It was hoped that this would prevent further bloodshed by either alarming or humbling them. But in this we were mistaken, for they sallied

From I. Schapera, ed., *Apprenticeship at Kuruman: Being the Journals and Letters of Robert and Mary Moffat, 1820–1828,* London: Chatto & Windus, 1951, pp. 92–95, 105.

forth with increased vigour, so as sometimes to oblige the Griquas to retreat, though only to a very short distance, for the enemy never attempted to pursue above 200 yards from their cattle. Though the firing was without any order, it was very destructive, each taking a steady aim. Though many of their chief men fell victims to their own temerity, they nevertheless manifested an undaunted spirit, boldly treading over the bodies of their slain companions. Ammunition being scarce, it was resolved to endeavour to draw the men out, by the horsemen retreating, and then to gallop in between them and the main body. This was once effected, and many fell, which deterred the others from making the same effort.

It appeared evident that many women, etc., were killed, which to avoid attempts were made to drive or take the cattle (which they seemed to hold dearer than life itself), it being hoped that the men would pursue, which they took care not once to attempt. They were constantly mingling with the groups of women, which rendered it extremely difficult to avoid shooting the latter.

Soon after the battle was commenced, the Bechuanas came up, and united in playing on them with poisoned arrows. A few of the enemy, *however,* soon made them take to their heels, and it appeared evident that twenty of them would have put thousands of the Bechuanas to flight.

After two hours and a half combating, the enemy began to give way, by taking a westerly direction. The horsemen, however, intercepted them, when they *immediately* descended the declivity towards the ravine, which they crossed, but they were again intercepted. On turning round they seemed desperate, but were soon repulsed with considerable slaughter. *Great confusion existed at this moment, the descent being very stony, which rendered it difficult to manage the horses. The enemy then* directed their course northwards towards the town, which was in possession of a tribe of the same people, still more numerous.

After both parties came together, they set fire to the town, and appeared to be taking their departure, proceeding in an immense body northward. After they were quite clear of the town, and *while we* were going slowly through the passes, the enemy threw out their right and left wings, apparently with the intention of enclosing us among the houses, which were then bursting into flames. Whatever were their intentions, they were soon defeated. At this moment the scene was very striking, while *we were* under the lee of the town, the *clouds of* smoke rolling over our heads, and the dust arising from the confusion before us. The Griquas continued to pursue them to about eight miles east of the town, when they left them, apparently filled with terror at the enemies with whom they had been fighting.

But, to resume the subject where the battle commenced. As soon as the enemy retired from their station, the Bechuanas, like voracious wolves, with their spears and war axes began despatching the wounded men and butchering the women and children. As fighting was not my province, I of course avoided discharging a single shot. The only place of safety was to mingle with the commando; but seeing the savage ferocity of the Bechuanas, killing the inoffensive women and children, *and* severing the head from the body, for the sake of a few paltry rings, I turned my attention to those objects of pity, who were flying in consternation to all directions. By galloping in amongst them, they were generally prevented from their barbarous purposes. It was *truly* affecting to see the mother and infant rolled in blood, and I more than once saw the living infant in the arms of a dead mother. All ages and sexes were lying prostrate on the ground. Shortly after the enemy began their retreat, many of the women, seeing that mercy was shown them, instead of flying generally sat down, baring their bosoms [and] exclaiming, 'I am a woman', 'we are women'. It seemed impossible for the men to yield, There were several instances of a wounded man being surrounded by fifty Bechuanas, but it was not till life was almost extinct that a single one would allow himself to be conquered. I saw more than one fighting boldly, with ten and twelve spears, and a number of arrows, fixed in his body.

Though the noise and confusion was great, yet the wounded and dying did not manifest those marks of sensibility which their situation was calculated to draw forth. The cries of infants who had fallen from their mothers, who were fled or slain, were distinctly heard, but all the others seemed thoughtless of their woeful situation. Several times I narrowly escaped the spears and war-axes of the wounded while I was busy rescuing the women and children. The men struggling with death would sometimes raise themselves from the ground and discharge their weapon at any one of our number within their reach. The spirit of revenge seemed only to cease when life was extinct. Instead of laying down their arms and suing for life, some actually fought on upon their knees, their legs being broken. The whole course *which* the enemy took, as far as the Griquas pursued, was thickly strewed with karosses, victuals, utensils, ornaments, and weapons, which the Bechuanas eagerly gathered up.

Contemplating this savage battle, we cannot but admire the providence of God, that not one of our number was killed, and only one slightly wounded. One Buchuan lost his life, perhaps from too much boldness in plunder. *The slain of the enemy was between 400 and 500.*

I shall conclude this day's proceedings with a few general observations. This barbarous people were extremely numerous, both sexes amounting to at the very least near 50,000. The men were tall and robust, perfectly black, being smeared with charcoal and grease. Their features resemble the Bechuanas, which, except the thick lips, is like that of the European, and their real colour if anything darker than the Bechuanas. Their dress consists of prepared ox-hides, hanging double over their shoulders, and the lower dress of the women is much inferior to that of the Bechuan. The men, during the engagement, were naked except *for* a small skin round their middle. Their ornaments are large copper rings, sometimes six and eight in number, *worn* round their necks, with numerous arm, leg, and ear, rings of the same material. They have porcelain, iron, and copper beads, etc. Some of the men have very large ear-plates, and on their heads round cockades of black ostrich feathers. Their weapons are war-axes of various shapes, spears, and clubs. In many of their knob-sticks are *inserted pieces of* iron, resembling a sickle, but more curved, *sometimes to a circle,* and sharp on the outside. Their riches seemed only to consist in their ornaments and cattle; they had neither sheep or goats. I saw many of their picks, which were rather different *in shape* to those used by the Bechuan. Their language appears only to be another dialect of the Bechuan; so much so, that I understand them almost as well as the people among which we live.

Upon the whole, they appear to be a much more barbarous people than the tribes [in] this quarter, rude and savage in the extreme. Most of them seem suffering from want, so that, in the heat of battle, the poorer class seized pieces of meat with the utmost avidity, tearing and eating it raw. After the battle (which lasted seven hours), when Mr. Melvill and myself were engaged collecting the women and children to bring them to a place of safety, it was with the utmost difficulty that we could get them onward. They willingly followed us till they fell in with *a piece of* meat, when *nearly* all *of them* halted to tear and devour it. Threatenings and entreaties were alike ineffectual, which obliged us to leave many behind.

Robert Moffat to James & Mary Smith, Dukinfield

GRIQUA TOWN
23 July, 1823
(C. A. Archives. M.9/1/5. Doc. 3/1823)

. . . Four of the prisoners are inmates of our family. They are as follows: Mahonn or Mahum, a woman, about 25 years of age; Moshanee, also a woman, rather older; Fahaange, a boy, about eight years old; and a girl, about four. Mary has made Mahum cook, and Moshanee nurse and washerwoman; and the boy, who seems clever, I shall find very useful. Considering their former savage state, they do exceedingly well. Moshanee makes a good nurse, and helps to wash very well. This is a great comfort to Mary, as washing is her greatest hardship in this climate. They seem very happy in their new situation, and pleased with their clothes . . .

2.   Andrew Smith Recounts a Conversation with Moshoeshoe, Founder of the Lesotho Kingdom, 1834

Moshoeshoe reigned as one of the greatest South African leaders of the nineteenth century. In the 1830s he gathered groups of refugees from the Mfecane wars and provided them with resources and defensible positions

From William F. Lye, ed., *Andrew Smith's Journal of His Expedition into the Interior of South Africa, 1834–1836,* Cape Town: A. A. Balkema, 1975, pp. 64–66. Reprinted by permission of A. A. Balkema (Pty), Cape Town.

in the Caledon River valley and the mountains to the east. Here, he founded his kingdom of Lesotho, a state more loosely structured than the centralized military states of Shaka or Mzilikazi. He led the kingdom until his death in 1870, all the while facing pressure from the trekkers of the Orange Free State, with whom he fought several wars. Although he was never decisively defeated, Moshoeshoe gradually lost his best valley land. Nevertheless, the kingdom's location and its leader's brilliant diplomatic skills shielded Lesotho from the strengthening forces of white imperialism. Thus Lesotho avoided colonial annexation and instead gained separate annexation by the British Empire.

The conversations and events recorded in Andrew Smith's account paint a vivid picture of Moshoeshoe's abilities.

Just after we had returned from a ramble in the vicinity of the station and commenced some investigation relative to the tribe, our progress was suddenly interrupted by the entrance of a messenger to announce the approach of Moschesh [Moshoeshoe], the chief of the tribe, and on issuing from the tent, a mounted party was observed in the distance advancing at a rapid pace. The European mode of announcing certain arrivals had actually travelled this far. When within a moderate distance of the camp, the royal attendants alighted from their steeds, fired a salute, them remounted and approached in the rear of their king. Taking it for granted that Mr. Cassilis was with us, Moschesh passed the mission house with a call and advanced slowly towards our tent where he dismounted, and approaching with an air of freedom and an appearance of delight, shook us by the hand with a warmth indicating that the best of feelings dictated the ceremony, the effect of which left us no room to suspect he had fingers devoid of joints, as we used sometimes to suppose was the condition of some of the colonists.

Though he generally prefers his native dress, the occasion as well as the circumstance of his having travelled on horseback probably induced him this day to lay it aside. Before us he appeared clothed in the common dress of a colonial farmer, and though not particularly comely, he was by no means awkward. What his figure and his air were not calculated to excite, his face was well adapted to supply, and in the good natured smile and satisfied expression of his countenance we could readily imagine the character of the person with whom we had to communicate.

He was immediately invited into a tent and on a seat being offered him he replied, "ya" (yes), and immediately seated himself. "Ya, hoendag." (good day), and one or two other words comprised all he yet knew of the Dutch language.

While he rested, his principal follower together with a number of the inhabitants of Morija who had flocked to the spot where the king was, apparently satisfied that they were now more entitled to visit us, took up their positions around the door of the tent, and while the majority were occupied in frivolous conversation a few of those most conveniently situated were with their heads within the door actively occupied in surveying the interior of the white house, as they designated the tent, and the utensils it contained, more than in attending to the conversation.

We soon made Moschesh acquainted with the object of our journey and with the course we proposed to pursue. To all the items of information he remarked, it is good, until we arrived at that which made him understand we were to visit Mosilikatzie. To that he replied in a different strain—declared without hesitation his disapprobation—and added if we went to him we should never return. On my laughing at this declaration and asking him how it happened that I had escaped from Dingaan, who was a more awful character than the other, he remarked more awful he might be in some respects yet he was the friend of the *white man* and, moreover, not so treacherous as Mosilikatzie [Mzilikazi]. The latter from nothing had been forced to raise himself into importance and was therefore more conversant with deceit and evil designs than Dingaan and more in the habit of practicing them. And in support of what he affirmed he added that Mosilikatzie sends messengers to smooth the road for his successes by professing friendship when he means next hour to appear the enemy, while the other, when he means evil, shows it at once in the attack of his warriors. Nothing we could urge appeared to have the slightest effect in diminishing his aversion to the projected visit and, as we afterwards discovered, it was not without reason that he entertained such a hatred and suspicion of the man.

After some farther conversation on the subject, we spoke to him of the sympathy the white people felt for the uncivilized man and of the interest they took in the welfare of the natives of South Africa. He replied it must be so; he had a proof of it. He had Mr. Cassilis sent by them to teach him and his people that now they were happy. In consequence of the latter remark I took an opportunity to suggest it as possible that his friend might require to leave him, in order to see how far he really valued the boon which had been conferred. The hint roused him in an instant, his eyes beamed with excitement and he repudiated the idea of such an occurrence, He spoke of the benefits which were conferred upon him and his people by the residence of the missionaries. Among them, said he, was now a man he had like the other tribes white men living with him and his people, and like the other, could now learn. Besides he felt himself more in security against enemies knowing, he said, there was less chance of being attacked when supplied with missionaries than when without them and that under that conviction he intended soon to abandon his mountain and repair to Morija in order to protect his good friends and see that his people attended to their instructions. Observing him so excited and believing it injudicious to keep his fears so alive I told him to his great relief that there was little chance of what I had promised happening if they only attended to the instructions they received and abstained from evil practices.

This called forth a detail of all he had lately done and of certain steps he had taken against some of his people and, among others, one of his own brothers, who had been discovered to have stolen horses from some of the colonial farmers.

"When I first found him," observed he, "prepossessed in favour of thieving from the colonists I confined him for a year under surveillance after which, on promises of good conduct, I permitted him to return to his kraal and to his people. Now that I have found him not to have observed his promise, I have instructed him he must return and live with me for the remainder of his days as it is no longer possible to leave him as a man." This is but one of the many circumstances which he advanced as proof of his desire to suppress crime, and there was every reason to believe he was sincere in his professions, only he has that knowledge which every savage ruler possesses and which inculcates that reformations must not be enforced too quickly nor punishment inflicted too rigidly else he would soon be a king without people.

It is to the liability of chiefs to being forsaken by their subjects that the latter owe their principal privileges and, in one sense, it is fortunate for the lower classes that such liability exists, as were it otherwise, there would be no protection for them against tyranny and oppression. On the other hand again, as may be easily conceived, it proves often most detrimental to the peace of the country as well as to the internal comfort of the tribe. It enables the mass of the population to act often in direct opposition to the inclinations and interests of the chief and as the crimes committed are not recognized as crimes by the laws of the tribe and by universal consent, the infliction of punishments, merely because it happens at the moment to be the interest of the chief, is calculated to lessen his domestic influence in a greater proportion than can be compensated for by any advantages to which it may entitle him from without.

This peculiar position of the rulers of savage clans has never been sufficiently considered and the Cape Government has acted entirely without regard to it in its transactions with the tribes upon the colonial borders. Instead of having ascertained the political condition of these tribes and devising something to improve it and render the chief less dependent on the caprice of subjects, the government has attempted to make them single handed perform a duty which, if strictly discharged, would occasion one of the very consequences which all are anxious to avoid. Even the direct evidence of Gaika [Ngqika] at a time when he was treated as the sole king of Kaffirland was not sufficient to arouse a suspicion that the policy was as a matter of course ineffective. When he was imperatively required to punish everyone who stole cattle from the colonists, he alleged that if he and he alone was to be made responsible, he would soon not have a man under his banner whom he could employ to execute his orders as all his people were leaving him to become subjects of neighbouring chiefs merely because he was made to punish what the others tolerated if not encouraged.

It is not so easy a matter for a civilized government to manage a savage tribe as may be supposed. The character and constitution of such tribe must first be thoroughly understood before a line of policy at all likely to prove successful can be devised. The position and power of the chief ruler must be distinctly comprehended rather than taken for granted. A barbarian clan is to a certain extent under the rule of some one principal. Yet, in many respects, a great portion of it is in no way liable to his control and if he aspires to an unlimited sway he must generally maintain it by force of arms. In matters involving the interest of the entire tribe his authority will generally be recognized, but in the management of divisions of the community over which some particular chief presides, the latter, according to established custom, will arrogate to himself the right of governing the division because the inhabitants thereof have attached themselves to him as their feudal lord. This ought to show the necessity of beginning a system of intercourse by effecting an alteration in the character of the constitution of a tribe and when that has been done, then and only then the principal chief may be regarded as an instrument ofr maintaining order throughout the tribe. In making these remarks we must be understood as speaking of the savage tribes which inhabit the country neighbouring upon the Cape Colony.

After Moschesh had passed nearly two hours in the tent, during which time we were much pleased with his candour and honesty, he proposed to leave us for a time to visit his people. When he took his departure a portion of the individuals who had squatted themselves outside, as already mentioned, who had remained there during the time he passed in the tent, immediately sprung up and joined with his personal attendant in forming his train. Not one remained behind. Their removal was an indication of respect for Moschesh and some of them when afterwards questioned on the subject asked, "Is it not proper for a child to follow its father?" Though they profess to do this from reverence for the persons they follow, and perhaps even at the moment are sincere, it is the expectation of the feasts which generally accompany the movements of the chief that gains him so many followers.

Though a regard to self predominates in all states and conditions of society perhaps in none is it more decidedly manifested than among the natives of South Africa. I have often observed that give then what you may and then ask any trifle in return, it will either be refused or granted with apparent reluctance though it might have been readily purchased for half of the articles which had been presented. If upbraided for a want of generosity under such circumstances, they will rarely argue the point; a simple remark amounting to nothing more than that they are poor and you are rich is considered to be the most judicious reply.

Scarcely could Moschesh have reached the residence of his son, the chief of the station, when a young ox, which had no doubt been directed to be in readiness was seen proceeding from thence in the direction of our camp and ina few minutes it was paraded before me as the gift of the king. In this there was nothing extraordinary, it being a custom for the chiefs to make such presents to visitors of any importance whether whites or blacks under an idea that food is to be supplied them while they sojourn with him. Though it be a custom, however, which is yet very generally observed, many exceptions are to be found and those principally occur among tribes who have acquired modified views from their intercourse with civilized men. The whole of the Amakosa country, or what is commonly called Kafirland, may be traversed without any such indications of friendship being offered. Nay, we may even go farther and include all the districts in which missionaries reside. This has arisen no doubt partly from inability to supply every visitor who repairs to countries so circumstanced and in some degree from their observing how generously the traveller is now entertained at the tables of the hospitable missionaries.

Though I have often refused to accept such proofs of friendship when I was satisfied they could not be offered without inconvenience, and might perhaps have attempted the same here had the chief been present. Yet, as it was otherwise and I was not sure how he might view the refusal, directed the animal to be taken in charge and dispatched the messenger to thank the king for the proof he had given us of the *whiteness of his heart,* an expression common among them and synonymous with friendship.

As the present was accepted with the determination of adhering to the custom usually observed on such occasions, the animal was immediately slaughtered and the breast together with one of the hinder legs and certain portions of the bowels, were directly forwarded as a present to the chief and for which he tendered his thanks. This observance is invariably expected and though its omission will not be regarded more than as an indication of ignorance of their customs, the practice of it ensures consideration and advantages which might be lost by its neglect.

An ox so presented is expected to be consumed at one meal, or at least the greater part of it, and the congregation which takes place upon such a donation being conferred sufficiently indicates that many expect to be partakers of the bounty of the donor. Such, in fact, is the intention of the latter, and at a time when I did not understand so much of savage customs it was distinctly communicated to me in a message from Dingaan, king of the Amazooloo [Zulu]. After having sent an ox in the evening he repeated the present next morning, but as I found the major part of the first yet unconsumed, I sent him word that it was unnecessary as we were still well provided. His reply was he did not expect that I or my people would be able to eat all he might send—his object was to enable me to be generous to his people in order that they also might love me. Here was a man thoroughly acquainted with human nature— he knew well from experience that nothing secured the attachment of such persons as those he had to rule so effectually as an ample allowance of food. And it was from his liberality in that respect that he rendered his own residence, which on other accounts was the spot [undeciphered], specially desirable to his warriors.

3.   A Praise Poem for Letsie I, 1800s

Letsie I (ca. 1811–1891) was Moshoeshoe's eldest son. Although Letsie ascended to the throne in 1870 on his father's death he proved unable to control his brothers or to orchestrate the affairs of the kingdom as had Moshoeshoe. He lived at the mission station of Morija, where Casalis and

From M. Damane and P. B. Sanders, eds., *Lithoko: Sotho Praise-Poems,* Oxford: Clarendon Press, 1974, pp. 107–110. Reprinted by permission of Oxford University Press.

Arbousset preached, but he never became a Christian. When Lesotho went to war in 1879 to retain its firearms (the Gun War), Letsie favored turning in the weapons and keeping the peace. Despite the praises of the following poem, he was never known for military valor.

The praise poem touches many historical events. African oral literature, however, is elusive as historical evidence. To understand it fully, the reader needs to bring historical knowledge to it rather than expect to gain accurate details from it. Such a poem is not valued so much for its recounting of events as it is for its power to rally political support, its ruminations on leadership, and its ability to confirm political authority.

Father of Lerotholi, the Locusts' repeller,
Repeller, repel, please, the wretched little Bushmen,
Repel Gert's Bushmen, and make them return.
The Bushmen ran, they left their round buttocks,
Their tortoise-like buttocks they left behind!
Father of Lerotholi the Locusts' thief,
The thief is a robber, father of Lerotholi,
When Moroka came he stinted him,
He stinted him, he gave him no people at all!
They came, did the people of 'MaNthatisi,
They tried to extinguish the fires in our hearths;
The old men stripped off their karosses to fight them,
The cattle came back, we people lived!
The extinguisher of fire of the people from Mokhachane's
Extinguished the fire of the Likonyela,
And, even as to lighting it, they no longer light it,
They go away weeping to the land of the Whites.
What a narrow escape it was, Kora youngster,
When you got away from us Man-Eaters!
The devourer of the cattle of Mjaluza, the man who is full of invention,
Letsie devours no Sotho's cattle,
Letsie devoured the Ndebele's,
He's devoured those of Tyopho and Mjaluza,
Mashapha's have been devoured with their baggage.
The cattle of the millet have slipped away,
They slipped away, they returned to Mhlambiso's.
The surpasser of those who surpass the peoples,
Mafa, I can surpass both you and your uncle,
And your uncle, your father's brother:
You brandish your mighty sticks
That have just been cut at Masite, at the rapids.
The lizard, the serpent of the waters, Letsie,
He licked, he blew away the villages at Hlatsing:
Lethala he was afraid to lick,
He's afraid, because he's old, this Siea,
He's afraid of the wailing at home,
He's afraid of the crying from the depths of the hut,

He's afraid of the crying of Letuka Tlhabeli.
It hasn't any milk, any thick milk, the roan cow,
It belongs to those who fight battles:
It doesn't produce any milk for 'MaSenate.
Stamper of the stampers, husband of Mokhali,
Stamp the ground, the sorcerers are asleep,
Maqatela and 'Mota are asleep.
The mantis is smeared with white clay, the Hound,
I, the girl from the school at Kholu's, I've entered the pass!
The complainer as he eats of the people of Mokhachane's,
The complainer as he eats lacks food for the journey,
They say that the food is enough for the warriors!

4.   Chief Mokgatle Takes a New Wife

Naboth Mokgatle was born in the first decade of the twentieth century and wrote his autobiography in the 1950s, drawing on knowledge that came down through his family from nearly a century earlier.

The selection below tells the story of the marriage of Naboth's grandfather, Chief Mokgatle of the Transvaal village of Phokeng, to Naboth's grandmother, Paulina. The reading reveals a great deal about marriage customs among the people of Phokeng.

First Marriage

The fighting which took place between my grandmother's tribe and the Dutch settlers under Piet Potgieter resulted in confusion and great distress. Cattle, sheep and goats were missed by the inhabitants of KwaMukopani, as well as men, women and children. No one knew whether they were killed during the fighting or whether they were merely missing. My grandmother, it is said, was still a child of about two or three years old, and was one of those missing when the fighting ended. As a daughter of the Chief, a great search for her was undertaken but she was found nowhere. In the end, like many missing persons who could not be found, she was presumed dead. The people of KwaMukopani were sad because they did not see the dead body of their Chief's daughter, and no one could testify that he or she saw her dying.

The tribe's suspicion that she was not dead was true; she was alive, having been taken away by one of Potgieter's followers to the western end of the

Transvaal province, in the Rustenburg district. With the Dutch family which took her away from her people, grandmother went to live in strange lands amongst strange people. They passed the town of Rustenburg, crossed the Magaliesberg mountains and settled to the south-west of them where the Dutch family began farming. The place was about twelve or fourteen miles from Phokeng, our headquarters, and my grandfather, Paramount Chief Mokgatle, was the ruler of the tribe. I tried hard to discover the name of the family or the man who took grandmother away and kept her as a slave, but failed. The only name I got was the nickname the Africans gave that man— KaMongoele, which means 'on the knees'. I shall therefore refer to that man as KaMongoele.

From his nickname, I guess that he was a deeply religious man, who must always have ordered his children and those who were under his care and guidance to go on their knees and pray. Every European, even today, who has daily dealings with the Africans has a nickname, and the Africans amongst themselves call him by that name. If he wears a beard he is nicknamed beard, if he is fat he will be called Mafutha, which means fat, if he is a man with a big nose he will be called Rangko, if he has large eyes, Ramatlho.

Although my grandmother grew up in the household of a Dutch farmer, working without pay as a slave, and had been taken away from her tribe at a very early age, she did not forget her language. She remembered well the names of her parents but did not know where she could find her people. She learned to speak Dutch, which is today called Afrikaans, but because there was no school for her could not read or write it. She remembered, too, that her tribal name was Matlhodi, the daughter of Chief Kekana of Kwamukopani.

I did not think that she was ill-treated, because that would not have been in the interest of KaMangoele and his family. KaMangoele and grandfather Paramount Chief Mokgatle became friends, paid each other visits and gave one another presents. According to legend, Mokgatle's greatest gifts to his friend KaMangoele were honey. Each time KaMangoele visited grandfather at Phokeng he returned to his farm with large quantities of honey and other gifts he liked very much. It is said that each time KaMangoele arrived at Phokeng he brought presents to his friend, and through those presents their friendship deepened. According to legend there was no feeling of a white man meeting a black man, one thinking that the other was not his equal, but man meeting another man and accepting him into his household.

Grandfather saw the young slave girl, who later became his wife, grow into a pretty young woman, but I wonder whether grandfather asked his friend where he got the little slave girl whom he saw working in his house. When grandmother was old enough to become a cook for KaMangoele's household, the task of working in the house and cooking for the family became her routine. She was not only the cook, but waited as well on her master's family and all friends who visited the family. KaMangoele's family gave grandmother a European name, Paulina. As a cook in a European house she learned a great deal about the art of preparing European food, and each time grandfather visited his friend he could not leave without a meal and expressing thanks to the one who did the preparations. For a long time grandfather thought that the cooking was done by his friend's wife or one of his daughters. It was only at KaMangoele's home that grandfather could enjoy European food, and he developed a liking for it, but to go to his friend's home meant that he had to be away from the tribe for the whole day.

I do not know precisely how many wives my grandfather Paramount Chief Mokgatle had. Some people said he had more than forty, others say less. Whatever the figure, like all polygamous Paramount Chiefs, he had many wives. At the head of his wives there were three top ones who were expected to provide the tribe with a ruler, in case one of them was childless. They were numbers one, two and three. Number one was the one expected to bear the future ruler of the tribe. The law and custom was that number one's male child should become Chief, his juniors following in succession if death or insanity deprived the elder one of the chance to become the ruler of the tribe. And so on with wives numbers two and three.

Wife number one is called Mohumagadi (queen, or mother of the tribe) and all the Chief's wives are under her and look to her for advice, and follow her lead whenever the women of the tribe were to do something which particularly concerned women. I do not know the name of my grandfather's number one wife, but I do know that in the tribe she was called by the name of her first son who became Paramount Chief after grandfather's death. The son's name was Dumagole and thus his mother was called Madumagole.

The name of wife number two, who was the closest to me, was Nkhubu, but like number one she was popularly known by her first son's name, Dikeledi (tears): I do not know why he was so named, but I can imagine that at the time of his birth there must have been something which saddened the grandfather or the whole tribe. One other thing which surprises me is why he was given the name Dikeledi, since the name belongs to females. Nkhubu was therefore called Madikeledi, Dikeledi's mother.

Grandfather's wife number three was also called by the name of her first son, who was named after grandfather's grandfather, Sekete. Sekete's mother was called Masekete. Those were grandfather's chief wives, who had great influence in our tribe. Their sons, too, became very powerful and influential during grandfather's reign and after his death. They called each other brother, one calling the other 'my elder brother' and referring to others as 'my younger brothers'. Dumagole led, Dekeledi followed him, and Sekete followed both of them.

Other wives and their houses were important, but were referred to as minor wives or minor houses. Today in our tribe there are many families which bear the surname Mokgatle, and all are descendants of Paramount Chief Mokgatle. All of them know their positions in the tribal line and follow the rule as it was laid down for them by their grandfather. Dumagole too had several wives and his number one wife provided the tribe with the ruler after his death, and the procedure has been followed till today, when Dumagole's descendant Lebone (the lamp) is the Chief.

While grandfather and the Dutch farmer KaMangoele were great friends, offering each other gifts, receiving each other as equals in their households, and Paulina my grandmother cooked tasty European food which Mokgatle enjoyed enormously, grandfather asked his friend to allow him to marry Paulina, so that she could cook him European food at his headquarters, Phokeng. KaMangoele agreed but reminded grandfather that his marriage to Paulina must be performed according to his law and customs, so that Paulina could acquire social standing in his tribe. Grandfather readily consented, and this meant that grandfather must pay KaMangoele dowry (*bogadi*) which would make her grandfather's legal wife. On his return to the tribe, grandfather reported his intentions to the tribal Council and the negotiations he had had with KaMangoele. The tribal Council approved and later a number of messengers were sent to KaMangoele's home to ascertain what amount of dowry he required for Paulina's release, so that she could marry grandfather.

All the formalities were agreed to and finalised. A number of cattle were delivered to KaMangoele as dowry for my grandmother, and once delivered she was married to Mokgatle, and all that was left for Mokgatle to do was to take her to his tribe.

Grandmother, married to Mokgatle and given away by her master KaMangoele, began her second journey, that time from KaMangoele's farm to Phokeng to join the circle of Paramount Chief's wives. She was a young woman, beautiful, speaking the Dutch of that time and Sintebele, her tribal language. On arrival she found herself again in a strange land amongst strange people, with whom she had only the colour of her skin in common. She still did not know where her people were, and how she could get in touch with them. She had no choice; all that concerned her was that she was alive and married to a Paramount Chief.

At the time when her marriage was being negotiated, Mokgatle's second wife Madikeledi, Nkhubu, was sick, and immediately before grandmother arrived in the tribe she died, leaving three sons, Dikeledi, Dikeletsane (small tears) and Ramarata, and two daughters, Malengena and Theko, a name which indicates that she was born when grandmother's dowry was paid to Kamangoele. Theko means tariff or price. Dikeledi and his two brothers were still young and their sisters were very small, and all needed care. Instead of giving grandmother a home, fields and cattle of her own, like all married women in the tribe, grandfather decided that she should move into Nkhubu's house to care for the children who had lost their mother. That gave her the right to use Madikeledi's house and her fields, as well as her animals. Grandmother's four children were born in Nkhubu's house, and regarded Madikeledi's children as their true brothers and sisters. They looked upon Madikeledi's properties as their mother's properties. I think that grandmother's arrival, Nkhubu's death and the drafting of grandmother into the second main house in the tribe placed grandfather and the tribal councillors in a dilemma. Here was a woman, legally married, but also the last to be married, given the honour of living as, and caring for the children of, the second most important woman of the tribe. Was she replacing Nkhubu in status? What was her status in the tribe, the second or the last? What position would her children occupy in Kgotla (the royal court)? If these questions were asked, they were never settled. A vacuum existed and still exists. . . .

Second Marriage

All the time that my grandmother's marriage to grandfather Paramount Chief Mokgatle was being arranged and performed by the man who had taken her away without consent from her people, and when she left the Dutch farmer's house for her new home on Phokeng, her people had no idea that their daughter was still alive somewhere in Africa, perhaps less then two hundred miles from her birthplace. They had given up hope that one day they would hear of her whereabouts, let alone see her, in possession of her body, flesh, blood and soul.

In Phokeng she gave birth to four children, [including the author's father]. . .

After the discovery of diamonds in the Cape Province of South Africa at Kimberley in 1870, money became an attractive object in the eyes of Africans, and with it they found that they could buy things they needed from the Europeans who introduced it. The claim owners at Kimberley needed labour and the only people who could provide them with it were the Africans. There was stiff competition for labour among the claim owners, which made them pay more.

African men from all parts of South Africa made their way to Kimberley, travelling for days or weeks on foot to get there, to offer their services in return for money. Six months was a long period for men to be away from their homes. When they returned, they brought back with them large amounts of money which they used to buy themselves cattle and to buy presents or beautiful things for their wives, mothers, sisters or sweethearts. It became a source of pride for it to be known that a young man had been to Kimberley, and no one who had been to Kimberley was expected to be a poor man with no money or the other things needed to make life easier.

One man from my tribe whose name I do not know also reached Kimberley to search for riches. While he was there he met another man who was Ntebele, or Leteble, from my grandmother's tribe. Both worked for one claim owner and they got to know each other well. One day, the legend goes, the man from our tribe had an argument with the other, and for the first time he heard the language Sintebele spoken. It sounded to him like the way grandmother spoke when angry. Thus started a new chapter in grandmother's life. The man from our tribe told his friend that the language he spoke sounded like that spoken by one of his Paramount Chief's wives. During their time together they told each other stories about their people and tribes, and as a result the man from her tribe got to know that grandmother was alive.

The man from our tribe told the Ntebele one that when grandmother was annoyed by the people with whom she lived, she time and again reminded them that she was not a simple person as they thought, but the daughter of a Chief and her name was Matlhodi-a-Kekana. That cleared all the Ntebele man's doubts that the woman described by his friend was the one his people had been searching for and had presumed dead.

After a time, when both were satisfied that they had earned enough money to get some of the things they needed most, they returned to their respective tribes. Our tribesman thought that the story has ended at Kimberley, but the man from grandmother's people went back with a story to tell his people, that by sheer chance he had discovered the whereabouts of grandmother. After arriving home he passed on his information to the head of his clan (*induna*), who thereafter took him to the Chief's place so that he could relate the news himself. He had also gathered some information about our place Phokeng, that it was to the west of them, though he lacked knowledge how many miles away it was.

His story was so convincing that his people began to prepare to send a group of men including himself to search for Phokeng, and to ascertain whether it was really true that Matlhodi was alive and a married woman. The story is that they travelled on foot through wild areas, asking people they met for directions to Phokeng. Eventually, after spending days on the way, they reached our capital. On arrival, the man who had brought the information from Kimberley asked where he could find his friend. Before long his friend was surprised to see him with a number of men calling on him at his home. After receiving the visitors our man reported them to the head of his clan, as was the procedure, and the next day they were taken to the Chief's place to be introduced, so that they could explain themselves thoroughly and why they were there.

As it was the rule in those days, once strangers were introduced to the Chief they became the Chief's visitors. For several days, the legend goes, they stayed at grandfather's place as his guests, being interviewed by councillors and others who were interested to find out who they were and the purpose of their visit. Their feet first had to be cooled off, since it was said, 'Never speak to a visitor while his feet are still hot; give him food, all hospitality, allow him a chance to relax and then ask him to open his bag', which meant, 'Give him strength to relate his story.' When the day had arrived for them to tell their tale, though grandfather, together with those who were close to him, knew the purpose of the Ntebeles' or Matebeles' visit, he called his councillors together to hear the news for themselves.

The leader of the Matebeles, who I understand was related to grandmother and was a man of high social standing in their tribe and was also a Kekana, told my people who they were and that they were searching for a lost child whom they had presumed dead. They were not sure, but had information that the person they were searching for was living with us. Eventually grandmother was produced before them and they were asked whether she was the person they were searching for. As she was no longer a child, but a woman with children, they had lost recognition of her and some members of their delegation had never seen her before, so they all said that they were not sure that she was the one they were looking for. Grandmother was asked whether she recognised any of the men who stood before her, but she shook her head, saying they were complete strangers to her. The leader of the delegation from KwaMukopani then said that the only means by which they could identify her was by speaking to her in her own tribal language, Sintebele. That was allowed, and they began to talk to her in their own language, and were surprised that grandmother still spoke it well. That cleared all the doubts and for the first time grandmother came face to face with her own people. At home her parents had died, but very close relatives were still alive. The delegation, being satisfied that they had found what they were sent out to search for, spent a week or two in Phokeng and they were given great honour and hospitality.

On the day of their departure, I learnt, they were given a dignified and exciting send-off, because both sides were satisfied that everlasting friendship between the two tribes had been established. No doubt grandmother became homesick when she saw the people she knew going back to her birthplace. There was nothing she could do, since she was already married to the Paramount Chief of the Bafokeng tribe. At that time my father was a young boy of about three or four years old.

On their return home the Matebele delegation, pleased with the results of their mission, reported to their Chief and people with pride that their presumed dead daughter Matlhodi-a-Kekana was alive, married and the mother of four children, two of whom died in infancy. The Matebele thereafter began discussions amongst themselves, whether or not they recognised her marriage to the Bafokeng tribe. Guided by their laws and customs, they agreed that since her marriage was not negotiated with them, they were not party to her marriage. They had not received dowry, or given her away to the Paramount Chief Mokgatle of the Bafokeng tribe. They were bound to declare that, according to their law and custom, grandmother was not legally married, therefore they did not recognise her marriage.

Two years after the delegation's return from Phokeng, another stronger delegation, led by grandmother's paternal uncle, was sent off to Phokeng, with a message to thank the Bafokeng tribe for having looked after and protected grandmother since she came to live amongst them, but to declare firmly that her marriage was not recognised by her people. In support of their argument, they cited a legal standpoint that the dowry the Bafokeng claimed to have paid was not paid to them but to a Dutch farmer, KaMangoele, who took her away from the people who gave birth to her without their knowledge and consent and had no legal right to keep her, demand dowry for her, and to give her away.

In addition, they were told to make it plain to the Bafokeng and their Chief that it was up to them, if they desired to keep her, to negotiate a new marriage. As for the dowry they paid to KaMangoele, this was a matter which the Matebele could not discuss or go into, but one to be solved by the Bafokeng and their friend KaMangoele, the Dutch farmer.

Apparently, at the time when the Dutch people arrived at KwaMukopani, the land of my grandmother's people, now called Piet Potgietersrust, the lands were roamed by herds of elephant. Grandmother's people's tribal symbol was and is still an elephant, which I think they inherited fron the main body of the Zulu nation, which they broke away from under the leadership of Musilikazi,

[Mzilikazi] the founder of the Matebele [Ndebele] in Matebeleland in Rhodesia.

I was told that when the second delegation arrived in Phokeng to tell grandfather and his people that grandmother's marriage was not recognised at KwaMukopani, they brought with them large quantities of elephants' tusks and other gifts for grandfather. Again, the legend goes, they were received with great honour and dignity because at that time it was a visit not only of friends but of brothers-in-law. After resting for two days the delegation, led by grandmother's uncle, opened its bag by breaking the news that the Matebeles of KwaMukopani did not regard their daughter as being legally married. They therefore proposed that if grandfather's people wished to start fresh marriage negotiations all over again, they were ready to talk. Before grandfather and his people had time to consider their proposal, which seemed astonishing to other people in our tribe, they gave a warning that if grandfather and his people did not agree to their proposal, there was no alternative but that, after their return home, another delegation would come to fetch her together with her children.

At that time, I was told, grandmother was in the family way, expecting Uncle Setlhatsana. Some councillors, without considering the proposal well, told the Matebele delegation that a second marriage was out of the question since, as far as they were concerned, grandmother was married and was their Paramount Chief's wife. It is said that grandfather reserved his views and made no comments. A few days later the Matebele delegation returned home to report how their proposal was received by the Bafokeng tribe. Several months elapsed, and after second thoughts and with grandfather's influence, a Bafokeng delegation left for KwaMukopani to say that they were willing to enter into marriage negotiations. Their arrival, I was told, was a colourful one. Before they opened their bag to say why they had come, the Matebeles could guess that they brought good news with them.

The arrival of the Bafokeng delegation at KwaMukopani, her birthplace, marked the beginning of grandmother's second marriage. The delegation was authorised to conclude all the arrangements so that the marriage could attain legal status. The Matebeles, knowing that they had the advantage over the people of my tribe, named the number of cattle they needed, so that my grandfather's people should know that, after all, grandmother had people who had the right to marry her off, and give her away. The Bafokeng delegation agreed to the number of cattle demanded.

After spending several days in KwaMukopani they returned home, leaving a promise that before long the cattle demanded would come. This would bar grandmother's people from going to Phokeng to fetch her. Back in Phokeng, they reported the agreement they had reached with the Matebeles about their daughther. I do not know how many cattle went to KwaMukopani as grandmother's second dowry, but the name of the man who led the delegation which took the cattle to grandmother's people was Ramotsoagole Nameng. The cattle were exactly as the Matebeles had asked, and they became the stamp and seal of grandmother's legal marriage.

The celebrations for grandmother's marriage at her birthplace took place in her absence before the Bafokeng delegation left. Following the tribal customs, many beasts lost their lives to feed those who were still alive in her tribe as well as to provide the Bafokeng delegation with food to eat on their way back home. At Phokeng, too, the wedding was celebrated with the slaughter of many beasts to feed the people and to make known to them that from that day Matlhodi-a-Kekana was married to their tribe with the consent of her people and was the legal wife of their Paramount Chief. Grandmother's marriage established a friendship with the Matebele of KwaMukopani. It also gave her pride that the people to whom she had been married as a slave by KaMangoele, the Dutch farmer, now knew that she had people who could demand to know her fate should something unpleasant happen to her. She knew that those in our tribe who used to tell her that she ought to thank her lucky stars that she was married to their Chief, who had given her status in life, would not repeat their rudeness. The second dowry paid to her people earned her the nickname of the most expensive woman in the tribe. . . .

General Botha during the Anglo-Boers War

PART 3

Toward a White-Dominated State,

1851–1936

The period from 1851 to 1936 saw the unfolding of many complex and intertwined developments in South Africa. Two major themes dominate the period; a South African industrial revolution and the building of a white-dominated unified state. Related to both of these changes are cultural, political, and economic transformations in the lives of Africans. To understand the workings of the new society, we need to consider all of these strands together.

The process of industrialization drove the period. In the 1850s and early 1860s, South Africa comprised a few miles of railway tracks, a scattered European settler population, a meager stream of immigrants, and a few weak exports. However, the discovery of diamonds in Griqualand West in 1867 and of gold on the Witwatersrand in the Transvaal in 1885 attracted waves of immigrants from the rest of the region and from all over the world. These mining industries stimulated a myriad of related subsidiary activities, especially the building of railways, the provision of transport, retailing, agriculture, and financial services. The new prosperity unleashed huge quantities of local capital and spurred advances in manufacturing, urbanization, education, and government services. From a depressed and scattered set of settlements, South Africa blossomed into a modern capitalist economy. This metamorphosis was gradual, however, and by 1936 South Africa, along with other western capitalist countries, floundered in the worldwide economic crisis.

Earlier analyses of this period emphasized the transformation of white politics: the moves toward the political unification of the subcontinent under a government free from British control. Although white politics still serves as an important theme in this era, it needs to be considered in conjunction with the economic changes outlined above. In the early 1850s, the white settlers of South Africa lived under four political units. The largest was the Cape Colony, the earliest settlement, ruled by Britain since 1806. In 1852 a new constitution established the Cape Parliament, whose powers increased with the granting of responsible government in 1872. Under this system, ministers controlling internal affairs answered to a majority of the elected members of Parliament, and the British-appointed governor was in turn bound by their advice. For affairs beyond the boundaries of the Cape, the governor acted as high commissoner, wielding the full political authority of the British imperial government.

Weak as it was, the Cape dwarfed the other settlements in Natal, the Orange Free State, and the Transvaal. Natal, a British colony since 1843, had a small settler population living among a vast majority of Africans. After 1860 the sugar industry, which imported indentured labor from India, somewhat buoyed the frail Natal economy, but the white population remained small. The Natal settlers did not achieve responsible government until the 1890s. In the interior, the trekker communities overcame their shortfalls and division sufficiently to form two republics, the Orange Free State and the Transvaal, or South African Republic. Both republics achieved virtual autonomy under general British hegemony through the Sand River Convention of 1852 and the Pretoria Convention of 1854.

As the economic revolution gathered momentum, the need for political unity became obvious. But who would sponsor the creation of a general government, and who would control it? Not surprisingly, the settlers did not question the assumption that they would dominate a new government. After Sir George Grey's abortive scheme for unification in the 1850s, Lord Carnarvon, British secretary of state for the colonies in Disraeli's cabinet, took the first major initiative toward unity by seizing control of the Transvaal from its feeble government in 1877.

This attempt to unify South Africa under imperial auspices misfired with Disraeli's fall and with the Transvaal Boers' rebellion in 1881. After the Boers' 1881 victory, the Transvaal's independence was reestablished by the Pretoria Convention of 1881. Yet its citizens still chafed under the vague and onerous "British suzerainty" asserted in the convention, and their nationalism intensified in the ensuing years. The rush for Witwatersrand gold in the later 1880s suddenly empowered the Transvaal to challenge the Cape's regional domination and question British authority in general.

Paul Kruger, president of the Transvaal in the 1890s, embodied this intransigent Afrikaner nationalism, with its goals of complete republican independence and Afrikaner dominance. Kruger resisted both British imperial control and other versions of South African patriotism that embraced both English and Afrikaner settlers. Nevertheless, his exclusivist nationalism did not hold sway among the Afrikaners of the Cape Colony or in the Orange Free State. Instead, the more inclusive South African settler patriotism accommodated a partnership between Afrikaners and English politicians, yet it too sought to minimize imperial control and to extend local self-government.

Thus in the 1890s, a conflict brewed in South African white politics that centered on rival views of South Africa's future. On the surface the debate pitted the Transvaal against imperial and Cape interests concerning customs duties, transportation routes, and citizenship questions. At the center of controversy swirled the issue of Uitlander grievances. The Uitlanders—immigrant miners, workers, and businessmen who flooded the Transvaal after the gold discoveries—quickly outnumbered the republic's Afrikaner population. The Transvaal government kept the Uitlanders disfranchised by making naturalization difficult while squeezing as much revenue as possible out of the mining industry. The tension surrounding these issues undermined moderate opinion and strengthened extremists on all sides. In a key event—the Jameson Raid of 1895—Sir Leander Starr Jameson, an associate of Cecil Rhodes, led a force of British South African Company police into the Transvaal. Jameson expected to coordinate his invasion with an Uitlander rebellion, but the uprising never materialized and the raiders were rounded up and arrested. The fiasco discredited Rhodes and set the stage for the outbreak of the Anglo-Boer War in 1899.

The 1899–1902 war between the British Empire and the two Boer republics is crucial for understanding twentieth-century South African white politics. In the first phase of the conflict, republican forces besieged British garrisons in such places as Mafeking, Kimberley, and Ladysmith. During the second phase, reinforcements from Britain crushed the Boer forces and occupied the republican capitals. By 1900 the war seemed to be over, but hostilities would grind on for two more years. Small forces of Afrikaner soldiers waging guerrilla warfare harassed and demoralized the imperial forces. The British responded by segmenting the entire countryside into barbed-wire enclosures, removing or destroying Afrikaner crops and cattle, and ultimately placing much of the Afrikaner population in concentration camps. By 1902 these strategies forced the Boers to sue for peace, negotiated at Vereeniging. Even then, the Boers were divided between "handsuppers" (Afrikaner soldiers who surrendered near the end of the Anglo-Boer War) and "bitter-enders" (Afrikaner soldiers who wanted to fight on). Twenty-six thousand detainees, mostly women and children, had died in the concentration camps, and Afrikaner farms lay in ruins. "It is the bitter end," mourned Afrikaner general Jan Smuts in signing the peace terms.

With the Boer republics subdued and annexed, Lord Milner, governor and high commissioner, launched elaborate reconstruction plans to get the mines back into production and to achieve other economic and political goals. As one of the fruits of victory, he expected Britain to set the terms for a unified South Africa. However, the war had evoked a troublesome reaction in Britain: a large segment of the public, including much of the Liberal party, opposed the war and proclaimed itself "pro-Boer." Indeed, Sir Henry Campbell-Bannerman, the Liberal leader, decried the antiguerrilla campaign as "methods of barbarism." In the election of 1905, the Liberals defeated Lord Balfour's Conservative government and took office at the beginning of 1906. The pro-Boer Campbell-Bannerman became prime minister and gave Anglo-Boer reconciliation the highest priority. Within a year, the Liberals moved to grant responsible government to elected white governments in the former republics and thus surrendered to South African politicians the right to negotiate the terms of union.

In the short run, this gesture benefited moderates, those who held the old Cape Colony ideal of partnership between English and Afrikaner. The shape of the new Union of South Africa was negotiated, passed by the British Parliament, and put into effect by 1910. The constitution guaranteed the equality of Dutch and English, and South Africa received "dominion status"—the same autonomy achieved by Canada and Australia. The Boer War generals Louis Botha, Jan Smuts, and J.B.M. Hertzog took office under the new constitution.

Nevertheless, the old tensions still simmered under the surface. Within two years General Hertzog had formed a separate National party, asserting that official "equality" still left the Dutch far behind within South Africa and that South African autonomous status provided insufficient protection against imperial meddling. He continued to nurture dreams of an independent republic rather than a parliamentary constitutional monarchy tied to Britain. The Boer War had consigned a large proportion of the Afrikaner population to poverty, and the Nationalists concerned themselves with the plight of these poor whites. Destitute Afrikaners provided a fertile recruiting ground as the party built political support.

The Botha-Smuts South African party held power until 1924, with Smuts serv-

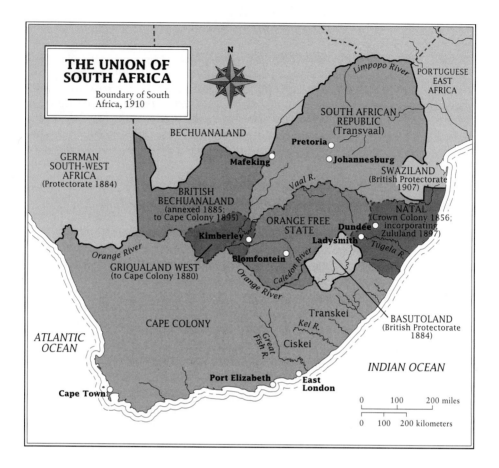

ing as prime minister after Botha's death in 1919. Campaigning on issues of South African autonomy and national status, Hertzog's Nationalists defeated the Smuts government in 1924. Hertzog strengthened his campaign by attacking the government's handling of the great Witwatersrand strike of 1922, in which Smuts had sided with the large mining companies and used military force to squelch the uprising. Allying with the small, largely English Labour party, Hertzog defused the ethnic issue by agreeing to defer his quest for a republic.

As prime minister, Hertzog pursued his nationalist goals of educational advancement for Afrikaners, apprenticeships for poor whites, and reformed civil-service rules to give Afrikaners access to power. He won the adoption of a new flag that displayed the symbolism of the Boer republics. Hertzog scored successes in imperial relations as well. By the time of the imperial conference of 1926 and the passage of the Statute of Westminster by the British Parliament in 1931, Hertzog had secured an unambiguous assurance of South African immunity from imperial interference.

Although South Africa was not a republic and still maintained the British connection, Hertzog felt satisfied, and the reasons for his original break with Smuts evaporated. Now, to ease the economic crisis, Smuts joined Hertzog in a fusion government in 1932, and several years later their parties merged to form the United party.

A few diehards who remained dissatisfied with South Africa's international status and with Afrikaners' social position formed their own "Purified" National party. They drew on the work of the Afrikaner Broederbond, a cultural organization founded in the 1920s that eventually became a secret society pledged to advance the interests and status of Afrikaners. The Purified National party would gain power in South Africa in 1948.

This terse sketch of white politics has so far omitted all reference to Africans and to white attitudes or policies toward them. Yet clearly these vital issues are connected at every point in the story. Here we separate the two strands to clarify those connections. The period 1850–1880 witnessed the last generation of African political independence. As we have seen, autonomous chiefdoms and kingdoms were giving way to increasing settler pressure. However, during the early years of the mining revolution, which coincided with the last years of African independence, many Africans used their wages to purchase firearms and sometimes pooled their earnings to buy land. In the Eastern Cape and later in other areas, they also grew produce or provided wagon haulage for white migrants traveling to the diggings. Thus some Africans enjoyed lucrative opportunities in the new economy, even as many others suffered dispossession.

Beyond economic concerns, other aspects of African life shifted in these years, albeit unevenly. In the Eastern Cape, in Natal, among the Tswana, and elsewhere, increasing numbers of Africans had converted to Christianity and attended school. A small elite, a few thousand at most, became teachers, ministers, journalists, and soon lawyers and doctors. Some Kholwa (converts) broke away from the missions to form separatist or "Ethiopian" churches. Many others rejected both Christianity and schooling and retained their traditional culture.

Variety characterized African economic life as well. In some areas, Africans retained substantial blocks of land and cattle and practiced something close to their traditional economy. Others were squatters on white farms, where they farmed on the shares with some success—although they proved vulnerable to being expelled or reduced to wage labor as white agriculture modernized. A few Africans lived on land that they or missionary societies had purchased. In addition, more and more Africans traveled to the mines and cities to seek wage labor, sometimes by choice, at other times driven by government policies that denied them alternative means of livelihood. Thus the changes revolutionizing African society were both uneven and incomplete. A few Africans benefited, but more suffered brutal hardship. Even those whose lives seemingly remained untouched found that change insidiously altered the context in which they practiced their traditions.

These three themes of South African history—economic revolution, white politics, and the transformation of African life—coalesced in the ceaseless discussion of what contemporaries called the "native question," or how can Africans be controlled and subordinated in a white-dominated state and economic system? One aspect of the question concerned the extent and form of African political rights. In the Cape Colony's constitution of 1852, a few Africans and Coloured people (the mixed-race descendants of European settlers, Khoikoi, and slaves in the Cape Colony) had the right to vote based on property and literacy tests. Would this limited system extend to all of South Africa under the terms of union, or would it be eliminated? Ultimately, the franchise was retained only in the Cape. Like the provision that made the Dutch and English languages equal, the Cape's system was entrenched, and thus harder to amend than other constitutional provisions.

The ongoing debate also raised the issue of land policy and eventually led to the Native Land Act of 1913, which separated the country into white and black areas. Finally, the "native question" asked how Africans could be made to provide sufficient labor at low wages, without their presence disrupting the life of European communities. The requirement that Africans outside the reserves carry passes and the restriction of Africans' access to the cities, as stipulated in the Native (Urban Areas) Act of 1923, reflected this concern.

Debates over these and other facets of white policy towards Africans—especially regarding education, religion, and interracial social relations—sprang up in legislative hearings; during the sittings of royal commissions of the imperial, colonial, and Union governments; and in newspapers and innumerable pamphlets. Three distinct positions emerged, which we may term baaskap, segregation, and liberalism. Baaskap *advocated simple white domination with no pretense of concern for African welfare. The attitude pervaded South Africa but especially typified white farmers who wanted a reliable supply of labor. In brief,* baaskap *held that an African wearing shoes and a hat who remained on a public sidewalk in the presence of a white man must be knocked down.*

The word segregation*—first used in the early twentieth century, although the practice was older—also had proponents from all areas of South Africa. It was perhaps best typified in Natal where the Zulu dwelling in the large contiguous reserves lived separately from the small European population. The idea of segregation in part expressed white fears of black domination. On a more sophisticated level, the doctrine claimed to offer a means of protecting African as well as European interests. At its center lay the belief that the preservation of African leadership, social structure, culture, and an independent economic base in their own land was vital to controlling the population and maintaining white security.*

Liberalism found a voice among a few missionaries, educators, and self-styled "friends of Africans," again throughout South Africa but especially in the Cape Colony and province. Starting with the premise of the spiritual equality of all human beings before God, liberalism assumed not the racial inferiority of Africans but their cultural backwardness. The liberals urged the assimilation of Africans into European culture through a gradual and paternally guided process. The few Africans who qualified by their educational, economic, and moral progress eventually would gain admittance to political participation.

From the 1850s to 1936, proponents of all three positions debated the "native question." Of course, they seldom presented their arguments in pure form. For example, some proposed segregation as a way of achieving baaskap, *and the cultural arrogance detected in liberalism often dovetailed with ordinary claims of racial superiority. Liberals also echoed segregationists' claims that Africans would benefit from the protection and tutelage of segregated institutions.*

According to an old saying, South African political debate is an argument among whites about what to do with blacks. This, of course, is not quite true, for Africans participated in the debates throughout these years. The example of Indian political activity in Natal in the 1890s and 1900s helped to shape the principal African political organiziation, the South African Native National Congress, later the African National Congress (ANC) founded in 1912. This organization stood largely in the liberal camp, and the educated elite who founded it came from a background of mission education.

In the early decades of the Union, down to the 1940s, the ANC, with its small elite membership, adopted a cautious, moderate approach, relying on petitions, legislative testimony, a close cooperation with white liberals. Its leaders participated, for example, in the Bantu-European Joint Councils that were set up in some cities in the 1920s to discuss such matters as housing, municipal services, and education. Some ANC members even clung to the obsolete hope of appealing to England for help.

Africans possessed other forums for expressing their political views. At the grass roots, in the countryside, African protests sometimes took a more militant form. After the Zulu rebellion of 1906–1908, however, rural protest was isolated and easily suppressed and often passed unnoticed in national discussions. Labor organizing among urban and mining workers played a more important role, but the ANC failed to address workers' concerns consistently after 1921. The Industrial and Commercial Workers Union (ICU), which amassed a huge membership in the Eastern Cape and in Natal in the 1920s, stepped into the vacuum.

The long debate on the position of Africans in a white-dominated South Africa wore on from the 1850s until 1936, when benchmark legislation recast the entire issue. In that year African hopes for better conditions in the urban workplace and on the rural reserves shattered. The repeal of the African vote in the Cape province decisively checked liberalism, and the African elite's traditional reliance on cooperation with white liberals was questioned.

The End of African Autonomy and the White-Domination Debate

1. Khoikhoi-Coloured Peoples Debate Rebellion, 1851

The Eastern Cape frontier war of 1850–1853 was the most destructive ever and substantially broke the power of the Xhosa people. The Khoikhoi and mixed-race communities also became involved in the conflict. The Kat River Settlement, sponsored and supported by missionaries since 1829, had provided a buffer and support for colonists in case of conflict with the Xhosa. However, the colored communities occupied valuable land in the settlement, and thus in this war it, too, was attacked and expropriated. In the following selection, one of the settlement leaders calls on the Griqua of the northern Cape districts for help, but to little avail.

Anskola, June 11, 1851

Much-esteemed Messieurs Adam Kok and H. Hendricks

Forasmuch as we the poor oppressed Hottentot race are objects of the present war which is going on here, who have now been for a considerable time oppressed by the unrighteous English settlers, who have so continually petitioned the Government, by memorials, for consent and execution of irregular and oppressive laws, such as vagrant laws, which tend to oppression and complete ruin of the coloured and poor of this land, a land which we, as natives, may justly claim as our mother land, it is my aim and object, by this opportunity, esteeming it my duty, owing to all who are there as nation and family of one house (although long delayed and neglected therewith), to give information that this war which is going on here, is declared against us Hottentots because we defend ourselves against above-mentioned laws, or will not let them pass. Thus it is my earnest wish and request to you (since the poor and ruined of our race here have employed me to represent to you this their

---

From "Correspondence Related to the State of the Kaffir Tribes and to the Recent Outbreak in the Eastern Frontier," British Sessional Papers, 1852, xxxiii [1428], pp. 448–449.

deplorable condition) to hear your determination regarding this matter as a nation, and who ought to bear and feel with one another in hardship; and what your plans and intentions are, as the principal portion of our nation have earnestly requested me to entreat from you to favour them as soon as possible with an answer or decision.

It is already five months that we have been engaged in this war, and consequently we have suffered much loss of human life and property, and we greatly lament that we could not inform you of this matter sooner, for there was no opportunity, as the outbreak of this war came very unexpectedly upon us, which exposed us to great danger, and also occasioned many of our people to be still amongst the settlers, and obliged us for safety's sake to join ourselves to the Kaffirs of Sandilli, Macomo, Botman, and others, for they were also on our side.

Beloved, rise manfully and unanimously as a nation and children of one house to engage yourselves in this important work, a work which concerns your mother country, for not a single person of colour, wherever he may be, will escape this law. Trust, therefore, in the Lord (whose character is known to be unfriendly to injustice), and undertake your work, and he will give us prosperity—a work for your mother-land and freedom, for it is now the time, yea, the appointed time, and no other.

Kat River, our home, and the refuge of all the poor races, is utterly destroyed and burnt, Shiloh, or Klipplaats, likewise. We are now in the Amatola, and the people of Shiloh in Zuurberg.

I am, your obedient servant,

(Signed) Willem Uithaalder

P.S.— We have wholly excluded the English Government in our present war, because the Government has no fault about this war, and we perceive that the Government has hitherto abstained from lending aid to the settlers in carrying it forward; therefore we (that is, the Kaffirs and me) leave them out till we see further.

I am also charged to request you further to communicate, as speedily as possible, our knowledge of this matter, by a commission to the highly-esteemed Mr. Watterboer, also a part of our nation.

Help, in all respects, is of the greatest necessity. The esteemed Mr. Walsbrom, whom I have requested to be the medium of delivering to you these letters, will also be so good as to relate to you every circumstance connected with this matter.

Your faithful servant,

(signed) Willem Uithaalder

To Mr. Willem Uithaalder, Amatola

Philippolis, August 27, 1851

Sir,

I have received your letter of the 11th June, and in answer thereto I must state to you my opinion candidly and plainly.

My heart is very sorrowful on account of the condition in which many of the Hottentots of the colony now are. I much regret that they have taken such a step. I have not the slightest sympathy with the rebellion of the Hottentots. Instead of regarding you and your associates as the brave defenders of the Hottentot race, I cannot but consider you as the enemies of all the coloured people of South Africa, for by your rebellion you will impress a strong prejudice on the minds of all thinking people against the character, the rights, and the claims of the coloured classes. There may probably have been grounds for dissatisfaction among the Hottentots, but I am fully convinced that you had no sufficient grounds to take up arms against your Government; and believe me, as a friend and well-wisher to you all, you have adopted wrong methods to gain your rights. By your rebellion you will bring nothing but loss and misery on yourselves and your posterity.

As far as I and my people are concerned, you must not expect the least assistance from us. We even considered ourselves injured in our cause by your rebellion.

Any complaint that we may have against the English Government, we intend to bring forward in an honourable and just way, by letters and memorials, and we feel a confident hope that justice will be done us.

In case you will receive any advice from me, I would recommend you and your associates most earnestly to lay down your arms and to seek forgiveness from your Government for the great evil you have done. Possibly there may still be mercy shown you. I cannot have anything to do with your affairs, consequently I must refuse to forward your message to Waterboer or Pretorius or Moshesh. But respecting Waterboer, I can assure you that his feelings are altogether in accordance with mine, as I have expressed them in this letter.

I remain your faithful servant,
(Signed) Adam Kok, Kaptyn

2.   An African Clergyman Reflects on Africans' Future, 1865

Tiyo Soga (1829–1871) studied theology in Scotland, where he married a Scottish woman named Janet Burnside. He worked as a missionary on the Eastern Cape frontier and often bore the brunt of settler racism. He thus saw his position as one of constant ambiguity. Even as he worked to convert the Xhosa to Christianity, he was a proud African who extolled African achievements and recorded some of the earliest written statements of Xhosa cultural values.

In the following selection, a letter to the editor of the King William's Town Gazette *and* Kaffrarian Banner, *he defends the progress made by the African peoples, urges patience in awaiting the impact of Christianity on Africa, and expresses his belief in a shining future for Africans.*

King William's Town Gazette and Kaffrarian Banner

11 May 1865

What Is the Destiny of the Kaffir Race?

To the Editor: Sir,—It is only lately that an article with the above title appeared within the columns of your journal. A one admirable trait in the character of a true Englishman, is his love of 'fair play,' I trust you will have no objection in giving space to an unpretending rejoinder to that startling production. I would have sent it to the Kaffir periodical from which, I believe, it was taken by your paper, but difficulties have, in the meantime, suspended its republication.

I openly at the outset avow myself to the writer of that article to be one of those who hold the very opposite of the views he has given forth to the public, on the important question of the extinction of the Kaffir race. If he had said that the three reasons he has advanced to prove his case, form some of the difficulties in the way of elevating this people, I would have understood him clearly. But when he draws from them the astonishing conclusion of their extinction, that conclusion I cannot accept until it rests upon surer premises.

The article seems inconsistent with itself, and so to a certain extent the ill effects, which otherwise it could not have failed to produce, is neutralized. Few men would believe in the doom of any people, and then accept the illogical words of the two last paragraphs, which close the article.

But to enter more particularly into the examination of the views the author has advanced, I call your unbiassed attention to the glaring fact that the writer passes over in silence the results of missionary labours among the Kaffirs for the last fifty years. Is this fair? In the difficult and necessarily slow

From Reverend Tiyo Soga, "What Is the Destiny of the Kaffir Race?", Donovan Williams, ed., *The Journal and Selected Writings of the Reverend Tiyo Soga*, Cape Town: A. A. Balkema, 1983, pp. 178–182. Reprinted by permission of A. A. Balkema (Pty), Cape Town.

work of elevating men, surely the smallest results are worthy of appreciation. Has nothing then, as a set off to the gloomy picture, been done among this people this fifty years? Without seeking to enter into details, I hold that mission stations would return to the question the emphatic answer that something has been done, and is doing, yea, that a great deal has been done, for which missionaries thank God and take courage. But here is a point which the author must verify for himself. Take a nation—any nation in the exact circumstances of the Kaffirs of South Africa—compare the Kaffirs with that nation (for it is futile and unfair to compare him to a European with the advantage of a civilisation and christianity of 15 or 18 centuries), give that nation the same number of years—fifty,—during which the experiments of civilizing and christianizing have been tried, let this work among that nation have had to contend with the difficulties of three ruinous wars, and with the introduced views of civilization, and he will find that the Kaffirs or rather the results of Christian labours among them, will stand nobly the test of the comparison.

The sentence which ends the first large division of Reason I, evinces an unpardonable ignorance of facts, and of the recent history of the people, the knell of whose doom of extinction the writer has rung. It does monstrous injustice to a class of natives who amid much that is against them have been striving to rise and to improve. The historical facts I shall purposely set aside, but what does he make of three or four hundred Kaffirs and Fingoes who have bought 80 acre lots from government? And of many now ready to buy if they could get the chance? Are these men unworthy of notice? If they are, then that I may give up all controversy, and accept the theory of the doom of the Kaffir race, will the writer inform the public what the usual length of time is, allowed by those who compute these things, for the appearance of the first signs of improvement in education, in christianity, and in civilization, beginning from the first day of their introduction among a people? Until he can show that the Kaffirs have outstepped the limits of the boundary line of improvement, I cannot take it absolutely that there are no signs of better things among them, and I shall not believe in their extinction.

The concluding sentences of Reason II will meet with the approbation of those who wish nothing well to the Kaffir race; but it is wide of the truth. Here a part is taken for the whole, the exception for the rule. The many hundreds of native young men, in Mission Stations, members of churches, and teachers in Sabbath Schools, do they answer to this flowery description? Did those before them as young men answer to it? I mean men, who for consistency of christian character, considering the 'Slough of Despond' out of which christianity had lifted them, will compare with the multitudes of their white brethren, who can boast of greater advantages. Here is a large class of christian young men in mission institutions, made in this gaudy description to suffer for the few who are not well-doers. And why should there be no ill-doers among young men in Mission Stations? What wonder is there, if there are? Are there not many such among our European youths in our cities and towns?

I have already, Sir, referred to the concluding paragraphs of the article in question. The first begins, 'a golden opportunity, &c;' the second, 'Here are a people capable of being exalted, &c.' Now what good can 'a golden opportunity' do for men who are doomed? Is there really a golden opportunity for such? And then they are 'capable,' are they? And yet doomed? The writer will please forgive me for it, I cannot reconcile this. The Kaffirs are 'indolent,' 'drunken,' averse to change; then 'doomed to extinction,' and yet 'capable.' If I take the other terms, or rather facts, the last cannot follow—impossible.

Permit me, Sir, before I close to make some general observations, embodying some humble views of your correspondent on this momentous question. When the writers of the article 'What is the Destiny of the Kaffir Race' overturns these views by other arguments than those with which he has favored the public, I shall then believe in the doom of the Kaffir Race.

And here I remark that the author does not state whether he limits this doom to the small section of the Amakosa Kaffirs, including the Gaikas, the Galekas, and Slambies, or whether it extends to the numerous and powerful tribes of the Fingoe Kaffirs, the Tambookie Kaffirs, the Amampondo Kaffirs, the Amapondomisi Kaffirs, the Zulu Kaffirs, and the Amaswazi Kaffirs. I find the family of the Kaffir tribe extending nearly to the equator; along this line I find them taking the north-eastern coast of Africa, the dominant and the governing race; they are all one in language, and are one people—for language is that which decides the difference between one race and another. Now, I venture to say that if this doom includes all these tribes, the process of its extinction will be very long indeed.

Here is another view. Africa was of God given to the race of Ham. I find the Negro from the days of the old Assyrians downwards, keeping his 'individuality' and 'distinctiveness,' amid the wreck of empires, and the revolution of ages. I find him keeping his place among the nations, and keeping his home and country. I find him opposed by nation after nation and driven from his home. I find him enslaved—exposed to the vices and the brandy of the white man. I find him in this condition for many a day—in the West Indian Islands, in Northern and Southern America, and in the South American Colonies of Spain and Portugal. I find him exposed to all these disasters, and yet living—multiplying 'and never extinct.' Yea, I find him now as the prevalence of christian and philanthropic opinions on the right of man obtains among civilized nations, returning unmanacled to the land of his forefathers, taking back with him the civilization and the christianity of those nations. (See the Negro Republic of Liberia). I find the negro in the present struggle in America looking forward—though still with chains in his hands and with chains on his feet—yet looking forward to the dawn of a better day for himself and all his sable brethren in Africa. Until the Negro is doomed against all history and experience—until his God-given inheritance of Africa be taken finally from him, I shall never believe in the total extinction of his brethren along the southern limits of the land of Ham. The fact that the dark races of this vast continent, amid intestine wars and revolutions, and notwithstanding external spoliation, have remained 'unextinct,' have retained their individuality, has baffled historians, and challenges the author of the doom of the Kaffir race in a satisfactory explanation. There has been observed among these races the operation of a singular law, by which events have readjusted themselves when they threatened their destruction. I believe firmly that among the Negro races of South Africa events will follow the same law, and therefore neither the indolence of the Kaffirs, nor their aversion to change, nor the vices of civilization, all of which barriers the gospel must overthrow, shall suffice to exterminate them as a people.

I take another ground. How does the extinction of the Kaffir race tally with the glowing prediction—the sheet-anchor of the Church of Christ, and of the expectations of the toil-worn African missionary—'Ethiopia shall soon stretch her hands to God? The total extinction of a people who form a large family of races to whom the promise applies, shall not, surely, precede its fulfilment. In this manner, I for one shall adhere to the declaration of the 'old book' before I accept the theories of men.

To the same effect. Can a nation sunk in the barbarism of the Kaffirs,—the barbarism of the ages—elevate itself? Is it an easy thing for them to go out of the hut, along which their habits, customs, and prejudices, have for ages moved? What other nation has done this easily and at once? Civilization and christianity have in the first instance to be introduced among such a people. Then time, comprising generations—centuries—is allowed before they are expected to leaven the whole mass. Now among these doomed Kaffirs christianity has been introduced, and it is yet to be shown that among other races in circumstances exactly similar, it has accomplished more in the same space of time. But as for civilization and education, they have never been carried on among them as systems and great means of elevating a people. This has never been done to any extent worthy of being spoken of by any person at all acquainted with the history of Kaffirland. With regard to education, missionaries have never been able to do more than introduce only the elements. With but one or two exceptions they could attempt nothing that ever came up to their most ardent wishes. Had the silver and the gold of the world been theirs, they would have done vastly more, and with greater results. Is it not a fact known to the writer himself that neither of their great benefactors, the missionaries, nor the parents, have adequate means to make of many a sober and promising native youth anything better than grooms and wagon drivers. Would that the Government of Great Britain, the Father of its many people, would come forward with aids worthy of the Greatness.

The writer admits that the 'outlaws and refuse' of the mother country have introduced vices among the Kaffirs. Well, then, all that is wanted to conserve the life, and to advance the alternate elevation of aboriginal races is to give the Gospel by itself and christian civilization by itself.

Defensor

3.   A School Principal Assesses the Progress of Education for Africans, 1880

James Stewart (1831–1905) had worked with David Livingstone (the English writer and lecturer who traveled to central Africa and called for the establishment of Christian missions there) as a missionary in Central Africa. Stewart later became principal of Lovedale school in the town of Alice, where many early westernized African leaders were educated. A strong proponent of African education against the hostility of the generally racist settler society, Stewart nevertheless was stern and paternalistic in his treatment of his African students. Moreover, he bowed to settler prejudices by stressing the practical aspects of African schooling and diluting the academic curriculum.

For myself it has been a constant daily study, as the years go on, to watch and ascertain accurately what results have been gained by the amount of education already enjoyed by the natives of this country. These results are far beyond what some men not black, are willing to admit. That a certain number have abused their education and become more worthless in consequence is undoubtedly true. But that is by no means a sin peculiar to the natives of South Africa. I have seen men of other countries, not a few of my own country,—whose wickedness or weakness was augmented by the education they had received, who had become more worthless, more vile in consequence. I have seen quite as much of that, in men whose bodies were clothed in white skins, as I have seen among those whose skins were black; and I have seen men in black skins make as good a use of their education as the average of white men make. Colour, then, has just as little to do with the use or abuse of education, as it has with the right to obtain it at first.

But what I have noticed, is the opinion growing among the few educated native young men of the country that they, or, if not they, the native people are much further advanced than they really are:—that they are ready for certain changes and for the use of certain privileges, for which in reality they are not ready. I have noticed a considerable ambition without the ability, which makes a just ambition, a force and power towards the acquisition of the objects coveted. I have noticed a desire to have positions granted, while no corresponding effort and activity have been put forth, to warrant the expectation that such can yet be gained. What I mean is, that the wider and more complete education,—the kind of education a man gives to himself, has not been reached by many native young men who entertain or express these views. . . .

From James Stewart, *The Educated Kaffir, an Apology; and Industrial Education, a Sequel: Two Valedictory Addresses,* Alice: Lovedale Press, 1880, pp. 8, 10–15.

Test of Education and Ability

I would ask any educated native to make the following experiment, as a test of his qualification. Let him, with all the past advantages he has enjoyed, and with all the advantages of present circumstances, of quiet, plenty of time, and freedom from interruption, sit down and write a paper on any public question, relating to the country, or to Native affairs. Let him try to make it of such a kind and quality, as will attract attention, and suggest something new, or even solve practically and really any old difficulty, and would lead those who read it, or should know of it to say, "Well, here is a man who has ideas. He can propose solutions for real difficulties, which other men recognise as true solutions."

If any young man aspiring to a public position feels (and he will probably feel if he tries) that he cannot write such a paper, he may be perfectly sure he could not speak one, in the midst of a not over-friendly audience of older men, some of whom, if not at all, have been trained to practical views of life, to keen debate, and prompt action on important questions. Now the conclusion we reach is one that hardly requires to be stated, that native education is at a much lower level than it is supposed to be: that it is much lower even than it is believed to be, by the very few proportionally who have received some education.

The second ground on which this statement rests, is that the preparatory work is not being done. There are very few young men who are training themselves by voluntary work, by extensive reading and study, for anything beyond the position they secure immediately on leaving this, or any similar Institution. There are various kinds of work in which native young men might engage, for the benefit of their own countrymen without going as far as Cape Town. I will give you an instance, and it is not an unfair test.

There is a native newspaper—the longest lived of its race—which has now been ten years in existence and is kept going by men, whose skins are not black. Its name is the *Isigidimi Samaxosa*. It is published at Lovedale. It would have served my purpose equally well had it been published anywhere else, and its history been the same as it is. And it is not because it is a Lovedale production that I refer to it, but because I have no other such instance as an example.

Now, with the exception of the papers written or drawn out in outline by white men who have contributed; and by the native editor, Mr. Makiwane; and one or two papers by the Rev. Tiyo Soga, there has not appeared in ten years in that paper for the natives, any thing written by native men of a kind to warrant the belief that they have ideas beyond the average; or if they have them, that they can put them into proper form and expression.

I do not say that the educated native young men have not got these ideas. I only say that they have not appeared that for lack of active support in the shape of contributions from educated Kaffirs—and from lack of support of another kind, in the shape of subscriptions, from those who read, but cannot write, the paper is a heavy piece of work, and a cause of anxiety to those who have to provide printers' ink and paper and printers' wages to keep the

Isigidimi in existence. Neither do I say that the *Isigidimi* is all that it ought to be, and that all the failure lies outside of the paper itself. I simply state that as an educator, it has not as yet taken its proper place; and before the educated portion of any people is qualified for public positions, there is generally a previous period of preparation, by the spread of intelligence and information; and that one of the agencies for that purpose is the Newspaper. And so far as I am able to judge, that period of preparation has barely yet begun. And in so far as it has been begun, and is being carried on, that it is chiefly by white men; and that the educated native young men of this country with one or two rare exceptions, have not thrown themselves into the preliminary work of diffusing information, or of qualifying themselves for higher positions, or of preparing their less educated countrymen for exercising a right, and obtaining a privilege they may reasonably expect one day to enjoy. It is too early yet to speak of using such privileges. But it is not too early to prepare; and I have pointed out in what ways it may be done.

Your truest friends are not always those who flatter you, but those who give the soundest advice and the wisest counsel, whether it be exactly the advice most relished or not.

Now if those views which I have spoken in your hearing be correct, and it will be difficult to controvert them, how do they bear on a certain debate which took place in the Society during this session; and on the vote which followed that debate. The subject was "Should the Education of Native young men be chiefly Industrial?" The majority I understand voted in favour of education without industrial training. I am not going to re-open the question, but the wisdom on that occasion was, as it not unfrequently is, on the side of the minority. If the subject ever comes to be discussed again, let us hope that the result of the vote will be very different.

Connection of Education with Christianity and the Material Progress of the Country

I have been dealing mainly to night with the subject of Native Education; the position it has reached; the position it may reach; and the results that may follow, provided it is wisely used, and not like unripe fruit, plucked too early. I want also to show its relation to missionary work, that is to the progress of Christianity, for the two expressions mean the same thing: and second to the civilization and progress of the country. The progress of the native people under missionary teaching depends very largely on the way the natives themselves deal with these three forces, or powers, or ideas which are offered to them—namely Education, Industry, and the Gospel. . . . Education, Industry, and Wealth,—that is the sound view as regards the mere civilization of the country; quite as true as the connection between Christianity and education. Now if these connections are true—and I think you will search the world through, in order to find a country with wealth and without industry and education, certain conclusions follow, from which escape is impossible. One of these is:—That every Government which desires the material progress of the country it administers, will foster and encourage education by every means—and amongst all classes of the population. This is the low economic ground, and it leaves the moral duties of administrators—for they have these—out of account at present. Out of the wants of the individual, when these individuals become numerous, the industries of many countries are benefitted. I am not about to give you a Political Economy lecture. It is not necessary. You can see the whole truth on this subject illustrated on the road, a Kaffir flitting, any day, when you meet a native woman from a kraal, quite untouched by either the Gospel or education. Stand still and observe, the next time you meet her. On her head she carries the whole household effects, moveable property, and gear of the family. It consists of a couple of grass mats, one or two clay pots, and two or three calabashes, and one or two skins; total value to a purchaser, five shillings or half a crown. No retail trader in the district, no merchant in any of the ports; no shipper or shipowner at home; no manufacturer of any description of goods in Manchester, Birmingham or Glasgow; no grower of raw produce in any colony, dependency, or foreign country has been benefitted by the wants of her household; and the Revenue itself—that mighty river of many rills—has never received from her a single drop to swell its volume. But let education come, and taste developes, and wants arise, and work is sought for, and the demand for goods is created. Now education and the Gospel have been in South Africa the chief awakeners of these wants, though that is but a lower kind of result, and subordinate to the one great result which we are always anxious for, and often press upon you. A change of heart, or in other words, conversion, is the one great hope we have, as the power to enable you to turn your education to real use. Whether you believe us or not now, you will yet see the meaning and the truth of all that has been urged upon you for your acceptance on this point. I have never met with it more exactly put than thus:—'Religious training with its best results, *conversion*, is the proper door into the kingdom of knowledge, as well as into the kingdom of heaven; and those who climb up some other way, add in many cases to their weakness or their wickedness just as much as they do to their power or goodness'—if the intellect merely is trained, and the heart and the conscience left entirely untouched.

This is the ground and reason for the connection between religion and education, as carried on in missionary institutions: and taking the nature of human beings as we find it, whatever be their colour, it seems to be a better way than any other that has yet been proposed.

4.   Sir Theophilus Shepstone Disagrees with the Orange Free State President, 1892

Sir Theophilus Shepstone (1817–1893), the son of an 1820 settler, for many years served as the chief "native administrator" of Natal. As one of his major tasks, he brought the Zulu kingdom under colonial authority after 1879. In 1892 an article by President Francis William Reitz of the Orange Free State sparked the following reply from Shepstone, and others soon entered the debate. Reitz had proposed abolishing chiefdoms, breaking up African locations, and putting Africans to work. Shepstone's contributions to this debate, while not detailed policy proposals, provide interesting theoretical statements with segregationist implications.

The Editor proceeds to say: "Having thus brought the natives within the pale of civilisation, let us then proceed to raise them gradually and steadily, by means of well applied technical education." If by the establishment at present, of what he suggests as something new, we should bring our natives "within the pale of civilisation," Natal may fairly claim, upon the Editor's own showing, and despite his condemnation, that it achieved this more than 40 years ago. As to the techinical [sic] education which he recommends, a little more definition would have made his meaning clearer; but as I understand it, I must ask where is the colony to get the thousands upon thousands of pounds sterling that would be annually required for such a gigantic enterprise? And in the light of that question I am bound to decide that the suggestion is chimerical in the extreme. For such instruction the colony must depend, as it ever has depended, upon the thousands of points of contact that take place daily between the races in their capacities of employer and employed. This is the most practical and therefore the most useful technical education that can be given; because it will enable the natives ultimately, if they are capable of doing so, to rise naturally and healthily to the conditions of a more civilised and artificial life. It is the business of the Government to regulate this in so far only as not to interfere with the healthy development of the process. The great teachers are, and ever will be, the colonists themselves.

One more point I wish to notice; the Editor seems to believe that so long as the natives continue under their present form of government they are a huge organisation, and that until they have advanced very much further out of their barbarism they will continue to be a constant element of danger. I cannot [help] thinking that if the Editor would look at the matter in the light shed by daily facts in Natal, he would think a little differently. All tribes are, like families, minor organisations. They cherish the special rivalries, jealousies, and feuds which usually exist between them; and bitter enough these frequently are. They are kept within bounds by the central authority to which they all

From Sir Theophilus Shepstone, "The Native Question: Sir Theophilus Shepstone and His Local Critics," *Natal Mercury*, April 1, 1892, pp. 14–17, 28–30.

look up. It is obvious that so long as this lasts the only power that could give coherence to any "huge organisation" among the tribes must be that central authority. This authority can be superseded only by a feeling, or apprehension strong enough to overwhelm tribal aversions. Such a condition could be brought about by some huge mistake or injustice, or by the provocation produced by a policy, the obvious aim of which was their oppression as a race, so that the bringing about of such a condition is very much in our own hands. It would, therefore, be the wildest of experiments to attempt to break up their tribal organisation. A state of tutelage such as theirs is, requires more or less of special control. Their tribal organisation places this in the hands of the Government. Our system of civilised laws supplies no such facility. . . .

When a civilised government is called upon to undertake the control of an inferior race, and that race is found to be possessed of an organisation, built up by its own needs; suited to its ideas, habits, and circumstances, including the most effective machinery for its internal control, and easily adaptable to our civilised methods; when, moreover, it is optional with such government to take into its own hands that organisation, and to ensure that the control it affords shall be wielded by itself, it seems the height of folly to reject it for the illogical reason that its methods are not those of our higher civilisation. How long the organisation should last must depend upon its value and the use that can be made of it. The object being always to replace in it that which, from time to time, may become obsolete or decayed, by what civilisation may judge wise and prudent, the methods in it repugnant to civilisation having been eliminated from the beginning. One thing is beyond doubt that to suppress native management by their own laws in Natal would be to release every native in it from all the special personal control that he fully understands, that he so much needs, and that he has all his life looked up to. Civilisation is advancing with rapid strides in these days. When its methods are found more suited to changed circumstances, the natives themselves will be glad to adopt them. Tribalism and chieftainship having become unnecessary and inconvenient to all concerned may then be left to die out for lack of use. . . .

I hold that so long as the social condition of the natives is what it is chieftainship and tribalism are necessary. They are necessary to give us proper control of them, and proper control they must have. I do not believe in the efficacy of violent measures to destroy prejudices; to efface barbarism, or to commend civilised ideas and habits to a barbarous race. Such means are only the loading of shells with shorter or longer timefuses.

Their ancient institutions may be faulty, but they are efficient, and can be made so for the purposes of enlightened government. Reform them and use them so long as they answer that purpose. Civilisation will undermine them by the gradual but sure process of enforcing the fitness of things. They will become obsolete; useless to the natives themselves, and the practical extinction of them will take place when they are no longer of use to you.

The only "serious outcome" that Mr. Grant adduces against the Tribal System is "faction fights." If he can instance nothing worse, or if he rightly classes these among the worst, there is not much harm in the Tribal System.

Faction fights may be between tribes or between sections of one tribe. The causes are invariably local, or personal, or both. They have no connection with the politics of the country, and are of no political significance, except to show that those who compose the factions are much more ready to quarrel among themselves than with us.

Mr. Grant's observations on the tendencies of the rising generation of natives I fully agree with; they are, as he says, growing up with all the liberty our protection affords, and are far less amenable to law and order than their forefathers were; and he very rightly remarks that "any hesitation or flabbiness in dealing with them will certainly produce disaster." It is in the nature of things that it should be so. During a period of 16 years when corrective measures were most needed, the legislative power was in a state of collapse. A period long enough to give a generation a wrong bias has thus been lost. Meanwhile deteriorating influences daily increased in strength and number. Mr. Grant will probably be surprised to hear that no class feels and complains of this more than the chiefs themselves.

Mr. Grant quotes a scheme propounded to him by a member of the Cape Parliament, and an influential member of the Bond, for the universal apprenticeship of native youths under a certain age in the colony. Whether this is likely to cure the evil complained of, or to be successfully carried out I need not to discuss. We shall at least gain experience if the attempt is made.

I can understand a condition of things in which State reasons might justify a civilised government in applying some indirect, but efficient pressure to minimise the mischiefs of barbarous idleness; but it would have to be fenced about with many precautions. . . .

5.   Africans Give Their Views on Their Own Laws and Customs, 1883

As Europeans began to rule more and more Africans, the native marriage and family customs, especially polygyny and lobola, *or bridewealth, catalyzed controversy. Lobola, a payment from the groom to the bride's family at the time of a marriage, set up a pattern of obligations and tied the families together. The payment was usually in the form of cattle. Europeans regarded this custom as tantamount to the purchase of women, and many colonists deemed these customs immoral and a threat to the colonists. They also believed that the customs cultivated "laziness," a concern for whites who worried about reliable supplies of African labor.*

Cape of Good Hope, South Africa, *Commission on Native Laws and Customs, Report and Proceedings, with Appendices: Presented to Both Houses of Parliament by His Excellency the Governor, January 1883*, Cape Town: W. A. Richard, 1883. From Minutes of Evidence, October 14, 1881, pp. 303–307.

When some Africans converted to Christianity, they began to question their traditional customs as well, creating controversy among all Africans.

Kamastone, 14th October, 1881

Present:

W. E. Stanford, Esq.   E.S. Rolland, Esq.

Zulu, Xayimpi, Pombani, Tisani, Jacob Pateni, Zoudani, Klaas Dondola, James Matshoba, Samuel Sokaba, Petrus Matshingele, John Maqutzana, Joshua Lishuha, Jantje Buge, Hendrik Goza, Jan Nyingiza, Utonga and others, Fingo headmen and residents of Kamastone and Ox Kraal, examined.

5476. Mr. *Stanford.*] You are Fingoes who have been for many years resident in the native locations of Kamastone and Ox Kraal?—

Samuel Sokaba: Yes; the tribes to which we belong originally lived across the Tugela River, under their chiefs, but we were driven away by wars and wandered down into Hintza's country, where the missionaries found us, and we met the Rev. Mr. Ayliff, with whom we came into the colony. Part of our people went to Fort Peddie District with Mr. Shepstone, and others scattered about the country amongst the farmers seeking service. I took service with farmers, and worked my way down towards Graham's Town, and then I joined Mr. Shepstone's mission station and came down here with him. A considerable number of Fingoes came down with Mr. Shepstone to this part. Kama was living here, having had this country given him by the Tembus. After we had been here a little time, I don't know how many years, the war of 1850 broke out. After the end of the war of 1850 Kama went away to the lower country, and we remained in the district.

5477. Do you continue the customs of polygamy and ukulobola [lobola]?—

John Maqutzana: In the old times we married many wives and paid cattle for them. We still pay cattle for our wives. The school people do not pay cattle for their wives.

April May: The school people do not pay cattle for their wives. We still approve of ukulobola.

James Matshoba (Christian): I have given up ukulobola, because I was convinced it was not right. I am a Christian.

Samuel Sokaba: I am going to say what two venerable missionaries told me, Mr. Shaw and Mr. Shepstone, that as far as they could judge the custom among the natives was a good one, that it was a bond of friendship between the two families, and that where we married without ukulobola the woman had no place of refuge in case of desertion by her husband or destitution. Among ourselves we never heard of it as being the sale and purchase of a woman. That view has only been taken of ukulobola by Government.

Petrus Matshingele (Christian): I say that ukulobola partakes of the nature of a sale, because a man gets a wife for cattle, and when he ill-uses her he brags about the cattle he paid for her. A man of good character would not take this view. He would remember that although he sent cattle to his wife's relatives it was only to strengthen the bond between them; and amongst us, if a man has not paid anything for a wife, he is very much despised by his wife's relatives. Therefore, when a man gives cattle to his wife's relatives, it causes him to receive respect from those relatives. We see evil days arrive when men of bad character pay for their wives, it gives them greater authority to ill-use them. In many cases the cattle have been disposed of by the wife's relatives, and even where the parties would like to dissolve the marriage they cannot command sufficient stock to return the husband the cattle he has paid. Therefore we Christians, accept the Gospel and consider it a bad custom, and only make presents to the father of the bride after marriage, perhaps two or three head of cattle, simply as a gift from his son-in-law by his own free will. He is not asked by the father of the bride for the present, and we have never yet had a case of a son-in-law attempting to recover this cattle in the event of any trouble with his wife, though, I should remind you, that this practice of which I speak has but lately come.

5478. By whom are cases arising out of ukulobola settled?—Ukulobola cases are arbitrated on by our superintendent where we cannot arrange them among ourselves.

5479. Do you consider this practice of ukulobola a good one?—

Pombani (headman) states on behalf of the heathen natives: This ukulobola is a very good thing. We believe that cattle are given in consideration of the trouble, expense and anxiety of parents in rearing the children, and when the girl is married it is only natural that the father should ask his son-in-law for some bread. It is not a sale, because where a husband and wife disagree the wife can return to her relatives, and that is a proof that there is no sale. Where a husband dies the woman returns to her relatives, therefore there can have been no sale. A husband buying a wife has no right to sell her again, and if you beat her the case is "talked" and settled at the kraal of her relatives. If you buy a horse, and have a quarrel with him, would you think of bringing the cause about it to the person from whom you bought it. For this reason I also say the woman is not bought. I say it is giving the father of the girl some bread. I say it is not right that this custom should be abolished. If it is to be done away with let it be so by the word, not by legislation. I say that the custom should not be abolished by law, but let the people abandon it of their own accord under the influence of Christianity, of moral teaching. In giving our daughters in marriage we do not look alone to the cattle but to the character and standing of the man to whom we give her. We do not allow a girl to choose a husband for herself, we choose for her. Now the girls are giving us trouble in this respect, and this trouble arises through a thing called love. We parents do not comprehend this at all. In regard to the treatment of the woman much depends on the character of the man. Even where ukulobola is not paid the treatment may be good, though it is sometimes not so. Ukulobola may be paid and the treatment may be unkind, but it is worse where ukulobola has not been paid. A man can turn round on his wife and say "You are only a cat, I did not pay for you." A cat is the only living animal which we natives never buy, and cats are passed among ourselves as presents. In former days we used to compel our daughters to marry the man we selected for them. Now we have learned this is not right and the girls wishes are consulted. Of course, I cannot answer for everyone, because it might create anger. But one evil which we see resulting from leaving the choice of a husband to the girls is, that they are very often seduced, and that after seduction it may appear that the man is not a fit man to marry the girl, and so we have to keep the girl at our kraals. If we complain we are told what colonial law is, that it was by mutual consent, and the girls say it is by love. No fine is imposed on the man. According to our own laws, when a man has seduced a girl, she is depreciated in value and becomes a *idikazi* [a widow who is going to remarry]. It is not right, in our opinion, that this should be so, and the man who seduces a girl should be fined, because a father cannot get cattle for her, and he would have done so had she not been seduced. There was never a parent who allowed his daughter to be seduced. In the old time, even since living in this country, girls were carefully looked after, and were examined frequently by older women, and if anything wrong was observed it was reported to the father, and, in consequence of this supervision, when any attempt was made by a man on a girl she at once reported it. Now the girls never report it, they say it is love, and this thing is spreading all over the country. I say this is owing to the fact that the man is not punished, as he used formerly to be.

5480. Can you suggest any remedy for this state of things?—It is not my place to furnish a remedy, I merely state the evil.

Klaas Dondolo (Christian) states: In the days when seduction was punishable by fine the evil was not so great as it is now, but since this thing love has been introduced, it appears to us that the sin is acquiring chieftainship amongst us and spreading everywhere. It appears to us that the opening of the gates in this way has allowed the thing to grow freely amongst us, there being no checks imposed. We are for the Government, and cannot say that we wish our own laws to be restored. We mention this matter and it is for the Government to say what is to be done. We state what we see amongst us, and it must be for the chiefs to decide. The seduction of girls is becoming far more common amongst us than in former times.

5481. How are the cases of adultery dealt with?—

Pombani (heathen) states: In regard to adultery cases we settle them at present among ourselves. Where the evidence is not complete the case stands over. The case is settled by fine, and is arranged between the plaintiff and defendant, but the fine is not fixed. Sometimes a man pays one head of cattle, and sometimes two or three, according to the rank of the husband. If he is a man of high rank, more cattle would be paid. We find men of all ages and classes committing adultery, from greyheads downwards. I consider that the majority of our women do not have paramours. I cannot speak very positively about this because I do not live with them all.

5482. Do you consider that these cases should be entertained by the resident magistrates?—Yes; we think that the courts of resident magistrates should entertain cases of adultery amongst ourselves, and punish by fine.

5483. You would not imprison?—We do not know about imprisonment for cases of adultery. We think a fine would perhaps be best, and that the cattle should go to the husband. If the man has no cattle to pay, he is a wolf, and he cannot help it. You cannot cut his body open, but if he has only one beast he must pay it. . . .

Joshua Lishuba continuing said:—We have also this to bring to the notice of the Commission. We are under the Government and we are pleased with the laws of the Government. The grievance we have is that when we go into the field to fight for them we do not receive the same privileges as the other Government people, although we die the same death as the white man. When one of our number falls his body remains there where it fell. This is a very sore matter with the Fingoes. We say that the Government is our chief and in this respect treats us differently from the rest of her children. We are under one Government and one law, and cheerfully submit to that law. We are under the same Governor and the same Queen. When we serve in the field we receive two or three shillings a day, but the white forces receive five shillings or six shillings a day. In the matter of details we were not paid by the commander personally, but by the captains. We say that our leading men should receive officer's rank. Many men went to the front leaving their occupations, by which they gained money, behind. They went to uphold the fame of Government and lost money by so doing, and no regard is paid to their losses in this respect. Among ourselves, as good officers could be found as those who were placed over us, and with reference to the last war, we should have preferred, had we been responsible to you, Mr. Stanford, direct, instead of having officers between you and ourselves.

Klaas Dondola said:—I wish again to return to the titles. We have been waiting for the final decision as to what the amount charged would be upon these titles. We do not care to pay up without having been called together and fully understanding what that amount would be. It may have appeared that we were constantly troubling our superintendent, Mr. Jeffery, in regard to this manner. We have been told what the final decision of the Government is, and that we hear. This continual change in regard to the cost of the titles made us feel discontented in the same way as the gun question has done. I say we were afraid in regard to the payment for the title-deeds. It was very much like the gun question. We were told to do certain things in regard to our guns, and now we are told that we gave up our guns by our own choice. And so in regard to these titles, we might be told that we had chosen to give them up. Leaving the questions of titles and the guns I say that we elect Europeans here to go to parliament. They go to parliament but they never return and tell us what has been done about ourselves in parliament, therefore it appears to us that we might just as well be without these representatives in parliament. Our grievance in regard to the guns still troubles us, and not knowing what our representatives have done for us in parliament, we should like them, on their return, to call us together and tell us what has taken place.

Utonga said:—I have only one word to throw among you. We thank you for the joy you have caused us because you have given us hope in regard to the law. Our fathers served the Government, and we were born under the Government. To-day we have grey heads under the Government. We came to the Government dust of the earth. When we came to the Government from the very beginning, Government inquired as to our wishes and principles, thereby treating us in a manner different to that of the tribes we have passed through. Government appeared, therefore, to us as our father. When it asked who were our leading men our fathers told the Government who were our leaders. Government then gave all orders through them. We grew up under the laws of Government, and became its children in every respect. There are new things now, sir, which have come among us, since we have grey heads, which things have caused much soreness. Then we began to question about Government, and to ask how many Governments there were. Where is that Government at whose feet we grew up? In any work which we undertook we always had great hopes because it was Government work. It would appear then that the Government would give orders to the men we put forward, and tell us how far the Government had ordered. We would then speak, as we should, on the orders given us and the work to be performed. Then it would appear at the conclusion of our work, that the Government was pleased with us and gave us thanks, and then we would prove, by the thanks given us, that we were the Government's children, and we ourselves had no desire for anything beyond the order by Government with reference to our laws and customs, and we were satisfied with the laws of Government, as they appeared to be the laws of a father and mother to their children; and all this time the Government had not forgotten those men put forward as our leaders. Now, in these later times, the Government has reduced these men whom we respected and looked up to, and appointed other men in their stead, and even the orders appear to come from different directions. We were confused, and now we do not know what order to believe, and we begin not to understand what the Government mean or what we should do. When the Gcaleka war broke out, the war began as other wars had commenced. We did not know the origin of these wars; all we knew was that Government told us war had broken out in a certain quarter, and we went there, and when we went we hoped, as usual, when we returned, there would be thanks given us on the part of Government. But, on our return, the Government did something which caused us trouble and anxiety. On our return from active service we were told to surrender our arms. We said to the Government, is the war over yet. The Government said yes, the war is over, there is peace everywhere. Shortly afterwards war broke out again. When war broke out again Government spoke to us. We said "Chief, give us our guns back again," and these guns have never been returned to us. Many of our people were killed in Fingoland without arms in their hands. While we were still in this state, we heard that accusations were made against us that we were going to join the rebels. We said, "who says we are going to fight, and why do they say so?" We know that if anyone was accused of sedition that he would be arrested, and we waited to see if there was any accuser. We have known that, according to the old custom, when a man was charged with sedition, that he was arrested, and brought before the magistrate, and his accusers had to appear against him, but to this day we have never seen before us the man who made the accusation against us of sedition. These are matters which are grievances among us, and we wish to bring them before the Government, not because we are dissatisfied with the laws of Government, but because we wish to make these things known.

Mr. Stanford, in bringing the meeting to a close, said:—In thanking you for your attendance here to-day, I have to state that our duty has been to examine you on the important subject of your marriage and inheritance laws, and your land tenure. With regard to the complaints you have made about the accusation of sedition brought against you and never substantiated, that charge was sufficiently answered by the good service you rendered under my command, in the movements of Commandant Frost's column in Tembuland and Griqualand East. You should not pay attention to idle report. I am glad that you have spoken freely. It is better for men to say out what is in their hearts. These grievances you have brought forward are not for this Commission to inquire into. You should represent them through the officer who is in charge of you, Mr. Jeffreys, and I feel confident that any representation you make respectfully to Government, through him, will receive due consideration.

SECTION
B

Defining Africans' Place in a Unified South Africa

1. James Bryce Attacks British Imperialism, 1900

The struggle between Afrikaner and British for control of white South Africa foreshadowed subsequent debate over blacks' place in a unified South Africa. It especially raised the question of who would sponsor and control such a move to union. As victims of British imperialism, the Afrikaner residents of the republics attracted sympathy among the so-called pro-Boers within the British Liberal party and in the United States and continental Europe.

In the following selection, James Bryce challenges Britain's rationale for subjugating the Afrikaners.

The whole Transvaal issue hinges on one question: Have the Boers the right to govern themselves as they choose; or, rather, have the English the right to interfere with the form of government, administration, and life that the Boers have chosen for themselves? The answer to this query involves considerations of public and international law which are of great importance.

It is the practice of those Powers who have embarked on colonization to occupy territories belonging to savage or semi-savage populations, without much reference to the lawfulness of the operation. In this way, England, France, Germany, ill-advised Italy, and, recently, the United States have spread their dominion over immense tracts of country. Challenged to prove the justifiableness of their conduct, they will begin by solemnly invoking the clauses of conventions concluded with local potentates; and, when the flimsiness and utter hypocrisy of this line of defence are denounced—for we all know the part that intimidation and gin play in these transactions—they fall back on the plea that they are acting in the name of higher interests of humanity; nay, some say, and they have said it in verse (*vide* Kipling's poem on "The White Man's Burden"), that they are *sacrificing* themselves in behalf of a high notion of

From James Bryce, et al.; *Briton and Boer: Both Sides of the South African Question*, New York and London: Harper & Brothers, 1900, pp. 82–92.

duty. Thus, quite a new doctrine has sprung up. Undoubtedly the substitution of enlightened European or American rule for the primitive and too often ferocious modes of savage administration benefits mankind and the natives themselves, for whom it is not much of a gain, but still again, to die from gin instead of murdering one another. . . .

From being applied only to the savage populations of Africa and Asia, the principle of the rights of superior races and civilizations has come, by a steep incline, to mean also that it has reference to countries like the Celestial Empire and the Boer Republic. Between the Zulus and the Boers, what is the difference? Only one of degree. Fine reasoning clears the way for the perpetration of any outrage on the liberty and sovereignty of minor or weak States.

I do not mean to contradict my former statement, which is sincere, notwithstanding the irony it seems to contain, regarding the general profit arising from the substitution of civilization for barbarism—especially when the barbarism is of a sanguinary kind—and the justification of transfer of territory in such cases; but what I want to point out is that, invented in an hour of need, a principle has been laid down which is false, because it is loose in its aim and wording, and thus leaves the door open to abuse. We are thus confronted with the angry claims of the English to govern in the Transvaal—enfranchisement means nothing else—followed by threats of war if they are not satisfied.

The demonstration of the inferiority of the Boers is eagerly undertaken by Mr. Brooks, who calls the situation in the Transvaal "almost too fantastic for serious presentation." On the one hand, we are presented with a bright sketch of the qualities and achievements of the Uitlanders; on the other, with a sombre picture of the Boers, which represents them as being in a semi-barbarous condition. Mr. Brooks says:

> "A half-nomad people, of sullen and unsocial temperament, severed from Europe and its influences for other two hundred years, living rudely and contentedly on the vast, arid holdings where their sheep and cattle are pastured—each man as far as may be from his neighbor—disdaining trade, disdaining agriculture, ignorant to an almost inconceivable degree of ignorance, without music, literature, or art, superstitious, grimly religious, they are in all things, except courage and stubbornness of character, the very antithesis of the strangers settled among them."

And yet, *horribile dictu*, these strangers are kept "in complete subjection to their bucolic task-masters." Thus, out of the superiority of the Uitlanders arises a demand for a share in the legislation of the Transvaal; and, because this is opposed, it becomes an additional grievance—the principal one.

Now, what are the specific grievances originally formulated by the Uitlanders? Mr. Brooks speaks of bad administration, as illustrated by the absence of sufficient police and sanitary arrangements, by the prostitution of the law-courts to the whims of the Legislature, and by the adoption of prohibitive measures against commerce and industry, and the spread of the

English language. Even if this is a correct representation of the state of things in the Transvaal—and it may be, except in its reference to justice, which is susceptible of reservations—the English cannot make it a plea for the suppression of Boer government, because that government, although primitive and slowly progressive, as I can afford to admit it is, does not come within the class of institutions which are an outrage to the moral feelings of mankind and provide the only excuse a State can invoke for the suppression of another State. No Englishman, I hope, will deny that the essential notions of morality, if not of civilization, pervade the Transvaal State. What is missing in it is a set of institutions and ideas productive of well-being and luxury. The faculty of a people to dispense with these calls forth the frequent commendation of the English themselves in their political and social literature, as well as in their current talk, with the help of expressions such as "healthy simplicity of life," "freedom from the enervating and corrupting influences of civilization," and so forth. Besides, the unfriendliness of the soil, as well as the geographical situation of the Transvaal, together with other circumstances, conspired to maintain the Boer community in the state of primitiveness to which it adhered as a matter of temperament, as well as of social and religious principle. If, even after the discovery of the gold-mines, it did not adopt the Anglo-Saxon ideal of a State, it was—supposing there be any necessity to justify a belated form of existence in a nation on other grounds than that of its right to shape its destinies as it pleases, provided it does not tend to become a source of immorality—it was, I say, because, by opposing the spread of what is called civilization within its confines, it hoped to discourage the influx of foreigners, in whose presence, especially in that of the English, it immediately detected the germ of a great danger to its independence. In fact, the inertia of the Boers in the matter of reforms, and their activity in creating obstacles to the development of industry and commerce and to the use of the English language, are inspired as much by this thought as by their constitutional aversion to what the English are free to call "the blessings," and what *they* are free to call "the curses," of civilization. If there is one duty to which a State is more particularly pledged than to any other, it is the obligation to maintain its existence, and to prefer its own interests to those of other Powers. With this object in view, the Boers are distinctly justified in overlooking the complaints of the British; and there are States which have gone a much greater length in their indifference to the choice of means in devising plans for the national safety, without international law allowing of interference on the part of their neighbors. . . .

Because they cannot obtain redress, through the Boers, for their imaginary grievances, the English claim a share in the government of the Transvaal, insisting that they have a right to be represented in the Raad [legislature]; and, being denied this privilege, they make it their principal grievance. On what is this claim founded? Certainly not on the doctrine or practice of other States. I defy anybody to prove that any State or, for that matter, any theory of international law, considers it an "obligation" for governments to enfranchise aliens, however great their services to the country in which they reside, however great their contributions to its exchequer, however marked their superiority over the natives. Representation, where it exists, is a consequence of citizenship. . . .

2. Dudley Kidd Argues Against African Suffrage, 1908

Dudley Kidd (1863–1921) migrated to South Africa from England in 1889. He was a missionary but spent much of his time traveling in African areas and studying African life. His books were widely accepted as authorities on race-relations policies and were still being cited after the mid-twentieth century, yet they reflect the paternalism and racism of early twentieth-century South Africa.

When it is said that the Kafirs have not asked for the franchise, reference is only made to the raw natives. In recent years the civilised Kafirs, who have broken entirely with all clan-relationships, and who have now become a small and exclusive party of their own, have been agitating on the subject of the franchise. If we may judge by the violence and intemperance of their language, this handful of educated Kafirs wants the franchise very badly. It would, however, be folly to listen to the clamour of these men who make extravagant demands, for they do not quite know what they want, and would soon be more discontented than ever if they got what they demanded. Our difficulties would be enormously increased if we were to exploit the interests of a clique to the detriment of the whole community. A nation must rise as a whole, and those who form the vanguard must not lose touch with the main body. That cannot be a racial demand which is unknown even in name to the majority of the people. The question can be reduced to its true proportions by asking whether in England we should alter our entire constitution because *half a member* kept creating a continual disturbance in the House of Commons.

The Kafirs are not fitted to profit by the franchise even if it were granted to them, for democracy is a conception alien to their past thought. The natives have a sententious proverb, which says that height is not reached in a hurry. This is their own shrewd remark that is addressed to all young men who are in great haste. I have more hope than many have with regard to the future of the Kafir, and for that reason I feel anxious that the natives should not be led into a *cul-de-sac*. If they are left to follow their own natural political development, the result arrived at will be more stable and will have a more permanent value than the outcome of any impatient patchwork of our own. It is of the

Dudley Kidd, *Kaffir Socialism and the Dawn of Individualism: An Introduction to the Study of the South African Native Problem,* London: A. & C. Black, 1908, pp. 114-116, 121 (Negro University Press facsimile reprint).

utmost importance that the Kafirs should not get their attention artificially turned to futile topics. There are far more important things than the franchise for the educated natives to think about. At present it is largely the bizarre and the fantastic that appeal to them, and every crack-brained idea that is mooted is apt to occupy their thoughts unduly. They are not yet capable of taking long views on the problems that arise from the contact of the races, and, like children, would gaily sacrifice the future for the present. The natives are quite capable, so long as they are not in contact with Europeans, of managing their own affairs: but they cannot steer their course aright when they are brought into contact or competition with white races. It is agreed on all sides, on the side of the Kafir no less than on that of the European, that a social fusion of the races is impossible: why then should we seek to bring the Kafirs into the stress and turmoil of our political life? It is difficult to conceive a more risky thing for the future of South Africa than to throw two races, which are entirely distinct socially, into violent conflict on political matters. Even the educated natives are better off attending to the things that concern their own progress than they would be in meddling with matters that do not concern them by carrying on a race-warfare at the Polls. They have more than sufficient work before them in attending to education, industry, and the evolution of their race. The granting of the franchise would not only distract the attention of the natives from urgent to trivial matters, but it would certainly lead to accentuated race-animosity: it would throw the respective interests of the races into conflict, and it would make racial problems perennial. If only this question could be settled once and for all, then the various parties would recognise the fact that it was useless to pit race against race; they would then bury the subject of their differences and turn their attention to the next thing. If we insist on keeping alive racial conflict by endless conflict at the hustings [polling or political-discussion place], we must be prepared for the inevitable consequence; racial problems will then remain an open sore, for as long as a man looks at a grievance it worries and chafes him. The very machinery of political life would stir up race-hatred owing to a great increase of racial contact; and it would do this at a time when both the parties had their passions inflamed by frothy eloquence. At present the white men are, on the whole, well disposed towards the natives; but any granting of the franchise would be certain to stir up slumbering fires. There are plenty of white men keen on the welfare of the Kafirs, and who will see that no injustice is done to them. And as for the natives, they are happier, more contented, and generally better off under parental government than they would be when frittering away their time in fighting the white man on the political platform. . . .

It is not necessary to enter into a lengthy description of the various schemes of native representation that have been suggested. These range from the formation of a Council or Debating Society of Hereditary Chiefs—with no executive power—with which the white Government might consult, up to a representation of black men by their full numerical proportion of Kafirs who should actually be in Parliament. Every conceivable compromise between these extremes has been suggested, though no one seems to have sought to show that the movement could be stayed anywhere short of the logical conclusion in which there would be at least five black men to every white man in Parliament. Neither representation of black men by white men, nor representation by two or three black men, nor representation by men chosen by the Governor to watch native interests, would have the remotest chance of satisfying any sense of need such schemes might awaken. We do not usually give children just a little taste of a thing we know they will eat to excess. And the worst of experimenting in a subject of this sort is that, should the scheme prove impracticable, the recall of such a privilege would stir up every evil passion.

3. Maurice Evans Defends an Active, Paternalistic Policy Toward Africans, 1911

Maurice Evans (1854–1920) actively pursued a career as an expert on the "native question." He served in the Natal legislature and was a member of the Native Affairs Commission of 1904–1906. A paternalist segregationist, he nevertheless proved a moderate by the standards of white South Africa at the time, stressing that white domination should be exercised to benefit Africans. He made comparisons between South Africa and the United States, and some of his ideas were influential in America.

It was the fashion in past years, even among churchgoing Europeans, to decry the Christian native and to compare him, much to his disadvantage, with his heathen brother. I am afraid that the standard by which both were judged was not the benefit or otherwise to the native, not whether he himself was intrinsically improved, but whether he came up to the standard of what a black man should be in the eyes of a white man. And the relation was that of employer and employed, and to make a "good nigger," in this sense, the employed should be always deferential, willing to accept what was regarded as sufficient for a black man in regard to housing, feeding, and wages, and above all free from any airs or assumptions. In these respects the raw native was perfect, his tribal training ensured this, whilst the mission boy was, too often, self-conscious and not too well-mannered. Any other virtues or acquirements were either non-regarded or considered as unbecoming in a native, and he was judged on his little unpleasantness, which would have been tolerated or thought quite natural in a European. I think too little attention was paid to manners in their education; but there were numerous instances in which, to the natural politeness and respect of the raw Zulu, the Christian native added

From Maurice Evans, *Black and White in Southeast Africa*, London: Longmans, 1911, pp. 102–109, (Negro University Press facsimile reprint).

acquired virtues which were worthy of all praise. And at the time when this dictum was most in vogue, every native wearing more than the ragtag accoutrements of the kraal native, when he came into town to work, was accounted a Christian, and the mission system charged with his faults and deficiencies even though he had never been under instruction in his life.

Another generalization which obtained popular currency was that, however a native was educated, at the first opportunity or relaxation of control, he threw off the habiliments of civilization and reverted to the mutya and blanket and all his old barbarous customs—the call of his savage nature was too strong for him. That this did happen in cases is true. All who know the Abantu [Bantu] are fully aware how strong is their attachment to their ancient life—their history during the last fifty years shows this; it is the virtue of a strong race, and the temptation to reversion must be, in some cases, overwhelming. The wonder is that such instances are so few, for in comparison to those who stand fast they are few indeed.

It is quite a common thing in Natal to hear it said that the Amakolwa, or some individuals who come under this name, have gone back, are lazy, immoral, unclean. Laziness, even immorality, are matters of evidence, degree, and opinion, and such a general charge is easy to make and often difficult to disprove. During the inquiry of the Natal Native Commission, extending over nearly twelve months, I made a point, in every part of Natal and Zululand, to try and elucidate this aspect of the case. To make my inquiry definite I confined it to natives who were exempted from native law, and who, in nearly every case, were professed Christians. I also limited it to the one question of reversion to polygamy, on which a clear and definite answer could be given, and it was put to those who favoured Missions and exemption, and those who opposed both. My definite question was, Do you, of your own personal knowledge, know any exempted natives who have fallen back into polygamy? From the answers received it was made clear to me that such cases were remarkably few. It should be borne in mind that if a native lapses into barbarism the greatest temptation thereto would be to obtain a plurality of wives.

Unfortunately too, it is the fact that when an educated and nominally Christian native turns out badly, and uses his acquirements for his sensual gratification or unlawful personal gain, a chorus of condemnation goes up, not against the individual native, but against the system which makes such a product possible. These unfortunate instances are quoted and emphasized in any general conversation about Missions far more frequently than are the many cases in which the Amakolwa live exemplary lives. The backsliding of professed Christians, the abuse of education to low and selfish ends, are not unknown among ourselves, but these instances are not deemed to utterly condemn Christianity and education. Let us be fair, and take into full consideration the far greater difficulties of the native, and especially those due to race and environment, and after due entry of debit and credit, try to strike a just balance.

I have spoken of the self-consciousness and lack of respect sometimes displayed by station natives, and compared it with the almost invariable defer-

ence shown to Europeans and superiors which is so conspicuous a characteristic of the real kraal native. This is probably the chief failing of the educated
man in the eyes of the average colonist. Actuated by the frequency of this and
similar charges, so often made against mission natives, the Rev. Mr. Le Roy of
the American Zulu Mission in Natal compiled a list of some ninety-one
natives, who had been educated and trained by them, and who had left their
stations to work for themselves. The inquiry was directed to those who had
actually employed the boys, and included questions concerning their general
attitude and behaviour. Most of the employers replied, and the answers as far
as these natives went were conclusively in their favour, not only with reference
to their ability and industry, but also as regards behaviour. Many of these
answers were characteristically colonial, such as "best I ever had," "a rattling
good boy," "would engage him again to-morrow," and so on. To give accurate
figures. Out of forty-seven working in Durban, unqualified approval was
given in the case of forty-four, and not one was charged with disrespect; out
of forty-four working in Johannesburg, thirty-eight received excellent characters from their employers, and again no complaint was made of bad behaviour
or disrespect. The old uneducated and uncontaminated Zulu could not have
earned a better character.

To summarize, I think it can be shown that the once generally accepted
formula, which is not yet dead, stigmatizing Christian natives as useless and
below the standard of the raw native, is one of those generalizations, accepted
without due inquiry and thought, which have done so much in the past to
obscure the true facts and issues of our question.

One of the highest services rendered to the State by the missionaries must
now be mentioned, and the more so because I have not heard it claimed by
them, and it is certainly not recognized by the public. Underlying the evidence
given by the natives before the Natal Native Commission was a feeling, not
often directly expressed, but unquestionably ever present, of a shaken confidence in the desire of Europeans in general, and the Government in particular, for their well-being. The old faith in the good intentions of the
Government, and their belief that it was animated by a desire to protect and
help them, was seldom expressed with any real conviction. The rock in a
thirsty land no longer gave shade to them. In place was a feeling of suspicion,
sometimes amounting to a fixed idea, that the white man was ever concocting
deep-laid schemes for their exploitation, was planning to make money out of
them. Confidence in us, not only in our justice but in our fatherliness, is essential to true success with the Abantu. In a time when doubt as to our good
intentions was rife, when confidence in our goodwill was shaken, the
unselfishness and altruism of the missionary stood fast, as a pledge to the
native that the white man still desired his good, still stood as a father to him,
and that cash, or its value in material things, was not the only bond between
black and white. A bulwark to a shattered and fast-disappearing faith were
and are these men, and it is a service to the State and to their race which can
hardly be too highly estimated.

Many of those who are hostile or apathetic to the work now undertaken by the missionaries, are willing to tolerate some teaching of religion, but are opposed to giving the natives education. "An educated nigger is a spoiled nigger," say such. Before I enter into the question of education, literary and industrial, and how that education should be formulated and applied to suit the peculiar needs of the position, I would like briefly to state the present position of affairs, and put a definite question to the objectors.

We have, among us, an overwhelming preponderance of these people, we are a white speck in a black mass. They live in two camps of unequal size, the vast majority as did their fathers as tribesmen, the minority, more or less educated, and following at greater or less distance, our life. We have so far broken in upon them as to notably decrease, in some cases to entirely kill, much that in the old time made up their interest in life. Before we arrived and in the early days of our occupation their lives, though easy, were not vacant, they had many interests and congenial occupations. Their share in their own government was limited, but they knew what was going on and were not ignored; from time to time they were called up to the kraal of the chief, and indirectly, their opinions had weight and formed custom and law. Under a tyrant they could not become lethargic or apathetic, the danger of some arbitrary action kept them on the alert, but their position was not irremediable, for they could and did rise, directly or by proxy, and assert their rights. The witchcraft which they dreaded, prevented them from stagnating, and folk lore and myth gave interest to their lives. Their strong physical natures found vent in warlike expeditions and tribal fights, the country was full of game, and hunting was a frequent exercise which worked off their hot blood. Their weapons and utensils were simple enough, but all had to be made by hand from raw materials which had to be found, and the manufacture gave scope to considerable ingenuity and some little artistic effort.

All this we have changed. The pride of the Zulu in his king is limited to a tribal head under control of the magistrate. His laws are ready-made for him by the European, and his opinion thereon is never asked, his interests have degenerated into grievances. The great and absorbing game of war is forbidden him, and even faction fights are severely (too severely) punished. The great herds of wild animals have gone, and hunting, as his fathers knew it, with its thrilling dangers, is a thing of the past; at best he is called out as beater to a European shooting harmless buck. The weapons and utensils, to the making of which he had to devote time, patience, and skill, are now bought at the store of the Asiatic or white man. The old customs, the stories, folk lore and myth, with knowledge of woodcraft and plant, all of which stimulated the mental powers and imagination, are rapidly being forgotten.

As I cannot too often reiterate, they are, though outwardly little changed, undergoing inward changes, and the whole process amounts to bewilderment. The young people are getting out of hand; the simple interest their fathers had in their natural surroundings and social life is dwindling, and they look for excitement in more frequent visits to town and in beer drinking. This casting down of restraint and sanctions, coupled with the comparative monotony of their lives, is leading rapidly, in the opinion of nearly all observers, to deterioration of character. Neither the colonists in their private capacity, nor the Government as representing them, are replacing the old activities with any adequate substitute, and for the old recognized and accepted control familiar to them, is put the policeman. Laws without end are made to prevent their injuring the white man, but few which aim at their own benefit.

Briefly summarized this is the position to-day.

I ask the objectors this question: If they are left to work out their own salvation in these altered and unfamiliar surroundings what will be the result? Did we retire from the scene there is little doubt but that through some turmoil and bloodshed they would readjust themselves, and the majority congratulate themselves they were rid of the white man. But we remain, and in our presence and under our government can they satisfactorily heal the wounds, and rebalance the parts of the organism, at present injured and out of gear, so that it shall work in the future with a minimum of friction and a maximum of good? I doubt it—the change is too rapid and violent; they are learning what is extraneous and often vicious, the characteristics and habits of which the white man is himself ashamed; the deeper life, the inward sanctions are not seen. The obvious gratifications and the vices they copy, the self-restraints and the virtues are hidden from them. If I am right in my statement of the present position, and I feel I have the general support of those who know, I must ask the opponents of missionary work and education what they have to suggest? Surely to leave these people, the old discipline and salutary activities removed, learning the vices of a stronger race in a bewildering and ever-changing environment, to welter through it all untaught and without guidance, is to prepare to reap the whirlwind, and is utterly unworthy of us and of the race to which we belong. What sane man, recognizing the position as I have tried to draw it, would remain to live his home life in a country with such an outlook as this before him? If the Abantu were people of a race akin to our own in such a condition, the remedy for hopelessness would be to create and stimulate an intelligent interest in life by giving them an object, such as better material conditions, for which to work,—for ignorance, education; for immorality, religious and moral instruction. If this is the best we could offer to those of our own race, is it not our duty as the responsible governors to give our best to those who, largely through our advent, are in this condition? I have made it abundantly clear, that exactly what would suit the white man may not apply to the black man; that insight and discrimination are needful, and our remedies must peradventure be modified, even profoundly modified, to meet his racial peculiarities and needs. In our ignorance we may make mistakes; but again I ask, is it not due to us to give our best to balance the worst these people are at present receiving at our hands? If so, what is the best those who denounce the missionary and his works would give?

I have put the question many times, often without answer, and at best have been told that our policy would be to keep him in his place. Yes, but his place is a shifting one; we ourselves are altering the plane; what was his place yesterday may not know him to-morrow. This means, in other words, repression with an appeal to the rifle. If this is the only policy, the white man will solve the problem himself by leaving South Africa. The strain will gradually become too tense for all but the strongest, and South Africa will never become a home for our race. To my mind this is impossible. . . .

4.   A White Farmer Deems Blacks Inferior, 1904

The South African Native Affairs Commission, generated by the South African rather than the imperial government, held investigations from 1903 to 1905 to explore the question of Africans' position in a unified, capitalist, white-dominated South Africa. Some testimony addresses labor issues, but all aspects of African life and of race relations come under the commission's purview, as the following document reveals.

41,791. Are there any particular subjects on which you would like to express your views?—The subject that I would like to say a few words about is as regards the franchise for Natives. I have not studied the matter, but it is important, I think, for the country to have it fully discussed.

41,792. Do you think that it is a desirable thing at present to grant that?—No, I do not.

41,793. Will you give us your reasons?—My reasons are these. I am the son of a missionary who came out in 1838. I was born in the Cape Colony in 1844, and in 1853, when the British left the Orange River Colony, which was then under the British Sovereignty, my father was a missionary at Bethany. I went, as a child, at the end of 1853, with the deputation to England, with Mr. Murray and Dr. Fraser, who were sent as a deputation by the inhabitants of the country between the Vaal and Orange River to ask the British Government not to abandon this country. The reason we had was only one—the Native. They were in such numbers that they would be able to demolish us at any time, seeing that all the soldiers were leaving the country. The reason for this was that the Natives were getting obstreperous and would not work. The missionaries wanted to build a church for their benefit, and they had to make their own bricks, as the Natives would not work.

41,794. Even in those days?—Even in those days. Then there was a little disturbance with the Natives. This was reported to Berlin by the missionaries, and they had a reprimand from headquarters, which eventually led to the resignation of some of the missionaries, and the question then arose whether the people here in South Africa were not better able to judge as to the management of the Native than the people at Home. They considered any interference from Europe as to the treatment of Natives (mostly of the Koranna tribe)

Testimony of C. G. Radloff, Orange River Colony Farmer, Before the South African Native Affairs Commission, October 7, 1904, pp. 620–623, 626.

could only lead to rupture. This brings me to the point of the franchise. We have lived in this country all our lives, and had to do a lot with Natives, and are, therefore, better acquainted with them than the people in Europe. In my capacity as an old Justice of the Peace of the late Free State, and a member of the Volksraad, I came a good deal in contact with Natives, and I found, on the whole, that they are really an inferior class of humanity, and cannot be expected to be put on the same level as the white man. Therefore, if the Native gets the franchise, and has the right, as we have, to vote, it would place him on an equal footing, and it would bring him into prominence in many respects. He would be able to vote in towns for municipalities, would get a seat perhaps in the Councils, and would become appointed a Justice of the Peace. There are some clever men among them who have been educated, but I think it is our duty in Africa to try and keep a distinct separation between black and white. During the war I had the opportunity of residing in Basutoland for about 18 months, and I had occasion to meet the son of a certain Chief. He received me very well, and sent me some books, gave me a hut, as shelter, and then he came over. He had a blanket on. I said to him, "How it that? You have been in Europe." He replied, "I have had a good education. I read these papers, but since I have come back to my kraal I want to fall back to the old blanket, Kafir customs, and so on." He had a nice house, which had just been built by his father, and he said, "I prefer living in a hut." That showed me that although he was well educated, moved in good society, and was treated very well, being the son of a Chief who was a good loyal man, he did not act up to the higher standard that was expected from an educated man.

41,795. You were saying that although he had received a high education, and had associated with civilised people, he had relapsed into the old barbarous habits?—Yes; when I allude to barbarous habits, I mean, for instance, that he had already two wives, and was about to get a third wife. For these reasons, and the general experience that I have had with Natives, being a farmer for many years, I think that they are an inferior race, and ought not to be put on the same level as the white man. Many Europeans, who have come out to reside in South Africa, have entirely changed their views in regard to the treatment of Natives after having had some experience, and admit that the born South African white man, with a few exceptions, understands the character of a Native better, and knows how to handle him, so that he soon finds he is not on the same level with his master, and shows obedience and civility far more to him than to the man just fresh from Europe.

41,796. Do you mean to include all Natives, whether they are educated, or whether they have been raised to any higher standard, within that?—Yes. I think it has always been a difficulty to classify what is a Native, but I think it would be the wisest plan to say a Native is a man of black descent, and call him a Native. I know the difficulty is very great about this question. There are many good Natives half white, who are respectable, and classification is very difficult. But I say that for this country we ought to class every man who has black blood in him as a Native, and exclude him from the franchise.

41,797. You do that on race lines?—Yes.

41,798. *Mr Samuelson.*] I would like to ask you, in connection with what you have just said, if every person who has black blood in him should be excluded from the franchise?—Yes.

41,799. Do you mean to include the legitimate offspring of black and white in that?—Yes.

41,800. The lawful offspring?—Yes, a lawful marriage between a white and a black, on either side.

41,801. Your object in that is really to put a stop, if possible, to the inter-marriage of white people with black people?—Yes. That ought not to be allowed.

41,802. And with illicit intercourse between white people and black peo-ple?—Yes, that is my feeling about it. I do not know whether it will be neces-sary to say anything about the marriage laws. I think in Basutoland no attempt has been made to stop cattle marriages between the Natives, the giving of so many cattle for a wife. This is, of course, against Christian policy, but I do not think even in Basutoland that the Government endeavoured to put a stop to it, because it involved a great many questions going against Native principle, so I think it is better not to say anything about it.

41,803. *Chairman.*] Will you speak of South Africa as a whole, not of Basutoland? What have you against the principle?—I have this, that this mar-riage among Natives ought not to take place in the way it is done: bargaining for cattle, giving the wife away to a man who gives most cattle. There ought not to be any handing over of stock in payment for the wife. I think that is a principle which ought to be done away with.

41,804. How would you regulate Native marriages if you did away with this old system?—They would have to go before the Magistrate, I think, and get legally married and registered. Christian Natives could go before the min-ister like the white people do, but other Natives could go before the Magistrate and have their marriage registered. There would then be a means of finding either party in case of misbehaviour.

41,805. Do you mean that in South Africa you would break down the present system that exists of cattle marriages, and substitute for it marriages to be registered by law?—Yes, now the country is under the British flag.

41,806. Do you mean to say you would do that by an act of legislation?—I could not say how it is to be done.

41,807. Would you do it summarily?—It ought to be discussed, I think. It will take years before it can be altered, I think, because there will be some trouble about it.

41,808. That is a thing you think should be aimed at? Do you think the effect of these cattle marriages upon the Natives is bad?—I think so; that is my impression.

41,809. Do you mean morally?—Yes, it leads to marriages that are not, as we would say, out of love; it is a speculation, and they cannot be considered to last in a happy state—those people that are united like that.

41,810. You mean to say that Natives when married are not kind and affectionate towards each other in their married life?—Yes, I have seen it.

When they are married for love, so to speak, they are happy, and have been so for years, but I have seen a lot of cases where the marriage was forced and very unhappy. The women have run away and have been caught again, and have had to be thrashed, and all that kind of thing, or the husband's father demands cattle paid for such a wife back.

41,811. So far with regard to cattle marriages. Are there any other customs which you think should be interfered with in this manner?—As regards the education and religion of Natives: I was always in favour of it formerly, but I have lately changed my opinion, because I find that it does not do the good to the Natives which the European population think it does, especially religion. It seems to me that when they get religion and go to church, that they leave work alone. I have found many Natives who are very fond of going to church, neglecting their work, and always sitting with their Bible. Some are very fond of reading. If the missionary were to adopt the system of making them work and educating them at the same time, it would be a very good thing, and I know one man—the Reverend Father Douglas, who is dead—who was the man who went as far as to say to the Natives that they must work and be educated at the same time, that they should work six days, and rest on Sundays, and go to church. But I have often found that on mission stations the Natives spend most of their days in idleness, occupied with books, and so on, which I think ought not to be so. Even white people have to work six days, and rest on the seventh. But this is a very difficult question. I have not found that education has done the Native much good on the whole in South Africa, and many think it best to leave them uneducated altogether.

41,812. Would you deny them education?—I would not say that. No, I would like them educated to a certain extent, but at the same time, they must be made to work.

41,813. Work during their education, or afterwards?—During their education, like white boys, who go to a school and learn, but still are taught to work. The Native has not got the advantage in this country of a boarding school where he is looked after. He goes from school back to his hut. Now he prefers that kind of education, because it is a lazy life.

41,814. Are not a good many of the boys, who go to school in that way in the morning, employed in herding their father's cattle in the afternoon?—Yes.

41,815. That is a form of labour is it not?—Yes.

41,816. That is what you advocate, that they should do some labour while they were being educated?—Yes. As to the labour question, I was very much opposed to the Chinese importation, as we have so many Natives in South Africa, but one good feature in the whole thing was that the Chinese coming to South Africa would make the Natives work. My impression was that the Natives throughout South Africa, especially in the Orange River Colony and the Transvaal, having done very well during the war and made money, were independent, and that is why we could not get labour, especially at Johannesburg. Now, the Chinese coming in will force them to say, "Well, the white population can do without us; we must go and work." The money that they have earned will not last them very long, and then they will have to work.

If I am not mistaken, the Government have put a tax on the Native of, I think, something more than it used to be, and that will perhaps also force them afterwards to go to work. I find that in South Africa, where the black race outnumbers the white so much, that we have to make them pay something toward keeping up the Government. They live in the country and get protection, and if they are through the taxation forced to work, that is a good thing.

41,817. Do I understand the gist of your remarks to be that they will have to work to get the money? You think it is desirable that all Natives should have to work?—Yes, it is a broad question. It comes to this, if they are not obliged to work they might go on farms and lie there as squatters, which is to the disadvantage of the white population.

41,818. You are against squatting?—Yes.

41,819. In the Orange River Colony, where you come from, I suppose it does not exist?—No, we did away with that.

41,820. Do you think the Orange River Colony is better in consequence of having done away with squatting?—Yes, I can give you an instance in the Harrismith district. Complaints came from there that there were large farm owners, resident in Europe, who allowed Natives to live on the farms, for a certain payment, which brought them in a nice little income. These Natives were doing a lot of harm to the neighbours. Complaints were made, and then a law was passed, allowing each farmer so many heads of families to live on his farm, and this did away with the squatting system.

41,821. You have given us your views about squatting and labour?—Yes, I see something here about the liquor traffic, but I think that is strict enough. I do not think a Native is entitled to go into a place here in Pretoria, or anywhere, to get a glass of liquor. In the Orange River Colony it is the same; I do not think a Native is even allowed to go and buy liquor. That does not prevent the Native from making his own beer, or stronger stuff, "utyala," and getting drunk on it. I believe the law is also strict on that, because where they make it in a large quantity they have to have a licence, and dare not sell it. When they give a party the Native must take out a licence, and then he is allowed to give this party. At any rate, that was the case in the olden times.

41,822. Is this a good law, do you think?—Yes. You cannot check them from using this stuff that they make themselves; besides, it is an income to the Government, and there is a certain restriction on them, because they only get this licence for two days. . . .

41,858. Then, you said, you have noticed a good deal of idleness amongst Natives living on mission stations?—Yes.

41,859. What was the age of the Natives you speak of in that case?—From, I may say, 16 up to 30 years.

41,860. You do not think that boys who are attending school, and who are being educated at the mission schools, should be compelled to go out to work whilst they are doing so. You do not recommend that they should be really deprived of any education by being forced to go away to the labour market?—It is very difficult to answer that question. The Native who can afford to give his child an education should be allowed to let him be at school, but the missionary, or whoever may be in charge of the establishment, can not look after this child as is the case with white boys who live in a boarding establishment, and where there is no mission school such boys go for a few hours to the school, and then they are left on the veld, and idle in that time.

41,861. You approve of Natives being educated to a certain extent?—Yes, if a system were adopted to make them understand that they must be educated to work at the same time. The education need not be of any high standard.

41,862. And you do not think that they should be deprived of that education by any law which would compel them to go out to work before a certain age?—They must be taught in the schools to work.

41,863. Up to what age do you think a boy should be exempt from a sort of coercive measure for turning him out to work?—He ought to commence to work from the age of fourteen.

The Union, the Native Land Act, and Stirrings of African Political Power

1. The Chief of Edendale Mission Urges Land Ownership for Africans, 1904

The South African Native Affairs Commission made extensive use of black witnesses, and their testimony provides a rich source of African opinion on this period. Edendale was a mission-centered settlement of "rich [black] peasants" from which many prominent Africans skilled in music, literature, and politics came.

DURBAN, WEDNESDAY, JUNE 1st, 1904

Present:—

Mr. Sloley (Acting Chairman).

Hon. M. Campbell	Mr. Hamilton
Capt. Dickson	Mr. Samuelson
Mr. Krogh	Mr. Thompson
Mr. De La Harpe	

Stephen Mini, Chief of Edendale Mission station; *Stephen Kuzwayo, Solomon Xaba, Jabez Molife*, followers, examined; (Mr. Samuelson, by request, acting as interpreter).

33,886. *Acting Chairman.*] We understand that you wished to come before this Commission and give some evidence. We are glad to see you to-day to give you an opportunity of doing so, and we hope you will express your views freely. Which of you will act as spokesman?—*Stephen Mini:* I wish to speak,

---

Testimony of Stephen Mini, Chief of Edendale Mission Station, also Stephen Kuzwayo, Solomon Xaba, Jabez Molife Before the South African Native Affairs Commission, June 1, 1904, pp. 963–964, 967–969.

but I take it that my companions may be allowed to say something if they wish to do so.

33,887. On the question of land tenure, what would you like to say about that?—What I wish to speak about first is about lands which were formerly in the possession of Natives, and which are not now in their possession; I mean Mission reserves. The original object with regard to these lands, so far as I know, was that the land should be set apart for such Natives as wished to leave heathenism and the life of the heathens, and come to live on lands under the instruction and guidance of the Missionaries, and get enlightenment and civilisation. I think that was done more than 50 years ago. That is a thing which I regard as having been a very good thing done by the Government; but what I see to-day, as the result of recent legislation, is a change, inasmuch as the land has been taken away from the trustees, in whom it was vested and put into the hands of others. It was the Government which gave, and it is the Government which now has taken back; and this is a thing which I do not view with pleasure. My view is that the persons who have for many years occupied these lands, on the former conditions, who have planted trees and improved their lots by gardening and in other ways, should now have allotments made to them as individual holdings. It is now the third generation since the lands were vested in the trustees, as I have said. The original Natives who were there when the lands were so vested have died; some of their children have died; many live; it is now their grandchildren who are in occupation of these lands. The views I have stated are prompted by the wish that I would like to see our Natives getting closer and closer to the Government we love so well, and not to be removed from it by the resumption of those lands by the Government. I will go now to another class of land tenure. I have two or three classes of land to speak about; and I will next speak about lands which have been reserved for Natives, which lands are called locations. The lands I refer to are those which the Government hold for the Natives on them. The Natives on these lands are now living on them in a state of nervousness; they do not quite know whether these lands may not possibly be taken away from them. In respect to these lands, I have a small opinion of my own. I say also, with respect to these lands, that the Natives who reside on them have been on them for a very long time, in fact, I may say that a good proportion of them were found occupying these lands when the good Government took over the country. With respect to the Natives on these lands, too, I think, in order that they should have courage to improve their houses, their methods of occupation and cultivation, they should have these lands divided up for them and given into their possession, so that they might be encouraged to raise themselves and to be more affectionate and loving to the Government, knowing that the Government has in that way secured to them for all time these lands in personal holdings, so that the Natives living on them may understand and know that by these lands, and by their occupation and use, they will be in that way elevating, holding up, and supporting the Government which is over them. I will go on to another question about land. I will speak now of those Natives who bought land for themselves. I look with great favour on what the

Government did there in allowing the Natives to buy land for themselves. When I look on the Natives who live on the lands that they have bought for themselves, and compare them with the other Natives, who do not live on such lands, I see that they are not like these other Natives; they are better, on account of their ownership of land. From what I have heard of the opinion of such Native land-owners, I have ascertained that they are grateful to the Government for having so permitted them to become land-owners, and it has improved their love and their affection to the Government, and made them more loyal and affectionate at heart on that account. In speaking of this, I compare the present state of things with that existing in the time of our fathers, who are no longer living now; the time when our fathers left darkness and heathenism, with the Reverend Mr. Allison, and came into the Colony, and where he is, at the very commencement, assisted them to buy lands and become owners of their own lands. From what I have seen amongst the people of the community I refer to, who are owners of land, I find that they have been more willing and more ready to share the burdens and the responsibilities of the Colony with the Government, and that they have not been backward; in fact, they have always been ready to shed their blood in the service of the Government more than Natives who were not so possessed of land. Our fathers, as I have said, have transmitted that feeling of loyalty and affection to us, their children. I close there with reference to land matters. . . .

33,932. *Acting Chairman.*] We have heard and understand, Stephen. What is your next point?—The next point is in regard to the laws of succession and inheritance amongst Natives. I have something to say about those laws, but first of all, with regard to the Native Courts, I wish to say something. I find that the law of Christian marriage applying to us Natives puts those who are married under it into a two-fold position: one leg is under Native law, and the other leg is under the ordinary law. The Natives themselves, when they become married, are under Native law, but the marriage places them partly under European law, so that, should anything happen in regard to the marriage, or any question rise in connection with the marriage, the case would have to be heard under the ordinary law, the white people's law, although at the same time they are still under Native law in other respects. I look upon that as a not satisfactory state of things. When we look at these things, we wonder, because, in our opinion, the law of the ruler is the law which should be followed in all things; that is, the law of civilisation. I think that, inasmuch as the law for the marriage of Natives by Christian rites brings the spouses in such marriages under the ordinary laws in relation to the questions of marriage, the Natives at the same time should be brought entirely under the white man's law. I will now refer to marriages according to Native custom in the presence of official witnesses. I think that marriages according to Native usage are instrumental in causing a good deal of misunderstanding, too. Natives nowadays may agree—a man and a girl—and the marriage may take place in the presence of an official witness, although only two head of cattle as "lobolo" may have been given. The agreement is made between the parents of the man and girl, the contract is concluded, and that is the end of that part of it. The agreements made in respect of marriage and the effect of marriage itself are then reported at the Magistrate's office, and when they get to the Magistrate's office, they state there that the "lobolo" has been paid, whereas, as a matter of fact, at home it is known that the "lobolo" was not given in full. I look upon that as caused by that section of the Code, which says that the "lobolo" must be given before the day of marriage. Therefore, I say, at the present time there are a large number of marriages which take place in that way, where only two or three head of cattle have been given, and where there are large balances still to be given, and where the Magistrate's books show that the full amount has been given. Therefore, I go on to say that the Government has made limitations and regulations with regard to the matter—the matter of "lobolo" and marriage—which did not exist among the Natives originally, and which are not in accordance with their original usages. That is a matter the Government should not have interfered with or made any law about. The original customs of the Natives in regard to these matters should have been left alone, so that if the parties agreed to let the marriage go for one beast, or for no beast at all, only for food, or some bags of mealies, or something like that, the marriage should take place; there should have been no interference. To look at this matter, my opinion is that the Government should not by legislation have adopted or at all taken over any of those uncivilised customs of Natives as law, or restricted them. They should have left the Natives to practice their customs and usages in these matters, and not have adopted them in any measures as their own.

33,933. What is your next point?—In respect of the administration of local affairs, I have recommended what I think should be done here as far as the land is concerned, on locations and Mission reserves.

33,934. You have not said anything about the formation of Councils, which, I take it, in this administration of local affairs, is more directly alluded to?—I will go on to the question of the franchise now. I look upon the exercise of the franchise as the right thing for us. I think we Natives should be treated in that respect in exactly the same way as the white man is treated. When I say so, I mean a land-owner, a person who owns land, and also a person who has a certain income in the year, or has certain property, in accordance with the laws affecting the franchise. I say so because that enables the Native who may be an elector to be a participator in the framing and enacting of laws affecting him. I think that Native land-owners should have the same right as white men, and should participate in the election of whatever European is nominated to represent them in the electoral district. I say that that would elevate the Native who enjoyed the franchise and make a man of him, and make something of him in the country. That is why I say that every Native owner of land in this Colony and every Native who fulfills the stipulations or the qualifications required by the franchise laws, should have the right of being placed on the voters' list in the same manner as the Europeans. That is what I have to say on that point.

33,935. *Mr Thompson.*] Would you not be satisfied by representatives nominated by the Government, that would be one, two, three, or four white men representing purely Native interests, and voting only for Native interests in Parliament; would that not meet your case?—I do not think that would do because in that case the man would not have the mandate of the people to represent them. He would not be sent by the people to represent them, but he would be a man thrown out to the people, or given them by the Government; whereas what I am in favour of is a person elected by the people.

33,936. Would you be in favour of four white men, for instance, elected by the Natives to represent them in Parliament, and to vote only on Native questions?—No, I object to that, too, because that would bring about a separation between even the members of Parliament. This would be a sort of dividing line between the Native race and the white men. I would like the people to be united, to be one in this respect.

33,937. Would you like to send a Zulu to Parliament?—No, that time has not come yet.

33,938. For the present you would be content to have a white representative, and have no ambition to send a black man to Parliament?—We know the white people, and those whose sympathies are with the Native race.

33,939. *Acting Chairman.*] As to the franchise; suppose at an election you Natives were trying to get one man in, and the white men were trying to get another in, would not the election itself be something that would divide you and make you quarrel?—I do not personally think so. The persons requisitioned by the European population to stand, may be two, and may be three, and when they have received requisitions, and have accepted, we Natives will then know who the men are who are standing, and will decide in our own minds as to which one is the one we should vote for, and who would be the best one to represent us.

33,940. Might it not happen sometimes that you would choose quite a different person, one who was not requisitioned by the Europeans?—No, we do not wish to do that; we want to be united, to be one people, and of those who are requisitioned by the Europeans to stand for them, we will select amongst ourselves who is the best one, and we will vote for him. We want to be all the same under the rule of the King. The white people themselves, when they vote, are divided; some vote for one man, and some for the other; we want to be just the same. I should like now to speak about education and Christianity. With regard to education, I say it is a very good thing. Education and Christianity have wrought very great things amongst us Natives. These are things more than any others which have, under the reign of His Majesty King Edward, made us to feel that we have interests in common, and are one with the white people, and which have brought us out from our homes to share in the battles, and share in the troubles of our rulers. Education shows the subject his proper place in the country, and it also makes him understand and know the position of those who are over him. It teaches us to exercise humility, and to keep ourselves in a position of subservience and obedience. Education and Christianity are things which teach us how to live in this world, how to obey the authorities that are over us, and it also teaches us how we are to live, in view of the future life, and what our position will be then. It teaches us to know that there is another Ruler who is over all other rulers here; and education teaches us to know that the rule and the government of the English race is that of a Christian government. Therefore, in these matters, we get strength and encouragement from education and Christianity. And in this connection I feel that it is right for me to-day to express my gratitude and the gratitude of our people to the Missionaries who came out to us, and gave us the education and Christianity which we have amongst us, and also the Government. We thank the Government for having enabled the Missionaries to help them to do this work amongst us, and we look forward to the time in these matters when the Government will go further still, and make it compulsory for our children to be sent to school. The Government would not be doing a wrong thing, should it do that. It would be a good thing for the children; it would be like giving a child a taste of castor oil, which might be unpleasant at the time, but which would work a benefit and help that child. I do not wish, by what I have said, to limit education only to head work and the improvement of the mind. I say that we should also be taught industries. We have cases amongst us already where industrial training has been a great benefit to those who have obtained it; those who can build houses amongst us; those who can make their own wagons now, and do their own blacksmith's work. I have said all I wish to say on that head. I would like to speak on the laws affecting the Natives, and their administration. There are matters with regard to administration, and as affecting the sizes of the tribes, some small, some large, and the administration of their affairs by the heads of those tribes, on which I wish to speak. Chiefs have been appointed over their respective tribes in the Colony, and have been placed there as the eyes and ears of the Government. I look upon these as men in whom the confidence of the Government has been reposed, and when I look upon these Chiefs, I feel that the Government has reduced their ability to be of assistance to the Government, and to keep down and detect wrong doing. There have been faction fights between members of different tribes, and cases have been heard and tried by the Courts in connection with these tribal disturbances, but I have never known a case where the heads of those tribes have been called up by the Government to be asked what they had to do with it, or how they came to have anything to do with it, or what their conduct was in connection with those cases. I know of only one case, which took place many years ago, where the people of two Chiefs had fought, and there had been disturbances, and the Chiefs themselves were called up by the Government and taxed with the conduct of their people. The two Chiefs and heads of the tribes were punished after an enquiry, and since that time there has been no more trouble between those tribes; they have lived together as if they were one family. I feel that men like Chiefs have been taken into the confidence of the Government, by being appointed and made Chiefs and that when there are matters like that between their tribes, or other misconduct, they should be brought up and charged with the responsibility of these things, and made aware of what their position is. Although I speak of that system of Chiefs, I do not say that that is a system which will bring about the advancement and civilisation of the Natives. The very fact that the Government of this country has made two laws, one for the white people and one for the Native, is one which makes it doubtful what is the future object or what is the future end of the Native population. I think that that system is one which brings about and gives birth to a feeling of mutual distrust, and want of co-operation, and I do not think anybody can say that there is some other place, where the same state of things prevails amongst the Natives in respect of their own laws. We know that when a race conquers another, that the law of the conquering race is made the law of the conquered people, and for all times is made the law of the conquered people; but any local customs or usages amongst the people themselves are left; they are not interfered with. That is why I am of opinion to-day that if this divided state of things continues for long, so also will distrust and want of mutual confidence increase and grow in the country. What I feel would give satisfaction and pleasure to the people is that all the people should live and be under the same laws as the laws governing the white people, and the expressions I have hard amongst the people would cease—which are as follows: that when laws are made, they make laws for themselves and they make laws for us black people, laws that they would not on any account have over them. To put an end to all these conflicting feelings and dissatisfied feelings in the country, there should be one country, one ruler, one law; but I do not say interfere or abrogate any of the local customs that they may have amongst them.

2.   African Workers Discuss a Variety of Concerns, 1904

The following testimony, from the South African Native Affairs Commission, gives African workers' views on schools, land-purchase rights, housing conditions, and life in the city.

Paulus Molatje and eight others; also *Saul Msane* (Compound Manager) and *Solomon Kumalo* (Assistant Compound Manager), examined (through an interpreter). . . .

44,353. Besides this matter of the location, is there any other matter you wish to speak of?—There are many things which I can speak about to the Commission. There is the way in which we live in this town of Johannesburg. The treatment is very bad for us in the location and everywhere where we live. Sometimes when we sit in our houses we simply see a policeman walk in, pushing the door open; and sometimes in the middle of the night when we sleep lots of policemen come round the location and take everybody out of

Testimony of Paulus Molatje and Eight Others (Basuto Committee); Saul Msane, Compound Manager, and Solomon Kumalo, Assistant Compound Manager, Before the South African Native Affairs Commission, October 17, 1904, pp. 853–860.

their houses to the square in the location. Here in the town also we have very bad treatment under the pass law.

44,354. Do you think that you can do without the pass law?—We cannot live without passes, but the pass law is very heavy for us. I will be pleased if the Commission will see some other way to give a pass to the Native people; the way we have got now is very heavy.

44,355. Is there not a law by which some people are not obliged to carry passes which the Natives have to take out every month?—There are laws like that, but we cannot find out about them; we cannot say anything about that, because we have not seen anything good about it.

44,356. Do the people who are here this afternoon hold exemptions or certificates which make it unnecessary for them to have monthly passes?—I cannot answer that; each one can say what he wishes to say.

44,357. Have you yourself an exemption pass?—Yes.

44,358. And does that not make it less heavy for you?—The one that I have got is better than the one the Natives have to take out every month.

44,359. What else is there?—Another matter I wish to speak about is the taxes paid at the outside stations. Some very young people have to pay taxes, and that we do not understand. Some boys who are quite young and who are not yet able to work have to pay the tax. The father must pay, and the youngsters must pay too.

44,360. Do you know a young boy who has had to pay a tax?—Yes; my sister has a boy here, and I pay a tax every year for him. Every year I pay £2 for him, and £2 for myself too. I have got all the receipts of the taxes which have been paid.

44,361. Is he at work?—No, he is in school; he is too young to work, but he has to pay the tax.

44,362. What school is he at?—He is in the Wesleyan school.

44,363. Have you complained about this payment of the tax by this boy?—No; this is the first time.

44,364. Are you referring to a municipal tax, or to the tax that all the people in the country have to pay?—I speak for the country generally.

44,365. What else is there you wish to say?—There is another complaint which I wish to bring before the Commission, regarding the treatment we receive. The Commission knows that we are all working men, and that we are in employ every day. The nine o'clock bell is very hard for us. When we leave work at nine at night, sometimes we have to go and do some work at the Church; it may be a concert is being given, and we cannot get the right to go to that concert.

44,366. That is on account of what is called the Curfew Law; you have to be in by nine o'clock at night?—Yes, and it is heavy, because we are the whole day at work.

44,367. Can you be out after nine if you get a special pass from your employer?—Yes, but he cannot give it every day; he may give it one day.

44,368. So you do not like this law by which you have to be in by a certain hour?—No.

44,369. Would you like to be able to walk about all night?—Yes; sometimes if I have no time to go where I wish to go I wish to go through the whole night.

44,370. *Mr. Sloley.*] Do you not know how many Natives there are in Johannesburg?—I cannot tell the total. I know there are Basutos and Shangaans and Zulus, and some other nations which I do not know.

44,371. I mean how many thousands are there?—I could not tell.

44,372. It is about 150,000: Do you think it would be possible to keep good order in the town with all the vast number of people here unless there were special and strict laws to regulate them?—The law must let them have that right, because they are a people which live.

44,373. Do you not see among those many thousands of people there are a great many who are bad people—I do not mean that they are all bad, but there are many who are bad—and those bad people who are going about would do things which would get the whole of the black population into trouble?—It is so, but the law has got police and a gaol in which to lock up those people; the law is there to see about those people who do not do right.

44,374. What is your trade?—I work under my employer.

44,375. What is he?—I work under Messrs. Lewis and Marks. I have an office.

44,376. As to the tax which you are complaining about, what do you pay yourself?—I pay for my pass and for my taxes.

44,377. What taxes; how much?—I pay £2 for my tax for the year and £1 for my pass.

44,378. As to this young man you pay for, who is he?—He is my sister's son.

44,379. You pay for him also?—I pay for him also.

44,380. Are these the only two members of your family for whom you pay tax?—I pay altogether £5 every year for the boy and for myself.

44,381. Do you pay municipal taxes also to the Town Council?—No, I pay nothing to the municipality because I have no house; I live at my employer's place. I am not married yet, and I am not living in a location yet.

44,382. *Mr. De la Harpe.*] How many years have you been paying for this youngster you speak of?—Two years.

44,383. Do you know his age?—I cannot tell you his age; he is a young boy. . . .

Saul Msane:

44,395. Where is your land?—In Natal.

44,396. Did you buy the land?—Yes.

44,397. Would you like that all the people should be allowed to buy the land in that way?—Yes, I would like all individuals that can buy to buy.

44,398. Speak, if you wish to talk upon this subject?—I wish to speak on the franchise.

44,399. What do you wish to say about that?—I think the Natives should not be altogether shut out of it; the English should admit civilised Natives to the franchise.

44,400. Have you got the vote in Natal?—I have not the vote in Natal.

44,401. Could you get it if you asked for it?—By exemption. I know some of my people who have got a vote.

44,402. Do you think you all ought to get the vote?—Not in the mass.

44,403. What is a civilised man, in your opinion?—A civilised man is a man who is born and brought up under the influence of Europeans and educated.

44,404. You think all such persons should have the franchise?—The educated and well-conducted people.

44,405. Have you anything to say on that subject?—No. . . .

44,414. What you want is schools?—Yes.

44,415. Do you mean all over the country, or just in the towns?—Schools in appointed places, where Natives could be sent for education. For instance, it would not be a bad idea if schools among the mines were established; that is, to educate the Natives to be useful, educate them how to labour, and things of that sort. It would help very much the labour question.

44,416. Do you mean to educate them in trades?—In anything that will make a Native useful.

44,417. Are you referring to those boys who work in the mines?—I would not exclude those. If they wanted to join the school and attend it, I think, so much the better.

44,418. But they could not go to work in the same mines all day and then go to school and learn trades at the same time?—There are such things as night classes.

44,419. Do you think the Natives in the mines would be able to keep awake and attend night schools?—Yes, some of them go from our mine all the way to the City and Suburban, because there is a night school there, to learn.

44,420. Many of the boys work at night, they go down at sundown, do they not?—When it is their time for day shift then they will get the night to themselves. When they are on the night shift then they will have the day, and they cannot go that week.

44,421. Is there anything more about education?—No.

44,422. Is there any other subject that you have omitted?—I do not remember the subjects now.

44,423. *Captain Dickson.*] Are there many boys attending these night schools on the mines?—I would not say many, but a few are attending.

44,424. Are there more than 100 attending?—I could not say. I do not know how many are attending.

44,425. How long have you been working on the mines?—I am in my tenth year now.

44,426. Continuously?—Yes.

44,427. What are you?—I am the compound manager.

44,428. Of what mine?—Of the Jubilee.

44,429. How much leave have you taken within the ten years? How long have you been away from the mines within the ten years?—Putting it together, not more than three months.

44,430. Are there many other Natives on the mines who have worked for long periods?—Not many. There are some who have been there 15 years.

44,431. *Mr. Campbell.*] What salary do you receive?—At the present time?

44,432. Yes?—£26 10s. per month.

44,433. Have you got charge of the whole of the Natives in that compound?—I have.

44,434. Have you any white man over you, as far as the compound is concerned?—The General Manager.

44,435. You have full charge?—Yes.

44,436. How long have you held that position?—Since 1895.

44,437. *Mr. Samuelson.*] Are you exempted from the operation of Native law in Natal?—No.

44,438. Do you think that men who have reached the same stage of education and civilisation as yourself, even if they are under Native law, should have the franchise?—I do.

44,439. If total prohibition of liquor were to operate against your getting the franchise, would you approve of it then?—I do not like liquor at all.

44,440. You would rather go without the franchise and keep the prohibition?—I would keep it.

44,441. Have you anything to say about the pass regulations? Do they affect you in any way?—I hold an exemption.

44,442. I do not mean here particularly, I mean generally?—Of course, with the masses it is quite necessary that we should have a pass law. One objection to the operation of the pass law here is that it gives the officials the right to enter anyone's room in the night when they are asleep, and they can do it forcibly. That is the only objection that I have to the pass law: giving a right to a man to interfere with another man when he is in his own castle.

44,443. Have you bought land in the Transvaal?—No; I have tried to, but the law was against me.

44,444. Did you pay for it?—We had already started to pay for it, but we had to go, because it was stopped. The owner was told not to sell it to the Natives.

44,445. Who by?—By the Commissioner for Native Affairs.

44,446. Did you get your money back?—I took it back.

44,447. There is nothing you wish to tell the Commission now that you can think of that you have left unsaid?—It is merely that we would like to have the privilege of buying land. We all agree on that point.

44,448. Is there anything else you would like to say? It is your only chance, and if you have anything to say, say it?—I wish I had seen the questions; they took me rather by surprise, because none were sent to me.

44,449. You do not think of anything more to-day. I will ask you this question. You remember the Edendale community near Maritzburg?—Yes.

44,450. That community is under a Chief, is it not?—We call him Induna ourselves.

44,451. But he has the same powers and the same jurisdiction as any other man of his standing —any Chief?—Yes.

44,452. Why do you Christians have Chiefs if they are not so opposed to Christianity and progress?—We should not have them at all. All we want is an Induna.

44,453. An Induna with the same powers as the Chiefs?—No, not exactly.

44,454. Would you like to be entirely free from Chiefs and put under the Magistrate?—Yes, that is quite sufficient.

44,455. You, with your education and civilisation, have preferred to remain under Native law rather than to come out of it and come under the ordinary law?—What really stopped me from exempting myself at the time in Natal was because it then admitted a raw man, an uneducated man, and I knew of so many that were exempted that really it was no inducement to be exempted. It seemed rather as if it was lowering oneself to do it. I thought if my education was not good enough to carry me through without, exemption could not do it.

44,456. That was your reason?—That was my reason.

44,457. Have others neglected to be exempted for the same reason?—I could not say. When it came about here in the Transvaal we had to produce certificates of our education. I had got that. I was the first to apply for it.

44,458. *Mr. Campbell.*] What salary were you receiving when you came here first?—I started at £8.

44,459. What were you doing then?—I was compound manager.

44,460. And you have worked yourself up to £26 10s.?—Yes, I have worked myself up to that.

44,461. *Captain Dickson.*] Which exemption law do you prefer —the exemption law of the Transvaal, or the exemption law of Natal?—I hold an exemption pass of the Transvaal.

44,462. Do you think the law is better here than in Natal?—Inasmuch as it is attained by those who are fitted.

44,463. And you think no exemption should be obtained except by education and fitness?—I think so.

44,464. *Chairman.*] Letseleba, what do the Basuto deputation say about liquor? Are they in favour of it? I refer to the law which prohibits the sale or purchase of spirituous liquors?—*Letseleba:* I think they have a right to get what they want. Drink is medicine. It is to help many people sometimes when they are in sickness, therefore I say they should be allowed.

44,465. Do you say this for yourself, or is it what the others think?—All say so. They say that it is medicine.

44,466. All those who are in favour of being able to buy drink stand up?—(*All, except Saul Msane, stood up.*) *Solomon Kumalo:* I am in favour of it, but not altogether. I think that Natives who conduct themselves and who are civilised should be privileged to buy liquor, but they must satisfy the officials or the Native Affairs Department as to their conduct before they can obtain that privilege, which privilege may be cancelled at any time should the person enjoying the privilege misuse it, or abuse it in any way, or contravene the laws affecting liquor.

44,467. So that any man who got permission to buy drink and got drunk should lose the right of getting any more?—If he contravenes the liquor law. If I am granted the privilege of purchasing liquor, and I go to my fellow countrymen and supply them with drink, I think my privilege ought to be cancelled altogether.

44,468. *Mr. Samuelson.*] You are exempted from the operation of Native law in Natal?—Yes.

44,469. You had not the privilege of buying liquor through that exemption, had you?—No.

44,470. Natives exempted from the operation of Native law are subject to the Liquor Act of Natal?—Yes, they are subject to the Liquor Act of Natal.

44,471. But under the Liquor Act they can be specially exempted from the operation of that Liquor Act?—They can.

44,472. You petitioned the Governor, as an exempted Native, to be exempted from the operation of the Liquor Act?—I did.

44,473. And you got the Governor's certificate of exemption?—I have it.

44,474. Has the exemption done you good? Are you as strong and healthy a man now as you were before your exemption?—It has done me no harm.

44,475. Before you were exempted you were a strong healthy Native, were you not—very vigorous and able; is not that so?—I think I am just about the same.

44,476. Do you think so?—Yes.

44,477. You are not a bit the worse for it?—No.

3. Reverend James Dwane Reassures Europeans About the Direction of African Churches, 1903

In the early twentieth century, white South Africans were alarmed by the African religious movement toward separate and independent Christian churches. Whites believed these institutions would spawn agitation, unrest, or political opposition. The Native Affairs Commission was especially concerned about influences from black America. Dwane partly agrees with and confirms white fears about separatists, but he insists that his own religious influence is responsible and safely free of political involvement.

Afternoon Sitting

Reverend James Mata Dwane, examined.

9678. *Chairman.*] You are a missionary, I believe?—I am.

Testimony of Reverend James Mata Dwane Before the South African Native Affairs Commission, November 12, 1903, pp. 708–711, 714.

9679. Where were you brought up?—Amongst Kama's people, Middledrift.

9680. In the Cape Colony?—Yes.

9681. What are you by nationality?—I am a Kafir of the Amatinde tribe.

9682. Where were you educated?—Healdtown.

9683. What were you brought up to?—First as a schoolmaster.

9684. Then did you perform the duties of a schoolmaster?—Yes.

9685. For how many years?—For three years.

9686. Under whom?—Under the Wesleyan Missionary Society.

9687. Did they bring you up?—Yes.

9688. How long did you remain with them?—I remained with them until the end of the year 1895.

9689. Altogether, how many years?—Well, I could not say exactly, as I went there as a heathen boy. I was brought up by Mr. Lamplough, one of the leading Wesleyans.

9690. At any rate, you remained for some years?—For many years.

9691. As a schoolmaster, or a missionary?—As a missionary.

9692. Now you are ordained?—I was ordained in 1881.

9693. Then after a time you left the Wesleyan Mission?—I left it at the end of 1895.

9694. And what became of you then?—Then I connected myself with what is known as the "Ethiopian movement."

9695. How did you connect yourself with it?—After my resignation, which took place at the end of the year 1895, a deputation of Native men who belonged to that movement came down from the Transvaal to meet me at Queenstown, where they asked me to join them and help them. We had a long discussion about the matter at Queenstown, about the month of December, 1895, and they told me that their intention was to unite with the American Negro Organisation, of which I knew nothing at that time, and I told them that it did not look to me as a good thing. I said: "If you unite yourselves with a purely Native organization the people in this country will take you as anti-English," but they assured me that such was not the case; that their intention was simply to try and do good in connection with that Society. After a long discussion I consented and I went up to Pretoria to attend their conference. At that conference I was appointed, with two others, as a deputation to go to the United States, and confer with the authorities of that body, namely, the African Methodist Episcopal Church. I visited several States in United America, inspecting their work, conferring with their Bishops, and examining things, and I returned to this country after effecting union with that body. Then Mr. Turner, the Senior Bishop, came to Africa to see what the work was, and met a conference in Queenstown and Pretoria to complete the arrangements. During his visit to Africa he consecrated me at Queenstown as an Assistant Bishop, and requested me to visit America again. During my second visit to America I examined things more closely, read several books, standard works, of their Church, among which there was one in particular named the "Polity of Methodism," by Bishop Turner himself. This book I read carefully through, and after reading it, with other books, I found that this body, the African Methodist Episcopal Church of America, traced their origin, and the validity of their Orders, to the fact that when Richard Allan, their first Bishop, was consecrated in America, there was one Priest, named Absolom Jones, a coloured priest, who was himself ordained by Bishop White, of the Anglican Church of America, and they laid a great stress on that fact, that one minister belonging to the Church of England took part in the consecration of their first Bishop, and hence the validity of their Order. That led me to examine the question more closely, and, to make the whole thing short, I came to the conclusion that they were not satisfied with the validity of their Orders and their Church. Of course, I found that out in conversation with them. I presided over a large number of their Annual Conferences in America myself. Another thing I found in America which did not please me, the feeling between the whites and the blacks was very bitter; not only that, but I found amongst the coloured themselves that the darker ones were looked down upon by the lighter-coloured ones—of course, there are a great deal of half-castes—and this was carried to such an extent, that in appointing a minister, it became a very difficult matter. The lighter ones would not have a very dark man as their minister, and so at the Conferences I told the coloured people of America that I did not think it would be a good thing for them to come out here. I told them that repeatedly in my public addresses. I said, in Africa it is just the other way. We are satisfied, and contented with our colour; in fact, if such a thing could be done, we would rather keep our colour than change it, whereas in America it is the other way—they are doing all they can to get white, and so, on the whole, I came back, and said to my people, "I am not satisfied; as I told you when you came down to Queenstown, when you had an interview with me, I did not believe this thing would answer. You should have applied to the people on the spot, who brought the Gospel to you; you should have gone straight to them, and if you wanted an organization of your own—it is not wrong—you should have gone to them and asked them to give you one." And so that led me to write to the Archbishop of Cape Town in August, 1899, making certain proposals, and asking him and the other Bishops of the Church of the Province of South Africa to give us an organization of our own, a distinct organization, within the Church, and be allowed to try and do as much good as we can amongst our people in Africa. The correspondence took a long time, and at last the Archbishop wanted to know if the people sided with me, so I convened a Conference at Queenstown, and we discussed the matter. Of course, it was during the war, and the people of the Transvaal and the Orange River Colony could not attend the Conference, but all the ministers in the Cape Colony attended, and, with the exception of about four men, they all voted in favour of appealing to the Church of the Province. The four immediately left the Conference. In August, 1900, the Bishops called a Synod of their own in Grahamstown, and at the same time I called a Conference of the Ethiopians in Grahamstown, and both meetings were held there to discuss the whole question. A document was drawn up by the Bishops—there were about eight of them there: there was the Archbishop of Cape Town, the

Bishop of Grahamstown, the Bishop of Pretoria, and others the names of whom I do not remember—and the document was sent to us at the Conference. I read the document and the proposals of the Bishops, and we all agreed that an Order within the Church of England should be formed, to be called the "Order of Ethiopia," and that we should have our conferences, our laws, and try and manage our own affairs. We were to be subject to the Archbishop of Cape Town, and the Diocesan Bishops who perform the duties of Bishop to the Order; but we have a definite order that our schools, rooms, and other Church property are held by Provincial Trustees for the use of the Ethiopian people. I think that is the short history of the movement with which I am connected, and I am Provincial of that Order, and we have congregations in the Colony, and, I believe, in the other Colonies.

9696. You have told us something about the Order of Ethiopia, which you now belong to; will you tell us something of the aims and objects of the African Methodist Episcopal Church, to which you belonged, and which you have left?—I am afraid I could not say much about it—it would not be fair for me to do so.

9697. Is there anything in the methods or policy which are politically objectionable?—Yes.

9698. Do they go beyond that—is there nothing more than that?—I am afraid the teaching and everything is calculated to bring about an undesirable state of things in the country; that is as much as I can say.

9699. Is there that in the teaching which might tend to disturb the good relations between the Natives of South Africa and Europeans?—In the printed doctrines and teaching, and all that, you would not find much that is objectionable; but in the practical teaching and training the tendency is to set the black race against the white race.

9700. Teaching in school?—Yes; and especially in America. I had to speak very plainly to them about it, so much so, that some of them were displeased with me in the United States. I said: "Now we are living in peace in Africa, and if you attempt to do the same as in America, I believe it would bring the whole country into trouble."

9701. Would you describe their teaching as mischievous?—Yes, I would.

9702. Would you go further, and say that if the teaching were to be continued it might lead the Natives of South Africa into trouble?—If they were to go on and do as they were doing in America, I am certain it would. . . .

9745. Then I take it that the Commission may gather from this expression of your views that while you think the time has arrived for a beginning to be made in the establishment of a Native Church, under Native control, your desire is that such Church should be entirely loyal to the Government of this country?—Yes.

9746. *Mr. Sloley.*] Do you know what were the motives which induced those people in the Transvaal to seek connection with the American Church?—I found that in some way or other they got hold of the newspaper called "Voice of Missions" which was published in America by Bishop Turner, and a book of discipline and so on. Who sent them the book I do not know, but when I went up to Pretoria I found them in possession of it.

9747. But what was the motive that induced them to seek connection with the American Church: were they dissatisfied with the churches and missions of this country?—They were dissatisfied, I believe, or they would never have left them. One Nehemia Tile was the first to move, and then several joined him, including Jonas Goduka, J. Gqamana and others, and then it was started in the Transvaal by M. Mokone. . . .

4.   Gandhi Designs a Campaign Against Discriminatory Laws, 1906

M. K. Gandhi (1869–1948) spent about twenty-one years in South Africa where he originally intended to practice law on behalf of the merchant community. He eventually became involved in politics, founded the Natal Indian Congress, and developed his nonviolent political technique of satyagraha. *In 1907 he protested the oppressive legislation passed by the British colony of the Transvaal, which had come under British rule after the end of the Anglo–Boer War. The territory received full internal self-government in 1907. However, instead of easing restrictions on Indians living in the territory, the Transvaal government tightened them, despite the loyalty of Indians in South Africa in times of crisis. The administration passed an Asiatic Registration Bill, which required Indians to be fingerprinted and to carry registration certificates or face jail, fine, or deportation. Under Gandhi's leadership, the Indian community launched a protest campaign against the injustice of being singled out in this way. Through this campaign, Gandhi developed and refined his techniques of political organization and protest, and his efforts in turn spurred the maturing of African politics in South Africa.*

476. Johannesburg Letter

Miracle of Gaol [Jail]-Going

In the Transvaal and, if I am not mistaken, all over South Africa, Indians are discussing the gaol-going resolution. They feel certain that the Transvaal Indians will court imprisonment. Some say that gaol is a palace; others look upon it as a beautiful garden. Yet others consider it paradise. Again there are some who think that gaol will prove to be a key which will unshackle the Indians. Some others hold that, through the gaol gates, we shall pass from our present bondage to freedom. Thus in their several ways, people have shown

From Mohandas K. Gandhi, Johannesburg Letters, 1907, *The Collected Works of Mahatma Gandhi,* Vol. 6 (1906–1907), The Publications Division, Ministry of Information and Broadcasting, Government of India, Ahmedabad: Navajivan Trust, 1961, pp. 485–491.

enthusiasm about going to gaol. There are also some who, when the enthusiasm wanes, start worrying about what will happen to this person or that, and get into a panic. I have received a few letters of this kind and the questions they raise do deserve not to be rejected out of hand. For if we are to achieve success in the end, we should provide for the difficulties that are being felt. *Indian Opinion* as well as the Association has received some letters to this effect. I reply to them all in this letter and, on behalf of the Association, I apologize to the writers for its inability to answer them individually. I do not refer to the writers by name as this is unnecessary.

What Should Traders Do?

An Indian writes that his shop is run by him and his son, and that he has debts to pay. What should they do if they are both arrested? To this question there can be many answers. First, let me give the one that comes readily to mind.

Reply 1. Going to gaol is a great adventure, which will benefit not only the person concerned, but all the Transvaal Indians and, in fact, the Indian community as a whole. To win such great benefits, one must put up with whatever loss may occur. I believe that going to gaol will please Khuda or Ishwar. The Creator always helps us in anything we do in fear of Him. We reap the fruit of our labour in proportion to our faith in Him. The Prophet Mahomed and his disciples were once in a cave. A whole army was marching towards them. The disciples cried out in fear: "O Prophet! We are only three, and the army consists of hundreds of men. How shall we save ourselves?" The Prophet replied, "We are not just three. God, Who is a match for all, is also with us." It was owing to such superhuman faith that the Prophet succeeded in all that he attempted. The enemy could not do him the least harm. They passed the cave by; it did not occur to them even to look in. Likewise, if we turn to the Hindu scriptures, we find Prahlad, a steadfast devotee of God, who remained unharmed even when made to embrace a red-hot pillar, because he too had unshakable faith in God's help. In the same way, for an Indian who undertakes this adventure with Khuda as witness, there is nothing more to think about. The great God, the protector of the faithful and the preserver of their honour, is present everywhere and at all times. This reply implies reliance on fate. But, as we know, fate without human effort is of no avail. Hence, we need to think of other things too.

Reply 2. While thinking of human effort, we have always to bear the first reply in mind. For those who cannot fully and sincerely trust in God, there is a remedy indicated by Mr. Coovadia: that is, even if all the men working in a shop are arrested simultaneously, they should go to gaol. After returning from gaol, someone—not the proprietor of the shop—might take out a permit (not with the intention of obeying the law, but with that of getting it repealed) and run the shop. Every person will thus come out of gaol well trained.

Reply 3. If anyone finds it difficult to act up to Reply 2, permits for all persons other than the proprietor of the shop may be taken out on the last day fixed in the *Gazette* for the purpose.

Reply 4. The reader will remember what I said earlier: before it becomes necessary for an Indian to go to gaol, he will receive a notice to quit the Transvaal. He will be arrested after the expiry of the notice-period, then sentenced to pay a fine and to imprisonment in case of default. One must then go to gaol instead of paying the fine. It will thus be possible for the trader, during the notice-period, to make over his goods to his creditors. For the small trader this will be the best remedy. He is unlikely to find any difficulty in earning his daily bread after release from gaol.

What of Women and Children?

The Act gives [the Government] no power to arrest women, and children under sixteen. They will thus have to suffer nothing more than separation from husband or father. As for their maintenance, the answer had already been given that the Indian community will look after them. It is to be remembered that all the thirteen thousand Indians will not have to go to gaol at the same time. If, however, this should happen, our deliverance would be immediate. Since all the Indians will not be going to gaol at the same time, there will always be a few people outside to look after one another.

What Is a Valid Permit?

A correspondent has raised a further query. Anyone who has obtained a permit after making a true affidavit and whose permit bears his signature or thumb-impression is the holder of a valid permit, irrespective of whether or not he is a refugee. Only these [that is, holders of valid permits] are to live on in the Transvaal and court imprisonment.

What Will Happen to Men in Small Villages?

This question has been asked by a correspondent from Belfast. The answer to this is contained for the most part in the foregoing replies. If, however, the villages come in for attack first, Mr. Gandhi will very probably rush there. Even if he happens to be busy in another part of the Transvaal, the people need not at all be afraid. When an officer comes to investigate, whatever permit one holds should be shown to him. He should be told that taking out a new permit is humiliating to us and that it would never happen. If he asks for any finger-prints other than the thumb-impression, these should be flatly refused. If a notice is served on anyone, information should be immediately sent to the Association with particulars, such as name, address, etc. On the expiry of the notice-period, he should appear before the court and accept whatever gaol sentence is awarded. If a fine is imposed, it should not be paid. It is necessary that every Indian everywhere should communicate these instructions to those who may not know about them.

Boys Over Sixteen

Questions on this subject have been asked from Pietersburg. No boy, as long as he is under sixteen, will be arrested. Boys who are over sixteen, whether or not they hold permits or other documents, are in the same situation as the holders of valid permits.

What Will Happen to Existing Permits?

A correspondent from Lindleyspoort seeks to know what will happen to those who hold permits now, but go to India on business while the struggle is on, and then wish to return. He asks whether their permits will hold good then. For those who are preparing to go to gaol, this question will not arise. For no one can tell what the end of the struggle will be. However, generally speaking, the reply to this question is that such a permit-holder will probably find no difficulty in returning.

How to Act during Police Investigation

A correspondent from Volkstroom asks: what are the police to be told when they come to investigate? What is to be done if the police forcibly take away the permits? The answer to these questions is only this: produce the permit when they come. If required, give one thumb-impression only. If asked to take out new permits, refuse to do so, and say that you have no intention at all of taking out one, and that, if, for not doing so, the Government sends you to gaol, you will be ready for it. The police do not have the authority to take away permits by force. Therefore, if they threaten you in any way, reply boldly that you will not give up the permit. If any such thing happens, report it to the Association.

The same person also inquires what arrangements will be made for the dependents of those who go to gaol according to the Fourth Resolution, and whether the Association will pay the counsel's fees, etc. Answers to these questions have already been given above.

Curtis's Letter

Mr. Curtis has addressed a letter to *The Times* of London. A comment on it has already appeared in this journal. The whole letter is reproduced in *The Star.* It is not necessary to offer a translation of it, as most of the facts in it are a matter of history. There are, however, some points in the letter that deserve to be noted. For Mr. Curtis is a member of the Council, and importance will always be attached to his statements. Every Indian will therefore have to think about the matter.

Mr. Curtis says:

(1) that Englishmen and Indians ought never to have equal rights;
(2) that the law which has been enacted lays down quite properly that their rights are not equal;
(3) that this law is only the beginning of a series of many similar laws to come; and
(4) that Lord Selborne's promise that no new Indian would be allowed into the Transvaal should be honoured.

Mr. Curtis goes on to make other points, but those mentioned above are sufficient to put the Indian community on its guard. The letter shows that the Transvaal Act is intended not merely to provide for registration, but to humiliate us also, to show that we are not their [the whites'] equals in any way, and to brand us as slaves. From the letter one thing at least becomes certain: if the Act comes into force, and if we submit to it, instead of fresh rights being granted to us, we shall be deprived of what little remains to us, not merely in the Transvaal, but all over South Africa. We shall, therefore, do well to remember what kind of law this is. It will be better for every worthy son of India to leave the Colony or commit suicide than to submit to a law with such dire consequences. Mr. Polak, the editor of this journal, has given Mr. Curtis a biting and powerful reply. There is no time for translating it here. But it may be read in the English section. . . .

Threat by "The Star"

The editor of *The Star* was somewhat piqued that the Klerksdorp Indians should have held a meeting about gaol-going. Mr. Polak therefore replied to him that not only in Klerksdorp but in Germiston and other places also such meetings had been held and that news was coming in from all over concerning the gaol-going resolution. This has enraged the editor all the more. He has said in his comment that there were only a few leaders who were inciting the Indian community, and that, if they were deported, the other Indians would not utter a word but would cheerfully accept the new Act. Mr. Gandhi has replied to him as follows:

Gandhi's Reply

> You say in your leaderette that those who oppose the Indians would not be sorry if their leaders were deported. But I ought to point out to such opponents that there is no law authorizing the Government forcibly to deport anyone. If that is to be done, another law will have to be passed. Then the Transvaal Government will be able to deport those Indians who are ready to serve their country and even the Government. You say that, if the leaders are deported, the remaining Indians will obey the Act. They will then realize how the Act protects them and how they had been misled about it. It is readily seen that, in saying this, you cannot appreciate the feelings of Indians. You are mistaken if you think that there is a single Indian who takes the Act as being meant for his protection. I have repeatedly gone through the Act without coming across any section which might protect Indians. Moreover, there can be no question of misleading any Indians in this regard for what has been placed before them is a very simple matter: the new Act only insults Indians by branding them as slaves. In several ways the Act reduces Indians to the position of slaves since it is an attack on them as a community.
>
> They have therefore been advised not to forego in any circumstances the existing rights by submitting to the new Act. If the new Act comes into force, I believe that the Indian community will be reduced to that position.
>
> To ward off this deadly blow, I have advised people to do three things as under:

(1) They should not take out new registers.

(2) As the Indians residing in the Transvaal have no right to vote, the resolution about going to gaol is the only means they have to oppose any particular law. They should not take out a permit, nor leave the country, nor pay a fine; the only straightforward and effective course for them is to go to gaol.

(3) If they do this, they should have nothing to do with the Permit Office, and should also write to their friends to persuade them not to ask for new permits, whether temporary or permanent.

If anyone should say that, by doing so, they would be doing just what the whites wanted, let the whites think so. This will prove what I have always said, viz., that that Indian community is not out to save its trade in the Transvaal, but to stay here with honour. The Indian community will not sacrifice its good name just for the sake of a living. . . .

5. An ANC Founder Prophesies the Rise of African Power, 1906

Pixley ka Isaka Seme, one of the founders of the African National Congress, delivered this speech while a student at Columbia University. After completing his studies, he returned to practice law in Johannesburg and became the first treasurer of the ANC.

I have chosen to speak to you on this occasion upon "The Regeneration of Africa." I am an African, and I set my pride in my race over against a hostile public opinion. Men have tried to compare races on the basis of some equality. In all the works of nature, equality, if by it we mean identity, is an impossible dream! Search the universe! You will find no two units alike. The scientists tell us there are no two cells, no two atoms, identical. Nature has bestowed upon each a peculiar individuality, an exclusive patent—from the great giants of the forest to the tenderest blade. Catch in your hand, if you please, the gentle flakes of snow. Each is a perfect gem, a new creation; it shines in its own glory—a work of art different from all of its aërial companions. Man, the crowning achievement of nature, defies analysis. He is a mystery through all ages and for all time. The races of mankind are composed of free and unique individuals. An attempt to compare them on the basis of

Pixley ka Isaka Seme, "The Regeneration of Africa," *The African Abroad,* April 5, 1906, from Thomas Karis and Gwendolyn M. Carter, eds., *From Protest to Challenge: A Documentary History of African Politics in South Africa, 1882–1964, Vol. 1: Protest and Hope, 1882–1934,* ed. by Sheridan Johns, III. Stanford: Hoover Institution Press, 1972, pp. 68–71.

equality can never be finally satisfactory. Each is self. My thesis stands on this truth; time has proved it. In all races, genius is like a spark, which, concealed in the bosom of a flint, bursts forth at the summoning stroke. It may arise anywhere and in any race.

I would ask you not to compare Africa to Europe or to any other continent. I make this request not from any fear that such comparison might bring humiliation upon Africa. The reason I have stated,—a common standard is impossible! Come with me to the ancient capital of Egypt, Thebes, the city of one hundred gates. The grandeur of its venerable ruins and the gigantic proportions of its architecture reduce to insignificance the boasted monuments of other nations. The pyramids of Egypt are structures to which the world presents nothing comparable. The mighty monuments seem to look with disdain on every other work of human art and to vie with nature herself. All the glory of Egypt belongs to Africa and her people. These monuments are the indestructible memorials of their great and original genius. It is not through Egypt alone that Africa claims such unrivalled historic achievements. I could have spoken of the pyramids of Ethiopia, which, though inferior in size to those of Egypt, far surpass them in architectural beauty; their sepulchres which evince the highest purity of taste, and of many prehistoric ruins in other parts of Africa. In such ruins Africa is like the golden sun, that, having sunk beneath the western horizon, still plays upon the world which he sustained and enlightened in his career.

Justly the world now demands—

"Whither is fled the visionary gleam,
Where is it now, the glory and the dream?"

Oh, for that historian who, with the open pen of truth, will bring to Africa's claim the strength of written proof. He will tell of a race whose onward tide was often swelled with tears, but in whose heart bondage has not quenched the fire of former years. He will write that in these later days when Earth's noble ones are named, she has a roll of honor too, of whom she is not ashamed. The giant is awakening! From the four corners of the earth Africa's sons, who have been proved through fire and sword, are marching to the future's golden door bearing the records of deeds of valor done.

Mr. Calhoun, I believe, was the most philosophical of all the slaveholders. He said once that if he could find a black man who could understand the Greek syntax, he would then consider their race human, and his attitude toward enslaving them would therefore change. What might have been the sensation kindled by the Greek syntax in the mind of the famous Southerner, I have so far been unable to discover; but oh, I envy the moment that was lost! And woe to the tongues that refused to tell the truth! If any such were among the now living, I could show him among black men of pure African blood those who could repeat the Koran from memory, skilled in Latin, Greek and Hebrew,—Arabic and Chaldaic—men great in wisdom and profound knowledge—one professor of philosophy in a celebrated German university; one corresponding member of the French Academy of Sciences, who regularly transmitted to that society meteorological observations, and hydrographical journals and papers on botany and geology; another whom many ages call "The Wise," whose authority Mahomet himself frequently appealed to in the Koran in support of his own opinion—men of wealth and active benevolence, those whose distinguished talents and reputation have made them famous in the cabinet and in the field, officers of artillery in the great armies of Europe, generals and lieutenant generals in the armies of Peter the Great in Russia and Napoleon in France, presidents of free republics, kings of independent nations which have burst their way to liberty by their own vigor. There are many other Africans who have shown marks of genius and high character sufficient to redeem their race from the charges which I am now considering.

Ladies and gentlemen, the day of great exploring expeditions in Africa is over! Man knows his home now in a sense never known before. Many great and holy men have evinced a passion for the day you are now witnessing— their prophetic vision shot through many unborn centuries to this very hour. "Men shall run to and fro," said Daniel, "and knowledge shall increase upon the earth." Oh, how true! See the triumph of human genius to-day! Science has searched out the deep things of nature, surprised the secrets of the most distant stars, disentombed the memorials of everlasting hills, taught the lightning to speak, the vapors to toil and the winds to worship—spanned the sweeping rivers, tunneled the longest mountain range—made the world a vast whispering gallery, and has brought foreign nations into one civilized family. This all-powerful contact says even to the most backward race, you cannot remain where you are, you cannot fall back, you must advance! A great century has come upon us. No race possessing the inherent capacity to survive can resist and remain unaffected by this influence of contact and intercourse, the backward with the advanced. This influence constitutes the very essence of efficient progress and of civilization.

From these heights of the twentieth century I again ask you to cast your eyes south of the Desert of Sahara. If you could go with me to the oppressed Congos and ask, What does it mean, that now, for liberty, they fight like men and die like martyrs; if you would go with me to Bechuanaland, face their council of headmen and ask what motives caused them recently to decree so emphatically that alcoholic drinks shall not enter their country—visit their king, Khama, ask for what cause he leaves the gold and ivory palace of his ancestors, its mountain strongholds and all its august ceremony, to wander daily from village to village through all his kingdom, without a guard or any decoration of his rank—a preacher of industry and education, and an apostle of the new order of things; if you would ask Menelik what means this that Abyssinia is now looking across the ocean—oh, if you could read the letters that come to us from Zululand—you too would be convinced that the elevation of the African race is evidently a part of the new order of things that belong to this new and powerful period.

The African already recognizes his anomalous position and desires a change. The brighter day is rising upon Africa. Already I seem to see her chains dissolved, her desert plains red with harvest, her Abyssinia and her Zululand the seats of science and religion, reflecting the glory of the rising sun from the spires of their churches ad universities. Her Congo and her Gambia whitened with commerce, her crowded cities sending forth the hum of business, and all her sons employed in advancing the victories of peace—greater and more abiding than the spoils of war.

Yes, the regeneration of Africa belongs to this new and powerful period! By this term regeneration I wish to be understood to mean the entrance into a new life, embracing the diverse phases of a higher, complex existence. The basic factor which assures their regeneration resides in the awakened race-consciousness. This gives them a clear perception of their elemental needs and of their undeveloped powers. It therefore must lead them to the attainment of that higher and advanced standard of life.

The African people, although not a strictly homogeneous race, possess a common fundamental sentiment which is everywhere manifest, crystallizing itself into one common controlling idea. Conflicts and strife are rapidly disappearing before the fusing force of this enlightened perception of the true intertribal relation, which relation should subsist among a people with a common destiny. Agencies of a social, economic and religious advance tell of a new spirit which, acting as a leavening ferment, shall raise the anxious and aspiring mass to the level of their ancient glory. The ancestral greatness, the unimpaired genius, and the recuperative power of the race, its irrepressibility, which assures its permanence, constitute the African's greatest source of inspiration. He has refused to camp forever on the borders of the industrial world; having learned that knowledge is power, he is educating his children. You find them in Edinburgh, in Cambridge, and in the great schools of Germany. These return to their country like arrows, to drive darkness from the land. I hold that his industrial and educational initiative, and his untiring devotion to these activities, must be regarded as positive evidences of this process of his regeneration.

The regeneration of Africa means that a new and unique civilization is soon to be added to the world. The African is not a proletarian in the world of science and art. He has precious creations of his own, of ivory, of copper and of gold fine, plated willow-ware and weapons of superior workmanship. Civilization resembles an organic being in its development—it is born, it perishes, and it can propagate itself. More particularly, it resembles a plant, it takes root in the teeming earth, and when the seeds fall in other soils new varieties sprout up. The most essential departure of this new civilization is that it shall be thoroughly spiritual and humanistic—indeed a regeneration moral and eternal!

> O Africa!
> Like some great century plant that shall
>   bloom
> In ages hence, we watch thee; in our dream
> See in thy swamps the Prospero of our
>   stream;

Thy doors unlocked, where knowledge in
    her tomb
Hath lain innumerable years in gloom.
Then shalt thou, walking with that morning
    gleam,
Shine as thy sister lands with equal beam.

6. An Account of the Squatters' Bill, 1912

The newspaper Imvo Zabantsundu *(Native Opinion) was founded by John Tengo Jabavu in 1884. The paper gave voice to black political opinion in the Eastern Cape at a time when the narrow African-educated elite had amassed a significant number of African voters. The following article describes a meeting between African voters and the white member of Parliament who is sympathetic to their concerns. In the meeting, the participants discussed the Squatters' Bill, an abortive measure that preceded the more sweeping Native Land Act of 1913.*

The Cape Peninsula Native Association inaugurated its campaign against the proposed Squatters' Bill of the Union Government the other day at a meeting called by it in the Ashley Hall, Cape Town. There was a full attendance, with the Rev. Nyombolo in the chair.

The Rev. Chairman said he was very glad to attend anything which marked a spirit of real progress and enlightenment among their people and he heartily thanked them on forming such an Association as that which had called them together that evening. He sincerely desired to see it go and prosper if it continued to watch over the rights, privileges and social and political welfare of their people. (Hear, Hear.) These were very worthy objects and he must again congratulate them. He would ask one of the Executive officers of the Association to explain fully the purport of their gathering.

Mr. T. Zini (President of the P.N.A.) said he would not detain them for any great length of time but it was necessary to explain their attitude to the Squatters' Bill, and their reasons for adopting that attitude. Turning to the more immediate subject they were met to discuss—the Squatters' Bill which it was proposed to introduce into the coming session of Parliament—he would ask them to bear in mind that they were commencing a campaign which would be a strenuous one. The harder the struggle the better they should fight. (Hear, hear.) It was simply and solely in the interests of the farmers and miners and of no other section of the community. He had been at some pains to

From Thomas Karis and Gwendolyn M. Carter, eds., *From Protest to Challenge: A Documentary History of African Politics in South Africa, 1882-1964, Vol. 1: Protest and Hope, 1882–1934*, ed. by Sheridan Johns, III. Stanford: Hoover Institution Press, 1972, pp. 82–84.

make himself acquainted with the provisions of the Bill, and he could assure them that all he could find it to contain was indifference to the interests of the bulk of the community, and the oppression of the Natives. It was a most iniquitous measure, and they should oppose it to the very last. If, unhappily, they were not successful in preventing its becoming law, they would at least have it on record that from first to last they had entered an emphatic protest against it. He was certain all Natives would combine in that. (Loud applause.) The whole measure was one gigantic invasion of their liberties. It would most adversely affect hundreds of thousands of Native families which had, up till then, lived on landed estates and farms, paid rents to the owners, and tilled the soil for a subsistence, happy and contented in their way of life. Why, in the Zoutpansburg district of the Transvaal alone there were 168,000 families thus living. Think what it would be to them and to all so living, if that mischievous proposition became law. They would be driven into locations with the sole object of forcing them to work in the mines or on the farms. If the former, they could hardly fail to prove victims of that terrible scourge, miners phthisis, while if they went on farms they would be subject to the treatment for which the great majority of the farmers were notorious in their dealings with the Natives. (Indignation.) The Bill took the cruellest harshest form of assailing the sacred right of every man to choose for himself in what manner he should earn his daily bread, and use the mental and physical attributes God has endowed him with. And yet the Ministry in power was never tired of proclaiming that it was the real friend of the Native and would see to it that he had justice. Yes! Miners phthisis "justice" or the "justice" of the farmers, the greatest sweaters of labour in South Africa. Such was what was proposed to be done by the men who made £2,000 a year each—very largely from the Natives, by the way. That most unjust and iniquitous measure would form one of the subjects for discussion at the Native Congress at Johannesburg on the 8th January. Many other important matters affecting the Natives would also be thought out, and he appealed to them to see that the P.N.A. was represented there by a delegate. (Hear, hear.)

Mr. B. Abrahams reminded his hearers of the very important feature of the proposed legislation, that it shamelessly sought to benefit the large gold mining companies and the big land owners at the price of the ruin of the health of the Natives, and with an utter disregard of all other sections of the people. The Government really played into the hands of the capitalists in Europe who held gold mining shares or owned vast tracts of undeveloped country—men who had never even seen South Africa, in many cases, but whose already bloated money bags the Government wished to swell to a still greater extent. (Indignation.) In no other country in the world did the Government seek to condemn men to contract a fell disease, saying (for that was what it meant) if they did not do that they must work for the farmers, at the expense of their future happiness and with no prospect of advancement. He (the Speaker) knew of nothing more unjust or tyrannical, a greater pandering to the capitalistic few at the expense of the many. (Applause.)

Mr. Umlamlelli asked them to remember General Botha's professions. The

General had said time and again that he was going to assist the Natives to rise in the social scale, to be happy and contented. And what was the result of it all? He now sought to rush through Parliament a measure which would destroy their health and be detrimental to the State. Was that the Act of a sincere well-wisher of the Natives or of a wise far-seeing statesman? (No! No!) A more obnoxious manner of interfering with the freedom of the subject as to the disposal of his labour he could not conceive. Worse still: it made them court death at the instance of the mining community with the alternative of being hewers of wood and drawers of water all their lives at 10s. or 6s. a month. In one hand death; in the other slavery. (Indignation.)

Mr. T. H. Mobutha characterised the proposed legislation as cruel and diabolical. He trusted they would let their protest against be a most emphatic one, ringing from end to end of the land. (Applause.) It was a callous and shameful playing with their lives, happiness, and all their future welfare. ("It is.") It was bad enough, nothing could be worse, to so affect those who worked in the mines or on the farms, but the Natives were mistaken if they thought those would be the only people it would affect. It concerned them all. The returning men from the mines would bring the seed of disease with them, to spread it far and wide among their people. (Fierce indignation.) Where was the vaunted superiority of the white man, if the Government thought it necessary to so unjustly and cruelly bolster him up against the competition of the Native? (Hear, hear.) Their people were to be pushed into the gutter for the only reason that they happened to have the unfortunate colour—black. The farmers complained of shortage of labour, but it was they themselves who were to blame. They drove labour away. Men were to work for them each day and every day, from sunrise to sunset on poor food and a miserable pittance, too often filched from them on one pretext or another. And when their hard labour had made them physical wrecks, old before their time, they were to be turned adrift to starve. (Renewed indignation.) The Native was not lazy; he was a willing worker, if fairly treated. Look at the Diamond-fields! Was De Beer's ever short of labour? No! Was German West Africa ever short of labour? And why? Because at both places the men were treated fairly. The Natives asked for nothing but fair treatment. The farmers were harming themselves by their oppression and injustice, for they humbug the Native once, but never again—he was built that way. (Laughter and applause.)

A speaker, whose reason for wishing his name withheld from print was accepted by the Chairman as valid, thought that, consciously or unconsciously, the Government was playing into the hands of the capitalists. In his opinion it was not the backveld farmer who wished for an Act of this description of the Squatters' Bill. At the present time there were thousands of Natives on their farms, Natives paying rent in money or kind, and it was not they who desired to drive them into locations. Some hundreds of thousands of Natives had done nothing else but farm all their lives; it was their work, and they were perfectly willing to rent suitable land from the white landowners, and so live there free, contented and peaceful lives. But now came this Bill to drive them into the locations where it would be impossible for them to live the lives for which alone they were suited, and to which alone they had been accustomed from their earliest years. The idea was that with the impossibility of existence in the locations, they would be forced into the mines. They would earn good wages there, no doubt, but at what a terrible risk?—a risk not only to themselves, but as had been pointed out by a previous speaker, to their whole people when they should return to the Native territories broken down in health and disseminators of the disease which had seized hold of them. (Hear, hear.) The alternative to the mines was to go on the farms to be treated like dogs, to work hard for a miserable pittance. (Cries of "true, true".) One could not understand some of our legislators. They were like so many acrobats, continually turning bewildering somersaults. (Laughter.) The speaker was indebted for the phrase "legislative acrobats" to perhaps the greatest of all in that line, the Right Hon. J.X. Merriman. (Renewed laughter.) You never knew where to have these people or what side of them they would show next. There was, too, the ex-Premier of Natal, Sir Frederick Moor. In England Sir Frederick had been their very good friend, he would do this, that and the other for the Natives; he would see to it that justice was done to them. Well, as he had said, that was in England. In Natal a few days ago he had openly expressed himself in favour of driving them into locations, and had laid it down as his policy that the Native should never be anything else than the servant of the white man. What did he really mean? Were it not so serious, it would be too funny for anything. (Loud laughter.) And when they turned to the members of the Cabinet, they saw the same sort of gymnastics even more wonderfully done.

The Chairman, in bringing the meeting to a close, had only one regret that the lateness of the hour made it impossible to do otherwise. He must again congratulate the Association. Its members showed an energy altogether to be praised, and conducted their meetings in a reasonable manner. They did not ask for impossibilities and for anything out of the way. All they urged was that the Natives should be treated fairly and justly. That was as it should be, and he hoped the Association would gain in strength and always watch over, safeguard and advance the interests of the Natives. (Applause.) When the speaker first heard that a Squatters' Bill was to be introduced into Parliament he had high hopes that it would prove an entirely satisfactory way of dealing with one phase of the Native problem. He could not help but regret saying that he was thoroughly disillusioned. To him it appeared that the Bill simply means pauperising thousands of Natives, and consigning them to untold misery. . . .

7.   Dr. A. Abdurahman Decries the Coloured Peoples' Plight, 1913

Dr. Abdurahman, one of the few nonwhites to hold elected office, was the leader of the Coloured-people in Cape Town. The predominantly Coloured African People's Organization (APO) existed alongside the early ANC as an outlet for petitions, protests, and scrutiny of government policies toward Africans.

In Dr. Abdurahman's address to the APO, he criticizes white treatment of Coloured people. The occasion was the tenth annual meeting of the APO, the main coloured organization, in 1913. The mayor of Kimberley presided.

Duty of Europeans

What is the duty of Europeans towards the coloured races of the country? Take the oft-repeated assertions of Europeans themselves. Their leaders are fond of talking of their responsibilities to us. They have everlastingly had, or used to have until quite recently, on their lips these nice-sounding phrases about 'our duties and our responsibilities to our coloured brothers'. But are such phrases not hollow and meaningless? If Europeans have duties towards the coloured people, what else is implied than the need for humane dealings, and endeavours to ameliorate their lot and uplift them in the scale of civilization. If that is what their duties mean, let us ask how far they have fulfilled them.

Instead of kindly, humane treatment, we find barbarous cruelty and inhumanity. Instead of ameliorating our lot they endavour to accentuate its bitterness. Instead of aiming at our upliftment they seek to degrade us. Instead of lending a helping hand to those struggling to improve themselves they thrust them back remorselessly and rigorously. Instead of making it possible for them to enjoy the blessings of an enlightened Christianity and a noble civilization, they refuse them the right to live, unless they are content to slave for farmers or descend into the bowels of the earth to delve the gold which enslaves the world, and before whose charms all freedom flies. In short, the object of the white man's rule today is not to develop the facilities of the coloured races so that they may live a full life, but to keep them forever in a servile position. The spirit that underlies this view of governing coloured races spread into this colony with the Union, and is now universal throughout South Africa.

The coloured people resent this, and one cannot be astonished at the feeling of violent hostility that has sprung up. It is a natural result. And, in the words of Carlyle, it may be said that 'to whatever other griefs the coloured

From Solomon T. Plaatje, *Native Life in South Africa*, Johannesburg: Ravan Press, 1982 (first published in London, 1916), pp.160–164.

people labour under, this bitterest grief—injustice—super-adds itself: the unendurable conviction that they are unfairly dealt with, that their lot in this world is not founded on right, nor even on necessity and might, is neither what it should be, nor what it shall be.' The coloured people are sentient beings. Their souls smart under the stigma of injustice. They are nursing a sullen revengeful humour of revolt against the white rule. They have lost respect for the white man, and are refusing to give their best to the country.

The duty of Europeans is plain. Show the coloured people that the Government is for the good of all, not for the privileged class. Prove that the first aim is not to keep us as hewers of wood and drawers of water to men who have the power. Engage the coloured races by their affection. Grant them equal opportunities. If you do so, then the happy harmonization of the whole community will be achieved, and you may be sure of receiving the grateful return of the affection and respect of the coloured races.

The treatment we might reasonably expect from the dominant race is just what they themselves would expect were they in our position. We have as much right to the land of South Africa as they. We have as much right as they to be governed on the same basis of humanity. In the language of one of England's greatest statesmen, Europeans themselves would have been shut out from all the blessings they enjoy, of peace, of happiness, and of liberty if there had been any truth in these principles which some gentlemen have not hesitated to lay down as applicable to the case of Africa. 'Had those principles been true, we ourselves,' said William Pitt, 'had languished to this hour in that miserable state of ignorance, brutality, and degradation, in which history proves our ancestors to have been immersed. Had other nations adopted those principles in their conduct towards us; had other nations applied to Great Britain the reasoning which some of the Senators of this very Island now apply to Africa, ages might have passed without our emerging from barbarism; and we, who are enjoying the blessings of British civilization, of British laws, and British liberty, might at this hour have been little superior either in morals, in knowledge, or refinement, to the rude inhabitants of the coast of Guinea.'

Such were the words of Pitt in a speech he delivered in 1792 in the course of a debate on the Slave Trade. His opinions were vastly different from those of our South African Premier, who only refrains from using the sjambok, so he has told us, on no other ground than that it might also hurt himself, and who is determined to allow no native representative in the Union Parliament as long as the Almighty spares him to be overlord. He does not look forward as Pitt did to the day when 'We [British] might behold the beams of science and philosophy breaking in upon Africa, which, at some happy period, may blaze with full lustre.' But this policy of repression cannot last much longer. If a handful of Indians in a matter of conscience can so firmly resist what they consider injustice, what could the coloured races not do if they were to adopt this practice of passive resistance? We must all admire what these British Indians have shown, and are showing, in their determination to maintain what they deem to be their rights. The inhumanity of the Free State has driven our women to resist the law. Numbers of them went to jail rather than carry passes. The coloured races applaud the noble actions of those brave daughters of Africa. I am convinced that if our people as a whole were prepared to suffer likewise we could gain redress of our most serious grievances while General Botha is still alive. Are we to be driven to that course? Europeans should ask themselves that question, and ask it promptly. For example, if the 200,000 natives on the mines were, in the language of the white Labour Party, to 'down' tools, and prefer to bask in the sun than to go down the mines; if the farm labourer at harvesting time refused to work for one shilling and sixpence a day, the economic foundation of South Africa would suddenly shake and tremble with such violence that the beautiful white South Africa superstructure which has been built on it would come down with a crash, entailing financial ruin such as the world has never witnessed before. If Europeans wish to prevent such a calamity in this country, they must pursue the right course and encourage the coloured people of South Africa to improve their position and become more useful citizens than they have ever been. They will themselves participate in the blessings that spring from our improvement and prosperity, and they will receive 'ample recompense for their tardy kindness (if kindness it can be called) in no longer hindering' our progress.

We also should urge Europeans to go back to the path of justice, to retrace their steps along the route they appear to have been travelling of late. They can influence the legislature. Whatever Parliament does is done in the name of the white people, and whites should, if they wish to see South Africa a happy, prosperous and peaceful country, check their Parliament in its mad career. It is worse than insensate folly to pursue that path any further. Many people have revolted at less oppression than we have had to suffer. At present we have no other course than to endure in silence the persecution of our tyrants, and conform to the servitude imposed on us. We may well exclaim that this is a country where

The wanton whites new penal statues draw

Whites grind the blacks, and white men rule the law. Nevertheless, it is not too late to mend. The estrangement between the two races is not irreconcilable. Europeans could, with advantage to the country, if they would only be men, show the coloured people that the white man's rule is for the good of all, not for the privileged class only. If they grant the coloured races equal opportunities, and do not penalize them on account of race or colour, they may see a happy realization of the dreams of the wisest statesmen that all classes should be contented, and should work together for the good of all.

8. Solomon Plaatje Observes the Impact of the Native Land Act, 1913

Plaatje (1876–1932) was a pioneer African journalist, novelist, and first secretary of the African National Congress. He traveled in England and the United States working for ANC causes. He also labored to develop Setswana as a written medium—creating new words as needed and establishing rules of spelling and grammar—in part by translating at least one Shakespeare play. His Native Life in South Africa *focuses on the impact of the Native Land Act of 1913 on Africans. In this excerpt Plaatje describes the plight of African sharecroppers who have been expelled from European farms as a result of the Native Land Act of that year.*

One farmer met a wandering native family in the town of Bloemhof a week before our visit. He was willing to employ the native and many more homeless families as follows: A monthly wage of £2 10s. for each such family, the husband working in the fields, the wife in the house, with an additional 10s. a month for each son, and 5s. for each daughter, but on condition that the native's cattle were also handed over to work for him. It must be clearly understood, we are told that the Dutchman added, that occasionally the native would have to leave his family at work on the farm, and go out with his wagon and his oxen to earn money whenever and wherever he was told to go, in order that the master may be enabled to pay the stipulated wage. The natives were at first inclined to laugh at the idea of working for a master with their families and goods and chattels, and then to have the additional pleasure of paying their own small wages, besides bringing money to pay the 'Baas' [boss] for employing them. But the Dutchman's serious demeanour told them that his suggestion was 'no joke'. He himself had for some time been in need of a native cattleowner, to assist him as transport rider between Bloemhof, Mooifontein, London, and other diggings, in return for the occupation and cultivation of some of his waste lands in the district, but that was now illegal. He could only 'employ' them; but, as he had no money to pay wages, their cattle would have to go out and earn it for him. 'Had they not heard of the law before?' he inquired. Of course they had; in fact that is why they left the other place, but as they thought that it was but a 'Free' State law, they took the anomalous situation for one of the multifarious aspects of the freedom of the 'Free' State whence they came; they had scarcely thought that the Transvaal was similarly afflicted.

Needless to say the natives did not see their way to agree with such a one-sided bargain. They moved up-country, but only to find the next farmer offering the same terms, however, with a good many more disturbing details—and the next farmer and the next—so that after this native farmer had wandered from farm to farm, occasionally getting into trouble for travelling with

From Solomon T. Plaatje, "One Night with the Fugitives," *Native Life in South Africa,* Johannesburg: Ravan Press, 1982 (first edition, London, 1916), pp. 78–87.

unknown stock, 'across my ground without my permission', and at times escaping arrest for he knew not what, and further, being abused for the crimes of having a black skin and no master, he sold some of his stock along the way, beside losing many which died of cold and starvation; and after thus having lost much of his substance, he eventually worked his way back to Bloemhof with the remainder, sold them for anything they could fetch, and went to work for a digger.

The experience of another native sufferer was similar to the above, except that instead of working for a digger he sold his stock for a mere bagatelle [trinket or trifle], and left with his family by the Johannesburg night train for an unknown destination. More native families crossed the river and went inland during the previous week, and as nothing had since been heard of them, it would seem that they were still wandering somewhere, and incidentally becoming well versed in the law that was responsible for their compulsory unsettlement.

Well, we knew that this law was as harsh as its instigators were callous, and we knew that it would, if passed, render many poor people homeless, but it must be confessed that we were scarcely prepared for such a rapid and widespread crash as it caused in the lives of the natives in this neighbourhood. We left our luggage the next morning with the local mission school teacher, and crossed the river to find out some more about this wonderful law of extermination. It was about 10 a.m. when we landed on the south bank of the Vaal River—the picturesque Vaal River, upon whose banks a hundred miles farther west we spent the best and happiest days of our boyhood. It was interesting to walk on one portion of the banks of that beautiful river—a portion which we had never traversed except as an infant in mother's arms more than thirty years before. How the subsequent happy days at Barkly West, so long past, came crowding upon our memory!—days when there were no railways, no bridges, and no system of irrigation. In rainy seasons, which at that time were far more regular and certain, the river used to overflow its high banks and flood the surrounding valleys to such an extent, that no punt could carry the wagons across. Thereby the transport service used to be hung up, and numbers of the wagons would congregate for weeks on both sides of the river until the floods subsided. At such times the price of fresh milk used to mount up to 1s. per pint. There being next to no competition, we boys had a monopoly over the milk trade. We recalled the number of haversacks full of bottles of milk we youngsters often carried to those wagons, how we returned with empty bottles and with just that number of shillings. Mother and our elder brothers had leather bags full of gold and did not care for the 'boy's money'; and unlike the boys of the neighbouring village, having no sisters of our own, we gave away some of our money to fair cousins, and jingled the rest in our pockets. We had been told from boyhood that sweets were injurious to the teeth, and so spurning these delights we had hardly any use for money, for all we wanted to eat, drink, and wear was at hand in plenty. We could then get six or eight shillings every morning from the pastime of washing that number of bottles, filling them with fresh milk and carrying them down to the wagons;

there was always such an abundance of the liquid that our shepherd's hunting dog could not possibly miss what we took, for while the flocks were feeding on the luscious buds of the haak-doorns and the blossoms of the rich mimosa and other wild vegetation that abounded on the banks of the Vaal River, the cows, similarly engaged, were gathering more and more milk.

The gods are cruel, and one of their cruellest acts of omission was that of giving us no hint that in very much less than a quarter of a century all those hundreds of heads of cattle, and sheep and horses belonging to the family would vanish like a morning mist, and that we ourselves would live to pay 30s. per month for a daily supply of this same precious fluid, and in very limited quantities. They might have warned us that Englishmen would agree with Dutchmen to make it unlawful for black men to keep milk cows of their own on the banks of that river, and gradually have prepared us for the shock.

Crossing the river from the Transvaal side brings one into the province of the Orange 'Free' State, in which, in the adjoining division of Boshof, we were born thirty-six years back. We remember the name of the farm, but not having been in this neighbourhood since infancy, we could not tell its whereabouts, nor could we say whether the present owner was a Dutchman, his lawyer, or a Hebrew merchant; one thing we do know, however: it is that even if we had the money and the owner was willing to sell the spot upon which we first saw the light of day and breathed the pure air of heaven, the sale would be followed with a fine of one hundred pounds. The law of the country forbids the sale of land to a native. Russia is one of the most abused countries in the world, but it is extremely doubtful if the statute book of that empire contains a law debarring the peasant from purchasing the land whereon he was born, or from building a home wherein he might end his days. . . .

It is doubtful if we ever thought so much on a single bicycle ride as we did on this journey; however, the sight of a policeman ahead of us disturbed these meditations and gave place to thoughts of quite another kind, for—we had no pass. Dutchmen, Englishmen, Jews, Germans and other foreigners may roam the 'Free' State without permission—but not natives. To us it would mean a fine and imprisonment to be without a pass. The 'pass' law was first instituted to check the movement of livestock over sparsely populated areas. In a sense it was a wise provision, in that it served to identify the livestock which one happened to be driving along the high road, to prove the bona fides of the driver and his title to the stock. Although white men still steal large droves of horses in Basutoland and sell them in Natal or in East Griqualand, they, of course, are not required to carry any passes. These white horse-thieves, to escape the clutches of the police, employ natives to go and sell the stolen stock and write the passes for these natives, forging the names of magistrates and justices of the peace. Such native thieves in some instances ceasing to be hirelings in the criminal business, trade on their own, but it is not clear what purpose it is intended to serve by subjecting native pedestrians to the degrading requirement of carrying passes when they are not in charge of any stock.

In a few moments the policeman was before us and we alighted in presence of the representative of the law, with our feet on the accursed soil of the district in which we were born. The policeman stopped. By his looks and his familiar 'Dag jong' ("Hello, young man") we noticed that the policeman was Dutch, and the embodiment of affability. He spoke and we were glad to notice that he had no intention of dragging an innocent man to prison. We were many miles from the nearest police station, and in such a case one is generally able to gather the real views of the man on patrol, as distinct from the written code of his office, but our friend was becoming very companionable. Naturally we asked him about the operation of the plague law. He was a Transvaler, he said, and he knew that Kaffirs were inferior beings, but they had rights, and were always left in undisturbed possession of their property when Paul Kruger was alive. 'The poor devils must be sorry now,' he said, 'that they ever sang "God save the Queen" when the British troops came into the Transvaal, for I have seen, in the course of my duties, that a Kaffir's life nowadays was not worth a—, and I believed that no man regretted the change of flags now more than the Kaffirs of Transvaal.' This information was superfluous, for personal contact with the natives of Transvaal had convinced us of the fact. They say it is only the criminal who has any reason to rejoice over the presence of the Union Jack, because in his case the cat-o'-nine-tails, except for very serious crimes, has been abolished.

'Some of the poor creatures,' continued the policeman, 'I knew to be fairly comfortable, if not rich, and they enjoyed the possession of their stock, living in many instances just like Dutchmen. Many of these are now being forced to leave their homes. Cycling along this road you will meet several of them in search of new homes, and if ever there was a fool's errand, it is that of a Kaffir trying to find a new home for his stock and family just now.'

'And what do you think, Baas Officer, must eventually be the lot of a people under such unfortunate circumstances?' we asked.

'I think,' said the policeman, 'that it must serve them right. They had no business to hanker after British rule, to cheat and plot with the enemies of their Republic for the overthrow of their Government. Why did they not assist the forces of their Republic during the war instead of supplying the English with scouts and intelligence? Oom [respected uncle] Paul [Kruger] would not have died of a broken heart and he would still be there to protect them. Serve them right, I say.'

So saying he spurred his horse, which showed a clean pair of hoofs. He left us rather abruptly, for we were about to ask why we, too, of Natal and the Cape were suffering, for we, being originally British subjects, never 'cheated and plotted with the enemies of our Colonies,' but he was gone and left us still cogitating by the roadside.

Proceeding on our journey we next came upon a native trek and heard the same old story of prosperity on a Dutch farm: They had raised an average eight hundred bags of grain each season, which, with the increased stock and sale of wool, gave a steady income of about £150 per year after the farmer had taken his share. There were gossipy rumours about somebody having met someone who said that someone else had overheard a conversation between the Baas and somebody else, to the effect that the Kaffirs were getting too rich on his property. This much involved tale incidentally conveys the idea that the Baas was himself getting too rich on his farm. For the native provides his own seed, his own cattle, his own labour for the ploughing, the weeding and the reaping, and after bagging his grain he calls in the landlord to receive his share, which is fifty per cent of the entire crop.

All had gone well till the previous week when the Baas came to the native tenants with the story that a new law had been passed under which 'all my oxen and cows must belong to him, and my family to work for £2 a month, failing which he gave me four days to leave the farm.'. . .

Liberalism and Segregation:
Africans Between the World Wars

1. Ernest Stubbs Deems Race Mixing a Threat, 1925

The debate over segregation, which had begun before the First World War, grew ever more elaborate and theoretical after the conflict. White supremacists, who openly advocated keeping Africans down, and apologists who claimed that their policies would benefit blacks, locked horns over the issue. The debate became more and more linked to actual legislation as J. B. M. Hertzog's government, elected in 1924, introduced a flurry of bills in 1926 to "settle" the African question. The legislation sparked discussion that ground on from 1926 to 1936, when a series of important measures finally passed.

In the following document, Ernest Stubbs makes one case for segregation: that race mixing threatens whites.

III

The Poor White is the product of a Black economy. In any other than a mixed Black and White State the individual whom we know as a Poor White would find a place in the ranks of the labouring classes. In South Africa his only place is a limbo between the White Aristocracy and the Black Proletariat, to both of whom he is equally an object of contempt. The System will not permit him to do "Kaffir's work" and he preserves a fancied superiority to the producing Native at the cost of losing every quality that is of value to the state. From unemployed he becomes unemployable and a mere incubus. In time he will lose even that remnant of self-respect which prevents him now from admitting the Natives to social equality; he will inevitably mix with them and our problems will be further complicated by the creation of a new racial entity.

Up to the present time, it may be broadly stated, the Poor White has been recruited from a class of persons who are incapable of any but rough manual

From Ernest Stubbs, *Tightening Coils: An Essay on Segregation,* n.p., n.d., Rustenberg: the author, 1925, pp. 3–9.

labour. But there are already indications that the competition of Natives is reducing even skilled workmen to the condition of Poor Whites; and this too is the direct and inevitable result of our economic system. It is no use disguising the fact that the Native possesses all the qualities necessary for proficiency in the manual arts and that there is no barrier which will prevent him from setting up serious competition with the white artisan. And the danger lies not so much in the increasing efficiency of the Native as in the debasement of his White Masters, who, in their characters of aristrocrats, tend more and more to lean upon their servants and, so doing, to lose the only qualities which entitle them to mastery. It is an open secret that the white workman especially on the Mines, is only too ready to leave work of a skilled and responsible nature to Native assistants who are intended only for rough manual labour.

The South African slave-economy is slowly destroying the fibre of the white race while it is developing the efficiency of the black.

IV.

There is another and, in some respects, even a blacker side to the picture, revealing the dangers of the intimate social contact of Black and White. Our system requires the presence of the Native in our midst, creating contacts at innumerable points. Contacts lead to fusion and the process, necessarily slow, almost imperceptible in detail, is already discernible in the slums, where the worst elements of White humanity live cheek by jowl with Natives, and in the remoter rural areas, where the white man is deprived of the restraints of civilised life.

There are degrees of colour prejudice in South Africa, and the danger to the White race lies in the breaking-down, by a gradual process of attrition, of a sentiment which, in the last resort, is the mainspring of white sovereignty.

The fusion which is now taking place in the slums and elsewhere might well extend to the higher orders of society if the conditions of intimacy existing in South Africa to-day are perpetuated. Indeed, such fusion is being facilitated by the education and christianisation of the Native people, the deliberate act of the White race itself.

The South African slave-economy, necessitating contact of Black and White, is tending to fusion of Black and White, and, by reason of the overwhelming preponderance of Black, to the absorption of White in Black—something which, in the view of the best elements of the White population, is the ultimate degradation.

V.

There is a tragic irony to be found in the fact that the White Race is not only itself forging the weapon which seems destined for its destruction, but is forging it with such thoroughness and devotion. Slave though the Native may be in the economic sense, he is receiving at the hands of his white masters almost every advantage, short of political and social equality, to make of him a formidable antagonist. Prohibited from indulging their natural inclination to make war upon and exterminate each other, and living in peace and personal freedom, the Native races have been enabled to grow into the Colossus which is threatening the existence of the White population. Freed from the insidious influences of intoxicating spirits which are reserved for the destruction of his betters, hardened by manual labour and the life of the open veld the Native has remained the physical superior of the White man. Educated and christ-ianised, uplifted morally and intellectually, who knows of what he may in time be capable? He has thriven on his contact with civilisation and he is being fit-ted slowly but surely for full economic and political freedom. And the time must come in a South Africa constituted as it is to-day, when he will demand and seize that freedom. An integral part of our economic system, trained by ourselves into an efficient human factor and swarming at our very doors, how indeed can the Native be resisted?

Surely, no people has been faced with a crueller dilemna than the White people of South Africa.

VI.

The danger in which we live as the result of the conditions that have been described is real and urgent. It is being forced at last upon important sections of the white population, but there is still a very considerable number of peo-ple who are blind to the implications of the present system. They fall roughly into two classes, firstly, those who are resigned to an ultimate absorption of the White in the Black population, and who may be dismissed at once as unworthy members of a race whose fundamental characteristic is its instinc-tive combativeness for permanence, and, secondly, those who, relying upon some imaginary and undefined virtue in the Aryan race, which is believed to confer upon it in perpetuity the sovereignty over inferior populations, scoff at the suggestion of danger.

Whatever virtue there may be in the Aryan decays without the proper stimulus and never so rapidly as when he is brought into intimate contact with an inferior race can he hope to survive. The pitiful remnants of the Greek Civilisation, squatted upon and defiled by a people still essentially squalid and barbarous in temper, furnish an example of the fate that may overtake the highest order of human beings. The Aryan Armenians, the Aryan Georgians, the Arian Tadjies of Central Asia constitute in their several communities an inferior and despised caste.

History has the knack of repeating itself; and it is well for us to remember that even an Aryan may be an object of contempt.

VII.

The foregoing brief analysis of the relations of Black and White in South Africa reveals the primary factor which is at work upon the destruction of the White race—namely, the contact of the two races, with its innumerable dam-

aging reactions upon the White. It is contact in the industrial field that has created and is creating more and still more White unemployment and that is sapping the supremacy and prestige of the White race. It is contact at almost every
point in the life of South Africans that is familiarising the two races and imper-
ceptibly but very surely breaking down the barrier of colour and race prejudice. It is contact that makes the preponderating Native population a real and
ever-present menace to the security of the White. It is contact that gives a suicidal flavour to every step taken by the White race for the mental and moral
improvement of the Black.

Continued contact means the utter and irretrievable ruin of the White
races of South Africa.

Their salvation lies in the creation of separate areas for the exclusive occupation of Black and White, maintained severally on the basis of an all-black
and an all-white economy.

We cannot have an all-white South Africa. We can have, with all the elements of permanency a White South Africa and a Black South Africa, side by
side.

2.   D. D. T. Jabavu Advocates Liberalism over Segregation, 1928

*D. D. T. Jabavu, the son of John Tengo Jabavu, was a professor at Fort
Hare, the college for Africans founded in the Eastern Cape in 1916. He
played an active role in missionary and education circles and was a moderate in the ANC. Jabavu worked closely with scholarly liberals such as
W. M. Macmillan in the Bantu-European Joint Councils of the 1920s. These
organizations sponsored discussions on such topics as African urban
problems. In addition, they made recommendations and offered expert
testimony to government commissions and parliamentary committees.*

The key to the whole Native Question is territorial segregation. If the white
people of South Africa were Christian enough to do the Bantu justice in a
thorough-going scheme of territorial segregation then the future would be
promising. But unfortunately Christianity has not yet been practised to that
extent. The first attempt we have had of territorial segregation is that of the
Natives Land Act of 1913. This Act confirmed the Natives in the sole occu-
pancy of their reserves in which they were already overcrowded, proposed the
setting aside of additional areas in which Natives could purchase land and forbade them to purchase in other areas except with the special permission of the

From D. D. T. Jabavu, "Cross-roads of Native Policy," *The Segregation Fallacy and Other Papers (A
Native View of Some South African Inter-Racial Problems)*, Alice Ciski: Lovedale Institution Press,
1928, pp. 99–105. Reprinted by permission.

Government. This Act satisfied no one. The Natives naturally objected to the restriction of their right to purchase and the Europeans were unwilling to have their farms set aside for Native occupation. Two commissions were appointed to recommend the areas which should be set aside but their suggestions have never been accepted. The Act is now thirteen years old, but no additional areas have been opened for Native occupation. On the contrary the evictions of Native tenants who have nowhere to go have been rigorously carried out by the farmers with harrowing results. Both General Smuts and General Hertzog as Prime Ministers have proudly owned this Land Act as their first step towards a segregation policy, to the amazement of the Natives who expected the Act to be either repealed or carried out to its reasonable conclusion. Of all grievances harboured by the Natives against European rule the greatest is this Land Act. Native confidence in the white man has been further undermined by the present Government which within twelve months lays claim to the doubtful record of having introduced a greater number of anti-Native bills in Parliament than any other previous Government: A tax on blankets used only by Natives; the Colour Bar Bill; the increase of Native taxation in three of the provinces; the attempted resuscitation of two defunct odious Pass Laws against Transvaal Native women and Transkei Native voters respectively; the civilized-labour policy that has displaced Native workers by white workers in railways and other industries and other projected anti-Native measures like the Masters and Servants Bill. The present Government are showing the world that their first care is the protection of the white race even at the cost of injustice to the Bantu, their candour has thrown the favourite political expression, "making South Africa a white man's country," into bold relief. We Natives are equally frank in our belief that present-day Christianity is not going to prove influential enough to induce Parliament to provide the land needed for Native development. Hence our lack of faith in the new Hertzog solution. We have no option but to judge it by its stern deeds and not by honeyed words.

Our lack of equal economic opportunity, now confirmed by the legal colour bar, is a stern reality. No cure is offered by the Churches to assuage our ills. We have been further disappointed that General Smuts, who has played an important part in European councils of world policy, has, in his native land, proved helpless in constructive measures of Native policy.

The most influential economic group in the country is that of European farmers. Their clamant need is cheap Native labour to operate their farms. They are solidly opposed to any scheme of segregation calculated to provide more land and independence for black men. These farmers control the government of the country. They rely for their labour on the black man who is squeezed out from his tribal location by the prevalent intolerable congestion. European farmers own large estates, in many cases of five thousand to fifty thousand acres each, while black men are herded together, between thirty and a hundred souls to the square mile of Native-owned land. The belief of the white farmers is that additional land provided for the Natives will react detrimentally on their labour market. This is where the Hertzog compromise breaks down.

What then is our hope? In our view the Cape liberal policy proves itself best. It has stood the test of time, giving the maximum satisfaction to both white and black. The Transvaal policy satisfies only the Northern party and engenders an anti-white feeling in the hearts of the Natives, a feeling that will ultimately recoil disastrously on the whole country. The black man does not ask for much, only for justice, justice in land distribution, justice in economic opportunity and justice in political representation. This is no excessive demand. Historically it has been natural for all races from the time of the Greek helots and Roman plebs. There will never be any inter-racial goodwill in the country until it is granted willingly by the authorities. We Natives deliberately stand or fall by the Cape policy because we know it. The Hertzog compromise we do not know; nor do we see any likelihood of its materialization under existing circumstances and in the light of our knowledge of the psychology of the white South African. Our conviction is that the Hertzog conception of segregation is chimerical. It has no parallel in the world. What we observe in actuality is the complete racial, territorial, and political segregation of France, Italy and Portugal. If we were allowed to live in our own autonomous Crown Colony, like Basutoland or the Bechuanaland Protectorate, extracted from the Union of South Africa and governed direct from Downing Street, then we would heartily say: "Yes." But the day of such a system of segregation has passed irrevocably.

The farmer-politicians of the northern provinces of South Africa are not prepared to make any sacrifices for the purposes of enlarging the supply of Native land, for that would work against the interests of those who depend on Native labour for their farms and industries. Some apposite comments are made in the Report of the Government Economic Commission (published February 1926) with reference to this argument:—"The contact of the Native and the European has lasted too long, and the economic co-operation is too intimate and well established, for the Native to be excluded from European areas and European industries. The provision of adequate Native reserves has been delayed too long for it to be possible for the present Native population of the Union to live without dependence on outside employment, and it was far too long the policy of the Union to drive the Native by taxation and other devices to work for Europeans for it to be possible now to exclude him from the field of employment he is occupying."

We should have thought that the white South African could have realized, in his personal and business interest if from no nobler motive, that the economic development of the five million Bantu was a paying proposition for his markets. It is a curious spectacle to see one million and a half white settlers transporting all sorts of products to foreign markets and neglecting the five million potential consumers in their own country. In fact the lack of progress among the Natives is manifestly an economic hindrance to the white commercial community. Booker T. Washington was correct in saying that you cannot keep the black man down in the gutter without keeping yourself there too. The one process inevitably involves the other.

The application of legislative machinery, such as the Colour Bar legislation, by a modern civilized people for the purpose of repressing a backward race must be the despair of the rest of the civilized world. To quote again from the Report: "To the Commissioners it appears to be an unsound policy to exclude by legislation a class which has no representation in the legislature from the economic developments at present open to them, for the benefit of a politically privileged class. The white man has less to fear from an improvement than from a deterioration in the economic status of the Native. . . . The Commissioners declare that a market for South African manufactures, from which much is hoped to be found, is the growing demands of the Native population, but any growth will be checked by a policy that restricts the Native's opportunities for employment and so keeps down his wages."

Our last hope lies with the world of the Chruch and its inculcation of higher ethical standards among the rulers of South Africa, where the underlying belief is that the application of Christianity to economics spells suicide. To believe this is to confess that Christianity is a failure. A Transvaal farmer-politician in commenting upon the Hertzog proposals on Native policy says: "A solution is impossible. It can only mean the extermination of the Native, and such a solution the white man will strenuously oppose, not because he loves the Kafir so much, nor because he needs the Kafir so badly, but simply because there is such a thing as right and justice, and because our deep-rooted Christian civilization prevents us from flying to remedies which are elemental, even if we had the power or strength to make use of them. Indeed, it is just this ingrained conception of fairness and equity that makes the problem so difficult. We wish to apply Christian principles, but apparently we cannot do so without committing suicide."

We do not believe that the application of the principles of Christianity to economics is suicidal, but the duty of proving and preaching this falls to the Church. The most influential Church in South Africa is the Dutch Reformed Church, inasmuch as it claims the great majority of our rulers. We Natives are not in a position to bring any influence to bear directly within the councils of this Church, but we highly appreciate the recent important European-Bantu Conference convened by this Church at Johannesburg in 1923. Therefore we urge that the sister Churches should intercede in our behalf and pray with us that a new heart be created in our rulers. We trust to the Almighty God to help us out of our gloom. Laymen can help us through their Rotary Clubs and Round Table Conferences. We can do our share in the existing Joint Councils, Native Welfare Associations and other inter-racial conferences (such as the European-Bantu Conference) which have proved effective to a considerable degree in bringing together the moderate leaders of all sections and races, dispelling much mutual ignorance and suspicion and creating knowledge and good understanding.

3. A Leading Liberal Asks, Will White Policies Allow Black Self-Development, 1935

Alfred Hoernle (1880–1943) was a professor of philosophy at the University of Witwatersrand and a leading liberal, although a strand of idealism wound through his thought. He was one of the founders and the primary theorist of the South African Institute of Race Relations, a major liberal organization and center for research on race relations in South Africa from the 1930s on.

The famous French statesman, Talleyrand, is credited with the epigram that 'language was given to man to conceal his thoughts.' If Talleyrand had been even more of a cynic than he actually was, he might have said, just as fittingly, that most men use language as a substitute for thinking, and that if they conceal anything by it, they conceal from themselves the fact that they are not thinking at all, but only making meaningless noises. We all acquire, in greater or less degree, the fatal habit of using verbal formulae which have an emotionally satisfying ring, but which express no live thinking, no grasp of reality at all.

This general principle is admirably illustrated by the slogan, so fashionable just now in discussions of the 'Native Problem,' viz., give the Natives the chance 'to develop along their own lines.' It sounds so eminently right—so exactly like what we want for ourselves—that it does not seem necessary to stop and think what, if anything, it really means. What more could the Natives reasonably ask? What more could we possibly give? Yet, when I ask the apostles of Native self-development to explain in detail just what these 'lines' are which are the Natives' very 'own,' and what are we doing, or ought to do, in order to help them develop along these lines, I can get no intelligible answer.

Here are some undeniable facts:—

(a) Every Native who is ambitious to better his position and qualify for wider opportunities and better pay, is trying to get an education of the European type for himself, or his children.

(b) We, on our side, because we need Native servants and workers, and want them as efficient as they can be taught to become, are drilling and moulding them to our requirements, to the European pattern of doing things.

(c) The efforts of the Missions to christianize the Natives are profoundly transforming their religious beliefs and practices and their social institutions (cf., e.g., the substitution of monogamy for polygamy, or the missionary objections to lobola).

From Alfred Hoernle, "Can South African Natives Develop Along Their Own Lines?", *Race and Reason*, Johannesburg: Witwatersrand University Press, 1945, pp. 87–93.

(d) Our Government, by demanding taxes to be paid in money, compels Natives to earn wages and imposes on them a money-economy utterly foreign to their 'own' system; and by its methods of administration and by its courts it introduces among them European ideas and standards, even when it professedly administers 'Native law.'

Yet, against facts such as these the Natives are told to 'develop along their own lines'!

When confronted with these, and other, evidences of the overpowering impact of Western civilization on the Natives of South Africa, the defenders of self-development generally remember, with a sigh of relief, that the Natives have, at any rate, one thing which is their very own, viz., their language. Here, then, is a line of their own to develop: let there be instruction in the vernacular, or the mother-tongue, in Native schools!

Apart from its intrinsic educational soundness, this is a principle which, I find, is readily supported by my Afrikaans-speaking friends who, having successfully struggled for the recognition of Afrikaans as an official language and for its development from a patois into a genuine 'kultuur-taal,' adequate to the expression of the whole content of Western civilization, are anxious to encourage a corresponding development of the Native languages.

Certainly, this development has begun and will continue. Look, e.g., at our Native newspapers, one of which, *The Bantu World,* regularly appears in five, and often in six, languages, thus bearing witnss to the growing number of Natives who not only speak, but read and write, their own languages. And there is a small, but growing, band of Native authors who, like W. B. Vilakazi, are exploring and developing the resources of their mother-tongue both for verse and for prose composition.

But, this does not alter the fact that the Native who would count as 'educated' in South Africa, or even who would merely hold his own in the bitter struggle of the economic underdog for mere existence, must learn English and/or Afrikaans, as well as his own language. In the Native Reserves he can get on with his own language only: but as soon as he comes out (as most of them must, sooner or later) into a White area and has to fend for himself in the labour-market, he is handicapped in proportion to his ignorance of the two European languages. They are, after all, the 'official' languages through which he is governed and tried in the courts. They are the languages through which his employers give him their orders, often bellowing them at him with a blustering rudeness intended to remind him of 'his place' as a social inferior. (Note, e.g., the tone in which many officials in post offices and pass offices speak, or rather roar, at Natives.) How many White employers can explain to a Native in his own language what they want him to do? He can give satisfaction in his work only by understanding their language. And, often he finds it necessary to know both European languages, for there are Afrikaners who resent being spoken to by a Native in English, just as there are English-speaking South Africans who lose their tempers when a Native addresses them in Afrikaans. And, lastly, if the Native wishes to make his own something of the knowledge of the world around him, some geography, or science, or history, or if he wishes to understand something of the principles and ideals of his rulers, he must learn the European languages in order to have access to their literatures.

Thence results the paradox that, whereas White experts are enthusiasts for the principle of mother-tongue instruction in Native education, many Natives look upon the principle with suspicion, because they fear that, under the cloak of encouraging the use of their own languages, they are going to be deprived of access to the languages of their rulers and employers. Nor do they fear only the resulting economic handicap and political helplessness: even more they fear that language segregation will mean their exclusion from the White man's knowledge and civilization. There may be no just ground for such suspicion at all. Yet, who of us Whites, if he had the misfortune to be born a Native of South Africa, would not approach every seeming boon offered from the White side in the spirit of the Vergilian: *Timeo Danaos et dona ferentes?* [Fear the Greeks, especially bearing gifts]

In any case, language is, after all, mainly an instrument of expression. What does the concept of the 'Natives' own' mean when we look beyond language at the content of culture?

Certainly, there is such a thing as Bantu culture; and for all that it was dubbed 'savage' and 'heathen' by the Europeans who first came into contact with it, it has, as those who know it at first hand bear witness, many admirable features—admirable even by White standards. Much of that culture still survives even after more than a hundred years of contact with Whites—more of it in the Reserves than among the Natives in White rural areas and in urban locations. Are not over three million Natives in the Union's official Year-Book classed as 'having no religion,' because to the Christian compilers of that book the Natives' 'own' religion is not a 'religion'?

Well then—is this original, officially religionless, Bantu culture to be developed as being the Natives' 'own lines'? And, if so, in what direction? By striving to undo all the changes in it due to European influences? By restoring it, as far as possible, to what it was in pre-European days? By keeping it stereotyped thus, and fending it off from all further infiltration of European culture elements? That would, indeed, be splendid! We could then advertise to overseas tourists, not only our Game Reserve with its lions and elephants, but also our Native Reserves—a sort of human zoo—with its specially preserved specimens of black-skinned savages and primitive cultures.

When I read the familiar diatribes against making the Natives into 'imitation Europeans,' I cannot help wondering whether this is perhaps what is meant. For, if in any way Natives are to be allowed, and even encouraged, to acquire European learning and culture, I am quite unable to discover where the advocates of this view would draw the line between 'imitation' and 'reality.' Does 'imitation' consist in adopting European clothes (prominent item on most missionaries' programme)? Is conversion of Christianity at bottom nothing but 'imitation'? Is it learning to read and write? Is it living in a location-house, sleeping on a bed, cooking on a stove, instead of living in a hut, sleeping on the floor, cooking at an open fire? Is it riding a bicycle or driving a car? Is it learning, in mine and factory, to wield European tools and handle European machines? I repeat, for I want to know: what is here imitation and what reality? May I, to bring the point home, ask those who inveigh against imitation and 'caricature' Europeans, whether they employ Native men for domestic service. If they do, are they aware that the work which Native men do in White houses is, in traditional Native culture, women's work? And yet we talk glibly of 'letting the Native develop along his own lines'!

Alternatively, there is the policy of giving the Natives access to whatever of European civilization they feel they need and wish to have. Their 'own,' then, will mean, not only what they have, or had, apart from contact with White civilization, but also all that in this contact they have acquired or are struggling to acquire—all, in fact, which they can make their own. Look at the development ('progress') of Japan, as an analogy. Are the Japanese 'imitation' Europeans because they have made their own European science, European (or American) factory methods of production, and, above all, European military organization and weapons of destruction?

We have to choose between these two senses of 'own'—the sense in which only that is the Natives' own which is different from what is European; and the sense in which their 'own' is all that they can make their own, and indeed must make their own, if they are to survive at all under the conditions which European conquest and overlordshop, economic and political, impose upon them. Whether they like it or not, whether we like it or not, historical events which we cannot, and do not want to, undo, have drawn the Natives into the orbit of Western civilization, and the lines of their development must be within that orbit. The only real question is, whether under the conditions of life which we Whites impose upon them, they have a chance to make their own the best or the worst of Western civilization.

I conclude with a final reflection: The complementary aspect of the 'develop-along-their-own lines' slogan is the out-cry against 'assimilation' and 'detribalization.'

Let us look these words in the face, allowing their meaning to be illuminated by the facts.

The most completely assimilated and detribalized Natives I have come across here in Johannesburg belong to the so-called 'Oorlam' group. They claim to be descendants of Natives who either came up from the Colony with the Voortrekkers as their servants, or who were, as children, 'apprenticed' to Voortrekker families, and later, as grown-ups, remained permanently with their White masters as domestic servants or farm-hands. Often their ancestors had been apprenticed so young that they had only a child's knowledge of their 'own' language. In any case, they all learnt Afrikaans, and adopted it as 'their own' speech so thoroughly that it became, and often still is, the literal 'mother-tongue' of their descendants. Their ways became European ways;

their standard of life—at their social level as servants—a European standard of life. From Native culture and tribal affiliations they became completely divorced. Of course, there was for them 'no equality in church or state'; they had no political rights; they were members of a distinct Sending Kerk, organized as a separate entity on Dutch Reformed principles; they were, as servants, excluded from social equality with their masters. But, for all that, they were detribalized, Europeanized, indeed Afrikanerized, in virtue of their assimilating their masters' language and European ways of life. And I find that they are proud of the fact and consider themselves, not without reason, as an *élite* among their fellows whose contact with White civilization has not been as long or as intimate as theirs.

For me the moral is: culture is essentially assimilable and communicable, and will be imparted or acquired simply through human contacts and relationships, whatever be the political and social barriers and discriminations by which these contacts and relationships are regulated.

I say therefore: what happened to these Oorlams when they were integrated into the social structure of Voortrekker South Africa, and when they there assimilated, within the limits of their status, the language and the ways of their White masters, that same thing is happening at the present day, and will continue to happen in the future, to vastly greater numbers of Natives under the conditions of the vastly more complex, and above all industrialized, type of Western civilization which has taken root in South Africa since Voortrekker days.

It is in the context of facts, such as these, that the phrase 'let the Natives develop along their own lines,' must be interpreted, if it is to have an intelligible meaning at all. Hence, to the question in the title of this paper, 'Can the Natives develop along their own lines?' there is—if 'their own lines' are to be 'lines fundamentally different from those of White South Africans'—only one answer: 'They cannot.' Placed as they are in South Africa, they cannot develop untouched by, nor apart from, Western civilization. And what is more, they do not want to. What they will retain of their traditional past will colour what they acquire from Western civilization, just as the folkways of the different peoples of Europe are now but nuances within the general type of a uniform civilization. With our help, or against our wish, they will take over from us and make their own, to the best of their ability and opportunity, whatever in Western civilization they need and desire most. And we can't say them 'Nay.'

4.   Clements Kadalie Explains the Aims of the I.C.U., 1928

Clements Kadalie (1896–1951) came to South Africa from Malawi. His Industrial and Commercial Workers Union played a prominent role in African protest during the 1920s, when the ANC proved relatively quiescent. From his start as a Cape Town dock activist in 1919, by 1928 Kadalie led about one hundred and fifty thousand I.C.U. members, especially in rural areas in the Eastern Cape and Natal. The movement eventually split over the question of finances and communist influence and crumbled under government pressure.

'That this Conference most respectfully requests the government to recognize its decisions to exclude agricultural labourers and domestic servants from the scope of the wage bill, and to acknowledge the injustice of such exclusion and the overwhelming claims of agricultural labourers to the advantages sought to confer upon the workers in general under this bill. Further, this conference submits that the agricultural labourer is the hardest worked servant in point of length of working day, and should therefore come first for consideration in any scheme for improvement of wages and conditions of employment. And further that this conference elect a Wages Committee to proceed to Cape Town with a view to give evidence before the Select Committee of the House of Assembly, and that the Minister of Labour should be acquainted with this request.

'That this Conference congratulates the Government on the introduction of the Wage Bill now before the Parliament and which augurs as well for the future of all industrial workers, but we would humbly suggest the necessity of so amending the provisions of Section I of the bill as to categorically define industrial spheres to which the Act will apply and to insert an enabling section for the minister to extend its scope by an amending act, thus according an opportunity for full discussion of the merits of the measure from time to time in the interests of those concerned. Should the Bill become law in its present form, the conference fears that party political considerations may act as a brake upon the Minister in his exercise of the powers conferred by Section (I) of the Bill.

'That while fully realizing that replacement of Natives by Europeans in State undertakings is the settled policy of the government, and therefore without entering into any futile discussion of the pros and cons of the policy, this conference of the organized African workers most respectfully submits to the government that in the absence of a definite scheme of land settlement as a compensatory measure the enormity of injustice indicated upon the victims of this one-sided policy is incalculable and will positively provoke a deep-seated sense of resentment which the country can ill afford to ignore.

From Clements Kadalie, "The Aims and Methods of the I.C.U.," *My Life and the I.C.U.*, London: Frank Cass & Co. Ltd., 1970, pp. 75–77. Copyright © 1970 by Frank Cass & Co., Ltd. Reprinted by permission of Frank Cass & Co., Ltd., 890-900 Eastern Avenue, Ilford, Essex, England.

'That this conference of the Industrial and Commercial Workers' Union of Africa, requests the employees of labour in the dock areas throughout the union ports, to introduce a scale of wages with that which prevails in the Cape Town Docks. Further, that employees in the docks be paid accordingly, since the custom at present in vogue of engaging labourers in the Cape Town docks and discharging them at any moment, and paid for hourly and one-quarter day, is determined to the interest of the workers in those areas, whose work is mostly that of serving the general public, and that this conference authorizes the Executive Council to approach the Minister of Labour with a view to obtaining his support in bringing about the proposed condition.

'That this Conference of organized Native and Coloured is the opinion that Passes, no matter what shape or form, are nothing more or less than an institution of the present capitalist system of government to reduce the African workers to a state of abject servility so as to facilitate their utmost exploitation, and further, this conference condemns the proposals of the joint council of Europeans and Natives intended for submission to the prime minister, but in the opinion of this conference the only alternative is abolition of the Pass System.

'That this Conference requests the Government to introduce into the House of Assembly a short Bill so amending the Industrial Conciliation Act No. II of 1924 as to include Native Miners and Colliers in the definition of "Employee". Further, the conference considers it is a grievous wrong to keep those workers entirely out of the pale of the Act while other classes of labourers are having the benefit of the machinery provided thereunder for consultation and conciliation and in the event of a clash of interest arbitration and meditation.

'That in view of the fact that there are so many complaints from the Natives about the Natives working under contracts in the Mines, the position of a recruited Native working under contract being no better than that of a convict who is not in a position to choose his working place, his class of work, his sleeping place, his kind and quality of food and his wages, this conference considers that the time has arrived when the government should consider the amendment of the Native Labour Regulation Act, of 1911, in so far as it affects recruiting systems. This conference requests the Minister of Labour to arrange for a conference with the representatives of this Union with a view to arriving at a system by which the natives should be enabled to reach the working centres, and further, this conference views with alarm the practice followed by the mine companies of compelling the voluntary Natives to work under contracts as though they were recruiting workers.

'That while desirous to avoid embarrassing the government in its laudable attempts to devise effective means of settling industrial disputes in times of emergency, this conference wished to call the attention of parliament and the public to the fact that the powers conferred on the Minister under Section II (I) of Emergency Powers Bill are constitutionally too enormous, and virtually obviates the necessity of an Indemnity Bill, which affords an opportunity, if not the only constitutional means known to modern democracies, of examining in detail the actions of a Parliamentary Executive on occasions of public disorders; indeed the section constitutes the sapping of the foundations upon which rests the constitutional doctrines of the rule of the law.

'That this Conference of organized Natives and Coloured workers gratefully records its appreciations of the material improvement of compensation benefits to the Native mine workers contemplated under Section 35 of the Miners Phthisis Acts Consolidation Bill, but we wish to draw the attention of the Minister to the urgent need of increasing the amount of compensation payable on death from the paltry sum of £10.'

5. The Hymns of Isaiah Shembe, 1911–1926

Isaiah Shembe (1870-1935) founded the Zulu's Church of the Nazarene, a prophetic healing institution. Shembe's order became the largest of the African separatist churches and one of the biggest denominations in South Africa. When Shembe died in 1935, his son, a graduate of Fort Hare, replaced him as leader.

The separatist churches exerted a profound impact on African life. Although the prophetic healing or "Zionist" churches had their own political agendas, they tended to steer their members away from secular concerns.

The following hymns were written between the founding of the church (1911) and 1926.

Hymn No. 17

1. He who is beaten is not thrown
                                    away
let him not despise himself,
rise up, rise up
Ye Africans.

2. The form of the doorway
causes you to bend,
Rise up, rise up
Ye Africans

3. The enemies of Jehova
rise up against you
rise up, rise up
Ye Africans.

4. Those are given kingly authority
upon the mountain,

From G. C. Oosthuizen, *The Theology of a South African Messiah: An Analysis of the Hymnal of the Church of the Nazarites,* Leiden: E. J. Brill, 1967, pp. 159–160, 164. Copyright © 1967 by E. J. Brill, Leiden, The Netherlands. Reprinted by permission.

Rise up, rise up
Ye Africans.

5. They already want to deprive
the eternal kingly authority,
Rise up, rise up
Ye Africans.

Hymn No. 24

1. See he comes by way of the
                              clouds
He will come to call his people,
even those who are asleep will
                              wake up
from the dust of the earth
Amen Halelujah
Praise ye all.

2. It is coming, it is coming
Ukuphakama
it comes with the saints
of the *iNkosi* of heaven.
Amen Halelujah
Praise ye all.

3. *iNkosi* himself in person
will come down from heaven
Coming with the many
of Ekuphakameni.
Amen Halelujah
Praise ye all.

4. Those who went out, we being
                              disappointed.
Ekuphakameni,
today they are coming
clothed with victory alone.
Amen Halelujah
Praise ye all.

5. Today rejoice ye,
Ye keepers of the laws.
You are going to be anointed
                              to sufficiency
though having (fulfilled)
      accomplished the laws.
Amen Halelujah
Praise ye all.

6. What shall ye be rewarded with
Ye transgressors of the laws,
Put your ears and hear
the din of the saints.
Amen Halelujah
Praise ye all.

Hymn No. 60

1. Praise Jehova
because He is righteous
because His kindness remains
                forever
because He is righteous.

2. He remembered Africa
because He is righteous,
He did not forget his people
because He is righteous.

3. He created the heaven
and also the earth,
it is the work of His hands
because He is good.

4. You remembered your people
whose hips are naked.
You sent them Isaiah, your Servant
because He is good.

5. During those days
the deaf will hear
that which is preached in this
                book
because He is righteous

6. Those who put on nothing
on their feet,
He prepared them to enter
in a place which is holy.

7. Even those who shave heads
shave the heads on the side,
Even those who shave chins
through breaking of the laws.

8. And those who enter with shoes
in the house of Jehova
turning it into a house of play
through the breaking of the laws.

**Scene at Sharpeville,
March 21, 1960**

PART 4

The Rise of the Apartheid State,

1936–1976

*T*he course of South African history from 1936 to 1976 is one of sweeping and complex transformation. At the beginning of the period, South Africa had begun to industrialize, yet it was basically a poor country. The African majority had lost a large proportion of its traditional land and resources and was only partially integrated into the modern wage economy. Many Africans had to participate in both modern and traditional economic sectors to earn even an inadequate living. The few who had gained a prosperous foothold in the modern economy were increasingly undermined by hostile government legislation. But poverty also touched large elements of the white population. By 1976 South African destitution had not been eliminated but redistributed. Poverty among whites had substantially vanished, but it had deepened among wide segments of the burgeoning black population.

Meanwhile, a vast bureaucratic state had grown up, one dedicated to broad control of the entire society. This surge to centralized wealth and power was accompanied by intensifying white domination. Although segregation, racial prejudice, and oppression had long been a fact of life, white rule in the second half of the twentieth century became efficient, thorough, and often brutal. In particular, whites increasingly denied the aspirations of the small but growing African elite.

We can cast such changes in terms of the defeat of liberalism. White liberals took a paternalist, gradualist, legalist, and optimistic approach to defending African interests. Their paternalism led them to counsel Africans against militant action, lest African protest inflame white opinion and frustrate the liberals' task. Their gradualism offered token political and social rights for Africans only after a long, slow process of acculturation. Their admonishment to Africans, "not now," did not immediately differ from what the supporters of baaskap told Africans: "Never." Their emphasis on legal procedures revealed a determination to work within the system, no matter how biased it was against nonwhites. Their optimism led them to accept such defeats as the passage of the Native Trust and Land Act and Representation of Natives Act in 1936, even though these measures segregated South Africa more thoroughly than ever, further closed the land market to Africans, and repealed the limited African vote in the Cape Province.

Despite these setbacks, the period of the Second World War (1939–1945) gave liberals a glimmer of hope. Faced with wartime labor needs, the government dropped some restrictions on African economic opportunity, and African movement into urban jobs accelerated. Segregation, said Prime Minister Jan Smuts, had fallen on evil days. But white liberals in the United party—the coalition party that had formed in 1934 out of Smuts's South African party and Hertzog's National party—could not sustain these advantages after the war.

By the mid-1940s, the old African National Congress alliance with white liberals had come under heavy attack from within ANC ranks. A new generation of activists, led by Nelson Mandela and Oliver Tambo, founded the Congress Youth League and challenged the older leadership. In 1949 a compromise candidate, Dr. J. S. Moroka, replaced the old-guard figure, Dr. A. B. Xuma, as president of the ANC; three years later, Chief Albert Luthuli began his fifteen-year presidency committed to decisive protest action. By then the ANC had fully rejected the gradualist and legalist counsels of white liberals, though it retained its full commitment to nonviolence. It sought full exercise of political and civil rights for all Africans. At the same time, a strong strain of "Africanism" in the Congress Youth League implied that Africans might reject the universalist principle of liberalism that presumed a common basis for the rights of all human beings. Throughout the 1950s, a struggle between Africanism and universalism would rage within the ANC. The group's 1955 Freedom Charter signaled a decisive victory for universalism, as the ANC remained committed to an alliance between like-minded people of all races. The opponents of this universalist commitment seceded in 1959 and formed the Pan Africanist Congress (PAC).

During these years, Afrikaner nationalists had grown more militant. When the National and South African parties fused in 1934, not all Nationalists had agreed to this merger. A small group instead formed the "Purified" National party. Closely associated with it were other Afrikaner organizations, especially the secret Afrikaner Broederbond and the Ossewa Brandwag (Oxwagon Sentinel), which later became a quasimilitary, profascist organization. During the Second World War, Afrikaners in the Broederbond and Ossewa Brandwag worked for the victory of Nazi Germany. (A number of leaders within the two groups, including Hendrik Verwoerd, had been educated in Nazi Germany and admired Nazi ideas.)

In 1948 the National party stunned South Africa by taking power in that year's general elections. The key campaign slogan of the election encapsulated in a new word, apartheid. At first no one fully knew what the term would mean, but planners and theorists at Afrikaner universities and within the Broederbond were working to define it. In the forty-two turbulent years from 1948 to 1990, apartheid became synonymous with racist oppression. It was that and much more: a complex system of social engineering created by a vast network of laws and bureaucratic mechanisms. Apartheid provided for systematic racial separation to be applied to all imaginable aspects of life. Based on a version of Calvinist theology, apartheid ostensibly offered Afrikaners—and, theoretically, peoples such as the Zulu or Sotho—a free space to enjoy full national rights within South Africa.

As enacted in legislation in the thirty years after 1948, the apartheid system enveloped all aspects of South African life. The keystone of the system was the

Group Areas Act of 1950, which built on earlier land legislation and separated the entire country into unequal black and white areas. The forcible relocation of people under its provisions formed one of the most oppressive aspects of the system. A second crucial piece of legislation came with the Population Registration Act of 1950, which required every person over the age of sixteen to register and carry an identity card as a member of a particular race. A huge bureaucracy carried out and enforced this system.

The secret to enforcing this system of racial groups and group areas lay in the pass laws, which required Africans to carry a reference book to prove their right to be in areas of the country set aside for whites. Africans found in white urban areas without passes were sent back to the countryside, or "endorsed out"; the government carried out three hundred thousand or more pass-law prosecutions annually during the height of apartheid. In addition, an elaborate system of job allocation reserved skilled and highly paid jobs for whites.

In the quest for thorough separation of the races, the government between 1951 and 1956 attacked and destroyed the remaining common-roll franchise of the Cape Coloured people. At the same time, the National party government abolished remaining indirect representation of Aricans in the government by proposing to give Africans full political rights outside the white-dominated state. The administration proceeded to develop the African reserves into homelands, which would eventually become separate independent nations for Africans. Thus members of African nations, such as Xhosa or Zulu, would lose their South African citizenship and become citizens of their homeland nations. The chief architect of this plan, Henrik Verwoerd, first as native minister (1948–1958) and then as prime minister (1958–1966), contended that this policy would provide liberty and justice for all. Critics pointed out the fraudulent nature of this independence, which established "countries" for over 80 percent of the population on only 13 percent of the land area of South Africa.

The social engineers of apartheid took over the entire system of mission education of Africans and consigned it to the Bantu Affairs department. Bantu education sought primarily to give Africans sufficient training so that they could satisfy the labor needs of the white-dominated economy. Nevertheless, primary education—and eventually secondary and higher educational institutions—were extended on a "tribal" basis to serve the needs of the "independent" nations being developed in the homelands.

The apartheid system also regulated interracial social contacts. The Immorality Act of 1950, which strengthened an earlier law, proscribed interracial sexual relations, and the Prohibition of Mixed Marriages Act (1949) outlawed marriages between individuals with different racial classifications. These laws were an important expression of white fears, but for Africans they proved relatively minor irritants in the overall system of oppressive legislation. In the mixed neighborhoods of the Western Cape, however, where racial identities were ambiguous, these laws at times inflicted considerable personal hardship.

Apartheid's creators defended the system as a manifestation of the will of God and dealt with their opponents harshly. Under a sequence of mandates—the Suppression of Communism Act (1950), the Terrorism Act (1967), the Internal Security Act (1976), and others—all avenues of legal recourse were closed off for anti-apartheid organizations. The first act not only outlawed the Communist party but created a vague standard for the prosecution of individuals whom the government deemed to be furthering the goals of communism. Later provisions established the principle of banning* for individuals and organizations and repeatable six-month imprisonment in solitary confinement without charges. Eventually, the enforcers of apartheid went beyond such oppressive rulings to assume powers with no basis at all in statute law.

Despite such harsh and determined measures, apartheid did not go unchallenged. The ANC-led Defiance Campaign of 1952 ended with the government's enacting draconian punishments for any symbolic breaking of the law. After 1952 the struggle continued in many arenas: resistance to the destruction of urban neighborhoods, such as Sophiatown, Cato Manor, and District Six; bus boycotts; demonstrations against the application of the pass system to women; and protest against the repeal of the Cape Coloured vote in the Cape Province. When the ANC-led Congress Alliance† met in 1955 to draft the Freedom Charter, the fundamental statement of principle for the anti-apartheid movement, the government responded immediately by accusing one hundred and sixty-two people of high treason. Even though they were all acquitted, the trial tied down the opposition in legal battles for six years.

In 1960, following the split between the ANC and the PAC, the PAC launched its anti-pass campaign. The government responded with force, killing sixty-eight demonstrators at Sharpeville on March 21. But the campaign pressed on, quickly swamping the prisons and straining the capacity of the state to control the unrest. The government was forced to suspend the pass laws. At first the protest seemed to succeed, but the government quickly turned the tables by banning the PAC and ANC and by assuming new powers. In secret deliberations after being banned, both the ANC and PAC, deprived of all legal means of protest, reluctantly decided to initiate armed struggle. Neither organization had much success in their early sabotage campaigns, and when the government caught and arrested some important ANC leaders at their hideout in Rivonia farm in 1964, the government gained the upper hand decisively. Resistance ground on throughout the 1960s and early 1970s, but to no avail.

The official version of Afrikaner history in this period emphasized triumph. It focused on the progressive defeat and scattering of the enemies of apartheid, the successive electoral successes of the National party by increasing majorities, the burgeoning prosperity of South Africa, the phasing out of "poor whiteism,"†† and finally, the achievement of the long-sought Republic with South Africa's separation from the British Commonwealth.

Another version of South African history would emphasize neither the anti-apartheid opposition's struggle nor government victories but simply life under

---

*banning: the outlawing of organizations; when an individual was banned, he or she could not publish, be quoted by any publication, or congregate with more than two other people at once. A banned person could not leave a prescribed district and had to report to the authorities periodically.

† Congress Alliance: the alliance, under the leadership of the African National Congress from the 1950s onward, of organizations opposed to apartheid and in pursuit of a democratic South African society; these included the mainly white Congress of Democrats, which included many former members of the banned Communist party, the Indian Congress, and the Colored People's Organization.

†† poor whiteism: the phenomenon of deep poverty among large numbers of whites, especially rural Afrikaners, in twentieth-century South Africa; its eradication was a priority of all South African governments after scholars studied the problem in the early 1920s.

apartheid and the emerging contradictions of the system. Verwoerd had predicted that by the mid-1970s the movement of Africans to urban areas would see substantial reversal. But with rapid population growth and the surging labor needs of the growing economy, quite the opposite happened. More and more Africans moved toward the cities, and full-time efforts to "endorse out"—to send back to the countryside—"surplus" Africans had little impact. By the early 1970s, the growing light-manufacturing sector needed African workers and wanted the freedom to negotiate with responsible union leaders; it also desired African consumers with purchasing power. The old assumptions of baaskap were becoming obsolete for an increasing proportion of the white public, including the ruling Nationalist elite.

In the meantime, a generation and more of Africans had grown up under apartheid and had been educated by the Bantu education system. Deprived of the role models of the banned, imprisoned, exiled leaders of the ANC, the new generation started over. In student organizations and church discussion groups, young Africans worked out a philosophy of "black consciousness." They had no intention of challenging the government's policies immediately, but instead hoped to pursue projects of consciousness raising, self-help, identity, and pride. Would the government allow them this? It incessantly reassured its critics around the world that Africans had free space for such development. The black consciousness movement called its bluff.

The government quickly demonstrated its unwillingness to allow Bantu Education to produce independent thinkers. In 1976 students violently rejected new government educational policies that required that certain subjects be taught in Afrikaans. After more than a decade of quiescence, African opposition exploded in 1976. It was not the older, banned, and exiled organizations who took the lead this time, but the township dwellers, especially the schoolchildren, who rose up spontaneously against the new government regulations. The disturbances started in Soweto in June and halted Bantu Education all over South Africa for the next two years. Although not inspired or led by the ANC, these events provided the occasion for the organization to recover its strength and resume effective leadership in the anti-apartheid struggle.

Another piece of the South African puzzle in this period concerns the country's international standing and reputation. In the 1930s, South Africa had been virtually in step with the colonial policies of the rest of the Western world. The major colonial powers—Britain, France, Belgium, and the Netherlands—were still committed to long-term colonial "responsibilities," which they pursued in ways not markedly different from those of South Africa. But after the Second World War, Britain moved toward colonial development and rapid decolonization while South Africa proceeded in the opposite direction. In the United Nations, newly independent India quickly became a critic of South Africa, and South Africa's application to move from League of Nations Mandate to United Nations Trusteeship authority over South West Africa was refused.

The beginnings of the Cold War had coincided with the victory of the vigorously anticommunist National party in 1948. Indeed, the Western powers and South Africa were concerned about growing communist influence in Africa and the colonial world in general. Britain pursued a policy of preempting communists by transferring power to responsible nationalist leaders. The South African government tended to believe, by contrast, that nationalist leaders were the communists and that decolonization constituted an abject surrender to the enemies of "Western civilization." Thus, as decolonization proceeded and African states

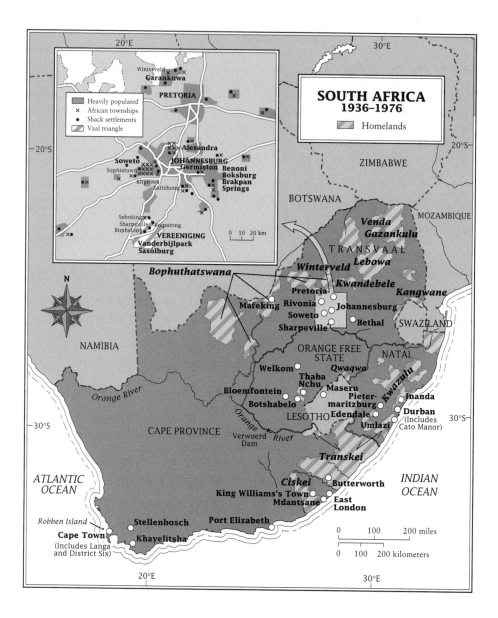

became independent, a gap in policy toward the Third World widened between South Africa and the Western powers. Nevertheless, although Western powers criticized apartheid, they did not yet seek to punish or isolate South Africa. South Africa, in fact, was an important ally of the West in the Cold War.

From 1948 to the 1970s, both the South African government and the growing anti-apartheid movement in Western countries waged major campaigns for support from opinion. Government propaganda trumpeted economic progress for all South Africans, the region's value as a trading partner producing scarce resources, the supposed benefits to Africans of homeland self-government, and South Africa's role as a bulwark against communism.

At the same time, the Western countries gradually became acquainted with oppression in South Africa through books. Leading the way in fostering outside awareness of conditions in South Africa was Alan Paton's Novel, Cry, the Beloved Country *(1947). Father Trevor Huddleston's* Naught for Your Comfort *(1956) recounted the destruction of Sophiatown. Journalists' records, especially works by Basil Davidson* (Report on Southern Africa, *1952) and Anthony Sampson* (Drum, *1956) also played a major role in spreading news about apartheid. The novels of Andre Brink and the works of Nadine Gordimer also awakened Western interest in South Africa, though both authors were far from anti-apartheid polemicists.*

The reporting of the events of 1960, especially the Sharpeville massacre, reflected a quantum jump in international criticism of South African racial policies. UNESCO and International Defense and Aid Fund publications on the sufferings of Africans under apartheid quickly garnered increased circulation. Organizations tied to the American civil-rights movement kept South African issues alive, and apartheid became a continuous concern rather than an occasional issue linked to big news stories. The 1976 Soweto disturbances received prime-time news coverage across the globe. Soon international concern about apartheid seemed powerful enough to shape conditions within South Africa. The tensions within that country and the mounting chorus of international criticism combined to make 1976 a decisive turning point, as the end of the apartheid regime drew near.

Apartheid in Theory and Practice

1. The Limits of Liberalism, 1939

Edgar Brookes was a moderate liberal and a white Native senator who spoke out for African interests in the Upper House. He opposed the contemporary agitation for increased segregation, but his opposition fell well short of the aspirations starting to find expression among young educated Africans.

In the document that follows—part of a speech that Brookes gave in Parliament in 1939—the senator warns against the dangers of segregation.

Senator Brookes: Most racial or colour legislation is like anti-Semitism, a cheap and nasty substitute for careful thought on economic questions . . . We are a fallible people, and the Indian people are fallible too. What are the faults of those Indian traders [whose licences to trade are being 'pegged']. Examine them one by one and if there are genuine faults, legislate not only against the faults of Indian traders, but also those of other traders. Legislate for example against indiscriminate credit, which constitutes a serious South African problem, but do not sidetrack by talking of segregation. Legislation against excess profits.

The Minister of the Interior: I never suggested they were making undue profits; I criticised the 'undue': they make profits; of course they do.

Senator Brookes: That is inevitable in commerce. I think my main line of argument is fair enough; if there are faults to be found in the Indian trader, these faults ought to be dealt with along with other faults in connection with our economic legislation, and not by this method of government by incantation. We need not use legislation as a means of emotional release. We feel 'fed up', so we pass a law to relieve our feelings. Legislation for emotional release is a

---

Edgar H. Brookes, Speech in Parliament, June 9, 1939, Phyllis Lewsen, ed., *Voices of Protest: From Segregation to Apartheid, 1938–1948,* Craighall, South Africa: A. B. Donker, 1988, pp. 84–86.

dangerous course for a nation to embark on, and I feel in this Bill [to 'peg' Indian trading licences and sites in the Transvaal] that we have the first step to what afterwards may prove a complete disaster.

We are building on wrong foundations. We are building a caste system in South Africa. Race and colour are being treated as a contamination, almost a crime. Legitimate and wise separation is one thing; rigid, harsh, unreasoning segregation, raised to the level of a religious dogma, is another. Keep your national life to some extent fluid; provide for the right kind of contacts across the colour line, and do not rule out all exceptions. Such, after half a lifetime of study of the colour problems here, in the United States of America and in India, is my earnest advice to South Africa, advice backed by thousands of thoughtful men whose votes helped to put the Government into office, and whose patriotism to South Africa is beyond all doubt.

The present agitation is part of a general agitation for segregation, and against inter-racial goodwill. It affects Bantu, Coloured, and Indian; it may affect Jews; its result will be to divide South Africa into hostile camps with the Europeans a heavily-armed, fear-ridden minority. This is the government's first step down the slippery slope. Do we want to produce within our borders the fears and rivalries of modern Europe on a small intensive scale? Or has the Minister not rather the ambition to show Europe how, by goodwill, the spirit of consultation and care for minority rights and sentiments, a splendid and durable peace may be built up in a land which is a miniature replica of a troubled racially-divided world. This small Bill becomes so regarded, a test case in the struggle for freedom and peace.

I appeal to the Minister. I have purposely refrained from any personal attack on him. I recognise his good will and his good intentions. I recognise the pressure that has been brought to bear upon him. But I ask him, does he not realize that men have looked to him as the senior representative in the cabinet of the best in the old Cape tradition and outlook. Surely he does not want his name to go down to posterity as that of an unfaithful steward. I know that it is an excess of the conciliatory spirit rather than malice aforethought that has led him to foster this Bill. But are his more conservative back-benchers the only people to be conciliated? Is there no place for liberal thinkers in the United Party? I, like many others, voted for it with high hopes, as a National Government finding a place for all schools of thought that agreed wholeheartedly on the principle of co-operation between the two white races. Is it after all only a Conservative party? Does it really want to drive some of the best brains and most loyal hearts in South Africa permanently into the wilderness?

I appeal to this House, a House which has a peculiar responsibility to defend the interests of the unrepresented and underrepresented, a House which ought to interpose delay in the case of hurried legislation, with regard to which there is a reasonable doubt, a House which as one of the last acts of a dying Senate might well help us to call a halt to racial legislation, and to re-check our policies. And if I fail I still appeal, from this House to the people of South Africa, to their calm and reasonable judgement, for fair play, statesmanship, and good will.

2.   The United Party Reviews Race Relations, 1946

*In the Fagan Commission, the government of Jan Smuts followed the tra-
ditional line of liberal paternalism, with extensive concessions to the prejudices of white voters. The Smuts government claimed that sufficient segregation was already in place. Thus the recommendations of the commission, full of compromises, were made to seem wishy-washy in contrast
to the fixed purposes claimed for National party proposals. In the following extract, the commissioners assess the evidence that they gathered
and dwell on the complex nature of the issues.*

28. From what we have already said it should be clear, firstly, that the idea of
total segregation is utterly impracticable; secondly, that the movement from
country to town has a background of economic necessity—that it may, so one
hopes, be guided and regulated, and may perhaps also be limited, but that it
cannot be stopped or be turned in the opposite direction; and, thirdly, that in
our urban areas there are not only Native migrant labourers, but there is also
a settled, permanent Native population. These are simply facts, which we have
to face as such. The old cry, "Send them back!"—still so often raised when
there is trouble with Natives—therefore no longer offers a solution. A policy
based on the proposition that the Natives in the towns are all temporary
migrants—or can be kept in the stage of temporary migrants—who, in the
words of the Stallard Commission of 1921, "should only be permitted within
municipal areas in so far and for so long as their presence is demanded by the
wants of the white population" and "should depart therefrom when they cease
to minister to the needs of the white man", would be a false policy, if for no
other reason, then because the proposition itself has in the course of time
proved to be false. It is, however, precisely this proposition of the Stallard
Commission which, as has already been noted by the Young-Barrett
Committee of 1935, lies near the root of many provisions of the legislation
relating to Natives in urban areas and has had far-reaching effect in the administration of that legislation throughout the Union. An admission, therefore,
that it is an untenable proposition—and that is an admission which is simply
forced upon us by hard facts—makes it necessary for us to find a new formula
which may serve as a guide in respect of our suggestions for revision of the
existing legislation.

29. From the side of the Natives strong representations were made to us
for the repeal of all discriminatory laws, for the removal of all restrictions on
the movement of Natives, and for direct representation of Natives on town
councils. There were European witnesses, too, who supported these claims, or
one or more of them. The fact, however, that there are settled Native-com-
munities in the urban areas is not the only circumstance that has to be taken
into account in determining a policy. There are other facts as well, equally rel-

From South Africa Department of Native Affairs, *Report of the Native Laws Commission, 1946–48,*
Pretoria: Government Printer, 1948, pp. 19–21.

evant and important, to which, in our opinion, the advocates of the view we have just referred to either do not pay attention or attach insufficient weight.

There is the fact, already mentioned, that, judged according to the extent to which they have adapted themselves to European civilisation, the Natives are by no means a homogeneous group. Side by side with the settled Natives there are very many who are simply migrants. Among these are numbers of raw kraal Natives, who are strangers to European ideas of sanitation, cleanliness and hygiene, to European morals and customs, to the requirements of a European community, and to European tradition and mentality in respect of the exercise of civic rights and the discharge of civic duties. This does not mean that there are not order, cleanliness and morality in Native tribal life, but they are moulded on a different pattern and spring from other conditions, other institutions, other customs and traditions. There are large numbers of Natives in a transitional state, who are partly urbanised but have not yet broken their ties with the Reserves; and we find not only these people, but also the settled urban Natives in varying stages of development. The difference between the European way of life, on the other hand, and that of the Native on the other, simply has to be taken into account.

The movement of Natives across the country in search of employment is confused and often to no purpose. In their own interest as well as that of the community as a whole it ought to be given direction. This question will be more fully discussed at a later stage.

Housing and municipal services of Natives must nearly always be provided at sub-economic rates, and their own contribution in the form of direct taxation is relatively very small. From their side it is argued that the fault lies with their low wages, and that it is their labour no less than that of the Europeans that sustains the industries of the town and helps to earn the profits out of which the rates are paid. That may be; but the man who is directly answerable for payment is more acutely and responsibly alive to financial interests and obligations; he considers—probably not without good reason—that his management is much more cautious and much better; he sees a danger in the claim that others, who may ultimately contribute but who cannot be held directly liable, should participate in the control; and he vigourously resists such a claim. It is obvious that the clash on this point would be so much the more vehement where the economic and the racial divisions coincide.

This brings us to another objection that has been raised against representation of Natives on town councils (whether it be representation by Natives themselves or by Europeans elected by the Natives), viz. the danger of divisions and consequent clashes on racial lines, resulting in both bad feeling and bad administration. At present the Natives complain that the advisory boards which function in the locations are useless because they are purely advisory and their recommendations are disregarded by the town councils. The town councils say that the advisory boards do not evince a sufficient sense of responsibility, but are often controlled by agitators who put forward preposterous claims. Have we reason to expect that direct representation would get over this conflict? That from both sides only moderate men, who are intent on watching over the interests of all races, and on promoting good accord between them will be returned to the Council? And that, if divisions on racial lines do arise, the minority will not experience the same feeling of frustration and dissatisfaction now being expressed by advisory boards?

It must be borne in mind that we are here on ground where sentiment and emotion play as great a role as—perhaps a greater one than—cold reason and logic. The point is not whether any particular sentiment is one to be approved or disapproved. We have already said that people will not let a commission dictate to them what their feelings ought to be. As individuals each of us may have and keep his own opinion and feelings about this matter; officially, as a Commission, we can and must simply state the fact that nearly all the municipalities that submitted memoranda to us objected to direct Native representation on the town council. Nor can the matter be settled simply by weighing the merits of one sentiment against the other. When we are concerned with schemes for the co-operation of two groups it would be futile to propose a scheme on which *both* groups are not prepared to co-operate. The only course then is to try to devise a scheme that will ensure both the most efficient administration and the greatest measure of co-operation that can be attained under the circumstances. It is worthy of note that the Stallard Commission made an objection to the granting of the municipal franchise to Natives the starting-point of the reasoning which led up to the proposition that the permanent residence of Natives within municipal areas should not be permitted. We are referring to the following portion of the Report of that Commission (paragraph 42, also quoted by the Young-Barrett Committee):— . . .

42. The differentiation on the grounds of colour—by confining the franchise to Europeans—is one of a serious character, and raises at once the future of the black races in white urban areas.

If the Native is to be regarded as a permanent element in municipal areas, and if he is to have an equal opportunity of establishing himself there permanently, there can be no justification for basing his exclusion from the franchise on the simple ground of colour.

Some coloured persons and Natives are possessed of property and brains, and have educational qualifications not inferior to some enfranchised Europeans; many carry on trades and are their own employers, and it cannot be denied that they have special and peculiar needs not at present being met.

The process of degradation of the Natives now going on in the white urban areas is set forth in Chapter III, paragraphs 260 to 266.

If, as we consider, it is to the public advantage that all sections of the permanent community should be represented in government, on what ground is the franchise withheld from the Natives?

We consider that the history of the races, especially having regard to South African history, shows that the commingling of black and white is undesirable. The Native should only be allowed to enter urban areas, which are essentially the white man's creation, when he is willing to enter and to minister to the needs of the white man, and should depart therefrom when he ceases so to minister.

Precisely the same reasoning—though couched in different words—came up repeatedly in representations made to our Commission. Let us analyse it. Commingling of black and white is undesirable. The granting of the municipal franchise to the Natives as well as to the whites would be a case of undesirable mingling. This second point is not put in express words, but is conveyed by implication—there is otherwise no connection between the various points of the argument. Conclusion from these premises also clearly implied: the Native should not have the multiple franchise. But if he is a permanent resident in the municipal area, there can be no justification for excluding him from the franchise on the simple ground of colour. *Ergo,* he may not become a permanent resident. It is clear from this analysis that, on a purely logical test, the argument breaks down. It puts the cart before the horse. If it is undesirable that white and black should have the same franchise, then surely that is a reason for excluding the Native from the European voters' roll, whether he is a permanent inhabitant or not, and for seeking an alternative arrangement which will do justice to both races without putting them on one common roll. And to deny a home to the Native because he may not have the vote along with the white man, and then to base his exclusion from the franchise on the fact that the town is not his home, is a most transparent camouflaging of the true reason for his exclusion. The real reason is still the racial difference, and the faulty reasoning we have analysed above merely leads to other privileges also being withheld from the Native in order to provide an apparent reason for his exclusion from the franchise. And if the difference in race is indeed the real reason for excluding him from the franchise, why not say so? Then the other questions can be dealt with on their merits; the question whether he may have a home in the urban area or as a fact already has one; the question, if he is a settled resident, what rights and privileges should accrue to him as such; and the question whether there cannot be alternative arrangements which will give him those rights without undesirable commingling between the races.

Now—twenty-five years later—we cannot get away from the fact that there is indeed a considerable Native population permanently settled in the urban areas, and that an argument about the desirability or undesirability of that state of affairs is purely academic—it is a state of affairs that is going to remain and that simply cannot be altered.

3.   The National Party Native Minister Explains Apartheid, 1950

Hendrik F. Verwoerd, the major theorist of apartheid, had been educated in Nazi Germany. He was the first Native minister and third prime minister (1958–1966) of the post-1948 National party government and fervently believed in his brand of Calvinism. Verwoerd believed—to the point of claiming divine inspiration—the justice of his policies. He survived one assassination attempt but then was fatally stabbed by a parliamentary messenger in 1966.

Next, I wish to accede to the wish which, I understand, has long been felt by members of this council, namely that a member of the Government should explain the main features of what is implied by the policy of Apartheid.

Within the compass of an address I have, naturally, to confine myself to the fundamentals of the Apartheid policy and to the main steps following logically from the policy. Further details and a fuller description of the reasons and value of what is being planned will have to remain in abeyance today. Properly understood, however, these main features will elucidate what will be done and how this will be as much in the interests of the Bantu as in those of the European.

As a premise, the question may be put: Must Bantu and European in future develop as intermixed communities, or as communities separated from one another in so far as this is practically possible? If the reply is "intermingled communities", then the following must be understood. There will be competition and conflict everywhere. So long as the points of contact are still comparatively few, as is the case now, friction and conflict will be few and less evident. The more this intermixing develops, however, the stronger the conflict will become. In such conflict, the Europeans will, at least for a long time, hold the stronger position, and the Bantu be the defeated party in every phase of the struggle. This must cause to rise in him an increasing sense of resentment and revenge. Neither for the European, nor for the Bantu, can this, namely increasing tension and conflict, be an ideal future, because the intermixed development involves disadvantage to both.

Perhaps, in such an eventuality, it is best frankly to face the situation which must arise in the political sphere. In the event of an intermixed development, the Bantu will undoubtedly desire a share in the government of the intermixed country. He will, in due course, not be satisfied with a limited share in the form of communal representation, but will desire full participation in the country's government on the basis of an equal franchise. For the sake of simplicity, I shall not enlarge here on the fact that, simultaneously with the development of this demand, he will desire the same in the social, economic and other spheres of life, involving in due course, intermixed residence, intermixed labour, intermixed living, and, eventually, a miscegenated popula-

From A. N. Pelzer, ed., *Verwoerd Speaks: Speeches, 1948–1966,* Johannesburg: APB Publishers, 1966, pp. 23–29.

tion—in spite of the well-known pride of both the Bantu and the European in their respective purity of descent. It follows logically, therefore, that, in an intermixed country, the Bantu must, in the political sphere, have as their object equal franchise with the European.

Now examine the same question from the European's point of view. A section of the Europeans, consisting of both Afrikaans- and English-speaking peoples, says equally clearly that, in regard to the above standpoint, the European must continue to dominate what will be the European part of South Africa. It should be noted that, notwithstanding false representations, these Europeans do not demand domination over the whole of South Africa, that is to say, over the Native territories according as the Bantu outgrow the need for their trusteeship. Because that section of the European population states its case very clearly, it must not be accepted, however, that the other section of the European population will support the above possible future demand of the Bantu. That section of the European population (English as well as Afrikaans) which is prepared to grant representation to the Bantu in the country's government does not wish to grant anything beyond communal representation, and that on a strictly limited basis. They do not yet realize that a balance of power may thereby be given to the non-European with which an attempt may later be made to secure full and equal franchise on the same voters' roll. The moment they realize that, or the moment when the attempt is made, this latter section of the European population will also throw in its weight with the first section in the interests of European supremacy in the European portion of the country. This appears clearly from its proposition that, in its belief on the basis of an inherent superiority, or greater knowledge, or whatever it may be, the European must remain master and leader. The section is, therefore, also a protagonist of separate residential areas, and of what it calls separation.

My point is this that, if mixed development is to be the policy of the future in South Africa, it will lead to the most terrific clash of interests imaginable. The endeavours and desires of the Bantu and the endeavours and objectives of *all* Europeans will be antagonistic. Such a clash can only bring unhappiness and misery to both. Both Bantu and European must, therefore, consider in good time how this misery can be averted from themselves and from their descendants. They must find a plan to provide the two population groups with opportunities for the full development of their respective powers and ambitions without coming into conflict.

The only possible way out is the second alternative, namely, that both adopt a development divorced from each other. That is all that the word apartheid means. Any word can be poisoned by attaching a false meaning to it. That has happened to this word. The Bantu have been made to believe that it means oppression, or even that the Native territories are to be taken away from them. In reality, however, exactly the opposite is intended with the policy of apartheid. To avoid the above-mentioned unpleasant and dangerous future for both sections of the population, the present Government adopts the attitude that it concedes and wishes to give to others precisely what it demands for itself. It believes in the supremacy (baasskap) of the European in his sphere but, then, it also believes equally in the supremacy (baasskap) of the Bantu in his own sphere. For the European child it wishes to create all the possible opportunities for its own development, prosperity and national service in its own sphere; but for the Bantu it also wishes to create all the opportunities for the realization of ambitions and the rendering of service to *their* own people. There is thus no policy of oppression here, but one of creating a situation which has never existed for the Bantu; namely, that, taking into consideration their languages, traditions, history and different national communities, they may pass through a development of their own. That opportunity arises for them as soon as such a division is brought into being between them and the Europeans that they need not be the imitators and henchmen of the latter.

The next question, then, is how the division is to be brought about so as to allow the European and the Bantu to pass through a development of their own, in accordance with their own traditions, under their own leaders in every sphere of life.

It is perfectly clear that it would have been the easiest—an ideal condition for each of the two groups—if the course of history had been different. Suppose there had arisen in Southern Africa a state in which only Bantu lived and worked, and another in which only Europeans lived and worked. Each could then have worked out its own destiny in its own way. This is not the situation today, however, and planning must in practice take present day actualities of life in the Union into account. We cannot escape from that which history has brought in its train. However, this easiest situation for peaceful association, self-government and development, each according to its own nature and completely apart from one another, may, in fact, be taken as a yardstick whereby to test plans for getting out of the present confusion and difficulties. One may, so far as is practicable, try to approach this objective in the future.

The realities of today are that a little over one-third of the Bantu resides, or still has its roots, in what are unambiguously termed Native territories. A little over a third lives in the countryside and on the farms of Europeans. A little less than a third lives and works in the cities, of whom a section have been detribalized and urbanized. The apartheid policy takes this reality into account.

Obviously, in order to grant equal opportunities to the Bantu, both in their interests as well as those of the Europeans, its starting-point is the Native territories. For the present, these territories cannot provide the desired opportunities for living and development to their inhabitants and their children, let alone to more people. Due to neglect of their soil and over-population by man and cattle, large numbers are even now being continuously forced to go and seek a living under the protection of the European and his industries. In these circumstances it cannot be expected that the Bantu community will so provide for itself and so progress as to allow ambitious and developed young people to be taken up by their own people in their own national service out of their own funds. According as a flourishing community arises in such territories, however, the need will develop for teachers, dealers, clerks, artisans, agricultural experts, leaders of local and general governing bodies of their own. In other words, the whole superstructure of administrative and professional people arising in every prosperous community will then become necessary. Our first aim as a Government is, therefore, to lay the foundation of a prosperous producing community through soil reclamation and conservation methods and through the systematic establishment in the Native territories of Bantu farming on an economic basis.

The limited territories are, however, as little able to carry the whole of the Bantu population of the reserves of the present and the future—if all were to be farmers—as the European area would be able to carry all the Europeans if they were all to be farmers, or as England would be able to carry its whole population if all of them had to be landowners, farmers, and cattle breeders. Consequently, the systematic building up of the Native territories aims at a development precisely as in all prosperous countries. Side by side with agricultural development must also come an urban development founded on industrial growth. The future Bantu towns and cities in the reserves may arise partly in conjunction with Bantu industries of their own in those reserves. In their establishment Europeans must be prepared to help with money and knowledge, in the consciousness that such industries must, as soon as is possible, wholly pass over into the hands of the Bantu.

On account of the backlog, it is conceivable, however, that such industries may not develop sufficiently rapidly to meet adequately the needs of the Bantu requiring work. The European industrialist will, therefore, have to be encouraged to establish industries within the European areas near such towns and cities. Bantu working in those industries will then be able to live within their own territories, where they have their own schools, their own traders, and where they govern themselves. Indeed, the kernel of the apartheid policy is that, as the Bantu no longer need the European, the latter must wholly withdraw from the Native territories.

What length of time it will take the Bantu in the reserves to advance to that stage of self-sufficiency and self-government will depend on his own industry and preparedness to grasp this opportunity offered by the apartheid policy for self-development and service to his own nation.

This development of the reserves will not, however, mean that all Natives from the cities or European countryside will be able, or wish, to trek to them. In the countryside there has, up to the present, not been a clash of social interests. The endeavour, at any rate for the time being, must be to grant the Bantu in town locations as much self-government as is practicable under the guardianship of the town councils, and to let tribal control of farm Natives function effectively. There the residential and working conditions will also have to enjoy special attention so that the Bantu community finding a livelihood as farm labourers may also be prosperous and happy. Here the problem is rather how to create better relationships, greater stability, correct training and good working conditions. Apart from the removal of black spots (like the removal of white spots in the Native areas), the policy of apartheid is for the time being, not so much an issue at this juncture, except if mechanization of farming should later cause a decrease in non-European labourers.

Finally, there are the implications of the apartheid policy in respect of European cities. The primary requirement of this policy is well known, namely, that not only must there be separation between European and non-European groups, such as the Bantu, the Coloured, and the Indian, shall live in their own residential areas. Although considerable numbers of Bantu who are still rooted in the reserves may conceivably return thither, particularly according as urban and industrial development take place, or even many urbanized Bantu may proceed thence because of the opportunities to exercise their talents as artisans, traders, clerks or professionals, or to realize their political ambitions—large numbers will undoubtedly still remain behind in the big cities. For a long time to come, this will probably continue to be the case.

For these Bantu also the Apartheid policy and separate residential areas have great significance. The objective is, namely, to give them the greatest possible measure of self-government in such areas according to the degree in which local authorities, who construct these towns, can fall into line. In due course, too, depending on the ability of the Bantu community, all the work there will have to be done by their own people, as was described in connection with the reserves. Even within a European area, therefore, the Bantu communities would not be separated for the former to oppress them, but to form their own communities within which they may pursue a full life of work and service.

In view of all this, it will be appreciated why the Apartheid policy also takes an interest in suitable education for the Bantu. This, in fact, brings in its train the need for sufficiently competent Bantu in many spheres. The only and obvious reservation is that the Bantu will have to place his development and his knowledge exclusively at the service of his own people.

Co-operation in implementing the apartheid policy as described here is one of the greatest services the present leader of the Bantu population can render his people. Instead of striving after vague chimeras and trying to equal the European in an intermingled community with confused ideals and inevitable conflict, he can be a national figure helping to lead his own people along the road of peace and prosperity. He can help to give the children and educated men and women of his poeple an opportunity to find employment or fully to realize their ambitions within their own sphere or, where this is not possible, as within the Europeans' sphere, employment and service within segregated areas of their own.

I trust that every Bantu will forget the misunderstandings of the past and choose not the road leading to conflict, but that which leads to peace and happiness for both the separate communities. Are the present leaders of the Bantu, under the influence of Communist agitators, going to seek a form of equality which they will not get? For in the long run they will come up against the whole of the European community, as well as the large section of their own compatriots who prefer the many advantages of self-government within a community of their own. I cannot believe that they will. Nobody can reject a form of independence, obtainable with everybody's co-operation, in favour of a futile striving after that which promises to be not freedom but downfall. . . .

The Years of Nonviolent Protest

1. Professor Z. K. Matthews Assesses African Reactions to the Second World War, 1941

Z. K. Matthews, a professor at Fort Hare College in the Eastern Cape, was one of the older generation of ANC leaders and a member of the Native Representative Council until that body dissolved itself as a protest against government policies in 1946. His statement represents a stage of transition from the prewar cautious and conservative ANC to the more militant posture being urged in the Congress Youth League.

This is not the first war in which Africans, as 'British subjects', have taken part. But, it is the first war about which Africans—at any rate, in the Union—are finding it difficult to make up their minds. Formerly, it was sufficient to say of any conflict that the King of England, a descendant of Queen Victoria, was involved, to evoke a ready response from all Africans. The King's enemies were their enemies, and the enthusiasm with which they responded to appeals for assistance was almost embarrassing.

Since the World War of 1914–18, great changes have taken place in African opinion about both British Colonial Policy and Union Native Policy, with the result that now there are various schools of thought among Africans regarding their attitude to the war. We still have with us, of course, the 'die-hards' who are prepared to out-British the British in their unquestioning patriotism and support for any cause espoused by His Majesty's Government. But, other sections are less single-minded in their loyalty. . . .

It is true that, at the outbreak of the war, all the important Native public bodies—both the official bodies like the Native Representative Council and the General Councils of the Transkei and the Ciskei, and the unofficial bodies like the African National Congress and the All-African Convention—were unanimous in affirming their loyalty to the Crown and in expressing their willingness to serve in the armed forces of the King. But, against these public

From Phyllis Lewsen, ed., *Voices of Protest: From Segregation to Apartheid, 1938–1948*, Craighall, South Africa: A. B. Donker, 1988, pp. 92–96.

affirmations must be set the fact that the response of the Africans to recruiting for the various services open to them, has, especially in certain areas, been disappointing; and that appeals for War Funds and Gifts and Comforts for both black and white troops have not aroused the enthusiasm which might have been expected. Obviously the attitude of Africans to the war requires further elucidation in order to be comprehended.

What does the African man-in-the-street mean by 'loyalty' to the Crown in this war?

Firstly, he means that he will not engage in subversive activities in league with the King's enemies. He will not sabotage the war effort of the Government. He refuses to become a dupe of fifth column activities. To the bulk of the African people, the promised Nazi millenium is a tale 'full of sound and fury, signifying nothing.' Moreover, their own past history has taught them that to support one European group against another brings upon them the enmity of the group to which they were disloyal, without earning them the friendship of the group to which they were loyal. As they put it, 'Europeans may fight one another during war-time, but when peace comes they remember that blood is thicker than water and they combine against us.'

Secondly, by their loyalty Africans mean they do not intend to exercise pressure on the Government during the war to secure rights which have thus far been withheld from them. Undoubtedly, some among them look upon the present crisis as a golden opportunity for bargaining, but perhaps because of that patience of the African which a famous South African statesman once described as 'asinine', the bulk of the people do not believe that advantages extorted out of an unwilling Government during a period of crisis can be regarded as permanent. This does not mean, of course, that Africans abandon their just claims, but they refuse to use the war as a lever to support their excellent case.

On the other hand, it is necessary also to consider what the African does *not* mean by his loyalty.

In the first place, it does not imply that he endorses the pre-war native policy of the Government, nor that he takes without a pinch of salt official propaganda about the issues involved in this war. Statements like 'this is a war between good and evil and we are on the good side and the Germans on the evil side'; or 'we are fighting for freedom and democracy and the Germans for world domination', leave him utterly cold. The African has experienced so little of the good that is on our side and so little of the freedom and democracy for which we are fighting, that he is tempted to ask, 'In which cheek has the white man got his tongue when he makes such statements to us?' He has not forgotten that the last war which was fought to make the world 'safe for democracy', was followed by the entrenchment of the segregation principle in the Union's land policy, by the financial strangulation of native education, and by the abolition of the old Cape Native franchise—none of which measures can be regarded as expression of a democracy worth fighting for.

Moreover, Africans are not impressed when they are told that 'if the Germans win this war, your position will be worse', for this requires them, by implication, to continue accepting the evils to which they are at present subjected. It may well be that a German victory will lead to a worsening of the position of the Africans, but, then, he is not a German subject and has no special claim upon the solicitude of the German Government. What he wants to know is, rather, whether a South African victory will lead to the betterment of his position. In all the schemes for post-war reconstruction, what sort of place will the African have in the South African, not the German 'New Order'? It has not escaped his attention that there is a deathly silence on this point which can hardly inspire him with confidence regarding the future.

What about the African's readiness to take up arms? He looks upon South Africa as the only country in which he has a stake. Consequently, he thinks that, if the country is in danger, no one is more entitled than he to take up arms in its defence. The refusal of the Government to accept his offer of the highest form of service, in order to placate certain white sections, is regarded by him as a direct declaration of the permanent denial of citizenship rights to him. The rumour that he might be armed when he gets beyond the borders of the Union only makes matters worse, and the sooner that is given up as a form of propaganda the better.

Another shock to Native sentiment has been the quibbling over the military pay of Africans on active service, low enough as it is in all conscience [1s.6d. a day]. That there should have been a debate about a paltry sum which would not have made much difference to the total cost of the war, has further strengthened the African's belief that they are regarded as butting in where they are not wanted.

All this does not mean that Africans are indifferent to the war. How could they be, when the war is affecting so many different aspects of their lives? Nor are they mindful of the tremendous suffering which it is causing in Europe. Their sympathy and admiration for the courage of the British people are beyond question. They share the hope of all right-thinking men that out of this upheaval will come a new world in which justice and fair play will be the rule rather than the exception, and in which war will be outlawed forever. But, as a subject people, they are, frankly, not enthusiastic about participation in this war, because for them neither the native policy of the Union, nor British colonial policy, nor indeed the colonial policy of any other Power, represent a cause worth fighting for. As the present writer has said elsewhere, 'We hope that one of the results of this war will be that everywhere and not least in South Africa, men will learn that the best way of defending freedom and democracy is to extend them during peace time to all sections of the community in the fullest measure and to remove every hindrance to the spread of these achievements of the human spirit.'

2.   The Congress Youth League's Case for Africanism, 1946

*Anton Lembede (1914–1947) was an influential ideologue of Africanism,
a doctrine that never captured the mainstream of the ANC but that
proved a powerful current in the 1950s. With many ANC leaders banned
or imprisoned, Africanists gained control of some local ANC branches.
The struggle continued within the organization until 1959, when the Pan
Africanist Congress split away. Africanism in some form has endured in
African politics in South Africa but is still rejected in official ANC policy.*

The history of modern times is the history of nationalism. Nationalism has
been tested in the people's struggles and the fires of battle and found to be the
only effective weapon, the only antidote against foreign rule and modern
imperialism. It is for that reason that the great imperialistic powers feverishly
endeavour with all their might to discourage and eradicate all nationalistic tendencies among their alien subjects; for that purpose huge and enormous sums
of money are lavishly expended on propaganda against nationalism which is
dubbed, designated or dismissed as 'narrow', 'barbarous', 'uncultured', 'dev-
ilish' etc. Some alien subjects become dupes of this sinister propaganda and
consequently become tools or instruments of imperialism for which great service they are highly praised, extolled and eulogised by the imperialistic power
and showered with such epithets as 'cultured', 'liberal', 'progressive', 'broad-
minded' etc.

All over the world nationalism is rising in revolt against foreign domination, conquest and oppression in India, in Indonesia, in Egypt, in Persia and
several other countries. Among Africans also clear signs of national awakening, national renaissance, or rebirth are noticeable on the far-off horizon.

A new spirit of African nationalism, or Africanism, is pervading through
and stirring the African society. A young virile nation is in the process of birth
and emergence. The national movement imbued with and animated by the
national spirit is gaining strength and momentum. The African National
Congress Youth League is called upon to aid and participate in this historical
process. African nationalism is based on the following cardinal principles:

1) *Africa is a blackman's country.* Africans are the natives of Africa and
   they have inhabited Africa, their Motherland, from times immemor-
   ial; Africa belongs to them.

2) *Africans are one.* Out of the heterogeneous tribes, there must emerge
   a homogeneous nation. The basis of national unity is the nationalistic
   feeling of the Africans, the feeling of being Africans irrespective of

---

Anton Lembede, "Policy of the Congress Youth League," in *Inkundla ya Bantu,* May 1946, from
Thomas Karis and Gwendolyn M. Carter, eds., *From Protest to Challenge: A Documentary History of
African Politics in South Africa, 1882–1964: Vol. 2: Hope and Challenge, 1935–1952,* ed. by Thomas
Karis, Stanford: Hoover Institution Press, 1973, pp. 317–318.

tribal connection, social status, educational attainment or economic class. This nationalistic feeling can only be realised in and interpreted by [a] national movement of which all Africans must be members.

3) *The Leader of the Africans will come out of their own loins.* No foreigner can ever be a true and genuine leader of the African people because no foreigner can ever truly and genuinely interpret the African spirit which is unique and peculiar to Africans only. Some foreigners Asiatic or European who pose as African leaders must be categorically denounced and rejected. An African must lead Africans. Africans must honour, venerate and find inspiration from African heroes of the past: Shaka, Moshoeshoe, Makana, Hintsa, Khama, Mzilikazi, Sekhukhuni, Sobhuza and many others.

4) *Cooperation between Africans and other Non-Europeans on common problems and issues may be highly desirable.* But this occasional cooperation can only take place between Africans as a single unit and other Non-European groups as separate units. Non-European unity is a fantastic dream which has no foundation in reality.

5) *The divine destiny of the African people is National Freedom.* Unless Africans achieve national freedom as early as possible they will be confronted with the impending doom and imminent catastrophe of extermination; they will not be able to survive the satanic forces, economic, social, and political unleashed against them. Africans are being mowed down by such diseases as tuberculosis, typhus, venereal diseases, etc. Infantile mortality is tremendously high. Moral and physical degeneration is assuming alarming dimensions. Moral and spiritual degeneration manifests itself in such abnormal and pathological phenomena as loss of self confidence, inferiority complex, a feeling of frustration, the worship and idolisation of white men, foreign leaders and ideologies. All these are symptoms of a pathological state of mind.

As a result of educational and industrial colour bars, young African men and women are converted into juvenile delinquents.

Now the panacea of all these ills is National Freedom, in as much as when Africans are free, they will be in a position to pilot their own ship and, unhampered, work toward their own destiny and, without external hindrance or restriction devise ways and means of saving or rescuing their perishing race.

Freedom is an indispensable condition for all progress and development. It will only be when Africans are free that they will be able to exploit fully and bring to fruition their divine talent and contribute something new towards the general welfare and prosperity of Mankind; and it will only be then that Africans will enter on a footing of equality with other nations of the world into the commonwealth of nations; and only then will Africans occupy their rightful and honourable place among the nations of the world.

6) *Africans must aim at balanced progress or advancement.* We must

guard against the temptation of lop-sided or one-sided progress. Our forces as it were, must march forward in a coordinated manner and in all theatres of the war, socially, educationally, culturally, morally, economically, and politically. Hence the Youth League must be all inclusive.

7) *After national freedom, then socialism.* Africans are naturally socialistic as illustrated in their social practices and customs. The achievement of national liberation will therefore herald or usher in a new era, the era of African socialism. Our immediate task, however, is not socialism, but national liberation.

Our motto: *Freedom in Our Life Time.*

3. The ANC Programme of Action, 1949

This document was adopted at the ANC annual conference of December 1949. It is in part a response to the anticipation that government policies would be markedly less favorable to Africans under the newly elected National party government of D. F. Malan. More important, it represents the fruition of several years of struggle within the ANC to revive the organization by extending its appeal and turning from petition to protest.

In contrast to the later Freedom Charter, the Programme of Action also implied endorsement of Africanist goals.

The fundamental principles of the programme of action of the African National Congress are inspired by the desire to achieve National freedom. By National freedom we mean freedom from White domination and the attainment of political independence. This implies the rejection of the conception of segregation, apartheid, trusteeship, or White leadership which are all in one way or another motivated by the idea of White domination or domination of the White over the Blacks. Like all other people the African people claim the right of self-determination.

With this object in view in the light of these principles we claim and will continue to fight for the political rights tabulated on page 8 of our Bill of Rights such as:

(1) the right of direct representation in all the governing bodies of the country—national, provincial, and local, and we resolve to work for the abolition of all differential institutions or bodies specially created for Africans, viz. representative councils, present form of parliamentary representation.

From Thomas Karis and Gwendolyn M. Carter, eds., *From Protest to Challenge: A Documentary History of African Politics in South Africa, 1882–1964: Vol. 2: Hope and Challenge, 1935–1952,* ed. by Thomas Karis, Stanford: Hoover Institution Press, 1973, pp. 337–339.

(2) to achieve these objectives the following programme of action is suggested:—
   (a) the creation of a national fund to finance the struggle for national liberation.
   (b) the appointment of a committee to organise an appeal for funds and to devise ways and means therefor.
   (c) the regular issue of propaganda material through:—
       (i) the usual press, newsletter, or other means of disseminating our ideas in order to raise the standard of political and national consciousness.
       (ii) establishment of a national press.
(3) appointment of a council of action whose function should be to carry into effect, vigorously and with the utmost determination the programme of action. It should be competent for the council of action to implement our resolve to work for:—
   (a) the abolition of all differential political institutions the boycotting of which we accept and to undertake a campaign to educate our people on this issue and, in addition, to employ the following weapons: immediate and active boycott, strike, civil disobedience, non-co-operation and such other means as may bring about the accomplishment and realisation of our aspirations.
   (b) preparations and making plans for a national stoppage of work for one day as a mark of protest against the reactionary policy of the Government.
(4) *Economic.*
   (a) The establishment of commercial, industrial, transport and other enterprises in both urban and rural areas.
   (b) Consolidation of the industrial organisation of the workers for the improvement of their standard of living.
   (c) Pursuant to paragraph (a) herein instructions be issued to Provincial Congresses to study the economic and social conditions in the reserves and other African settlements and to devise ways and means for their development, establishment of industries and such other enterprises as may give employment to a number of people.
(5) *Education.*
   It be an instruction to the African National Congress to devise ways and means for:—
   (a) Raising the standard of Africans in the commercial, industrial and other enterprises and workers in their workers' organisations by means of providing a common educational forum wherein intellectuals, peasants and workers participate for the common good.
   (b) Establishment of national centres of education for the purpose of training and educating African youth and provision of large scale scholarships tenable in various overseas countries.

(6) *Cultural.*
  (a) To unite the cultural with the educational and national struggle.
  (b) The establishment of a national academy of arts and sciences.
(7) Congress realises that ultimately the people will be brought together by inspired leadership, under the banner of African Nationalism with courage and determination.

[signed by G. I. M. Mzamane and D. W. Bopape]

4.   Albert Luthuli Is Removed as Chief of the Umtoti Mission Reserve, 1952

Albert Luthuli served as chief of the Umtoti Mission Reserve in Natal, a salaried position under the Native Affairs Department. In 1952 he became president of the ANC. Because the Defiance Campaign of 1952 signaled the ANC's new militancy, membership in the organization was, in the eyes of government, no longer compatible with service under the Native Affairs Department. Luthuli was removed from his chiefship, as recounted here in his autobiography. As president of the ANC through the next decade, Luthuli was in turn banned, tried for treason, and exiled. In 1960 he received the Nobel Prize for Peace.

At N.A.D. [Native Affairs Department] headquarters, when I presented myself, I was ushered into the presence of the Secretary for Native Affairs, Dr. W. W. M. Eiselen, who was flanked by the Deputy Secretary and by the Natal Chief Native Commissioner.

"We have called you here," began Dr. Eiselen, "to discuss your Congress activities. I want you to realise at once that so far as the Native Affairs Department is concerned we have no complaints—you've worked efficiently and conscientiously and have seen to the welfare of your community. We have noted this and appreciated it. We look on to you as one of our best chiefs.

"Now, before we come to the subject of your own participation in the A.N.C., we'd like to ask you some general questions. To begin with, why does the A.N.C. oppose Government schemes for land rehabilitation? It seems to us that any educated person should appreciate schemes to restore the land and prevent erosion."

"I shall speak for myself," I replied, "not for the A.N.C. Nobody, in a normal context, would oppose the prevention of erosion. Nobody. If I had a farm of my own, I would keep no more stock than the farm could carry. You

From Albert Luthuli, *Let My People Go,* New York and Cleveland: Meridian Books, 1970 (originally published, 1962), pp. 120–123.

realise of course, all the same, that preventing erosion, by cattle-culling, strikes at the only wealth—cattle—which rural people believe in. In theory, however, the principle of limiting the livestock to what the land can carry is sound. But in practice here is the factor which you ignore; the overcrowding of African areas by man and beast is the direct result of the 1913 and 1916 Land Acts—it is imposed on us. Your solution is to take our cattle away to-day because you took our land yesterday. We are not prepared to co-operate with you in applying this sort of remedy. If you remove the root cause of the trouble—the Land Acts—our co-operation in saving the land would be immediate. As it is, your solution is just another expression of the oppressive and restrictive legislation under which we suffer."

The Deputy Secretary put his question: "Why do you oppose Influx Control?"

"As you operate this system, it goes right against the usual understandings in Trade Union circles. Workers must be free to seek out the best market and sell their toil there. We do not accept a system in which huge, half-starved labour reserves are dammed up in order to keep the price of labour down."

"But," said the Deputy Secretary, "we're doing this to protect the urban natives." He went on, to my utter amazement, to harp on the evils of migrant labour—evils which the very system under discussion causes. Only labourers are allowed to join the influx, while the rest of the family is left behind. The family is effectively crippled. For a while I was speechless with amazement.

"You know, sir," I chipped in eventually, "we don't like migrant labour either. We didn't invent it. I approve of having the workers near their work and earning a living wage, I approve of the establishment of townships—provided the families can live with the breadwinners, and provided rural people can have the chance to acquire land and make a decent livelihood. But to go back: I have never heard that one urban African has opposed the influx of rural people to the cities. This is the first intimation. If my people have no complaint, why legislate as though they had?"

Dr. Eiselen apparently thought it was time to get down to business.

"You are a chief," he said, "yet you ask people to break the laws of the land. You are an officer whose work is to keep the law and order, yet you encourage people to defy the law. What do you say about that?"

I remember that I paused to arrange my thoughts. "I do admit without hesitation, sir, that I'm engaged in furthering the policy of the A.N.C. The course we have chosen is the only way open to us of showing our opposition to laws which have no moral basis. I have not asked people to become criminals or to act in a criminal way. Our motive is political. This is the only way we have of highlighting our plight, and our refusal to consent to being governed by criminal laws. Our hope is that white people will look into our grievances, take us seriously, realise that we are serious about this. The Defiance Campaign is a *political* demonstration against discriminatory laws."

"No!" said the Secretary. "You are asking people to break the law. You are asking people to break the law!"

"No, sir," I replied, "not to break the law. To signify in this way our rejection of a particular kind of law."

"And how do you reconcile the encouragement you give to people to break the law," somebody asked, either the Secretary or the Deputy, "with your duties as a chief?"

"As far as that is concerned, I have never experienced any conflict. My policy has been to keep my commitments distinct. I have never discussed Congress matters in tribal councils—in fact I have excluded such discussion when others have begun it. But my duties as a chief do not conflict in me with Congress activity. Congress has not yet been declared subversive."

"We have not called you here," said Dr. Eiselen, "to talk you out of belonging to the A.N.C., because you are asking people to break the law of the land. You can't be a Jekyll and Hyde."

I thought this remark revealing. It seems to imply that chiefs, who are indeed concerned with maintaining and dispensing law, must have split personalities before they can possibly object to the immoral laws, whose main purpose is to uphold white supremacy, a repugnant creed. In point of fact, I was in Congress not in spite of being a chief but partly, anyway, *because* of the things to which chieftainship had opened my eyes.

Dr. Eiselen drew the interview to its close: "I must make it clear to you that this Department cannot have you acting this way. Go away now and think it over, and let us have your reply in a week."

"I think that a matter of this kind needs a little time," I said. "There is the possibility of my ceasing to be chief. It is a matter which needs talking over with the tribe."

"With the tribe?" said Dr. Eiselen. "Must you?"

"Well, sir, I ought to discuss it with my headmen at least."

"Sir, isn't a week rather short?" asked the Natal Chief Native Commissioner.

"I leave that with you," said Dr. Eiselen.

The interview ended there. I had already made up my mind about what course to follow, but I said nothing of that for the moment. I was, however, distressed at the suggestion that I should act without consulting my people, possibly relinquishing office unknown to them. It might be the way of the Native Affairs Department, but it is not the way of the Zulus and nor is it mine.

I felt inhibited, all the same, by Dr. Eiselen's "Must you?" and for that reason I did not convene a tribal gathering. Seeing nothing further to add to what I had said in Pretoria, I refrained from writing to Dr. Eiselen. I still saw no conflict between the Defiance Campaign and my place as a chief, but that is perhaps because I failed to see my position in Groutville as a favour bestowed by the Native Affairs Department. I discussed the situation with my church ministers and awaited developments.

After a couple of weeks a letter came requiring my reply to the question posed in Pretoria. I replied neutrally, stating that I had no intention of resigning either from A.N.C. leadership nor from the chieftainship, since the two did not contradict one another. At this stage I forwarned my headmen of what was about to happen.

In due course the Native Commissioner asked me to call on him. "Pretoria says that from now you cease to be chief of the Umvoti Mission Reserve.". . .

5.   Mr. Drum Reports on Labor Conditions for African Farm Workers, 1952

During the 1950s the newspaper Drum, *under the editorship of Anthony Sampson, portrayed African life under apartheid in a lively and informative way. Though white owned, the paper boasted a talented staff of African journalists and benefited from an extended circle of interracial contacts and friendships. By 1961 the government, unable to tolerate either the contents of the paper or its staff's interracial camaraderie, cracked down on the newspaper with press restrictions and banning orders against the reporters. "Mr. Drum," most often Henry Nxumalo, was an investigative reporter who exposed the everyday hardships of African life.*

In order to discover the truth about the way contracts are signed, Mr Drum himself decided to become a farm recruit. He was soon picked up outside the Pass Office by one of the touts or 'runners' who look out for unemployed Africans, and are paid for each man they collect for the agencies. He was taken to an employment agency, where he did not, of course, give his real name, Mr. Drum, but adopted the name of GEORGE MAGWAZA. He said he had no pass, and, with many others, was told that he would be given a pass if he signed a contract to go and work out of Johannesburg: this is the normal way of dealing with people without passes, He chose to work on a farm in Springs, and was sent to—'s compound, where he waited nearly a day until he could sign the contract.

When the contract came to be signed the interpreter read out a small part of the contract to a number of recruits together, while the attesting officer held a pencil over the contract. No one asked the age of any of the recruits (they should have consent of parents if under eighteen), and Mr Drum was told nothing about whether his pay would be monthly or deferred, what food he was entitled to, or what length of shift he would work.

N A D African Clerk (calling roll of everyone on the contract sheet): You're going to work on a farm in the Middelburg district: you're on a six months' contract. You will be paid £3 a month, plus food and quarters. When you leave here you will be given an advance of 5s. for pocket money, 10s. 5d.

From Motholi Mutloatse, comp. & ed., *Reconstruction: 90 Years of Black Historical Literature,* Johannesburg: Ravan Press, 1981, pp. 135–144.

for food, and 14s. 5d. for train fare. The total amount is £1 9s. 5d. and this amount will be deducted from your first month's wages. Have you got that?

Mr Drum and other recruits: Yes.

Clerk: You will now proceed to touch the pencil.

Mr Drum: But I was told before that I was going to be sent to a farm in Springs. Why am I now going to Middelburg?

Clerk: I'm telling you where you're going, according to your contract sheet, and nothing else.

So Mr Drum refused to touch the pencil when he reached the attesting officer, and was told to wait outside for his pass.

The other recruits then ran past the attesting officer, each holding the pencil for a moment, which was not even touching the paper.

Mr Drum, who can read and write English, had no opportunity either to sign his name or read the contract—but on his way out, he succeeded in obtaining a contract. As a result of holding a pencil for a second (50 recruits were attested in a few minutes), the recruits were considered to be bound to a contract. But in fact the contract had not been signed and had not been fully understood. So it seems that none of the contracts 'signed' in this way are valid at all (Native Labour Regulation Act of 1911, as amended 1949).

To find out what happened after the contracts had been signed, Mr Drum went to Bethal to obtain the facts at first hand. With a good deal of difficulty and sometimes at some risk, Mr Drum succeeded in talking to a large number of people most closely concerned with farm conditions, and carefully compared and checked the different accounts. Sometimes the farmers themselves were friendly, and at one farm Mr Drum was presented with a sack of potatoes. Mr Drum was very careful not to cause any trouble or enmity on the farms, and never tried to influence what people said.

Out of over 50 labourers interviewed on eight farms stretching from Witbank to Kinross, not a single labourer admitted that he was satisfied with the conditions. Those who did not express this view refused to comment altogether, for fear that they might be victimised.

Two thirds of those consulted said they were sent to Bethal under false pretences: they were either promised soft jobs in Johannesburg or on dairies in the Springs district, but they subsequently found themselves being made to alight at Bethal Station and told they were going to work there.

A man from Nyasaland described how the touts employed by a certain labour agency in his country worked. There was a certain boundary which many people crossed in order to get to the Union. The touts lay in wait there to intercept, and when they saw one trying to cross the area they immediately pounced upon him and threatened him with arrest for trespass if he did not accept the offer of a contract to work in South Africa as a waiter. The victim only realised on arriving in the Union that he had been tricked and contracted to work on a farm.

Joseph—, who said he was 14 years old, told me he was recruited by X's agency, in the Northern Transvaal to work in a clothing factory at Springs. He was given an advance of 10s. for food and a train ticket, only to discover at Springs that he was going to work on a farm at Bethal at £2 a month.

Mzuzumi—(30) says he was recruited in Natal by Siz'Abafane Employment Agency, given a 10s. advance and told he would work in Johannesburg. He had no pass then and accepted the six months' contract as a solution to his problem. Siz'Abafane's guide got their party to alight at Bethal Station in the dead of night and told them that is where they were going to work.

The pay on the farms is between £2 and £3 a month, and the food consists mainly of porridge, with meat sometimes once a week, if that.

Months are calculated on the basis of 30 full working shifts, excluding non-working days such as Sundays and public holidays, and the wages for the first month are spent in repaying train fares and money advanced to the labourers as a loan on recruitment.

For example, R— F— (60), employed on the farm of Mr B, was recruited by Z's Agency, of Johannesburg. He earns £3 a month and has a wife and four children to support at home.

His fare to Johannesburg was £1 6s. 11d., and his whole wages for the first month repaid this sum. He will have £15 3 s. 1 d. to his credit at the end of his six months' contract. But if he decides to return home he will be minus another £2 16s. 11d. when he reaches Louis Trichardt, which means that he will be left with £12 6s. 2d. in cash, or even less should he ask for tobacco or clothes on credit from his employer before that time, to say nothing of what he will spend on his journey home. And that for half a year's work.

Labourers admitted that farmers are always willing to give them credit when their clothes give in, and although few farmers have their own shops, labourers told Mr Drum that farmers keep large supplies of khaki clothes which they sell to their labourers on credit at the exorbitant price of £1 12s. a shirt and £2 10s. a pair of trousers. Older men prefer to wear sacks in which holes have been cut for head and arms, and sleep on sacks instead of blankets rather than incur more debt.

Very often the boss boys, themselves Africans, are tough and ruthless with the labourers, for if they are not they lose their jobs. Most boss boys are old employees who have acquired the important status of permanent squatters on the farms, where they live with their families and repay the farmer by working for him free of charge. They enjoy certain facilities, such as the use of a horse when they supervise the labourers.

At Bethal Hospital I found Casbert Tutje, from Cetani, Cape Province, who, together with three other friends, was also recruited by Siz'Abafane Agency in Natal.

From there they were sent to the farm of Mr X at Bethal, to work as labourers at £3 a month each. This happened in November, 1950.

The foursome was invited by a family squatting on the farm to a beer drinking party on Christmas Day, but, as the farmer would not grant them permission to attend, they left the compound without leave that morning. The boss boy had left the compound gate open.

The farmer sent for them and they were severely punished, then handed over to the police. They were brought before the Court on a charge of desertion and sentenced to two months each. The farmer then arranged that their terms of imprisonment be served on his farm, where they were again thrashed by the boss boys severely.

It was in the course of this that Casbert sustained serious internal injuries which resulted in his being admitted to hospital from time to time. He gradually became weak and sickly, and spent more of his time lying in hospital than working on the farm. Before his contract expired in 1951 the doctor advised that he was unfit for farm work and should be sent home.

The farmer refused to pay Casbert his wages, however, stating that he had not completed his contract and still owed money for an overall purchased on credit; he would not give him his pass either. Casbert was given the sum of 10s. for food and told to leave the farm. And when he reported the matter to the Native Commissioner he was told that nothing could be done about it. His next alternative was to seek employment on another farm, with a view to obtaining a new pass and getting money to pay for his fare home.

Here, too, he had to sign another contract. He is not home yet. He has been a patient at Bethal Hospital since September, 1951, and is now diagnosed as a pulmonary T B case with little hope of recovery. He still has the new contract to complete.

Another farm in the Bethal area is probably the only one with a compound modelled on the same lines as a Reef mine compound; with the exception that it is dirtier.

A unique feature of it is that it has its own private hospital, a crowded, dirty, small brick building with iron beds and sick labourers lying on mattresses without blankets and vice versa. They sleep in their dirty working clothes, and I was told by the man in charge, P— T—, that the men are sent to Bethal Hospital if they do not improve after receiving treatment from a local doctor. P—has been working on the farm for 32 years and is better known by the name of 'doctor'. He is probably the best-paid African farm labourer: he earns £8 plus a bag of mealie meal a month, and has his family living with him on the farm. He told me that his treatment for sick farm labourers consisted mainly of regular doses of Epsom salts.

Next to the 'hospital' is the compound and the kitchen. Besides Emmanuel, the cook was the only other person wearing boots on the premises, the others being bare-footed. But the cook's clothes were as filthy with grease as those of an oil engine fitter who has not changed his overalls for many months. The filth shone at a distance.

The men ate out of improvised zinc containers which they made themselves. One labourer told me that he could not afford to buy himself a proper dish at that stage of his contract; but this was an improvement on what I saw on some farms at lunch-time, where the labourers not only wore sacks but ate on them.

I met the European in charge of the farm on my second visit, but he refused to allow Mr Drum to take pictures of the compound and stated that I had erred by asking his men about working conditions on the farm on my first visit there, without his permission. He said he did not want a repetition of what Michael Scott did.

People living in Bethal tell of labourers who died of cold while deserting or simply while living in the compounds, and there are farmers who, probably because of their ruthlessness or otherwise, are known by such names as Mabulala (the Killer) and Fake Futheni (Hit Him in the Marrow), and so on.

Most of the compounds I saw look much like jails. They have high walls, they are dirty and are often so closely attached to a cattle kraal that the labourers breathe the same air as the cattle at night. Some labourers told Mr Drum that they are locked in at night.

There are a few private schools on farms at Bethal, but the biggest school in the area is the Bethal United High and Senior School at Bethal Location, which has an enrollment of over 1,300 children.

Mr. Wycliffe Khayiyana, the principal, who identifies himself with the hardships and sufferings of the local community, told me that the so-called Trek Pass system was dealing a bad blow to the education of the children. When squatters are made to vacate a farm they take their children with them; quite often this happens in the middle of the school term. Over 100 children a year leave school in this way, either during the first term in the year or before the examinations at the end of the year. Not only is the schooling span of the children shortened by this, but other children who would benefit by attending school and are kept out of it because of lack of space are made to suffer unnecessarily.

In an endeavour to have at least one out of three children educated, a Bethal widow recently moved on to a farm for the first time with only two children, leaving the other at a boarding school. But the farmer found out about him when he was home on holiday, and that was the end of his school career—he was made to work on the farm too.

Last December the Bethal branch of the African National Congress invited Dr H F Verwoerd, Minister of Native Affairs, to visit the area in connection with the deteriorating position of the African farm labourers. The Minister replied through his private secretary that he was unable to do that before the present parliamentary session; at any rate, he was kept fully informed on matters in the Bethal area, and the information at his disposal was the same as that given by the chiefs who recently visited the area, namely, that the workers were 'generally well treated by their employers, and had no real grievances.'

But Congress officials deny all knowledge of these chiefs and their visit to Bethal, and hardly anyone at Bethal knew anything about them.

We wish to emphasise that while the Industrial Revolution is causing as much chaos in South Africa as it caused in 19th-century Europe no lessons have been learnt from the industrial past whatever. The same abuse of labour is repeated in the same style.

Farm prisons and contracted labour by-pass the normal need to attract men by improved working conditions and higher wages. They depend upon compulsion, not persuasion.

Most men who touch the pencil for a farm contract are hungry, ignorant and urgently in need of work. Once they have touched the pencil they have handed themselves over to an unknown area under largely unknown conditions.

It is obvious that care has been taken by the authorities to protect these people and equally plain that they have failed. For once men have 'signed' themselves away, itself often a trick, they are taken to an isolated farm where they are at the mercy of the farmer and his boss boys; brought back by the police if they run away; and liable to every abuse with no chance of being able to protect themselves.

We ask, when farm life is so often satisfactory, what are the conditions which have given Bethal so fearful and exceptional a history—and we reply: it is the system, the farm contract system that has had so vile a result.

6. Nat Nakasa Depicts the Narrow Confines of Interracial Social Life, 1952

> *Nat Nakasa (1937–1965) was a journalist for* Drum *and subsequently the first African journalist on the staff of the* Rand Daily Mail. *In 1964 he received a Niemann fellowship to study journalism at Harvard. When the South African government refused him a passport, he left the country on an exit permit, which precluded his return. After his Harvard stay, he practiced journalism in the United States. He committed suicide in July 1965. "I can't laugh any more—and when I can't laugh I can't write."*

Aunt Sally's shebeen [speakeasy; illegal beer hall] was doing excellent business, customers spending lavishly. Two white journalists, perched nervously on a bench, looked like business executives in a brothel.

Suddenly, from outside, Aunt Sally pulled the door with all the might in her round, fat arms. 'Make quick,' she screamed. 'The police! Lock top and bottom!' Someone jumped for the door and bolted it.

The man let out a shout announcing that he had locked. 'All right,' answered Aunt Sally, 'then shut up, close your mouths.' The man returned to his drink. The two journalists couldn't help laughing; although somewhat terrified by the prospect of being marched to a police station.

After a while the doors were flung open, and in stepped Aunt Sally with a thin, naughty-girl's smile on her face. Apparently, she had spotted a 300lb. police sergeant propelling himself in the direction of her place. 'But it's all fixed up now,' she assured us all.

For my two journalist friends, this was their first taste of life on 'the fringe'. Life in a 'No-man's Land' where anybody meets anybody, to hell with the price of their false teeth, or anything else.

"Between Two Worlds," from Essop Patel, ed., *The World of Nat Nakasa*, Johannesburg: Ravan Press, 1975, pp. 9–14.

My two white mates had not seen such things happen before. Yet they happen all over the Union. In Johannesburg and Bloemfontein, Durban and Cape Town. In the swanky homes of white suburbia, as well as in the slums of Cato Manor, District Six or Alexandria Township.

Some people call it 'crossing the colour line'. You may call it jumping the line or wiping it clean off. Whatever you please. Those who live on the fringe have no special labels. They see it simply as LIVING.

Dating a girl. Inviting a friend to lunch. Arranging a party for people who are interested in writing or painting, jazz or boxing. Or even apartheid, for that matter. I once organised such a party for talks with Afrikaner nationalists from Pretoria University. Among them was the son of a very senior Cabinet Minister. We talked apartheid and religion. We were just talking and drinking, not 'crashing' anything. We didn't see it that way anyhow.

'It's a question of having friends who are white when you are black,' Henry Sono summed it up. 'You've got to live with them, somehow, somewhere. It's against human nature to say "sorry, can't be friends" to a person you like, simply because your nose is longer than his, or because he is darker than you.'

It's easy to understand what Henry Sono meant. Just the other day there was a wedding in Dunkeld, that sinfully smart suburb of Johannesburg. It turned out that Arthur Henkins and Rosemary Bird had invited nearly all their friends in town for the occasion.

And there they were, on the green lawn for the wedding reception. Close to a hundred guests. Rosemary's little hand went into a clinch with a Zulu's hand, then a Jewish friend's, and everyone else.

It was a smooth afternoon. No fat messengers of justice rushing about. Not a grouse from the neighbours. We even got blessings from Father Dennis Sahj who had, earlier, conducted the wedding service with two African altar boys helping. Yes, there are men of God as well on the fringe. Father Huddleston was one.

Some outsiders look at the fringe-dwellers and wonder 'what is the world coming to?'. Others blink and twist their faces in disgust. There are those who take a look and decide, 'it is not any of my business how other people choose to live.'

Until recently, the Crescent Restaurant in Fordsburg, Johannesburg, ran jazz sessions every Sunday night. Jazz cats from the University of Witwatersrand and from every quarter of Johannesburg gathered there and listened to some of the best jazzmen at work. Jonas Gwangwa, Kippie Moeketsi, Lenny Lee and others. Every session at the Crescent was a delicious experience. Like getting a bit of sunshine on a winter day—with the knowledge that soon, very soon, it would all be gone.

Fringe men knew that sooner or later officialdom would stop the sessions on the grounds—and there's a strange irony here—that 'there is bound to be trouble when blacks mix with whites.' But it was good while it lasted. Good—and quite without trouble!

It was reminiscent of the jazz nights at the Goodwill Lounge, in Durban.

The Goodwill opened its doors once or twice a week and jazz addicts piled into the back rooms where Dalton Khanyile and other Durban jazzmen belted their instruments.

One Sunday night an Afrikaner policeman came to a session at the Crescent. Still draped in uniform, this cop sat pounding the piano to a background of wild, black and white hand-clapping. On the following Sunday, the man of Justice brought his sister along to sing while he played the piano. 'Dig those cats,' yelled a member of the crowd, 'they're real gone man, real gone. There's a cop who digs us real deep!'

Once, an American film producer visited Sophiatown shortly before it was demolished by officialdom.

It was during one of those evenings when 'Soft-town' listened to jazz, and Shakespearean plays. There were a few young citizens of Sophiatown and several young women from the white suburbs. Suddenly, police materialised with their heavy knocks at the door.

'One minute, Sergeant,' Bloke said, turning to his gram to put on *Julius Caesar*. Immediately after, he opened the door with a smile which looked perfectly normal, although it was a put-up job.

'Do come in Sarge,' Bloke said. 'Can I help you at all?'

The Sergeant's face turned pink instantly. The floor was covered with liquor. He stammered at last, 'We're searching for drink, you're not keeping any liquor illegally here, are you?'

Realising the helplessness of the man, Bloke picked up a glass and poured out a stiff one for the Sergeant. 'This is just a gathering of my friends, Sarge, and I'm sure you have noticed that yourself. You really ought to go further down.'

Bloke and his friends got away with it then. They had much less difficulty than the English young man who visited a friend in Sophiatown, and found only the sister at home. While the girl was explaining to the visitor that her brother was out, the police arrived.

Not knowing what to do, the girl ordered the English visitor to conceal himself behind a curtain. 'The cops can charge you with anything here,' she told him, 'you never know.' The Englishman took the girl's advice and stood behind the thick curtain like a queen's guard.

To his untold disgust, it turned out that the police were not raiding, but were after liquor to drink. They ordered some from the girl, and settled down to drink for the best part of the evening. And, for five hours, the Englishman was standing behind a curtain.

An Afrikaner woman complained: 'Believe me, my own sister and her husband will never enter my shop because too many of my customers are black and I'm too friendly with them.

'They would sooner go next door and ask for a lavatory there instead of using mine because, they say, I fill the place with kaffirs.'

How long will this woman hold out against the community that says she's abnormal and insane? How long will the black men on the fringe hold out against insults and police hounding which often costs a house, a job or the freedom to live without tension?

These are the questions that drag even the jazz-hunters into political talk, however apolitical they may wish to be. Legislation for the separation of people according to racial or colour groups makes life nearly impossible on the fringe.

They pick up newspapers and read with a deep sense of pity and scorn, about ministers of the Dutch Reformed Church landing in jail for acts of 'indecency' with black women.

Yes, people on the fringe have long conversations about this. Practically none of them is ever in court for any immorality. They generally credit this to the openness and naturalness with which they lead their lives.

There isn't the 'forbidden fruit' urge. When a black fringe-man meets a white woman, there is no question of the couple jumping into a clinch or into the nearest garage.

A young African writer put it into a few lines in a recent short story. The story is of two young men, a black one and a white one. A policeman stops the two men in a Johannesburg suburb and asks the black one why he is walking around in the white man's area instead of going to enjoy himself in the Bantu areas with his own people. 'Who are my people?' the black man asks, challenging the classification.

The man said all there is to be said about the fringe. The fact of being born into a tribe, be it Afrikaner or African, does not matter on the fringe. These people who are neither proud nor ashamed of it, are the emergent group in South Africa.

That new South Africa is being preceded by bold discussion and action. During a press conference, an executive of the South African Broadcasting Corporation was extolling the virtues of his pride in being an Afrikaner. 'Aren't you proud of your own tribe?' he asked an African journalist. 'No, I'm not,' said the journalist. 'I see nothing to be proud or ashamed of there.'

There is perhaps one of the hardest concepts to get through to Afrikaners and Africans. The idea of 'my own people' is deeply entrenched in the two groups. Much more so in the case of the Afrikaner people, whatever the historical reasons may be.

I found this feeling in an Afrikaner Nationalist's home. I was having dinner with Jannie Kruis and his pretty wife. Jannie gave me a drink, offered me a room in his house and asked me to see him more often. When I asked how he could make all these offers and still vote for segregation, he answered simply, 'I have to vote for my people's party. How can I desert my people?" He wouldn't be shaken from his stand.

An advocate spoke of his early days in the Orange Free State. 'I grew up with African boys and girls,' he says. 'But when I went to boarding school, there were only white children around me. So that when I came back home I couldn't even shake the hands of my childhood playmates. I had been taught it was wrong. I had been ordered to live by the values of separation.'

Drum's Cape Town man, Frank Barton, describes the recent restaurant campaigners as 'a courageous band of men and women—black, brown, and white—who are getting their shoulders to the door of apartheid.

'They are just ordinary decent people who believe that it is all very well to condemn the stupid colour barriers of South Africa, but that if things are to change, then somebody has got to start doing something about it.'

But others have been working in the same direction. Like a fringe hipster, J B, who once became fast friends with a luscious blonde in Cape town. 'The public gave us the usual stares,' J B recalls, 'but we got used to them, and discovered various ways of getting round all other difficulties.'

J B could not travel with his blonde friend by train, except on the third class coaches. In the second class the guard would tell her to get out because she was white, and in first class J B was not let in because the guard said he was black. 'But we managed to travel third class, because the guard does not come there,' J B says.

Yes, the restaurant campaigners are not treading virgin ground. Someone has been at it before.

7.   The Destruction of Sophiatown, 1955

The Johannesburg suburb Sophiatown was a slum area; nevertheless, Africans held significant property there. When the South African government condemned Sophiatown under the Group Areas Act, an intense but unavailing struggle was unleashed. After Sophiatown's destruction, the area became the site of the white district of Triomf.

Trevor Huddleston (1913–), a Church of England priest, lived in South Africa from 1943 to 1956, serving the people of Sophiatown and placing himself at the center of the Sophiatown controversy. His book was one of the first to reveal the conditions in South Africa under apartheid to Western readers.

It is the morning of February 10th, 1955. I stand once again where I have stood so many times before, at the low altar step in St. Mary Magdalene's chapel in the Church of Christ the King, Sophiatown. We begin the Preparation: "I will go unto the altar of God . . . even into the God of my joy and gladness. . . . Our help standeth in the name of the Lord. . . . Who hath made heaven and earth. . . ." I notice it is Michael who kneels beside me to make the responses . . . how many times has he knelt just there in the past years? . . . And behind me, I know without looking, there will be Seth Pilane, who never misses his daily Mass, there will be perhaps ten or fifteen members of the Guild, there will be the Sisters and some of the servers. . . . It is still dark outside, for it is only five o'clock and another hour to sunrise. Normally I would know exactly the appearance of the street outside, the familiar sounds of dawn in Sophiatown; the first steps of men walking down the hill to the bus stop; the clop-clop of the horses as they draw old Makudu's cart out of his yard for another day's coal-hawking; a baby crying, a cock crowing, distant voices as people greet each other in the half-light.

But to-day is not normal: not at all. In fact, I am saying Mass an hour early because it is "the Day"; because it is the beginning of the end of Sophiatown: because from now nothing will ever be the same again in this little corner of South Africa: because to-day the great removal is beginning, and all the people I know and the houses they live in will soon be scattered, and Sophiatown itself will crumble into dust.

"The Word was made flesh and dwelt among us, and we beheld His glory, the glory of the only begotten by the Father, full of grace and truth." I walk back to the sacristy and unvest; say my thanksgiving for this blessed and most strengthening food, then out, into the street. By the gate there is already a little group of men, waiting. They are African correspondents of many of the British and overseas newspapers. There seem to be dozens of cameras, though it is still so dark that a photograph would be hard to get. A light rain is falling. Suddenly, from the corner out of sight, where Edward Road meets Ray Street down the dip, there comes a sound I have never heard in Sophiatown before. It is the noise of men marching. The staccato "Hep, Hi, Hep . . . Hep, Hi, Hep . . ." getting louder; and in a moment they breast the hill and draw level with us. A flash-bulb goes off. A detachment of African police under European command marches raggedly but purposefully past us, down the hill. People appear from their houses in the darkness and stand, chattering but subdued, to watch this new and unfamiliar sight.

I walked with Douglas Brown of the *Daily Telegraph* and Leonard Ingalls of the New York *Times,* down Victoria Road to see what was happening. It was beginning to get light, but the rain was coming down hard. The bus queues were already forming, and as we passed, many of the men gave the Congress sign, and greeted me cheerfully. One or two others ran across the road and shook me by the hand. It all looked very normal. It was only when we got to Toby Street that we began to understand how things were shaping: that we knew for certain that the REMOVAL, so long talked about, so often and so fiercely debated, had actually begun. On the broad belt of grass between the European suburb of Westdene and Sophiatown (we called that strip "the Colour Bar") a whole fleet of Army lorries was drawn up: a grim sight against the grey, watery sky. Lining the whole street were thousands of police, both white and black: the former armed with rifles and revolvers, the latter with the usual assegai. A few Sten guns were in position at various points. A V.I.P. car, containing the Commissioner of Police and a mobile wireless unit (which we afterwards discovered was in hourly contact with the Minister in Cape Town) patrolled up and down. "Where are they beginning?" "In the yard opposite the bus station, at the bottom of Toby Street. . . . Let's go." It was a fantastic sight. It looked more like a film-set for an "atmospheric" Italian film than anything real. In the yard, military lorries were drawn up. Already they were piled high with the pathetic possessions which had come from the row of rooms in the background. A rusty kitchen stove: a few blackened pots and pans: a wicker chair: mattresses belching out their coir-stuffing: bundles of heaven-knows-what, and people, soaked, all soaked to the skin by the drenching rain. Above this strange and depressing crowd, perched on top of the van of a police truck, were more cameras filming the scene below. I deliberately put my arm around Robert Resha's shoulders and looked up at the camera. "Move away there . . . you've no right here . . . get out, I'm telling you . . . clear out of this yard." One officer was in a furious temper. Perhaps it was the rain, but I think it was the sight of me, with my arm on an African shoulder. This man made a rush at one of the cameramen who was trying to get a shot of him: pushed his camera away and might easily have broken it. We walked up the street. Whenever I stopped a little group of Africans gathered round me. They were OUR people. But as soon as I started chatting, a policeman would come up and order me to move on. The Minister of Justice had imposed a ban on all gatherings. A chat in the street with a few friends was a gathering. I moved on, and the process was repeated a hundred yards farther on. . . .

The first lorries began to move off for Meadowlands eight miles away to the west. The rain poured down. The removal was definitely under way. Two thousand police, armed; many foreign correspondents; dozens of photographers; a total ban on all gatherings, including (as was thought at the time) attendance at a church service. All this, to effect a slum-clearance scheme which would be of lasting benefit to the "natives"; all this to carry through a plan which anyone could see to be a good plan; all this excitement and fuss and publicity over a project which, to any sensible European in South Africa was a crying necessity if white civilisation was to be preserved. What was it all about? What were the principles involved? What was the Western Areas Removal Scheme anyway? These questions must be answered here in view of the immense interest shown in this matter by the world at large. Nothing, since Michael Scott's revelations about farming conditions at Bethal, has made so great an impact on the international Press. Yet to-day, when the removal of 60,000 people to Meadowlands is proceeding rapidly, and Sophiatown begins to look like a blitzed area in London, the moral and ethical implications of this scheme are barely understood, and if once they were debated, they are now forgotten. Yet I believe that the Western Areas Removal Scheme—to give it its offical name—will one day be recognised as a major issue of race-relations in South Africa. We would do well to learn the lessons it has to teach.

In the first place, the Removal Scheme is no new idea. It was not even the invention of the Nationalist Government. It emerged as soon as the white suburbs of Johannesburg began to spread westward and to make their first contact with old Tobiansky's "mixed" estate. It is now fifty years since Sophiatown was first occupied by Africans. It is over forty since Newclare (which is part of the Western Areas) was established and whites were specifically restricted from residing in the Township. It is nearly forty years since the Johannesburg Town Council was so convinced of the non-European nature of that part of the city that it built its own location, the Western Native

Township, in the heart of the area, and ringed it with an iron fence. By 1920, no one would have questioned the fact that Sophiatown, Martindale, and Newclare were and always would be black. And by 1920 the industrial expansion of Johannesburg had also begun, and the Africans drawn into the city as its labour force needed homes. They found them, as they must, in Sophiatown and its neighbourhood. What was more important to many of them, they found an opportunity—rare indeed in urban Africa—for investment in real estate. Instead of living in a municipally-owned location, they could live on their own plot in their own homes. And their children and their children's children could live there too. Freehold rights, even if amenities were lacking, were worth having. That was undoubtedly one of the great attractions of Sophiatown. The other was its nearness to the city. Instead of spending time and money on transport, as those who lived way out at Pimville Location had to do, they were within cycling distance of their work. Altogether it was a good place to be, combining the freedom of the country with the convenience of the town. And it was healthy, too, for it stood high on a ridge of rock and you could look away towards Pretoria over open, rolling country, where fresh breezes blew. The only problem, as the years passed, was that of overcrowding. Industry continued to expand, particularly when South Africa went off gold. Labour was needed for the factories and the business houses of the city in a big way. And it had to be black labour, for that alone was both cheap and plentiful. Unfortunately it did not occur to Johannesburg citizens that the labour force also had to live somewhere, had to have houses. One of the effects of the race situation in South Africa has always been that blindness. Labour is labour: it is not human, if it is black. It must be there, standing ready in your factory or your kitchen, or your office, but it must make no demands for the necessities of life: a roof-tree or an income large enough to support the home. It must have strong muscles for the job: but how they are to become strong is its own concern. It must have clean clothes and a tidy appearance in your home: but it doesn't matter where or how it is to get the water for washing or the space for drying. So Johannesburg built its factories, its flats and its fun-fairs: it forgot to build houses for its African citizens. And Sophiatown, with its eighteen hundred "stands," began to crack at the seams with its growing population. There was some relief when another municipal location at Orlando was started. But that was needed far more rapidly than it was built. The density of population in Sophiatown continued to increase every year, even though new families moved into Orlando as soon as the houses were finished: even though there was soon a waiting-list of thousands registered with the civic authorities for vacant homes.

The expansion of Johannesburg was not restricted to its non-European labour force. The white population, too, increased, drawing men from the country by the same economic forces which have operated in every part of the world since the industrial revolution. And it chose to spread westward. New suburbs sprang up beyond Ferreirastown. Brixton, Newlands, Westdene: an encirclement of the non-European area had begun. White artisans occupied these suburbs for the most part: and in Westdene they were predominantly

Afrikaners. By a strange irony, the group most strongly anti-African (because it has most to fear from African competition) occupied houses only a few years from the last street in Sophiatown and looked across a strip of grass at the homes which had been established there. By 1937 the first sounds of battle were heard, and by 1939 a city councillor whose constituency abutted on Sophiatown demanded the total removal of all non-European "settlements" in the Western Areas. But in view of the total failure of the City Council to build houses fast enough anywhere in Johannesburg to meet the needs of the African labour force, and also in view of the demands made on the country by the war, nothing was done. In 1944, a year after my arrival in Sophiatown, the Council approved in principle the removal of all Africans and coloureds from the area. But no attempt was made in the following years to implement the scheme, and no attempt was made either to proceed with slum-clearance or to build sufficient houses for those who desperately needed them. It was during the period 1944-1949 that the shanty town emerged, and it was during that period also that the number of African families without any proper home reached catastrophic proportions. The idea of uprooting sixty thousand people who at least had a roof over their heads became ludicrous in view of the vast mass of the homeless who had to make do with shacks and shanties all round the western perimeter of the city.

The "problem" of the Western Areas was added to all the other "problems" of South Africa. But basically the issue was dead simple. It was just this: that white Johannesburg had encroached upon black Johannesburg, and so, naturally, black Johannesburg must move on. MUST MOVE ON. That is why the Western Areas Scheme is so terribly important to the Christian: or rather, why it ought to be. An African freehold township, established for fifty years, can be uprooted and totally destroyed, because it is contiguous with a European suburb. The question of right or wrong does not have any relevance. The story of Naboth's vineyard rings no bell. Arguments soundly based on economics, or town-planning and on history, have no meaning whatsoever. If a black township stands where a white suburb wants to stand, the township must go. We can think up a justification for it afterwards.

When the Malan Government was returned to power in 1948, it wasted no time in elevating the Western Areas Scheme to the level of national importance. Mnr. Mentz, M.P., speaking in the House of Assembly, stated solemnly that "there is not a single strand of barbed wire between my constituency (Westdene) and Sophiatown." Obviously such an appalling danger to European security could not be allowed to continue any longer. The City Council was ordered to get a move on, and to implement its recommendations of 1944.

It should not be forgotten that during the long years when the removal scheme was under discussion by the authorities, it was never once discussed with the people who were going to be removed; with the ratepayers of Sophiatown who, though they paid their rates, had no other contact with the municipal authorities to whom they paid them than the privilege of paying. For nearly twenty years the threat had hung over the Western Areas. Those who had invested their savings in homes for themselves and their children might lose everything: those who wanted some security, some assurance of a future, dared not risk basing it on such shifting foundations. Always, in those years, we were living in a place which was besieged by the forces of fear and uncertainty. It was this, added to the overcrowding, which imposed slum conditions on an area which, in every possible respect, was most suited to be and to remain an African suburb. It is not much of an encouragement to improve your property if, any morning, you open your newspaper and see headlines, "Western Areas Plan Approved: Black Spots to be Removed." I am convinced, from my experience in Sophiatown, that a great deal of the crime and of the juvenile delinquency was directly due to this sense of insecurity. If you're going to lose what you've got anyhow, why worry too much about other peoples' rights and property? But that is another story.

Our chief difficulty in fighting the removal was twofold. In the first place we had to demand, and to go on demanding, a genuine slum-clearance scheme. That is to say, the building of houses in a sufficient number at Orlando or elsewhere to make it possible for the sub-tenants of Sophiatown to move out and thus reduce the density of population to reasonable proportions. On the other hand, we had to keep the citizens of Johannesburg awake to the plain truth that the Government's scheme was not slum-clearance but robbery: robbery carried out in the interests of and under pressure from the neighbouring white suburbs: a political manoeuvre. The South African Institute of Race Relations called a conference in August, 1953, to which fifty-one organisations sent representatives. The Government and the City Council were also invited to attend. Both refused. "Such a conference," said the Secretary of State for Native Affairs, "should not take place... it will not in my opinion serve any useful purpose." Obviously, as in every other issue affecting the African people, the Government had no intention of consultation and no desire to hear their point of view. THEY MUST MOVE. Being natives, the Government always knows what is best for them, and does it. . . .

"But after all this, Padre," said a B.B.C. correspondent sent to make a recording for his programme, "you must admit that Sophiatown was a slum. It was a jolly good thing it was cleared away. And I've seen Meadowlands: it's fine. They're quite happy. What are freehold rights anyway? Surely the principle isn't as important as that? And most of the property in Sophiatown was mortgaged too. Don't you think all the fuss was a bit of a mistake? Was it fair? Is the Government always wrong?" I should have liked to answer those questions over the air. But apparently that was not considered desirable. Now, when the removal is to most people a thing of the past, it is a little late to make comments. Yet, late or not, I must try for the sake of the future, and for the sake of truth itself.

Sophiatown WAS a slum. Those of us who have lived there would never wish to deny that. We have seen with our own eyes the heroism of so many of our own Christian people in their battle to fight and to overcome their environment. It would be treason to them to deny that Sophiatown was a slum. But slum conditions can be removed without the expropriation of a whole area. Indeed the greatest experts in town-planning would agree that only in the last resort should you uproot people from the place they know as home: for in such uprooting you destroy not only the fabric of their houses, you destroy a living organism—the community itself. Sophiatown, then, could have been replanned and rebuilt on the same site: a model African suburb. It could have been, but for the pressure of three things. First, the pressure of white opinion and the political force it represented; secondly, the existence of freehold tenure, and the threat of permanence which it implied; thirdly, that which underlies every event of any racial significance in South Africa: the assumption that white "civilisation" is threatened by the very existence of an African community in any way similar to itself. The African in the kraal is in his right place: so is the African in the kitchen. But the African in a "European" suburb, in a "European" house which he himself owns and is proud of: he is a menace: he must be removed. . . .

8.   The Freedom Charter of 1955

The Freedom Charter was drafted by a "Congress of the People," which met at Kliptown on June 25 and 26, 1955. All races were represented. The ANC and the Congress of Democrats, a mainly white organization formed after the banning and dissolution of the Communist party, dominated. Many of the charter framers were accused of and tried for treason, and their trials pervaded the second half of the 1950s.

The Freedom Charter is one of the most important documents of the anti-apartheid struggle. It remained the major statement of ANC goals as late as the end of the apartheid regime in the 1990s. Moreover, it defined the struggle as not against whites themselves but against the racist system of white domination. The anti-apartheid effort thus could unite all opponents of that system under ANC leadership. The Freedom Charter should be compared to the 1949 Programme of Action and to the 1994 South African Constitution.

The Freedom Charter

We, the people of South Africa, declare for all our country and the world to know:

- that South Africa belongs to all who live in it, black and white, and that no government can justly claim authority unless it is based on the will of all the people;
- that our people have been robbed of their birthright to land, liberty and peace by a form of government founded on injustice and inequality;

From Francis Meli, *South Africa Belongs to Us: A History of the ANC,* Bloomington: Indiana University Press, 1988, pp. 210–213.

- that our country will never be prosperous or free until all our people live in brotherhood, enjoying equal rights and opportunities;
- that only a democratic state, based on the will of all the people, can secure to all their birthright without distinction of colour, race, sex or belief;

And therefore, we, the people of South Africa, black and white together—equals, countrymen and brothers—adopt this Freedom Charter. And we pledge ourselves to strive together, sparing neither strength nor courage, until the democratic changes here set out have been won.

The people shall govern!

Every man and woman shall have the right to vote for and to stand as a candidate for all bodies which make laws.

All people shall be entitled to take part in the administration of the country.

The rights of the people shall be the same, regardless of race, colour or sex.

All bodies of minority rule, advisory boards, councils and authorities shall be replaced by democratic organs of self-government.

All national groups shall have equal rights!

There shall be equal status in the bodies of state, in the courts and in the schools for all national groups and races.

All people shall have equal right to use their own languages, and to develop their own folk culture and customs.

All national groups shall be protected by law against insults to their race and national pride.

The preaching and practice of national, race or colour discrimination and contempt shall be a punishable crime.

All apartheid laws and practices shall be set aside.

The people shall share in the country's wealth!

The national wealth of our country, the heritage of all South Africans, shall be restored to the people.

The mineral wealth beneath the soil, the banks and monopoly industry shall be transferred to the ownership of the people as a whole.

All other industry and trade shall be controlled to assist the well-being of the people.

All people shall have equal rights to trade where they choose, to manufacture and to enter all trades, crafts, and professions.

The land shall be shared among those who work it!

Restrictions of land ownership on a racial basis shall be ended, and all the land redivided amongst those who work it, to banish famine and land hunger.

The state shall help the peasants with implements, seed, tractors and dams to save the soil and assist the tillers.

Freedom of movement shall be guaranteed to all who work on the land.

All shall have the right to occupy land wherever they choose.

People shall not be robbed of their cattle, and forced labour and farm prisons shall be abolished.

All shall be equal before the law!

No one shall be imprisoned, deported, or restricted without a fair trial.

No one shall be condemned by the order of any Government official.

The courts shall be representative of all the people.

Imprisonment shall be only for serious crimes against the people, and shall aim at re-education, not vengeance.

The police force and army shall be open to all on an equal basis and shall be the helpers and protectors of the people.

All laws which discriminate on grounds of race, colour or belief shall be repealed.

All shall enjoy equal human rights!

The law shall guarantee to all their right to speak, to organise, to meet together, to publish, to preach, to worship and to educate their children.

The privacy of the house from police raids shall be protected by law.

All shall be free to travel without restriction from countryside to town, from province to province, and from South Africa abroad.

Pass Laws, permits and all other laws restricting these freedoms shall be abolished.

There shall be work and security!

All who work shall be free to form trade unions, to elect their officers and to make wage agreements with their employers.

The state shall recognise the right and duty of all to work, and to draw full unemployment benefits.

Men and women of all races shall receive equal pay for equal work.

There shall be a forty-hour working week, a national minimum wage, paid annual leave, and sick leave for all workers, and maternity leave on full pay for all working mothers.

Miners, domestic workers, farm workers and civil servants shall have the same rights as all others who work.

Child labour, compound labour, the tot system and contract labour shall be abolished.

The doors of learning and of culture shall be opened!

The Government shall discover, develop and encourage national talent for the enhancement of our cultural life.

All cultural treasures of mankind shall be open to all, by free exchange of books, ideas and contact with other lands.

The aim of education shall be to teach the youth to love their people and their culture, to honour human brotherhood, liberty and peace.

Education shall be free, compulsory, universal, and equal for all children.

Higher education and technical training shall be opened to all by means of state allowances and scholarships awarded on the basis of merit.

Adult illiteracy shall be ended by a mass state education plan.

Teachers shall have all the rights of other citizens.

The colour bar in cultural life, in sport and in education shall be abolished.

There shall be houses, security and comfort!

All people shall have the right to live where they choose, to be decently housed, and to bring up their families in comfort and security.

Unused housing space to be made available to the people.

Rent and prices shall be lowered, food plentiful and no one shall go hungry.

A preventative health scheme shall be run by the state.

Free medical care and hospitalization shall be provided for all, with special care for mothers and young children.

Slums shall be demolished, and new suburbs built where all have transport, roads, lighting, playing fields, creches and social centres.

The aged, the orphans, the disabled and the sick shall be cared for by the state.

Rent, leisure and recreation shall be the right of all.

Fenced locations and ghettos shall be abolished, and laws which break up families shall be repealed.

There shall be peace and friendship!

South Africa shall be a fully independent state, which respects the rights and sovereignty of all nations.

South Africa shall strive to maintain world peace and the settlement of all international disputes by negotiation—not war.

Peace and friendship amongst all our people shall be secured by upholding the equal rights, opportunities and status of all.

The people of the protectorates—Basutoland, Bechuanaland and Swaziland—shall be free to decide for themselves their own future.

The right of all the peoples of Africa to independence and self-government shall be recognised, and shall be the basis of close co-operation.

Let all who love their people and their country now say, as we say here:
"These freedoms we will fight for, side by side, throughout our lives, until we
have won our liberty."

Adopted at the Congress of the People, Kliptown, South Africa, on 26 June
1955.

9.   A Treason Trial Defendant Is Questioned About Communism and Violence, 1960

The prosecution in the treason trials concentrated on trying to prove that
the one hundred sixty-two defendants conspired to use force and violence
to overthrow the government of South Africa. They also sought to tie
them to a communist conspiracy. If defendants had predicted that relent-
less oppression could lead to violence, they were accused of advocating
violence. In addition, the mildly socialist prescriptions of the Freedom
Charter struck prosecutors as evidence of its framers' communist
purposes.

Masabalala Yengwa, whose testimony follows, had been Natal secre-
tary of the Congress Youth League and was an opponent of Africanism
and a strong supporter of the Freedom Charter. He had been instrumen-
tal in persuading Chief Albert Luthuli to stand for the ANC presidency.

Mr. Trengove: How much land held by Europeans at the moment would have
to be expropriated or confiscated in terms of that clause [of the Freedom
Charter]?

M. B. Yengwa: Now you're using the word 'expropriated' or 'confiscated.' I don't think either of them—I don't think here there is a question of
any particular portion, or a particular percentage of the land—it's merely a
question of seeing that the land is equitably distributed. The mechanics of distribution would have to be worked out in the future; I don't think it is dealt
with here.

What did the African National Congress have in mind; how are you going
to get hold of the large portion of the 87% of the land in order to distribute it
equally?—Well, to get hold of it is a matter of an arrangement with the people
in the country. I think any man—I don't think it matters who it is—there will

Treason trial testimony of M. B. Yengwa, from Thomas Karis and Gwendolyn M. Carter, eds., *From
Protest to Challenge: A Documentary History of African Politics in South Africa, 1882–1964: Vol. 3:
Challenge and Violence, 1953–1964,* ed. by Thomas Karis and Gail M. Gerhart, Stanford: Hoover
Institution Press, 1977, pp. 611–614.

be a stage where I think the people of South Africa will realise that this inequality is wrong; they'll find a way, as a group—as a multi-racial nation—as a common nation they'll find a way of distributing this land. It isn't a question of just Africans alone just grabbing the land; it's a question of agreeing between themselves and saying "Look, this is no good; 87% of the land belongs to about only 25% of the people".

Mr. Yengwa, before people agree to this they'll want to know what they're going to lose. Now what did the—?—You mean in terms of money?

In terms of land?—In terms of money, in terms of land?

How much land would have to be transferred to the non-white people. Surely that was considered by the African National Congress?—My lords, this is a question that involves a lot of other things; it involves goodwill, it involves a change of heart of the people, it is not only a question of shillings and pence. People are prepared to lose a lot in terms of shillings and pence for other greater things in life, and I think that is the way I personally look at it; that if it's a question of saving South Africa, it's a question of making South Africa a better place for all of us—then we have to appeal to the higher motives and higher values in the human being. And I think even the white man will ultimately have to see it this way, that it isn't just a question of his shillings and pence, it's a question of sacrifice for the common good, for the greater good.

You would expect a change of heart on behalf of the Europeans?—A change of mind more than a change of heart. A change of mind, a change of mental attitude towards the whole problem of South Africa.

Why not a change of heart, Mr. Yengwa?—Well, because I'm perhaps putting it in a way where only sentimentality only takes place; it is much more; I mean it's a real problem; it's not just a question of sentiment. For instance, I think the question of race prejudice is a question of heart, of sentiment only; there are other issues involved which I think will have to be taken into account by the people who have to live together.

Mr. Trengove: Would the races in any way be limited as to the amount of land they can hold?

M. B. Yengwa: The what?

The races in the country?— The races?

Yes?—No, there is no question of the races.

The Europeans—?—The point is, my lord, we are looking at the whole problem from a different angle because we are now racially oriented; we are looking at how much the African is going to get, how much the European is going to get. But in my own view that must die out as soon as we don't think in terms of Bantu, Englishman, Afrikaner—but think of South Africans, a common people with a common patriotism. That is how I look at it, so that actually the problems you are posing now apply now but they will never apply in a new society. They will have no place in a new society. In fact I look at the other man as a brother.

Mr. Yengwa, I want to put it to you that these details and these matters and these implications were never considered by the African National

Congress, as to how they were going to limit it, and what compensation they would have to pay, and all that kind of thing. They never thought of that?— My lord, the question of thinking about those details is a matter in fact which I think would have been wrong to think of at that particular time, because those are the details that must actually be worked out at a particular time when conditions are different; you don't have to work out details of something like this, because this is merely an ideal of what you think a future society should be.

I want to put it to you, Mr. Yengwa, that they didn't think of it because they never intended to negotiate; they intended to overthrow the ruling class and to seize power and to confiscate the land, the mines, the banks, the monopoly industries in a new society?—I say, my lord, there is no basis for that; that conclusion has no basis at all on the paper we see here. There is no basis for arriving at the conclusion that you've arrived at, my lord.

You wanted to destroy the old society; you wanted to destroy the capitalist structure of the society?—No, my lord, I don't agree with these assumptions that you are making now, of destroying the old society, destroying capital society. I don't agree with that. I don't know where you get that.

Mr. Trengove: Mr. Yengwa, apart from "Das Kapital" and "The Communist Manifesto", have you read any other works on Communism?

M. B. Yengwa: No, my lord.

No other works?—No, my lord.

And what did you mean when you said in your evidence you don't understand the Communist theory of revolution?—Well, I meant, my lord, that I have not read any particular—I've not read about the theory of revolution; I cannot tell you exactly the salient points, and the salient features of the Communist theory of revolution.

Mr. Trengove: Mr. Yengwa, you know very well that the Communists throughout the world are there to overthrow existing social conditions in non-Communist countries by force, by violence. You know that?

M. B. Yengwa: Well, my lords, I do not know; I don't know the whole history of Communism; I am not able to say that I know.

And I want to put it to you that the Communists in the Liberatory Movement in South Africa were working in that direction, and with that in mind?—That was not what I knew and that is not what they told us. As far as I knew they supported the Congress policy and that was all that was required of them in the Congress Movement.

You said yesterday that the Communists never opposed or criticised the non-violent policy of the African National Congress?—No, they never did.

I put it to you that they didn't because the African National Congress hasn't got a non-violent policy?— My lords, I've been repeating over and over again, and I want again to repeat that the A.N.C. policy is non-violent, and I have not been able to find anything at all from what the Prosecutor has said or shewn me, to show in support of his allegation, 'Here is the evidence to show that what you say is wrong'. He is only alleging and putting it to me, one hundred and one times, that the A.N.C. policy was violent, but without a shred of evidence to support his allegation, my lords.

Mr. Yengwa, I want to put it to you that the methods that you people consistently and systematically advocated in order to achieve your freedom, are completely in line with Communist policy; and is exactly what the Communists want?—I don't know, my lords, what the Communists want, but I do know what the African National Congress want.

Rumpff J: Isn't this argument, Mr. Trengove?

Mr Trengove: Mr. Yengwa, I want to put it to you that throughout the period of the Indictment, all your propaganda and all your campaigns, were directed at preparing the masses for the overthrow of the State by indoctrinating them with Communist propaganda?—I deny that, my lord, most emphatically.

And I also put it to you that your activities throughout this period were intended to be a softening up process against the State?—What do you mean softening up process?

A process to cause the disintegration and the break-down of the State, so that you could take over by violence, when the time was ripe?—That is ridiculous, my lords.

And I put it to you that apart from that your purpose—your campaigns served a purpose which enabled you to test the mood of the masses to find out whether they were ripe to move from one stage to another?—My lords, that is not correct at all, it is totally wrong.

Mr. Trengove: Is South Africa a Capitalist State?

M. B. Yengwa: As far as I'm concerned it has aspects of Capitalism, and it has aspects, too, of Socialism.

I want to know the African National Congress view?—The African National Congress view I think is the view that I'm giving you now.

Did they regard South Africa as a Capitalist State?—Both Capitalist and in some ways Socialist.

Did they regard South Africa as imperialist?—Yes, they do regard South Africa as having aspects of Imperialism.

Did they regard South Africa as Fascist?—They do regard South Africa as being Fascist.

Why?—Because the Government has very large powers over the lives of the people; in that way they regard South Africa as Fascist.

10.   The Ideology of Pan-Africanism, 1960

Robert Sobukwe, whose speech follows, led the Pan-Africanist Congress (PAC) after its split from the ANC in 1959. The PAC condemned the ANC's sympathy with communists and its adherence to the Congress Alliance,

From *Speeches of Mangaliso Sobukwe from 1949–1959 and Other Documents of the Pan-Africanist Congress of Azania:* A. A. C. Observer Mission to the UN, 1979, pp. 18–21.

which included radical white groups such as the Congress of Democrats. Sobukwe allied the movement with the emerging nationalism of tropical African territories such as Ghana and Nigeria just as these and other tropical African colonies were moving toward political independence. In an attempt to outbid the ANC for support, Sobukwe moved the PAC to challenge the government in the anti-pass campaign beginning in 1960.

In South Africa we recognize the existence of national groups which are the result of geographical origin within a certain area as well as a shared historical experience of these groups. The Europeans are a foreign minority group which has exclusive control of political, economic, social and military power. It is the dominant group. It is the exploiting group, responsible for the pernicious doctrine of white supremacy which has resulted in the humiliation and degradation of the indigenous African people. It is this group which has dispossessed the African people of their land and with arrogant conceit has set itself up as the "guardians", the "trustees" of the Africans. It is this group which conceives of the African people as a child nation, composed of Boys and Girls, ranging in age from 120 years to one day. It is this group which, after 300 years, can still state, with brazen effrontery, that the Native, the Bantu, the Kaffir is still backward and savage, etc. But they still want to remain "guardians", "trustees", and what have you, of the African people. In short, it is this group which has mismanaged affairs in South Africa just as their kith and kin are mismanaging affairs in Europe. It is from this group that the most rabid race baiters and agitators come. It is members of this group who, whenever they meet in their Parliament, say things which agitate the hearts of millions of peace-loving Africans. This is the group which turns out thousands of experts on that new South African science—the Native mind.

Then there is the Indian foreign minority group. This group came to this country not as imperialists or colonialists, but as indentured laborers. In the South African set-up of today, this group is an oppressed minority. But there are some members of this group, the merchant class in particular, who have become tainted with the virus of cultural supremacy and national arrogance. This class identifies itself by and large, with the oppressor but, significantly, this is the group which provides the political leadership of the Indian people in South Africa. And all that the politics of this class have meant up to now is preservation and defence of the sectional interests of the Indian merchant class. The down-trodden, poor "stinking coolies" of Natal who, alone, as a result of the pressure of material conditions, can identify themselves with the indigenous African majority in the struggle to overthrow White supremacy, have not yet produced their leadership. We hope they will do so soon.

The Africans constitute the indigenous group and form the majority of the population. They are the most ruthlessly exploited and are subjected to humiliation, degradation, and insult.

Now it is our contention that true democracy can be established in South Africa and on the continent as a whole, only when white supremacy has been destroyed. And the illiterate and semi-literate African masses constitute the key and centre and content of any struggle for true democracy in South

Africa. And the African people can be organized only under the banner of African nationalism in an All-African Organization where they will by themselves formulate policies and programmes and decide on the methods of struggle without interference from either so-called left-wing or right-wing groups of the minorities who arrogantly appropriate to themselves the right to plan and think for the Africans.

We wish to emphasize that the freedom of the African means the freedom of all in South Africa, the European included, because only the African can guarantee the establishment of a genuine democracy in which all men will be citizens of a common state and will live and be governed as individuals and not as distinctive sectional groups.

In conclusion, I wish to state that the Africanists do not at all subscribe to the fashionable doctrine of South African exceptionalism. Our contention is that South Africa is an integral part of the indivisible whole that is Africa. She cannot solve her problems in isolation from and with utter disregard of the rest of the continent.

Against multi-racialism, we have this objection, that the history of South Africa has fostered group prejudices and antagonisms, and if we have to maintain the same group exclusiveness, parading under the term of multi-racialism, we shall be transporting to the new Africa these very antagonisms and conflicts. Further, multi-racialism is in fact a pandering to European bigotry and arrogance. It is a method of safeguarding white interests irrespective of population figures. In that sense it is a complete negation of democracy. To us the term "multi-racialism" implies that there are such basic inseparable differences between the various national groups here that the best course is to keep them permanently distinctive in a kind of democratic apartheid. That to us is racialism multiplied, which probably is what the term truly connotes.

We aim, politically, at government of the Africans by the Africans for Africans, with everybody who owes his only loyalty to Africa and who is prepared to accept the democratic rule of an African majority being regarded as an African. We guarantee no minority rights, because we think in terms of individuals, not groups.

Economically, we aim at the rapid extension of industrial development in order to alleviate pressure on the land which is what progress means in terms of modern society. We stand committed to a policy guaranteeing the most equitable distribution of wealth.

Socially, we aim at the full development of the human personality and a ruthless uprooting and outlawing of all forms or manifestations of the racial myth. To sum it up, we stand for an Africanist Socialist Democracy.

Here is a tree rooted in African soil, nourished with waters from rivers of Africa. Come and sit under its shade and become, with us, leaves of the same branch and branches of the same tree.

Then Sons and Daughters of Africa, I declare this inaugural convention of the Africanists open! IZWE LETHU!!

The Republic of South Africa and the Armed Struggle

1. The Winds of Change

British prime minister Sir Harold Macmillan's speech before a joint session of the South African Parliament on February 3, 1960, pointed to the emerging gap between the policies of Britain and France, whose African colonies were moving to independence, and South African apartheid, which aimed to deny permanently the same aspirations to Africans of the Union. Macmillan's address marked a turning point: South Africa would shortly proclaim itself a republic and leave the Commonwealth.

In the twentieth century, and especially since the end of the war, the processes which gave birth to the nation states of Europe have been repeated all over the world. We have seen the awakening of national consciousness in peoples who have for centuries lived in dependence upon some other power. Fifteen years ago this movement spread through Asia. Many countries there of different races and civilisations pressed their claim to an independent national life. Today the same thing is happening in Africa, and the most striking of all the impressions I have formed since I left London a month ago is of the strength of this African national consciousness. In different places it takes different forms, but it is happening everywhere. The wind of change is blowing through this continent, and, whether we like it or not, this growth of national consciousness is a political fact. We must all accept it as a fact, and our national policies must take account of it.

Of course, you understand this better than anyone. You are sprung from Europe, the home of nationalism, and here in Africa you have yourselves created a new nation. Indeed, in the history of our times yours will be recorded as the first of the African nationalisms, and this tide of national consciousness which is now rising in Africa is a fact for which you and we and the other nations of the Western World are ultimately responsible. For its causes are to be found in the achievements of Western civilisation, in the pushing forward of the frontiers of knowledge, in the applying of science in the service of human needs, in the expanding of food production, in the speeding and multiplying of the means of communication, and perhaps, above all, the spread of education.

As I have said, the growth of national consciousness in Africa is a political fact, and we must accept it as such. That means, I would judge, that we must come to terms with it. I sincerely believe that if we cannot do so we may imperil the precarious balance between the East and West on which the peace of the world depends. The world today is divided into three main groups. First here are what we call the Western Powers. You in South Africa and we in Britain belong to this group, together with our friends and allies in other parts of the Commonwealth. In the United States of America and in Europe we call it the Free World. Secondly there are the Communists—Russia and her satellites in Europe and China whose population will rise by the end of the next ten years to the staggering total of 800,000,000. Thirdly, there are those parts of the world whose people are at present uncommitted either to Communism or to our Western ideas.

In this context we think first of Asia and then of Africa. As I see it the great issue in this second half of the twentieth century is whether the uncommitted peoples of Asia and Africa will swing to the East or to the West. Will they be drawn into the Communist camp? Or will the great experiments in self-government that are now being made in Asia and Africa, especially within the Commonwealth, prove so successful, and by their example so compelling, that the balance will come down in favour of freedom and order and justice?

The struggle is joined, and it is a struggle for the minds of men. What is now on trial is much more than our military strength or our diplomatic and administrative skill. It is our way of life. The uncommitted nations want to see before they choose.

What can we show them to help them choose right? Each of the independent members of the Commonwealth must answer that question for itself. It is a basic principle of our modern Commonwealth that we respect each other's sovereignty in matters of internal policy. At the same time we must recognise that in this shrinking world in which we live today the internal policies of one nation may have effects outside it. . . .

I am sure you will agree that in our own areas of responsibility we must each do what we think right. What we think right derives from a long experience both of failure and success in the management of our own affairs. We have tried to learn and apply the lessons of our judgement of right and wrong. Our justice is rooted in the same soil as yours—in Christianity and in the rule of law as the basis of a free society. This experience of our own explains why it has been our aim in the countries for which we have borne responsibility, not only to raise the material standards of living, but also to create a society which respects the rights of individuals, a society in which men are given the opportunity to grow to their full stature—and that must in our view include the opportunity to have an increasing share in political power and responsibility, a society in which individual merit and individual merit alone is the criterion for a man's advancement, whether political or economic.

Finally in countries inhabited by several different races it has been our aim to find means by which the community can become more of a community, and fellowship can be fostered between its various parts. This problem is by no means confined to Africa. Nor is it always a problem of a European minority. In Malaya, for instance, though there are Indian and European minorities, Malays and Chinese make up the great bulk of the population, and the Chinese are not much fewer in numbers than the Malays. Yet these two people must learn to live together in harmony and unity and the strength of Malaya as a nation will depend on the different contributions which the two races can make.

The attitude of the United Kingdom towards this problem was clearly expressed by the Foreign Secretary, Mr. Selwyn Lloyd, speaking at the United Nations General Assembly on 17 September 1959. These were his words:

> In those territories where different races or tribes live side by side the task is to ensure that all the people may enjoy security and freedom and the chance to contribute as individuals to the progress and well being of these countries. We reject the idea of any inherent superiority of one race over another. Our policy therefore is non-racial. It offers a future in which Africans, Europeans, Asians, the peoples of the Pacific and others with whom we are concerned, will all play their full part as citizens in the countries where they live, and in which feelings of race will be submerged in loyalty to new nations.

I have thought you would wish me to state plainly and with full candour the policy for which we in Britain stand. It may well be that in trying to do our duty as we see it we shall sometimes make difficulties for you. If this proves to be so we shall regret it. But I know that even so you would not ask us to flinch from doing our duty.

You, too, will do your duty as you see it. I am well aware of the peculiar nature of the problems with which you are faced here in the Union of South Africa. I know the differences between your situation and that of most of the other states in Africa. You have here some three million people of European origin. This country is their home. It has been their home for many generations. They have no other. The same is true of Europeans in Central and East Africa. In most other African states those who have come from Europe have come to work, to contribute their skills, perhaps to teach, but not to make a home.

The problems to which you as members of the Union Parliament have to address yourselves are very different from those which face the Parliaments of countries with homogenous populations. These are complicated and baffling problems. It would be surprising if your interpretation of your duty did not sometimes produce very different results from ours in terms of Government policies and actions.

As a fellow member of the Commonwealth it is our earnest desire to give South Africa our support and encouragement, but I hope you won't mind my saying frankly that there are some aspects of your policies which make it impossible for us to do this without being false to our own deep convictions about the political destinies of free men to which in our own territories we are trying to give effect. I think we ought, as friends, to face together, without seeking to apportion credit or blame, the fact that in the world of today this difference of outlook lies between us.

I said that I was speaking as a friend. I can also claim to be speaking as a relation, for we Scots can claim family connections with both the great European sections of your population, not only with the English-speaking people but with the Afrikaans-speaking as well. This is a point which hardly needs emphasis in Cape Town where you can see every day the statue of that great Scotsman, Andrew Murray. His work in the Dutch Reformed Church in the Cape, and the work of his son in the Orange Free State, was among Afrikaans-speaking people. There has always been a very close connection between the Church of Scotland and the Church of the Netherlands. The Synod of Dort plays the same great part in the history of both. Many aspirants to the Ministry of Scotland, especially in the seventeenth and eighteenth centuries, went to pursue their theological studies in the Netherlands. Scotland can claim to have repaid the debt in South Africa. I am thinking particularly of the Scots in the Orange Free State. Not only the younger Andrew Murray, but also the Robertsons, the Frasers, the McDonalds—families which have been called the Free State clans, who became burghers of the old Free State and whose descendants still play their part there.

But though I count myself a Scot, my mother was an American, and the United States provides a valuable illustration of one of the main points which I have been trying to make in my remarks today. Its population, like yours, is of different strains, and over the years most of those who have gone to North America have gone there in order to escape conditions in Europe which they found intolerable. The Pilgrim Fathers were fleeing from persecution as Puritans and the Marylanders from persecution as Roman Catholics. Throughout the nineteenth century a stream of immigrants flowed across the Atlantic to escape from the poverty in their homelands, and in the twentieth century the United States have provided asylum for the victims of political oppression in Europe.

Thus for the majority of its inhabitants America has been a place of refuge, or place to which people went because they wanted to get away from Europe. It is not surprising, therefore, that for many years a main objective of American statesmen, supported by the American public, was to isolate themselves from Europe, and with their great material strength, and the vast resources open to them, this might have seemed an attractive and practicable course. Nevertheless in the two world wars of this century they have found themselves unable to stand aside. Twice their manpower in arms has streamed back across the Atlantic to shed blood in those European struggles from which their ancestors thought they would escape by emigrating to the New World; and when the second war was over they were forced to recognise that in the small world of today isolationism is out of date and offers no assurance of security.

The fact is that in this modern world no country, not even the greatest, can live for itself alone. Nearly two thousand years ago, when the whole of the civilised world was comprised within the confines of the Roman Empire, St. Paul proclaimed one of the great truths of history—we are all members one of another. During this twentieth century that eternal truth has taken on a new and exciting significance. It has always been impossible for the individual man to live in isolation from his fellows, in the home, the tribe, the village, or the city. Today it is impossible for nations to live in isolation from one another. What Dr. John Donne said of individual men three hundred years ago is true today of my country, your country, and all the countries of the world:

> Any man's death diminishes me, because I am involved in Mankind.
> And therefore never send to know for whom the bell tolls; it tolls
> for thee.

All nations now are interdependent one upon another, and this is generally realised throughout the Western World. I hope in due course the countries of Communism will recognise it too.

It was certainly with that thought in mind that I took the decision to visit Moscow about this time last year. Russia has been isolationist in her time and still has tendencies that way, but the fact remains that we must live in the same world with Russia, and we must find a way of doing so. I believe that the initiative which we took last year has had some success, although grave difficulties may arise. Nevertheless I think nothing but good can come out of its extending contacts between individuals, contacts in trade and from the exchange of visitors.

I certainly do not believe in refusing to trade with people because you may happen to dislike the way they manage their internal affairs at home. Boycotts will never get you anywhere, and may I say in parenthesis that I deprecate the attempts that are being made today in Britain to organise the consumer boycott of South African goods. It has never been the practice, as far as I know, of any Government of the United Kingdom of whatever complexion to undertake or support campaigns of this kind designed to influence the internal politics of another Commonwealth country, and my colleagues in the United Kingdom deplore this proposed boycott and regard it as undesirable from every point of view. It can only have serious effects on Commonwealth relations, on trade, and lead to the ultimate detriment of others than those against whom it is aimed.

I said I was speaking of the interdependence of nations. The members of the Commonwealth feel particularly strongly the value of interdependence. They are as independent as any nation in this shrinking world can be, but they have voluntarily agreed to work together. They recognise that there may be and must be differences in their institutions; in their internal policies, and their membership does not imply the wish to express a judgement on these matters, or the need to impose a stifling uniformity. It is, I think, a help that there has never been question of any rigid constitution for the Commonwealth. Perhaps this is because we have got on well enough in the United Kingdom without a written constitution and tend to look suspiciously at them. Whether that is so or not, it is quite clear that a rigid constitutional framework for the Commonwealth would not work. At the first of the stresses and strains which are inevitable in this period of history, cracks would first appear in the framework and the whole structure would crumble. It is the flexibility of our Commonwealth institutions which gives them their strength.

Mr. President, Mr. Speaker, Honourable Ministers, Ladies and Gentlemen, I fear I have kept you a long time. I much welcome the opportunity to speak to this great audience. In conclusion may I say this? I have spoken frankly about the differences between our two countries in their approach to one of the great current problems with which each has to deal within its own sphere of responsibility. These differences are well-known. They are matters of public knowledge, indeed of public controversy, and I would have been less than honest if by remaining silent on them I had seemed to imply that they did not exist. But differences on one subject, important though it is, need not and should not impair our capacity to co-operate with one another in furthering the many practical interests which we share in common. . . .

2.   Nelson Mandela Explains the ANC Struggle, 1964

Nelson Mandela was already in prison on lesser charges when a police raid on the ANC hideout on Rivonia Farm netted authorities a store of documents revealing the plans of Umkonto we Sizwe, the newly founded military wing of the ANC. These documents implicated Mandela, who was then tried anew on additional charges and given a life sentence. The Rivonia trial statement below is one of the key documents of the ANC struggle against apartheid, and it states the goals and ideals to which Nelson Mandela still adhered after twenty-six years of further imprisonment.

I am the First Accused.

I hold a Bachelor's Degree in Arts and practised as an attorney in Johannesburg for a number of years in partnership with Oliver Tambo. I am a convicted prisoner serving five years for leaving the country without a permit and for inciting people to go on strike at the end of May, 1961.

At the outset, I want to say that the suggestion made by the State in its opening that the struggle in South Africa is under the influence of foreigners or communists is wholly incorrect. I have done whatever I did, both as an individual and as a leader of my people, because of my experience in South

From Thomas Karis and Gwendolyn M. Carter, eds., *From Protest to Challenge: A Documentary History of African Politics in South Africa, 1882–1964: Vol. 3: Challenge and Violence, 1953–1964,* ed. by Thomas Karis and Gail M. Gerhart, Stanford: Hoover Institution Press, 1977, pp. 771–777, 790–791, 795–796.

Africa and my own proudly-felt African background, and not because of what any outsider might have said.

In my youth in the Transkei I listened to the elders of my tribe telling stories of the old days. Amongst the tales they related to me were those of wars fought by our ancestors in defence of the fatherland. The names of Dingane and Bambata, Hintsa and Makana, Squngthi and Dalasile, Moshoeshoe and Sekukhuni, were praised as the glory of the entire African nation. I hoped then that life might offer me the opportunity to serve my people and make my own humble contribution to their freedom struggle. This is what has motivated me in all that I have done in relation to the charges made against me in this case.

Having said this, I must deal immediately and at some length, with the question of violence. Some of the things so far told to the Court are true and some are untrue. I do not, however, deny that I planned sabotage. I did not plan it in a spirit of recklessness, nor because I have any love of violence. I planned it as the result of a calm and sober assessment of the political situation that had arisen after many years of tyranny, exploitation and oppression of my people by the Whites.

I admit immediately that I was one of the persons who helped to form Umkonto We Sizwe, and that I played a prominent role in its affairs until I was arrested in August, 1962.

In the statement which I am about to make I shall correct certain false impressions which have been created by State witnesses. Amongst other things, I will demonstrate that certain of the acts referred to in the evidence were not and could not have been committed by Umkonto. I will also deal with the relationship between the African National Congress and Umkonto, and with the part which I personally have played in the affairs of both organizations. I shall deal also with the part played by the Communist Party. In order to explain these matters properly I will have to explain what Umkonto set out to achieve; what methods it prescribed for the achievement of these objects, and why these methods were chosen. I will also have to explain how I became involved in the activities of these organizations.

I deny that Umkonto was responsible for a number of acts which clearly fell outside the policy of the organization, and which have been charged in the Indictment against us. I do not know what justification there was for these acts, but to demonstrate that they could not have been authorised by Umkonto, I want to refer briefly to the roots and policy of the organization.

I have already mentioned that I was one of the persons who helped to form Umkonto. I, and the others who started the organization, did so for two reasons. Firstly, we believed that as a result of Government policy, violence by the African people had become inevitable, and that unless responsible leadership was given to canalise and control the feelings of our people, there would be outbreaks of terrorism which would produce an intensity of bitterness and hostility between the various races of this country which is not produced even by war. Secondly, we felt that without violence there would be no way open to the African people to succeed in their struggle against the principle of White supremacy. All lawful modes of expressing opposition to this principle had been closed by legislation, and we were placed in a position in which we had either to accept a permanent state of inferiority, or to defy the Government. We chose to defy the law. We first broke the law in a way which avoided any recourse to violence; when this form was legislated against, and when the Government resorted to a show of force to crush opposition to its policies, only then did we decide to answer violence with violence.

But the violence which we chose to adopt was not terrorism. We who formed Umkonto were all members of the African National Congress, and had behind us the A.N.C. tradition of non-violence and negotiation as a means of solving political disputes. We believe that South Africa belonged to all the people who lived in it, and not to one group, be it Black or White. We did not want an inter-racial war, and tried to avoid it to the last minute. If the Court is in doubt about this, it will be seen that the whole history of our organization bears out what I have said, and what I will subsequently say, when I describe the tactics which Umkonto decided to adopt. I want, therefore, to say something about the African National Congress.

The African National Congress was formed in 1912 to defend the rights of the African people which had been seriously curtailed by the South Africa Act, and which were then being threatened by the Native Land Act. For thirty-seven years—that is until 1949—it adhered strictly to a constitutional struggle. It put forward demands and resolutions; it sent delegations to the Government in the belief that African grievances could be settled through peaceful discussion and that Africans could advance gradually to full political rights. But White Governments remained unmoved, and the rights of Africans became less instead of becoming greater. In the words of my leader, Chief Luthuli, who became President of the A.N.C. in 1952, and who was later awarded the Nobel Peace Prize:

> "who will deny that thirty years of my life have been spent knocking in vain, patiently, moderately and modestly at a closed and barred door? What have been the fruits of moderation? The past thirty years have seen the greatest number of laws restricting our rights and progress, until today we have reached a stage where we have almost no rights at all".

Even after 1949, the A.N.C. remained determined to avoid violence. At this time, however, there was a change from the strictly constitutional means of protest which had been employed in the past. The change was embodied in a decision which was taken to protest against apartheid legislation by peaceful, but unlawful, demonstrations against certain laws. Pursuant to this policy the A.N.C. launched the Defiance Campaign, in which I was placed in charge of volunteers. This campaign was based on the principles of passive resistance. More than 8,500 people defied apartheid laws and went to gaol. Yet there was not a single instance of violence in the course of this campaign on the part of any defier. I, and nineteen colleagues were convicted for the role we played in organizing the campaign, but our sentences were suspended mainly because the Judge found that discipline and nonviolence had been stressed throughout. This was the time when the volunteer section of the A.N.C. was established, and the word 'Amadelakufa' was first used: this was the time when the volunteers were asked to take a pledge to uphold certain principles. Evidence dealing with volunteers and their pledges has been introduced into this case, but completely out of context. The volunteers were not, and are not, the soldiers of a Black Army pledged to fight a civil war against the Whites. They were, and are, the dedicated workers who are prepared to lead campaigns initiated by the A.N.C. to distribute leaflets; to organize strikes, or do whatever the particular campaign required. They are called volunteers because they volunteer to face the penalties of imprisonment and whipping which are now prescribed by the legislature for such acts.

During the Defiance Campaign, the Public Safety Act and the Criminal Law Amendment Act were passed. These Statutes provided harsher penalties for offences committed by way of protests against laws. Despite this, the protests continued and the A.N.C. adhered to its policy of non-violence. In 1956, one hundred and fifty-six leading members of the Congress Alliance, including myself, were arrested on a charge of High Treason and charged under the Suppression of Communism Act. The non-violent policy of the A.N.C. was put into issue by the State, but when the Court gave judgement some five years later, it found that the A.N.C. did not have a policy of violence. We were acquitted on all counts, which included a count that the A.N.C. sought to set up a Communist State in place of the existing regime. The Government has always sought to label all its opponents as communists. This allegation has been repeated in the present case, but as I will show, the A.N.C. is not, and never has been, a communist organization.

In 1960, there was the shooting at Sharpeville, which resulted in the proclamation of a State of Emergency and the declaration of the A.N.C. as an unlawful organization. My colleagues and I, after careful consideration, decided that we would not obey this decree. The African people were not part of the Government and did not make the laws by which they were governed. We believed in the words of the Universal Declaration of Human Rights, that "the will of the people shall be the basis of the authority of the Government", and for us to accept the banning was equivalent to accepting the silencing of the Africans for all time. The A.N.C. refused to dissolve, but instead went underground. We believed it was our duty to preserve this organization which had been built up with almost fifty years of unremitting toil. I have no doubt that no self-respecting White political organization would disband itself if declared illegal by a Government in which it had no say.

In some of the evidence the M. Plan* has been completely misrepresented. It was nothing more than a method of organizing, planned in 1953, and put into operation with varying degrees of success thereafter. After April, 1960,

---

*M-Plan. After the failure of the 1952 Defiance Campaign and the government's passage of punitive legislation against protest, including the banning of many individual leaders, Nelson Mandela worked out the M-Plan, designed to divide the ANC into small, discrete divisions of cells, zones, and wards. His hope was that in future protest campaigns the arrest of some activists would not compromise others. The plan itself was never carried out effectively, but similar policies were applied in the armed struggle by the 1980s.

new methods had to be devised, for instance, by relying on smaller Committees. The M. Plan was referred to in evidence at the Treason Trial, but it had nothing whatsoever to do with sabotage or Umkonto We Sizwe, and was never adopted by Umkonto. The confusion, particularly by certain witnesses from the Eastern Province, is, I think, due to the use of the phrase "High Command". This term was coined in Port Elizabeth during the Emergency, when most of the A.N.C. leaders were gaoled, and a Gaol Committee, set up to deal with complaints, was called the High Command. After the Emergency this phrase stuck and was used to describe certain of the A.N.C. Committees in that area. Thus we have had witnesses talking about the West Bank High Command and the Port Elizabeth High Command. These so-called "High Commands" came into existence before Umkonto was formed and were not concerned in any way with sabotage. In fact, as I will subsequently explain, Umkonto as an organization was, as far as possible, kept separate from the A.N.C. This explains why persons like Bennet Mashiyane and Reginald Ndube heard nothing about sabotage at the meetings they attended. But, as has been mentioned by Zizi Njikelane, the use of the phrase "High Command" caused some dissension in A.N.C. circles in the Eastern Province. I travelled there in 1961, because it was alleged that some of these so-called High Commands were using duress in order to enforce the new Plan. I did not find evidence of this, but nevertheless forbade it, and also insisted that the term "High Command" should not be used to describe any A.N.C. Committee. My visit and the discussions which took place have been described by Zizi Njikelane, and I admit his evidence in so far as it relates to me. Although it does not seem to have much relevance, I deny that I was taken to the meeting by the taxi driver John Tshingane, and I also deny that I went to the sea with him.

In 1960 the Government held a Referendum which led to the establishment of the Republic. Africans, who constituted approximately 70% of the population of South Africa, were not entitled to vote, and were not even consulted about the proposed constitutional change. All of us were apprehensive of our future under the proposed White Republic, and a resolution was taken to hold an All-In African Conference to call for a National Convention, and to organize mass demonstrations on the eve of the unwanted Republic, if the Government failed to call the Convention. The Conference was attended by Africans of various political persuasions. I was the Secretary of the Conference and undertook to be responsible for organizing the national stay-at-home which was subsequently called to coincide with the declaration of the Republic. As all strikes by Africans are illegal, the person organizing such a strike must avoid arrest. I was chosed to be this person, and consequently I had to leave my home and family and my practice and go into hiding to avoid arrest.

The stay-at-home, in accordance with A.N.C. policy, was to be a peaceful demonstration. Careful instructions were given to organizers and members to avoid any recourse to violence. The Government's answer was to introduce new and harsher laws, to mobilise its armed forces, and to send saracens [armored vehicles], armed vehicles and soldiers into the townships in a massive show of force designed to intimidate the people. This was an indication that the Government had decided to rule by force alone, and this decision was a milestone on the road to Umkonto.

Some of this may appear irrelevant to this trial. In fact, I believe none of it is irrelevant because it will, I hope, enable the Court to appreciate the attitude eventually adopted by the various persons and bodies concerned in the National Liberation Movement. When I went to gaol in 1962, the dominant idea was that loss of life should be avoided. I now know that this was still so in 1963.

I must return to June, 1961. What were we, the leaders of our people to do? Were we to give in to the show of force and the implied threat against future action, or were we to fight it, and if so, how?

We had no doubt that we had to continue the fight. Anything else would have been abject surrender. Our problem was not whether to fight, but was how to continue the fight. We of the A.N.C. had always stood for a non-racial democracy, and we shrank from any action which might drive the races further apart than they already were. But the hard facts were that fifty years of non-violence had brought the African people nothing but more and more repressive legislation, and fewer and fewer rights. It may not be easy for this Court to understand, but it is a fact that for a long time the people had been talking of violence—of the day when they would fight the White man and win back their country, and we, the leaders of the A.N.C., had nevertheless always prevailed upon them to avoid violence and to pursue peaceful methods. When some of us discussed this in May and June of 1961, it could not be denied that our policy to achieve a non-racial state by non-violence had achieved nothing, and that our followers were beginning to lose confidence in this policy and were developing disturbing ideas of terrorism.

It must not be forgotten that by this time violence had, in fact, become a feature of the South African political scene. There had been violence in 1957 when the women of Zeerust were ordered to carry passes; there was violence in 1958 with the enforcement of cattle culling in Sekhukuniland; there was violence in 1959 when the people of Cato Manor protested against Pass raids; there was violence in 1960 when the Government attempted to impose Bantu Authorities in Pondoland. Thirty-nine Africans died in these disturbances. In 1961 there had been riots in Warmbaths, and all this time the Transkei had been a seething mass of unrest. Each disturbance pointed clearly to the inevitable growth among Africans of the belief that violence was the only way out—it showed that a Government which uses force to maintain its rule teaches the oppressed to use force to oppose it. Already small groups had arisen in the urban areas and were spontaneously making plans for violent forms of political struggle. There now arose a danger that these groups would adopt terrorism against Africans, as well as Whites, if not properly directed. Particularly disturbing was the type of violence engendered in places such as Zeerust, Sekhukhuniland and Pondoland amongst Africans. It was increasingly taking the form, not of struggle against the Government—though this is what prompted it—but of civil strife amongst themselves, conducted in such a way that it could not hope to achieve anything other than a loss of life and bitterness.

At the beginning of June, 1961, after a long and anxious assessment of the South African situation, I, and some colleagues, came to the conclusion that as violence in this country was inevitable, it would be unrealistic and wrong for African leaders to continue preaching peace and non-violence at a time when the Government met our peaceful demands with force.

This conclusion was not easily arrived at. It was only when all else had failed, when all channels of peaceful protest had been barred to us, that the decision was made to embark on violent forms of political struggle, and to form Umkonto We Sizwe. We did so not because we desired such a course, but solely because the Government had left us with no choice. . . .

I turn now to my own position. I have denied that I am a Communist, and I think that in the circumstances I am obliged to state exactly what my political beliefs are.

I have always regarded myself, in the first place, as an African patriot. After all, I was born in Umtata, forty-six years ago. My guardian was my cousin, who was the acting paramount chief of Tembuland, and I am related both to the present paramount chief of Tembuland, Sabata Dalinyebo, and to Kaizer Matanzima, the Chief Minister of the Transkei.

Today I am attracted to the idea of a classless society, an attraction which springs in part from Marxist reading and, in part, from my admiration of the structure and organization of early African societies in this country. The land, then the main means of production, belonged to the tribe. There were no rich or poor and there was no exploitation.

It is true, as I have already stated, that I have been influenced by Marxist thought. But this is also true of many of the leaders of the new independent States. Such widely different persons as Gandhi, Nehru, Nkrumah and Nasser all acknowlege this fact. We all accept the need for some form of Socialism to enable our people to catch up with the advanced countries of this world and to overcome their legacy of extreme poverty. But this does not mean we are Marxists.

Indeed, for my own part, I believe that it is open to debate whether the Communist Party has any specific role to play at this particular stage of our political struggle. The basic task at the present moment is the removal of race discrimination and the attainment of democratic rights on the basis of the Freedom Charter. Insofar as that Party furthers this task, I welcome its assistance. I realize that it is one of the means by which people of all races can be drawn into our struggle.

From my reading of Marxist literature and from conversations with Marxists, I have gained the impression that Communists regard the parliamentary system of the West as undemocratic and reactionary. But, on the contrary, I am an admirer of such a system.

The Magna Charta, the Petition of Rights and the Bill of Rights, are documents which are held in veneration by democrats throughout the world.

I have great respect for British political institutions, and for the country's system of justice. I regard the British Parliament as the most democratic institution in the world, and the independence and impartiality of its judiciary never fail to arouse my admiration.

The American Congress, that country's doctrine of separation of powers, as well as the independence of its judiciary, arouse in me similar sentiments.

I have been influenced in my thinking by both West and East. All this has led me to feel that in my search for a political formula, I should be absolutely impartial and objective. I should tie myself to no particular system of society other than of socialism. I must leave myself free to borrow the best from the West and from the East. . . .

The Government often answers its critics by saying that Africans in South Africa are economically better off than the inhabitants of the other countries in Africa. I do not know whether this statement is true and doubt whether any comparison can be made without having regard to the cost of living index in such countries. But even if it is true, as far as the African people are concerned it is irrelevant. Our complaint is not that we are poor in comparison with people in other countries, but that we are poor by comparison with the White people in our own country, and that we are prevented by legislation from altering this imbalance.

The lack of human dignity experienced by Africans is the direct result of the policy of White supremacy. White supremacy implies Black inferiority. Legislation designed to preserve White supremacy entrenches this notion. Menial tasks in South Africa are invariably performed by Africans. When anything has to be carried or cleaned the White man will look around for an African to do it for him, whether the African is employed by him or not. Because of this sort of attitude, Whites tend to regard Africans as a separate breed. They do not look upon them as people with families of their own; they do not realise that they have emotions—that they fall in love like White people do; that they want to be with their wives and children like White people want to be with theirs; that they want to earn enough money to support their families properly, to feed and clothe them and send them to school. And what "house-boy" or "garden-boy" or labourer can ever hope to do this?

Pass Laws, which to the Africans are among the most hated bits of legislation in South Africa, render any African liable to police surveillance at any time. I doubt whether there is a single African male in South Africa who has not at some stage had a brush with the police over his pass. Hundreds and thousands of Africans are thrown into gaol every year under pass laws. Even worse than this is the fact that pass laws keep husband and wife apart and lead to the breakdown of family life.

Poverty and the breakdown of family life have secondary effects. Children wander about the streets of the Townships because they have no schools to go to, or no money to enable them to go to school, or no parents at home to see that they go to school, because both parents (if there be two) have to work to keep the family alive. This leads to a breakdown in moral standards, to an alarming rise in illegitimacy and to growing violence which erupts, not only politically, but everywhere. Life in the townships is dangerous. There is not a day that goes by without somebody being stabbed or assaulted. And violence is carried out of the townships in the White living areas. People are afraid to walk the streets after dark. Housebreakings and robberies are increasing, despite the fact that the death sentence can now be imposed for such offences. Death sentences cannot cure the festering sore.

Africans want to be paid a living wage. Africans want to perform work which they are capable of doing, and not work which the Government declares them to be capable of. Africans want to be allowed to live where they obtain work, and not be endorsed out of an area because they were not born there. Africans want to be allowed to own land in places where they work, and not to be obliged to live in rented houses which they can never call their own. Africans want to be part of the general population, and not confined to living in their own ghettos. African men want to have their wives and children to live with them where they work, and not be forced into an unnatural existence in men's hostels. African women want to be with their men folk and not be left permanently widowed in the reserves. Africans want to be allowed out after 11 o'clock at night and not to be confined to their rooms like little children. Africans want to be allowed to travel in their own country and to seek work where they want to and not where the Labour Bureau tells them to. Africans want a just share in the whole of South Africa; they want security and a stake in society.

Above all, we want equal political rights, because without them our disabilities will be permanent. I know this sounds revolutionary to the Whites in this country, because the majority of voters will be Africans. This makes the White man fear democracy.

But this fear cannot be allowed to stand in the way of the only solution which will guarantee racial harmony and freedom for all. It is not true that the enfranchisement of all will result in racial domination. Political division, based on colour, is entirely artificial and, when it disappears, so will the domination of one colour group by another. The A.N.C. has spent half a century fighting against racialism. When it triumphs it will not change that policy.

This then is what the A.N.C. is fighting. Their struggle is a truly national one. It is a struggle of the African people, inspired by their own suffering and their own experience. It is a struggle for the right to live.

During my lifetime I have dedicated myself to this struggle of the African people. I have fought against White domination, and I have fought against Black domination. I have cherished the ideal of a democratic and free society in which all persons live together in harmony and with equal opportunities. It is an ideal which I hope to live for and to achieve. But if needs be, it is an ideal for which I am prepared to die.

3.   Cosmas Desmond Deplores the Policy of Removal, 1971

Cosmas Desmond (1935–), a member of the Franciscan Order, migrated from England to South Africa in 1959 and later became a South African citizen. In the 1960s his investigations of the conditions of life in rural South Africa led the government to refuse him a passport on the grounds that he was a communist. The Discarded People trains a bright light on the suffering wrought by the government's policy of removing Africans to rural areas, a policy that the government preferred not to publicize.

Limehill has become symbolic of the plight of Natal's rural Africans. In the same way, Mnxesha has become a symbol for the Ciskei. As I travelled from Cape Town eastwards, the name kept recurring. Obviously conditions in this resettlement camp were more than usually atrocious.

When you have seen Morsgat, Weenen, Limehill, Stinkwater and so many others, it is difficult to be shocked or distressed by similar places. But one look at Mnxesha was sufficient to convince me that the reports I had heard had not been exaggerated and that here was grinding poverty, squalor and hardship equal to the worst places I had seen. There were the familiar, tiny one or two-room houses, many with a number of ragged, hungry-looking children or a bent old woman sitting outside. It was not quite true that I could no longer be shocked or disturbed. I was, in particular, by the sight of one tiny baby, a virtual skeleton, unable to move or even to cry and covered with flies. I have been through the children's wards in African hospitals throughout the country and over the past ten years have seen thousands of starving, dying children. But I doubt whether I have ever seen anything worse than this. I cut short my tour to take the child to hospital.

Mnxesha is about ten miles from Kingwilliamstown, on the road to Alice. From the main road you can see that there is some kind of settlement, but the worst parts are not visible. The first people were 'settled' there in December 1967 with the aim of eventually accommodating 1,800 families (about 10,000 people). But by July 1968 there were only about seventy families. The main influx took place between December 1968 and February 1969. This, I was told, was because once water had been laid on, the authorities in other areas pressed for the people to be sent to Mnxesha. The Minister of B.A.D. [Bantu Affairs Department] said in the House of Assembly on 4 March 1969 that 2,897 people, of whom 2,041 were children, had been moved there. Most of these had come from Middelburg (203 families), Burgersdorp (67 families) and Cape Town (39 families), with a few from a number of other towns. By May 1969, the official population figure was 3,400. My own estimate was much higher and seemed to be borne out by the numbers on the houses.

The first arrivals were put into wooden huts, with zinc roofs. The huts measured roughly 10 ft by 16 ft and 10 ft high, with no ceilings or floors.

From Cosmas Desmond, *The Discarded People: An Account of African Resettlement in South Africa*, Baltimore: Penguin Books, 1971, pp. 80–86. Copyright © 1971 by Cosmas Desmond. Reproduced by permission of Penguin Books, Ltd.

There are ninety-nine of these which are still in use. In one of them, chosen at random, there were three adults and four children; I was assured that some of the others contained more. These people are mainly pensioners and indigents who do not pay rent. Obviously such huts are extremely hot in summer and cold in winter and the earth floors become very damp, even wet, in the rainy season.

The bulk of the houses are two-roomed, cement-under-asbestos structures with no floors or ceilings. Some stand alone, others are semi-detached so that they appear to be four-roomed houses, but are in fact two-roomed ones. The rent for these is R3.42 a month, including rudimentary sanitation services. In one of them there were thirteen children whose mother was working in Cape Town. Many, if not all, of the houses are grossly overcrowded. Because of the number of widows and pensioners, the majority (53 per cent of the total in May 1969) of the householders are women. There are a few four-roomed houses for teachers and Government employees.

An official of the Information Office attached to the Chief of Bantu Affairs Commissioner's Office in Kingwilliamstown was quoted in the *Daily Dispatch* of 16 January 1969 as saying:

> Redundant people are being moved to Mnxesha. The township is the same as Ilingi near Lady Frere and Sada near Whittlesea. We house redundant people. The people would be of no particular age-group and could not render productive service in an urban area. Among such people were men who had lost their jobs and could not find new employment, old and infirm people and unmarried mothers. The Government would provide the children with one substantial meal a day and rations would be given to the old and infirm people. Able-bodied men would be able to enter into contracts for work on the mines, industries and other avenues of employment. The provision of employment in the new village is receiving the attention of the authorities.

How much attention they gave the matter we do not know, but they evidently decided against it. In the House of Assembly on 4 March 1969, the Minister of B.A.D. said that the Government was not contemplating establishing any industries in or near Mnxesha.

By May 1969, more people had arrived from Middelburg and others were still coming. These, and many of the others, were victims of the Government policy of moving all Africans to the east of the Kat-Fish Line. Since this had been the intention for some time it seems that little or no development of African locations in towns west of this line had been made. So, at Middelburg, the Government had built a large new coloured township, but had for many years done nothing about the African location where many people were living in tin 'pondokkies' [shack or shanty]. Conditions were thus far from satisfactory, but they did at least have better facilities than they found at Mnxesha. At Middelburg there were two established schools, a clinic with a permanent staff, lighting in some of the streets and a satisfactory water and sewerage system. Rents were R1.75 a month for a two-roomed house, R4 a month for a three-roomed house and R2 a month for a 'private stand'—at the time of the removal this was increased to R6 a month, presumably to encourage people to 'agree' to move. Many people at Mnxesha were quite adamant that they had been employed, reasonably housed and very much wanted to stay at Middelburg. But, as one said: 'You can't say no to a White man.'

They said they were told by an official that at Mnxesha they would have proper houses with a bath and a stove; there would be shops and other facilities and special bachelor quarters with their own kitchens and cooks. Others claimed they were told that if they did not move dogs would be set on them. Some were told to settle their families in Mnxesha and return to work in Middelburg. Those who owned their houses at Middelburg were promised compensation at the time of the removal, but some said they had received it several months after the move. The highest compensation that I heard of was R240 for a four-roomed house; others received between R25.25 and R80.

By the time of my visit the health facilities had improved considerably; previously, I was told, they were virtually non-existent. A qualified nurse was appointed in May 1969 to run a free clinic, with a doctor visiting once a week. Until that time a nurse from Mount Coke had visited once a week. But the charge was 20 cents, so most people could not afford treatment. There was also a T.B. clinic once a week. Free medical treatment was available in Kingwilliamstown but the return bus-fare of 40 cents was prohibitive. There was (and still is) a free ambulance service. But the African superintendent has to drive four miles to the nearest telephone to call it and this telephone does not operate in the evenings or at weekends. The district surgeon ran a clinic about three miles away. He normally charged R1.50 for an adult and R1 for a child, which was well beyond the means of most.

The signs of malnutrition are obvious throughout the settlement and there have been many deaths. In May 1969 there were over ninety graves, of which over seventy were children's. The bulk of the population only arrived in December–February 1969.

There are now taps in the streets. These first appeared in February 1969. Until then water was brought in once a day Monday to Friday, twice on Saturday and not on Sunday. The people were told to boil the water before drinking it. Pit latrines are provided but they appear to be very shallow and are prone to overflowing.

Almost half of the men are migrant workers. The only employment in the area is on the building of houses in the settlement, for which men are paid R16.50. Women are paid R6 a month for such work as planting grass in the settlement; this work is a form of poor-relief. In the beginning there was some employment in the settlement for one person from almost every house. But now there are many with no wage earner, who are provided with rations each month.

People complained that the rations were issued irregularly and that it appeared they were being cut down. Some said that the rations lasted them only two weeks: 'After that we have to pawn our clothes in order to buy food at the European store.' There are no shops in the settlement. The nearest one, which is White-owned, is about two miles away; there is another one and a Post Office about four miles away. The Border Council of Churches is subsidizing the sale of milk and soup powders. There is no fuel available in the area; I passed some children carrying wood four miles from the settlement. At first wood was being sold for 35 cents a bag and then for 25 cents. It is now being sold for 15 cents, the balance being paid by a relief organization. But even with this subsidy, wood was piling up with the distributor because the people could not afford it. A number of people have been fined R10 for trespassing while in search of fuel.

At Middelburg, and some of the other places from which they came, some of the people had been receiving maintenance grants of R5 a month for every child. But these grants are only applicable in urban 'Bantu areas', so they lost them on their removal to Mnxesha, which is a rural township. The Bantu Affairs Department in Zwelitsha had said that they would apply to Pretoria to make the grants applicable to Mnxesha.

A lower primary school was opened on 14 March 1969. Before that, the children had to walk about three and a half miles to school and often arrived exhausted, which was not surprising considering their undernourished state.

No matter how bad a settlement is there are usually some people, who have come from White farms, who prefer it; this is true even at Mnxesha. In general, the people from the towns did not want to move, but some said that, despite all the hardship, they were 'happy' because they felt that they had some security and were free from continual harassment about reference books. For example, at Middelburg many had to report every month to have their book stamped and they never knew when it would be the last time.

The sufferings of the people at Mnxesha are exemplified in the case of Mrs E.M. She arrived at Mnxesha from Burgersdorp in December 1968, with her six children. By May 1969 two of the children had died; two others, aged thirteen and six years, had 'gross pellagra' according to a doctor; another younger child was in hospital with malnutrition. She is a widow and was supporting herself in Burgersdorp doing domestic work; now she has no employment. She is only thirty-seven years old and so does not receive a pension. As Mnxesha is a rural area she cannot get a child maintenance allowance. Since she went to Mnxesha she has had no source of income apart from the few cents which she manages to earn by collecting wood from miles away and selling it in the settlement. She has taken her children to the nurse several times but because she did not have the 20 cents they were not attended to. She was receiving Government rations, which were obviously inadequate.

About one and a half miles from Mnxesha there is a growing settlement for pensioners and their families, called Emadakeni. In May 1969 there were sixteen mud huts, measuring about 10 ft by 15 ft; the roofs were also mud with a layer of tarpaulin in between. There were no windows, only two small openings. These huts housed more 'redundant' people from town locations. They did not pay any rent for the mud houses, which were certainly inferior to the normal farm house. There were no toilets provided and there was no sign of any having been built by the occupants of the sixteen huts. There was a water tank which was filled by a tanker. Some were building their own houses, for which they had been given doors and windows, a few yards away. Some of the people in the wooden huts at Mnxesha had been given plots at Emadakeni and told to build their own houses. A dozen or so wooden houses had recently been erected on this site.

4.   Praise Poems in Modern Politics, 1967

The traditional role of the praise poet or bard was not simply to praise or flatter but also to comment and criticize. As African communities came under pressure to accept and develop homeland institutions under the apartheid system, the resulting political conflicts were playing out in this medium. The poem below is from the Transkei.

. . . .

Be calm and composed, black multitudes.
You Poqo [Pan-Africanist Congress] members, you are excluded,
For you have acted stupidly and irresponsibly.
You have disgraced the whole black nation.
Discipline and self-respect must reign among us.
The Government will listen to your views in discussion.
Under the State of Emergency this is difficult to achieve,
For we are bottled up and we cannot hold open discussions.
We cannot advise one another on matters that affect us all.
Thieves, you are also advised to stop stealing because by so doing
You are creating ill-feeling and misunderstanding.
Go back to your normal behaviour, fellow-men, I beseech you.

We also appeal to you, grandson of Matanzima, to return to the senior
    Thembu chiefs.
Remember a single mind is more liable to stupidity and blunders.
Why must you press on at the peril of your own life?
Son of Mhlobo, you are not only ruining your future but also that of
    your children.
It is you today, and it will be your son tomorrow.
Be advised, abandon the course you have chosen;
Things are bad enough, as it is.
You are the weak link in the chain;
You are continually undermining our unity.
Return to the other Thembu chiefs, I appeal to you.

From Archie Mafeje, "The Role of the Bard in a Contemporary African Community," *Journal of African Languages*, 6, 3, 1967, p. 219.

5. The Ideology of Black Consciousness, 1971

Steve Biko (1946–1977) was the most prominent leader of the black consciousness movement, which flourished among African students from the late 1960s through the 1970s. Born in the Eastern Cape, Biko attended Catholic mission school in Natal and studied medicine at Natal University before devoting all his time to organizing the black consciousness movement.

The movement emerged among students who had been born after the late 1940s and spent their lives under apartheid. They came of age when earlier African political organizations were banned and struggling. Though influenced by militant ideas from black activists in the United States and Third World revolutionary ideologies, black consciousness supporters advocated self-help and racial pride, rather than confrontation with the government. Their clash with the authorities came after the 1976 uprising. The role of the black consciousness movement in that uprising is still much disputed.

White authorities later cited this article as an attack on whites, one which tended to foment hatred against them (an illegal act). Perhaps, instead, it is an analysis of the dynamics of mutual fear in poisoning South African life. Thus, liberals like Donald Woods at first thought Biko was a "reverse racist." Later Woods, at least, accepted Biko's position as an even-handed approach, fair to all groups.

It would seem that the greatest waste of time in South Africa is to try and find logic in why the white government does certain things. If anything else, the constant inroads into the freedom of the black people illustrates a complete contempt for this section of the community.

My premise has always been that black people should not at any one stage be surprised at some of the atrocities committed by the government. This to me follows logically after their initial assumption that they, being a settler minority, can have the right to be supreme masters. If they could be cruel enough to cow the natives down with brutal force and install themselves as perpetual rulers in a foreign land, then anything else they do to the same black people becomes logical in terms of the initial cruelty. To expect justice from them at any stage is to be naive. They almost have a duty to themselves and to their "electorate" to show that they still have the upper hand over the black people. There is only one way of showing that upper hand—by ruthlessly breaking down the back of resistance amongst the blacks, however petty that resistance is.

One must look at the huge security force that South Africa has in order to realise this. These men must always report something to their masters in order to justify their employment. It is not enough to report that "I have been to Pondoland and the natives are behaving well and are peaceful and content."

This is not satisfactory, for the perpetrators of evil are aware of the cruelty of their system and hence do not expect the natives to be satisfied. So the security boys are sent back to Pondoland to find out who the spokesman is who claims that the people are satisfied and to beat him until he admits that he is not satisfied. At that point he is either banned or brought forward to be tried under one of the many Acts. The absolutely infantile evidence upon which the State builds up its cases in some of the trials does suggest to me that they are quite capable of arresting a group of boys playing hide and seek and charging them with high treason.

This is the background against which one must see the many political trials that are held in this country. To them it looks as if something would be dangerously wrong if no major political trial was held for a period of one year. It looks as if someone will be accused by his superior for not doing his work. The strangest thing is that people are hauled in for almost nothing to be tried under the most vicious of Acts—like the Terrorism Act.

It is also against this background that one must view the recent banning and house arrest imposed on Mr. Mewa Ramgobin. No amount of persuasion by anyone can convince me that Ramgobin had something sinister up his sleeve. To all those who know him, Mewa was the last man to be considered a serious threat to anyone—let alone a powerful State with an army of perhaps 10,000 security men and informers. But then, as we said, logic is a strange word to these people.

Aimé Césaire [the French Caribbean poet, a founder of the Negritude literary movement] once said: "When I turn on my radio, when I hear that Negroes have been lynched in America, I say that we have been lied to: Hitler is not dead: When I turn on my radio and hear that in Africa, forced labour has been inaugurated and legislated, I say that we have certainly been lied to: Hitler is not dead".

Perhaps one need add only the following in order to make the picture complete:

"When I turn on my radio, when I hear that someone in the Pondoland forest was beaten and tortured, I say that we have been lied to: Hitler is not dead, when I turn on my radio, when I hear that someone in jail slipped off a piece of soap, fell and died I say that we have been lied to: Hitler is not dead, he is likely to be found in Pretoria".

To look for instances of cruelty directed at those who fall into disfavour with the security police is perhaps to look too far. One need not try to establish the truth of the claim that black people in South Africa have to struggle for survival. It presents itself in ever so many facets of our lives. Township life alone makes it a miracle for anyone to live up to adulthood. There we see a situation of absolute want in which black will kill black to be able to survive. This is the basis of the vandalism, murder, rape and plunder that goes on while the real sources of the evil—white society—are suntanning on exclusive beaches or relaxing in their bourgeois homes.

While those amongst blacks who do bother to open their mouths in feeble protest against what is going on are periodically intimidated with security visits and occasional banning orders and house arrests, the rest of the black community lives in absolute fear of the police. No average black man can ever at any moment be absolutely sure that he is not breaking a law. There are so many laws governing the lives and behaviour of black people that sometimes one feels that the police only need to page at random through a statute book to be able to get a law under which to charge a victim.

The philosophy behind police action in this country seems to be "harass them! harass them!". And one needs to add that they interpret the word in a very extravagant sense. Thus even young traffic policemen, people generally known for their grace, occasionally find it proper to slap adult black people. It sometimes looks obvious here that the great plan is to keep the black people thoroughly intimidated and to perpetuate the "super-race" image of the white man, if not intellectually, at least in terms of force. White people, working through their vanguard—the South African Police—have come to realise the truth of that golden maxim—if you cannot make a man respect you, then make him fear you.

Clearly black people cannot respect white people, at least not in this country. There is such an obvious aura of immorality and naked cruelty in all that is done in the name of white people that no black man, no matter how intimidated, can ever be made to respect white society. However, in spite of their obvious contempt for the values cherished by whites and the prices at which white comfort and security is purchased, blacks seem to me to have been successfully cowed down by the type of brutality that emanates from this section of the community.

It is this fear that erodes the soul of black people in South Africa—a fear obviously built up deliberately by the system through a myriad of civil agents, be they post office attendants, police, CID officials, army men in uniform, security police or even the occasional trigger-happy white farmer or store owner. It is a fear so basic in the considered actions of black people as to make it impossible for them to behave like people—let alone free people. From the attitude of a servant to his employer, to that of a black man being served by a white attendant at a shop, one sees this fear clearly showing through. How can people be prepared to put up resistance against their overall oppression if in their individual situations, they cannot insist on the observance of their manhood? This is a question that often occurs to overseas visitors who are perceptive enough to realise that all is not well in the land of sunshine and milk.

Yet this is a dangerous type of fear, for it only goes skin deep. It hides underneath it an immeasurable rage that often threatens to erupt. Beneath it, lies naked hatred for a group that deserves absolutely no respect. Unlike in the rest of the French or Spanish former colonies where chances of assimilation made it not impossible for blacks to aspire towards being white, in South Africa whiteness has always been associated with police brutality and intimidation, early morning pass raids, general harassment in and out of townships and hence no black really aspires to being white. The claim by whites of monopoly on comfort and security has always been so exclusive that blacks see whites as the major obstacle in their progress towards peace, prosperity and a sane society. Through its association with all these negative aspects, whiteness has thus been soiled beyond recognition. At best therefore blacks see whiteness as a concept that warrants being despised, hated, destroyed and replaced by an aspiration with more human content in it. At worst blacks envy white society for the comfort it has usurped and at the centre of this envy is the wish—nay, the secret determination—in the innermost minds of most blacks who think like this, to kick whites off those comfortable garden chairs that one sees as he rides in a bus, out of town, and to claim them for themselves. Day by day, one gets more convinced that Aimé Césaire could not have been right when he said "no race possesses the monopoly on truth, intelligence, force and there is room for all of us at the rendezvous of victory."

It may, perhaps, surprise some people that I should talk of whites in a collective sense when in fact it is a particular section i.e. the government—that carries out this unwarranted vendetta against blacks.

There are those whites who will completely disclaim responsibility for the country's inhumanity to the black man. These are the people who are governed by logic for $4\frac{1}{2}$ years but by fear at election time. The Nationalist party has perhaps many more English votes than one imagines. All whites collectively recognise in it a strong bastion against the highly played-up *swart gevaar* [black peril]. One must not underestimate the deeply imbedded fear of the black man so prevalent in white society. Whites know only too well what exactly they have been doing to blacks and logically find reason for the black man to be angry. Their state of insecurity however does not outweigh their greed for power and wealth, hence they brace themselves to react against this rage rather than to dispel it with openmindedness and fair play. This interaction between fear and reaction then sets on a vicious cycle that multiplies both the fear and the reaction. This is what makes meaningful coalitions between the black and white totally impossible. Also this is what makes whites act as a group and hence become culpable as a group.

In any case, even if there was a real fundamental difference in thinking amongst whites *vis-à-vis* blacks, the very fact that those disgruntled whites remain to enjoy the fruits of the system would alone be enough to condemn them at Nuremburg. Listen to Karl Jaspers writing on the concept of metaphysical guilt:

> There exists amongst men, because they are men, a solidarity through which each shares responsibility for every injustice and every wrong committed in the world and especially for crimes that are committed in his presence or of which he cannot be ignorant. If I do not do whatever I can to prevent them, I am an accomplice in them. If I have risked my life in order to prevent the murder of other men, if I have stood silent, I feel guilty in a sense that cannot in any adequate fashion be understood jurisdically or politically or morally . . . That I am still alive after such things have been done weighs on me as a guilt that cannot be expiated.
>
> Somewhere in the heart of human relations, an absolute command imposes itself: in the case of criminal attack or of living condi-

tions that threaten physical being, accept life for all together or not at all.

Thus if whites in general do not like what is happening to the black people, they have the power in them to stop it here and now. We, on the other hand, have every reason to bundle them together and blame them jointly.

One can of course say that blacks too are to blame for allowing the situation to exist. Or to drive the point even further, one may point out that there are black policemen and black special branch agents. To take the last point first, I must state categorically that there is no such thing as a black policeman. Any black man who props the system up actively has lost the right to being considered part of the black world: he has sold his soul for 30 pieces of silver and finds that he is in fact not acceptable to the white society he sought to join. These are colourless white lackeys who live in a marginal world of unhappiness. They are extensions of the enemy into our ranks. On the other hand, the rest of the black world is kept in check purely because of powerlessness.

Powerlessness breeds a race of beggars who smile at the enemy and swear at him in the sanctity of their toilets; who shout "Baas" willingly during the day and call the white man a dog in their buses as they go home. Once again the concept of fear is at the heart of this two-faced behaviour on the part of the conquered blacks.

This concept of fear has now taken a different dimension. One frequently hears people say of someone who has just been arrested or banned—"there is no smoke without fire" or if the guy was outspoken—"he asked for it, I am not surprised". In a sense this is almost deifying the security police; they cannot be wrong; if they could break the Rivonia plot, what makes them afraid of an individual to the point of banning him unless there is something—which we do not know? This kind of logic, found to varying degrees in the Afrikaner, the English and the black communities, is dangerous for it completely misses the point and reinforces irrational action on the part of the security police.

The fact of the matter is that the government and its security forces are also ruled by fear, in spite of their immense power. Like anyone living in mortal fear, they occasionally resort to irrational actions in the hope that a show of strength rather than proper intelligence might scare the resistors satisfactorily. This is the basis of security operations in South Africa most of the time. If they know that there are some three missionaries who are dangerous to their interest but whose identity is unknown, they would rather deport about 80 missionaries and hope that the three are among them than use some brains and find out who the three are. This was also the basis of the arrest of about 5,000 during the so-called "Poqo" raids of 1963. And of course the laws from which security police derive their power are so vague and sweeping as to allow for all this. Hence one concludes that the South African security system is force-oriented rather than intelligence-oriented. One may of course add that this type of mentality, in this country, stretches all the way from State security to the style of rugby whites adopt. It has become their way of life.

One will therefore not be surprised if it proves very difficult to accept that "there is room for all of us at the rendezvous of victory". The tripartate system of fear—that of white fearing the blacks, blacks fearing whites and the government fearing blacks and wishing to allay the fear amongst whites—makes it difficult to establish rapport amongst the two segments of the community. The fact of living apart adds a different dimension and perhaps a more serious one—it makes the aspirations of the two groups diametrically opposed. The white strategy so far has been to systematically break down the resistance of the blacks to the point where the latter would accept crumbs from the white table. This we have shown we reject unequivocally; and now the stage is therefore set for a very interesting turn of events.

6.   The Biko Inquest, 1977

Steve Biko was arrested in 1977 and died in police custody. He was the most prominent of the many young Africans killed while in detention in 1976 and 1977. The authorities uniformly proclaimed these deaths accidents or suicides.

Biko's death attracted unique international attention because he was so well known outside South Africa. Donald Woods's work exposed the conditions of Biko's death, and forced a detailed inquiry (for which Woods was put under banning orders). The Biko inquest lasted thirteen days and even became the inspiration for a play. Despite all the other evils that had surfaced about the apartheid state, the chilling nature of this evidence dealt a fatal blow to the regime.

The following passage includes part of the text of the inquest's third and fourth days, along with Donald Woods's summaries.

Day Three: Wednesday, November 16, 1977

Continuing the cross-examination of Captain Siebert, Mr. Kentridge asked him whether he had heard anyone tell his commanding officer (Colonel Goosen) that Mr. Biko had bumped his head against a wall during interrogation in Port Elizabeth on the morning of September 7.

Captain Siebert: I cannot remember.

Mr. Kentridge: You did not tell Colonel Goosen yourself that he had bumped his head?

Captain Siebert: It is a possibility.

Mr. Kentridge: You could have, but did you?

Captain Siebert: No, I cannot say that I did.

From Donald Woods, *Biko*, New York & London: Paddington Press, Ltd., 1978, pp. 193–198.

Captain Siebert said he did not mention to the investigating officer, Major-General Kleinhaus, that Biko had fallen twice during the interrogation because he stood by the statement he had made earlier to Colonel Goosen. In the statement to General Kleinhaus he had only replied to questions put to him.

On the morning of September 11, he and certain other officers had been told to take Mr. Biko to the Pretoria prison in a Land Rover for medical treatment.

Captain Siebert: I was told that as the doctors could not find anything wrong with him and the local hospitals did not have the necessary facilities, he had to be taken to Pretoria for observation and investigation.

Mr. Kentridge: Why was he not taken in an ambulance?

Captain Siebert: They tried to make arrangements for an aircraft to fly him to Pretoria, but no aircraft was available. Therefore the Land Rover was used.

Mr. Kentridge: Was the purpose that nobody outside your service could have access to this person?

Captain Siebert: No. He was seen by various doctors and in my opinion they would not have given permission for him to be transported if his condition did not allow it.

(Mr. Biko was put in the back of the Land Rover and lay on some cell mats.)

Mr. Kentridge: What was he wearing?

Captain Siebert: He was naked.

In reply to further questions, Captain Siebert said he understood Mr. Biko was in a half berserk state. In the limited space of the Land Rover, it would have been even more difficult to control him than it had been in the interrogation room.

Mr. Kentridge: Did considerations of common humanity not count with you?

Captain Siebert: Yes, I think so.

Mr. Kentridge: According to Colonel Bothma (of the Prisons Department in Pretoria) you told him Mr. Biko had studied medicine for four years, that he practiced yoga and that it was easy for him to mislead other people. Did you say that?

Captain Siebert: I could have said it.

Mr. Kentridge: Why did you take it upon yourself to tell Colonel Botha this?

Captain Siebert: I don't believe I said it was easy for him to mislead other people.

Captain Siebert said that he personally had believed Mr. Biko was shamming, but that he no longer thought so.

Mr. Kentridge: Another prison officer, Colonel Dorfling, made a statement that you told him Mr. Biko had been on hunger strike.

Captain Siebert: I said I saw him refuse to eat.

Mr. Kentridge: Colonel Botha also said you told him Mr. Biko had not eaten since his arrest.

Captain Siebert: I deny that. I only saw Mr. Biko for the first time on the 6th of September.

Mr. Kentridge: Colonel Dorfling also said you told him Mr. Biko was a medical student and that he practiced yoga. He understood that to mean Mr. Biko could pretend that he was sick.

Captain Siebert: He was examined by two doctors who could find nothing wrong.

Mr. Kentridge: I want to know why you went out of your way to tell the two colonels that Biko was shamming?

Captain Siebert's reply was inaudible.

Major Hansen then said he had made a statement and an affadavit after Mr. Biko's death about the incidents in King William's Town because he was asked to.

Mr. Kentridge: Did they ask you to describe the assault by Mr. Biko on Mr. Hattingh? Did they say they wanted it?

Major Hansen: Yes, but they didn't say why they wanted it. I was asked to describe his personality in the affidavit.

Mr. Kentridge: Mr. Biko was held in detention for 101 days and afterward no charge was laid. Do you know about that?

Major Hansen: I know that he was held, possibly for that time. No charges were laid.

Colonel P. J. Goosen, the head of the Eastern Cape Security Police, was the next witness. He said the Security Police, on the strength of the information they had, regarded Mr. Biko as nothing else than a terrorist leader in South Africa. Elaborating on an affidavit which he made on September 17, Colonel Goosen said: "At about 7:30 A.M. on September 9 Major Snyman reported to me that Mr. Biko had become very aggressive and had thrown a chair at him and had attacked Warrant Officer Beneke with his fists. A measure of force had to be used to subdue him so that he could be handcuffed again. I immediately visited Mr. Biko. He was sitting on the sleeping mat with his hands handcuffed and the leg irons fixed to an iron grille. I noticed a swelling on his upper lip. There was a wild expression in his eyes. I talked to him but he ignored me."

Colonel Goosen then immediately tried to get hold of the district surgeon, Dr. Lang, by telephone. After several other phonecalls he left a message for Dr. Lang who phoned him back later that morning. At about 9:30 A.M. Dr. Lang arrived at his office. Colonel Goosen continued: "I gave him a short sketch of Mr. Biko's personal background and asked him to examine the detainee. After Dr. Lang's examination he issued me with a certificate which reads as follows: 'This is to testify that I have examined Steve Biko as a result of a request from Colonel Goosen of the Security Police who complains that the above-mentioned would not speak. I have found no evidence of any abnormality or pathology on the detainee. Signed: Dr. Lang. Time: 10.10 A.M., September 7, 1977.'"

As a result of a report from Major Fischer, who headed a second interrogation team, at 9.15 P.M. on September 7 he again visited Mr. Biko, Colonel Goosen said. "I spoke to Mr. Biko. As before, he mumbled incoherently. At this stage I was honestly of the opinion that Mr. Biko was playing the fool with us as neither the district surgeon nor I could detect any scars or signs of illness. While I was in the office, I again asked whether Mr. Biko had partaken of any food or drink. It was reported to me that he flatly refused to eat or drink. On the morning of September 8, on arriving at my office, I immediately visited Mr. Biko. He was lying on the cell mats. I spoke to him. He mumbled. I immediately telephoned Dr. Lang and asked him to come and examine Mr. Biko again as he did not react to our questions. At about 12:55 P.M., the chief district surgeon, Dr. Tucker, and Dr. Lang reported to my office. I made a brief report to them on Mr. Biko's condition and again expressed concern because he did not eat or drink. Both doctors then examined Mr. Biko in my absence. After the examination I was informed by Dr. Tucker that neither of them could find anything physically wrong with Mr. Biko. Dr. Tucker suggested Mr. Biko be taken to a place where there were better facilities for a proper examination and that a specialist's opinion be obtained." (Arrangements were then made to take Mr. Biko to a prison hospital where he could be examined by a specialist, Dr. Hersch. Later that evening Mr. Biko was examined by Dr. Hersch and Dr. Lang.)

"After the examination Dr. Hersch informed me that he, like Dr. Lang and Dr. Tucker before him, could find nothing physically wrong with Mr. Biko. It was then agreed that Mr. Biko should be kept in the prison hospital for observation and that further tests, including a lumbar puncture, should be performed on him by Dr. Hersch on the morning of September 9. On September 9 Dr. Lang informed me by telephone that the lumbar puncture had been performed and that he would like to keep Mr. Biko in the hospital block for further observation. On September 11 Dr. Lang informed me by telephone that neither he, nor Dr. Tucker nor Dr. Hersch could find anything physically wrong with Mr. Biko and that I could remove him for futher detention in the police cells of Walmer. The necessary arrangements were made with Major Fischer. At about 2 P.M. on September 11 Major Fischer asked me by telephone to come to the Walmer police station, where a report was made to me. I visited Mr. Biko in his cell. He was lying on his cell mats and his breathing was reasonably irregular. A little foam could be seen around his lips. I immediately telephoned Dr. Tucker and asked him to come and examine Mr. Biko. Dr. Tucker examined Mr. Biko at 3.20 P.M. Both of us expressed concern, because the nature of any possible illness could not be diagnosed. It was mutually agreed to transfer Mr. Biko to an institution with all possible facilities for a proper medical examination. I informed Brigadier Zietsman of Security Police headquarters in Pretoria telephonically of the state of affairs. Instruction was received to transfer Mr. Biko to the central prison in Pretoria. However, I first had to ascertain whether any military aircraft were available. If not, I had to use road transport if the chief district surgeon had no objection.

"No military or other flights were available. I consulted Dr. Tucker, who had no objection to Mr. Biko being transferred to Pretoria by road provided we let him lie on a mattress or something soft. Brigadier Zietsman was again informed telephonically and the necessary arrangements were made for Captain Siebert, Lieutenant Wilken, Warrant Officer Fouche and Sergeant Nieuwoudt to transport Mr. Biko in this office's comfortable Land Rover to Pretoria as speedily as possible. At about 6:30 P.M. on September 11, Captain Siebert informed me telephonically that they were departing for Pretoria with Mr. Biko. Everything possible was done by me to ensure the comfort and health of Mr. Biko while in detention."

Mr. Biko had been held in chains and kept naked in police cells to prevent him from committing suicide or escaping, said Colonel Goosen. "What right have you to keep a man in chains for 48 hours or more?" Mr. Kentridge asked. Colonel Goosen said that as divisional commander he had authority to do so to a man detained under Section 6 of the Terrorism Act to prevent him committing suicide or injuring himself.

Mr. Kentridge: Where do you get your authority from? Show me a piece of paper that gives you the right to keep a man in chains—or are you people above the law?

Colonel Goosen: We have full authority. It is left to my sound discretion.

Mr. Kentridge: Under what statutory authority?

Colonel Goosen: We don't work under statutory authority.

Mr. Kentridge: You don't work under statutory authority? Thanks very much, Colonel, that's what we have always suspected.

Mr. Kentridge asked why Mr. Biko had been kept chained in the Security Police offices on the night of September 6 instead of being sent back to the Walmer police station cells. Colonel Goosen said there were adequate sleeping and toilet facilities at the offices, Mr. Biko might try to escape, and if he were transported there might be attempts to free him. Colonel Goosen added that Mr. Biko had been kept in chains because not all the offices had burglar-proofing.

Mr. Kentridge: Would you keep a dog chained up in this way for 48 hours? I want to know what sort of man you are.

Colonel Goosen: If I regarded him as absolutely dangerous, I would have done so.

Mr. Kentridge: We have been told Mr. Biko was kept naked at the police cells at Walmer. Can you confirm that? It has also been said this was by your order.

Colonel Goosen: That is so.

Asked about fears that detainees would use clothing to commit suicide by hanging, Colonel Goosen said there had been two examples recently of detainees hanging themselves by tearing up shirts and other articles of clothing.

Mr. Kentridge: Is there any reason why, for decency's sake, a man should have no underpants?

Colonel Goosen: For a specific reason. It is to eliminate suicide.

Mr. Kentridge: Have you ever had a man commit suicide with strips torn from his blankets?

Colonel Goosen: In twenty-three years I do not think I have had one occasion where that has happened. Blankets have been used for escapes.

Colonel Goosen said he was unaware of Special Branch allegations that men had hanged themselves with their blankets, and could not comment on whether he believed this was possible. The magistrate, Mr. Prins, then said: "The question is whether you ever thought it was possible for a man to commit suicide with a blanket." Colonel Goosen replied: "I have never thought about it." Asked whether he had given orders that Mr. Biko be kept naked in the prison hospital, Colonel Goosen said he could not remember giving such an order. Asked if he would accept that Mr. Biko had clothing at the prison hospital, Colonel Goosen said he was aware Mr. Biko had pajamas, among other items.

Colonel Goosen said that police investigations had connected Mr. Biko with the drafting, typing, duplicating and distribution of a subversive pamphlet distributed in Port Elizabeth black townships on the night of August 17. "Had he lived, serious criminal charges would most definitely have been laid against the deceased."

Colonel Goosen put forward the theory that Mr. Biko had sustained his fatal head injury while in Port Elizabeth prison hospital on September 8 or 9. He was aware that Mr. Biko had been found in the bath twice and on the floor in front of his bed there. He said: "If one takes into account that these incidents took place during the night of September 8 or 9, I wish to express the serious suspicion that the deceased possibly sustained the wound on his forehead and brain damage at the time of these incidents. The deceased was apparently determined on self-destruction, even with his method of breathing during his detention."

Colonel Goosen also said that Mr. Biko had deliberately breathed in an unnatural way, later observed and diagnosed by Dr. Lang as hyperventilation. This method, used by deep-sea divers to get as much oxygen as possible, could be dangerous, leading to light-headedness and even death, he had read in medical books. "This fact and the fact that the deceased was found in his clothes in a full bath of water in the prison in an apparent attempt at suicide could have resulted in his hitting his head hard, for example, against the bath, causing the brain damage," Colonel Goosen said.

(Adjournment)

**South Africans celebrate
unity at illegal rally at
Western Cape Union.**

PART 5

Toward a Democratic South Africa,

1977–the Present

In 1976 and 1977, the South African government under Prime Minister John Vorster brutally and decisively crushed the uprisings in Soweto and other townships. As in the resistance movements of 1952 and 1960, this action seemingly secured the regime's white-supremacist policies. From 1977 on, as if to consolidate this victory, the Vorster government used more than force to quell the unrest. It also stepped up efforts to gain allies and supporters for the system—internally and externally, among whites and blacks—through measures of concession and cooptation. Few observers saw any prospect of an end to apartheid.

In retrospect, however, the mid-1970s proved a turning point, and the apartheid regime unraveled inexorably from that time on. In just fifteen years came the release of Nelson Mandela from twenty-seven years of imprisonment, the lifting of the bans on the African National Congress and other resistance organizations, and the repeal of major apartheid laws. These moves set the stage for constitutional talks, agreements on a new constitution, and democratic elections lifted Mandela to the presidency in 1994.

This stunning dismantling of a near half-century of apartheid rule did not stem from a single factor such as an ANC military victory or a visionary leap in the dark by F. W. de Klerk. The dramatic events of 1990 and after grew out of a complex network of changes—political, economic, and demographic—unfolding throughout South African society and the rest of the world. We can separate various strands of the process, but the separation is inevitably artificial; each strand impinged on and interacted with the others. In fact, owing to these complex interactions, the measures by which the government attempted to regain control and prolong white supremacy always held unexpected consequences. Indeed, the very reform measures that the government initiated during this period to save and preserve the status quo were among the factors that ultimately led to the end of apartheid.

To get elected in 1948 and to stay in power, the National party had had to appeal to a virtually all-white electorate. Despite our interest in apartheid, we need also to note the importance of nationalist concerns in the early years, as the party proceeded to win over the voters. The unity of Afrikaners against previous English domination; their security and advancement in education, government services, and the economy; and the rescue of poor whites were the party's top priorities. The substantial achievement of these goals by the late 1970s yielded a number of important consequences, including the National party's ability to recruit English-speaking voters who supported its racial policies.

The party's successes also spurred professional, economic, and eventually ideological heterogeneity among Afrikaners. A growing class of Afrikaner businessmen, for example, had become comfortably prosperous and fully urbanized. To such men, the old nationalist agenda began to seem parochial, and they increasingly adhered to the liberal doctrine that apartheid policies such as influx control and job reservation were economically inefficient. By contrast, even though poor whiteism had substantially declined, some segments of Afrikaner society remained marginalized by the surging modernization of the country. These unfortunates were among the strongest adherents of apartheid, especially of its baaskap *aspects. The social diversity of Afrikaner society thus found parallels in a new ideological and political diversity. During the Vorster years (1966–1979), a division between the enlightened proponents of apartheid reform (*verligtes*) and the cramped supporters of the unalloyed Verwoerdian vision (*verkramptes*) climaxed finally in the formal breakaway of the Conservative party from the right wing of the Nationalists in 1982. Accusing the National party of heresy and claiming to be the true heirs of Afrikaner nationalism, the new party garnered enough electoral success to become the official opposition in the election of 1987.*

Other parties stood helpless as the Nationalists won each election by increased majorities. Despite its enormous majority during the Second World War, the United party simply disintegrated after 1948, though it remained the official opposition until 1977. Liberal members split away from the United party in 1953 to form the Liberal party, which disbanded when interracial parties were made illegal. Another group seceded in 1959 to form the Progressive party. For a number of years, the Progressives had only one member of parliament. By the mid-1970s, their supporters elected a small team of members—the Progressive Federal party—who became the only effective critics of apartheid in parliament.

Their critique of government policy was moderate, and they only gradually moved toward advocating full democracy for South Africa. Though the party received some significant defectors from the National organization in the 1980s, it never presented a major threat to the government.

Thus the National party's dominance in white politics was assured, leaving the government free to address other problems. In international affairs, for example, South Africa undertook vigorous damage-control measures after 1976. Its major problem came not from foreign governments but from the growing anti-apartheid sentiment in Western countries. In Scandinavia, Britain, the United States, and Canada, wider and wider swaths of the electorate called for action against apartheid South Africa. The general ban on South Africa's participation in international sports continued, even though the regime had begun to allow limited interracial sports. The human-rights rhetoric of the Carter administration, in particular, sounded a danger signal to South Africa's rulers.

South Africa took on the difficult task of repairing its image without giving up white supremacy. As one step, it restricted press coverage of South African events. It blocked international financial support for such black-consciousness groups as the South African Students' Organization (SASO) and the Christian Institute. In addition, Prime Minister Vorster sought "détente" with moderate African countries. Within South Africa, he carried the concept of Grand Apartheid to its logical conclusion by granting political independence to the Ciskei, Bophuthatswana, and other homelands. He could then boast of South Africa's commitment to decolonization and African freedom. However, no government except South Africa itself recognized these states, and their applications for UN membership were uniformly denied. Vorster even expressed a willingness to allow Namibia to become independent, though he intended the same kind of client-homeland independence already granted elsewhere. Such a dispensation of course would exclude the South West African People's Organization (SWAPO) rebels. He also offered to help broker independence for Zimbabwe, preferring stable African governments to armed rebellions on South Africa's borders.

Vorster's most ambitious effort to revive South African influence in the West came with the Information Project. In this scheme, a hidden information office spent large sums of secret and unaccountable money in buying newspapers and contributing to electoral campaigns in the United States. The project's aims were to defeat liberal senators in California, South Dakota, and Iowa in 1978 and to provide generous financial support for Ronald Reagan's presidential campaign. Although the secret funding unleashed the "Information Scandal" in South Africa, which brought down Vorster's government in 1979, American—and British—politics did take favorable turns for South Africa with Margaret Thatcher's Conservatives' gaining office in 1979 and Ronald Reagan's Republicans' winning in 1980.

These conservative victories helped South Africa, but only for a time. The high-water mark of cooperation between Reagan and the new South African government of P. W. Botha came during the transition period before Reagan took office. Indeed, just after Reagan's inauguration, South African liaison officers arrived in Washington uninvited and fanned out to several government departments. Although they were rebuffed, Reagan's South African policy, shaped by Chester Crocker at the African desk in the State Department, nevertheless featured "constructive engagement," by which the United States would both cooperate with the apartheid regime and press it toward reform. Billing their policies as anti-apartheid, both Reagan and Thatcher rejected calls for more radical actions, such as sanctions against South Africa, as irresponsible. They succeeded in delaying such action until 1986.

As Botha's ministers tried to mend their fences abroad, they also pursued reform at home, claiming to abandon apartheid. The government's reform efforts rested on the assumption that Africans were apolitical, innocent, and concerned only with surviving and improving their circumstances. In this interpretation, active resisters were labeled terrorists, communists, or agitators who must be isolated and defeated.

In reality, the regime eliminated only the word apartheid. *Reform still meant upholding white supremacy. This point needs underlining: Because the government offered unprecedented concessions in its attempt to coopt elements of African society and divide opposition, its actions struck some observers as genuine reform. The regime's reform policy had to seem genuine to fend off the still growing threat of anti-apartheid movements in the West.*

The new constitution of 1983 formed the center of Botha's reform efforts. The document accomplished two tasks. First, it created a strong state president, with Botha stepping into that office. Attached to the presidential office were new intelligence and security offices, independent of parliament and the cabinet. This arrangement put Botha in control of powerful new means for waging the "total strategy" against resisters. Second, the constitution established a tricameral parliament, with separate houses of parliament for whites, Coloured people, and Indians. Each house had authority over its own affairs, with the white parliament and the president wielding the decisive power in general affairs.

This obvious cooptation measure pointedly excluded Africans. Reforms for Africans were limited to municipal self-government in urban areas. Such policies represented a departure from the long-standing reliance on giving the homelands independence. Now urban Africans received elective councils for township government, and these councils were made responsible for raising revenues, providing services, and even enforcing influx-control measures. In addition, middle-class African job holders were secured in their urban status and even gained the opportunity to own their homes. These strategies clearly attempted to divide the African population and to siphon off the power of resisters by giving some Africans a stake in the system. The government hoped that the resulting expansion of an African middle class would not only foster loyalty and stability but also cultivate affluent African consumers for South Africa's growing manufacturing sector.

The government was trying to break a cycle in which unrest in the African townships fed international pressure while the erosion of outside confidence in South Africa hurt the economy. Economic decline in turn further intensified discontent in the townships. The Botha government hoped to stop this pattern by crushing resistance, rewarding loyalty, and impressing international critics with the success of its reforms.

For numerous reasons, by the mid-1980s the plan was clearly a failure. First, Botha and his associates misinterpreted African politics. Africans were not apolitical innocents manipulated by outside agitators. They had real grievances, which the reforms made worse. In addition, the township councils, manned by opportunists and collaborators, were forced to rely on higher and higher rents for revenue. Far from a gift of self-government, these councils became an increasingly oppressive part of the system and a focus of resistance. The violence of the government's efforts to crush opposition further undermined economic confidence. Finally, whether from reform policies or simply from the secular growth of the economy, some Africans did experience piecemeal improvements in education, wages, union rights, and housing. Rather than defusing African discontent, however, these small gains seemed to raise African expectations and frustrations still further.

Instead of fragmenting as the government hoped, African opposition burgeoned until a full-scale and sustained township insurrection erupted in 1984–1987. At its center, the people of the townships attacked the African police and township councillors, hounding them from office, burning their homes, and killing many. As one by-product of the violence, ANC fortunes revived. ANC members, whether in exile or imprisoned on Robben Island, off Cape Town, had snapped up and trained the refugees and detainees of the 1976–1977 disturbances. Now these recruits, for the first time in years, were able to give the armed struggle a real and sustained momentum.

In addition, in 1983 Allan Boesak and others founded the United Democratic Front (UDF), which opposed the new constitution and the Koornhof bills, those measures providing puppet self-government in the African townships. Accused of being an incarnation of the ANC, the UDF in fact served as an umbrella organization encompassing local sports clubs, church groups, and neighborhood associations in the townships. The organization had no fixed membership criteria or policy, but instead it supported and coordinated local efforts. The UDF was not the

ANC, but it was loyal to ANC ideals and increasingly would use ANC symbols and slogans. Though the government eventually banned the UDF and charged some of its leaders with treason, the real opposition was springing up in local townships all over South Africa, especially in the Vaal triangle—the cluster of African townships south of Johannesburg—and in the Eastern Cape.

The township violence developed another kind of cycle. The observation of anniversaries—the twenty-fifth of the Sharpeville massacre and the tenth of the Soweto uprising, in 1985 and 1986, respectively—triggered outbreaks of violence. When Africans held marches or demonstrations, police officers often killed some marchers. Declaring a state of emergency, the government would attempt to ban protest marches, but the murdered marchers' funerals themselves became protest rallies featuring speeches and singing. The police would intervene once again, and more people would die in a seemingly endless cycle of outrage. Within many townships, the government-imposed system of township councils was supplanted by local committees, who set up alternative governments, collected taxes, tried cases, and enforced boycotts against local white businesses. Faced with ruin from these boycotts, many business owners helped the African struggle by pressing the government to negotiate.

With this pattern creating a standoff by 1986, a distinguished group of Commonwealth statesmen—the Commonwealth Eminent Persons Group—attempted to negotiate a settlement between the government and the ANC. Their proposals closely resembled those finally accepted in President F. W. de Klerk's historic breakthrough of 1990. The recommendations seemed close to realization in 1986, but the "securocrats" of the Botha government set them aside and committed the government instead to one more campaign of violence, marked by raids on the townships, invasions in Angola and Namibia, and the bombing of frontline states.

Under these circumstances, the conservative administrations in Britain and the United States, though still eager to support South Africa, could no longer hold off the public's demand for sanctions. American sanctions were enacted over the veto of President Reagan in 1986. Private measures of economic boycott and divestment campaigns also accumulated. In a quiet but devastating move, Chase Manhattan Bank declined to roll over South Africa's short-term notes. For the first time, white South Africans paid for their privileges and for their government's intransigence—in high prices, political insecurity, and even the unavailability of standard consumer goods.

Although the election of 1987 implied a conservative swing, with the Conservatives supplanting the Liberal Progressives as the official opposition, increasing numbers of white South Africans accepted the need to negotiate with the ANC. Prominent businessmen, including Afrikaners, broke South African law to talk with ANC leaders in Lusaka. The prestigious Cape Times defied regulations by publishing an interview with Oliver Tambo, the exiled president of the ANC. Such openings undermined the government's ability to define its policy as a stand against so-called brutal terrorists.

President Botha suffered a heart attack in 1989 and withdrew first from the party leadership and then from the presidency. F. W. de Klerk replaced him in both offices. Within the year, de Klerk had announced his dramatic new policies: releasing Nelson Mandela; lifting the ban on the ANC, the PAC, and the Communist party; and instituting a process of negotiations toward a new constitution. In his earlier career, de Klerk had been a relatively conservative figure among National *party leaders; thus these measures were surprising. Perhaps they stemmed less from the particular commitment of one man—though the presidency was a powerful office—than from the logic of the situation. Options had been used up. Possibly the commitment to a democratic South Africa that emerged was not de Klerk's original intention. Rather, he may have planned to divide the opposition, meet international criticism, and still maintain significant white control. If so, events swept him into the Conference for a Democratic South Africa (CODESA), a new constitution, elections, and the Mandela presidency.*

The years 1990 through the election year 1994 witnessed as much turbulence as the previous periods of insurrection. Mandela and de Klerk were "chained together" by their common commitment to the negotiating process, but they remained deeply suspicious of each other. The ANC needed reassurance that negotiations could succeed before it was willing to suspend the armed struggle or endorse the lifting of international sanctions. It suspected de Klerk, in turn, of using the coercive apparatus of the state and sponsoring violent attacks on ANC supporters. Accusation and counteraccusation threatened to disrupt the negotiation process.

Mandela could not claim to represent all Africans, nor de Klerk all whites. For Mandela, the challenge lay not so much in the small PAC and AZAPO organizations, which refused to suspend their armed struggles or participate in the talks for two years, but in the posture of the Zulu-based Inkatha Freedom party, under the leadership of Mangosuthu G. Buthelezi. Buthelezi rejected the goal of a unitary state and a common society and instead stood for a federal system in which particularist Zulu interests would be safeguarded. For its part, the ANC touted itself not as a political party but as a freedom movement, implying that the organization represented everyone. Buthelezi, the ANC averred, was merely a "homeland leader," that is, a collaborator.

But Inkatha was better organized, wealthier, and more powerful than such a dismissive interpretation suggested. The chronic violence between the Inkatha and ANC supporters in Natal from 1991 into 1994 at times threatened to disrupt the peace process. The ANC charged that behind the Inkatha-ANC conflict lay a "third force." The government, or elements within it, they insisted, were supplying Inkatha with protection and arms to attack ANC adherents in Natal. After investigations headed by Justice Richard Goldstone, de Klerk was forced to admit that renegade police and army officers had, in fact, engaged in such activities.

President de Klerk also had difficulties with the white constituency. As he moved towards negotiations for a democratic South Africa, opponents accused him of going beyond the terms of his election. To meet such attacks, he held a whites-only referendum in early 1992, winning a decisive confirmation of sixty-nine percent support for his policy of negotiation. Yet white opponents of the process still made trouble. Andries Treurnicht's Conservative party refused to participate in the talks, and, more seriously, the quasimilitary Afrikaner Resistance Movement, led by Eugene Terre'Blanche, threatened to launch armed struggle against a democratic, unitary South African state. Its supporters attacked the CODESA site and tried to support the Bophuthatswana homeland government against a rebellion of its citizens. These groups could not stop the negotiations or the 1994 elections, but they remain a danger to South Africa's democratic future.

President de Klerk fought hard for minority rights and some reservation of authority over their own affairs for minorities (in particular whites). In the end, the ANC had its way in the creation of a united and democratic government. The

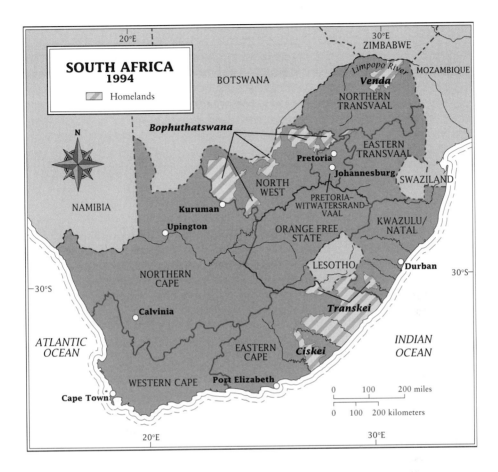

Inkatha Freedom party held out to the last moment but participated in the April 1994 elections, carrying the Natal region. President de Klerk's National party, with substantial support from Coloured voters, carried the Western Cape region. The ANC majority ultimately was not great enough for the organization to rule alone, and both Buthelezi and de Klerk have places in the new government. De Klerk predicts that after a term of ANC rule, the people of South Africa will want him back.

Nelson Mandela, the new president, took office in May 1994, acutely aware of the dangers facing South Africa, especially overly high expectations. His government must maintain racial peace while offering justice and opportunity to the victims of apartheid. To accomplish these tasks, Mandela needs the support of the international community to foster investment and economic recovery. He therefore cannot undertake any radical property redistribution or ruinously expensive social programs. Yet the young African men and women of the "class of '86," who sacrificed their education to the struggle, expect and demand effective action. They are not necessarily committed, in the long run, to the ideals of the Freedom Charter or to interracial reconciliation. If nothing is done for them, they could present a source of instability in the future. Mandela thus must make significant progress in African health, education, and housing, despite his limited resources. Failure could spur the renewal of racial strife, or possibly the emergence of a new multiracial elite ruling over an impoverished, bitter black underclass.

SECTION A

The Reform of Apartheid?

1. R. F. Botha Defends South Africa in the United Nations, 1975

In October 1975, Mauritius, Cameroon, Kenya, and Iraq introduced a draft revolution to expel South Africa from the United Nations. The reasons stated were South Africa's policy of apartheid, its refusal to withdraw from South West Africa, and its support for the renegade Rhodesian regime. The resolution was vetoed by Britain, France, and the United States. In the following document, Botha, the foreign minister, gives a standard set of arguments in defense of South African policy, which he saw as willfully misunderstood. The uprising that began in Soweto the next year decisively undermined the plausibility of such arguments.

Why is it if the position of the Blacks in South Africa is really so intolerable that hundreds of thousands of Black workers from other countries of Africa voluntarily come to South Africa for employment—many of them entering the country illegally for that purpose?

Why is it that according to figures as at 1 January 1972 released by the United Nations High Commissioner for Refugees there were a mere 300 refugees from South Africa out of a total of 988 000 refugees in Africa?

It can be denied that the wage gap between Black and White is being continually narrowed and that it is the Government itself which is taking an active lead in the matter? The figures will show it.

Is it denied that Black leaders chosen by majorities of their own people freely and often criticize the South African Government in public and in private on many aspects of its policies? This Organization seizes upon such criticism. But let such a leader come to the General Assembly as a member of the South African Delegation and he suddenly becomes a 'stooge' or a puppet.

Is it not manifest that millions and millions of Rands are spent in South Africa to provide free or virtually free medical services to the Blacks? In the

From F. R. Metrowich, ed., *Towards Dialogue and Detente*, Sandton: Valiant Publishers, 1975, pp. 56–61.

financial year 1972/73 US $282 million was expended by public undertakings on health services for the Black, Coloured and Indian peoples.

Need it be recorded that South Africa has never experienced famine? South Africa is virtually self sufficient in foodstuffs of a quality comparable with the world's best.

The school enrolment figures for Black pupils more than doubled from 1950 to 1960 and more than doubled again from 1960 to 1973 so that even in a period of rapidly increasing population the percentage of children of school going age increased from 45 per cent in 1954 to 75 per cent in 1974.

The combined rate of population growth of the Black peoples of South Africa is 3.23 per cent which is among the highest in Africa. We are accused of defying the U.N. and world opinion, of paying no heed whatsoever to resolutions of this Organization—indeed of adopting a provocative and challenging attitude towards the world body. This is just not so. We are receptive to constructive criticism or suggestions from any country or body in the world which is genuinely interested in the welfare of the peoples of South Africa and that includes the United Nations.

But would any Government anywhere react positively to the flood of accusations and condemnatory resolutions of the nature that I have mentioned when it must be realized even by circles in this Organization itself that the allegations on which they are based are exaggerated, untrue and even wilfully misrepresented?

Not for a moment do I wish to pretend that everything in our country is right. But to accuse us of the most evil designs and practices when we have improved the living conditions of all our peoples to the extent that we have, when my Government is making sincere and positive attempts to improve and develop the economic, social, and political conditions of all these peoples—not just some of them—and to safeguard their future engenders the strongest suspicion that what some members of this Organization aim at is not so much the advancement of the peoples of our region but the pursuance of their own selfish political ends. It is in regard to these very real efforts of ours that we consider that members of this Organization and in particular many of our fellow African states have displayed towards us an unjustified antagonism and a lack of tolerance of interest and of understanding our ultimate objectives. They have, we feel, not responded to nor given us any credit or recognition at all for what we are trying to do in order to give to every person in our country, Black and White, a fair deal from life. On the contrary many of these members simply ignore the important changes which have occurred and are occurring in South Africa—information about them seems sometimes to be deliberately suppressed.

I would be naive, Sir, to pretend that I do not know why it is that members of this Organization, especially the African members, display towards us this antagonism, this lack of goodwill. It is basically because these members think that the Whites of South Africa have some inborn hatred and prejudice against the Blacks, that they consider themselves to be superior to or in some way better than the Blacks and that on these grounds they discriminate against them in order to deny them fundamental rights and freedoms.

I shall return to this point. For the moment let me just state categorically that whatever the attitude of the White man to the Black man in the past might have been, that is not the attitude of the vast majority of White South Africans today.

I would first like to outline how our policy of multi-national development came about and on what it is based. I do so in order to put our policies in proper perspective.

Towards the middle of the 17th century the White and Black peoples of South African converged in what was then an almost uninhabited part of the continent. On the whole the tendency was for the White people as well as the various Black peoples to settle in distinct parts of the country. They were at different stages of development, all had their own institutions of government, land settlement and land ownership, traditions, cultures, languages and economies and for almost 150 years there was virtually no contact between Black and White. . . .

A historic movement called the Great Trek started in 1836 when White farmers of the Cape Colony moved northwards passing around the southern-most Black peoples and crossing the Orange and Vaal Rivers until they reached the Limpopo River in the North, the Kalahari desert in the West and Natal in the East.

The areas through which they trekked were for the most part completely uninhabited. This was due to what the Blacks of South Africa still call the "Mfekane" which means "the crushing". Over a period of 15 years from approximately 1820 terrible devastation of these areas had taken place as a result of wars between the various Black peoples. Mzilikazi, a lieutenant of the Zulu King Shaka, who had fled from his former master, subsequently completed this devastation and annihilated the African tribes living there.

The Trekkers did not by force or otherwise drive Blacks away from land occupied by them except in the case of Mzilikazi and his Matabeles [Ndebele] who fled to and settled in the present Rhodesia. In cases in which there was any doubt as to claims to land the Trekkers and later the Governments of the Orange Free State and the Transvaal Republics negotiated with the peoples concerned. . . .

In 1910 the Union of South Africa was created when an Act of the British Parliament united the four colonies of Natal, the Transvaal, the Orange Free State and the Cape. The British Act noted the fact that the three Protectorates of Basutoland, Bechuanaland and Swaziland formed an economic and geographic whole with the new Union. In fact it was generally expected that the three territories would one day become part of the Union. Constitutionally this Union was to a large extent an artificial creation. Excluded were the three Protectorates but included were nine other Black peoples and their territories as well as the Whites.

In regard to the remaining Black territories within the Union an Act was passed in 1913 to define and schedule some 8.9 million hectares of land in the four Provinces as inalienable Black areas. This was the recognition of a his-torical fact—it was not done for ideological reasons—just as Lesotho,

Botswana and Swaziland were not created for ideological reasons. In 1936 a further 6.3 million hectares of land were earmarked for addition to the Black territories.

It is true that the Black territories consist of only about 13 per cent of the land area of the present South Africa but it is also true that this area includes nearly half of the country's most fertile soil. And it is further true that if the total area of the former British South Africa is taken into consideration Black territories comprise almost 50 per cent of that area. The Black Africans for example never occupied the more than 250 000 km^2 of arid and semi desert areas known as the Karoo. The Karoo contrasts strikingly with for example the Tugela River system which flows for a considerable distance through the areas of South Africa's largest nation, the Zulus. It has been estimated that this river system has sufficient water to supply 14 cities the size of Johannesburg, leaving enough at the river's mouth to meet the needs of a city the size of Greater London. For a country like South Africa whose water is scarce this is considerable.

Large areas of the Black territories fall within the rich mineral belt ranging from the Northern Transvaal to the North Western Cape. In fact most of the Black territories are reasonably well endowed with a wide range of valuable mineral resources. Though the Xhosa areas of the Eastern Cape are less fortunate in this respect they have considerable agricultural potential.

On the basis of rainfall and climate 100 hectares of land in the Black territories have on average the potential of 147 hectares in the White part of South Africa.

In the light of these facts of history and geography, how, I ask, do members of this Organization reconcile the charges against my Government that the South African Government has driven the Black peoples into barren and desolate reservations in pursuit of a policy of racial oppression?

I mention these facts in bare outline. To really grasp South Africa's circumstances would require a far longer exposition of history. I mention these facts merely to indicate something of the historical background to our problems.

The divisions which exist in South Africa today thus came about naturally and historically through sociological affinities and not as a result of any ideology. We believe that the objective of self-determination for all our peoples will not be best achieved by attempting to force all of them into an artificial unity. Too often has the world seen the tragic consequences of attempts to force unity upon two or more divergent peoples and we see it still today.

A policy such as ours which is designed to avoid disaster, to eliminate friction and confrontation between different peoples, to eliminate domination of one group by another and to give to every man his due can surely not be said to run counter to civilized concepts of human dignities and freedoms.

Our policy is not based on any concepts of superiority or inferiority, but on the historical fact that different peoples differ in their loyalties, cultures, outlook and modes of life and that they wish to retain them.

Nor is our policy inflexible—it postulates a certain broad direction, the end of which is sovereign independence for the peoples concerned. There is no question of forcing together peoples who do not wish to be joined. Equally there is no question of keeping apart peoples who wish to come together. The real point at issue is therefore not one of objective but of method: the best practical way of ensuring self-determination and human development. We believe particularly in the light of events elsewhere in the world that our approach is better calculated to achieve the common objective than the alternative of forcing the different peoples of South Africa into an artificial entity which will lead to friction and strife not only between White and Black but also between Black and Black.

Let me put it clearly: The Whites of South Africa as well as the Government of South Africa are as much concerned about the implementation of human rights, human freedoms, human dignities and justice as any other nation or Government of the world. We fully realize that the well being of the Black man is as essential to the stability of Southern Africa as that of the White man.

2.   The Republic of South Africa Constitution Act, 1983

The centerpiece of P. W. Botha's attempts to reform the apartheid system was the constitution of 1983. It created a tricameral parliament, enfranchising Indian and Coloured voters along with whites, but it did not provide for African participation in the parliamentary system. The measure divided the powers of government into own affairs and general affairs by a principle called consociationalism. This principle retained its appeal for some whites in the constitutional talks of the early 1990s.

The 1983 constitution also created a strong state president, and Botha himself stepped from the office of prime minister to this new and more powerful executive position.

Own Affairs and General Affairs

Own Affairs

14. (1) Matters which specially or differentially affect a population group in relation to the maintenance of its identity and the upholding and furtherance of its way of life, culture, traditions and customs, are, subject to the provisions of section 16, own affairs in relation to such population group.

(2) Matters coming within the classes of subjects described in Schedule 1 are, subject to the provisions of section 16, own affairs in relation to each population group.

From L. J. Boulle, *Constitutional Reform and the Apartheid State: Legitimacy, Consociationalism and Control in South Africa*, New York: St. Martin's Press, 1984, pp. 236–237.

General Affairs

15. Matters which are not own affairs of a population group in terms of section 14 are general affairs.

Decision of Questions on Own or General Nature of Matters

16. (1) (a) Any question arising in the application of this Act as to whether any particular matters are own affairs of a population group shall be decided by the State President, who shall do so in such manner that the governmental institutions serving the interests of such population group are not by the decision enabled to affect the interests of any other population group, irrespective of whether or not it is defined as a population group in this Act.

(b) All such questions shall be general affairs.

(2) The State President may, if he deems it expedient, but subject to the provisions of section 31–

(a) express his decision on any question contemplated in subsection (1) by proclamation in the *Gazette;* or

(b) make his decision on any such question known for general information by such a proclamation, or make it known or cause it to be made known in such other manner as he may deem fit.

and shall advise the Chairman of each Ministers' Council of every such decision.

(3) When the State President assigns the administration of a law to a Minister of a department of State for own affairs of a population group under section 26 or 98 he shall do so in pursuance of a decision under this section that the law, in so far as its administration is so assigned, deals with own affairs of the population group in question.

Reference of Questions to President's Council for Advice, and Consultation on Certain Matters

17. (1) The State President may refer any question which is being considered by him in terms of section 16 to the President's Council for advice.

(2) (a) Before the State President issues a certificate under section 31 in respect of a bill or an amendment or a proposed amendment thereof, he shall consult the Speaker of Parliament and the Chairmen of the respective Houses in such manner as he deems fit.

(b) Paragraph (a) does not apply to the issue of a certificate in respect of a bill or an amendment thereof which has been altered as a result of the consultation in terms of that paragraph.

Validity of State President's Decisions on Own or General Nature of Matters

18. (1) Any division of the Supreme Court of South Africa shall be competent to inquire into and pronounce upon the question as to whether the provisions of section 17(2) were complied with in connection with a decision of the State President contemplated in those provisions.

(2) Save as provided in subsection (1), no court of law shall be competent to inquire into or pronounce upon the validity of a decision of the State President that matters mentioned in the decision are own affairs of a population group, or are not own affairs of a population group, as the case may be.

(3) For the purposes of subsection (2), the matters dealt with in any bill which, when introduced in a House, is not endorsed with or accompanied by a certificate contemplated in section 31, shall be deemed to be matters which are not own affairs of any population group by virtue of a decision of the State President.

Life Under Apartheid

1. Deaths in Detention, 1984

Deaths in detention are only one aspect of the brutal police enforcement of apartheid. Such deaths assumed prominence in the wake of the Soweto uprising, and many detainees were school-aged youths. In each case, the inquest concluded that no person was responsible for detainees' loss of life through any act of commission or omission.

Since 1963, when legislation first made possible the torture of political detainees, at least 60 people have died in the hands of the security police.

Name	Date of Death	Official Explanation of Death
1. Bellington MAMPE	1.9.63	causes undisclosed
2. Looksmart Ngudle SOLWANDLE	5.9.63	'suicide by hanging'
3. James TYITYA	24.1.63	'suicide by hanging'
4. Suliman SALOOJEE	9.9.64	'fell out of seventh floor window'
5. Nengeni GAGA	7.5.65	'natural causes'
6. Pongolosha HOYE	8.5.65	'natural causes'
7. James HAMAKWAYO	?.8.66	'suicide by hanging'
8. Hangula SHONYEKA	9.10.66	'suicide'
9. Leong Yun PIN	19.11.66	'suicide by hanging'
10. Ah YAN	30.11.66	'suicide by hanging'
11. Alpheus MALIBA	9.9.67	'suicide by hanging'
12. J B TUBAKWE	11.9.68	'suicide by hanging'

From *Torture Is Part of the System: State Violence in South Africa and Namibia*, London: ANC, 1984, pp. 14–15.

Name	Date of Death	Official Explanation of Death

13. An unidentified man died at an undisclosed time of an undisclosed cause at an undisclosed place. (Disclosed in parliament on 28.1.69.)

Name	Date of Death	Official Explanation of Death
14. Nichodemus KGOATHE	5.2.69	'bronchopneumonia following head injuries'
15. Solomon MODIPANE	28.2.69	'natural causes'
16. James LENKOE	10.3.69	'suicide by hanging'
17. Caleb MAYEKISO	1.6.69	'natural causes'
18. Michael SHIVUTE	16.6.69	'suicide'
19. Jacob MONAKGOTLA	10.9.69	'thrombosis'
20. Imam Abdullah HARON	27.9.69	'fell down a flight of stairs'
21. Mthayeni CUTHSELA	22.1.71	'natural causes'
22. Ahmed TIMOL	27.10.71	'fell out of tenth floor window'
23. Joseph MDLULI	19.3.76	'application of force to neck'
24. William TSHWANE	25.6.76	'gunshot wounds'
25. Mapetla MOHAPI	15.7.76	'suicide by hanging'
26. Luke MAZWEMBE	2.9.76	'suicide by hanging'
27. Dumisani MBATHA	25.9.76	'unknown illness'
28. Fenuel MOGATUSI	28.9.76	'suffocation'
29. Jacob MASHABANE	5.10.76	'suicide by hanging'
30. Edward MZOLO	9.10.76	causes undisclosed
31. Ernest MAMASILA	18.11.76	'suicide by hanging'
32. Thabo MOSALA	25.11.76	'internal bleeding'
33. Twalimfene JOYI	undisclosed	undisclosed
34. Wellington TSHAZIBANE	11.12.76	'suicide by hanging'
35. George BOTHA	15.12.76	'fell six floors down stairwell'
36. Naboath NTSHUNTSHA	9.1.77	'suicide by hanging'
37. Lawrence NDZANGA	9.1.77	'natural causes'
38. Elmon MALELE	20.1.77	'heart failure'
39. Mathews MABELANE	15.2.77	'fell out of tenth floor window'
40. Samuel MALINGA	22.2.77	'heart or respiratory failure'
41. Aaron KHOZA	26.3.77	'hanged himself'
42. Phakamile MABIJA	22.2.77	'fell from window'
43. Elijah LOZA	2.8.77	'natural causes'
44. Hoosen HAFFEJEE	3.8.77	'hanged himself'

Name	Date of Death	Official Explanation of Death
45. Bayempin MZIZI	15.8.77	'hanged himself'
46. Steve BIKO	12.9.77	'brain injury'
47. Bonaventura MALAZA	7.11.77	'hanged himself'
48. Mbulelo Rocky JAMES	9.11.77	'shot while escaping'
49. Mzukisi NOBHADULA	20.12.77	'natural causes'
50. Lungile TABALAZA	10.7.78	'fell out of fifth floor window'
51. Saul NDZUMO	9.9.80	'natural causes'
52. Sifundile MATALASI	20.12.80	'self strangulation'
53. Manana MGQWETO	17.9.81	undisclosed
54. Tshifhiwa MUOFHE	12.11.81	'beaten to death'
55. Neil AGGETT	5.2.82	'hanged himself'
56. Ernest DIPALE	8.7.82	'hanged himself'
57. Thembuyise MNDAWE	8.3.83	'hanged himself'
58. Molifi Paris MALATJI	4.7.83	'bullet wound'
59. Samuel TSHIKHUDO	20.1.84	?
60. J. Bonakele NGALO	15.7.84	?

The most common official explanation of death in detention has been suicide. The State has alleged that 20 detainees hanged themselves in their cells in the past 20 years. The death weapons, we are told, were items of clothing or bedding: a shirt torn into strips, a belt, a vest, or prison bedding ripped into shreds to make a "rope" thick enough for the exercise. There are no means of verifying the regime's claims. It is evident, however, that in the majority of cases, if the cause of death was, indeed, suicide, the detainees were desperate. Where individuals are driven to death it cannot be called suicide. Culpable homicide is more appropriate.

2. Frank Chikane Describes His Prison Ordeal, 1977

Frank Chikane, later a prominent exponent of liberation theology, was one of those swept up in the police dragnets in the year after the Soweto uprising. His crime was actively helping to locate the young people who disappeared during the uprising—some killed, some detained, some gone into hiding, and some gone into exile.

From Frank Chikane, "Detention and Torture," *No Life of My Own: An Autobiography*, Maryknoll, NY: Orbis Books, 1989, pp. 30–35. Copyright © 1989 by Rev. Frank Chikane.

Detention and Torture

Whenever the lawyers wrote to the police—and it was often, as many people and children had disappeared—they used my name as the person who had instructed them on behalf of the families. About six months later, on June 6, 1977, the police descended on the manse in the early hours of the morning and took me away after an extensive search. Midmorning of that day, my interrogation started.

From the nature of the questions, it became clear to me that the police were convinced I would not be helping these families without being involved with those who were detained or without knowing what they had been doing. If you minister to them, you must be party to their "crime," so went their logic. Secondly, from the evidence of one state witness in a trial started a year after these people had been detained, it was clear that they had tortured some of the young people to make them give statements incriminating me and so justifying their logic and conviction.

All this caused me to go through a six-week session of physical torture and interrogation. The torture involved being forced to remain in certain contorted positions for many hours until the body gave in. When I could not keep the prescribed position any longer, I was assaulted with fists and various other objects, like a broomstick. At times I was chained against other objects in a crouching position, handcuffs on my feet, and left in that position for a very long time. Once I was hung head down with my hands and feet over a wooden stick and assaulted in that position. I do not remember much of the details of the latter experience, as it looks like I lost consciousness.

Afterwards I was confused, with my whole body completely unstable. Walking was a struggle, and when I arrived at the prison where I was kept, I could not stand steadily as the warders checked me into prison. I remember the prison warders making a laughingstock of me, saying I had gone through some good "music" and that I was continuing to "dance." The last ordeal of my six weeks of torture had involved being kept standing in one spot for fifty hours continuously without sleep. I was chained against the bars of the heating system, underfed, interrogated and assaulted continuously by teams of interrogators who changed shifts every eight hours, twenty-four hours around the clock.

During this ordeal, I tried to make sense of the Gospel and the sermons I preached about loving your enemies. I began to ask questions as to what all this meant in this situation. I began to ask questions about God's power and concern. I began to wonder why God could could allow these people to do this to me. Does God really care? I began to ask whether the deeds of power of the times of Jesus and the early church were not applicable in our situation. And why?

One thing that kept me strong and made me survive was the experience of the Lord Jesus Christ: for the salvation of the world, it did not seem Jesus could have let the cup pass. He had to drink of the cup for our sakes. He was forsaken for our sakes. . . .

I said to them: "If I die now, I will be with the Lord. This is gain for me and even for the kindom." But if they let me live, I would still have to live for Christ, and it would mean continuing to challenge the evil apartheid system in South Africa. It was like using Mandela's words: "If you release me I will start where you stopped me as long as this evil system still exists."

My torturers had asked me in the course of this ordeal to make a choice between dying slowly in a painful way and cooperating by collaborating with them against those I am called to minister to. I told them that collaboration and cooperation with the evil racist system in South Africa was out for me. This to me was equal to a call for me to abandon the very fundamentals of my faith and calling. I told them that instead they had to decide whether to let me die or live, being conscious of the consequences of both options. Later, on rereading Paul, I realized that in verse 29 he was uncertain as to which option he would choose. But I did not have to make the choice; it lay in their hands. Through pain they made me feel at one stage that if I were to die, then the faster the better.

At one stage they suggested that I should commit suicide to speed up my death. My response was that Frank Chikane did not have the right to take his own life, and, anyway, I was not going to let them off the hook by terminating my own life and make them feel less guilty after what they had done. I felt that if they chose to do it, they must take the responsibility, and they must face the Lord on the day of judgment.

By the forty-eighth hour, I no longer felt normal enough to be able to continue intelligently answering their questions, and I decided to keep quiet after telling them about my position. I announced that I was not going to answer questions anymore. For two hours they tried every method to force me to talk, but in vain. On the fiftieth hour I was loosened and driven from Krugersdorp to Rustenburg prison, where I was dumped until around January 12, 1978.

When I arrived at the prison with my feet swollen and my whole body aching, I asked to see a doctor before I was locked up in a cell. I was taken to a prison doctor who looked at me, touched my swollen feet and said, "Just take him to the cell and let him rest. He will be okay." No medication was given and no records were made about my condition. I was shocked but I could do nothing. I was completely at their mercy. Although it was difficult that evening for me to sleep because of pain, when I did sleep I almost slept like a dead man.

Throughout my time in Rustenburg prison I was kept in solitary confinement without access to a lawyer or visits by the family. I was not allowed any reading material. The Bible that my younger sister, Thabile, smuggled into Krugersdorp prison was left there when I was transferred to Rustenburg. It took me about three months of arguing with the magistrates who visited me once every three weeks, according to the regulations, before I got a copy of the Bible. The security police's argument was that they would not give me a Bible because "*dit maak jou 'n terrorist*" ("it makes you a terrorist"). They felt that the Bible did not seem to help me. It is clear that for them, like all oppressive regimes, the Bible helps you only if it makes you submissive to the dictates of the oppressor. When, at last, they did give me a copy of the Bible, they gave me an Afrikaans one, maybe to force me to read their language. But nevertheless it was a blessing to have a Bible, whatever the language.

My release in January 1978 was very dramatic. They brought me to court with six other people, most of whom I was seeing for the first time. In court we were told that we were going to be charged with "public violence." I was surprised, because I was never asked questions about public violence during my entire detention, and I was never involved in such acts. But, nonetheless, we were granted bail of 200 Rand each and warned to appear in court six days later. There was no charge sheet and no indication of exactly what I was charged with.

At two o'clock in the morning of the day we were due to appear, I was redetained. This time I was assaulted right from the bedroom. My chief deacon, Isaac Genu, who stayed in the manse with his family, tried to intervene but was sent back to bed at gunpoint and told to stay there. I was taken away in my pajamas, with my clothes in my hand, and barely able to pull them on en route to the police station. Besides assaulting me with their fists, they pulled out my hair, and this continued at Kagiso police station, leaving clumps of hair scattered around. Afterwards I was ordered to collect every bit of it and put it in a garbage can. Next I was driven to Bethal, where the trial of some of those detained nearly a year before was in progress. Throughout the journey I was continuously assaulted. By nine o'clock, when we were expected to appear in court in Krugersdorp, we were in Bethal, miles away.

I have never understood why I was redetained that morning, assaulted so badly and driven to Bethal. On our arrival there those who brought us in were ordered to drive us back to Krugersdorp to appear in court. We arrived at 2:00 P.M. The courtroom was packed with members of my congregation, and there I was with my pajamas showing beneath my clothes. To say they were angry to see this unbelievable sight is to understate their real feelings. They were angry. But they became more angry after hearing the magistrate say, "*Daar is nie 'n saak met die man nie*" ("There is no case with this man"). Since that day my congregation was never the same again.

For about two months after this experience I was so upset that I could not sleep on one house for more than two days without feeling vulnerable. Every sound, sight or movement of a car or cars meant that they had come to detain me again, with a high probability of assault and torture. During this time my friends advised me to leave the country because they were convinced that I would not survive another detention, and there was a high possibility of my being killed by the police or other agents of the system. But I felt then that I was called to minster to victims of this very system and leaving the country seemed to me like abandoning the ministry. Although it looked foolish not to follow the advice of my friends, I just felt that God still had a purpose for me in this country and if we all left, no one would be there to minister to the bulk of people who have no option but to face the pain and misery of living under an oppressive, white minority, racist regime.

3. Prison Life on Robben Island, 1987

The prison on Robben Island off Cape Town was one of the best-known symbols of the oppression of apartheid. Nelson Mandela was held there for more than twenty years. The arrival of many 1976 detainees, who often came with a black-consciousness perspective, enabled Mandela and other ANC leaders to train them in ANC doctrines. For this reason, among others, the United Democratic Front of the 1980s, with numerous leaders of the 1976 generation, adhered closely to ANC ideals. Here Dingake describes some of the living conditions on the island.

Food

A favourite question from visitors to Robben Island was the food question:'What sort of food do they give you?' Our food was poor and unappetising. The authorities knew it. Consequently warders never allowed prisoners to answer the question. Yet the prison authorities insisted in their propaganda that prisoners enjoyed a balanced diet. The allegedly 'balanced' nature of the diet did not stop prisoners from going on hunger strikes in protest against both the quantity and quality of the diet from time to time.

Food, on Robben Island, was one of the unredressed grievances at the time of my release, in spite of major improvements in preparation, and promises of revised diet scales. In the mid-sixties when common-law and political prisoners were still mixed in the communal cells sections, the cooks were drawn exclusively from the common-law groups. The preparation of food was perfunctory and left much to be desired. The wardens who supervised the kitchen were equally indifferent. After all, the food was for 'Kaffer bandiets', 'hotnots' and 'koelies'. One chief warder was nicknamed 'Kaffer pap (Kaffir porridge)' from his habit of asking whether the 'Kaffer pap" was not ready yet.

The common-law cooks prepared better meals for themselves, from the same ingredients in separate pots. Corruption in the kitchen was encouraged by the wardens who, according to reports, were themselves corrupt. They were thieves, engaged in stealing some of the prisoners' food for their families. One warder was an exception to the corrupt kitchen practice: Warder Opperman, 'Phumasilwe (Come let's fight)' from his pugilistic challenges to his colleagues, was different. Every time he was on duty over the weekend, he took it upon himself to raid the kitchen. He invariably uncovered specially prepared dishes for the cooks. These, he would carry to the cells to distribute among the rest of the deprived inmates. Fried chickens, fried potatoes, puddings and other special dishes of which prisoners were not aware would come out of the kitchen on every raid by Phumasilwe. The kitchen staff was always caught unawares since they never knew in advance when he would be on weekend duty.

From Michael Dingake, *My Fight Against Apartheid*, London: Kliptown Books, 1987, pp. 204–213.

The major grievance against the prison diet however was that it was discriminatory. Coloured and Indian fellow-prisoners had one diet scale and the Africans, another. This, despite the fact that they were not segregated in the communal cells, nor were they, in the single cells section. How were the Coloured and Indian comrades to feel, when they enjoyed preferential food while their African fellow inmates sat next to them force-feeding themselves on boiled mealies? In the single cells sections, the initial reaction by Coloured and Indian prisoners was to reject this base discrimination and boycott any food that was not shared by all prisoners. The humiliation and embarrassment was palpable and prompted by this strong reaction.

After much discussion by all the inmates of the single cells sections, it was felt that the boycott was unlikely to achieve its purpose. The authorities would either ignore the protest completely and reduce the privileged diet scale to the less privileged level, or segregate the two groups and continue to enforce the discriminatory diet scale. All prisoners demanded an improved diet. Downgrading of existing official diet scales would not be in the short-term nor the long-term interests of any group of the prisoners. Moreover the principle of segregation of political prisoners was unpopular among the prison population. The correct strategy was to fight for uniform improvements without jeopardising existing privileges in spite of their sectionality. Africans were not entitled to bread. Coloureds and Indians were entitled to a 'katkop (cat's head)', about one quarter of a standard loaf for supper. After extensive discussion, Coloured and Indian comrades decided on a compromise of sharing their bread with their African fellow inmates.

A formula for sharing varied with gaol conditions. In the beginning, each 'D-diet' (privileged group) prisoner was assigned to cater for specific 'F-diet' (ie African) prisoners. The ratio of D-diets to F-diets was not conducive to equitable sharing. Some D-diets had to share with one other person, while others had to share with two. Not much could be done to arrive at a fair distribution, because at this stage sharing one's food with another prisoner was not only against the prison regulations but warders were vigilant, and would not hesitate to punish food-sharing culprits.

The sharing formula ensured that it could be done with the minimum detection. Later when conditions improved and the warders relaxed, a more convenient and fair formula was found. The bread slices were distributed from door to door by one member of the 'phaka span (dishing span)'. In that way the number of slices one received changed from day to day. One day it might be one and the following day two and so on and so forth. Although the wardens' supervising visits would not allow visited prisoners to answer questions on diet, the Minister of Prisons could not evade such questions when they were put to him in Parliament.

According to the 1970 *Survey of the South African Institute of Race Relations* here is a summary of his reply on prison diet (daily unless otherwise stated):

Item	Whites	Coloureds/Asians	Africans
Mealie meal or mealie rice or samp	4 ounces	14 ounces	12 ounces
Mealies	—	—	8 ounces
Bread	20 ounces	8 ounces	—
Meat or fish	7 ounces	6 ounces (4 × weekly)	5 ounces (4 × weekly)
Dried beans	—	4 ounces (meatless days)	4 ounces (on meatless days)
Vegetables	16 ounces	8 ounces	8 ounces
Soup/Protone/ gravy powder	1 ounce	4/5 ounces	4/5 ounces
Fat	1 ounce	1 ounce	1/2 ounce
Milk	3 ounces	—	—
Coffee or tea	Twice daily	Twice daily	Once daily
Puzamandla	—	—	1-7/9 ounces
Salt	1 ounce	1/2 ounce	1/2 ounce
Sugar	2 ounces	2 ounces	1-1/2 ounces

The scale is interesting for its fine distinction on both quantities and qualities. These fine distinctions, especially on quantity often led to controversial arbitrations when complaints were lodged by prisoners. On looking at his sugar, puzamandla or soup, an F-diet prisoner might honestly believe it was not the right quantity. Warders, generally, did not take kindly to prisoners' complaints. But just to demonstrate that he was keeping within the regulations, he might order the food-scale from the kitchen to weigh the item complained about. The result of such exercises invariably proved the prisoner wrong and authority right. The food the prisoner regarded as less than the right ration might be reduced further, on the basis of some deft manipulation or deliberate misreading of the scale. It was meant to intimidate prisoners against complaining about food. Prisoners were never intimidated however. They complained. They struck.

One wonders what criteria dieticians used to determine and distinguish nutritional needs of various groups. The prison authorities explained the differences in diet scales on traditional diet tendencies of the groups. Apparently on that basis, traditional Coloured, Indian and African diet did not include milk; Africans did not eat bread nor jam; Africans ate less meat than Coloured, and Coloureds and Indian less than Whites, etc, etc. Only an apartheid practitioner can follow the logic of this web of racial-diet theory. Of course it was never the policy of prison authorities to give honest and intelligent answers to prisoners. Prison officers from the lowest rank to the highest, are not trained nor do they have the inclination to discuss prisoners' complaints about policy—they respond in terms of unfamiliar regulation, prison practice, ideology and orders from above. The regulations says so and so! These are OC's orders! An order is an order, verstaan (understand)?

The new type of prisoner who complained and argued for his inalienable rights as a human being was 'hardegat (cheeky)', a 'terrorist', 'poqo' or a 'communist'. The vigorous and sometimes agressive manner of laying complaints or making requests was to pay dividends in the end. We delegated Comrade Raymond Mhlaba to take up the question of fruit for prisoners on one occasion. Ray was in his aggressive element: 'Look here,' he addressed the head of prison, 'we demand fruit. It is an essential food ingredient, even baboons in the wilds eat wild fruit . . . And we are not baboons whatever you think of us . . .' We did not get the fruit immediately. But the swelling representation to the authorities for fruit over the years was soon to have results.

The first consignment of peaches arrived without prior warning. We might have been a colony of Adams in the garden of Eden tasting the forbidden fruit. Perhaps the original Adam knew when to stop, before God and the rumbling tummy warned him of his transgression. Many of us did not know when to stop after all the years of deprivation and abstinence. Our overindulged tummies had good reason to rumble and run. Guavas followed later. It tasted like a new era in prison. The snag was that fruit rations were not regular but highly erratic. The authorities, to be fair, had indicated we could only get fruit when it was available. It was difficult to know what that meant. We had to guess that the supply would probably depend on the yield from Victor Verster prison orchard or some other such prison.

Occasionally we supplemented our food deficiencies from the veld, during working hours. Whenever we were out on time-killing weeding on the Island, we usually came across guinea fowl eggs. Except with very wicked warders, a friendly conversation in Afrikaans with the warder generally managed to secure the guinea fowl eggs for consumption by the work span. For pots, we used the same ones that brought our lunch from the kitchen. These had to be thoroughly scoured after the cooking so that they left no tell-tale remains of the day's contraband.

Along the sea-coast, correct approaches to warders also used to yield mussels and even crayfish. One day Lieutenant Terblanche, then head of prison, caught our pot of mussels on inspection. Unlike previous heads of prison he never seemed to trust his warders with prisoners. He suspected they smuggled things and did prisoners many favours. He personally body-searched night-duty warders to ensure they did not conceal newspapers and other contraband for prisoners. Moreover he was the only officer who seemed not to have a routine hour for his inspections. All this was deliberate and meant to catch warders during their fraternising moments with prisoners.

When Lt Terblanche appeared on the scene and walked to our steaming pot of mussels we were all petrified. He opened the pot, pulled one mussel out, tasted it and pronounced it 'smaaklik (tasty)'. And that was it. There was no confrontation with anybody. Unbelievable! From then on the consensus on Terblanche's personality was undermined. We no longer spoke in a single voice about him. He was still a pig to some. To others he was reasonable, even wonderful. Food 'supplements' from the veld and the sea coast were of course niggardly and far between.

Robben Island diet was monotonous. Extremely so. But contrary to my primary school lesson that 'monotony in diet leads to indigestion', I would not say the food on the Island led to such tummy malfunction. Tummies in Robben Island had to learn to squeeze nourishment from the least nourishing products. One got tired or had little time to masticate half-cooked mealie grains, and half the time one swallowed these grains chicken-style. Unendowed with the gizzard like a chicken, the prisoner relied solely on his one stomach to do the job.

Even over the Christmas festive season, the food remained the same. Monotonous. The little extra the prison department spoiled prisoners with was a mug of black coffee. Black coffee for Christmas in a Christian country! Some said it was not even real coffee, but something that looked like coffee without tasting like it. South African prison regulations however have some provision for the prisoner's palate for Christmas. Provided a prisoner could afford it, the regulations said he/she could buy three pounds of some delicacies: one pound of sweets, one pound of dried fruit and one pound of fruit-cake or biscuits. For many who had no funds, nothing could be done. Officially, they were supposed to watch those who could afford, enjoy their three-pound purchases. Whether one prisoner was prepared to spend his money on his fellow prisoner was immaterial to the authorities; the regulations stipulated that a prisoner had to spend his own money to enjoy the privilege, and that was it. It meant that any prisoner who dared share his Christmas buy, was breaking the prison regulations and subject to appropriate discipline. The prisoners as usual shared in defiance of the regulations. And perhaps in the spirit of Christmas, the warders turned a blind eye to the wholesale defiance. The three-pound limit on prisoners' Christmas shopping has not been amended as far as I know. At least up to the time of my release it still applied in its original form. . . .

The improvement in the prison food situation came when the preparation was improved. This happened after the transfer of the common-law prisoners. As a result of this transfer the political prisoners did their own cooking. Those selected for the kitchen had to undergo on-the-job training. The large-scale corruption of the past disappeared from the kitchen. Every ounce of fat was accounted for. The mealies became edible with the new magic touch of fat. The meat began to taste like meat. The only problem was one bit one's lip and fingers more than the meat because of its quantity. Vegetables became a delight to the palate, potatoes became mashed, fried or in their skins. Eggs were fried, scrambled or boiled. Although the quantity did not change, the better-prepared rations were more filling. Hunger-strikes still occurred from time to time but not as a protest against the food but against other grievances.

Eventually complaints about the diet centred around its discriminatory nature. The denial of certain food categories to some groups of prisoners did not make sense. Here, we lived together, played together, and worked together; so whence the discrimination? The argument that the food which Africans received in gaol was the sort of food they enjoyed in their homes was so much bunk. A deliberate lie!

In 1979 we were informed non-racial diet had been approved in principle by the policy-makers. It was not certain when full implementation of the decision would take place. There were disturbing reports that the transition from a discriminatory to a non-racial diet would be gradual. The Boers are firm believers in Darwinism. It does not matter that Darwin based his theory on the natural process, and they based theirs on the apartheid process, they believe if Darwin was right, they are right too. Things must take time. Evolution, not revolution. The equating of natural process with social process is a prostitution of analogies. Shortly before my release, the process of phasing out the apartheid diet was beginning to assume some amorphous shape. It was a shape without a shape.

The F-diets, ie Africans, had gone as far as one slice of bread in the morning. We continued to pool bread and distribute it in the old way. The morning F-diet slices were kept until the evening when they were thrown in with the D-diet slices and distributed on the arithmetic formula of X slices divided by Y inmates. The quotient did not rise sharply but rise it did by one. The sugar-scale was levelled at the bottom rung, ie the Coloured and Indian sugar-scale fell from two ounces to one and a half ounces. The same axe fell on the D-diet meat. I do not know whether the puzamandla was extended to Coloured and Indian prisoners because our section had imposed an indefinite boycott on this fortified apartheid diet.

The puzamandla boycott was forced upon our section by some authoritarian officer, without good reason. There was a time when puzamandla used to be mixed in the kitchen for us. We complained that the mixture was not to our taste. Since the amount of puzamandla powder each prisoner was entitled to was fixed, why couldn't the prisoners be given the powder to mix according to their individual taste? The prison administration then listened to our complaint and puzamandla came in powder form. Most of us preferred to accumulate our daily ration of puzamandla until we felt it was sufficient to make a delicious mug of drink. The arrangement seemed to suit everyone concerned.

Suddenly, here comes this new head, his head full of baaskap. Puzamandla to be mixed in the kitchen from now on! We tried to make this guy see things our way; no, he was adamant. His word was to be final. Okay then, can the quantity of water be reduced so that we get half a mug of thick stuff instead of a full mug of watery stuff; it is tasteless. No! The man was determined: a full mug was to our taste and flavour. To hell then! The puzamandla boycott was on. It went on for a long time. It was still in progress when I was released. The D-diets originally did not get milk. Somewhere before the talk of non-racial diet they had started getting milk. The F-diets joined them after the announcement of the principle of non-racial diet.

It seemed the process of implementing the new diet was to be multi-phased and slow. Moreover it was clear it would be at the expense of the privileged groups. The preoccupation of the prison administration appeared to be to juggle around with estimated figures of the various prison population groups without tampering with the total estimates in the prison food vote.

When we complained about the slowness of the experimental process, we were advised, 'have patience', for the dietician was busy, very busy, doing his best to expedite the whole process. We suspected that with so many departments likely to be interested, the process was going to evolve pitifully slowly. Imagine the accountants working out the budget, economists wary about rising government expenditure, racist anthropologists probably sceptical about the 'imposition of western dishes on primitive Bantu', ideologists arguing about the politics of introducing equality through the prison kitchen door. Mercy!

4. Joyce Sikakane Opens a Window on Soweto, 1977

The massive suburban sprawl of Soweto (South West Townships), with its unpaved streets and minimal plumbing, electricity, or business amenities, is one of the largest cities of South Africa. Developed after the destruction of Sophiatown, after 1976 it became one of the symbols of the oppression of apartheid and of the struggle against it. It also serves as a creative center of African culture, especially for music, poetry, and fiction.

Housing in Soweto

Soweto (jocularly called by its inhabitants "so-where-to") is the largest single modern ghetto in Africa. Soweto is a bastard child born out of circumstances following the dispossession of the African people and the discovery of gold in the Witwatersrand. It was born out of white greed and racism perpetrated against the Africans. Even its name is a bastard one, taken from its geographical location: **South West Townships.**

There are 26 locations which cover 85 square kilometres. The 108,766 red or grey brick houses with multi-coloured roofs that make up the smog-smothered ghetto are built opposite each other in straight single rows running parallel to a street. A common feature of the huge settlement is that fifty yards from each house is a backyard toilet separated by a wall from that of a neighbour's. Naked bulbs hanging on roughly installed electric cables cast a dim light inside some of the houses. Most homes use candles, paraffin or gas lamps for lighting. Coal stoves are used in almost all the homes.

From Joyce Sikakane, "Life in Soweto," *A Window on Soweto,* London: International Defence & Aid Fund, 1977, pp. 8–10.

The sizes of the houses vary. Some of the very first built locations consist of two or three tiny rooms with small verandahs. Their only water supply is through a tap attached to one of the walls of the backyard toilet. Then there are the army barrack shaped ones—three to four rooms, without bathrooms, but with a tap hanging outside each back wall. The four to five roomed houses of Orlando West are an exception to other four-roomed houses forming 98 per cent of the Soweto complex. These houses are exclusive in that each has an indoor shower room with a tap. Some are also provided with a kitchen sink or pantry. Scattered here and there in Soweto are a variety of small three-roomed enclaves whose walls, floors and roofs are all made of concrete blocks.

An average of six to seven people occupy Soweto homes of less than four rooms and four of these people being adults.

Only a quarter of the houses in Soweto have running cold water inside the houses. In all the others, residents fetch cold water by buckets from the outside taps. Only three in every hundred houses have running hot water. Only seven in a hundred have a bath or shower. Only fifteen in a hundred houses have electricity.

Situated in the heart of the slum are the attractive lodgings of Soweto's rich class. The select Dube Township, designed and created as a show piece of "African advancement" displays costly palatially-built houses forming a sharp contrast to the multifarious staid matchbox confines surrounding it. The creation of Dube Township in 1955 was a result of a tactical manoeuvre by the government so as to succeed with its segregated housing policy. At the beginning of 1955, Sophiatown, a suburb within the confines of the City in which Africans owned properties, was demolished. In order to succeed in removing African property-owners from Sophiatown the government created Dube Township. Here plots were made available for purchase by the aspiring moneyed Africans.

These underdeveloped plots were sold to the buyers on a 90-year lease basis. Purchasers bought plots and constructed stylish houses of their own choice. The township was named after Mr. John Dube one of the first distinguished African educationalists and principal of an African teacher training college in South Africa. Ironically Mr. Dube was also the first President of the African National Congress of South Africa. Residents of this glamorous township are composed of doctors, lawyers, teachers, nurses, highly paid white collar workers and businessmen. The ghetto dwellers generally refer to Dube Township as the home of "Situations" because it is choice situated, or as the place of the "excuse me's" because the African intelligentsia residing there prefer speaking English, or as the suburb of the "highbugs","tycoons" and "socialites" because some homeowners are businessmen and those who like the glamour of public life.

To the ordinary Sowetonian Dube Township gives a feeling of being out of place because it imposes a false picture of contentment, gaiety and affluence amidst a huge dissatisfied, gloomy, hardworking and poverty-stricken community. White tourists are taken to Dube to see how comfortably the "Bantu" live.

Separately built in some of the 26 locations are the most notorious and depressing barracks known as hostels. There are about a dozen of them. These long narrow-built compartments accommodate "single" men i.e. migrant workers. In Soweto alone 60,000 men are hostel dwellers. Indoors, the inmates share the dormitories in tribal groups, as required by government law. In each dormitory are moveable black-painted iron and steel beds, a common one-plate coal stove and iron bar lockers used by the occupants. Each dormitory has a common cold water shower room. Barbed wire fences divide the hostel premises from that of the locations. There are no dining-rooms, no visitors' rooms, no reading rooms, no recreation facilities, and absolutely no privacy for the inmates. Women are not allowed to venture into the hostel premises. Here in the hostels thousands of African men are caged after working hours.

Most of these "single" male occupants are migrant workers from the Bantustans. They consist of respectable married men forced by migratory laws to leave their wives and children in the homelands, of divorced men and widowers evicted from Soweto houses because they are without spouses. By government law, no single man or woman is allowed to rent a house in Soweto. Some of the men are bachelors from the homelands and from Soweto, the latter being men no longer qualifying to lodge with their parents as they are of working age.

For instance, Dube Hostel, one of the many hostels, houses over 6,000 male migrant workers, only 5 per cent of whom are short-term contract labourers, the other 95 per cent stay indefinitely irrespective of their marital status.

A hostel for single women was built in Mzimhlophe, just a stone's throw from a male one. This hostel houses 800 women. It consists of four-roomed blocks each with a common bathroom. Two occupants share a room. The "single" women inmates are mostly domestic servants, factory workers and office teamakers. They are women who, during the mass urban removals and resettlements, were found to be without spouses. Some of them are "push-outs" from the Soweto housing system. The latter group are girls of working age—16 years upwards according to the government law which compels African women to carry reference books, and thus if they are not at school should be employed. Widows and divorcees, orphans and unmarried mothers are also included. Mothers are not allowed to reside with their children in the hostels. Men are also forbidden into the hostel premises. No visitors are allowed. The hostel premises are fenced with barbed wire.

Rent for each inmate of these single-sex hostels varies from R7 to R8 a month. These single-sex hostels are hovels for men and women denied the right to lead creative lives.

Some of the houses which have family occupants have small gardens and Sowetonians take a pride in planting flowers and lawns, with a peach or apricot tree here and there. Streets in Soweto are narrow, dusty in winter and full of potholes. They turn into streams during heavy rains in summer. A few of the streets have dim electric lights. Only those leading to police stations, administration offices, bottle stores and the big Johannesburg City are brightly lit. By 1976 Soweto had only 39 public telephones—one for every 25,900 people. The 985 private phones are installed in police stations, administration offices, post offices, shops, doctors' consulting rooms and a few private homes.

5.   Sheila Sisulu Reviews Bantu Education, 1984

The closing of the mission-supported schools and their absorption into the government-controlled Bantu Education system largely reached completion by the 1970s. Thus a tradition of liberal education for an African elite was cut off. Nevertheless, African education, controlled as it was, became greatly extended, at least on the primary level. The graduates of Bantu Education were starting to have an impact on African life by 1970; many were perhaps better educated than Hendrik Verwoerd had intended. Sheila Sisulu reviews educational conditions and the options available to at least a few Africans.

Sheila Sisulu works for Sached—the South African Committee for Higher Education—which provides opportunities for 1,200 black students to study for a degree through the University of London.

'I grew up in Johannesburg—was born in Western Native Township. I went to a mission school just at the time when the government was starting the whole bantu education system, where we were segregated from whites and others, as before, but now had a new education that was considered "appropriate" for blacks. There were immediate protests, and in fact I remember being told by my brother not to go to school because we were part of a boycott movement. I was only 6 or 7 at the time and I don't think I really understood what was going on. There had already been demonstrations and clashes... the day I stayed home was "D-Day" and all those who didn't come were regarded as boycotting and immediately thrown out. You could say I was expelled at the tender age of 7! That was in the fifties. Congress set up schools—makeshift schools in halls, and we had older pupils trying to teach us. . . . I can't remember today whether it was in English or Sotho! This went on for about three months, but then I was allowed back into my own school after all; but of course the curriculum had changed... the inspectors were coming around to make sure the teachers taught in the children's mother tongue: we really started getting the third-rate education that was supposed to turn us into third-class citizens.

'Finally my parents decided they couldn't stand it any longer. Slap bang in the middle of the school year they sent me off to a mission school in Swaziland—they were fortunate, because they could afford to do that.

'They really felt everything was collapsing around us—that was true, certainly, for many of my friends. They never got beyond a primary school education, and the little they had was dreadfully poor.

From Beata Lipman, *We Make Freedom: Women in South Africa*, London & New York: Kegan, 1984, pp. 101–103.

We had been seventy-five to a class before I went to Swaziland—the teachers couldn't cope: they used to try and force people to leave, to bring the numbers down.

'It's still happening now—when they talk about compulsory education these days for blacks, they don't prepare for it and at the beginning of each school year they have such an influx they're quite overwhelmed.

'School starts at 7—you can't speak of compulsory education and then not provide the facilities. It links up with the peanuts that's being spent on black education generally; it may sound fine for the outside world, that phrase "compulsory education", but it doesn't mean very much when you see the desperately overcrowded reality.

'In Swaziland the classes were very much smaller and the teachers could really teach us something... after that I went to University in Lesotho to do a BA in English and philosophy, as well as an education certificate. When I came back to Soweto I began to teach in the high school—and found that numbers had grown to 150 pupils per class! Then the department decided I wasn't a fit person to teach anyhow because of course I'd learnt no Afrikaans in Swaziland or Lesotho. . . . That was in 1975, before the Soweto uprising; they said I could stay as an untrained teacher at the salary of 79 rand a month—I couldn't cope, so I looked for another job and left. But it was the numbers, not the money that decided me.

'The objection to bantu education is complex. Not on numbers, like me trying to teach 150 pupils the same thing, and not on money: it's very easy to see where the huge sums that go into white education are used. We only get a tenth of that, so parents have to pay for books as well as uniforms, when they can afford it. And of course when it comes to science courses it's quite impossible when you haven't got the equipment. All that is really straightforward—if the same amount was spent on schooling of every child in this country one of the objections to bantu education would go.

'In 1976 the language became such a big issue because it helped symbolise all the inferiorities. First the children start school learning in Sotho, or Zulu—then at high school they were told they had to learn through Afrikaans: it helps perpetuate the backwardness, the lack of education...

'On paper the syllabus is the same for whites and blacks. But it has an enormous bias—the only thing that matters is what the whites have done. Black history either doesn't matter or else it's put across in such a biased way: blacks are cheeky, whites are good. When it comes to English you'd think there's nothing that can be changed; after all, if you're teaching a verb, what else can you do? But I had a comprehension passage in an English textbook that contained "Yes, master, berry quiet, berry careful." And that whole book was a translation from Afrikaans into English—it sounded really clumsy, not English at all.

'We're supposed to want mother-tongue education. Every sociologist and educationist says kids should first learn through the language they know . . . we believe that the only way to get an equal education today in South Africa is to see that it's in English from the word go. That's not only political. So many families see it as a tool to escape poverty . . . sons and daughters are sent to school for many years right into their twenties, in the hope that they'll reach Standard 5 or 6. Some of them have time off in the middle to look after younger ones—they go to school in rotation—but the belief that this can change lives is really powerful and many stick at it. They try and stay on at school in spite of huge difficulties—no money, nowhere at home to do homework in peace, not enough textbooks. And then, at school, undertrained teachers and hardly any equipment. In winter they work by candlelight in the evening.'

6.   Family Life Under Apartheid: An Interview with Adeline Pholosi, 1984

"Section 10 rights," which gave some Africans the right to remain in urban areas despite influx-control regulations, proved elaborately complex. Establishing one's rights was difficult, and the claim had to be fully documented. The struggle for married couples to remain together with their children became one of the most onerous aspects of living under apartheid.

Miss Pholosi is a 39-year-old clerk in Johannesburg. She lives in Soweto. She has a son of 18 and a daughter of 13, both still at school.

'I was married by lobola to Mr Mohaka in 1960. I grew up in Soweto, so I'm a "Section 10" person—I've a right to be here. They can't make me leave at the moment unless I take a foreign nationality. I'm a Christian and a believer, but I got married by tribal custom because I was afraid about this nationality business: Mr Mohaka is a Sotho—would I have had to leave straight off if I took his nationality? Now my parents were very upset that I did not get married properly, as a Christian should, but to this day we have not done so. It's even more important now than it was in 1960. He's a foreign passport holder, like someone from the Transkei or Bophuthatswana; and I'm still wanting my children to be South Africans. So, if after all these years, if I were to marry him by civil rights as my parents still wish (and he now does, as well) I would have to

From Beata Lipman, *We Make Freedom: Women in South Africa*, London and New York: Kegan, 1984, pp. 8–10.

carry a foreign passport too. That would mean I couldn't have a house; I won't have what I want. I don't like to stay in Lesotho, I like to stay in South Africa.

'We've been married twenty-one years and we've never had a house together . . . in fact I haven't even got a house of my own. I'm on the waiting list, but there's no housing—I'll have to buy instead. I've been on that waiting list since 1971—me and 33,000 other people! Now I'm collecting my deposit to buy instead. Even so I'm only allowed leasehold . . . huh! I've been saving for that house. But one thing I don't understand: even though it's a 99-year lease the children are not qualifying for that house . . . when I'm dead they're going to take that house and then the children are going to to have to buy that house. Whatever I pay off, they will lose it: they will have to start again to buy that house, I'm putting away 50 rand a week because I have to have my house. . . .

'I'm still living at home in my parents' house. . . it's a four-roomed house . . . we are now eighteen people. Mr Mohaka and I have two children, my sister's got four children—she's not married—the other siter she's got four children; she's married and they are on the waiting list for their house. My brother who has divorced—he's got three children and then my mother's children are two, and they've got two children each.

'Some are sleeping in the kitchen—my sister with her four children and my brother's three children are sleeping in the kitchen on the floor. The grown-up boys are sleeping in the dining room with my brother. I'm sleeping in the small bedroom with my sisters and their children; my father in their bedroom with the three children.

'It means I haven't got, really, a life with my husband. He sleeps in the mines—he's a clerk there, but there's no room for us there. If I want to go to see him or I want to make love I must go to him to discuss where we can go and get the room outside the location, next to the mines. We do that after two months or after three months because everybody don't like that at all—the people where we ask for a room. We don't want to go often—it's awkward. Sometimes we want to discuss something and we can't speak because we find we are disturbing the people, and we find we can't talk and discuss this thing—even if we want maybe to shout or something we can't do that—we must go out and talk our secrets outside. He comes to my parents' home to visit once after two months or three months so we can go and ask somewhere to sleep. I also go to the mines . . . I last went to see him when our child was sick—the one who is at school at Lesotho. I went to discuss, but the children of that house where he was were in, for their school holidays, so we couldn't make love . . . we slept separately and he went back to where he's working.

'My whole married life has been like this—we have never stayed together in twenty-one years. If I can buy my house, if he's still working in the mines, because he likes to work in the mines—then at least he can come and visit me once a week or once a fortnight from the mines.

'There's no transport where he's working, just outside Johannesburg the transport is very bad—he starts to work early in the morning at half past four—so he has to live at the mine.

'I like always to be with him—and I can't understand how I can be married to my husband and then I never have the love of my husband. I don't even know what suits him, and he don't know what it is that suits me . . . and I always like to be with him . . . I'm not satisfied . . . that makes me cry a lot. I don't like to think about that, it upsets me. It would be easy to find love from another man, if I like, but—I have never had a full love to him: when I find him, it's always like a new love every time . . . it would be impossible to leave him and find somebody else.

'The children keep wanting to know—when are they going to have their own home, and whan are they going to be together with their father—they miss their father. Children need both parents there, to talk to them, to discipline them, to love them . . . they do, it's very important for children to have their parents next to them. That's the thing that makes me so cross—having no house, my husband not next to me. I don't know our love.'

She has had two holidays with him in all these years, believes his love for her has remained strong in spite of all these difficulties—believes too that he takes a lover now and then but has never taxed him with it because their difficulties are so great. The soft longing of her voice. . . .

Oppression and Struggle in the 1980s

1. The Founding of the United Democratic Front, 1983

Allan Boesak was the founding leader of the United Democratic Front, which was organized to resist the new Botha constitution of 1983. The UDF had little central organization but was an umbrella group comprising many local affiliated organizations—church groups, women's groups, sports clubs, and community organizations from the African townships. These groups pursued local goals, and the UDF did not enforce any particular policy.

Allan Boesak was president of the World Council of Reformed Churches. In the following address, delivered at the national launch of the UDF in Cape Town, he praises the goals of the new organization.

Peace in Our Day

We have arrived at a historic moment. We have now brought together under the aegis of the United Democratic Front the broadest and most significant coalition of groups and organizations struggling against apartheid, racism, and injustice in South Africa since the early 1950s. We have been able to create a unity among freedom-loving persons that this country has not seen for many a year.

I am particularly happy to note that this meeting is not merely a gathering of isolated individuals. No, we represent organizations deeply rooted in the struggle for justice, deeply rooted in the heart of our people. Indeed, I believe we are standing at the birth of what could become the greatest and most significant popular movement in more than a quarter of a century.

We are here to say that the constitutional proposals of the government are inadequate, and that they do not express the will of the vast majority of South Africans. But more than that, we are here to say that what we are working for is one, undivided South Africa that shall belong to all its people: an open democracy from which no South African shall be excluded; a society in which the human dignity of all shall be respected. We are here to say that there are rights that are neither conferred by nor derived from the state; you have to go back beyond the dim mist of eternity to understand their origin: they are God-given. And we are not here to beg for those rights; we are here to claim them.

In a sense, the formation of the United Democratric Front both highlights and symbolizes the crisis that apartheid and its supporters have created for themselves. After a history of some three hundred thirty years of slavery, racial discrimination, dehumanization, and economic exploitation, what the supporters of apartheid expected was acceptance of the status quo, docility, and subservience. Instead they are finding persons who refuse to accept racial injustice, and who are ready to face the challenges of the moment. . . .

For those of us, however, who are black and who suffer under this system there is no positive side to apartheid. How can we see something positive in a system built on oppression, injustice, and exploitation? What is positive about a system that systematically and deliberately destroys human dignity, that makes a criterion as irrelevant and unimportant as skin color the basis of society and the key to the understanding of human relationships, political participation, and economic injustice? How can apartheid be positive when in the name of Christianity it spawns policies that cause little children to die of hunger and malnutrition, that break up black family life and spell out a continuous, hopeless death for millions of blacks?

How can apartheid be positive when it keeps most South African children manacled in the chains of unfreedom and the others manacled in the chains of fear? The time has come for white South Africans to realize that their destiny is inextricably bound up with our destiny, and that they shall never be free until we are free. How happy I am that many of our white brothers and sisters are saying this by their presence here today.

Those who think their security and peace lie in the perpetuation of intimidation, dehumanization, and violence are *not* free. They will never be free as long as they have to kill our children in order to safeguard their overprivileged positions. They will never be free as long as thay have to lie awake at night wondering if, when white power will have come to its inevitable end, a black government will do the same to them as they are now doing to us.

We must also ask the question: What is positive about the new constitutional proposals of the government? In order that there should be no misunderstanding, let me, as clearly and briefly as possible, repeat the reasons why we reject these proposals:

1) Racism, so embeded in South African society, is once again written into the constitution. All over the world, persons are beginning to recognize that racism is politically untenable, sociologically unsound, and morally unacceptable. In this country, however, the doctrine of racial supremacy, although condemned by most churches in South Africa as heresy and idolatry, is once again enshrined in the constitution as the basis upon

which to build the further development of our society and the nurturing of human relationships.

2) All the basic laws, those that are the very pillars of apartheid, and without which the system cannot survive—laws concerning mixed marriages, group areas, racial classification, separate and unequal education—remain untouched and unchanged by the new proposals.

3) The homelands policy, which is surely the most immoral and objectionable aspect of the apartheid policies of the government, forms the basis of the willful exclusion of 80 percent of our nation from the new political deal. Indeed, in the words of the President's Council, the homelands policy is to be regarded as "irreversible." So our black African brothers and sisters will be driven even further into the wilderness of homeland politics. Millions will have to find their political rights in the sham independence of those bush republics. Millions more will continue to lose their South African citizenship, and millions more will be removed forcibly from their homes into resettlement camps.

4) Clearly the opression will continue; the brutal breakup of black family life will not end. The apartheid line is not at all abolished; it is simply shifted so as to include the so-called coloureds and Indians who are willing to cooperate with the government.

5) Not only is the present system of apartheid given more elasticity, making fundamental change even harder than before, but in the new proposals the dream of democracy for which we strive is still further eroded.

6) Whereas, then, the proposals may mean something for those middle-class blacks, who think that the improvement of their own economic position is the highest good, they will not bring any significant changes to the life of those who have no rights at all, who must languish in the poverty and utter destitution of the homelands, and who are forbidden by law to live together as families in what is called "white South Africa."

It cannot be repeated often enough that all South Africans who love this country and who care for its future—black and white, Jew and Gentile, Christian and Muslim—have no option but to reject these proposals.

Aparthied is a cancer in the body politic of the world, a scourge on our society, and an everlasting shame to the church of Jesus Christ in the world and in this country. It exists only because of economic greed, cultural chauvinism, and political oppression maintained by both systemic and physical violence, and a false sense of racial superiority. Therefore we must resist apartheid. We must resist it because it is in fundamental opposition to the noble principles of our Judeo-Christian heritage, and of the Muslim faith. We must resist it because it is a fundamental denial of all that is worthwhile and human in our society. It is in opposition to the will of God for this country. We must resist it because in its claim to be Christian apartheid is blasphemy, idolatry, and heresy.

To be sure, the new proposals will make apartheid less blatant in some ways. It will be modernized and streamlined, and in its new multicolored cloak it will be less conspicuous and less offensive to some. Nonetheless, it will still be there. Apartheid, we must remember, is a thoroughly evil system, and, as such, it cannot be modified, modernized, or streamlined. It has to be eradicated irrevocably. We must continue, therefore, to struggle until that glorious day dawns when apartheid will exist no more.

To those who ask why we are not satisfied and when we shall be satisfied, we must say in clear, patient terms; we shall not be satisfied as long as injustice reigns supreme on the throne of our land. We shall not be satisfied as long as those who rule us are not inspired by justice, but dictated to by fear, greed, and racism. We shall not be satisfied until South Africa is once again one, undivided country, a democracy where there will be meaningful participation in a democratic process of government for all the people. We shall not be satisfied until the wealth and riches of this country are shared by all. We shall not be satisfied until justice rolls down like a waterfall and righteousness like a mighty stream. . . .

As we struggle on, let us continue to sing that wonderful hymn of freedom: *Nkosi Sikilel i Afrika!* [Lord Bless Afrika] I know that today we are singing the hymn with tears in our eyes. We are singing it while we are bowed down by the weight of oppression and battered by the winds of injustice. We are singing it while our elderly languish in resettlement camps, and our children are dying of hunger in the "homelands." We are singing it now while we suffer under the brutality of apartheid, and while the blood of our children is calling to God from the streets of our nation.

We must, however, work for the day when we shall sing it as *free* black South Africans! We shall sing it on that day when our children will no longer be judged by the color of their skin but by the humanness of their character. We shall sing it on that day when even here in this country, in Johannesburg and Cape Town, in Port Elizabeth and Durban, the sanctity of marriage and family life will be respected, and no law will sunder what God has joined together. We shall sing it on that day when in this rich land no child will die of hunger and no infant will die an untimely death; when our elderly will close their eyes in peace, and the wrinkled stomachs of our children will be filled with food just as their lives will be filled with meaning. We shall sing it when here, in South Africa, whites and blacks will have learned to love one another and work together in building a truly good and beautiful land.

With this faith we shall be able to give justice and peace their rightful place on the throne of our land. With this faith, we shall be able to see beyond the darkness of our present into the bright and glittering daylight of our future. With this faith we shall be able to speed the day when all South African children will embrace each other and sing with new meaning:

> God bless Africa!
> Guide her rulers!
> Bless her children!
> Give her peace!
> O, give her peace!

2. Rian Malan Assesses Factionalism in the Townships, 1990

Rian Malan, a close relative of the first National party prime minister after 1948, grew up as a self-conscious dissident from Afrikaner norms. After a number of years in exile, he returned to South Africa to pursue a career as an investigative journalist. In the second half of My Traitor's Heart, *Malan examines the ways in which South Africans were killing one another in the mid-1980s. The following passage looks at conflict between those loyal to the ANC and the Freedom Charter and the followers of a Bikoist black-consciousness doctrine.*

In the nine years since I was last in Dhlamini, the place has brightened somewhat. Black people have finally been granted the right to permanent residence in "white" South Africa. Many now own the houses they live in, and with ownership has come a measure of pride. Every second or third residence has been expanded or modified in some fashion. There are splashes of color here and there—a house brightly painted, a flowering rose garden, a new car in some lucky man's driveway—but the backdrop remains dreary and depressing. The ranks of matchbox houses run down toward a stretch of reedy marshland, where a rubble-strewn patch of land serves as a makeshift soccer field.

It is deserted today, but in a more innocent time a group of black schoolboys in their early teens might have been playing soccer down there. Those soccer games were a daily after-school ritual for the schoolboys of Dhlamini 1 and its adjoining zone, Dhlamini 2. They took their games seriously and always played to win, but they were good friends off the field. They lived within hailing distance of one another, and often attended the same schools. They were all black, all sons of struggling parents, all victims of apartheid's atrocious Bantu Education, dished out in overcrowded classrooms by teachers barely educated themselves. And they were all to some degree politicized. Some of the boys were members of Azapo, and some belonged to the UDF, but they were still playing soccer together in the afternoons a year or so ago. Today, they're trying to kill each other.

I locate the house I'm looking for and knock on the door. A firebomb has recently exploded on this very doorstep. A month or two hence, a teenaged son of the household within will be waylaid as he's coming home, stabbed with garden forks and burned alive. Right now, however, the street seems peaceful. Even so, I feel apprehensive and cast fearful glances in the direction from which danger will come, if it comes. I usually work with a black interpreter, but nobody would accompany me on this particular mission. They all said it was too dangerous.

The door opens, and I find myself shaking hands with a teenager in a T-shirt and skintight designer jeans. The boy's skin is golden-brown and he's still carrying a little baby fat on his plump face and frame. This is Vuyisele Byron Wauchope, age fifteen. Alongside him stands his friend and ideological mentor, Vuyo Kapa, age nineteen. Through an open doorway I catch a glimpse of Byron's Uncle George, the general secretary of Azapo, sleeping the sleep of the utterly exhausted in a bedroom piled with clothes and other belongings. He is a refugee now. He and his wife and children no longer have a home. Their home has burned down, which means that Byron is homeless too.

Byron leads me through into the dining room, and we sit down at the table to talk. Vuyo joins us. Vuyo is a desperately serious young man. He has a goatee like Trotsky's, and some ideas to match. He is here to keep vigil over the utterances of young Byron, who is too young to have truly mastered the party line. Byron has only just turned fifteen, and he's still inclined to squirm and giggle nervously in the presence of a strange adult. It's hard to see him as a player in the deadly game of township politics, but that's how things were in the great uprising of the mid-eighties. In some ways, it was a Children's Crusade.

Byron is the son of George Wauchope's sister, but he was raised in the BC leader's household and seems to have racial politics in his bones. One of his earliest memories is of visiting his famous uncle in prison during one of George's periodic detention spells. Byron's relatives used to carry him to BC rallies and congresses before he could walk or talk. "I joined politics when I was five," the boy says proudly. Shortly thereafter, he was teargassed for the first time, at a rally commemorating Steve Biko's death in detention. At the age of twelve, he became a card-carrying member of the Biko youth movement, and soon rose to be treasurer of the Dhlamini 1 branch of Azasm. His best friend, Fana Mhlongo, was the branch's mascot. Fana was by no means the youngest comrade, but he was one of the smallest, short and fat like a snub-nosed revolver. That's why they called him Gunman—comrade Gunman Mhlongo, a soldier at the age of fourteen.

Fana lived just up the road, and he'd been Byron's best friend since 1983. The boys were inseparable in all things, not just politics. They attended the same primary school, played on the same soccer team in those afternoon pick-up games. They liked the same TV shows—*Knight Rider, The A-Team* and Bill Cosby—and the same pop groups: Stimela, The Big Dudes, Yvonne Chaka-Chaka. Their favorite film stars were "James Bond" and Chuck Norris. Their favorite movies were *Rambo, First Blood,* and *Wild Geese,* a luridly racist action adventure in which white mercenaries kick hell out of a caricatural African despot. And their favorite game, Byron added, was Monopoly. I thought the next thing to emerge from his young mouth would be some kind words about Ronald Reagan or Margaret Thatcher, but Byron Wauchope was actually a revolutionary socialist. His friend Fana was one, too.

"We wrote a freedom song," said Byron. It was called, "Strive Tirelessly for a Socialist Azania," and it went like this: "If you can fight fearlessly, I'll meet you on the freedom day. I shall fight for Azania, Azania, my beloved country."

Impressed, I asked Byron why he and Fana had opted to join the Azanians, as opposed to the UDF.

"Well," Byron answered, "the UDF says, 'Mandela it's our father,' but we say, 'Biko it's our father.'"

"Yes," I said, "I understand that, but what I'm really asking is, Why do you prefer BC? What is Black Consciousness?"

He thought about that, and then he said, "Steve Biko was a man, and Abraham Tiro says there is no struggle without casualties."

The late Abraham Tiro was a prominent BC leader in the seventies, but even so, it was not the most illuminating reply. My line of questioning was clearly incorrect, so I tried another tack. Instead of asking what was right about BC, I asked what was wrong with the UDF.

"They are trying to confuse the masses," said Byron.

"How so?" I wondered.

"When they saw we were too powerful," he said, "they said you will get free money and free T-shirts if you join the UDF."

At this point, Vuyo stepped in to offer a more coherent statement on the boy's behalf. "Biko was trying to boost the morale of the exploited masses of Azania," Vuyo began. His discourse lasted ten minutes and touched on several hair-raising conspiracy theories, one of which was that the American CIA was funnelling funds through the ANC to the UDF, which was using the money to bribe Biko followers over to the Mandela side. He concluded on a familiar note: Only the BC movement was "fighting for socialism and the total liberation of all blacks and oppressed people" and would not rest until victory was achieved. It was very interesting, but Byron's remark about the T-shirts stood and deserved to be heard.

In the beginning, to hear young Byron tell it, being a comrade was quite exciting. They held meetings and workshops in their homes after school while their parents were away at work. They discussed apartheid and the fight against it. Older members of the organization delivered lectures on ideology and tactics. Once the struggle got underway in earnest, they declared Dhlamini 1 a "liberated zone" and drew up plans to defend it. Every comrade was given a list of names and phone numbers to keep beside his parents' telephone, if they had one, so that he could raise the alarm in the event of an attack. They also divised codes to baffle the system's ubiquitous spies. If a comrade said "Bring the Kentucky!" for instance, it really meant, "Bring the gun!" Many comrades were so young that they'd stub out cigarettes when they saw their parents coming, but some carried pistols or revolvers in their socks.

The guns were intended for defense against the system, of course, not against people like Paulos Madonsela. Paulos lived three doors down from Byron and often played soccer with him and Fana after school. Paulos was a year or two older, and inclined to play rough. Indeed, he once tackled Byron so hard that he accidently broke his arm, but that was part of the game. The boys remained friends in spite of everything. Even when Paulos succumbed to alleged CIA blandishments and donned the yellow T-shirt of the rival UDF, he and Byron stayed friends. "We all shared a pain for Soweto," Byron explained. But then Senator Kennedy came to South Africa, and nothing was ever the same again.

As the BC comrades saw it, the American senator's visit would only raise false hopes and foster illusions among Soweto's dowtrodden people. "The Charterists were telling people who doesn't know anything that someone from the USA is coming to deliver a speech," Byron said. "So people who are not educated thought maybe this man is having good news, coming from the States. But BC said, 'There's nothing like that. Kennedy will deliver nothing. He's out of order. We don't want Kennedy here.'"

Paulos disagreed. He and his fellow Charterists were planning to roll out the red carpet for the famous American. One day Paulos saw Byron in the road and called out mockingly, "Come and listen to this man! Maybe you can be liberated!" Byron just laughed. "Paulos," he replied, "you are still young in politics. You are an amateur."

On the appointed day, all the comrades in Dhlamini marched down the hill to Regina Mundi cathedral, where Kennedy was scheduled to speak. Thousands of people were waiting, plus scores of reporters and TV cameras from all over the world. Paulos and the Charterists stood at the front of the hall. Byron, Fana, and the rest of the BC contingent stood at the back. And Bishop Tutu stood on stage with his hands in the air, begging the seething factions to make peace. It didn't help. The BC comrades were determined not to let Kennedy speak. Indeed, they put on such a show of force and fury that Tutu lost his nerve and advised his friend Kennedy to stay away. It was a humiliation for the UDF, and there would be a price to pay.

One day, not long after, the slogan "One Azania, One Nation" appeared on a transformer housing at the entrance to Dhlamini 1, marking the zone a Zim-zim stronghold. Few whites knew the term Zim-zim, and it seldom if ever appeared in the copy of foreign correspondents. It was becoming an important word in Soweto, though. In Soweto, youngsters who said Biko were dubbed Zim-zims, in honor of all the -isms in their ideological arsenal: socialism, racism, capitalism, colonialism. Those who said Mandela, on the other hand, were called Wararas, a corruption of the Afrikaans *waar-waar*, meaning "where-where." In the estimation of Zim-zims, anyone who believed the UDF's nonracial doctrine was very confused. They were groping around in the dark in search of their true enemy, crying. "Where? Where?" Dhlamini 1 became a Zim-zim stronghold, and Dhlamini 2, just across the road, became Warara turf. Much of the rest of Soweto was similarly divided, in preparation for the coming war.

To the best of Byron's recollection, the first casualty, was Sipho Mngomezulu, a young man who "preached BC" in a part of Soweto called Emdeni. The Wararas abducted him from his home in full view of his helpless parents, dragged him to a vacant lot and stoned him to death. I tried to ask the Wararas for their version of this event, but I couldn't contact them. They were hiding from the Zim-zims, or on the run from the police. If I had reached them, though, I daresay they might have claimed that Mngomezulu was executed in retaliation for the recent abduction and torture-murders of three teenaged Wararas. The Zim-zims, in turn, denied complicity in those killings, claiming that they were actually carried out by the maKabasa, a criminal gang that just happened to live in a Zim-zim stronghold and probably took orders from the white secret police. Such knots are never unraveled, not in South Africa.

All that is certain is that Sipho Mngomezulu was abducted and killed in broad daylight. To add insult to injury, a mob of Wararas invaded the wake, set fire to Sipho's coffin, and demolished his parents' home with a hijacked bulldozer. The Zim-zims managed to save the coffin and bury it, but there was a second killing after the funeral. This time, the victim was Martin Mohau, age twenty-nine. Mohau was a hero of the struggle against apartheid and another "graduate" of Robben Island, the political prison in Table Bay. He was also a Zim-zim. A mob of Wararas waylaid him on his way home from Sipho's funeral and necklaced him—put a car tire around his neck, poured gasoline on him, and burned him alive.

"After that," Byron continued, "everyone chose sides." Wararas started "expelling" Zim-zims from schools in their strongholds. Teenagers with dissident politics were threatened or beaten up by their classmates. Some were doused with petrol, put inside car tires and given a choice: "Say Mandela or die." Or: "Say Biko or die."

Fana's school was Ibongho High, a bad place to be BC. One morning, leaders of the dominant Warara faction ordered their teachers and headmaster to go sit in the staff room. Then they summoned the students to an assembly. All Zim-zims were ordered to step to the fore and recant. Several did, but not Comrade Gunman Mhlongo. "He was ready to die for BC," young Byron told me. So Fana and approximately twenty fellow BC stalwarts were banished on pain of death. "If we ever see you here again," the Wararas warned, "tell us what size car tire you wear." Then the Zim-zims were chased away. Fana was a fat boy and couldn't run very fast. He dropped his school bag while making his getaway, and that was the end of his education.

A few days later, a similar incident took place at Byron's school. A group of Wararas led by his old friend Paulos burst into Byron's classroom, looking for him. "Where is he?" the Wararas demanded. "We want to necklace him." Byron was lucky; he'd had a premonition and stayed at home that day.

Appalled by the image of a gang of sixteen-year-olds invading a higher-primary-school classroom to murder a fifteen-year-old, I asked Byron how the teacher responded. "He just shut his mouth," the boy giggled, "because he knew that if he opened it they would kill him, too. But after they left, he phoned my house and told me I must not come back to school."

And so Byron and his best friend Fana stayed home, with nothing to do all day. They listened to Radio Bop, beaming in from the quasi-independent homeland of Bophuthatswana. They played Monopoly, or fooled around on Uncle George's tape, recording themselves singing freedom songs. One day, on their way to the shops, they were attacked by a band of Wararas. Fana fended off a knife-thrust with his bare hand, and one of his fingers was virtually severed. After that, the BC comrades always traveled in a group. They started sleeping in groups too, staying one night at one comrade's house, the next at another's. They wanted to be together in case of an attack.

Outside, the killing continued. A BC comrade's home was damaged by a Soviet limpet mine. In apparent retaliation, Zim-zims hijacked a bus and crashed it into the home of a Warara leader. In counterstrike, the Wararas started kidnapping and killing Zim-zim next-of-kin. A well-known Soweto sports personality and church leader was abducted and murdered by Wararas hunting his son. The aging grandmother of a Zim-zim met a similar fate. A UDF street committee ordered her to produce her grandson; when she failed to comply, she was killed. A few days later, someone from the other side was bundled into a car, shot thrice, and his body dumped in a coalyard. And so it carried on.

In this war, as in all wars, there were no innocent parties and no innocent bystanders, but the Zim-zims were clearly on the losing end. Azapo seemed to be disintegrating, its members resigning in fear of their lives, its leaders driven underground. There came a time when no one was safe anymore, least of all the Wauchope family. George Wauchope had been one of Steve Biko's closest allies, but this did not entitle him to mercy. First there were phone calls, anonymous voices warning George that his time was running out. Then someone rammed a stolen van into the front of his house. A few nights later, a firebomb was hurled at George's home. It smashed against an outside wall, causing little damage, but still, these incidents left him unnerved. George had a family to think about—a wife, two young children, an ailing mother and a teenage nephew. That's why he went into hiding, hoping to draw the Wararas away. And that in turn is why there was no man in the house at 1454 Dhlamini when the Wararas returned to burn it down.

They came at three in the morning, and this time they came in force. Byron was wakened by a great crashing of glass, and the whomp of igniting gasoline. In his estimation, at least twenty Molotov cocktails came in through the windows simultaneously. One landed right on top of his cousin Ephraim, setting his clothes and bedding afire. It was bright as day from the flames, but the house soon filled with smoke. The family milled around in terror. Byron groped his way to the door, but it wouldn't open. Someone was holding it closed from the outside. The flames were mounting, and the Wauchopes thought themselves doomed to burn. They were lucky, though. Their screams roused the neighbors, who came to see what was going on. At that, the Wararas melted away into the night. The door suddenly gave, and the Wauchopes staggered outside, choking and gasping for air.

Nobody was seriously injured in the fire, but the Wauchopes lost almost everything they owned. In the aftermath, young Byron telephoned Uncle George at his place of hiding and told him to come and see. The BC leader arrived just as the fire brigade was dousing the last flames in the smoldering ruins of his home.

"He didn't day anything," Byron told me. "He just looked down at the ground."

3. Kidnapped from Swaziland: An Interview with
    Grace Cele, 1986

Not only did African communities within South Africa suffer raids, but all of the frontline countries were affected as well. Moreover, such raids swept up many people who were not resistance activists but only bystanders. The authorities frankly admitted that such practices were necessary for the maintenance of South African security. After 1976 it became more and more clear that despite the earlier moral pretensions of apartheid (as expressed, for example, by Hendrik Verwoerd), the regime was morally bankrupt, even by its own account. South African leaders pursued security for its own sake.

Grace Cele was married to a South African working in Swaziland. He died in 1980, leaving her with five children, four boys and a girl. At the time of this interview, her eldest son and her daughter were away studying in the United States. The three younger boys—Sipho, Mfana, Zanele—live with her in Ottawa.

I was living in Swailand; it was in the night of 12 December. I was kidnapped by the South African commandos. My apartment was bombed—I thought it was an explosion from the refrigerator. I wanted to get up, but I didn't have time. I was pulled out of my bed and there were these men who asked me who I was. And I told them that I was Grace; and they said, 'Grace who?' And I said, 'Grace Cele.' I thought I was dreaming, I thought it was a nightmare. It was the middle of the night.

So they took me out of my bed, I was handcuffed. And as I went out I thought I was dreaming, and I called one of my children: 'Sipho!' and there was no response. So I was taken out, bundled into a car and it ran away. I was blindfolded. The car stopped—I didn't know where it was, until one of these guys—they were laughing then—he said, 'Please use your ashtrays to prevent forest fires.' Then I knew that we were on the road to Mhlambanyati, because there's a sign there in the forest, a manmade forest. They got out of the car and they were talking to somebody who was outside the car, and they were using these walkie-talkies. And the other one said: 'Oh, that was quick.' And the one said: 'Ja, it was quick. But next time they mustn't give us the same cars.'

And when they took off again we were just in a convoy; we were following other cars, two. And at one stage they tried to push me down, and one said: 'There's a truck coming.' You see, that road from Mhlambanyati it's used by loggers, usually during the night when there's no traffic. So they pushed me down and the other one said, 'No, they mustn't see that we've got something here.' So the truck passed. I was . . . I was defenceless because I was blindfolded; I had a nightie on, just my nightie, nothing else. My hands were crossed like this [indicating] just like this, and tied. And they were just . . . they

From Hilda Bernstein, *The Rift: The Exile Experience of South Africans*, London: Jonathan Cape, 1994, pp. 199–205. Copyright © 1994 by Hilda Bernstein. Reprinted by permission of Sheil Land Associates.

were trying to touch me and I was trying to protect myself—I think if they had time they would have raped me and killed me; and they would have said I was trying to resist arrest. But they didn't have time, because they were saying, 'At such-and-such a time we should be at the border.'

Then they must have got lost, because somebody said: 'No. This is not the turning we are supposed to take.' So they reversed again, they followed, and we stopped somewhere—I have no idea where. And I thought to myself, oh, I think now they are going to kill me. But I heard . . . it was just . . . it wasn't a sharp sound . . . I don't know how to call it, but it wasn't sharp; no, it was sort of deadly . . . how do I describe it? No, they were shooting at something, but it wasn't sharp; it was as though it was snuffled, ja. Muffled. I thought, well they are shooting at somebody.

I heard gates open, and the car went in. And next thing I was told to get out. So I got out and I heard this guy talking in Afrikaans: 'Is the gate open?' 'Ja, I have the key.' Now I assumed that we were on the South African side now. So he opened the gate and I was pushed through. Then I heard a Kombi [armored police vehicle] and it came this Kombi and I was the first one who was thrown in. And immediately when they threw me in, I was handshackled. You see this Kombi I think it was specially made to take people, because there were these bars where I was tied. My feet were chained on to the bars and my hands were chained at the back, and I was left like that. Still blindfolded.

There were others who were thrown in too. And it took off. On the way, I heard these people talking—I thought they were talking German—and the police, well, these bandits kept on saying: 'Shut up!' And then they would keep quiet; and then start talking again. Then I was trying to think, now what is happening because we have got Germans here; who are these other people? But they drove on and on, it seemed we were just driving for all eternity.

We came to a place I don't know where, and these two whites were taken out. And the lady started crying and they said to her: 'No don't cry. If you co-operate, we won't harm you.' So they moved them, put them into another car; and we proceeded. Later I met these two—it turned out it was Corinne Bischoff and Danny Schneider. I found that out afterwards.

So we just moved on and on. There was this man who kept crying and saying: 'I want to pee.' And they kept on saying: 'Shut up!' But he kept on saying: 'I want to pee.' And I heard them say in Afrikaans: '*What van die?* What about this one?' They whispered to each other, and I heard them pull something; it was as though it was a sack, heavy sack of sand. Then I said to myself, whatever it is it must be dead.

Before we took off, when they had taken out that couple, I said to one of them; 'Excuse me, could you please make me comfortable'—I was all bruises because I was knocked all over the place. So they came, put me up straight; they made me sit this time and my hands were still behind me. So we went on. Then we came to this place where we stopped, and they took this guy out—the one who was asking to pee. And I was left there. I can't recall how long . . . it could have been for ten minutes, it could have been two, three hours or whatever. Just sitting in that van.

Eventually they came for me and they took off the foot shackles, ja, but my hands were still tied, and they said I should walk. I couldn't walk; I was swollen all over. So they picked me up—there were two—and they told me: 'Now, listen! We are going up the stairs now. Start walking.' So they tried to lift me up, up, and I went to the top floor whatever it was, and I was just thrown into a . . . I discovered afterwards it was just a long passage. I was thrown there and left there.

After some time they came again and removed the bandage from my eyes. And these two guys came again—I think they were the ones who had done this operation—and put me into a room. It was full of these Boers, and they were just hurling insults at me. Then I saw September. I was shocked when I saw him. September had been in Swaziland; I knew him as a refugee who had been arrested and put into Mangayane Prison. We had then heard over the news that the prison was broken into and some of the refugees were gone, so we thought they must have broken out. But it turned out the South African bandits came for these guys and took them over. I didn't know then that September was alive—I thought he was dead. He says: 'You're surprised I'm alive? I'm alive and I would advise you to just co-operate with these guys; they will give you a lot of money.' I couldn't believe it, because I thought, you know, September was a staunch ANC member. And I looked at September . . . I was confused. And I said, 'What?' He says, 'No, later on we'll talk anyway, we'll talk. But there's a lot of money involved, Grace. Just do as they say.'

By that time I was in pains; and one of the guys said, 'Ay, just look at her.' Now I didn't know what they meant when they say look at me—whether they meant how I looked; because I was bruised, the face, the head, I was swollen just everything. So I thought maybe he meant about my swollen feet, swollen hands, swollen face. And I heard the other one said, 'Oh, you'd better go and get her something to dress.' So one guy went; and they took me to a lean-to thing, and I was made to get in there and wash myself. That's when I was trying to take off my nightie that I discovered that I had blood all over my back, it was just a big stain of blood. I didn't know where that blood came from. But I learned later that one of the ANC members, Maphumulo, had been shot; he was taken from Manzini, put into the car. And I think he was the person I was sitting next to. Dead. It was that person they were pulling. It was Maphumulo.

I came back. They had brought me an overall; and they started asking me questions, 'Do you know ANC people?' Then I said, 'No. But I do have friends who are refugees.' They say, 'No. ANC.' You see, with the Boers if you say refugee, no, they don't want to accept that; you have to identify and say ANC. Then I said, 'Well as far as I know, my friends are refugees.' Then they said, 'Oh ja, we know a lot about you. And we are asking you, as a South African, to help us get these ANC people.'

Then I turned to September—you see I didn't understand. I said, 'September, they say I'm a South African now, but I'm a Swazi. I'm a Swazi citizen now. I know at home I've never been considered a South African by the Boers, so how can I be a South African?' He says, 'You are not a Swazi.'

So I kept on saying, 'No, I'm a Swazi'; they said, 'No, you are not a Swazi; you are a South African.' Then I said, 'Well, I'm a South African conveniently.' That's when they started beating me up. 'Don't talk! We are the ones who are going to do the talking. You only talk when we want an answer from you.'

So they left me. And September said to me, 'No, please listen. You see that one? He said I should talk to you because I told them that I know you. And he said I should talk to you, and there's a lot of money involved.'

But I was not interested then, I was in pain. They took me, put me in a cell, and locked me up there. After two days they came again. So they used to come . . . sometimes they would come every day, sometimes they would stay for three, four days, not appearing, and I'm left in that cell all by myself. All I see is people giving me food through the iron bars. I remember, it was the second day they came with a piece of paper, and this guy said to me, 'Oh sign here.' I said, 'What for?' He says, 'Well Colonel Verster says he arrested you at the border with a car full of arms of war.' And I said, 'No, I'm sure I'm dreaming—did he say he found me?' He says, 'Yes.' Then I said, 'No, I'm not going to sign that.' He says, '*Ek sal jou drap*! I'm going to beat you up.' Then I took the paper, I flipped it over, and I signed on the Afrikaans side because they maintained that I didn't know Afrikaans. So at the back of my mind I was saying, Oh let me sign in Afrikaans. In case they ask me, then I'll say, 'This was Afrikaans, I did not know.' Then I said, 'Now what is this Section 29 you are telling me about?' He says, 'No, you were found with arms of war, and you are state security or something like that. How do they call it? Section 29 . . . ' [Laughs]

I was asked to identify refugees—yes, they brought piles and piles of photos. And before he started, he says, 'Now Grace, I'd like to know where you are working, how much do you earn?' So I told them. He said, 'Now listen, that's peanuts. We can give you five times, seven times what you are earning. And we can give you, if you give us a big fish, a bonus for that. And we can give you a car of your choice.'

They told me where my children were schooling and they were asking me to verify. So I thought, no, I'm not going to lie because I don't know what they know. So I told them. They said, 'Ja, we can take care of your children, we can educate them, you don't have to pay anything.' Then I said to them, 'What about my place that was bombed?' They said, 'No, that was nothing. We can look after that; if you still want payment for that we can do that easily. But you can get a better place.' And September was harking, kept on saying, 'Grace there's lots of money, lots of money here.'

Then I said to myself, I know in Swaziland a lot of people have been killed by the system after they have done whatever they wanted them to do, and when now they couldn't give more information. So I said, 'No.' This time I thought, I don't know how I'm going to do it God, but please help me. Because really I was at their mercy.

They beat me with fists, with clubs, what they call it, sticks, ja. I still have scars here on the legs and you can see some of them here, here. Ja, there are still some of them here and here; it's never been right since that time. I didn't know what I was capable of saying or doing. And at one stage, I don't know, I think . . . I must have fainted, or I can't describe it because there was a time when I couldn't feel pain. You know, during these beatings I couldn't feel pain, so I don't know whether I fainted or it was the body mechanism trying to protect me. I don't know.

They would come, sometimes three would come and get me, sometimes two, sometimes one. And I remember one time they said to me, 'You keep on saying you don't know these guys, but they know you.' I was confused now, when they say, 'They know you.' Who were they talking about? Were they talking about the people they kidnapped from Swaziland and who were trying to save their skins? I had no idea. Then I got a very serious beating when they said, 'Oh, they know you, and you say you don't know them?' Then I said, 'Ja, you're right. It's like the Minister of Justice Vlok, ja.' I said, 'It's like me saying I know Vlok; and when you ask Vlok he says he doesn't know me.'

And I . . . I decided then, that I'm not going to say anything. I didn't want to eat their food because of the stories we hear about people being poisoned. So I was scared to eat anything. And they would come and they would find the food stacked there. And they said to me, 'Are you on a hunger strike?' And I wouldn't answer them because it wasn't a hunger strike, it was fear more than anything. And at one stage they asked me, 'Is your hair permed?' Then I said, 'No it's not.' Then I heard him saying to this guy, 'Ja, she's lucky. Because I was going to set light to that hair!'

I don't know what to say, there's so many things. Some time during my stay in the cell there were people in cells on both sides; and they would shout to each other, 'No, just get on the toilet seat.' They were not talking to me. Then I said to myself, oh boy, all along I should have done this thing—get on the toilet seat and look outside. But I went to the toilet seat and I look over, and I saw there were two Kombis, and children coming out of these Kombis. Then I said to myself, now, what are these children . . . what are they doing here? And I heard this other guy in the next cell saying, 'Oh, those are the children that have been taken from all over the country.'

One day I heard them opening doors. Usually they used to give me food through the iron bars. They opened and I saw this child, he was about eight or nine. Then I looked at this guy who was bringing my food, and I said to this child, 'Hey, what do you want here?' And then he started crying. He said, 'Oh I was taken from Soweto. Please I want to go home, I was taken from so-and-so'. And this guy said, 'Shut up! You are telling a lie! You were trying to chop somebody with a machete. You are telling a lie!' He says, 'No, I'm not telling a lie. I've been taken from Soweto!' That's the first and the last time they brought anybody around, but sometimes I would hear people crying. I heard one crying and she says, 'No, I'm telling the truth! I'm telling the truth!' But they were just beating up these kids, just beating them up. She says, 'No, I'm not lying! I'm telling the truth!'

So the guy came again who was bringing me food. I said, 'Now who is this one crying? What is happening?' He says, 'Oh no; that one is mad. Ja,' he says, 'he's a mad person. He's mad.' But I could hear the beatings up.

One day I was taken to a doctor because now I was getting sick. The doctor says, 'Now you are very sick; you have got kitons in your urine because you don't eat right. Right now you should have been in a coma, why aren't you eating? Are you on a hunger strike?'

I said, 'No. I'm not on a hunger strike. I don't know why I'm here; and my children have been killed.' They said, 'No, your children haven't been killed.' I said, 'I called to them when they took me, and they didn't respond; it has never happened with my children that when I called out to them, they don't respond.' The doctor talked to one of the police, said, 'Find out if her children are OK, are alive.' He went, came back and said, 'Oh, we called your house and there was nobody.' I said, 'Of course. You've killed my kids! Do you expect the ghosts to answer the telephone?' Then they said, 'Who can we get in touch with?' I remembered a friend of mine who was working for UNDP, so I said, 'Oh, call Doreen.' I gave them the number, and he came back and said, 'Doreen says the children are OK.' I said, 'I don't trust you. I'll only believe when I talk to Doreen.' But at that time I was hysterical, I was crying. They said, 'No, try to keep quiet; then you'll be able to talk to Doreen.'

So I spoke to Doreen. I was warned before, 'Don't tell Doreen where you are, what we are doing; just ask about the children and that's all. And don't cry.' So I said, 'Doreen, it's Grace.' Then she started crying over the phone, 'Where are you? What are you doing? Where are you?' Then I said, 'Are my children OK, Doreen?' Says, 'Ja, they are fine; somebody is taking care of them.' And then she said, 'Oh your cousin just called from Ermelo.' I don't have any cousin.

The doctor said, 'Now you can eat.' But I never ate a morsel of food for all the time I was held there. That was sixty-eight days, ja; and my teeth were sort of getting loose. And they called the doctor again and the doctor said, 'No Grace, you'd better eat.' And he prescribed some tablets. I was afraid again to take those tablets because I'd heard that people are given slow poison. They would bring these tablets and they would look at me, then I would put them under my tongue; as soon as they go, then I would spit them out! But when the doctor came a fortnight later and told them, 'I've given her these vitamin tablets but there's no improvement,' I nearly kicked myself. And after that, faithfully each time I would take these vitamin tablets. But I never ate their food.

During that time a number of people would come. One said he was from the Minister of Justice to ask if I have any complaints. And I said, 'You've been coming here I don't know how many times, asking about my complaints. I've asked you, and I'll still ask you: if I've done anything wrong let me be charged. If I haven't done anything wrong, let me be released and put back into Swaziland.' 'I'll convey your message to the Minister!' And another day there was one who came and said, 'I'm the Prosecutor here.' I said, 'Prosecutor here— where is here?' Says, 'Oh, never mind; but I was told to come and see if you have any needs and so on.' I said, 'Oh, could you please try and get me a toothbrush and some toothpaste, and soap.' Because they gave me a carbolic soap and I used it and I just got burned. But he never brought me soap.

Until one day, they just came and said, 'You are going home.' I cried all night. I cried all night because I was thinking: now home, it means they are going to kill me; it's their way of talking, they are going to kill me. So . . . that was Friday when they told me. Nothing happened. Saturday nothing happened. And they came on Sunday morning with a nailclipper—my nails were this long, I'd been asking for a nailclipper and they refused. But that particular morning, when I was supposed to go home, they brought a nailclipper, said, 'OK. You can cut your nails and make yourself presentable, so that they shouldn't think that we are ill-treating you.'

Just before I was told I was going home, somebody came and said, 'I'm sent by the Minister to check if you have any fresh scars and wounds. Did you have any beatings?' That's when I was told that I can go home. They came at about 5 p.m. and said, 'Now we are taking you home. But never ever utter a word to anybody where you were held, what we did to you, what we asked you to do for us. Because if you do, we know where your children are.'

I wasn't scared so much for myself. I was scared for my children. And I know how brutal they are.

So I was released. They said, 'You shouldn't be interviewed by anything—media, television, nothing, nobody. Because we will be watching you.' This is why, when I was released, I didn't talk to anybody. I asked my children, 'If the telephone rings you'd better answer it.' They would call and ask to talk to Grace; my friends would say, 'She's not in.' I kept quiet. I stayed away from the media.

But I was scared. And as soon as I got home I had made up my mind that I'll just organise my children and run away. But I didn't know where to.

Debating the New South Africa

1. Nomavenda Mathiane Considers the Meanings of Freedom, 1987

Ms. Mathiane started her career in journalism with Drum *publications in 1972, and then became assistant editor of* Frontline *in Johannesburg. She is thus a successor of the original* Drum *journalists of the 1950s, such as Henry Nxumalo, Nat Nakasa, and Can Themba. In the following selection, Mathiane records the hopes, fears, and expectations of Africans as the apartheid regime drew to its end.*

Our Future: Meanings of Freedom

Saturday Morning in the township. Suddenly the car ahead comes to a grinding stop. You slam on your brakes, and so does the person behind you. There is no movement. Tempers begin to flare. Motorists start hooting. On investigation, you discover that two taxi drivers travelling in opposite directions have decided to hold a conversation right in the middle of the road.

On such occasions, powerless and disgruntled motorists and taxi passengers throw their hands in the air and mutter, "What can we do, these chaps are a law unto themselves." It is at such incidents that one hears the remark, "So that is the freedom that black people are fighting for! The freedom to stop anywhere, and inconvenience anyone."

At the Zimbabwe independence celebrations, I was walking with a group of South Africans back to our various hotels from the stadium. Our hearts were heavy and we were all asking ourselves the obvious question: when was it going to be our turn? Then we came across a group of Zimbabweans seated on the pavement drinking Shibuku. They offered us some but we declined. One of them sauntered up to us, and with a drunken slur said, "We have long been liberated, freedom we have just had."

That statement hit me hard. I realized for the first time that freedom and liberation were two concepts whose meanings I barely understood. How much we were being bombarded with the two words and how everybody took them for granted. Recently I tried to find what they mean.

At a party I spoke to a woman who had been entertaining us about her problems with her colleagues, and how her blackness stopped her from being free and equal with them. She was on the ball and we were spellbound with her anecdotes. But then I asked her, "What is your perception of freedom? At what stage in your life will you say you are free?"

One would have thought I had said something terribly rude. She paused for a long time and when she spoke she said, "Freedom, what is freedom? I don't know." She tried to smile while groping for an answer, looking around at her friends for reassurance. That simple question messed up the laughter and the joking. People wanted to joke about how problems are because of our lack of finding freedom. What if we should acquire our freedom and then still have problems? That is not something to be thought of.

At a shebeen [speakeasy] I asked some guys what they understood to be freedom. "The right for us to move into white areas and for poor whites to move into black areas," was one reply which got the approval of most.

Probing into the mechanics of arriving at that situation, I was told that perhaps not many blacks were financially qualified to go to white areas, but that many whites were sheltered by the privileges accrued by being white.

"As a whitey, you can get a loan to buy a house, a farm or start a business. The type of job you do puts you immediately in a good earning bracket and from there a number of privileges roll in. Whereas, if you are black, before you can qualify for a housing loan you have to meet certain obligations.

"There are many negating issues. So the government that we will put into power will have to cater to our needs as voters, or the struggle will continue," said one of the men.

Another said: "In the South African situation it means the whites relinquishing power to blacks." Another: "That we can do whatever work we are qualified for and live wherever we want to, like the whites."

The biggest argument was about whether poor whites should be brought to live in black areas. Some said there was no way whites could want to live in Soweto. Whether under Mandela or Mlambo, ghettos will always be there for poor blacks, not for whites. Some pointed out that in Africa there were no poor areas where one could find poor blacks living door to door with whites. A classic example was Zimbabwe, where only blacks have moved up and not the other way round. "Have you heard of a single white who now lives in Rufaro township? They have kept to their lifestyles even if the standards may have dropped. Do you envisage a time when there will be whites who live on pap and spinach? Even the liberals who are always telling of their love and empathy for blacks do not want to live with us."

Just as the thought of black freedom conjures up many ideas to whites, so it does to blacks. There seem to be two levels of freedom. There is the one level where people see Mandela, Sisulu and Mbeki back home and all the men and women in exile reunited in jollity. Beyond that is a curtain. People know there is something terribly wrong about the present system, but what shape a different one will take is something they cannot explain, at least not in words.

To some, freedom means the turning of the tables where the black man will be on top of the white man. There are many stories about what will happen when blacks take over. One woman maintains she will hunt down all the whites who were responsible for black suffering, lock them up at Voortrekkerhoogte and be their warder. On Sunday, her prisoners will go without shoes, winter or summer. Similar stories are common, half in jest and half serious.

Some see freedom as suddenly acquiring money and moving into white areas, while others see the disappearing of the police and casspirs [armored cars] in the township. To others the release of Mandela will be freedom. "As long as Mandela is in prison I will keep on fighting. I am not afraid to die. I have nothing to lose. But the day he is free, then I will be afraid to die," said an activist.

To others, Mandela's release means nothing. Nor does the scrapping of apartheid. "So what, we will still have to contend with a staff reductions, price increases, retrenchment and all the constraints which black people have to live with." Whereas if the whole system is changed, including property relations and the abolition of large-scale private ownership, then we have a new order where the government will make employment available to the people, where people have the right to work and working ceases to be the privilege of a few.

For a domestic worker in Jabavu, it is very different: "Things are getting better now. Even our wages have been improved, it is just that the cost of living has gone very high. If only the government can allow our children better education, I would say that we are free. Look, as blacks what can we do for ourselves? Without the white man and his ways we are useless. Lately the white man has gone a long way to improve things for us. I only wish blacks could stop killing each other."

"What is freedom?" asks Joe Khoza, who has spent sixteen of his fifty years on Robben Island. "We want to be free from oppression, but then what?"

He would like to see certain black attitudes change. "Freedom, to too many blacks, is the power to grab. To be able to get things. That to me is not freedom. Freedom is being responsible. It is the ability to keep time, to make an airplane fly and the lifts work. To be able to be honest with whatever duty is entrusted to one, and not to have whitey behind with the whip all the time to keep things moving." He further spoke of changing people's complacency. "So many black people know that their land was taken by whites, but have given up on themselves."

J. Cebekhulu of the Lembede Mda Foundation, which is based on self-reliance, maintains, "Freedom is the expression by the people of control of the land's resources." It is not the accumulation of wealth or education. For Mpho Mashinini of Operation Hunger, freedom is the right to participate in the governing bodies of the country from the grassroots level. "That is the one way which will ensure that everybody's interests are secured."

"Freedom is relative," says a Wits student. "What might be freedom for Dr. Motlana is certainly not freedom for my mother in Senaoane. Motlana is self-employed; he does not need to pander to whites and accept abuse from any white person. But my mother, who is a factory worker and is entirely dependent on whites, must swallow all they throw at her."

Writer Sej Motau feels strongly. "We know about flag freedom, where people suddenly find themselves free and don't know what to do. Some people equate independence with getting manna from heaven. What freedom actually means is the right to do certain things, allowance to do certain things. Freedom is more costly than oppression. Freedom has small print which people ought to read carefully."

To many, South Africa is seen as the last bastion of colonialism. Stories abound of how, in some parts of Africa, when the "natives" got independence they rushed into offices with pens behind their ears all wanting to be clerks. That does not seem to be a factor in South Arica. Many blacks have taken a look at what brought about the downfall of a number of independent African countries.

It may be true that some blacks think that come Uhuru then all will be hunky-dory, but there are many responsible down-to-earth people who only want jobs and education opportunities, and as one says: "laws made not by white people only, laws that will be made by us too."

There are some who expect these laws to mean changes in earnings. A nightwatchman says the present laws are double standards. "Look at my salary, I get peanuts. To me it really does not matter that I am uneducated. The fact of the matter is I watch over this building for fourteen hours and the owner is hardly ever here. But at the end of the month, he collects a huge check which he hasn't worked for and I go away with peanuts. Is it fair that he should steal from me by not paying me properly? He is protected by the laws made by his fellow men."

"I don't care for politics," said one typist. "All I know is the country is not run right. The whites are not happy, the blacks are also not happy. I do not even understand the freedom you are talking about because, if a black government takes over, there will be even more bloodshed. To me a black government is not the answer to our problems. We blacks need a person, be he black or white, who will put our case across in parliament. Someone whom we will vote in, not the stooges that the government gives us."

Her colleague did not agree. She strongly felt a black person has to represent the interest of blacks in parliament. "How can a white person represent us? What does he know about our plight?"

Although people had different ideas of freedom, they knew there was a lot they did not like about the system. Education featured top on the list of things they wanted to acquire. Housing and wages were also among the issues to be tackled if they were free. Voting came in also as a priority. The scrapping of the Mixed Marriages Act and debate about the Group Areas Act were non-issues to them.

But the more people I spoke to the more I realized how abstract a noun freedom was. If we had more understanding about what was at stake, perhaps there would be less fears, as well as less dreams.

August/September, 1987

2. The Kairos Document, 1985

Drafted in 1985 by one hundred and fifty clergymen of all races and denominations, the Kairos document proclaims the duty of Christians to oppose tyranny. It thus rejected the theological arguments by which Dutch Reformed churches had defended apartheid, and it criticized the passivity of English and other churches in the face of oppression. A landmark document in the emergence of new possibilities in South Africa, it demoralized the supporters of apartheid.

Critique of 'State Theology'

The South African apartheid State has a theology of its own and we have chosen to call it 'State Theology.' 'State Theology' is simply the theological justification of the status quo with its racism, capitalism and totalitarianism. It blesses injustice, canonises the will of the powerful and reduces the poor to passivity, obedience and apathy.

How does 'State Theology' do this? It does it by misusing theological concepts and biblical texts for its own political purposes. In this document we would like to draw your attention to four key examples of how this is done in South Africa. The first would be the use of Romans 13:1-7 to give an absolute and 'divine' authority to the State. The second would be the use of the idea of 'Law and Order' to determine and control what the people may be permitted to regard as just and unjust. The third would be the use of the word 'communist' to brand anyone who rejects 'State Theology'. And finally there is the use that is made of the name of God.

Romans 13:1-7

The text reads as follows:

1. You must all obey the governing authorities. Since all government comes from God, the civil authorities were appointed by God.

2. And so anyone who resists authority is rebelling against God's decision, and such an act is bound to be punished.

From Vernon February, *The Afrikaners of South Africa*, London and New York: Kegan Paul International, 1991, pp. 229–236.

3. Good behaviour is not afraid of magistrates; only criminals have anything to fear. If you want to live without being afraid of authority, you must live honestly and authority may even honour you.

4. The State is there to serve God for your benefit. If you break the law, however, you may well have fear: the bearing of the sword has its significance. The authorities are there to serve God: they carry out God's revenge by punishing wrongdoers.

5. You must obey, therefore, not only because you are afraid of being punished, but also for conscience's sake.

6. This is also the reason why you must pay taxes since all government officials are God's officers. They serve God by collecting taxes.

7. Pay every government official what he has a right to ask—whether it be direct tax or indirect, fear or honour (Rom. 13:1-7)

The misuse of this famous text is not confined to the present government in South Africa. Throughout the history of Christianity totalitarian regimes have tried to legitimise an attitude of blind obedience and absolute servility towards the State by quoting this text. 'As soon as Christians, out of loyalty to the Gospel of Jesus, offer resistance to a state's totalitarian claim, the representatives of the State or their collaborationist theological advisers are accustomed to appeal to this saying of Paul, as if Christians are here commended to endorse and thus to abet all the crimes of a totalitarian state.'

But what then is the meaning of Rom.13:1-7 and why is the use made of it by 'State Theology' unjustifiable from a biblical point of view.

'State Theology' assumes that in this text Paul is presenting us with the absolute and definitive Christian doctrine about the State, in other words an absolute and universal principle that is equally valid for all times and in all *circumstances.* The falseness of this assumption has been pointed out by numerous biblical scholars.

What has been overlooked here is one of the most fundamental of all principles of biblical interpretation: every text must be interpreted *in its context.* To abstract a text from its context and to interpret it in the abstract is to distort the meaning of God's Word. Moreover the context here is not only the chapters and verses that precede and succeed this particular text nor is it even limited to the total context of the Bible. The context includes also the *circumstances* in which Paul's statements were made. Paul was writing to a particular Christian community in Rome, a community that had its own particular problems in relation to the State at that time and in those circumstances. That is part of the context of our text.

Many authors have drawn attention to the fact that in the rest of the Bible God does not demand obedience to oppressive rulers. Examples can be given ranging from Pharoah to Pilate and through into Apostolic times. The Jews and later the Christians did not believe that their imperial overlords, the Egyptians, the Babylonians, the Greeks or the Romans, had some kind of divine right to rule them and oppress them. These empires were the beasts described in the Book of Daniel and the Book of Revelations. God *allowed* them to rule for a while but he did not *approve* of what they did. It was not God's Will. His Will was the freedom and liberation of Israel. Rom. 13:1-7 cannot be contradicting all of this.

But most revealing of all is the circumstances of the Roman Christians to whom Paul was writing. They were revolutionaries. They were not trying to overthrow the State. They were not calling for a change of government. They were what has been called, 'antinomians' or 'enthusiasts' and their belief was that Christians and only Christians, were exonerated from obeying any state at all, any government or political authority at all, *because* Jesus alone was their Lord and King. This is of course heretical and Paul is compelled to point out to these Christians that before the second coming of Christ there will always be some kind of state, some kind of secular government and that Christians are not exonerated from subjection to some kind of political authority.

Paul is simply not addressing the issue of a just or unjust state or the need to change one government for another. He is simply establishing the fact that there will be some kind of secular authority and that Christians as such are not exonerated from subjection to secular laws and authorities. '*The State is there to serve God for your benefit*', says Paul. That is the kind of state he is speaking of. That is the kind of state that must be obeyed. In this text Paul does not tell us what we should do when a state does not serve God and does not work for the benefit of all but has become unjust and oppressive. That is another question.

If we wish to search the Bible for guidance in a situation where the State that is supposed to be 'the servant of God' betrays that calling and begins to serve Satan instead, then we can study Chapter 13 of the Book of Revelations. Here the Roman state becomes the servant of the dragon (the devil) and takes on the appearance of a horrible beast. Its days are numbered because God will not permit his unfaithful servant to reign forever.

Consequently, those who try to find answers to the very different questions and problems of our time in the text of Rom. 13:1-7 are doing a great disservice to Paul. The uses that 'State Theology' makes of this text tell us more about the political options of those who construct this theology than it does about the meaning of God's Word in this text. As one biblical scholar puts it: 'The primary concern is to justify the interests of the States and the text is pressed into its service without respect for the context and the intention of Paul.'

Law and Order

The State makes use of the concept of law and order to maintain the status quo which it depicts as 'normal'. But this *law* is the unjust and discriminatory laws of apartheid and this *order* is the organised and institutionalised disorder of oppression. Anyone who wishes to change this law and this order is made to feel that they are lawless and disorderly. In other words they are made to feel guilty of sin.

It is indeed the duty of the State to maintain law and order, but it has no divine mandate to maintain any kind of law and order. Something does not become moral and just simply because the State has declared it to be a law and the organisation of a society is not a just and right order simply because it has been instituted by the State. We cannot accept any kind of law and any kind of order. The concern of Christians is that we should have in our country a just law and a right order.

In the present crisis and especially during the State of Emergency, 'State Theology' has tried to re-establish the status quo of orderly discrimination, exploitation and oppression by appealing to the consciences of its citizens in the name of law and order. It tries to make those who reject this law and this order feel that they are ungodly. The State here is not only usurping the right of the Church to make judgement about what would be right and just in our circumstances; it is going even further than that and demanding of us, in the name of law and order, an obedience that must be reserved for God alone. The South African State recognises no authority beyond itself and therefore it will not allow anyone to question what it has chosen to define as 'law and order'. However, there are millions of Christians in South Africa today who are saying with Peter: 'We must obey God rather than man' (human beings) (Acts 5:29).

'State Theology' further believes that the government has the God-given right to use *violence* to enforce its system of 'law and order'. It bases this on Rom. 13:4 'The authorities were there to serve God: They carry out God's revenge by punishing wrongdoers'. In this way *state security* becomes a more important concern than *justice,* and those who in the name of God work to change the unjust structures of society are branded as ungodly agitators and rebels. The State often admonishes church leaders to 'preach the pure gospel' and not to 'meddle in politics', while at the same time it indulges in its own political theology which claims God's approval for its use of violence in maintaining an unjust system of 'law and order'.

The State appeals to the consciences of Christians in the name of 'law and order' to accept this use of violence as a God-given duty, in order to re-establish the status quo of oppression. In this way people are sacrificed for the sake of laws, rather than laws for the sake of people, as in the life of Jesus: 'The sabbath was made for man (the human person); not man (the human person) for the sabbath' (Mark 2:27). The State's efforts to preserve law and order, which should imply the protection of human life, means the very opposite for the majority of the people, namely the suppression and destruction of life.

The Threat of Communism

We all know how the South African State makes use of the label 'communist'. Anything that threatens the status quo is labelled 'communist'. Anyone who opposes the State and especially anyone who rejects its theology is simply dismissed as a 'communist'. No account is taken of what communism really means. No thought is given to why some people have indeed opted for communism or for some form of socialism. Even people who have not rejected capitalism are called 'communists' when they reject 'State Theology'. The State uses the label 'communist' in an uncritical and unexamined way as its symbol of evil.

'State Theology' like every other theology needs to have its own concrete symbol of evil. It must be able to symbolise what it regards as godless behaviour and what ideas must be regarded as atheistic. It must have its own version of hell. And so it has invented, or rather taken over, the myth of communism. All evil is communistic and all communist or social ideas are atheistic and godless. Threats about hell-fire and eternal damnation are replaced by threats and warnings about the horrors of a tyrannical, totalitarian, atheistic and terrorist communist regime—a kind of hell-on-earth. This is a very convenient way of frightening some people into accepting any kind of domination and exploitation by a capitalist minority.

The South African State has its own heretical theology and according to that theology millions of Christians in South Africa (not to mention the rest of the world) are to be regarded as 'atheists'. It is significant that in earlier times when Christians rejected the gods of the Roman Empire they were branded as 'atheists'—by the State.

The God of the State

The State in its oppression of the people makes use again and again of the name of God. Military chaplains use it to encourage South African Defence Force, police chaplains use it to strengthen policemen and Cabinet Ministers use it in their propaganda speeches. But perhaps the most revealing of all is the blasphemous use of God's holy name in the preamble to the new apartheid constitution.

In humble submission to Almighty God, who controls the destinies of nations and the history of peoples, who gathered our forebears together from many lands and gave them their own; who had guided them from generation to generation; who has wondrously delivered them from the dangers that beset them.

This god is an idol. It is as mischievous, sinister and evil as any of the idols that the prophets of Israel had to contend with. Here we have a god who is historically on the side of the white settlers, who dispossesses black people of their land and who gives the major part of the land to his 'chosen people'.

It is the god of superior weapons who conquered those who were armed with nothing but spears. It is the god of casspirs and hippos, the god of tear gas, rubber bullets, sjamboks, prison cells and death sentences. Here is a god who exalts the proud and humbles the poor—the very opposite of the God of the Bible who 'scatters the proud of heart, pulls down the mighty from their thrones and exalts the humble' (Lk 1:51-52). From a theological point of view the opposite of the God of the Bible is the devil, Satan. The god of the South African State is not merely an idol or false god, it is the devil disguised as Almighty God—the Antichrist.

The oppressive South African regime will always be particularly abhorrent to Christians precisely because it makes use of Christianity to justify its evil ways. As Christians we simply cannot tolerate this blasphemous use of God's name and God's Word. 'State Theology' is not only heretical, it is blasphemous. Christians who are trying to remain faithful to the God of the Bible are even more horrified when they see that there are Churches, like the white Dutch Reformed churches and other groups of Christians, who actually subscribe to this heretical theology. 'State Theology' needs its own prophets and it manages to find them from the ranks of those who profess to be ministers of God's Word in some of our churches. What is particularly tragic for a Christian is to see the number of people who are fooled and confused by these false prophets and their heretical theology.

South African 'State Theology' can be compared with the 'Court Theology' of Israel's kings, and our false prophets can be compared with the 'Court Prophets' of Israel, of whom it is said:

'They have misled my people by saying: Peace! when there is no peace. Instead of my people rebuilding the wall, these men come and slap on plaster. I mean to shatter the wall you slapped with plaster, to throw it down and lay its foundations bare. It will fall and you will perish under it; and so you will learn that I am Yahweh' (Ezekiel 13:10, 14).

3.   The Inkatha Freedom Party Challenges the ANC Leadership, 1990

If AZAPO and other forms of Africanism posed the most plausible and likely challenge to ANC leadership in the early 1990s, the Zulu-based Inkatha Freedom party, under the leadership of Mangosuthu G. Buthelezi, presented the most powerful and immediate one. Having taken office under the homeland system, Buthelezi was widely accused of collaborationism, both abroad and within South Africa. But he regarded himself as a serious and effective opponent of apartheid. As the Zulu leader representing the largest single group in South Africa, he felt entitled to a major voice in negotiating South Africa's future. He rejected the ANC's claims as a freedom movement that represented all South Africans, including the Zulu.

Postscript Negotiations Now—Who Will Make or Break Them?

I see real dangers in the kind of politics that attempt to intimidate and force South Africans into specific party-political and ideological camps. People must be free to choose, they must be free to differ. Now, instead of this, those

From Mangosuthu Buthelezi, *South Africa: My Vision of the Future*, London: Weidefeld and Nicolson, 1990, pp. 130–139. Copyright © 1990 Mangosuthu Buthelezi.

who do wish to stand their own ground face deliberate attempts to annihilate them politically.

Certain journalists, for instance, write openly that some black leaders who ignore overtures to align themselves with the ANC 'risk being swept aside ignominiously and dumped into the historical rubbish bin.' (Patrick Laurence, *The Star,* March 3, 1990) This is not the thinking on which democracies are founded.

Mr Terror Lekota, of the United Democratic Front, told reporters outright in Washington recently that the ANC/UDF was out to 'kill' me politically and that the collective leadership of the 'Mass Democratic Movement' was not in favour of any meetings between myself and Dr Mandela.

So there we have it. The gauntlet, to some extent, has been thrown down. Black unity, for certain people, is not a priority and it is clear that they intend to attempt to crush individuals and organisations that do not toe their line. All the signs are already with us.

I state now that this is not a situation of my own choosing or Inkatha's. How others wish to face the onslaught is up to them; I cannot speak or act for them. Some I know to be frightened men and women and the way things are going they have every reason to be. Their voices will be silenced; they will not be heard from again.

Inkatha holds out a hand of friendship to all while having the strength and the determination to continue to advocate its beliefs openly. We seek to work in the broader and democratic political context of having an equal right to put our aims and objectives to all the people of this country along with everybody else. Attempts to 'smash' us and 'deprive Inkatha of its political base' (as stated objectives in official ANC documents) have only hardened our resolve to seek a real multi-party system of government for our country.

We ask all organisations and leaders to see the need for across-the-board valuable input into the negotiations that lie ahead. We simply cannot comprehend that this will not be in the best interests of South Africa. This is not diverting the struggle for liberation, as we have been accused. We see it as a way of ensuring meaningful consensus and lasting national peace and stability. But, then again, Inkatha is not playing winner-takes-all politics.

As I write this I have just returned from abroad and from meetings with Prime Minister Margaret Thatcher and President George Bush. A Press conference was held on my arrival.

The questioning from some reporters was not how I and Inkatha saw our contribution to the emerging process of negotiations in this country but, instead, aggressive queries (almost accusations implying traitorous behaviour) as to why Inkatha had not 'joined' the African National Congress. There is a perception being peddled by some that only the ANC can negotiate a new South Africa into existence.

I pose the question: Is the ANC prepared to join a political process in which they will be one of a number of political parties negotiating with the Government? I further question whether it would be in the best interests of South Africa for there to be a bi-polar ANC/S. A. Government negotiating situation. Too few are really analysing why the ANC is insisting on their Harare Declaration which gives them ground to adopt confrontational positions and why they are still clamouring for the retention of punitive measures against South Africa.

Somewhere along the line the point is being missed by many here and abroad that national unity in South Africa does not have to be based on obedience to a specific party. What has happened so recently in the Eastern bloc and in the Soviet Union are lessons that have not, to date, been learnt by some here. It will be to our cost if they are not.

The Harare document is the first example of what could become a dangerous trend during the politics of negotiation in South Africa. The ANC met in Harare and drew up the Harare Declaration. It took this Declaration to the Organisation of African Unity and had it endorsed there. It was then taken to the Non-Aligned Countries and again it was endorsed. Finally, it was taken to the United Nations where its substance was endorsed with minor reservations.

The ANC is now tabling this Declaration as a document which purports to have real international acclaim and support. This is not a people's document. It has not been endorsed by the people of South Africa. It makes assumptions about the supremacy of the ANC and was drawn up to reflect the assumption that the only negotiations of any importance in South Africa will be negotiations between the ANC and the S. A. Government.

The ANC is a party among parties in South Africa. Attempts to create a perception of negotiations between the Government and the ANC, with all other Parties lining up behind one or the other, must be thwarted now. If this is insisted on, it will bedevil the whole political process of change in South Africa.

If it does continue to be the case, I warn now of troubled times ahead. I warn in the sense of the old Zulu folk tale of a herdboy who tells a passing stranger that there is a deadly snake around the next bend and to be careful that it does not rise up and strike him. The fact that the herdboy knew of the danger did not mean that he put the snake there.

There is an urgent need for Western governments to do everything that diplomacy can do to support developments in South Africa in which party political interests are bent to serve the interests of the State and of all South Africans. I am convinced that only a multi-party democracy, supported by both black and white, will survive in South Africa.

A lack of compromise and unwillingness to share and give-and-take on the part of some is already taking on ominous proportions. Violence throughout the country has exploded anew in some areas and continues unabated in others. It appals me. I completely denounce violence. I will go to my grave believing that non-violence and peaceful aims and objectives are primary, decent and worthwhile objectives which should be inculcated into the hearts and minds of all at all times.

Dimensions of a winner-takes-all conflict by those who are determined to eliminate opposition now in their quest for ultimate power are emerging daily.

It is a tragic and extremely worrying situation. Calls, pleas and outright begging for calm, discipline and unity have not prevailed to any degree whatsoever. The killing, the arson, the looting continues.

As I greatly feared the myth of the 'armed struggle' of the ANC and the so-called 'right' of some to dispatch the 'enemy' as they see fit, has now reached over our borders and into our townships and cities.

The 'enemy' for many has become fellow blacks, who are being battered to death and intimidated for political, criminal and socio-economic reasons. Shops, homes, factories—all manner of facilities—are being burned to the ground in an orgy of spreading destruction. Battle zones and territories have been drawn. Families are fleeing their homes seeking refuge, safety and protection elsewhere. Many call for the police and the Army to move in. Others say they must stay out.

Thousands more breadwinners are now out of work because their places of employment are in ashes. This means that tens of thousands more who rely on the wages of these workers have no money to buy food, pay for rent and so on. Millions are now without any means of support in South Africa due to vast unemployment caused by economic and other conditions and considerably exacerbated by sanctions and disinvestment.

Some businessmen prepare to 'pack for Perth' while others frantically place billions of Rands off-shore far beyond the reach of those who talk of nationalisation and their understanding of the causes of the violence.

Behaviour once encouraged by the ANC as integral to the struggle for liberation (it was all right and often a duty to murder 'collaborators' and opponents, including town councillors, policemen, people like myself and anybody else targetted for assassination for whatever reason) is now reaping anarchy.

Violent youth, unemployed adults and others caught up in the chaos are out of control and even if the ANC does, at some stage, admit to regretting its militaristic stance, too much damage will already have been done. Smoke is in the air.

The simple facts are that no organisation can speak with two tongues. On the one hand the ANC says its armed struggle will continue (however ineffectually) and on the other it calls for guns and knives to be thrown into the sea in pursuit of black peace and unity. It talks of democracy while some of its spokesmen clearly attempt to force adherence to its views—quite certainly insofar as Inkatha is concerned. It can' t work like that and now is the time for straight talk.

I had hoped to play down, in my earlier writing, the divisions between black leaders and organisations in the hope that once negotiations were made possible we would all concur and agree to abide by the tenets of fair play in politics as practised to a considerable degree in democracies throughout the world. I am not saying that the usual cut and thrust of competition will not play a part as they do everywhere. I am talking here of basic rights to put political options to the people for their ultimate acceptance or rejection. I had hoped, and still do, that multi-party strategies would quite naturally be acceptable to all. I hoped for too much as far as some people are concerned.

Now we will all have to wait and see. Democracy is waiting in the wings and the following is clear: wars are not won and the one-party States are not established by playing marbles.

Business confidence is not encouraged by calls, for nationalisation and the spectacle of burning buildings, butchered bodies, coups and out-of-control mob scenes. A vision of black and white getting on now with creating a new South Africa is rocked to the core and confusion and mistrust abounds when call continue to be made, as Dr Nelson Mandela did in Stockholm, for world governments to drastically intensify sanctions and impose total diplomatic, cultural and sporting isolation on South Africa.

How will this pressure, as he claimed, Pretoria into accepting a peaceful negotiated settlement? Pretoria has already made it quite clear that it wants a peaceful, negotiated settlement. This is a task for us all to achieve.

I express now grave concerns about the consequences we will all suffer if far too many regard the struggle for liberation as a way of life and are not preparing themselves for the kind of politics that we will see around us in 1990. I warn about black leadership that is remote from the people who are crying out for peace and growing prosperity. Ultimately it is only real progress around the negotiating table which will defuse violence in South Africa and create equal opportunities for all.

The prime actors for negotiations have already been created by history and politics. The central stage on which they can act is already there. The audience is already seated and waiting.

What I am saying could perhaps provocatively be engineered to precipitate a confrontation between Dr Mandela and myself. This I do not want. In interviews Dr Mandela refers to me as his friend of many years and that is absolutely true. He has certainly had my friendship ever since I was a young man and he still has it. We will remain friends even if we do hold different positions at this juncture of South African political development. Even then it is only on a few issues on which I believe that we must agree to disagree.

When Dr Mandela talks about the need for the armed struggle to continue; when he talks about the need for nationalisation; when he likens Israel to South Africa; when he calls for intensified sanctions against South Africa and continued international pressure, he is not attacking me *per se.*

When I question these things, I am not attacking him *per se.* My respect for Dr Mandela is very profound. All I say is: 'My friend, you are very wrong on these issues. You are wrong for yourself, you are wrong for the ANC and you are wrong for South Africa. That is all. It does not diminish my love and respect for you and for the sacrifices that you have made for all of us.'

While Dr Mandela and I differ on some issues, and differ fundamentally on others, there is a great need for dialogue because there are some things that both he and I must be joined together in preserving. He has, for example, spoken sincerely of the need for black unity.

There is a broad South Africanism which will now emerge as friendly to democracy and Dr Mandela and I need to make quite sure that what either of us does separately, or what perchance we can do together, nurtures this new South Africanism.

Dr Mandela is now a free man and his own person and he can pursue his own tactics and strategies and set his own priorities. I am just as free and I can do just the same. If, however, the areas where we differ preclude dialogue and discussion of fundamental differences between us, then our several and joint under-achievement must only be laid at our own feet.

Differences between black and black are primarily differences about how to achieve and how to secure the values we hold in common and they are differences about what circumstances would best suit the preservation of the things we value in common. There are politically sound reasons why there must be black unity based on the acceptance of a multi-strategy approach. There are some things which if we do not either tackle together or help preserve together will run out of hand to be a danger to both of us.

Black South Africa has yet to get its act together and every action taken now by all concerned will have vast implications.

This is a time, I believe, for looking forward towards a Government of national unity and reconciliation. When I started writing this book nearly a year ago I had no idea of how quickly things would move. Nobody did. Some were caught completely off-guard and are now scrambling around trying to formalise and establish negotiating structures and positions. They harbour illusions of capturing the political high ground when in reality it should belong eventually to all South Africans.

I am in the fortunate position of standing right where I have always been and not having to move: in the middle ground along with the silent majority seeking decency and democracy and a peaceful end to racism. Inkatha has not had to make any adjustments to remain relevant to centre-stage politics. Its policy remains entirely intact and will not have to be changed for participation in this period of negotiation for which we have been working.

The ruling National Party and the S.A. Government have shifted precisely and directly towards our thinking in embracing and acting on the majority of the obstacles to negotiation Inkatha has outlined and articulated *ad nauseam* over the years. They talk now, as we have always done, of negotiations to end apartheid and of a multi-party, free-enterprise, democratic South Africa in which there will be equality of opportunity for all. Apologies are being made for the evils of apartheid; admissions of squandered, corrupt and ruthless power.

On the other side, the ANC and its affiliates can no longer talk in grandiose terms of seizing power and returning as a government from exile. They too appear to be moving, however, reluctantly and gradually, towards the political centre-field where the real dynamics of purposeful will emanate.

If they do not participate in negotiations they will be out-manoeuvred and they know it. They can only attempt to smash them for their own needs. The irony is that the 'enemy' is forcing them (however subtly) to—as the saying goes—'put up or shut up.' A whole new ball game has been put into play.

I say take the ball and run with it. There's no chance of being trapped by apartheid now. The State President cannot now go back on his word because if he did so it would unleash a tidal wave of anger and violence.

Let's get on with making people happy, making them secure in all ways. The ANC, instead, calls for continuing the armed struggle from abroad while in fact they can't even control uprisings and ongoing black violence (even though they claim superior support from the masses) within the country. Their plan to make South Africa ungovernable has sown bitter and unpalatable seeds. Whites are now looking with very wary eyes at the barbarous behaviour of some blacks and clearly wish they hadn't heard the political and economic pronouncements of others.

As I write this the ANC is seeking huge international financial backing to launch them on the road to building power bases and structures within South Africa. Whether similar resources will be forthcoming for fair contest and for other diverse political structures, including Inkatha, is another matter altogether. The West must be wary of loading the dice against multi-party choices being freely available to all South Africans.

If the world continues to support the politics of confrontation despite the fact that the South African Government has taken a giant step into the politics of reconciliation, I really do fear a white backlash.

However much the ANC and their publicists will shout and scream at the following assertion, they *are* being forced at present to move inch by inch, step by step, to where I stand—ready to participate in negotiations. This they cannot do while holding rifles in their hands and limpet mines in their briefcases. Sooner rather than later they will have to put their cards on the table. They will either be prepared to participate as equals or they will embark on a smash-and-grab campaign. Already supporters such as Archbishop Desmond Tutu and President Kenneth Kaunda have urged them to cease using violence as a political weapon, unfortunately to no avail. We have early indications. We have early warnings.

The ANC's idea of negotiations and mine differ drastically but, unlike me, they will sooner or later have to abandon the military accoutrement of their past power bases if they do indeed seek free and fair negotiations. I have always advocated jaw-jaw not war-war. They will have to do likewise or turn to unleasing hell on earth on this country. The West must analyse events and political posturing very carefully.

The ANC's Harare document clearly spells out the ANC's intention not to negotiate equally alongside the South African Government and others about the future of South Africa. They want the future to be decided in some kind of Constituent Assembly arrangement with the ANC as the dominant black factor. What the Harare document amounts to is a demand for the laying down of power by the South African Government and the ruling National Party taking its place as a party among parties. Political history has lessons in this regard which some have not read.

What they call for must be the end product of South African politics. It is an end, however, that must be negotiated to conclusion. South Africa is not Zimbabwe and I repeat, as I said elsewhere, that a Lancaster House-type conference will not be accepted by white South Africa. Likewise, South Africa is not Mozambique or Angola. Whites in South Africa, as noted earlier, have vast economic power, have superior military might. They control, whether we like it or not, the treasury and all manner of government and all other structures. They are talking of a desire to share that power, because they know they will eventually have to. They are thinking in terms of a process which will lead us to power-sharing.

We cannot risk a white backlash, caused by black ineptitude, halting the policies of negotiation. We cannot risk a black backlash caused by white ineptitude. Black South Africa, in the end, will get all that it wants and more if it plays its cards right.

There is something which runs very deep in my political soul and it is a real appreciation that political power based on anything other than acting out real mandates honestly received in real democratic consultations with the people, can only be passing power.

4.   The *Constitution of the Republic of South Africa Bill*, 1993

> *This bill is the outcome of the CODESA talks between the ANC, the government, and other parties. A number of important groups—the Conservatives, the PAC, and the Inkatha Freedom party boycotted the talks all or part of the time.*
>
> *This document formed the basis for the elections of April 1994. It should be compared with the Freedom Charter and the Botha Constitution of 1983.*

Now therefore the following provisions are adopted as the Constitution of the Republic of South Africa:

Chapter 1

Constituent and Formal Provisions

Republic of South Africa

1.   (1) The Republic of South Africa shall be one, sovereign state.

(2) The national territory of the Republic shall comprise the areas defined in Part 1 of Schedule 1.

✳ ✳ ✳

Languages

3.   (1) Afrikaans, English, isiNdebele, SeSotho sa Leboa, SeSotho, siSwati, Xitsonga, Setswana, Tshivenda, isiXhosa and isiZulu shall be the official

South African languages at national level, and conditions shall be created for their development and for the promotion of their equal use and enjoyment.

(2) Rights relating to language and the status of languages existing at the commencement of this Constitution shall not be diminished, and provision shall be made by an Act of Parliament for rights relating to language and the status of languages existing only at regional level, to be extended nationally in accordance with the principles set out in subsection (9).

(3) Wherever practicable, a person shall have the right to use and to be addressed in his or her dealings with any public administration at the national level of government in any official South African language of his or her choice.

(4) Regional differentiation in relation to language policy and practice shall be permissible.

(5) A provincial legislature may, by a resolution adopted by a majority of at least two-thirds of all its members, declare any language referred to in subsection (1) to be an official language for the whole or any part of the province and for any or all powers and functions within the competence of that legislature, save that neither the rights relating to language nor the status of an official language as existing in any area or in relation to any function at the time of the commencement of this Constitution, shall be diminished.

(6) Wherever practicable, a person shall have the right to use and to be addressed in his or her dealings with any public administration at the provincial level of government in any one of the official languages of his or her choice as contemplated in subsection (5).

(7) A member of Parliament may address Parliament in the official South African language of his or her choice.

(8) Parliament and any provincial legislature may, subject to this section, make provision by legislation for the use of official languages for the purpose of the functioning of government, taking into account questions of usage, practicality and expense.

(9) Legislation, as well as official policy and practice, in relation to the use of languages at any level of government shall be subject to and based on the provisions of this section and the following principles:

(a) The creation of conditions for the development and for the promotion of equal use and enjoyment of all official South African languages;

(b) the extension of those rights relating to language and the status of languages which at the commencement of this Constitution are restricted to certain regions;

(c) the prevention of the use of any language for the purposes of exploitation, domination or division;

(d) the promotion of multilingualism and the provision of translation facilities;

(e) the fostering of respect for languages spoken in the Republic other than the official languages, and the encouragement of their use in appropriate circumstances; and

(f) the non-diminution of rights relating to language and the status of languages existing at the commencement of this Constitution.

(10)(a) Provision shall be made by an Act of Parliament for the establishment by the Senate of an independent Pan South African Language Board to promote respect for the principles referred to in subsection (9) and to further the development of the official South African languages.

(b) The Pan South African Language Board shall be consulted, and be given the opportunity to make recommendations, in relation to any proposed legislation contemplated in this section.

(c) The Pan South African Language Board shall be responsible for promoting respect for and the development of German, Greek, Gujerati, Hindi, Portuguese, Tamil, Telegu, Urdu and other languages used by communities in South Africa, as well as Arabic, Hebrew and Sanskrit and other languages used for religious purposes.

Supremacy of the Constitution

4. (1) This Constitution shall be the supreme law of the Republic and any law or act inconsistent with its provisions shall, unless otherwise provided expressly or by necessary implication in this Constitution, be of no force and effect to the extent of the inconsistency.

(2) The Constitution shall bind all legislative, executive and judicial organs of state at all levels of government.

Chapter 2

Citizenship and Franchise

Citizenship

5. (1) There shall be a South African citizenship.

(2) South African citizenship and the acquisition, loss and restoration of South African citizenship shall, subject to section 20 read with section 33 (1), be regulated by an Act of Parliament.

(3) Every person who is a South African citizen shall, subject to this Constitution, be entitled to enjoy all rights, privileges and benefits of South African citizenship, and shall be subject to all duties, obligations and responsibilities of South African citizenship as are accorded or imposed upon him or her in terms of this Constitution or an Act of Parliament.

The Franchise

6. Every person who is—
   (a) (i) a South African citizen; or
       (ii) not such a citizen but who in terms of an Act of Parliament has been accorded the right to exercise the franchise;
   (b) of or over the age of 18 years; and
   (c) not subject to any disqualifications as may be prescribed by law. shall be entitled to vote in elections of the National Assembly, a provincial legislature or a local government and in referenda or plebiscites contemplated in this Constitution, in accordance with and subject to the laws regulating such elections, referenda and plebiscites.

Chapter 3

Fundamental Rights

Application

7. (1) This Chapter shall bind all legislative and executive organs of state at all levels of government.
   (2) This Chapter shall apply to all law in force and all administrative decisions taken and acts performed during the period of operation of this Constitution.
   (3) Juristic persons shall be entitled to the rights contained in this Chapter where, and to the extent that, the nature of the rights permits.
   (4) (a) When an infringement of or threat to any right entrenched in this Chapter is alleged, any person referred to in paragraph (b) shall be entitled to apply to competent court of law for appropriate relief, which may include a declaration of rights.
       (b) The relief referred to in paragraph (a) may be sought by—
           (i)   a person acting in his or her own interests;
           (ii)   an association acting in the interest of its members;
           (iii) a person acting on behalf of another person who is not in a position to seek such relief in his or her own name;
           (iv)   a person acting as a member of or in the interest of a group or class of persons; or
           (v)   a person acting in the public interest.

Equality

8. (1) Every person shall have the right to equality before the law and to equal protection of the law.
   (2) No person shall be unfairly discriminated against, directly or indirectly, and, without derogating from the generality of this provision, on one or more of the following grounds in particular; race, gender,

sex, ethnic or social orgin, colour, sexual orientation, age, disability, religion, conscience, belief, culture, or language.

(3) (a) This section shall not preclude measures designed to achieve the adequate protection and advancement of persons or groups or categories of persons disadvantaged by unfair discrimination, in order to enable their full and equal enjoyment of all rights and freedoms.

(b) Every person or community dispossessed of rights in land before the commencement of this Constitution under any law which would have been inconsistent with subsection (2) had that subsection been in operation at the time of the dispossession, shall be entitled to claim restitution of such rights subject to and in accordance with sections 121, 122, and 123.

(4) *Prima facie* proof of discrimination on any of the grounds specified in subsection (2) shall be presumed to be sufficient proof of unfair discrimination as contemplated in that subsection, until the contrary is established.

Life

9. Every person shall have the right to life.

Human Dignity

10. Every person shall have the right to respect for and protection of his or her dignity.

Freedom and Security of the Person

11. (1) Every person shall have the right to freedom and security of the person, which shall include the right not to be detained without trial.

(2) No person shall be subject to torture of any kind, whether physical, mental or emotional, nor shall any person be subject to cruel, inhuman or degrading treatment or punishment.

Servitude and Forced Labour

12. No person shall be subject to servitude or forced labour.

Privacy

13. Every person shall have the right to his or her personal privacy, which shall include the right not to be subject to searches of his or her person, home or property, the seizure of private possessions or the violation of private communications.

Religion, Belief and Opinion

14. (1) Every person shall have the right to freedom of conscience, religion, thought, belief, and opinion, which shall include academic freedom in institutions of higher learning.

    (2) Without derogating from the generality of subsection (1), religious observances may be conducted at state or state-aided institutions under rules established by an appropriate authority for that purpose, provided that such religious observances are conducted on an equitable basis and attendance at them is free and voluntary.

    (3) Nothing in this Chapter shall preclude legislation recognising—

    (a) a system of personal and family law adhered to by persons professing a particular religion; and

    (b) the validity of marriages concluded under a system of religious law subject to specified procedures.

Freedom of Expression

15. (1) Every person shall have the right to freedom of speech and expression which shall include freedom of the press and other media, and the freedom of artistic creativity and scientific research.

    (2) All media financed by or under the control of the state shall be regulated in a manner which ensures impartiality and the expression of a diversity of opinion.

Assembly, Demonstration and Petition

16. Every person shall have the right to assemble and demonstrate with others peacefully and unarmed, and to present petitions.

Freedom of Association

17. Every person shall have the right to freedom of association.

Freedom of Movement

18. Every person shall have the right to freedom of movement anywhere within the national territory.

Residence

19. Every person shall have the right freely to choose his or her place of residence anywhere in the national territory.

Citizens' Rights

20. Every citizen shall have the right to enter, remain in and leave the Republic, and no citizen shall without justification be deprived of his or her citizenship.

Political Rights

21. (1) Every citizen shall have the right—
      (a) to form, to participate in the activities of and to recruit members for a political party;
      (b) to campaign for a political party or cause; and
      (c) freely to make political choices.
    (2) Every citizen shall have the right to vote, to do so in secret and to stand for election to public office.

Access to Court

22. Every person shall have the right to have justiciable disputes settled by a court of law, where appropriate, another independent and impartial forum.

Access to Information

23. Every person shall have the right of access to all information held by the state or any of its organs at any level of government in so far as such information is required for the exercise or protection of any of his or her rights.

Administrative Justice

24. Every person shall have the right to—
      (a) lawful administrative action where any of his or her rights is affected or threatened;
      (b) procedurally fair administrative action where any of his or her rights or legitimate expectations is affected or threatened;
      (c) be furnished with reasons in writing for administrative action which affects any of his or her rights or interests unless the reasons for such action have been made public; and
      (d) administrative action which is justifiable in relation to the reasons given for it where any of his or her rights is affected or threatened.

5.   Nelson Mandela Delivers His Presidential Inaugural Address, 1994

Mandela's numerous speeches were interrupted by a twenty-seven-year silence. His addresses since his release from prison in 1990 echo those he gave before his imprisonment, most notably his Rivonia Trial Statement of 1994. Mandela's inauguration as president seemed to offer the prospect of fulfilling these ideals for all South Africans—a shining vision. Although South Africans have accomplished much that seemed impossible only a few years ago, enormous obstacles remain.

Mandela's Address: 'Glory and Hope'

Your majesties, your royal highnesses, distinguished guests, comrades and friends:

Today, all of us do, by our presence here, and by our celebrations in other parts of our country and the world confer glory and hope to newborn liberty.

Out of the experience of an extraordinary human disaster that lasted too long must be born a society of which all humanity will be proud.

Our daily deeds as ordinary South Africans must produce an actual South African reality that will reinforce humanity's belief in justice, strengthen its confidence in the nobility of the human soul and sustain all our hopes for a glorious life for all.

A Sense of Renewal

All this we owe both to ourselves and to the peoples of the world who are so well represented here today.

To my compatriots, I have no hesitation in saying that each of us is as intimately attached to the soil of this beautiful country as are the famous jacaranda trees of Pretoria and the mimosa trees of the bushveld.

Each time one of us touches the soil of this land, we feel a sense of personal renewal. The national mood changes as the seasons change.

We are moved by a sense of joy and exhilaration when the grass turns green and the flowers bloom.

That spirtual and physical oneness we all share with this common homeland explains the depth of the pain we all carried in our hearts as we saw our country tear itself apart in terrible conflict, and as we saw it spurned, outlawed and isolated by the peoples of the world, precisely because it has become the universal base of the pernicious ideology and practice of racism and racial oppression.

Guests Are Thanked

We, the people of South Africa, feel fulfilled that humanity has taken us back into its bosom, that we, who were outlaws not so long ago, have today been given the rare privilege to be host to the nations of the world on our own soil.

We thank all our distinguished international guests for having come to take possession with the people of our country of what is, after all, a common victory for justice, for peace, for human dignity.

We trust that you will continue to stand by us as we tackle the challenges of building peace, prosperity, nonsexism, nonracialism and democracy.

We deeply appreciate the role that the masses of our people and their democratic, religious, women, youth, business, traditional and other leaders have played to bring about this conclusion. Not least among them is my Second Deputy President, the Honorable F. W. de Klerk.

A Pledge of Liberation

We would also like to pay tribute to our security forces, in all their ranks, for the distinguished role they have played in securing our first democratic elections and the transition to democracy, from the bloodthirsty forces which still refuse to see the light.

The time for the healing of the wounds has come.

The moment to bridge the chasms that divide us has come.

The time to build is upon us.

We have, at last, achieved our political emancipation. We pledge ourselves to liberate all our people from the continuing bondage of poverty, deprivation, suffering, gender and other discrimination.

We succeeded to take our last steps to freedom in conditions of relative peace. We commit ourselves to the construction of a complete, just and lasting peace.

Issue of Amnesty

We have triumphed in the effort to implant hope in the breasts of the millions of our people. We enter into a covenant that we shall build the society in which all South Africans, both black and white, will be able to walk tall, without any fear in their hearts, assured of their inalienable right to human dignity—a rainbow nation at peace with itself and the world.

As a token of its commitment to the renewal of our country, the new Interim Government of National Unity will, as a matter of urgency, address the issue of amnesty for various categories of our people who are currently serving terms of imprisonment.

We dedicate this day to all the heroes and heroines in this country and the rest of the world who sacrificed in many ways and surrendered their lives so that we could be free.

Their dreams have become reality. Freedom is their reward.

We are both humbled and elevated by the honor and privilege that you, the people of South Africa, have bestowed on us, as the first President of a united, democratic, nonracial and nonsexist South Africa, to lead our country out of the valley of darkness.

We understand it still that there is no easy road to freedom.

We know it well that none of us acting alone can achieve success.

We must therefore act together as a united people, for national reconciliation, for nation building, for the birth of a new world.

Let there be justice for all.

Let there be peace for all.

Let there be work, bread, water and salt for all.

Let each know that for each the body, the mind and the soul have been freed to fulfill themselves.

Never, never, and never again shall it be that this beautiful land will again experience the oppression of one by another and suffer the indignity of being the skunk of the world.

The sun shall never set on so glorious a human achievement!

Let freedom reign. God bless Africa!

Brief Biographical Guide

Bambatha village chief in Natal, leader of the Zulu rebellion of 1906–1908, in its first phase

Biko, Steve leader of black consciousness movement from the late 1960s; died in police custody, 1977

Boesak, Allan served as President of the World Council of Reformed Churches; one of the founders of UDF; represented South Africa at the UN in the 1994 Mandela government

Botha, Louis Afrikaner general, prime minister of Union of South Africa, 1910–1919

Botha, P. W. Prime Minister of Republic of South Africa, 1979–1983, State president, 1983–1989

Buthelezi, Mangosutho Zulu political leader, as head of Inkatha Freedom Party, he ruled the KwaZulu homeland in the later years of apartheid

de Klerk, F. W. State president, 1989–1994

Dingane Shaka's half brother, who assassinated him and ruled the Zulu kingdom, 1828–1840; defeated by trekkers in 1838

Dube, John L. Zulu educator, one of the founders of the ANC and its president, 1912–1917

First, Ruth Journalist and South African communist leader; murdered by South African agents, 1982

Fischer, Bram Afrikaner lawyer, communist, defended activists charged under apartheid laws; died in prison, 1975

Galant leader of slave rebellion in the Cape colony, 1825

Hertzog, J. B. M. Afrikaner general, prime minister, 1924–1939

Hintsa 1789–1835; leader of the Transkei Xhosa in the early nineteenth century; fought the British in the war of 1834–5

Huddleston, Trevor 1913– Anglican priest, served in the African suburb of Sophiatown and supported the African struggle to preserve Sophiatown

Jabavu, John Tengo 1859–1921; African journalist and politician in the Cape colony and province

Kadalie, Clements labor leader from Malawi; founded and led the ICU during the 1920s

Khama (Kgama) Ngwato king in Botswana; converted to Christianity and led his people into British alliance; ruled 1875–1923

Kok, Adam and Cornelis Griqua leaders; the first Adam Kok escaped from slavery and settled on the borders of the Cape Colony in the eighteenth century; Cornelis, and the two succeeding Adam Koks, maintained Griqua independence under missionary influence down to 1875, by migrating to Griqualand East in 1862

Kruger, Paul Afrikaner president of the South African Republic (Transvaal), 1883–1900

Lembede, Anton 1914–1947; member of the Congress Youth League; theorist of Africanist ideology

Lobengula second Ndebele king ruled 1868 to 1893, when the kingdom was conquered

Luthuli (Lutuli), Albert President of the ANC, 1952–1967; winner of the Nobel Peace Prize

Malan, D. F. National party leader, prime minister of South Africa, 1948–1954

Mandela, Nelson 1918– Congress Youth League, 1944; founder and initial leader of Umkhonto we Sizwe, 1961; imprisoned, 1962–1990; President of ANC, 1990–; President of South Africa, 1994–

Merriman, John X. 1841–1926; liberal politician of the Cape colony and province, one of the architects of the Union of 1910

Moshoeshoe (Moshesh) founder of kingdom of Lestho, 1830s, ruled until 1870; brilliant statesman

Mpande, Shaka's half brother, third Zulu king; ruled from 1840 to 1872, gave way to his son's Cetshawyo's regency after

Mzilikazi founder of the Ndebele kingdom, in Transvaal in the 1830s, migrated to southern Zimbabwe in late 1830s: ruled until 1868

Naude, Beyers Dutch reformed church leader, Afrikaner nationalist, broke from party to found Christian Institute in opposition to apartheid policies

Nongqawuse young woman whose prophesies led to the Xhosa cattle killing of 1857

Ngqika (Gaika) Xhosa leader in the Ciskei; collaborated at times with the British in tortuous attempts to maintain land and cattle

Oppenheimer, Ernest 1880–1957; industrial and mining magnate, head of the Anglo American Corporation

Plaatje, Sol 1876–1932; African journalist and writer; Secretary-General of the ANC, 1912–1917

Ramaphosa, Cyril 1952–, Secretary-General of National Union of Mineworkers (1982–1991), founder of Congress of South African Trade Unions (COSATU); member of 1994 Mandela government

Rhodes, Cecil 1852–1902; built a fortune in diamonds; prime minister of Cape Colony, founder of British South Africa Company, by which he became the colonizer of Rhodesia

Retief, Piet 1789–1838; leader of trekkers out of Cape colony to Natal; killed by Dingane, 1838

Sachs, Solly General Secretary of the Garment Workers Union, and interracial union, 1930s

Sandile 1820–1879; son of Ngqika, chief of Ciskei Xhosa during the last generation of independence; killed in war of 1878–1879

Sarhili 1809–1892; son of Hintsa, chief of the Transkei Xhosa during the last generation of independence; fought the British in 1846, 1850–1852, 1877–1888

Sekhukune Pedi leader of the northern Transvaal; fought against the Transvaal and the Swazi in 1876–1877, and against the British in 1878–1879; deposed and exiled, killed by rivals on his return home in 1882

Shaka, Chaka founder of the Zulu kingdom, ruled as king, 1818–1828

Shembe, Isaiah founder of the Church of the Nazarene, a large Zulu prophetic church; d. 1935

Shepstone, Sir Theophilus Natal administrator of African affairs from the 1840s to the 1870s; presided over the dissolution of the Zulu kingdom after the conquest of 1879

Sisulu, Walter 1912– Senior ANC leader; imprisoned 1964–1989

Slovo, Joe 1926–1995 South African communist leader; head of Umkhonto we Sizwe; minister of housing in the 1994 Mandela government

Smuts, Jan Afrikaner general, prime minister, 1919–1924, 1939–1948

Sobukwe, Robert founder of the PAC, which split from the ANC in 1959 to pursue Africanist goals

Soga, Tiyo 1829–1871; Xhosa missionary, ordained in Scotland; returned in 1857 as LMS missionary

Strijdom, J. G. Prime minister, 1954–1958

Suzman, Helen opposition member of South African parliament, 1953–1989; in the early 1960s was the only Progressive party MP

Tambo, Oliver 1917–1990 President of the ANC, 1967–1990; represented the ANC overseas during the years it was banned

Treurnicht, Andries Afrikaner nationalist politician; founder of Conservative party, 1982

Tutu, Desmond Archbishop of Cape Town; appointed 1981; Nobel Peace Prize recipient, 1984

van Riebeeck, Jan first VOC governor of Cape Town, served from 1652–1662

Verwoerd, Hendrik F. Native minister, 1948–1958, prime minister, 1958–1966; major architect of apartheid policy; assassinated

Vorster, John Prime Minister of Republic of South Africa, 1966–1979

Xuma, Dr. A. B. President of ANC, 1940–1949

Key Terms

Afrikaans   the language of the South African Dutch settler, developed from Dutch, with African, Portuguese and English influences; standardized as the medium of education, literature, and journalism in the twentieth century

African National Congress   ANC; founded in 1912 and remained a moderate, elite organization until after 1945; turned to mass membership and non-violent militant protest to 1960; banned, and launched the armed struggle from 1961; unbanned in 1990, and won power in general elections of 1994

African People's Organization   founded in 1902 as the organization of Coloured people who held the franchise in the Cape Province down to 1956; at times cooperated, at times held aloof from the ANC

Afrikaners   the descendants of Dutch settlers, with some French protestant and German settlers, who speak Afrikaans and have been classified as white in South African custom and law.

Afrikaner Resistance Movement   ARM; Afrikaner Weerstandsbeweging, a militant neo-Nazi organization founded by Eugene Terre Blanche in 1973, to oppose any weakening of white supremacy

Anglo-Boer War   fought between the British Empire and the Afrikaner republics, the Orange Free State and the Transvaal from 1899 to 1902; the war cast the Afrikaners (Boers) as victims of imperialism, and the British use of concentration camps left a legacy of bitterness

apartheid   the legal system of racial segregation in all aspects of life, enacted by the National party government and maintained from 1948 to 1990

Azanian People's Organization   AZAPO; Black Consciousness organization founded in 1978 to carry on the work of the banned black consciousness organizations led by Steve Biko until his death in 1977; maintained Africanist goals in contrast to the universalist goals of the ANC

baaskap   the doctrine and practice of naked white domination pursued for its own sake, in contrast to segregationist and liberal doctrines which claimed positive benefits for Africans

banning   the outlawing of organizations or individuals by government decree; banned individuals could not publish, be quoted by any publication, or congregate with more than two other people at any time, or leave a prescribed district; they had to report at regular intervals to the authorities

Bantu   vast language family reaching from Uganda in East Africa to the Cameroon's in West Africa and down to South Africa; black South Africans the iron age mixed farmers such as the Xhosa, Zulu, and Sotho are Bantu speakers; except as a term of linguistic classification, the term has become disparaging in South Africa through its association with the policy of apartheid

Bantu Education   a central part of the apartheid policy, designed to give Africans sufficient education to satisfy the labor needs of the white dominated economy; extended on a "tribal basis to serve the needs of the developing homelands; Bantu Education was removed from the Education Department and placed under the Bantu Affairs Department

Black consciousness movement   movement flourishing from the late 1960s through the 1970s, in which student organizations and church discussion groups promoted community development, racial pride, and identity; its most important leader was Steve Biko

Boer   Dutch settler or farmer; the term was standard in the nineteenth century but became derogatory; the accepted term today is Afrikaner

British South African Company   colonizing company, founded by Cecil Rhodes and chartered by the crown in 1889; founded Rhodesia, conquered the Ndebele in 1893, and governed the colony down to 1923

Broederbond   cultural organization founded in the 1920s which later became a secret society pledged to advance the interest and status of Afrikaners; it dominated the councils of the national party until leaks and betrayals reduced its effectiveness

Bushmen   stone age hunters of South Africa, who painted many vivid rock painting in South Africa; their technical name is *San;* a few still practice their traditional culture in the Kalahari desert

Cape Coloured People   group of mixed ancestry descended from Khoikhoi, imported slaves, and white settlers in the Cape colony, comprising today over three million people

Church Missionary Society   CMS; evangelical missionary organization associated with the Church of England, important in introducing Christianity to black South Africans in the nineteenth century

Conference for a Democratic South Africa   CODESA; series of multi-party meetings, dominated by the African National Congress and the National Party, to work out a new constitution for a democratic South Africa in the early 1990s

Congress Alliance   alliance under ANC leadership from the 1950s on, of white, Indian, and Coloured organizations; the mostly white Congress of Democrats contained many members of the banned communist party; the alliance was instrumental in drafting the Freedom Charter of 1955

Congress Youth League   CYL; organization formed in the 1940s within the ANC; it brought Nelson Mandela into prominence; the CYL pressed the moderate leaders of the ANC toward more militant action

Conservative party   Afrikaner political party led by Andries Treurnicht; split away from the National party in 1982, claiming that P. W. Botha's reforms meant that the National party had betrayed the apartheid ideals of Hendrik Verwoerd and no longer represented the Afrikaner nation; the conservatives became the official parliamentary opposition after the elections of 1987

Defiance campaign   non-violent campaign of 1952 in which ANC volunteers broke apartheid laws by entering whites only waiting rooms and entrances in order to court arrest, with the aim of discrediting the government's policies; the government enacted harsh penalties against such symbolic law-breaking, and the movement petered out after several months

Drakensberg   South African mountain range extending from the northern Transvaal to the Cape midlands; the range rises steeply from the coastal plain along the Indian Ocean, separating the subtropical coast from the High Veld; the tallest peaks are over 11,000 feet

"endorsing out"   the policy under the pass laws and influx control policies of removing Africans from urban centers in "white" areas of the country and sending them to the homelands in the countryside

Ethiopian churches   African Christian churches which broke away from white missionary control from the late nineteenth century on but retained orthodox Christian religious beliefs, in contrast to Zionist churches

free burghers   settlers given land grants by the VOC in 1657, and the class of private landholders who developed from that policy

Freedom Charter   1955; document drafted at Kliptown by the Congress Alliance under ANC leadership, proclaiming a mild socialism and the universalist principle that "South Africa belongs to all who live in it, black and white."

Great Trek   the migration of about 10,000 settlers from the eastern districts of the Cape colony across the Orange River to Natal, the Transvaal, and the Orange River region from 1836 on; the settlers created two new republics in the interior, the Orange Free State and the Transvaal; the trek provides formative myths to Afrikaner nationalist ideology

Griquas   mixed race communities settled along the Orange River under the auspices of the London Missionary Society in the early nineteenth century; they had called themselves "Bastaards"

Group Areas Act 1950 law consolidating earlier laws, dividing South Africa into unequal separate territories defined by race; one of the basic laws of the apartheid system

heemraden   subordinate local officials serving under the Landdrost in the early Cape colony

High Commissioner   in the late nineteenth century, the Governor of the Cape colony, while answerable to the Cape colony's cabinet for Cape affairs; as High Commissioner, he assumed control over British interests in the rest of southern Africa, and was answerable to the British Colonial Office

high veld   area of grasslands, some of it higher that 4000 feet above sea level, west of the Drakensberg mountains in the Transvaal and Orange Free State, giving way in the west to desert in Botswana

homelands   under apartheid, the African areas defined by ethnicity intended to become independent nations; most comprised many small pieces of territory; four of them received "independence" during the apartheid regime

Hottentot   old name for the Khoikhoi pastoralists of the Cape province, the people first contracted by European settlers at the Cape of Good Hope in the seventeenth century; the term Hottentot has become derogatory

Immorality Act   law forbidding interracial sexual relations, first passed in 1927 and made stricter by the apartheid government in 1950 and in subsequent amendments

impi   regimental unit in the Zulu military system

Industrial and Commercial Workers Union   ICU; mass labor movement of the 1920s, founded by Clements Kadalie; gained a large following in the eastern Cape and Natal, declined because of government harrassment, accusations of financial irregularities, and splits over Communist party influence

Information Project   secret plan to use unaccountable funds to influence overseas public opinion; worked to defeat liberal senators and support Ronald Reagan's presidential bid in the late 1970s; when the project became public, the ensuing scandal destroyed Vorster's government

Inkatha Freedom Party   Inkatha was founded in the 1920s as a Zulu patriotic and cultural organization; under apartheid and after, a political party machine controlled by Mangosuthu Gatsha Buthelezi; in the early 1990s it opposed the idea of a unitary state, and it participated in the 1994 elections only at the last moment

Internal Security Act   1976 law, extending and consolidating earlier laws, giving the police extensive powers of arbitrary arrest, solitary confinement, and banning, and preventing organizations from receiving funds from abroad

Jameson Raid 1895 plot for British raiders led by Sir Leander Starr Jameson to invade the Transvaal, and, in conjunction with an unprising of Uitlanders in the Transvaal, to overthrow Paul Kruger's republican government; the raid was a total failure and ruined Cecil Rhodes' Cape political career

Kaffir, Caffer, Caffre term for black South Africans, derived from the Arabic word for infidel, common usage through the nineteenth century; a highly derogatory, racist term in recent usage

Kat River Settlement a settlement for independent Coloured (mixed race) small holders set up in 1829, north of Grahamstown; it served as a frontier buffer zone, but was broken up in the frontier war of 1850–1853

Khoikhoi name, meaning "men of men," for the pastoralist inhabitants of the Cape province, whose ancestors have occupied the region for several thousand years; termed "Hottentots" in early documents

Kholwa term for African converts to Christianity in the nineteenth century

Koornhof bills 1983 bills providing for municipal self-governemt in African townships; African mayors and councillors who collaborated with the system had to enforce influx restrictions and collect rents; the bills were the focus of renewed African resistance

kraal term of Portuguese origin, related to "corral"; an African village

laager the defensive circle of pioneer wagons; metaphorically, the defensive attitudes of aparthied South Africa

landdrost district magistrate in colonial South Africa, down to 1828

Lesotho formerly Basutoland; landlocked kingdom, founded by Moshoeshoe in the 1830s; annexed by the British Empire in 1884, received its independence in 1966

Liberal Party formed in 1953 by a split away from the United Party; disbanded in 1968 when parties with multiracial memberships became illegal

liberalism in South African racial politics, the position of "friends of Africans," who defended the limited Cape African political rights; whose position was gradualist, paternalist, and founded on assumptions of European cultural superiority

lineage state before the early ninteenth century, southern Bantu peoples had not developed large centralized kingdoms; smaller states were based on the leadership of senior lineages but also incorporated nonkin dependents and clients

lobola bridewealth payment, usually in the form of cattle, from the groom to the bride's family at the time of marriage; the custom established mutual obligations, but nineteenth-century Europeans objected to the custom as tantamount to the sale of women

London Missionary Society LMS; interdenominational group backed by Presbyterian and Congregational churches

mfecane "crushing"; in historical interpretations current until recently, the series of destructive wars associated with the rise of the Zulu kingdom between 1800 and the 1830s

National party the original party was founded in 1912 by J. B. M. Hertzog; when Hertzog joined with Smuts to form the Fusion government in 1933, the small group that refused to join became the basis for the "Purified" National party that held power from 1948 to 1994

Native Land Act 1913; divided South Africa between black and white areas and restricted African land purchases in "white" areas of the country; restricted the previous practice of black squatters "farming on the share" on white farms

"native question" debate among whites in late nineteenth and early twentieth century South Africa about how to subordinate and control Africans and define their political rights, landholdings, and labor opportunities; "native" became a derogatory term in the twentieth century

Natives (Urban Areas) Act 1923; legislative attempt to limit the number of Africans entering the city to those who were working for whites or were temporarily present to seek work; the basis for many later attempts to control the influx of Africans into "white" areas

Ndebele Matabele kingdom formed in the 1830s under the leadership of Mzilikazi, who seceded from the Zulu kingdom and settled first in the Transvaal and later in southern Zimbabwe; lost its independence in 1893 during the reign of the second king, Lobengula

Nguni broad cultural classification of the southern Bantu living on the Indian Ocean coastal plain between Mozambique and the eastern Cape frontier, including Zulu and Xhosa

Ngwato Tswana kingdom with its capital at Palapye and Serowe; which under the leadership of King Khama after 1875 converted to Christianity and negotiated their annexation to the British Empire

Ossewa Brandwag Oxwagon Sentinel; Afrikaner nationalist organization of the 1930s and 1940, which led in the centenary celebrations of the Great Trek; paramilitary and pronazi in the Second World War

Pan Africanist Congress PAC; organization which split away from the ANC in 1959, stressing Africanism in contrast to the ANC's universalist alliance with sympathetic supporters from all races

pass laws apartheid mandates requiring Africans to carry a reference book to prove their right to be in regions of the country set aside for whites

poor whiteism the phenomenon of deep poverty among large numbers of whites, especially rural Afrikaners, in twentieth century South Africa; its eradication became a priority for all South African governments from the 1920s through the 1980s

Population Registration Act 1950; basic law of apartheid, by which all members of the society were given a racial classification, with every person over sixteen required to carry a racial identity card

Pretoria Convention 1881; agreement by which the British government restored the Transvaal's independence after the annexation of 1877; retaining a vague British suzerainty, it forbade settlement beyond the Transvaal's borders, kept British control of foreign relations and maintained the British right to safeguard African interests

Progressive Federal party white parliamentary opposition party formed in 1977 when the Progressive party joined with liberal elements of the defunct United party

Progressive party white parliamentary opposition party which seceded from the United party in 1959, representing free enterprise liberalism but falling well short of supporting full non-racial democracy; for some years, Helen Suzman was its only member of parliament

Prohibition of Mixed Marriages Act 1949; law making interracial marriages illegal in South Africa, based on South African legal definitions of race; one of the first apartheid laws passed after 1948

Purified National Party *Gesuiwerde Nasionale party*, 1934; party formed by those who refused to follow J. B. M. Hertzog into the Fusion government and United party, and who went on to gain power in 1948

responsible government system of self government in British colonies, in which elected members of the legislature take ministerial control over government departments, answering to a majority of the elected members, with the colonial governor in turn bound by their advice; these powers were granted to the Cape parliament in 1872

San hunting peoples of southern Africa, known for rock paintings found all over South Africa; also called Bushmen

satyagraha Mohandas Gandhi's technique of nonviolent resistance, developed during his twenty-one years in South Africa; the term means truth-force, or firmness in the truth

segregation system of racial division, widely discussed and applied in South Africa from the late nineteenth century on; the theory posited preservation of African leadership, social structure, culture, and a partially separate economic base as a way to control Africans and maintain white security; distinct from **liberalism** and **baaskap**

Sharpeville massacre March 21, 1960; the police killing of sixty-nine demonstrators and the wounding of one hundred eighty during the PAC's antipass campaign

Sotho broad cultural classification in contrast to Nguni, including the southern Bantu living on the high veld, west of the Drakensberg mountains, including the people of Lesotho, the Pedi of the Transvaal, and the Tswana; but many of these people, such as in Lesotho, specifically call themselves Sotho

South African Native National Congress original name for the ANC when it was founded in 1912

South African Students' Organization SASO; black consciousness organization founded in 1968 when black university students broke away from the nonracial National Union of South African Students (NUSAS); blaming the black consciousness movement for the Soweto uprising, the government banned the organization in 1977

South West African People's Organization SWAPO; South West African or Namibian guerrilla movement, active from 1966 on, centering its power in northern Namibia among the Ovambo people; it became the ruling party after Namibian independence in 1990

Soweto uprising 1976 uprising of students and township dwellers, starting in Soweto in June but spreading to townships all over South Africa in the remainder of the year

Statute of Westminster 1931 law passed in the British parliament, defining the status of self governing colonies such as Canada and South Africa as virtually independent states

Suppression of Communism Act 1950; outlawed the Communist party in South Africa, and provided powers for the government to ban or prosecute anyone the government "deemed" to be advancing the communist cause

Terrorism Act 1967; defining terrorism as "any act whatsoever with intention to endanger the maintenance of law and order" the act provided for indefinite periods of detention without trial

townships urban locations set aside for African workers living in the "white" areas of South Africa; previous areas where Africans had owned urban property had been destroyed; provision of township housing was always inadequate, and most had squatter camps and shanty towns on their edges

Tswana   Bantu speaking peoples of the Transvaal, Orange Free State and Botswana; in dry country they depend more on cattle than agriculture, and they live in sizeable towns instead of scattered rural settlements

Uitlanders   immigrant miners, workers, and businessmen who entered the Transvaal in the late nineteenth century to work the gold mines; their economic and political grievances were one element in the crises leading to the Anglo-Boer war of 1899–1902

Umkhonto we Sizwe   Spear of the Nation; the military wing of the ANC, founded in 1961 to wage the armed struggle, after the banning of the ANC and the failure of previous nonviolent campaigns

United Democratic Front   UDF; organization founded by Allan Boesak and others to oppose the 1983 constitution and the Koornhof bills; served as an umbrella organization encompassing local sports clubs, church groups, and neighborhood associations in the townships

United Party   party formed in 1934 by the fusion of Smuts' South African party and Hertzog's National party; it lost power to the National party in 1948 and disintegrated in 1977

Vaal triangle   cluster of African townships South of Johannesburg, including Sebokeng, Sharpeville, Evaton, and Bophalong; the center of violent insurrections in the middle 1980s

Vereenigde Ostindische Compagnie   VOC; the Dutch East India Company that founded the Cape colony in 1652 as a refreshment station on the route to Indonesia

Volksraad   the elected legislative assembly of any of the Afrikaner trekker republics, the Transvaal, the Orange Free State, or Natalia, during their years of independence

Witwatersrand   "ridge of the white waters"; area. Five to six thousand feet above sea level, of deep gold bearing reefs, comprising the largest goldfield in the world; with Johannesburg at its center, it is the industrial heart of South Africa

Xhosa   Bantu-speaking mixed farmers of the eastern Cape region of South Africa; they are the dominant population group in the Ciskei and Transkei areas

Zionist churches   African separatist churches; in contrast to Ethiopian churches, these churches often mix African and Christian elements, emphasizing prophesy and healing; they are often aloof from politics

Zulu   largest ethnic group in South Africa, with over six million people; their kingdom was founded in 1818 by Shaka; the kingdom was defeated and divided in 1879, but after the end of political independence, many groups excluded from the kingdom came to identify themselves as Zulu

Bibliography

1. Textbooks and General Histories

Beinart, William, *Twentieth Century South Africa,* New York: Oxford University Press, 1994

Davenport, T. R. H., *South Africa: A Modern History,* Toronto: University of Toronto Press, 3rd ed., 1987

Omer Cooper, J. D., *History of Southern Africa,* Portsmouth: Heinemann, 1987 [and later edition]

Thompson, Leonard M., *A History of South Africa,* New Haven: Yale University Press, 1990 [and later edition]

Wilson, Monica & Leonard Thompson, eds., *The Oxford History of South Africa I: South Africa to 1870; II: South Africa, 1870–1966,* New York: Oxford University Press, 1969, 1971

Worden, Nigel, *The Making of Modern South Africa: Conquest, Segregation, and Apartheid,* Oxford: Blackwell, 1994

2. South Africa in Comparative Perspective

Cell, John W., *The Highest Stage of White Supremacy: the Origins of Segregation in South Africa and the American South,* New York: Cambridge University Press, 1982

Denoon, Donald, *Settler Capitalism: The Dynamics of Development in the Southern Hemisphere,* Oxford: Clarendon Press, 1983

Fredrickson, George M., *Black Liberation: A Comparative Study of Black Ideologies in the United States and South Africa,* New York: Oxford University Press, 1995

Fredrickson, George M., *White Supremacy: A Comparative Study in American and South African History,* New York: Oxford University Press, 1981

Greenstein, Ran, *Genealogies of Conflict: Class, Identities, and State in Palestine/Israel and South Africa,* Hanover, N.H.: University Press of New England, 1995

Lamar, Howard & Leonard Thompson, eds., *The Frontier in History: North America and South Africa Compared,* New Haven: Yale University Press, 1981

3. Historiography and Reference

Saunders, Christopher, *The Making of the South African Past: Major Historians on Race and Class,* Totowa, N.J.: Barnes and Noble, 1988

Saunders, Christopher C., *Historical Dictionary of South Africa,* Metuchen, N.J.: Scarecrow Press, 1983

Smith, Ken, *The Changing Past: Trends in South African Historical Writing,* Athens: Ohio University Press, 1988

Thompson, Leonard, *The Political Mythology of Apartheid,* New Haven: Yale University Press, 1985

Wright, Harrison M., *The Burden of the Present: Liberal-Radical Controversy over Southern African History,* Cape Town: David Philip, 1977

4. Collections of Essays: Recent Research

Beinart, William & Colin Bundy, *Hidden Struggles in Rural South Africa: Politics and Popular Movements in the Transkei and Eastern Cape, 1890–1930,* Berkeley: University of California Press, 1987

Beinart, William, Peter Delius & Stanley Trapido, eds., *Putting a Plough to the Ground: Accumulation and Dispossession in Rural South Africa, 1850–1930,* Johannesburg: Ravan Press, 1986

Bonner, Philip, Peter Delius, & Deborah Posel, eds., *Apartheid's Genesis, 1935–1962,* Johannesburg: Witwatersrand University Press, 1993

Marks, Shula & Anthony Atmore, eds., *Economy and Society in Pre-Industrial South Africa,* London: Longman, 1980

Marks, Shula & Richard Rathbone, eds., *Industrialisation and Social Change in South Africa: African Class Formation, Culture and Consciousness, 1870–1930,* London: Longman, 1982

Marks, Shula & Stanley Trapido, eds., *The Politics of Race, Class and Nationalism in Twentieth Century South Africa,* London: Longman, 1987

Saunders, Christopher, ed., *Black Leaders in Southern African History,* London: Heinemann, 1979

Thompson, L. M., ed., *African Societies in Southern Africa: Historical Studies,* London: Heinemann, 1978

Vail, Leroy, ed., *The Creation of Tribalism in Southern Africa,* Berkeley: University of California Press, 1989

Worden, Nigel & Clifton Crais, eds., *Breaking the Chains: Slavery and its Legacy in Nineteenth Century South Africa,* Bloomington: Indiana University Press, 1995

5. Early Cape Settlement and Slavery

Eldredge, Elizabeth A. & Fred Morton, eds., *Slavery in South Africa: Captive Labor on the Dutch Frontier,* Boulder: Westview Press, 1994.

Elphick, Richard, *Kraal and Castle: Khoikhoi and the Founding of White South Africa,* New Haven: Yale University Press, 1977

Elphick, Richard & Hermann Giliomee, eds., *The Shaping of South African Society, 1652–1840,* Middletown: Wesleyan University Press, 1988

Ross, Robert, *Cape of Torments: Slavery and Resistance in South Africa,* London: Routledge & Kegan Paul, 1983

Shell, Robert C.-H., *Children of Bondage: A Social History of the Slave Society at the Cape of Good Hope, 1652–1838,* Hanover: University Press of New England, 1994

Watson, R. L., *The Slave Question: Liberty and Property in South Africa,* Hanover: University Press of New England, 1990

6. African Society and Politics, ca. 1800–1912

Bridgman, Jon, *The Revolt of the Hereros,* Berkeley: University of California Press, 1981

Bundy, Colin, *The Rise and Fall of the South African Peasantry,* Berkeley: University of California Press, 1979

Burman, Sandra, *Chiefdom Politics and Alien Law: Basutoland under Cape Rule, 1871–1884,* New York: Holmes & Meier, 1981

Chirenje, J. Mutero, *Chief Kgama and His Times: The Story of a Southern African Ruler,* London: Rex Collings, 1978

Chirenje, J. Mutero, *Ethiopianism and Afro-Americans in Southern Africa, 1881–1916,* Baton Rouge: Louisiana State University Press, 1987

Delius, Peter, *The Land Belongs to Us: The Pedi Polity, the Boers and the British in the Nineteenth Century Transvaal,* Berkeley: University of California Press, 1984

Guy, Jeff, *The Destruction of the Zulu Kingdom,* London: Longman, 1979

Keegan, Tim, *Rural Transformations in Industrializing South Africa: The Southern Highveld to 1914,* London: Macmillan, 1987

Marks, Shula, *Reluctant Rebellion: The 1906–1908 Disturbances in Natal,* Oxford: The Clarendon Press, 1970

Omer Cooper, J. D., *The Zulu Aftermath: A Nineteenth Century Revolution in Bantu Africa,* Evanston: Northwestern University Press, 1966

Peires, J. B., *The Dead Will Arise: Nongqawuse and the Great Xhosa Cattle-Killing Movement of 1856–7*, Bloomington: Indiana University Press, 1989

Peires, J. B., *The House of Phalo: A History of the Xhosa People in the Days of Their Independence*, Berkeley: University of California Press, 1982

Ranger, T. O., *Revolt in Southern Rhodesia, 1896–97: A Study in African Resistance*, Evanston: Northwestern University Press, 1967

Shillington, Kevin, *The Colonisation of the Southern Tswana, 1870–1900*, Johannesburg: Ravan Press, 1985

Switzer, Les, *Power and Resistance in an African Society: The Ciskei Xhosa and the Making of South Africa*, Madison: University of Wisconsin Press, 1993

Thompson, Leonard M., *Survival in Two Worlds: Moshoeshoe of Lesotho, 1786–1870*, Oxford: At the Clarendon Press, 1975

Vail, Leroy & Landeg White, *Power and the Praise Poem: Southern African Voices in History*, Charlottesville: University Press of Virginia, 1991

7. Colonial History, 1795–1910

Comaroff, Jean & John Comaroff, *Of Revelation and Revolution: Christianity, Colonialism, and Consciousness in South Africa*, Chicago: University of Chicago Press, 1991

Crais, Clifton C., *White Supremacy and Black Resistance in Pre-industrial South Africa: The Making of the Colonial Order in the Eastern Cape, 1770–1865*, New York: Cambridge Unversity Press, 1992

Davenport, T. R. H., *The Afrikaner Bond: The History of a South African Political Party, 1880–1911*, New York: Oxford University Press, 1966

De Kiewiet, Cornelis W., *The Imperial Factor in South Africa*, London: Frank Cass, 1965 (1937)

Denoon, Donald, *A Grand Illusion: The Failure of Imperial Policy in the Transvaal during the Period of Reconstruction, 1900–1905*, London: Longman, 1973

Galbraith, John S., *Crown and Charter: The Early Years of the British South Africa Company*, Berkeley: University of California Press, 1974

Galbraith, John S., *Reluctant Empire: British Policy on the South African Frontier, 1834–1854*, Berkeley: University of California Press, 1963

Goodfellow, C. F., *Great Britain and South African Confederation 1870–1881*, New York: Oxford University Press, 1966

Hancock, W. K. Smuts: *The Sanguine Years, 1870–1919*, Cambridge: At the University Press, 1962

Huttenback, Robert A., *Gandhi in South Africa: British Imperialism and the Indian Question, 1860–1914*, Ithaca: Cornell University Press, 1971

James, Wilmot G. & Mary Simons, *The Angry Divide, Social and Economic History of the Western Cape*, Cape Town: David Philip, 1989

Lewsen, Phyllis, John X. *Merriman: Paradoxical South African Statesman*, New Haven: Yale University Press, 1982

MacLennan, Ben, *A Proper Degree of Terror: John Graham and the Cape's Eastern Frontier*, Johannesburg: Ravan Press, 1986

McCracken, J. L., *The Cape Parliament, 1854–1910*, Oxford: Clarendon Press, 1967

Pakenham, Thomas, *The Boer War*, New York: Random House, 1979

Porter, A. N., *The Origins of the South African War: Joseph Chamberlain and the Diplomacy of Imperialism, 1895–99*, New York: St. Martin's Press, 1980

Pyrah, G. B., *Imperial Policy and South Africa, 1902–10*, Oxford: At the Clarendon Press, 1955

Ross, Robert, *Beyond the Pale: Essays on the History of Colonial South Africa,* Hanover: University Press of New England, 1993

Rotberg, Robert I., *The Founder: Cecil Rhodes and the Pursuit of Power,* New York: Oxford University Press, 1988

Thompson, L. M., *The Unification of South Africa, 1902–1910,* Oxford: At the Clarendon Press, 1960

Welsh, David, *The Roots of Segregation: Native Policy in Colonial Natal, 1845–1910,* New York: Oxford University Press, 1971

8. Mining, Business, and the Labor System

Clark, Nancy L., *Manufacturing Apartheid: State Corporations in South Africa,* New Haven: Yale University Press, 1994

Crush, J. S. *South Africa's Labour Empire: A History of Black Migrancy to the Gold Mines,* Boulder: Westview Press, 1991

Innes, Duncan, *Anglo American and the Rise of Modern South Africa,* New York: Monthly Review Press, 1984

James Wilmot G., *Our Precious Metal: African Labour in South Africa's Gold Industry, 1970–1990,* Bloomington: Indiana University Press, 1992

Kanfer, Stefan, *The Last Empire: De Beers, Diamonds, and the World,* New York: Farrer, Straus & Giroux, 1993

Lacey, Marian, *Working for Boroko: The Origins of a Coercive Labour System in South Africa,* Johannesburg: Ravan Press, 1981

Mendelsohn, Richard, *Sammy Marks: 'Uncrowned King of the Transvaal',* Athens: Ohio University Press, 1991

Moodie, T. Dunbar (with Vivienne Ndatshe), *Going for Gold: Men, Mines and Migration,* Berkeley: University of California Press, 1994

Pallister, David, Sarah Stewart & Ian Lepper, *South Africa Inc.: The Oppenheimer Empire,* New Haven: Yale University Press, 1987

Wheatcroft, Geoffrey, *The Randlords,* New York: Atheneum, 1986

van Onselen, Charles, *Studies in the Social and Economic History of the Witwatersrand, 1886–1914, I: New Babylon; II: New Nineveh,* London: Longman, 1982

Worger, William H., *South Africa's City of Diamonds: Mine Workers and Monopoly Capitalism in Kimberley, 1867–1895,* New Haven: Yale University Press, 1987

9. Afrikaner Society and Politics

Bloomberg, Charles, *Christian-Nationalism and the Rise of the Afrikaner Broederbond in South Africa, 1918–1948,* Bloomington, Indiana University Press, 1989

de Villiers, Marq, *White Tribe Dreaming: Apartheid's Bitter Roots as Witnessed by Eight Generations of an Afrikaner Family,* New York: Viking, 1988

du Toit, Andre, & Hermann Giliomee, eds., *Afrikaner Political Thought: Analysis and Documents. Vol. 1, 1780–1850,* Berkeley: University of California Press, 1983

February, Vernon, *The Afrikaners of South Africa,* New York: Kegan Paul International, 1991

Furlong, Patrick J., *Between Crown and Swastika: The Impact of the Radical Right on the Afrikaner Nationalist Movement in the Fascist Era,* Hanover, N.H.: University Press of New England, 1991

Goodwin, June & Ben Schiff, *Heart of Whiteness: Afrikaners Face Black Rule in the New South Africa,* New York: Scribner, 1995

Leach, Graham, *The Afrikaners: the Last Great Trek,* London: Macmillan, 1989

Moodie, T. Dunbar, *The Rise of Afrikanerdom: Power, Apartheid, and the Afrikaner Civil Religion,* Berkeley: University of California Press, 1975

O'Meara, Dan, *Volkskapitalisme: Class, Capital, and Ideology in the Development of Afrikaner Nationalism, 1934–1948,* New York: Cambridge University Press, 1983

Serfontein, J. H. P., *Brotherhood of Power: An Expose of the Secret Afrikaner Broederbond,* Bloomington: Indiana University Press, 1978

Stultz, Newell M., *Afrikaner Politics in South Africa, 1934–1948,* Berkeley: University of California Press, 1974

van Jaarsveld, F. A., *The Awakening of Afrikaner Nationalism, 1868–1881,* Cape Town: Human & Rousseau, 1961

10. White Politics, Segregation, and Apartheid, 1910–1976

Adam, Heribert, *Modernizing Racial Domination: The Dynamics of South African Politics,* Berkeley: University of California Press, 1971

Bose, Mihir, *Sporting Colours: Sport and Politics in South Africa,* London: Robson Books, 1994

Boulle, Laurence, *Malan to de Klerk: Leadership in the Apartheid State,* London: Hurst, 1994

Christopher, A. J., *The Atlas of Apartheid,* New York: Routledge, 1994

Dubow, Saul, *Racial Segregation and the Origins of Apartheid in South Africa, 1919–1936,* New York: St. Martin's Press, 1989

Hancock, W. K., *Smuts: The Fields of Force, 1919–1950,* Cambridge: At the University Press, 1968

Murray, Christine & Catherine O'Regan, eds., *No Place to Rest: Forced Removals in South Africa,* New York: Oxford University Press, 1990

Posel, Deborah, *The Making of Apartheid, 1940–1961: Conflict and Compromise,* Oxford: At the Clarendon Press, 1991

Rich, Paul B., *White Power and the Liberal Conscience: Racial Segregation and South African Liberalism, 1921–60,* Manchester: Manchester University Press, 1984

Simons, H. J. & R. E. Simons, *Class and Colour in South Africa, 1859–1950,* Baltimore: Penguin Books, 1969

Western, John, *Outcast Cape Town,* Minneapolis: University of Minnesota Press, 1981

11. African Society and Politics, 1912–1976

Bernstein, Hilda, *The World that Was Ours: The Story of the Rivonia Trial,* London: SAWriters, 1989

Bozzoli, Belinda, *Women of Phokeng: Consciousness, Life Strategy, and Migrancy in South Africa, 1900–1983,* Portsmouth, N.H.: Heinemann, 1991

Bradford, Helen, *A Taste of Freedom: The ICU in Rural South Africa, 1924–1930,* New Haven: Yale University Press, 1987

Cock, Jacklyn, *Maids and Madams: Domestic Workers under Apartheid,* London: Women's Press, 1989

Ellis, Stephen & Tsepho Sechaba, *Comrades against Apartheid: The ANC and the South African Communist Party in Exile,* Bloomington: Indiana University Press, 1992

Johns, Sheridan & R. Hunt Davis, Jr., eds., *Mandela, Tambo, and the African National Congress: The Struggle against Apartheid, 1948–1990: A Documentary Survey,* New York: Oxford University Press, 1991

Gerhart, Gail, *Black Power in South Africa: The Evolution of an Ideology,* Berkeley: University of California Press, 1978

Keegan, Tim, *Facing the Storm: Portraits of Black Lives in Rural South Africa,* Athens: Ohio University Press, 1988

Lewis, Gavin, *Between the Wire and the Wall: A History of South African Coloured Politics,* New York: St. Martin's Press, 1987

Lodge, Tom, *Black Politics in South Africa since 1945,* London: Longman, 1983

Marks, Shula, *The Ambiguities of Dependence: Class, Nationalism, and the State in Twentieth-Century Natal,* Baltimore: The Johns Hopkins University Press, 1986

Marx, Anthony W., *Lessons of Struggle: South African Internal Opposition, 1960–1990,* New York: Oxford University Press, 1992

Meli, Francis, *A History of the ANC: South African Belongs to Us,* Bloomington: Indiana University Press, 1988

Pogrund, Benjamin, *Sobukwe and Apartheid,* New Brunswick: Rutgers University Press, 1990

Roux, Edward, *Time Longer than Rope: A History of the Struggle of the Black Man for Freedom in South Africa,* Madison: University of Wisconsin Press, 1964

Sampson, Anthony, *Drum: The Newspaper That Won the Heart of Africa,* Boston: Houghton Mifflin, 1957

Sundkler, Bengt, *Bantu Prophets in South Africa,* London: Oxford University Press, 2nd ed., 1961

Van Onselen, Charles, *The Seed Is Mine: The Life of Kas Maine, a South African Sharecropper, 1894–1985,* New York: Hill & Wang, 1996

van Vuuren, Nancy, *Women against Apartheid: The Fight for Freedom, 1920–1975,* Palo Alto: R & E Research Association, 1979

Walshe, Peter, *The Rise of African Nationalism in South Africa: The African National Congress, 1912–1952,* Berkeley: University of California Press, 1971

Willan, Brian, *Sol Plaatje: South African Nationalist, 1876–1932,* Berkeley: University of California Press, 1984

Woods, Donald, *Biko,* New York: Henry Holt, 3rd rev. ed., 1991

12. South Africa in the International Context

Barber, James & John Barratt, *South Africa's Foreign Policy: the Search for Status and Security, 1945–1988,* New York: Cambridge University Press, 1990

Borstelmann, Thomas, *Apartheid's Reluctant Uncle: The United States and Southern Africa in the Early Cold War,* New York: Oxford University Press, 1993

First, Ruth, Jonathan Steele & Christabel Gurney, *The South African Connection: Western Investment in Apartheid,* Harmondsworth: Penguin Books, 1973

Hanlon, Joseph, *Beggar Your Neighbour: Apartheid Power in Southern Africa,* Bloomington: Indiana University Press, 1986

Johnson, Phyllis & David Martin, eds., *Frontline South Africa: Destructive Engagement,* New York: Four Walls Eight Windows, 1988

Klotz, Andre, *Norms in International Relations: The Struggle Against Apartheid,* Ithaca: Cornell University Press, 1995

Minter, William, *King Solomon's Mines Revisited: Western Interests and the Burdened History of Southern Africa,* New York: Basic Books, 1986

Nixon, Rob, *Homelands, Harlem, and Hollywood: South African Culture and the World Beyond,* New York: Routledge, 1994

Noer, Thomas J., *Cold War and Black Liberation: The United States and White Rule in South Africa, 1948–1968,* Columbia: University of Missouri Press, 1985

Shimoni, Gideon, *Jews and Zionism: The South African Experience,* New York: Oxford University Press, 1980

13. Autobiographies

Abrahams, Peter, *Tell Freedom: Memories of Africa,* New York: Collier Books, 1970

Benson, Mary, *A Far Cry: The Making of a South African,* London: Penguin Book, 1990

Breytenbach, Breyten, *The True Confessions of an Albino Terrorist,* New York: Farrar, Straus, Giroux, 1985

Chikane, Frank, *No Life of My Own: An Autobiography,* Maryknoll, N.Y.: Orbis Books, 1988

Head, Bessie, *A Woman Alone: Autobiographical Writings,* selected & edited by Craig Mackenzie, Portsmouth, N.H.: Heinemann, 1990

Heard, Anthony Hazlitt, *The Cape of Storms: A Personal History of the Crisis in South Africa,* Fayetteville: The University of Arkansas Press, 1990

Jabavu, Noni, *The Ochre People: Scenes from a South African Life,* New York: St. Martin's Press, 1963

Joseph, Helen, *Side by Side: The Autobiography of Helen Joseph,* New York: Morrow, 1986

Kuzwayo, Ellen, *Call Me Woman,* San Francisco: Spinsters/Aunt Lute, 1985

Levine, Janet, *Inside Apartheid: One Woman's Struggle in South Africa,* Chicago: Contemporary Books, 1988

Macmillan, W. M., *My South African Years: An Autobiography,* Cape Town: David Philip, 1975

Magona, Sindiwe, *To My Children's Children,* New York: Interlink Books, 1994

Magona, Sindiwe, *Forced to Grow,* London: The Women's Press, 1992

Mandela, Nelson, *Long Walk to Freedom: The Autobiography of Nelson Mendela,* Boston: Little, Brown, 1994

Mashinini, Emma, *Strikers Have Followed Me All My Life: A South African Autobiography,* New York: Routledge, 1991

Mattera, Don, *Sophiatown: Coming of Age in South Africa,* Boston: Beacon Press, 1989

Matthews, Z. K., *Freedom for my People; The Autobiography of Z. K. Matthews: Southern Africa, 1901 to 1968* [Memoir by Monica Wilson] Cape Town: David Philip, 1983

Modisane, Bloke, *Blame Me on History,* New York: Simon & Schuster, 1986

Mphahlele, Es'kia, *Afrika My Music: An Autobiography, 1957–1983,* Johannesburg: Ravan Press, 1984

Mphahlele, Ezekiel (Es'kia), *Down Second Avenue,* Garden City: Doubleday & Co., 1971

Ntantala, Phyllis, *A Life's Mosaic: The Autobiography of Phyllis Ntantala,* Berkeley: University of Califronia Press, 1993

Paton, Alan, *Towards the Mountain: An Autobiography,* New York: Charles Scribner's, 1977

Paton, Alan, *Journey Continued: An Autobiography,* New York: Collier Books, 1988

Suzman, Helen, *In No Uncertain Terms: A South African Memoir,* New York: Alfred A. Knopf, 1993

Woods, Donald, *Asking for Trouble: The Education of a White South African,* Boston: Beacon Press, 1980

14. South Africa Since 1976

Abel, Richard L., *Politics by Other Means: Law in the Struggle Against Apartheid,* 1980–1994. New York: Routledge, 1995

Baskin, Jeremy, *Striking Back: A History of COSATU,* London: Verso, 1991

Crapanzano, Vincent, *Waiting: The Whites of South Africa* New York: Random House, 1985

Davis, Stephen M., *Apartheid's Rebels: Inside South Africa's Hidden War,* New Haven: Yale University Press, 1987

Ellmann, Stephen, *In a Time of Trouble: Law and Liberty in South Africa's State of Emergency,* New York: Oxford University Press, 1992

Moss, Rose, *Shouting at the Crocodile: Popo Molefe, Patrick Lekota, and the Freeing of South Africa,* Boston: Beacon Press, 1990

Mufson, Steven, *Fighting Years: Black Resistance and the Struggle for a New South Africa,* Boston: Beacon Press, 1990

Murray, Martin J., *The Revolution Deferred: The Painful Birth of Post-Apartheid South Africa,* New York: Verso, 1994

Ottaway, David, *Chained Together: Mandela, de Klerk, and the Struggle to Remake South Africa,* New York: Times Books, 1993

Price, Robert M., *The Apartheid State in Crisis: Political Transformation in South Africa, 1975–1990,* New York: Oxford University Press, 1991

Sparks, Allister, *The Mind of South Africa,* New York: Alfred A. Knopf, 1990

Sparks, Allister, *Tomorrow Is Another Country: the Inside Story of South Africa's Road to Change,* New York: Hill & Wang, 1995

Stengel, Richard, *January Sun: One Day, Three Lives, a South African Town,* New York: Simon & Schuster, 1990

van Rooyen, Johann, *Hard Right: The New White Power in South Africa,* London: I. B. Taurus, 1994 Town: David Philip, 1975

15. Literature, Music, Photography

Attwell, David, *J. M. Coetzee: South Africa and the Politics of Writing,* Berkeley: University of California Press, 1993

Badsha, Omar, *South Africa: The Cordoned Heart [Essays by Twenty South African Photographers],* Cape Town: The Gallery Press, 1986

Ballantine, Christopher, *Marabi Nights: Early South African Jazz and Vaudeville,* Athens: Ohio University Press, 1994

Barnett, Ursula, *A Vision of Order: A Study of Black South African Literature in English (1914–1980),* Amherst: University of Massachusetts Press, 1983

Brink, Andre, *Writing in a State of Siege: Essays on Politics and Literature,* New York: Summit Books, 1983

Coetzee, J. M. *White Writing: On the Culture of Letters in South Africa,* New Haven: Yale University Press, 1988

Coplan, David B., *In Township Tonight: South African Black City Music and Theatre,* London: Longman, 1985

Couzens, Tim, *The New African: A Study of the Life and Work of H. I. E. Dhlomo,* Johannesburg: Ravan Press, 1985

Erlmann, Veit, *African Stars: Studies in Black South African Performance,* Chicago: University of Chicago Press, 1991

Goldblatt, David, *The Transported of Kwandebele: A South African Odyssey,* Aperture, in Association with the Center for Documentary Studies, Duke University, 1989

Gordimer, Nadine, *The Essential Gesture: Writing, Politics, and Places,* London: Jonathan Cape, 1988

Gordimer, Nadine & David Goldblatt, *Lifetimes: Under Apartheid,* New York: Alfred A. Knopf, 1986

Gunner, Liz, *Politics and Performance: Theatre, Poetry and Song in Southern Africa,* Bloomington: Indiana University Press, 1995

Jordan, A. C., *Towards an African Literature: The Emergence of Literary Form in Xhosa,* Berkeley: University of California Press, 1973

Kivnick, Helen, *Where Is the Way: Song and Struggle in South Africa,* New York: Penguin Books, 1990

Kunene, Daniel P., *Thomas Mofolo and the Emergence of Written Sesotho Prose,* Johannesburg: Ravan Press, 1989

Magubane, Peter, *Magubane's South Africa,* New York: Alfred A. Knopf, 1978

Shava, Piniel Viriri, *A People's Voice: Black South African Writing in the Twentieth Century,* Athens: Ohio University Press, 1989